D0939077

WITHDRAWN

With *Fast Track* Speed Notes

MASTERING VENTURA®

SECOND EDITION

Matthew Holtz

Through Version 2.0

For New & Experienced Users

Includes the Professional Extension

"Useful and very comprehensive"
Desktop Publishing Journal

MENU/SELECTION	EFFECT	PAGE
FILE		
New	Clears the displayed chapter from the screen so you can create a new one.	77
Open Chapter	Retrieves a chapter and its related files from the disk for editing.	43
Save (^S)	Saves the displayed chapter and its associated files.	77
Save As	Makes a copy of the displayed chapter by saving it on disk with a new name.	47
Abandon	Abandons the edits made to the current chapter and reloads the chapter from disk.	77
Load Text/Picture	Loads a word-processed text file or picture file and adds its name to the Assignment list.	86
Load Diff. Style	Retrieves a style sheet. Links it with the displayed chapter when the chapter is saved.	119
Save As New Style	Makes a copy of the style sheet in use by saving it with a new name.	47
To Print	Initiates the printing process using printer specifications in the Options menu's Set Printer Info.	184
DOS File Ops	Allows you to delete files from the disk and to make and remove DOS directories.	46
Quit	Brings the work session with Ventura to an end.	77
EDIT		
Cut (Del)	Deletes the selected text, frames, or graphics (depending on the mode) to the clipboard.	100
Copy (Shift-Del)	Copies the selected text, frames, or graphics (depending on the mode) to the clipboard.	103
Paste (Ins)	Inserts text, frames, or graphics (depending on the mode) from the clipboard.	104
Ins. Special Item (^C)	Leads to menu for inserting Box Character, Footnote, Index Entry, Fraction, Frame Anchor, Cross Reference	247
Edit Special Item (^D)	Allows you to edit above items.	249
Remove Text/File	Allows you to remove a text or picture file from a frame or from the Assignment list.	88
File Type/Rename	Allows you to rename a text file or change its word-processed format.	90
VIEW		
Facing Pages View	Displays a two-page spread on the screen.	63

MENU/SELECTION	EFFECT	PAGE
Reduced View (^R)	Shows the document sized smaller than its printed versions.	63
Normal View (^N)	Shows the document the same size as its printed version.	61
Enlarged View (^E)	Shows the document twice the size of its printed versions.	62
Frame Setting (^U)	Activates Frame mode. Used to create and manipulate frames.	51
Paragraph Tagging (^I)	Activates Paragraph mode. Used to tag paragraphs and set up tag formats.	115
Text Editing (^O)	Activates Text mode. Used to edit text and assign text attributes.	94
Graphic Drawing (^P)	Activates Graphics mode. Used to manipulate Ventura graphics.	275
CHAPTER		
Page Size & Layout	Sets portrait/landscape; letter, legal, and so on; single/double sides.	72
Chapter Typography	For the chapter, sets Widows, Orphans, Column Balance, Move Down, Pair Kerning.	339
Update Counters	Sets numbering of Chapter, Page, Tables, Figures.	246
Auto-Numbering	Automatically inserts section numbers and sets their style.	387
Renumber Chapter (^B)	Updates the numbering defined by Chapter's Auto-numbering.	391
Re-Anchor Frames	Moves frames to the page on which their anchors appear.	249
Headers & Footers	Controls text appearing repeatedly at the top and bottom of each page.	344
Turn Header On/Off	Removes or redisplays headers (defined with Headers & Footers, above).	349
Turn Footer On/Off	Removes or redisplays footers (defined with Headers & Footers, above).	349
Footnote Settings	Controls the format of footnotes.	397
Insert/Remove Page	Inserts or removes pages of the document.	328
Go To Page (^G)	Displays the specified page or a page relative to the document or selected file.	91
FRAME		
Margins & Columns	Controls the margins and columns for underlying-page and standard frames.	55
Sizing & Scaling	Controls frame position, dimensions, padding, flow-around, picture scale, cropping.	68
Frame Typography	Set frame overrides for Widows, Orphans, Column Balance, Move Down, Pair Kerning.	458

This table continues at the back of this book.

MASTERING VENTURA

MASTERING VENTURA™

Second Edition

Matthew Holtz

SAN FRANCISCO • PARIS • DÜSSELDORF • LONDON

Cover design by Thomas Ingalls + Associates
Cover photography by Casey Cartwright
Series Design by Julie Bilski
Technical illustrations by Lucie Zivny

Library of Congress Card Number: 88-63712
ISBN 0-89588-581-6
Manufactured in the United States of America
10 9 8 7 6 5 4 3 2 1

To Barbara Gordon, *with thanks for the professionalism and patience.*

It is one thing to write, and another to publish.

—Edward George Earle Bulwer-Lytton

ACKNOWLEDGMENTS

Thanks to all those at SYBEX who assisted in the production of this edition, especially Eric Stone for editorial assistance. Thanks also to Hannah Robinson for the helpful input. Thanks to the following people for their efforts at all stages of the book: Jeff Giese, technical review; Bob Myren and Jocelyn Reynolds, word processing; Olivia Shinomoto, typesetting; Sylvia Townsend, proofreading; Charlotte Carter, paste-up and layout; and Sonja Schenk, screen reproduction.

Thanks to the folks at Blue Chip International for editorial assistance, especially Eric Delore. Thanks to Gene Brott for the special help.

Thanks especially to the following companies for providing hardware that assisted in the production of this book: Hewlett-Packard for the LaserJet Series II; Micro Display Systems, Inc. for the Genius Full-Page Display; and Princeton Graphics Systems for the LS-300 Image Scanner.

CONTENTS AT A GLANCE

TABLE OF CONTENTS

INTRODUCTION

AT LAST THE FULL POWER OF DESKTOP PUBLISHING, formerly the sole province of the Apple Macintosh, has come to the IBM PC and compatibles, in the form of Xerox's Ventura Publisher, or simply Ventura. This book is here to guide you through Ventura's many sophisticated features. It is an easy-to-follow tutorial that will teach you the program and then stay by your side for reference as you gain expertise.

WHAT MAKES VENTURA SPECIAL?

Ventura Publisher was the first full-featured desktop publisher available for the IBM personal computer and compatibles. It has been so successful in its features and design that it is now the standard with which other desktop publishers are compared.

Several covers of the most popular computer magazines have showcased Ventura. Periodicals have given it one rave review after another. Some have called it the best piece of software since Lotus 1-2-3. And now, feature articles are examining version 2.0 as a new milestone in desktop publishing

To many, Ventura accomplished what was thought impossible with an IBM. To get a sense of why Ventura garnered such high praises, let's take a quick look at its capabilities in the categories that are generally most important to users.

Pricing For around $1000, Ventura offers capabilities previously available only on machines costing upward of $200,000. At the same time, it has managed to keep hardware requirements to a minimum.

Performance Ventura has completely belied the prediction that desktop publishing with an IBM would be sluggish and severely limited. Now, with version 2.0, Ventura is even more efficient to operate. At the same time, it incorporates over 100 new features that make the program more capable and, indeed, faster to use.

Compatibility Ventura provides the common ground that allows your word processing and graphics packages as well as your hardware to perform in "symphony" in a way no other piece of software has been able to orchestrate (see Table I.1). In addition, especially with version 2.0, Ventura extends itself in anticipating the popularity of cutting-edge technology, such as color printing and big-screen displays.

Ease of Use As encompassing as the program is, Ventura's structure is logical, intuitive, and easy to grasp. Using the built-in *GEM user interface* (GEM stands for Graphics Environment Manager), the program presents itself to you with icons, a choice of drop-down or pull-down menus, dialog boxes, and other graphics displays that are the hallmarks of that interface system. This format—which originated on the Apple Macintosh computer—has a well-deserved reputation for ease of use, because its components are visually-oriented.

Version 2.0 enhances ease of use by offering over 250 help screens available from within the program, and a choice of how menus appear. The new version cleans up screen clutter by making some choices appear only as needed.

Table I.1: Software Packages Supported by Ventura

LINE ART	IMAGES	WORD PROCESSING
AutoCAD	DFX format	ASCII format
CGM	GEM	IBM DCA (DisplayWrite)
Encapsulated PostScript	MAC Paint	Microsoft WORD
GEM	PC Paintbrush	MultiMate
HPGL	Publishers Paintbrush	WordPerfect
Lotus 1-2-3	TIFF	WordStar
Macintosh PICT	VideoShow format	Xerox Writer
Mentor Graphics		XyWrite
Microsoft Windows		
VideoShow		

WHAT VENTURA CAN DO

Not only can Ventura integrate the creations of state-of-the-art programs into its documents, it also possesses its own exceptional features. Here are some of the operations you can perform with it:

- Captions
- Cut-and-paste
- Footnotes
- Headers and footers
- Hyphenation
- An index and a table of contents
- Page numbers
- Section numbering
- Sophisticated typography
- Tables

SYSTEM REQUIREMENTS FOR VENTURA

To step into Ventura's desktop-publishing sphere, of course, you'll need the Ventura software, distributed by Xerox Corporation. For version 2.0, you'll need a minimum of 640K of RAM on your computer. Your operating system must be MS-DOS or PC-DOS, version 2.10 or higher.

You'll also need to have a graphics card, such as the one manufactured by Hercules for monochrome display. Ventura supports a variety of graphics cards, including CGA and EGA cards for color display. Just be certain that the graphics card you get will work with your monitor, and that the resulting resolution is acceptable to you. You can have a computer dealer install it in your computer, or if you have a little computer savvy, you can install the board yourself.

In addition to at least one floppy drive, a hard disk is necessary. You cannot use Ventura if you have only floppy drives. Before you install Ventura, be sure that the hard disk has from 1 to 3 megabytes of storage available. The exact amount depends on the printer you will be using. In addition, after installation it's recommended that you have 2 to 3 megabytes available for storage of documents and additional fonts.

Xerox says that you will need a mouse. Because the program is designed to be used with a mouse, we will assume that you have one and will be using it with Ventura. While it is possible to use the program without a mouse, doing so is quite difficult, especially if you are new to the program. Appendix A provides information on the use of Ventura without a mouse.

To print your documents, you need a printer that Ventura supports. The list includes the Epson MX-80, RX-80, and LQ 1050; the Hewlett-Packard LaserJet Plus, LaserJet with F cartridge, and LaserJet Series II; the IBM ProPrinter; the Xerox 4020 Color and 4045 Laser printers; the NEC P series; the Toshiba P351SX; and any printer that uses the PostScript command language, such as the Apple LaserWriter. You can also use a JLaser card with a printer that's compatible with it, such as the IBM 4216 PostScript printer.

Support of the Epson LQ 1050, the NEC P series, and Toshiba P351SX printers are the additions to Version 2.0. The Epson LQ 1050 driver can be used for the IBM XL24 printer. Support for the direct-connecting IBM 4216 PostScript printer has also been added.

As your system and your skills in using Ventura become increasingly sophisticated, you may find that your normal screen is simply too small. That's because standard screens cannot display a full 8.5-by-11-inch page. To alleviate this problem, it's a pleasure to use a full-page display, such as the Genius from Micro Display Systems. With this ingenious piece of hardware, you can finally have a screen that displays a full 8.5 by 11 inches. If you've yet to purchase your hardware, you may wish to consider a full-page display. Some experts estimate that using such a display can double the efficiency of your desktop-publishing work. (If you purchase a full-page display, you'll also need to use a special graphics card.) As we proceed in this book, we'll occasionally use the Genius to display some of the examples.

There are even displays, such as one manufactured by Wyse, that are large enough to show a full size two-page spread. We'll use the term *large display* to indicate either a full-page or a two-page display.

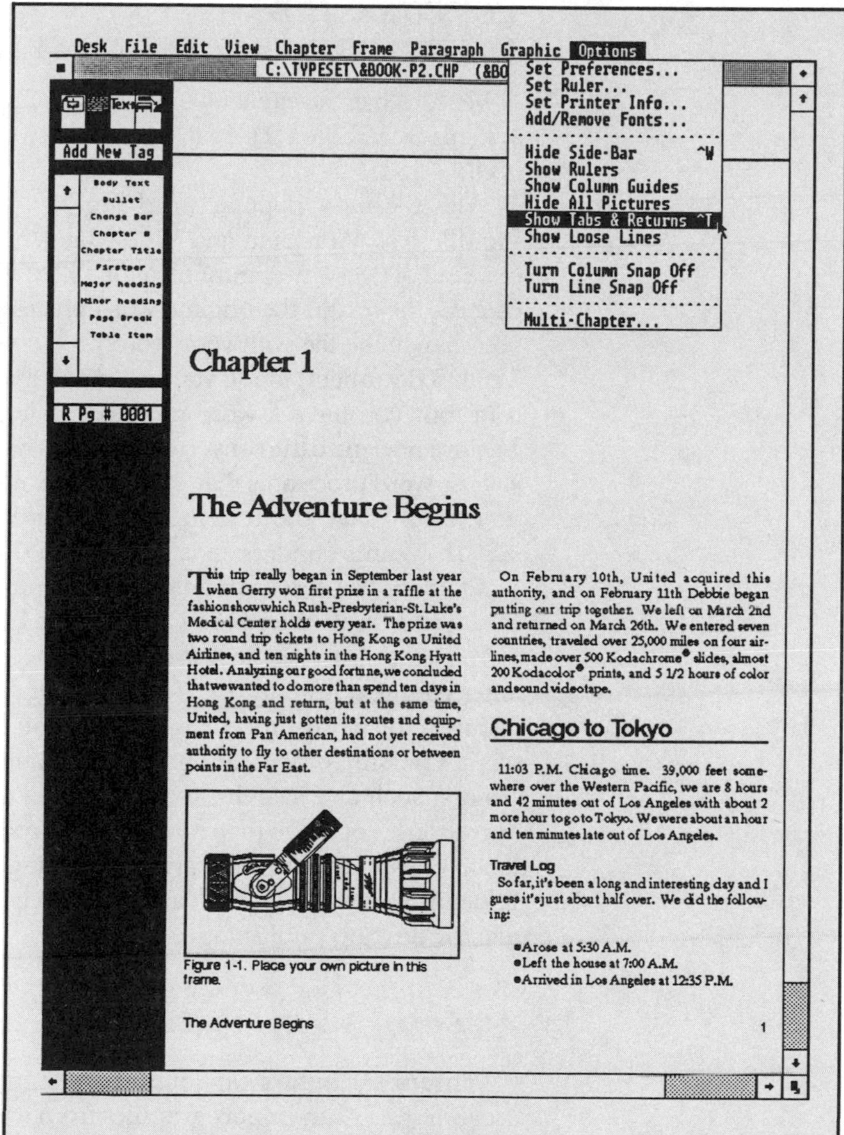

Figure I.1: Ventura on a Genius full-page display

VENTURA AND YOUR WORD-PROCESSING SYSTEM

Ventura has the capacity to work with a variety of word-processing systems (see Table I.1). It also has some word-processing capabilities itself.

With the most popular word processors (like Microsoft WORD, WordPerfect, WordStar, and MultiMate), Ventura Publisher is capable of a kind of two-way communication. That is, changing text in Ventura changes the text in the original word-processed file as well. Likewise, if you change the file with your word processor, the text changes in your Ventura document, too. If your word processor is not supported by Ventura, but you have a word-processor converter for it, you can have Ventura recognize the converter. If you do not have a converter, you can still use word processors that Ventura does not support fully. To do that, you simply save the text in IBM's standard, plain vanilla format: ASCII. Ventura understands ASCII and can save in that format, too. In addition, you can use data from other programs that have the ability to output in ASCII format. This includes Lotus 1-2-3 and dBASE IV.

You can also use the word-processing capabilities of Ventura to enter your text initially. Be aware, though, that the program does not feature a full word-processing system. You can use it to cut and paste, but it's missing other features that are standard with most word processors, such as a search capability and a spelling checker. For these operations, you have to use your word processor. This apparent limitation of Ventura, however, is an advantage rather than a drawback. It means that you needn't learn an entirely new word-processing system for desktop publishing.

GRAPHICS AND VENTURA

Ventura's graphics capabilities are similar to its word-processing capabilities. It can import graphics from a variety of sources. As with word processing, it can also create modest graphics, or fine-tune those that it imports. Ventura supports graphics created by Lotus, GEM, AutoCAD, and ZSoft, among others. It can also manipulate graphics imported by means of a scanner. If your graphics package is not supported by Ventura, but you have a converter for it, you can use the converter to gain support.

Even if you make changes to pictures that appear in your Ventura document, you can always restore the originals later. That's because Ventura always leaves the file containing the original art intact. If you accidentally cropped your boss's left ear in the company newsletter, it's simplicity itself to crop the picture differently and include the missing ear.

Ventura can also create lines, boxes, and circles. You can use its graphics and fonts, for instance, to add legends or text to an existing graphics file, or to expand upon text that is already there.

Version 2.0 significantly enhances Ventura's graphics capabilities. For example, to obtain quicker "draft" printouts of your document, you restrain Ventura from printing some or all pictures. Additionally, Ventura supports more graphics software formats than ever. And it enhances its own graphics, allowing you to draw perfect squares, circles, and angled lines more easily than ever.

HOW TO USE THIS BOOK

To assist you in mastering Ventura's features, both basic and sophisticated, this book describes all of Ventura's major procedures step by step, with illustrations and examples. The methods used allow you to practice these procedures in order to get to know them, or to reference them as your practical needs demand. A thorough index makes procedures quickly available.

This book makes liberal use of the extensive samples that Ventura provides with its software. By examining and dissecting these samples, you'll come to understand the innermost workings of Ventura. This means that you'll learn and see the program in action without typing in volumes of text. Using material at hand speeds the learning process.

If you've just acquired Ventura, begin with Appendix A. This appendix explains how you install the program on your computer. You can skip it if you (or someone else) have already installed Ventura. With Ventura installed, start with Chapter 1 if you haven't otherwise used Ventura before. Once you understand Ventura's fundamentals, you can use various chapters of this book as necessary. For example, if you are especially interested in incorporating 1-2-3 graphs into Ventura, you can simply consult Chapter 6. Each chapter contains cross-references to other chapters and appendices that contain related information.

A "Fast Track" section at the beginning of each chapter lists the most important tasks covered in the chapter and how to accomplish them. If you're in a hurry, or if you need a quick refresher on a feature you've learned before, this is the place to turn. To the right of each Fast Track entry, you'll find the page number to which you can turn for more details.

Sidelights

Throughout the text, we've used margin notes to provide sidelights for topics under discussion. Marked with the pointing hand as shown to the left, they also warn you of potential pitfalls that you may encounter as you work with Ventura.

! New for version 2.0

There is a special flag, shown to the left, that draws your attention to features that are new with Ventura 2.0. If you're looking to learn the new features, just scan the text for this marker.

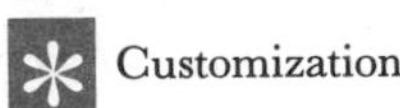

Customization

There are also margin notes that show you how to customize Ventura in ways that may assist you with the matter at hand. Such notes are marked with the symbol you see to the left. They refer you to material on custom installation, the Options menu, custom colors, and the Professional Extension (Ventura's add-on package).

There are two conventions this book uses in discussing various category labels that appear on the screeen. We capitalize each word of a label, such as the Relative To setting (even though the screen actually says "Relative to"). Also, periods are eliminated; thus we show the Text Attr button (though the screen says "Text Attr."). Following these conventions makes the text of this book easier to read.

Finally, if you find it useful to use the samples Ventura provides, you may wish to add to your library of sample documents and style sheets. Consider ordering the *Mastering Ventura* Samples Disk. A coupon and explanation of these samples appear at the end of this book.

WHAT THIS BOOK CONTAINS

Let's take a look at this book's contents, chapter by chapter:

Chapter 1, "Getting Started," examines the Ventura screen and the conventions Ventura uses to communicate to the user. It also examines Ventura's four operating modes, and provides an overview of how to use them.

Chapter 2, "Setting Up a Newsletter," is the first to work with one of the samples, showing you how you can adapt it to your needs. We examine using and saving files, and specifying the size of pages, margins, and columns. We'll also see how to create and adjust *frames,* Ventura's primary means of organizing the page.

Chapter 3, "Using Electronic Scissors and Glue," shows you how to use Ventura's editing abilities to rework text. We'll see how to electronically cut, copy, and paste frames as well.

Chapter 4, "Paragraph Tags and Text Attributes: Building Blocks for Formatting," examines a fundamental formatting tool in Ventura: the *paragraph tag.* You'll see how to set fonts and create italics, boldface, underlining, and other attributes. In this chapter, we'll also examine centering and justification, as well as hyphenation, indenting, spacing between lines, and various other formats you can apply to paragraphs.

Chapter 5, "Start the Presses: Printing and Other Output," explains how you can use Ventura to print your work. Although printing with Ventura is generally a simple and straightforward process, the program nevertheless provides many sophisticated printing abilities, allowing for a high degree of flexibility. The chapter contains a discussion of various printers, with sections on setting up printers, printing multiple copies, and so on. There is also a section on how to add fonts to your printer, as well as how to use Ventura for printing with a typesetter.

Chapter 6, "Adding Pictures from Lotus 1-2-3 and Other Sources," shows how you use Ventura's uncanny ability to integrate pictures from a variety of sources with word-processed text. We'll discuss the characteristics of the two kinds of pictures that Ventura uses and see how to adjust pictures to fit your needs. We'll also look at how text interacts with pictures, how to create captions, and how to keep a picture with its associated text as you edit.

Chapter 7, "Lines, Circles, and Boxes," is an examination of the graphics capabilities that are built into Ventura. You'll see how such graphics can be assigned to frames or paragraph tags. You'll see how to use Ventura's Graphics mode to create arrows, squares, circles and custom shapes as well. You'll also see how text works with these graphics in special ways.

Chapter 8, "Creating Tables," is a discussion of how to make tables of text in Ventura. To accommodate a variety of needs, Ventura provides you with four different ways to create tables. By using this chapter, you'll see how these methods differ, and so be able to choose the one that suits you best.

Chapter 9, "Working with Pages: Formats and Page Headings," provides a look at how to format the page and create headings that are automatically repeated on each page. We'll see how automatically generated pages differ from pages that you insert individually. We'll also see how to make material repeat on every page, and we'll look at some methods for speeding up the page-layout process.

Chapter 10, "Multichapter Features: Tables of Contents, Indexes, Footnotes, and Numbering," discusses the features you would usually press into service for long documents. We'll see how to make copies of chapters and publications, rearrange chapters, and create a table of contents and an index. We'll also see how to number and renumber section headings, as well as pages and chapters, automatically.

Chapter 11, "Using Other Programs with Ventura," provides a discussion of how to use word processors and other programs with Ventura. We'll see how you can use your favorite word processor to create text and assign formatting to Ventura documents. We'll specifically examine the use of Microsoft WORD, WordStar, and WordPerfect with Ventura. We'll also look at using macro generators with Ventura and see how to use word processors that Ventura supports to a lesser extent. The chapter also contains a discussion of the use of dBASE and other database systems for providing data for Ventura and creating "mail-merge" documents.

Chapter 12, "Typographical Elements and Effects," is an examination of Ventura's sophisticated typographical capabilities, many of which are new or improved for version 2.0. We'll see how to begin paragraphs with special effects and how to create reverse text and other unusual effects. We'll also show how to make adjustments to the spacing between letters and words, as well as between paragraphs. We'll see how fine-tuning like this can put the finishing touches on your Ventura documents.

Chapter 13, "Enhancing Ventura with the Professional Extension," examines features available in the optional Professional Extension available from Xerox. You'll see how it allows you to cross-reference material, improve hyphenation, streamline the creation of elaborate tables, and churn out sophisticated mathematical equations.

The appendices provide some supplemental information that you will find a useful reference as you work with Ventura. Appendix A tells you how to install Ventura and how to create alternative setups with the Options menu. Operating without a mouse, with a RAM drive, and under OS/2 are also covered. Appendix B is a listing of the sample documents provided with Ventura, along with a display of each and a discussion of their features. Appendix C contains a discussion of the DOS conventions that Ventura uses; you may wish to consult this appendix if you are unfamiliar with DOS, or if you need a brush-up. Appendix D is a listing of companies that provide fonts for use with Ventura. Appendix E contains a listing of unusual characters and special codes that Ventura makes available for additional typographical flexibility.

This edition of *Mastering Ventura* covers the features available in Version 2.0. To determine which version of Ventura you have, check the title line as you start the program (see Chapter 1).

Congratulations. You are about to participate in a technological adventure. Now the adventure begins.

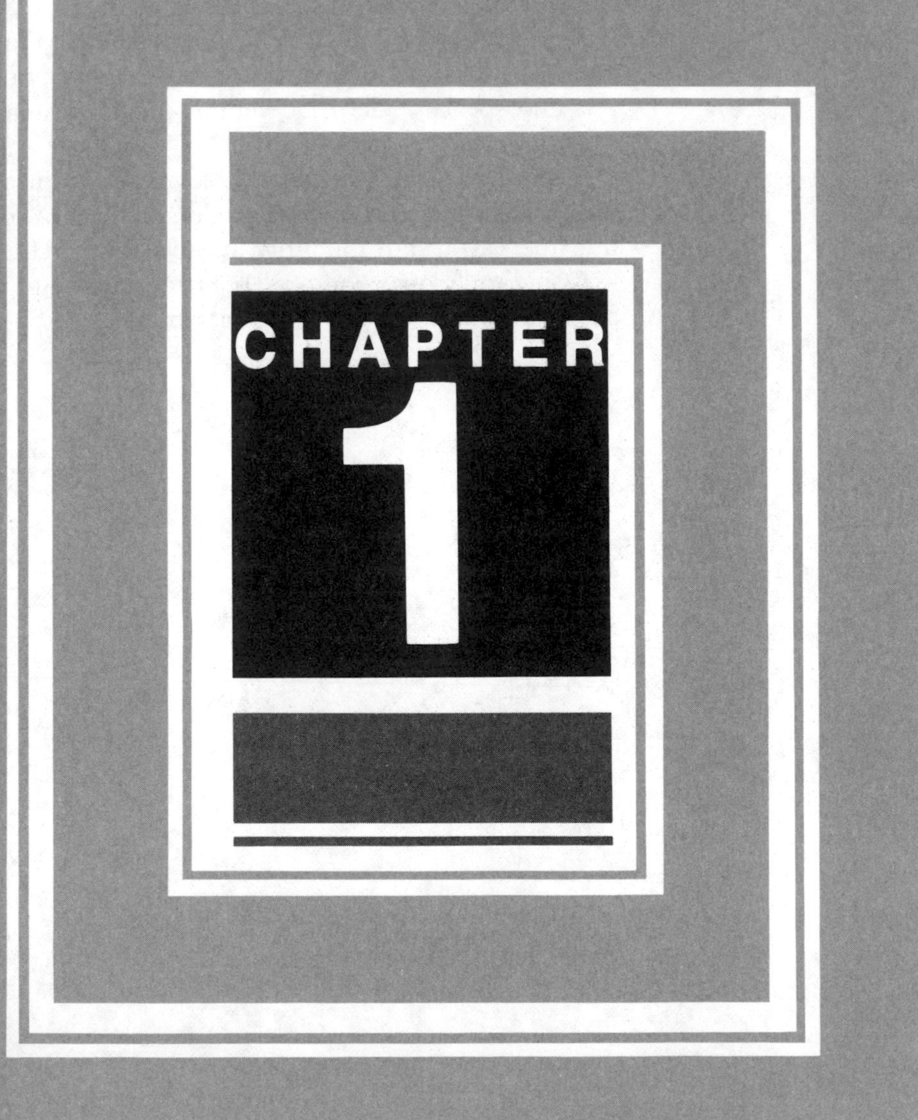
CHAPTER
1

Getting Started

Fast Track

Before using Ventura 4

you must install the program. If you have not already installed Ventura, refer to Appendix A.

To start Ventura 4

you type **VP** at the system prompt. If you have the Professional Extension, type **VPPROF**. Doing so displays Ventura's main screen.

To use the mouse 5

you move the mouse, and the mouse cursor moves on the screen in a corresponding fashion. You can click the mouse (press and release the button) or drag the mouse (press the button and hold it while moving).

Ventura's two cursors 5

are the mouse cursor and the text cursor. The mouse cursor comes in a variety of shapes. The text cursor is a slender vertical bar. You use the text cursor to enter text at the keyboard.

Ventura's main screen 9

is divided into

- the working area, where your document appears.
- the Side-bar, including the Mode selector, the Addition button, the Assignment list, and the Current box.
- scroll bars, which you use to move displayed material.
- the Title bar, which displays the name of the document and the style sheet.
- the Menu line, which you use to initiate procedures.

Dialog boxes 16

spring from certain commands on the drop-down menus. You can click buttons in the dialog boxes or use pop-up menus by pressing and holding the mouse. To register your choices, you generally click OK or press the Enter key.

Use Item Selector boxes 20

to indicate the files that you want to use in Ventura. You can fill in the fields lines yourself, or you can use the mouse to change directories and select your files.

In Frame mode 25

you create and manipulate frames—Ventura's containers for text and pictures. You can move frames with the mouse or with the Frame menu's Sizing & Scaling.

In Paragraph mode 27

you assign paragraph attributes to tags. Tags are Ventura's components that format paragraphs. Paragraphs sharing the same tag receive the same attributes.

In Text mode 28

you edit and enter text as you would with a word processor. However, Ventura's editing capabilities are less extensive than those of a word processor. You can also use text mode to change text attributes, and to cut, copy, and paste text.

In Graphics mode 29

you create and manipulate graphics directly within Ventura.

To use the four modes 29

you activate the appropriate mode, select the element that you wish to change (frame, paragraph, text, or graphic), and effect the change from the Assignment list, menu, or keyboard.

CHAPTER 1

VENTURA IS QUITE A SOPHISTICATED PROGRAM. Fortunately for us, its structure is exquisitely designed to give users *intuitive* access to the program's features; that is, the program operates in a fashion that seems natural and flows logically. Ventura's commands, for example, are categorized in menus whose names are easy to remember and locate. The menus have straightforward, descriptive names, such as Chapter and Paragraph. As you continue to work with Ventura, you may find yourself guessing the way in which an operation will perform, even before you learn it.

The first step in developing an understanding of the program's operations is to learn how they are compartmentalized. Ventura is divided into four *operating modes,* only one of which is active at any given time. The active mode controls the manner in which Ventura behaves and the way the screen looks to you, the user.

The purpose of this chapter is to give you an overview of the workings of Ventura. That way, you'll have a chance to explore the Ventura screen and see how the program's features operate before you actually try them out. As part of this overview, we'll provide you with a short tour of Ventura's four modes of operation.

STARTING VENTURA

If you have not yet installed Ventura, refer to Appendix A for instructions, and then return here.

* If you have the Ventura Professional Extension type **VPPROF** to load the program (see Chapter 13).

- Load Ventura from the root directory of your hard disk by typing

  VP

  at your system prompt and hitting the Enter key. The screen shown in Figure 1.1 appears, with the mouse cursor in the center of the screen.

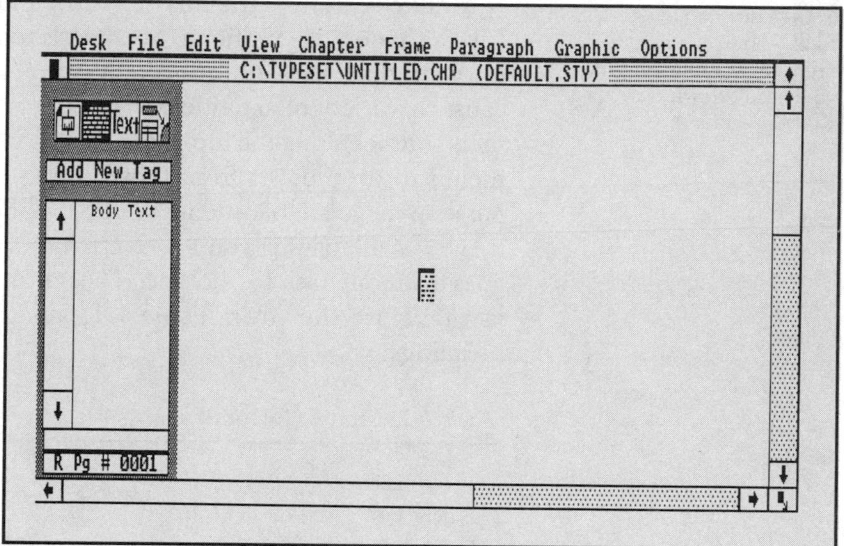

Figure 1.1: The main screen (without the Professional Extension)

If you or others have used Ventura on your computer you may see differences in the screen. For example, the panel on the left side may not appear; you can correct this by typing Ctrl-T. If necessary, see Appendix A for more information.

VENTURA'S TWO CURSORS

Ventura makes liberal use of the mouse.

- Try moving the mouse around.

You'll see an indicator on the screen moving in a corresponding fashion. This indicator, which Ventura calls a *mouse cursor,* changes shape depending on the operation of the program. We'll look at mouse shapes as we study Ventura's screen later in this chapter.

Ventura has two cursors, the mouse cursor and the text cursor. These two cursors act as your servants throughout the program. They open doors to Ventura's commands, so you can see what's available and instruct the program to do your bidding.

*You can change Ventura's menus from the drop-down type to the pull-down type. See Appendix A.

You've seen how the mouse cursor moves all around the screen. Like a shadow, its motion corresponds to movements that you make on your desk with the mouse. With a sometimes jerky action, it causes a variety of activities to occur. For example, as it passes over menu names along the top of the screen, it causes their corresponding menus to drop down from those names like a window shade. As it passes over available menu items, it darkens them, indicating that they're available for you to select. Also, its own shape changes as it goes from one task to another. The various shapes the mouse cursor can take are shown in Table 1.1, along with a summary of their meanings.

Table 1.1: Mouse Cursor Shapes

Mouse Cursor Shapes	Mode	Operation
+	Frame	
FR	Frame	Add new frame
	Frame	Resize frame
	Frame	Crop image
✥	Frame	Move frame
	Paragraph	
I	Text	
	Graphics	
Te	Graphics	Box text
	Graphics	Line drawing
⊕	Graphics	Circle drawing
┌	Graphics	Rectangle drawing
╭	Graphics	Rounded rectangle drawing
⊠	Waiting	

Note: The mouse cursor changes to ↖ when you make selections from pull-down menus, dialog boxes, and the Side-bar.

The other cursor in Ventura is the *text cursor* (or *keyboard cursor*). This cursor operates in a more staid manner than the mouse cursor. Its shape is always that of a slender vertical bar (see Figure 1.2), which blinks at certain times and at other times stays constant. The purpose of this cursor is straightforward. As you type at the keyboard, it simply marks the point at which the letters, numbers, and other characters that you type appear. To move the text cursor without entering characters, you use the arrow keys on the right side of the keyboard.

Although the mouse and text cursors differ completely in the way they perform, they cooperate fully and complement each other's activities. In fact, when you are working with one, the other often disappears. Like perfect servants, though, they return to the screen the moment you need them.

! New for Version 2.0

You can move the mouse cursor during loading and printing operations. In earlier versions of Ventura, the mouse froze until the operation was completed, making Ventura seem unresponsive.

USING THE MOUSE

In Ventura, you use the mouse to accomplish a wide range of tasks. Even if your mouse has more than one button, however, you'll use only the one on the left.

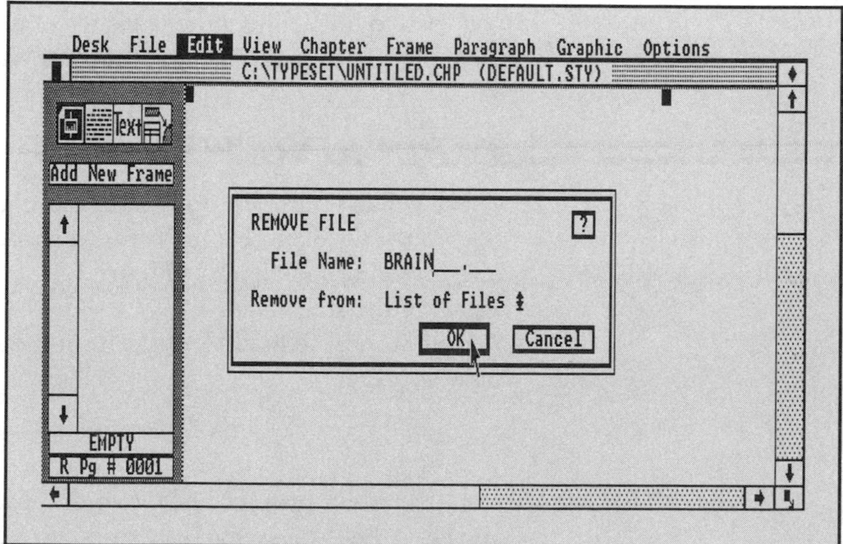

Figure 1.2: Using the text cursor to type a file name

You can use the mouse to select a designated item or feature by pointing to a choice on the screen and pushing the mouse button. Pushing and releasing the mouse button is often referred to as *clicking* the mouse. Pointing the mouse cursor at a choice and pushing the mouse button to select it is called *clicking the choice.*

To try it:

1. Move the mouse cursor to the four small boxes near the upper-left corner of your screen.
2. Click the mouse on each one in turn.

Notice how the screen changes as you click your choice. Later in this chapter, you'll learn what each of these choices means.

You can also use the mouse cursor to indicate where you wish to type next. By pointing to a certain spot and clicking, you can cause the text cursor to appear there. As you then start to type, your typing appears in that spot.

For other effects, you'll use a technique called *dragging* the mouse. To drag the mouse, you point to one spot and press the mouse button down. Then, with your finger still holding the mouse button down, you move the mouse to another location. When you reach the appropriate location, you release the mouse button. This action affects the area between the two points in some manner. For instance, should you wish to underline some text previously typed in, you would drag the mouse to indicate the text that you want underlined.

EXPLORING THE MAIN SCREEN

Let's take a moment to look at the main Ventura screen and see how to use it for access to Ventura's many features. Refer to your own screen or look back at Figure 1.1 as we discuss the different elements of the screen.

Remember, to load Ventura from the root directory of your hard disk, you type

```
VP
```

at your system prompt and press the Enter key. (Type **VPPROF** if you have the Professional Extension version.) Ventura's main screen appears.

THE WORKING AREA

The screen's main blank space is the *working area.* This is the area in which you'll lay out your document and see it take shape. It's here that you'll indicate your columns, insert your headlines and titles, position your illustrations, and view the results as you compose your document.

Besides the text cursor, there are six unusual symbols that you may encounter in the working area. They are shown in Table 1.2, and they will be explained in detail when they are first encountered.

THE SIDE-BAR

* You can have Ventura display the Side-bar or make it disappear with Ctrl-W on the Options menu. See Appendix A.

To the left of the working area is a panel with several boxes inside it. This area is the *Side-bar.*

THE MODE SELECTOR The first area of the Side-bar is the *Mode selector.* It consists of the four small boxes or *buttons* with which you were experimenting earlier in this chapter. We'll use the term *button* to describe any labeled box that you can use to change something. You "push" a button by pointing to it with the mouse and clicking. Generally, this causes the button to darken. Note that most button labels are short, as suits a button, but some are not; button labels can be up to a sentence in length.

The buttons of the Mode selector indicate which operating mode of Ventura is operating at any moment. A darkened button indicates the mode that is currently in effect or *active.* Earlier, when you were clicking these buttons, you were actually changing the operating mode—*activating* one mode or another. Later you'll see that there are other ways to change the operating mode. As you change the active mode, much of the Side-bar changes as well (Figure 1.3).

THE ADDITION BUTTON Below the mode selector is the *Addition button.* What appears inside it varies depending upon which mode is active.

- Click the different Mode selector buttons and see what happens to the Addition button.

Table 1.2: Working Area Symbols

SYMBOL ON THE SCREEN	NAME IN THE CURRENT BOX	HOW CREATED
¶	Paragraph End	Enter Key
↵ or ◄	Line Break	Ctrl-Enter
► or →	Horizontal Tab	Tab Key
	End of File	(Automatically)
␣	NoBreak Space	Ctrl-Space
	Em Space	Ctrl-Shift-M
	En Space	Ctrl-Shift-N
	Thin Space	Ctrl-Shift-T
	Figure Space	Ctrl-Shift-F
°	Box Character	Edit menu's Insert Special Item
	Footnote	Edit menu's Insert Special Item
	Index Entry	Edit menu's Insert Special Item
	Fraction	Edit menu's Insert Special Item
	Frame Anchor	Edit Menu's Insert Special Item
	Reference	Edit menu's Insert Special Item

As Figure 1.3 shows, it may say "Add New Frame," "Add New Tag," or "Set Font." You use the Addition button to add various elements to the document you're formatting in the working area.

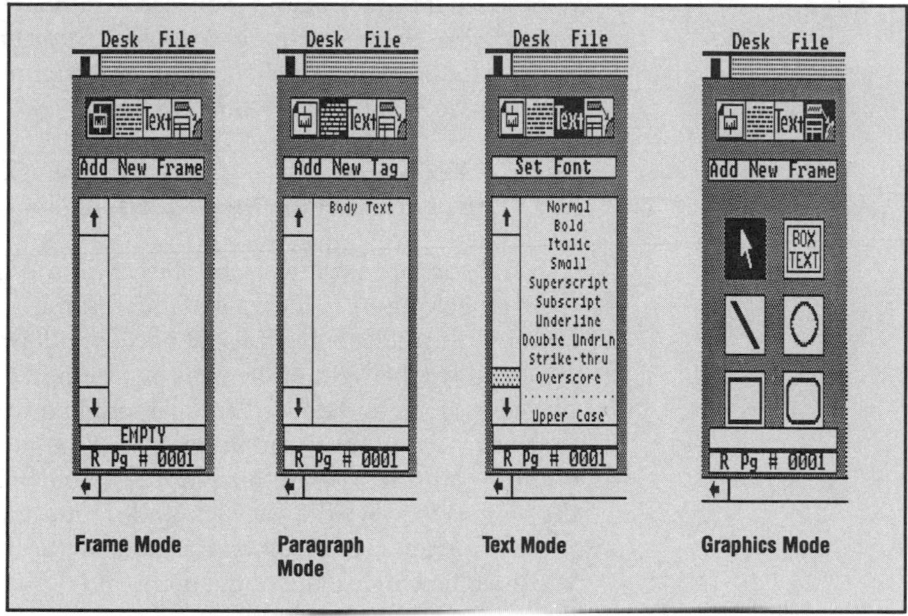

Figure 1.3: How the Side-bar changes with the operating mode

THE ASSIGNMENT LIST Generally, when you use the Addition button, you do so in conjunction with the elements that appear in the area below it. This area is called the *Assignment list.* A listing of the items that are available for assigning appears in this box.

The kinds of choices available depend upon the mode that's active. You may see the names of text files, paragraph tags that are available for formatting, or text attributes such as italic, bold, and underline. The Assignment list is not present when Graphics mode is active. We'll discuss the contents of the Assignment list further when we examine the various modes in detail.

SCROLL BARS To the left of the Assignment list is a *scroll bar.* You use scroll bars to bring hidden material into view. When the total number of available choices exceeds that which the Assignment list can accommodate, you can use the scroll bar to move the list up and down in order to view and select additional items.

A scroll bar with a shaded area indicates that there is more available than meets the eye. The amount of white area (as opposed to shaded) shows the relative amount that the display occupies as opposed to the amount that is unseen in either direction. If there is no shaded area, there is nothing to scroll. A scroll bar with a shaded area appears if there are enough items in the Assignment list that they cannot all be seen without scrolling.

- Observe the scroll bar next to the Assignment list as you click the buttons of the Mode selector.

Scroll bars appear in various places within Ventura. For instance, there are scroll bars to the right of the working area as well as below it. If you can't see the entire page at once, you'll want to use the vertical scroll bar (to the right of the working area). This bar moves the displayed page up and down. Vertical scrolling will probably be necessary unless you have a monitor with a large display, such as the Genius. You'll use the horizontal scroll bar (at the bottom of the screen) to move the page left and right as necessary.

The operation of scroll bars is similar throughout the program. We'll see how to use them in a moment.

THE CURRENT BOX The *Current box* appears below the Assignment list. It shows the current status of some elements in Ventura. Its contents, like those of the Assignment list, vary depending upon the active mode.

Note that the Current box is not a button, but simply an *indicator*; its contents are for display purposes only. You can't change the Current box by clicking it, as you can a button.

The top half of the Current box provides information about the current *selection.* As dictated by the mode, it identifies the contents of the frame, paragraph, text, or graphic that you have chosen to work on.

The bottom half of the Current box gives you information about the page that you have displayed in the working area. It indicates the page number and whether it is a left or right page.

THE TITLE BAR AND THE MENU LINE

The *Title bar* appears just above the working area. The Title bar displays the name of the *chapter* that's on the screen, along with the disk drive and directory that store it. Chapters are described in detail in Chapter 2. For now, it's enough to know that a chapter is a file that keeps track of everything in a Ventura document, such as word-processed and picture files. Until you assign a name, Ventura calls the document UNTITLED.CHP.

The Title bar also shows, in parentheses, the name of the *style sheet* you've assigned to the document. (You'll learn about style sheets in Chapter 4.) With a new chapter, Ventura initially assigns for you the same style sheet that you were last using.

At the right end of the Title bar is a small box called the *Full box.* This box and the box at the bottom-right corner of the screen (called the *Size box*) do operate, but they serve no useful purpose. They change the size of Ventura's display area (and you can use the Title bar to move a reduced Ventura display around the screen). Perhaps future versions of Ventura will make productive use of these boxes, which are vestiges of the GEM interface.

At the very top of the screen, the *Menu line* (Desk, File, Edit, View, and so on) displays the names of nine drop-down menus that you can expose with the mouse. This Menu line provides your main entrée into the operations of Ventura.

DROP-DOWN MENUS AND ASSOCIATED FEATURES

- Move the mouse cursor up to the Menu line.

It will take on an arrow shape. As long as the screen isn't displaying a *dialog box* or an *Item Selector box* (both of which we'll discuss shortly), the mouse arrow activates the drop-down menus associated with each of the names on the Menu line.

In this section we'll examine these menus and see how they operate. We'll also examine some commands, shortcuts, and other features that work hand-in-glove with these menus.

DROP-DOWN MENUS

Ventura's menus are called drop-down menus because they seem to drop-down from the menu name that you point at with the mouse.

- Point your mouse cursor at the word *File* on the Menu line.

Remember that you can specify drop-down or pull-down menus. Drop-down menus appear any time the mouse cursor is moved to the Menu line at the top of the screen. Pull-down menus appear only when the mouse button is depressed with the cursor positioned on the menu line. See Appendix A for more information. This book assumes that you are using drop-down menus, the method Ventura initially installs.

The File drop-down menu appears, as shown in Figure 1.4. The Addition button and Assignment list may be different from the one shown in Figure 1.4 if a different mode is active or a different style sheet is loaded.

Once a drop-down menu appears, you can use the mouse cursor—an arrow—to select one of the offered choices, which we'll call *commands*.

- Move the arrow down the drop-down menu.

Every command in dark letters will cause a darkened bar to appear as the mouse arrow passes in front of it. The commands that are not displayed in dark letters, New and Abandon, will not trigger a darkened bar. These commands are *ghosting*. You'll learn about this term shortly. To choose a darkened command, you click the mouse button.

- Move the arrow to the Save command on the File drop-down menu.

Notice how it is darkened and standing by, ready for selection (Figure 1.5).

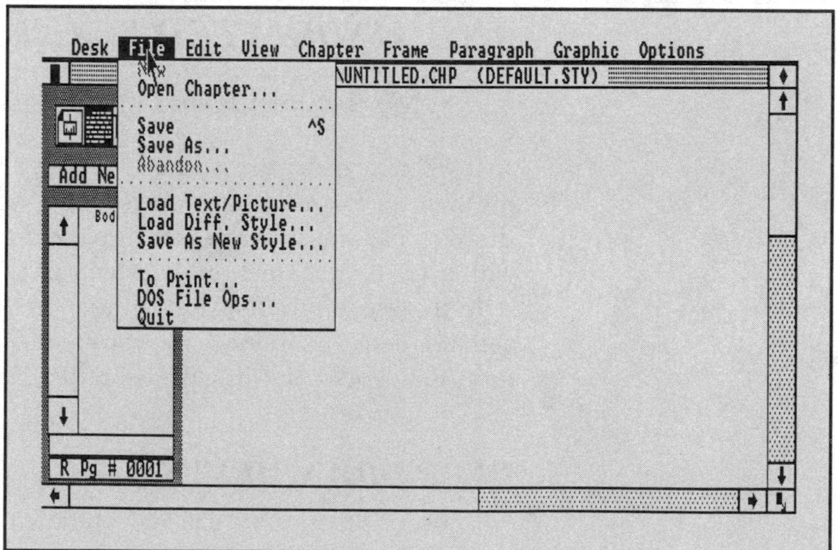

Figure 1.4: Activating a drop-down menu

KEYBOARD SHORTCUTS Notice, too, that ^S appears to the right of the darkened Save choice. This ^S is an abbreviation for Ctrl-S, a *keyboard shortcut.* Several of Ventura's commands have such shortcuts, which you may prefer to use.

Thus, in order to execute the Save command, you can drop down the File menu and click Save with the mouse, or you can simply type Ctrl-S at the keyboard. Both methods accomplish the same thing. The table on the inside front and back covers of this book shows Ventura's keyboard shortcuts alongside their drop-down menu counterparts.

GHOSTING ITEMS As you move the cursor arrow across the various items on the Menu line, you'll notice that some commands on the drop-down menus are lighter in type than others, and that as you move the mouse cursor over these lighter items, they do not darken as the others do. Such lighter items are sometimes said to be *ghosting.*

A ghosting item simply indicates that the item is not currently available for you to choose. This may be due to a variety of conditions. As you change the surrounding circumstances, the ghosting

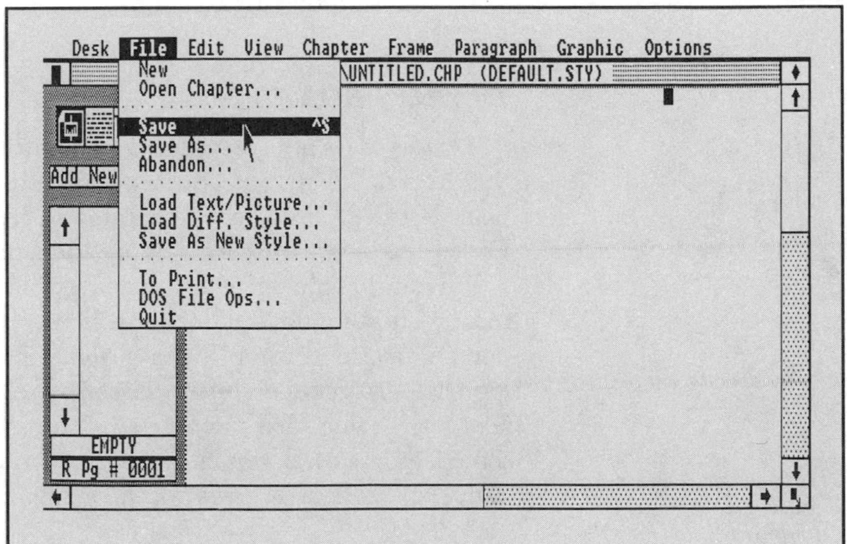

Figure 1.5: Selecting from a drop-down menu

item will appear in normal type, indicating that it is available for you to select.

For example, the New and Abandon commands in Figure 1.4 are ghosting. You use the New command to start work on a new document and the Abandon command to abandon the work you've done. Since you haven't started work on a document, you can't start work on a new one, and you can't abandon work since you haven't done any. Hence the two commands are unavailable and ghosting.

CLOSING DROP-DOWN MENUS If you decide you want to use a drop-down menu other than the one you've opened, just point the mouse cursor at the desired menu name (such as Edit) on the Menu line. The new menu will open and the old menu will close.

If you wish to close a menu without opening a new one, click the mouse when it's not pointing at a darkened (available) command. Thus, you can be pointing anywhere outside the drop-down menu, at any ghosting command, or somewhere between commands, in order to close a menu.

- Try closing the File menu on your screen.

DIALOG BOXES

A *dialog box* is a display that is generated by certain commands on the drop-down menus. Such commands are indicated by ellipsis points—three dots after the command (as in *Page Size & Layout...*). Dialog boxes let you select features and customize their operation.

! New for version 2.0

Previously, dialog boxes displayed all options for each feature, merely ghosting the options for which you hadn't clicked the corresponding feature button. Many users suggested redesigning the dialog boxes to reduce clutter and more clearly delineate Ventura's features. Dialog boxes in Version 2.0 hide the options available for some features until you click a corresponding feature button. Alternatively, Ventura displays pop-up arrows that lead to pop-up menus.

* You can make the pop-up arrows (↕) disappear from the dialog boxes. See Appendix A.

- Drop the Chapter menu and click Page Size & Layout.

You will see the Page Layout dialog box (Figure 1.6). Within it, you can view, choose, or change the various settings that affect the layout of the page.

New for Version 2.0

CHANGING POP-UP SETTINGS IN A DIALOG BOX You can use the Page Layout dialog box to see how pop-up settings operate. The dialog box indicates the current settings of various features. To change one of the features, you point the mouse cursor to the left of the pop-up arrow (↕). Then you press the mouse and hold. The pop-up menu will appear, with a check mark indicating the current setting. The setting you point to will darken. To change, point to a different setting and release the mouse.

Changing a setting will undo a different setting within the same category. For example, in the Page Layout dialog box, you could change the paper type from letter size to legal size by pointing to Letter, pressing and holding while you move the mouse to Legal, and releasing the mouse button. The Legal setting would appear for Paper Type & Dimension. (The page dimensions, shown after the word *Letter* or *Legal,* would automatically change as well.)

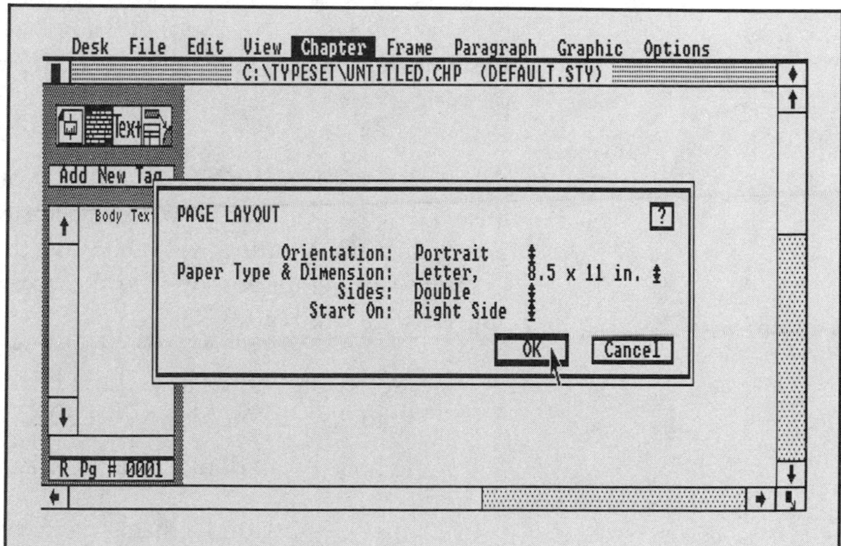

Figure 1.6: The Page Layout dialog box

New for version 2.0

Use the ? box to display and use Ventura's new Help pop-up menu. When you press and hold the ? box, you see several topics—related to the dialog box—pop up. For example, in this dialog box the topics are

General Info
Paper Type & Dimension
Sides
Start On

Drag the mouse to one of the topics and release to see a dialog box with some descriptive information on the topic.

- Use the ? box and display General Info about the Page Layout dialog box.
- After viewing the information, click OK or press the enter key to redisplay the Page Layout dialog box.

GIVING THE OK Once you change the settings, they don't take effect until you *give the OK*. Generally, there are two ways to do that. You can point to the OK button and click the mouse, or you can press the Enter key on the keyboard. Both methods register the features as you've set them in the dialog box. The heavy outline of the OK button indicates that clicking the button does the same thing as pressing Enter.

CANCELING YOUR CHANGES If you decide you don't want to make any changes after all, you can click the Cancel button instead of giving the OK. Ventura will then leave the settings in the dialog box as they were before you opened the box; that is, any resetting that you've done will not take place.

1. Go ahead and change some of the Page Layout settings on your screen, but don't click OK or press Enter.
2. When you're done, click the Cancel button.

New for version 2.0

Pressing Ctrl-X within a dialog box is the same as clicking Cancel. Pressing Ctrl-X when Ventura is not displaying a dialog box recalls the last active dialog box.

DISAPPEARING BUTTONS Consider another property of dialog boxes.

- Drop the File menu and select the Load Text/Picture option by clicking it.

You see the dialog box shown in Figure 1.7. Only one Type Of File button is darkened at a time. Depending on which one you click, the button in the grouping below them disappears and others appear. Often, previous selections you've made in the same dialog box determine which items are available. Ventura sometimes indicates unavailable buttons by ghosting, as we saw with the File menu. In Figure 1.7, the Text Cursor button is ghosting.

In the first group of choices, Type Of File is set for Text. For that reason, the Text Format grouping (Generated, ASCII, WordStar 3, and so on) appears. You can click any of these buttons. If, however, you set Type Of File to Line-Art, the grouping for Line-Art Format (GEM, AutoCAD .SLD, Lotus .PIC, and so on) will appear in place of the Text Format grouping, indicating that these new choices are now available to you.

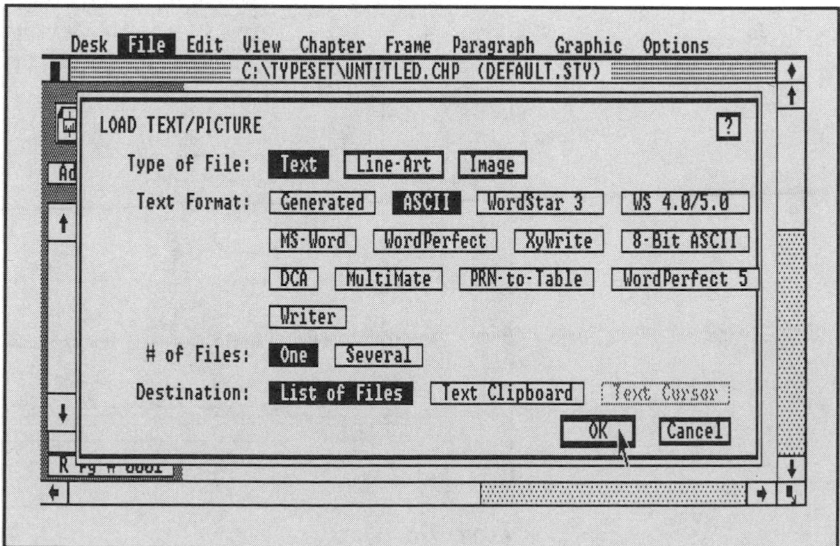

Figure 1.7: The File menu's Load Text/Picture dialog box

To experiment with this property of dialog boxes:

- Check what happens when you click the Image button.

ITEM SECTOR BOXES

Ventura also has a display that it calls the *Item Selector box.* An Item Selector box is very much like a dialog box. However, rather than showing settings for Ventura's features, an Item Selector box lists the names of files that are in a directory of your disk.

- In the Load Text/Picture dialog box, click Type Of File: Text and give the OK.

You see the Item Selector box shown in Figure 1.8. You use this box to retrieve a file of the type you've specified with the Load Text/ Picture dialog box. The Item Selector list will also display the names of available directories. A diamond-shaped character (◆) precedes directory names.

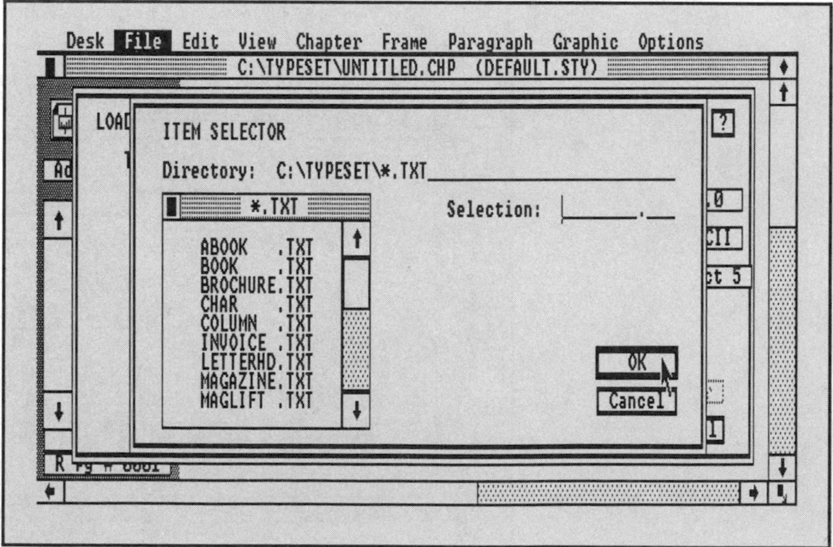

Figure 1.8: The Item Selector box

There are two ways to make a choice using the Item Selector box. You can use the "fill-in-the-blanks" method or the multiple-choice method. (These two techniques also work with many dialog boxes.)

THE FILL-IN-THE-BLANKS METHOD To fill in the blanks, you use the text cursor—the thin vertical bar that appears on one of the *fields* (horizontal fill-in lines) in the Item Selector box. (In Figure 1.8, the text cursor is to the right of the word *Selection.*) As you type at the keyboard, the characters you type appear at the text cursor.

One at a time, you can erase characters that appear in the field by pressing the Backspace key. You can wipe out all characters that are in a field by pressing the Esc key. Without erasing, you can move the text cursor back and forth over characters that appear by using the ← and → keys on the numeric keypad at the right of your keyboard.

You move the text cursor from one field to another in any of several ways. You can use the Tab key or the ↓ key on the keypad to move to the next field. To move back to the previous field, you can press the ↑ key or Shift-Tab.

You cannot use the Enter key to move to the next field, as you can with some programs. As in dialog boxes, pressing Enter has the effect of giving the OK to the selections that you've made.

You can also relocate the text cursor by using the arrow-shaped mouse cursor. Just move the mouse cursor to the field where you wish the text cursor to appear and click the mouse button. The text cursor will appear at the end of the field.

THE MULTIPLE-CHOICE METHOD The other way to make an item selection is to use the mouse. Just point to the file you wish to choose and click. The item you've chosen darkens, as it does with dialog boxes. Simultaneously, your choice appears in the appropriate field. If you wish, you can then edit the field, as you would with the fill-in-the-blanks method.

* You can customize Ventura's BAT file to indicate the disk drives that should appear. See Appendix A.

To change directories or disk drives, you use the Backup button—the small black box to the top left of the Item Selector list. Clicking it causes the name of the directory to appear, along with other directories and possibly files side-by-side. Repeated clicking will display the disk drives, which you can then select by clicking.

Once your choices are made, you can give the OK in the same way that you do with dialog boxes; that is, you can either click the OK button or hit Enter.

You can adjust the speed at which double-clicking operates. See Appendix A.

There is a third way to give the OK to the Item Selector box. When you point to an item you wish to select, you can choose the item *and* give the OK by clicking it twice in rapid succession. We'll work with this technique, which is called *double-clicking,* in Chapter 2.

SCROLL BARS IN THE ITEM SELECTOR BOX

As mentioned, the choices available in Item Selector boxes are files on disk. However, you won't always be able to see the names of all the files that you can choose. To see additional files, you may need to use the scroll bar that appears at the right of the directory list. This scroll bar operates in the same manner as the scroll bar used to manipulate the Side-bar's Assignment list.

Now you'll see the scroll bar in action.

1. Bring the mouse cursor to the *Down button,* which is the box with the ↓ symbol at the bottom of the scroll bar. You use the Down button when you want to scroll down the list.
2. With the mouse cursor on the Down button, press the mouse button and hold it down.

You'll see the list of directories and files move up the box. Notice that as the list of file names moves up, the white area of the scroll bar, like a counterweight, moves down. This action can be a little disconcerting at first, but you'll grow used to it quickly. At the top of the scroll bar there is an Up button that you can use to scroll up the list. With this button, the action is reversed.

You can also move the list by dragging the scroll bar, rather than moving it with the Up and Down buttons.

1. Point to the white area of the scroll bar, press the mouse button, and hold it down.
2. Move the mouse cursor up or down.

As you do, you'll see a ghost of the white area move along with you. There will be no change in the directory display until you release the mouse button (when the ghost is at the new, desired position). At that moment, both the scroll bar and the file display will jump to the new position.

There is a third way to move a scroll bar.

- Click one of the shaded areas on the scroll bar.

The white area will jump in the direction you indicate, and the display will be relocated in that direction. Each click of the shaded area moves the white area a distance equal to the size of the white area.

- Click Cancel to return to the main screen.

This completes our examination of the main screen and the kinds of operations that can be performed from it. Now let's take a look at your keyboard and how it operates in Ventura.

THE VENTURA KEYBOARD

Despite Ventura's sophisticated capabilities, its use of the keyboard is rather simple and straightforward. See Table 1.3 for descriptions of the operation of the important keys. You'll learn more about these keys as you use them to work through the examples in this book.

THE FOUR OPERATING MODES

Ventura has four main modes of operation. At any time, the program will be operating in one of these four modes. Each mode affects most operations in many basic ways. (By the way, the mode that is active when you start a work session with Ventura will be the same mode that was active when you last quit.)

We'll study all techniques for changing the operating mode in Chapter 2 when we begin to work with Frame mode. But for the present, just remember that you can change or choose a mode by clicking the Mode selector buttons at the top of the Side-bar, as you did earlier in the chapter. We'll see later that you can also use a drop-down menu or the keyboard to change modes.

Table 1.3: Important Keys in Ventura

KEY	ACTION
Alt with the keypad	Creates special characters.
Alt with the mouse	Crops pictures and constrains graphics.
Arrow keys on the keypad	Move the text (keyboard) cursor.
Backspace	Erases text as it backs up.
Ctrl with the mouse	Selects hidden frames or graphics.
Ctrl with various keys	Activates commands or creates special characters.
Ctrl-Hyphen	Inserts a discretionary hyphen.
Ctrl-Enter	Starts a new line but not a new paragraph.
Ctrl-Right Shift	Allows directional arrows to move the mouse cursor.
Ctrl-Space	Creates a NoBreak Space (a space that prevents text on either side from breaking across lines).
Del	Deletes (cuts) text to the right of text cursor or selected material.
End	Displays the end of the chapter.
Esc	"Re-inks" the screen in the working area. Erases a displayed entry field. Interrupts printing or a GoTo operation.
Home	Displays the beginning of the chapter.
Ins	Inserts (pastes) text or other clipboard material.

Table 1.3: Important Keys in Ventura (continued)

KEY	ACTION
PgUp, PgDn	Display the previous and next page, respectively.
Enter	Starts a new paragraph.
Shift-← and Shift-→	Kern selected text.
Shift-↑ and Shift-↓	Change font size of selected text.
Shift-Del	Copies text or other selected material.
Shift with the mouse	Selects multiple elements. Adds multiple frames or graphics.
Tab	Moves to the next tab stop in the paragraph or, in a dialog box, next field line.

Each of the four buttons of the Mode selector corresponds to one of the modes we'll now examine in turn. The first is Frame mode.

FRAME MODE

To lay out and set the various text and graphic elements of your documents, Ventura allows you to divide each page into box-shaped areas of varying dimensions. These areas are called *frames.* To create these frames, and to manipulate them, you use *Frame Setting mode* or simply *Frame mode.* You switch into Frame mode by clicking the first (leftmost) button on the Mode selector.

Once you create a frame, you can place text or a picture within it. Unless you choose to outline it, the frame itself is invisible when you print the document. All you see are its contents. Thus the elements that make up a page appear to be seamlessly integrated.

On the other hand, if you wish to outline the frame in your final document, you can have up to three lines above, below, or within the periphery of the frame. You can set the thickness and spacing of these lines in any way you wish. There is a great deal of flexibility in creating lines; we'll work with them in Chapter 7. You can also shade the background of a frame.

THE UNDERLYING-PAGE FRAME Initially, each page consists of a single frame. This main frame is the size of the page. Imagine pasting down on a page by conventional means; you would paste all other *standard frames* on top of this one. For this reason, the main frame is called the *underlying-page frame.* (By "standard frame," we mean any frame that is not the underlying-page frame.)

As you view the screen, you can imagine the underlying-page frame as being at the bottom—that is, farthest away from you, the viewer. You can place standard frames on top of it (closer to you). There is no apparent limit to the number of frames you can stack in this manner.

In many respects, the underlying-page frame is just a frame like the standard frames that might be laid on top of it. Many of the settings for Frame mode apply both to the underlying-page frame and to standard frames. In other ways, however, the underlying-page frame is special and different from standard frames. For instance, if you assign a text file to the underlying page frame, Ventura will generate as many pages as necessary to display all the text in the file. If, however, you assign a text file to a standard frame, Ventura will only display as much of the file as the frame allows.

MARGINS AND COLUMNS Each frame can contain up to eight columns. This holds true for the underlying-page frame as well as for any frame on top of it. Should it be necessary to create additional columns, you can add more standard frames, side by side, as the paper allows.

You can also specify margins for either kind of frame. Text will not appear in these areas of the frame.

You'll learn how to set margins and columns for your own documents in Chapter 2.

MOVING FRAMES There are two ways to relocate or change the size of a standard frame. One way is to grab the frame with the mouse and move the mouse. You can also drop down the Frame menu and change the various settings in the Sizing & Scaling dialog box. We'll see how to do this in Chapter 2.

IMPORTING PICTURES Ventura has the ability to import pictures into frames. You can create graphic designs with a variety of programs—AutoCAD or Publisher's Paintbrush, for instance. Or you can create graphic designs with a scanner. You can then use Frame mode to display the file you created with the graphics program. As mentioned earlier, any changes you make will not affect the original artwork.

PARAGRAPH MODE

The second of Ventura's operational modes is *Paragraph Tagging mode* or simply *Paragraph mode.* We'll study tagging in Chapter 4. Paragraphs, along with text attributes, constitute the main building blocks for formatting with Ventura.

You switch into Paragraph mode by clicking the second button from the left on the Mode Selector. Paragraph formatting controls the alignment (justification, indentation, and so on), tab settings, spacing, and other attributes of chunks of text. The size of these chunks is generally about the size of a paragraph. However, each chunk simply ends with a return; you do not have to use true paragraphs as these formatting components. A series of short lines—such as an address, for instance—may qualify as a paragraph for the purpose of formatting.

Alignment is one of the attributes handled with paragraph tags. This feature determines if a paragraph is ragged, justified, or centered. It can also indent (or outdent) the first line of each paragraph automatically. Spacing is another feature Ventura can set automatically; you set the distance between characters, lines, and paragraphs once, and Ventura adjusts all similar paragraphs simultaneously. Tab settings are also handled with paragraph tags, although there are other ways to create tables, as you'll see in Chapter 8.

In addition, paragraph tagging governs whether a paragraph should be kept together (not split between the bottom of one column and the top of the next, for instance). You can also use tagging to create lines or boxes around paragraphs, as you can with frames.

Initially, Ventura assigns a tag with the name *body text* to all paragraphs in the text. All the attributes that you assign to the body-text tag will affect all the paragraphs so designated. You can tag paragraphs with other paragraph tags that you create or that Ventura Publisher has created for you already. All paragraphs with the same tag will share the attributes that you have assigned. In Paragraph mode, tags appear in the Assignment list in the Side-bar. You assign them from the list with the mouse.

Ventura has two tools to assist in the tagging procedure. First, you can assign the ten function keys to various paragraph tags. Second, you (or others writing articles for you) can assign the tag directly with your word processor as you create or edit the text. You do this by typing in a special code along with the tag's name. Paragraph tagging is discussed in Chapter 4, and tagging with the word processor appears in Chapter 11.

TEXT MODE

As you work with Ventura, you're certain to find that you need to edit the text that appears on your pages. You can use your word processor to make the changes in the original text files. Alternatively, you can use Ventura's *Text mode* to edit. You switch into Text mode by clicking the third button from the left on the Mode selector.

The technique for editing is simple. Once you activate Text mode, you use the mouse cursor to place the text cursor in the text. Then you simply edit from the keyboard.

One beautiful aspect of Text mode is that as you type and eventually save the document, the changes you make are made in the original word-processed files as well. Thus, for instance, if you need to search for a string (remember that Ventura has no search capabilities), you can simply switch to your word processor and use its search command to find the string. Using a word processor to work on Ventura files is discussed in Chapter 11.

You can use Text mode to change some text *attributes,* such as boldface, italics, underline, and so on, for text that you designate. (Alternatively, you can use your word processor to insert such formatting. Ventura will then convert the word processor's formatting to its own system, and vice versa.) You can also capitalize a whole block of text, such as the title of a table, automatically without retyping it. You can use Text mode to type in special characters, such as accents and em dashes. You can set fonts selectively and *kern* (change the distance between character pairs) as well.

You can even use Text mode to enter the original text. The original text for this book, for instance, was created using Ventura's Text mode (with help from SmartKey).

Finally, you can use Text mode for cut-and-paste applications. You can move or copy text to any place in the chapter or from chapter to chapter. Ventura does not confine cut-and-paste operations to Text mode, however. You can also move and copy frames along with all their attributes in Frame mode.

All of these operations that you can perform with Text mode are discussed in more detail throughout this book.

GRAPHICS MODE

As if its impressive text capabilities aren't enough, Ventura has graphics capabilities, too. You can use Graphics mode to create modest graphics directly in Ventura. Often, publishers use these graphics to spruce up imported graphics. To switch into Graphics mode, you click the fourth (rightmost) button on the Mode selector. Ventura's graphics capabilities are discussed in Chapters 6 and 7.

USE OF THE FOUR MODES

Throughout Ventura, there is a consistent approach in the use of the various modes. To accomplish much of your work with the program, you'll find that you generally follow these steps:

1. Activate the appropriate mode (Frame, Paragraph, Text, Graphics).
2. Select the particular item that you wish to change; that is, use the mouse to click the appropriate frame, paragraph, piece of text, or graphic as it appears in the working area.
3. Make the change you desire. You can do this in one of three ways, depending upon the nature of the change:
    - Click the correct item on the Assignment list in the Side-bar.

- Activate a drop-down menu and make a selection from it.
- Use the keyboard.

! New for Version 2.0

You no longer need to tie graphics to a standard frame. Version 2.0 lets you select or draw a graphic tied to the underlying page frame. In addition, you can select frames and perform many frame operations with Graphics mode. This eliminates confusion and cuts down on time spent switching from mode to mode.

As we work with frames in the next chapter, you'll see Ventura's consistent approach in action. You'll see it in the work you perform with other modes as well. Now:

- Either exit Ventura by dropping down the File menu and clicking Quit, or go on to Chapter 2.

CHAPTER
2

Setting Up a Newsletter

Fast Track

A Ventura chapter 36

is the fundamental unit that you use to create a document. The chapter file coordinates other files, and multiple chapters combine to create a publication.

A style sheet 37

is a file that coordinates the typographic formatting characteristics of Ventura documents. It consists of modular formatting components called *tags,* which you assign by the paragraph. Style sheets also contain some fundamental page settings, such as the margins for the page.

To use a sample or other chapter file 41

load it using the Chapter menu's Open Chapter. Use the Item Selector box to display the TYPESET directory, and choose a file with the CHP extension.

To save a copy of the chapter file 46

you use the File menu's Save As. To save a copy of the style sheet, use the File menu's Save As New Style.

To select a frame 51

activate Frame mode, position the mouse within the frame, and click. The name of the file assigned to the selected frame appears in the Current box.

To set up margins and columns 55

activate Frame mode, select the frame whose margins and columns you wish to adjust, and select the Frame menu's Margins & Columns. In the resulting dialog box, click the button for the desired number of columns. Enter values for the column widths and gutters (distances between columns). Provide values for the space from the edge of the frame (or, with the underlying-page frame, from the edge of the page).

To create a new frame 64

activate Frame mode and click the Add New Frame button. Position the mouse at the desired top-left corner for the frame, drag to the bottom-right corner, and release. To add several new frames in succession, hold the Shift key as you add the frames, including the first one, and release it before creating the last one.

To relocate a frame with the mouse 66

position the mouse somewhere within the frame, drag to a new location, and release.

To resize a frame with the mouse 67

drag one of the frame's handles to a new location.

To relocate and resize a frame by providing values 69

use the Frame menu's Sizing & Scaling. Set Flow Text Around to On or Off. Set the X value for the distance of the frame from the left edge of the paper, the Y value for the distance of the frame from the top edge, and values for the frame's width and height. Set Horiz Padding and Vert Padding to keep surrounding text away from the edges of the frame.

To save a chapter 77

use the File menu's Save, or press Ctrl-S. To start work on a new chapter, select the File menu's New. To abandon changes you've made to a chapter and reload the previous version, use the File menu's Abandon. To quit, use the File menu's Quit.

CHAPTER 2

EFFECTIVE DESKTOP PUBLISHING CAN ORGANIZE SO many different elements that creating a complex newsletter is now a manageable task, even for nondesigners. With Ventura, you can align columns evenly, leapfrog stories over different pages, mix variably sized graphic and text elements, and number pages automatically. These elements, done right, can combine to catch the interest of readers, provide them with comprehensible copy, and create a coherent visual impression that stays with them long after they finish reading. Because of the variety of challenges a newsletter presents, its creation encapsulates many of the capabilities desktop publishing has to offer.

Designing a sophisticated newsletter has long been outside the realm of the conventional word processor. On the other hand, the prospect of doing it with scissors and glue is intimidating, to say the least. So up until recently, when it came to creating good-looking newsletters, the prospective do-it-yourselfer has done without or has had it done.

In this chapter we will begin to use frames to demarcate areas for a Ventura newsletter. Doing so will provide a good introduction to frames and how to use them. It will demonstrate how Ventura pours word-processed text to accommodate columns on the page automatically. It will also show how to make a copy of one of the standard chapters and style sheets provided with Ventura, in order to use them as a foundation for the design of your publication.

HOW CHAPTERS AND PUBLICATIONS COORDINATE MATERIAL

A *chapter* is Ventura's fundamental unit for coordinating files and other elements that go into creating a document. Multiple chapters combine together to make a *publication.* You can assign up to 128 files to a chapter or publication. Each chapter can contain up to 500 kilobytes of text.

To coordinate the composition of text and graphics, a *chapter file* locates the appropriate word-processed and picture files—as well as other files, such as one it uses to create and hold captions—on the disk. Then the chapter file positions their contents properly on the page. Figure 2.1 shows the relationship among these elements. (We'll discuss style sheets in a moment.) To hold and position these elements, Ventura uses containers that it calls *frames*. The chapter file presents the resulting page, consisting of frames that hold files, on the screen.

In turn, you (and Ventura) can then combine multiple chapters together. Ventura calls the resulting conglomeration a *publication*. In a publication, Ventura automatically coordinates printing of the various chapters.

This chapter will take you through the first steps in the creation of a newsletter. Remember, although you may consider your newsletter to be a "publication," in Ventura's terms it is a chapter.

STYLE SHEETS

A *style sheet* is a special kind of file that controls the formatting characteristics of a document that you prepare with Ventura. Unlike text and graphics files, style sheets are always created within Ventura, not some outside program. Every chapter must have a style sheet associated with it. However, more than one chapter can utilize the same style sheet. You can use the sample style sheets that Ventura provides or you can create your own. You can also customize the sample style sheets to suit your own needs. (See Appendix B to get a sense of what these style sheets are like.)

Style sheets contain specifications for such style elements as fonts, alignment, spacing, and tabs. You group these elements into modular components that Ventura calls *tags*. A group of tags, in turn, composes a style sheet. You can have up to 128 such tags to a style sheet.

Within your chapter, you assign tags by the paragraph. The name of a tag should signal the purpose of the paragraph. For instance, you may have tags for a headline, subheading, caption, and footnote. Every style sheet has at least one tag that is always present: Body

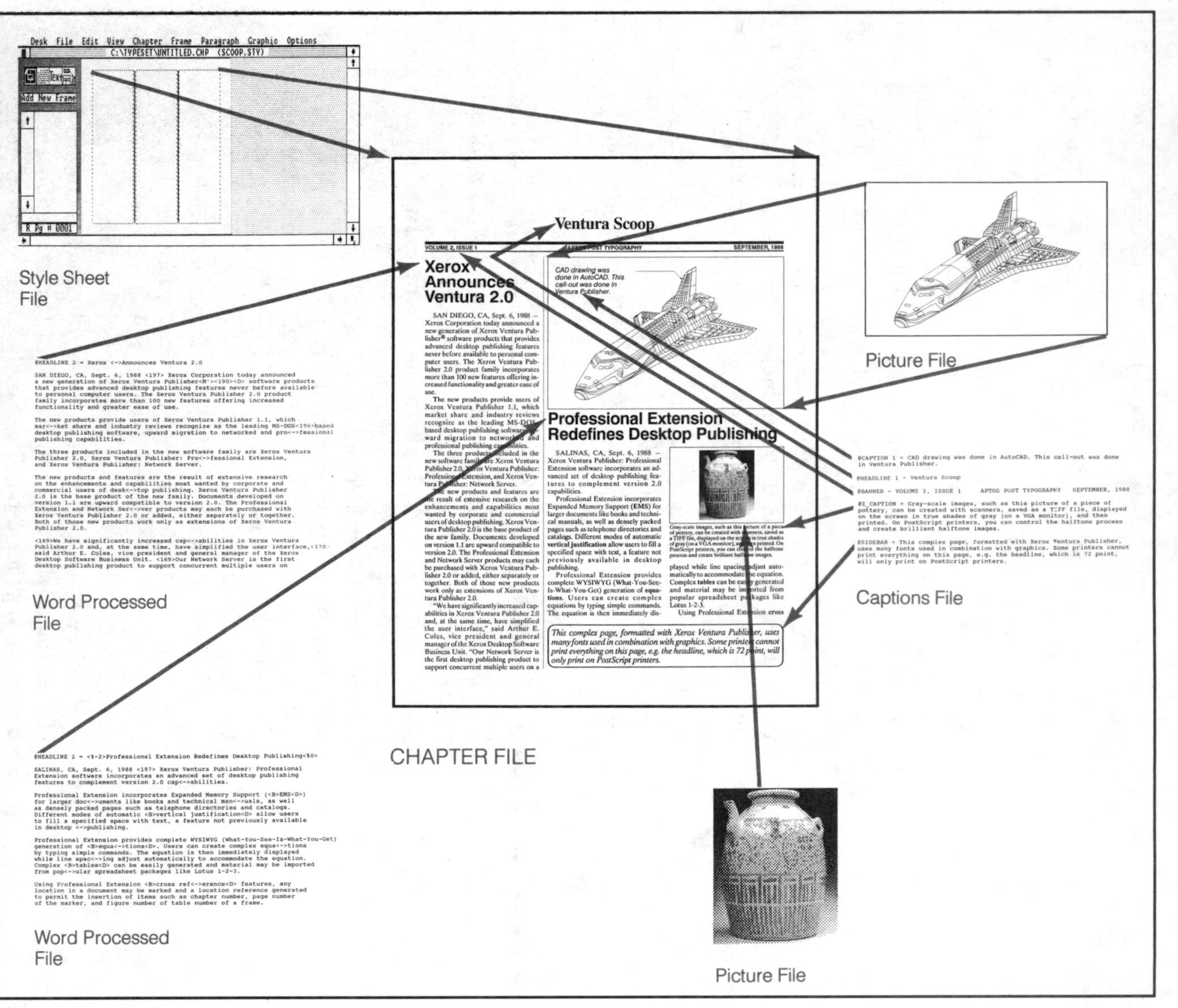

Figure 2.1: Chapters in Ventura

Text. You use this tag to format the most standard type of paragraph in the document.

By associating formats with tags, you guarantee a consistent format throughout your chapter. Each time the tag appears, the proper font size and style, paragraph alignment, spacing, and so on are set in place automatically. Style sheets also contain some fundamental page settings, such as margins and columns. Note that style-sheet file names have the STY extension unless you specify otherwise.

For now, you should not be concerned with creating or modifying style sheets. Our sample newsletter will use the style sheet that Ventura has assigned to it. As you work on the newsletter, observe how the style sheet governs the design of the Ventura chapter.

ADAPTING A SAMPLE

The first step in creating a good document with Ventura Publisher is to envision the final document in your mind's eye. Always have a good idea of where you are heading. It's especially important to consider how the pages will be laid out.

In this example, let's say that you want to create a newsletter on letter-size paper. This is because you want to copy the newsletter on your office copier, which has only letter and legal size, and you feel that letter size would be easier for your readers to grab and run with.

You want your newsletter to have a good-sized masthead at the top of the first page. You also plan to use headlines and subheads.

With Ventura you could create such a publication from scratch. You could select all the typefaces, column widths, margins, spacing, and so on, one by one.

However, you'll probably find chapter creation easiest, at least initially, if you build on the samples that come with the program. To do that, you just pick out one of the sample style sheets and one of the sample chapters and adapt them to suit your needs.

You can purchase an additional set of sample style sheets, direct from the author of *Mastering Ventura.* See the coupon at the back of this book.

The samples that come with the program are displayed in Appendix B. As you begin work on a new chapter, leaf through those samples. Find one that resembles the way you'd like your document to look. Then copy the sample and proceed to work on the duplicate.

Naming Conventions of Sample Style Sheets and Chapters Provided with Ventura

&NEWS-P2.STY

All files begin with the ampersand to identify them as samples provided with the program.

Three or four letters identify the use of the file as follows:

BOOK	Book
BRO	Brochure
INV	Invoice
LSTG	Listing
LTR	Letter
MAG	Magazine
NEWS	Newsletter
PHON	Phone listing
PREL	Press Release
PRPT	Proposal/Report
TBL	Table
TCHD or TDOC	Technical Document
VWGF	Viewgraph

Following the dash, one letter identifies the orientation of the paper:

P	Portrait (vertical)
L	Landscape (horizontal)

A single digit indicates the number of columns the underlying-page frame specifies. This sample has 2 columns.

Following the period, the extension identifies the type of file.

STY	Style sheet
CHP	Chapter

As you consider the sample, compare its purpose with yours. Take into account the page layout, type size and style, paragraph formats, and margins. Don't forget to consider your gut reaction to the style.

For this exercise, we'll say that you decide on the sample that's called &NEWS-P2.CHP, shown in Figure 2.2. It has the masthead and headline style you want, and it uses letter-size paper. Perhaps the small table of contents appeals to you, too.

LOADING A SAMPLE

It's important to protect the original samples against alteration. That way, if you want to use them again, they're sure to look like the samples in the back of this book. To accomplish this first important step, we'll make a copy of the samples we'll use, stored under different names.

The first thing you do is copy the sample chapter to a new file. Let's suppose that your publication is going to be called *The Brainstorm.* We'll call the new file BRAIN.CHP. Once the file is copied, you can substitute your headlines and articles for those in the sample.

You'll also want to copy the style sheet associated with the sample chapter, &NEWS-P2.STY. We'll assign the new style sheet the name BRAIN.STY. As you make formatting changes in the document, the new style sheet will store your specifications.

To make the copies of the sample chapter and style sheet, you first start Ventura. Then you load the original samples. Before you make any changes, save the chapter and the style sheet under new names. To perform these operations, proceed as follows:

1. If you quit Ventura at the end of Chapter 1, reload the program by typing:

   VP

   at the system prompt and hitting the Enter key. (Type **VPPROF** if you have the Professional Extension.)
2. From Ventura's main screen, point to File on the Menu line to drop down the File menu.

Widget World News

Views and News of Widget Manufacturing in the 80s

Software Salaries: How do you stack up?

by Joe Smith

How much your software professionals are paid is a function of many variables, and a subject of considerable interest to your organization.

Software salary pay scales

Because of the dynamic growth of the software industry over the last decade, the demand for experienced, qualified programmers has greatly increased, thus leading to a spiraling of salaries.

But what causes managers to pay one programmer more than another? Does the type of organization, its size, or location make a difference? What career path or programming specialty leads to the most remuneration?

To answer these questions, Acme Magazine recently conducted its third annual compensation survey for software professionals. This newsletter article presents the results of this study and explores what the findings may mean to you.

Acme Magazine asked Joe Smith, a compensation consulting specialist for the software industry, to design and conduct the survey. Twenty-four positions, representing four programmer job families plus management, were included.

Data was collected for base pay, bonus and incentive payments, and whether nor not incumbents received stock options or other forms of equity.

Questionnaires were sent to the data processing heads of 2,400 organizations throughout the United States.

Table of Contents

CD-ROM Breaks New Ground

Compact Disk Read Only Memory (CD-ROM) is a rapidly emerging new technology for the retrieval of vast amounts of information from an optical disk. This new peripheral device allows a totally new level of functionality in the use of microcomputers.

Physically, the CD-ROM device has a laser disk drive (or "player") the same size as a traditional 5 1/4" drive. The removable disk is 4 3/4", and has a capacity of 550M bytes (equivalent to 1500 360K floppy disks).

Theory of Operation

Information stored on a CD-ROM can be loaded into memory (RAM), displayed and printed, as with other media. While that data in RAM may be altered and stored to a conventional magnetic disk, the original information on the CD-ROM is unalterable, always ensuring the original copy is intact, making archiving easy.

The storage capacity, low cost, and read only feature of CD-ROM bring an enormous new capability to microcomputer users – that is, information retrieval of very large reference publications. How people receive and use information in the immediate and long term future will be dramatically changed by CD-ROM.

In addition to the huge capacity of raw information storage, specialized software for the search of that information is currently being introduced. This software allows searching the information in areas, methods and speeds not previously feasible.

It now becomes possible to electronically publish reference material more

Caption

March, 1987

Figure 2.2: A sample newsletter

3. Move the mouse cursor (shaped like an arrow) down the menu to Open Chapter. The command name darkens, as shown in Figure 2.3.
4. Click the mouse button while the arrow is on that choice.

When you do, the Item Selector box appears, as shown in Figure 2.4. Notice that the text cursor (the thin vertical bar) initially appears in the Selection field.

If Ventura Publisher has been properly installed, your hard drive is C, and no one has used the program yet, the directory and disk drive (in the Directory field) will say:

C:\TYPESET*.CHP

If it doesn't, you will need to make some changes. To change the directory:

1. Move the text cursor up to the Directory field. You can use the ↑ key, the Shift-Tab key combination, or the mouse.

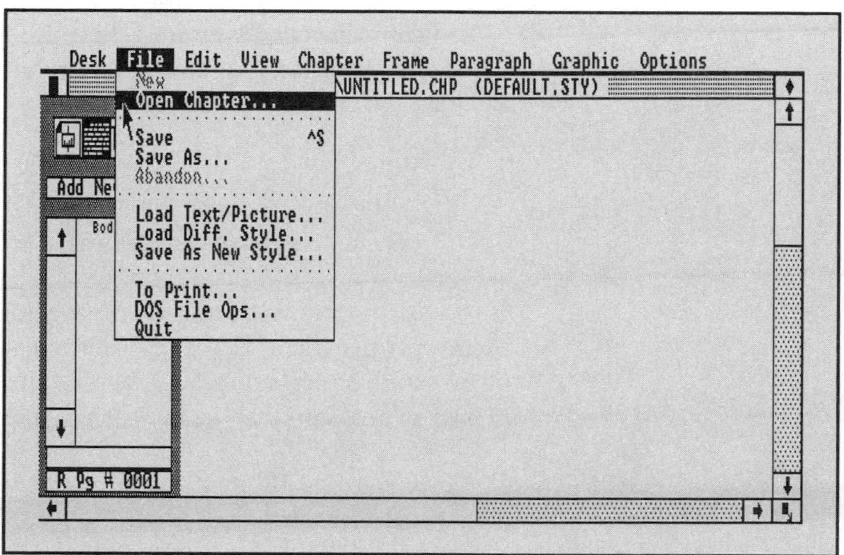

Figure 2.3: Dropping down the File menu and clicking Open Chapter

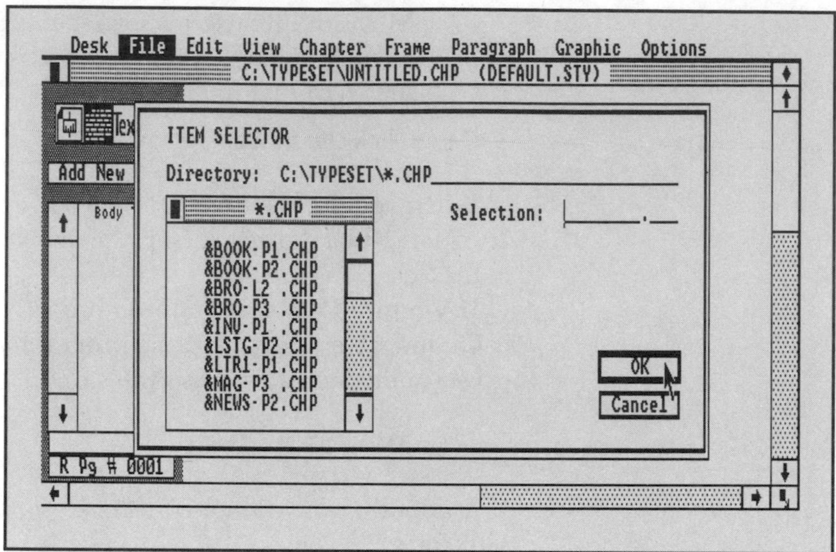

Figure 2.4: The Item Selector box for the File menu's Open Chapter

2. Once there, delete unwanted directory-line characters.

You can wipe out the entire field by hitting the Esc key, or you can delete one character at a time by using the Backspace or Del key. You can float the cursor over the characters by using the ← and → keys as well.

3. Type in your corrections. (Instead of typing, you can use the mouse to change directories, as we'll see shortly.)

If you had to change the directory, the items in the list would not yet be the proper ones, because Ventura would still be showing the incorrect directory's display. There is one more simple step that will make the program display the correct files:

4. Give the OK by hitting Enter or clicking the mouse on the OK button.

With that, the samples stored in the TYPESET directory will appear on the screen, as shown in Figure 2.4. The text cursor will move from the Directory field to the Selection field.

Next you must indicate the file for Ventura Publisher to load. Depending on the version, and if others have been using the program, the name of the sample file may not be in view.

1. If necessary, scroll down the list of file names. (Scrolling techniques are described in Chapter 1.)
2. Darken the name

   &NEWS-P2.CHP

   by pointing to it with the mouse cursor and clicking. You could also simply type in the file name, rather than picking it from the list.
3. Give the OK by clicking the OK button or by hitting Enter.

You can combine steps 7 and 8 by pointing to the file name and clicking twice in rapid succession. Doing so both selects the file and gives the OK.

You can adjust the speed at which double-clicking operates. See Appendix A.

Once you give the OK, Ventura flashes some "loading" and "hyphenating" messages on the screen. When they're done, you've successfully loaded the sample chapter into Ventura.

MAKING A NEW DIRECTORY

Before saving the files with new names, we'll create a special directory called MASTERVP. You'll use this directory to hold the exercises you work with in this book.

Judicious use of directories is an aid to categorizing the various files you use with Ventura. Some people like to create a new directory for each new document they compose. Others like to use directories to group similar elements, such as text, chapter, or graphics files, regardless of the document.

Whatever the strategy, it's wise to use your own directories. Don't just dump everything into the TYPESET directory, which Ventura uses to house its sample documents.

Here's how to make the MASTERVP directory with Ventura. (You can also use DOS's MD command to make directories.)

1. Drop the File menu.
2. Click DOS File Ops.

Doing so displays the dialog box for DOS File Operations. The File Spec field reads

C:*.*

You can also use this dialog box to delete files and remove directories from the disk. Use these capabilities to remove DOS files once you're done with a document. For more on DOS, see Appendix C.

3. Use the Backspace key to erase the *.* that's showing.
4. Type in **MASTERVP** as the name for the new directory. The dialog box now looks like Figure 2.5.
5. Click the Make Directory button.
6. To make the dialog box disappear, click the Done box or press Enter.

SAVING A COPY OF THE CHAPTER FILE

Now that we've created the special directory, save the chapter with a new name in that directory. This action will make a copy of the

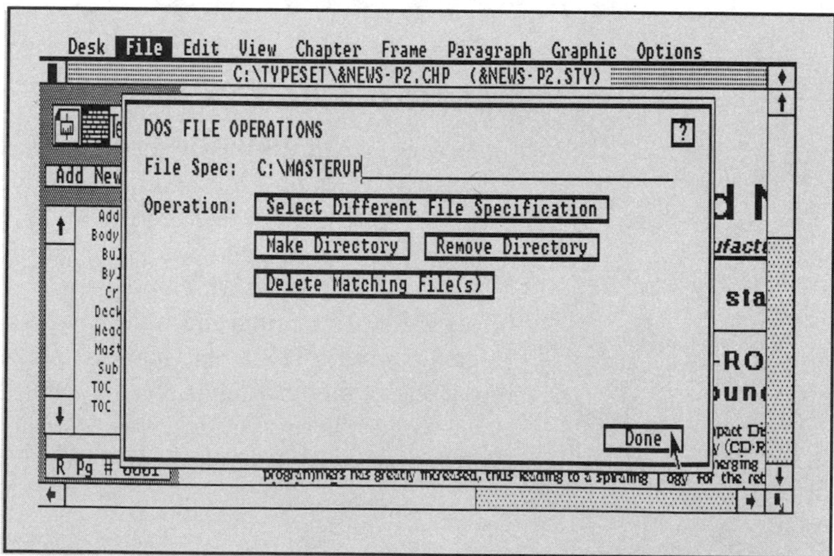

Figure 2.5: The dialog box for the File menu's DOS File Operations

chapter file on the disk. You can then make changes in the chapter specifications and save the changed version. The original is separate and will not reflect those changes. Note, however, that this does not copy text files that are loaded into the chapter. Doing that is a separate procedure we'll examine later.

To save the copy of the chapter file, follow these steps:

1. Drop the File menu and click the Save As command. The Item Selector box appears.
2. Change the directory or disk drive, if desired, either as specified earlier or by using the Backup button, which we'll describe in a moment. You may wish, for instance, to place the new files on a floppy disk in drive A.
3. Type in the name we're assigning to the copy of the chapter file:

   BRAIN

   Do not type a period or the CHP extension; Ventura will assign the CHP extension automatically.
4. Give the OK as discussed earlier.

You can customize the disk drives that appear in the Item Selector box. See Appendix A.

To change directories and drives using the Backup button, located in the top-left corner of the box of listings, simply click it. When backing out of a directory, the system will first change to the root directory (or the parent directory, which holds the directory the system is backing out of). Clicking the button again will cause the disk drives to be listed, as shown in Figure 2.6. At this point you can click a different drive, and then choose one of its directories, if necessary.

This and the previous procedure do not make copies of the text files that hold the newsletter articles. They only copy the style-sheet file, which dictates the format of the newsletter, and the chapter file, which coordinates the various elements of the document.

COPYING THE STYLE SHEET

Now that the chapter file is safe, to protect the original style sheet, you must save it with a new name as well. The procedure is basically the same as that used to save the chapter. Ventura Publisher has already loaded the style sheet along with the document, so all you need do is save it under a new name. To do that:

1. Drop the File menu.
2. Click Save As New Style.

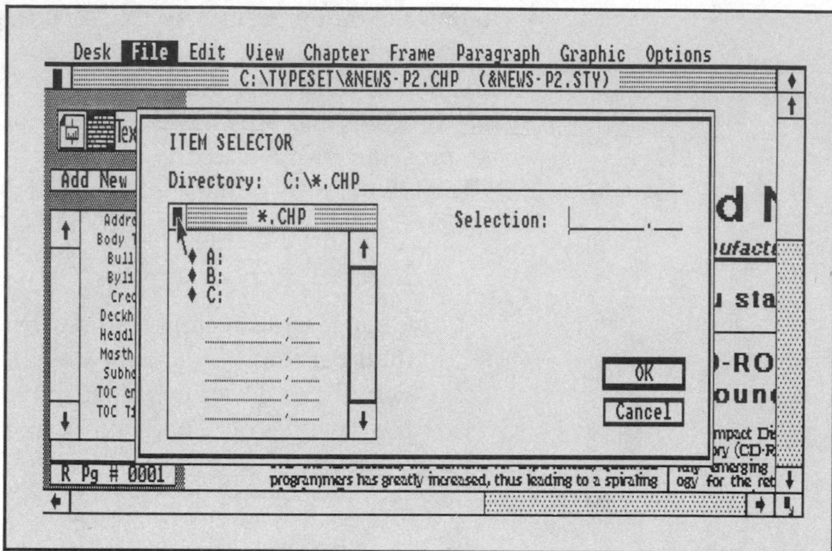

Figure 2.6: Backup button used to display disk drives in the Item Selector box

The Item Selector box that appears (see Figure 2.7) is similar to the one you saw when you saved the chapter. This time, however, the system assumes an extension of STY.

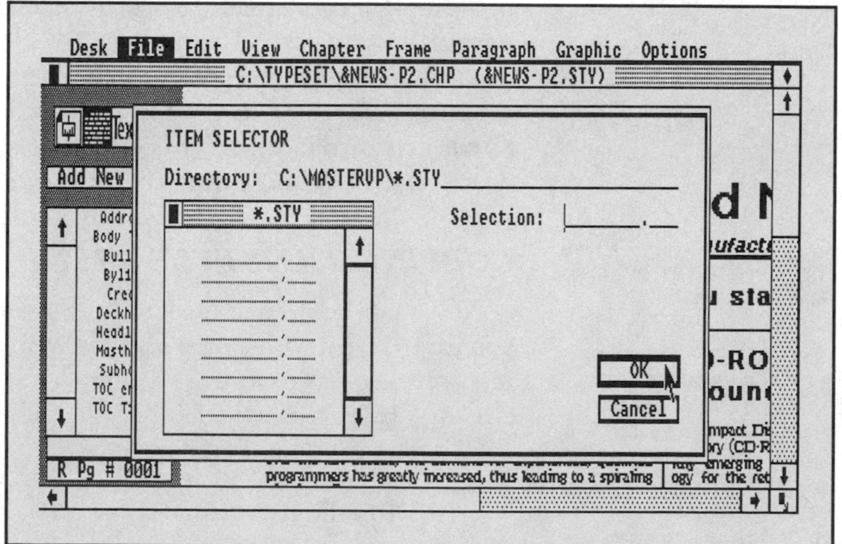

Figure 2.7: Saving a style sheet under a new name

3. Complete the Item Selector box. Use the name

   BRAIN

   Ventura Publisher will add the STY extension.

Let's discuss why we've saved the material before making any changes. You could have made the changes first and then performed the saves. However, saving them before you start to make changes guards against accidentally saving those changes with the original files.

If, however, you do change the originals accidentally, you can simply recopy them from the disk labeled "Examples" (disk #4 in version 2.0).

If you plan to make alterations in the content of these files, you must also save the text files under a different name to protect the originals. Alternatively, you can pull in new text files that you create with a word processor (Chapter 11). You can also use the Options menu's Multi-Chapter, discussed in Chapter 10, to copy all the material associated with a chapter, including text files.

We'll look at how to change the text as well as the layout presently.

SETTING UP MARGINS AND COLUMNS

Let's examine the frames that compose our newsletter sample. Then we'll consider which frame to alter and how to activate Frame mode to do it. In Figure 2.8, Frame mode is operational and you can see the frames. We used a Genius full-page display to create this figure, so you can study the page and its frames as a unit.

The sample page has nine frames in it. There is one around the masthead (*Widget World News* . . .) and one surrounding the headline (*Software Salaries* . . .). There's a frame set aside for a figure in the bottom-right corner, and one for a caption below it. Another frame holds the table of contents. The left and right halves of the main text area are each framed, and there's also a footer frame at the bottom. The last frame is the main one, the *underlying-page frame.* This is the frame you reset to change settings for the entire page. The underlying-page frame holds the other frames (*standard* frames) but, in this example, it does not contain any text itself.

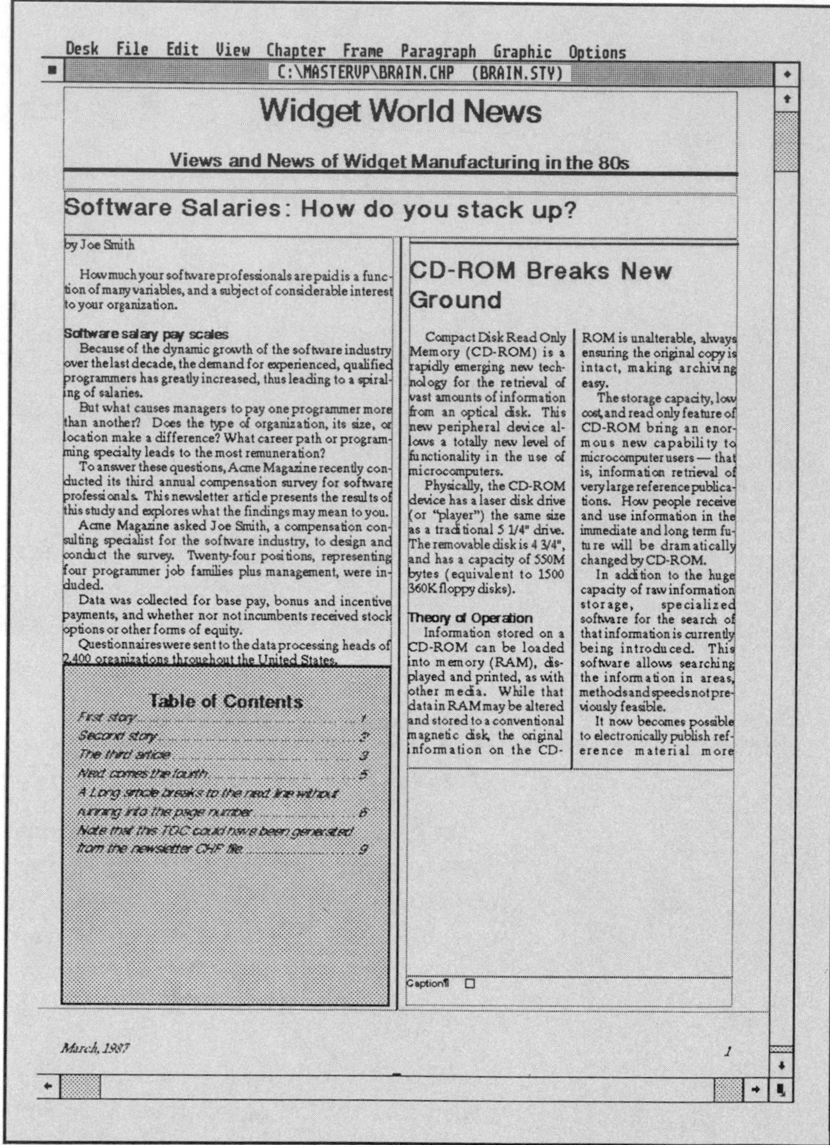

Desk File Edit View Chapter Frame Paragraph Graphic Options

C:\MASTERVP\BRAIN.CHP (BRAIN.STY)

Widget World News

Views and News of Widget Manufacturing in the 80s

Software Salaries: How do you stack up?

by Joe Smith

How much your software professionals are paid is a function of many variables, and a subject of considerable interest to your organization.

Software salary pay scales

Because of the dynamic growth of the software industry over the last decade, the demand for experienced, qualified programmers has greatly increased, thus leading to a spiraling of salaries.

But what causes managers to pay one programmer more than another? Does the type of organization, its size, or location make a difference? What career path or programming specialty leads to the most remuneration?

To answer these questions, Acme Magazine recently conducted its third annual compensation survey for software professionals. This newsletter article presents the results of this study and explores what the findings may mean to you.

Acme Magazine asked Joe Smith, a compensation consulting specialist for the software industry, to design and conduct the survey. Twenty-four positions, representing four programmer job families plus management, were included.

Data was collected for base pay, bonus and incentive payments, and whether nor not incumbents received stock options or other forms of equity.

Questionnaires were sent to the data processing heads of 2,400 organizations throughout the United States.

Table of Contents

First story 1
Second story 2
The third article 3
Next comes the fourth 5
A Long article breaks to the next line without running into the page number 6
Note that this TOC could have been generated from the newsletter CHP file 9

CD-ROM Breaks New Ground

Compact Disk Read Only Memory (CD-ROM) is a rapidly emerging new technology for the retrieval of vast amounts of information from an optical disk. This new peripheral device allows a totally new level of functionality in the use of microcomputers.

Physically, the CD-ROM device has a laser disk drive (or "player") the same size as a traditional 5 1/4" drive. The removable disk is 4 3/4", and has a capacity of 550M bytes (equivalent to 1500 360K floppy disks).

Theory of Operation

Information stored on a CD-ROM can be loaded into memory (RAM), displayed and printed, as with other media. While that data in RAM may be altered and stored to a conventional magnetic disk, the original information on the CD-ROM is unalterable, always ensuring the original copy is intact, making archiving easy.

The storage capacity, low cost, and read only feature of CD-ROM bring an enormous new capability to microcomputer users — that is, information retrieval of very large reference publications. How people receive and use information in the immediate and long term future will be dramatically changed by CD-ROM.

In addition to the huge capacity of raw information storage, specialized software for the search of that information is currently being introduced. This software allows searching the information in areas, methods and speeds not previously feasible.

It now becomes possible to electronically publish reference material more

Caption¶

March, 1987 1

Figure 2.8: Frames in Frame mode on a Genius monitor

CHANGING MODES

Let's say that you don't like the two narrow columns on the right side of the page. You'd like to change this frame to a single-column format. To work with a frame, you must first activate Frame mode.

The mode that was active when you (or someone else) last used Ventura will be the one that's active when you start a work session. You can tell which of the four modes is active by consulting the Mode selector at the top of the Side-bar (Chapter 1). The button on the left is for Frame mode. If it's darkened, Frame mode is active. Buttons for Paragraph, Text, and Graphics mode follow the Frame mode button in turn. If one of them is darkened instead—only one can be active at a time—its corresponding mode is active. If this is the case, you must change to Frame mode before proceeding.

There are three ways that you can change modes in Ventura. First, as you've learned, you can click the appropriate button in the Mode selector at the top of the Side-bar.

The second method is to choose from the View drop-down menu. The lower four choices on this menu are the four modes, in the same order as they appear at the top of the Side-bar. A check mark to the left of a menu choice indicates which mode is active, in the same way that the darkened button in the Mode selector does.

The third method of changing modes is the keyboard method. The key you use is indicated on the View drop-down menu. Thus, you type Ctrl-U to activate Frame mode. Notice that the four keys you use to change modes are positioned on the keyboard in the same order as the buttons in the Mode selector.

- Now use one of these three methods to change modes to Frame mode. All three accomplish the same end.

The methods are summarized in Figure 2.9.

Once you activate Frame mode, you'll notice that the mouse cursor changes to a plus sign. This serves as a reminder that Frame mode is active. As Figure 2.9 shows, each mode has a corresponding shape for the mouse cursor.

SELECTING A FRAME

Now that you have activated Frame mode, you must select the proper frame in the working area before you can alter it. Follow these steps to select the frame that contains the two columns on the right of the page:

1. Scroll the screen, if necessary, so that the frame we want is visible on the screen.

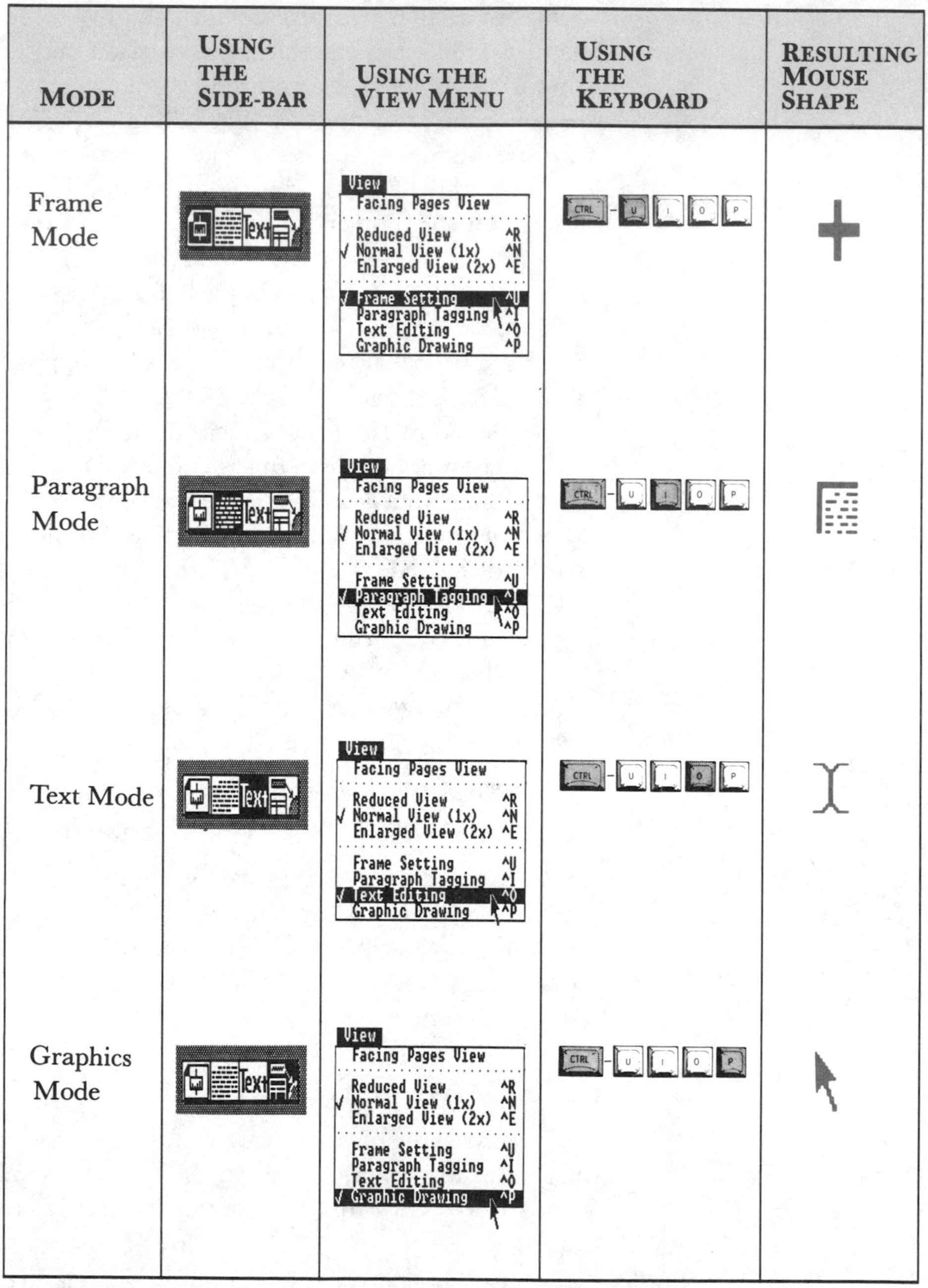

MODE	USING THE SIDE-BAR	USING THE VIEW MENU	USING THE KEYBOARD	RESULTING MOUSE SHAPE
Frame Mode	Text	View Facing Pages View Reduced View ^R √ Normal View (1x) ^N Enlarged View (2x) ^E √ Frame Setting ^U Paragraph Tagging ^I Text Editing ^O Graphic Drawing ^P	CTRL - U I O P	
Paragraph Mode	Text	View Facing Pages View Reduced View ^R √ Normal View (1x) ^N Enlarged View (2x) ^E Frame Setting ^U √ Paragraph Tagging ^I Text Editing ^O Graphic Drawing ^P	CTRL - U I O P	
Text Mode	Text	View Facing Pages View Reduced View ^R √ Normal View (1x) ^N Enlarged View (2x) ^E Frame Setting ^U Paragraph Tagging ^I √ Text Editing ^O Graphic Drawing ^P	CTRL - U I O P	
Graphics Mode	Text	View Facing Pages View Reduced View ^R √ Normal View (1x) ^N Enlarged View (2x) ^E Frame Setting ^U Paragraph Tagging ^I Text Editing ^O √ Graphic Drawing ^P	CTRL - U I O P	

Figure 2.9: Methods for changing modes and resultant mouse shapes

2. Double-check that Frame mode is active, as shown by the Mode selector at the top of the Side-bar.
3. Move the mouse cursor anywhere inside the frame.
4. Click the mouse button.

Ventura indicates that the frame is selected by displaying small black boxes along the edges of the frame, as shown in Figure 2.10. These boxes are called *handles*. Usually, there are eight handles to a frame. There may be fewer if the frame is too small to accommodate eight or if some of the frame is off the screen. Shortly, we'll see how you can grab these handles to manipulate a frame.

CHANGING THE SELECTED FRAME

If you wanted to select a different frame, you would just position the plus-shaped mouse cursor within the new frame and click. The handles appear on the new frame and disappear from the first one. This works well as long as the two frames are completely separate.

Frames can overlap, but this method also works if the first frame lies within the second frame. In that case, just move the mouse cursor

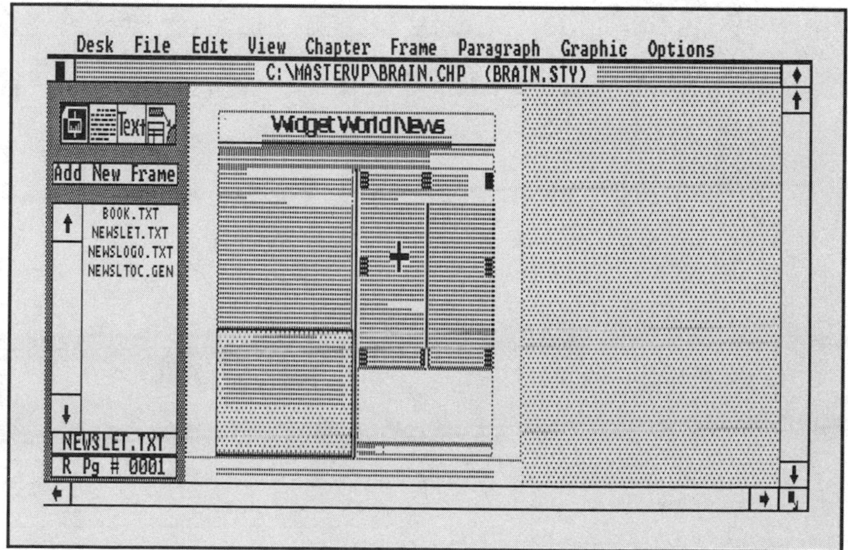

Figure 2.10: Handles on the selected frame

to a point that's within the second frame but not the first (see Figure 2.11). Then click. This is how you could select the underlying-page frame, for instance.

Changing back to the first frame is trickier, since the first frame is fully within the second. To select the first frame again, begin by selecting some third frame that doesn't contain these frames (Figure 2.12). Then you can select the first frame. (You may add a third frame temporarily just for this purpose—you'll learn how to create a frame later in this chapter.)

Alternatively, you could move the second frame away temporarily, so that it doesn't surround the first frame. Once you've completed your work with the first frame, you would move the second frame back in position. We'll see how to add and move frames shortly. There is a third method for selecting a frame within a frame. By holding down the Ctrl key as you click, you can select frames piled on top of each other. Each Ctrl-click successively selects a different frame in the pile.

Once you select a frame, the name of the text file that's assigned to the selected frame appears in the Current box (at the bottom of the Side-bar). The Current box in Figure 2.10 shows that the sample

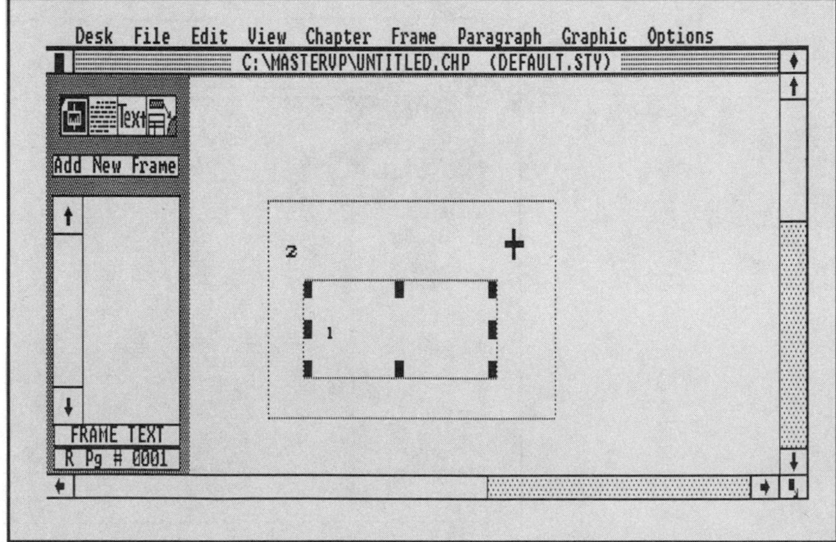

Figure 2.11: Selecting a frame that contains the currently selected frame

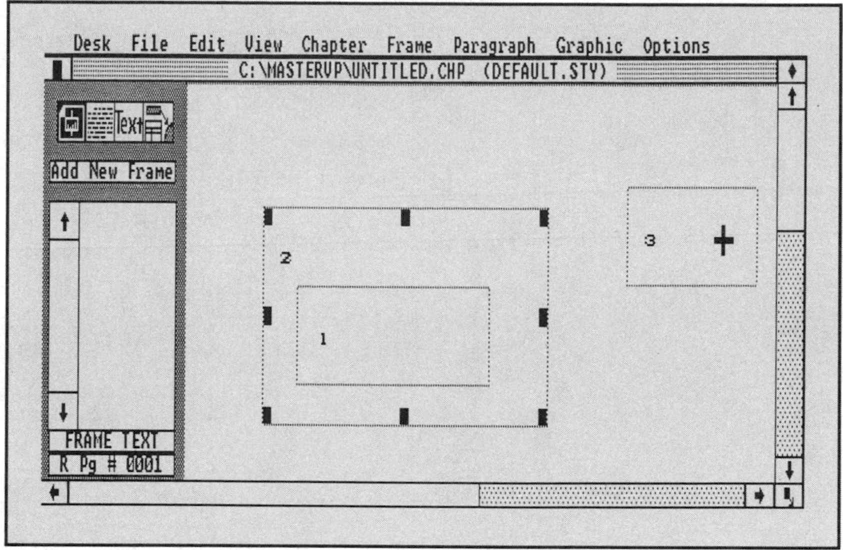

Figure 2.12: Using a third frame to select a frame within the currently selected frame

chapter is using the NEWSLET.TXT file to fill the two-column frame on the right.

When you use a sample's format, you'll undoubtedly want to exchange the text files that appear in the frames of the sample newsletter for the files containing the stories that are to appear in your newsletter. We'll see how to do that in Chapter 3.

DIALOG BOX FOR MARGINS AND COLUMNS

Now you're ready to change the margins and columns for the right half of the sample page. To do that, you'll use the Frame menu's Margins & Columns. Follow these steps to display this command's dialog box:

1. Make sure that Frame mode is active and you've selected the proper frame.
2. Display the Frame drop-down menu.
3. Click Margins & Columns.

The dialog box shown in Figure 2.13 should appear.

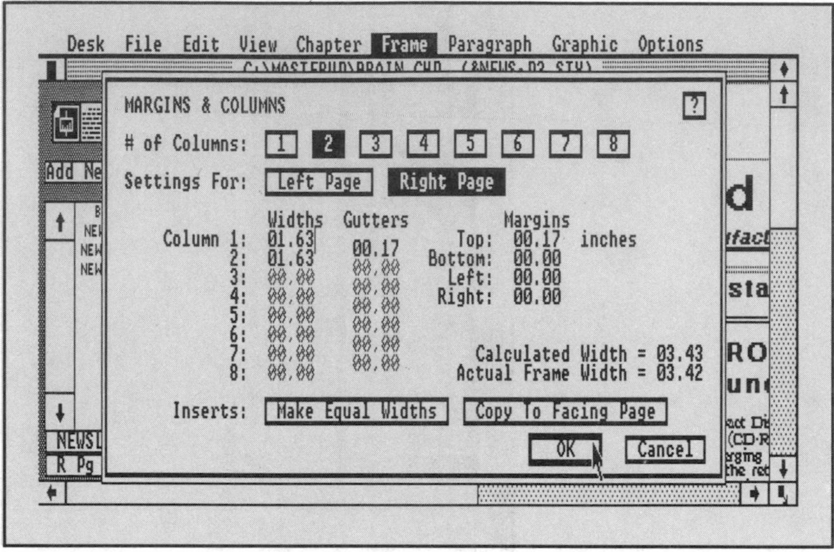

Figure 2.13: The Frame menu's Margins & Columns dialog box

The settings you provide in this dialog box will affect the selected frame. When you select the underlying-page frame, the settings apply to the entire page. In that case, they generally affect every page in the chapter, because you usually have only one basic page format to a chapter.

SETTING COLUMNS Notice that you can have from one to eight columns of text in the frame. To change the number of columns, simply click the button of your choice.

- Change our sample frame to single-column format by clicking the 1 button.

> ✻ You can determine whether Ventura displays columns on the page by using the Options menu. See Appendix A.

When you set columns, the appropriate number of Widths fields will darken automatically. You can then enter each column width individually or make them equal automatically, as we'll see.

Gutters in Ventura are the distances between the columns. As with column widths, you can set gutters individually or make them equal automatically.

Next look at the two fields labeled Calculated Width and Actual Frame Width. You cannot enter values for these fields, but it is important that you pay close attention to them as you set up your columns. The values in these two fields must be equal. Otherwise, you could cause formatting irregularities in your document.

Ventura computes the calculated width by adding values that you have specified in this dialog box. That is, it adds together the left and right margins, all the columns, and all the gutters. It gets the value for Actual Frame Width from the Sizing & Scaling dialog box, which also springs from the Frame menu. This box works in close connection with the Margins & Columns dialog box. We'll study the Sizing & Scaling dialog box later in this chapter.

CREATING EQUAL COLUMNS AUTOMATICALLY If you had set multiple columns and you wanted to make the columns and gutters for the frame equal in width, all you'd need do is assign a value to the first gutter width. Then, point to the Make Equal Widths button and click. Ventura fills in the correct values.

SETTING MARGINS Look at the Margins settings on the right side of the Margins & Columns dialog box. When you work with margins and columns, you'll probably find it easiest to set the margins first and then allocate column widths according to what's left. In our example, however, we don't need to change the margin settings.

The top, bottom, left, and right margin settings are the widths of the margins from their respective edges of the frame. (In the case of the underlying-page frame, these measurements are from the edge of the page.) Contents of the frame, such as text, will not be allowed in the margins, thus creating a blank area between the contents and the edges of the frame.

SYSTEMS OF MEASUREMENT In its dialog boxes, Ventura can display measurements in four ways. You can change the system of measurement that a dialog box uses.

In the Frame menu's Margins & Columns dialog box (Figure 2.13), notice that the word *inches* appears to the right of the top-margin setting. This label indicates the system of measurement Ventura Publisher is using to display values in the dialog box.

- Click the mouse cursor directly on the word *inches*.

The word *centimeters* replaces the word *inches,* and all measurements convert to centimeters (Figure 2.14).

- Click several times.

Ventura displays two other systems of measurement—*picas & points* and *fractional points*—in turn, before it goes back to inches. Typesetters can use picas and points for vertical and linear measurement of type. (There are about 6 picas in 1 inch, and there are 72 points in 1 inch.) With the picas & points setting, Ventura displays the number of picas, followed by a comma and the number of points. Thus, 1.25 inches, which is equal to 7 picas plus 6 points, would be displayed as

07,06 picas & points

Fractional points appear as the number of points, a decimal, and then fractions of points. Thus, the same value would convert to

90.00 fractional pts

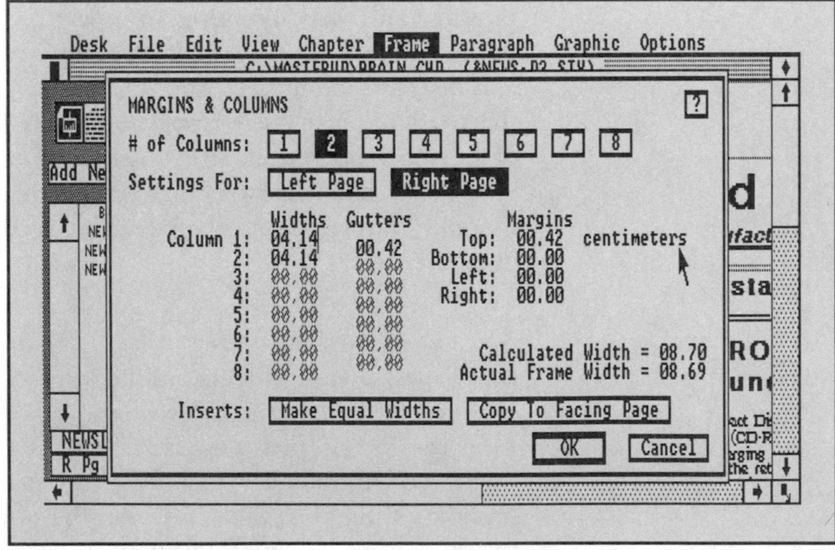

Figure 2.14: Changing the system of measurement to centimeters

Figure 2.15 shows the various systems of measurement that Ventura has available for you. The figure also shows how they correspond; as the figure is actual size, you can use it for measuring.

Once you convert a value, if the field in a dialog box is too small to display the resulting large value, a tilde (˜) appears in the field instead. To see the true value, simply click the measurement name, as we've discussed, to convert the value to a different system of measurement.

Be aware, too, that slight rounding errors may occur when you convert. This is normal and usually inconsequential.

COPYING SETTINGS TO THE FACING PAGE Now let's consider one final button in this dialog box, though we don't need to use it now. When you are working on the underlying-page frame, you can copy the margin and column settings to the page facing the one you're working on. For this to work, you must first have dropped the Chapter menu, clicked the Page Size & Layout command, and specified the Sides setting as Double in the resulting dialog box.

Then, with the underlying-page frame active, you would use the Frame menu's Margins & Columns dialog box to set your margins and columns, as discussed above. Then you would point to the Copy To Facing Page button and click.

Ventura changes the settings for the facing page to match those you've specified. You can check that the transfer was successful by clicking the opposite Settings For button, Left Page or Right Page. The settings that correspond to that button then appear. Ventura puts the settings into effect when you give the OK.

When you use this technique, the left and right margins are copied as mirror images on the opposite page. That is, the left is right and the right is left. Because of this, the pages' inside margins will match, as will their outside margins. This mirroring effect only occurs for the margins, not for the columns or gutters. That is, column 1 on the facing page is the same width as column 1 on the original page.

If you don't want to have the margins mirrored, change the settings for the opposite page *after* you copy them to that page. To do that, copy the settings and then simply click the opposite Settings For setting (Left Page or Right Page). Ventura will display the newly copied settings, and you can change them as you wish.

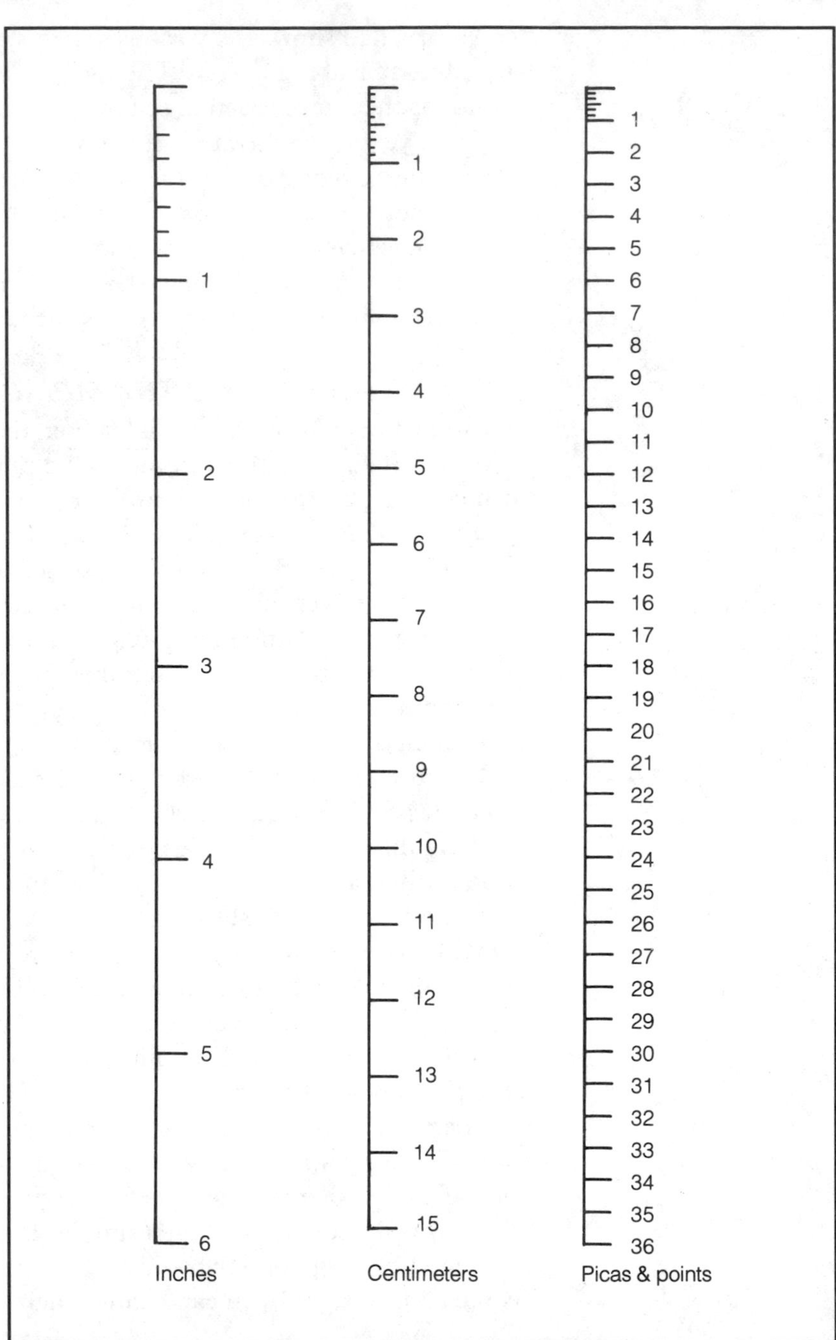

Figure 2.15: Ventura's systems of measurement

This completes our examination of the Frame menu's Margins & Columns dialog box.

- In the Margins & Columns dialog box, click OK or press the Enter key. Your new settings will take effect on the frame you selected before displaying the dialog box.

A CHANGE OF VIEW: ENLARGING AND REDUCING

Now that you've begun to make changes in the layout of your newsletter, you may find it necessary to have a magnified or reduced look at your work. Just as an artist does, you may wish to step in closer to perform some delicate detail work. Similarly, there will be times when you'd like to step back to take in a more removed view of the page. That way, you can check general layout and initial impact on the reader, as well as see how a headline, for instance, looks compared with the rest of the page.

To afford you alternative ways of scrutinizing your document, Ventura offers four different views: Normal, Enlarged, Reduced, and Facing Pages.

- Drop the View menu.

You can see these views as the first four commands (Figure 2.16). When you load Ventura, the program appears with the same view you were using when you quit.

NORMAL VIEW (CTRL-N)

Normal view is the view that most closely represents the true size and proportions of your document. The (1x) next to the command name indicates that Normal view is the same size as the printed version. Note that because of differences between the way a monitor and a printer operate, there may still be some difference in what is called the *aspect ratio*—the ratio of the height (of the screen or page) to the width.

Generally, you use the Normal view to read text and make changes in it. You can activate Normal view either by clicking Normal View on the View menu or by typing Ctrl-N at the keyboard.

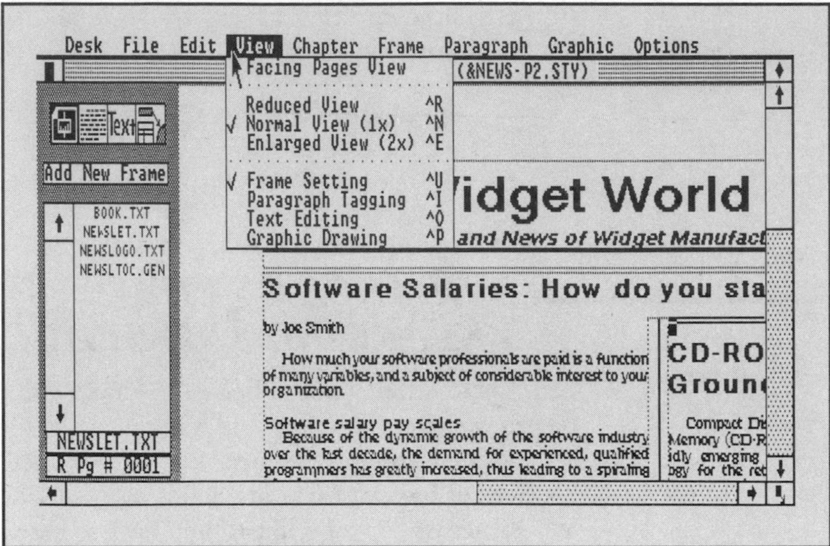

Figure 2.16: The View menu

The drop-down menu reminds you of this keyboard shortcut by displaying ^N next to the words *Normal View.*

ENLARGED VIEW (CTRL-E)

Like Normal view, Enlarged view can be triggered in either of two ways: by dropping down the View menu and clicking Enlarged View or by typing Ctrl-E. As indicated by the (2x) next to the command name, Enlarged view is twice the normal size of the layout. You'll find Enlarged view helpful when you want to check the details of pictures, or when you are working with very small type.

When you use a keyboard shortcut (such as Ctrl-E) to change to a larger view, Ventura takes the approximate location of the mouse cursor as its cue for positioning the top-left corner of the larger view. This feature makes the program operate efficiently: it's not necessary to use the scroll bars after you enlarge the view because the screen will be properly positioned. You cannot make use of this feature if you use the drop-down menu method.

- Change to Enlarged view with Ctrl-E or with the View menu's Enlarged View.

REDUCED VIEW (CTRL-R)

If you have a standard monitor, you'll find it helpful to use Reduced view to check the entire page at once. Of course with a full-page monitor, such as the Genius, you can usually see the entire page with Normal view.

When you use Reduced view, Ventura may *greek* some of the text; that is, substitute plain straight lines for some lines of text. By greeking text, the program can operate more quickly as you make changes that affect the page. (Due to the reduction in size, these lines of text would probably be too small to read anyway.)

* You can set the amount of text that Ventura greeks. See Appendix A.

Figure 2.17 shows how the displayed document appears with greeked text. The height and width of the greeked lines approximate the true dimensions of the actual text.

- Change to the Reduced view either with Ctrl-R or with the View menu's Reduced View.

FACING PAGES VIEW

Facing Pages view displays left- and right-hand pages simultaneously for documents that are so designed. This view allows you to

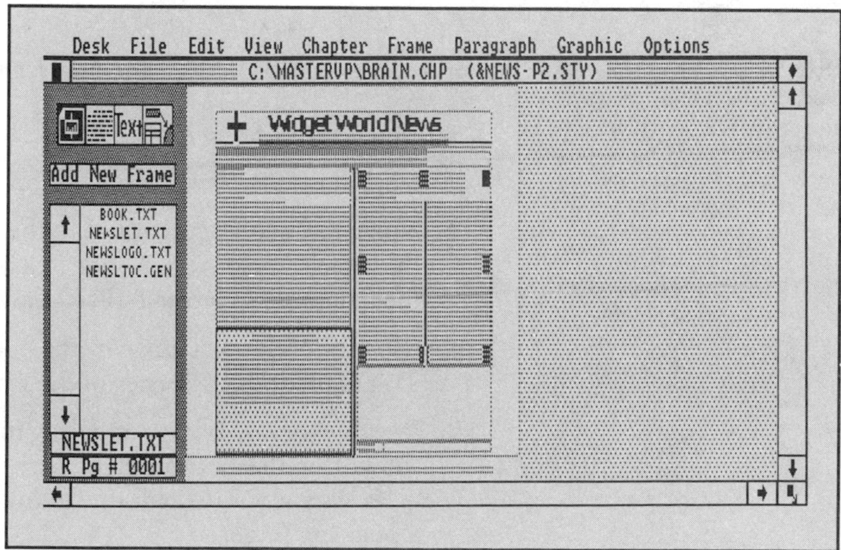

Figure 2.17: Greeked text in the Reduced view

assess the combined impact of the two pages that your reader will be viewing together. As with Reduced view, Ventura Publisher may greek some text. Note that there is no keyboard shortcut for triggering Facing Pages view.

As you construct your documents, use these four views freely to your advantage. For now, change Ventura back to Normal view:

- Return to Normal view with Ctrl-N or with the View menu's Normal View.

You probably noticed that besides these four views, there are four other commands available on the View drop-down menu. We'll examine these commands shortly, as we begin to adapt the newsletter.

MANIPULATING FRAMES

So far, we've discussed how to adapt existing frames for new uses. Naturally, there are times when it's necessary to create an entirely new frame. Let's say that you want to add some information about the author at the beginning of the first article. Doing this would call for a new frame.

CREATING NEW FRAMES

* To assist in placing a new frame, you may wish to show rulers, which are measuring sticks that can appear at the top and the left of the working area. These rulers each display a traveling marker that shows the position of the mouse cursor (see Appendix A).

Follow these steps to create the new frame:

1. Make sure Frame mode is active.
2. Click the Add New Frame button in the Side-bar.
3. Move the mouse cursor out to the working area. As you do, the mouse cursor will change to a bracket shape that includes the letters *FR* (Figure 2.18).
4. Move the mouse cursor to the spot shown in Figure 2.18. This is the top-left corner of the frame.
5. Press the mouse button and drag the mouse cursor to the spot shown for the bottom-right corner of the frame in Figure 2.19. As you *stretch* the frame in this way, the cursor looks like a pointing finger.

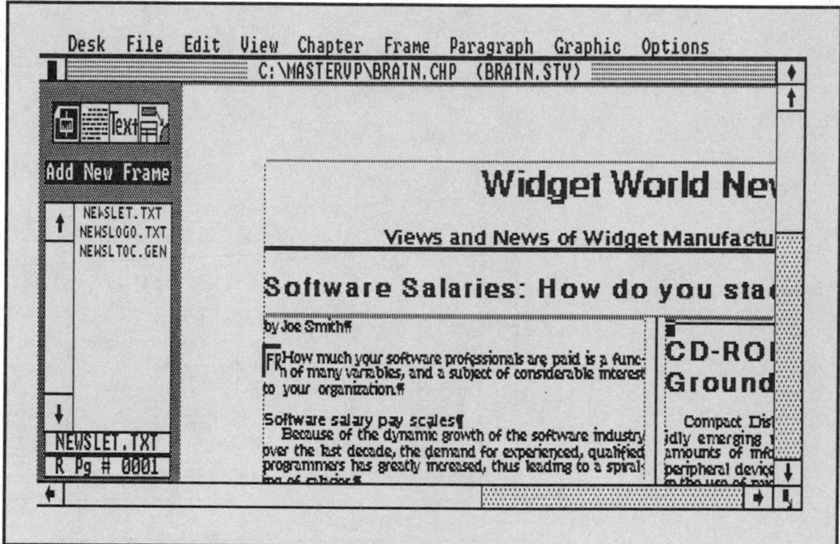

Figure 2.18: Starting to create a new frame

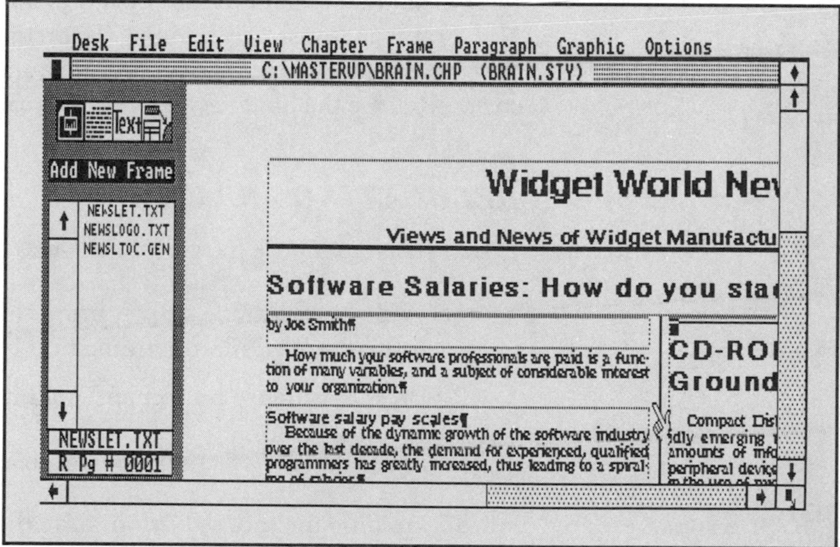

Figure 2.19: Defining the size of a new frame

6. Release the button to establish the new frame (Figure 2.20).

It's an empty frame for now, but in Chapter 3 you'll enter some text directly into the frame. Such text is called Frame text.

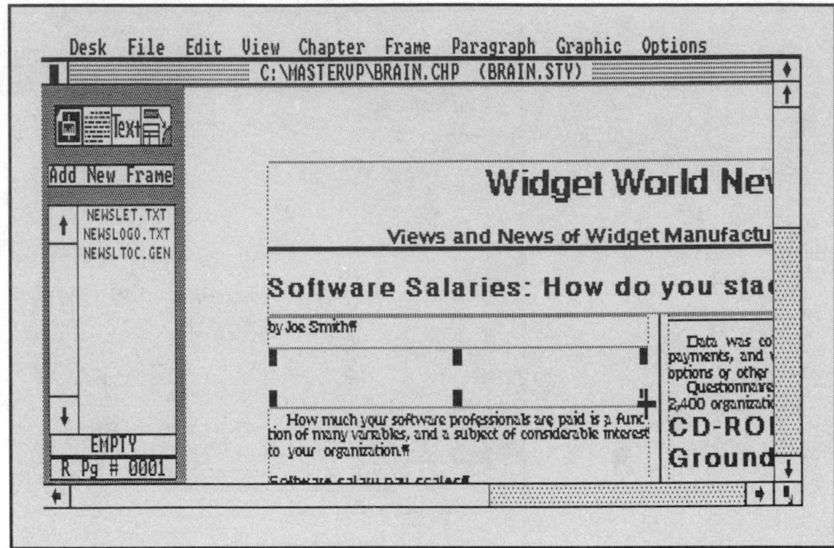

Figure 2.20: Finishing the creation of a new frame

You can add several frames in succession without clicking the Add New Frame button for each frame. To do that, hold down the Shift key as you create and stretch each new frame, including the first frame you create. Release the Shift key before you create the final frame.

RELOCATING FRAMES

Let's use the mouse to relocate a frame on the same page.

1. With Frame mode active, bring the mouse cursor to a point somewhere within the frame that holds the table of contents.
2. Press the mouse button and hold it down.

The mouse cursor will change to the cross shape (see Figure 2.21).

3. Holding the mouse button, drag the frame to a new location. As you do, you'll see a ghost of the frame move along with you. Release the button, and the frame will jump to the new location.
4. Repeat the procedure to return the table of contents to its original location.

* You can turn the Column Snap and Line Snap features on or off. Having these on causes frames to snap jerkily from one place to the next as you move them. See Appendix A.

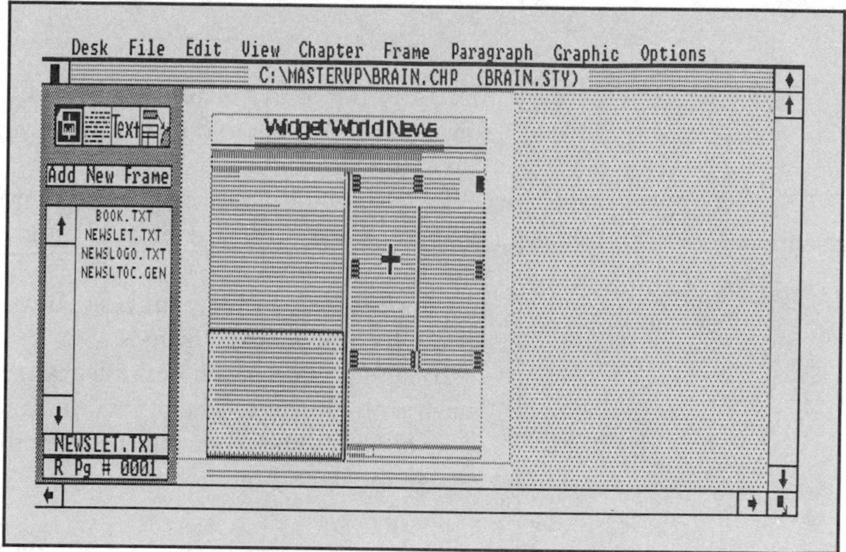

Figure 2.21: Relocating a frame

RESIZING FRAMES

You can also use the mouse to resize frames. To do so, grab the frame (once you've selected it) by one of its eight black handles. (Smaller frames will have fewer handles.) Press and hold the mouse button; the mouse cursor changes to the shape of a pointing finger, as it does when you are creating a frame. Drag the handle to a new location; the frame's ghost will stretch or shrink in the direction that you move the handle. When you reach the desired location, release the mouse button.

If you grab a corner handle, you stretch and contract both edges of the frame that meet at that corner. If you grab a handle in the middle of either the top or bottom of the frame, the top or bottom edge adjusts up and down. The action is rather like that of a window shade. If you use one of the handles centered along the left or right edge of the frame, the frame adjusts left and right, somewhat like a sliding door.

- Try resizing some of the frames of the sample newsletter on your screen, but restore them to their original size before you continue.

Selecting Multiple Frames

If you need to move or resize several frames in a similar fashion, you don't have to do so for one frame at a time. Instead, you can select *multiple frames.*

To select multiple frames, begin by selecting the first frame as usual. Then, press the Shift key and, as you hold it down, click the additional frames, one by one. Each frame will display its handles, and any moves you make with the mouse will affect all of the selected frames.

To deselect one of the multiple frames, shift-click the frame you wish to deselect. The others will remain selected. To deselect all the frames, just select some other frame as usual or change the operating mode.

SIZING AND SCALING FRAMES

As you resize or relocate a frame with the mouse, Ventura Publisher keeps accurate track of the frame's edges. It stores the values for their location in the Frame menu's Sizing & Scaling dialog box (see Figure 2.22). You can change these values directly in the dialog box, rather than by using the mouse on a frame. You may find it handiest to do your major moves with the mouse and fine-tune with this dialog box.

You can use the underlying-page frame's Sizing & Scaling dialog box to reduce the size of a page. Do this to accommodate odd-sized paper not provided for with the Chapter menu's Page Size & Layout (see below).

- Drop the Frame menu and click Sizing & Scaling. The Sizing & Scaling dialog box appears.

The Frame menu's Sizing & Scaling (S&S) dialog box works closely with its Margins & Columns (M&C) dialog box. The manner in which these values influence each other is summarized in Figure 2.23.

! New for version 2.0

The Column Balance feature, formerly contained in the Frame menu's Sizing & Scaling dialog box, has been moved to the Chapter menu's Chapter Typography dialog box in version 2.0. We'll study balancing columns in Chapter 4.

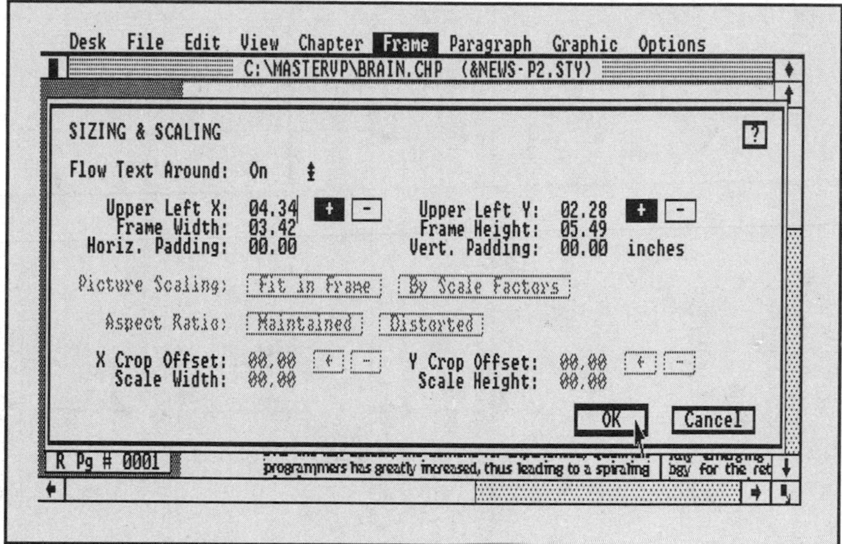

Figure 2.22: The Frame menu's Sizing & Scaling dialog box

TEXT AROUND A FRAME

The one on/off setting in the Sizing & Scaling dialog box, Flow Text Around, is usually set to On. When you add a frame on top of existing text, this feature makes the text flow around the new frame automatically, preventing the new frame from obscuring text that previously occupied the frame's space. You saw an example of this in Figure 2.20.

You may wish to change this setting to Off for certain graphic effects, as you'll see in Chapter 6. In Chapter 6, you'll also learn how to use other settings in the Sizing & Scaling box, those shown ghosting in Figure 2.22.

FRAME POSITION AND SIZE

The X value indicates the distance of the left edge of the frame from the left edge of the paper. The Y value is the distance of the top edge of the frame from the top edge of the paper. (If you are working with the underlying-page frame, these two values, naturally, will be zero; the underlying-page frame is the same as the page.)

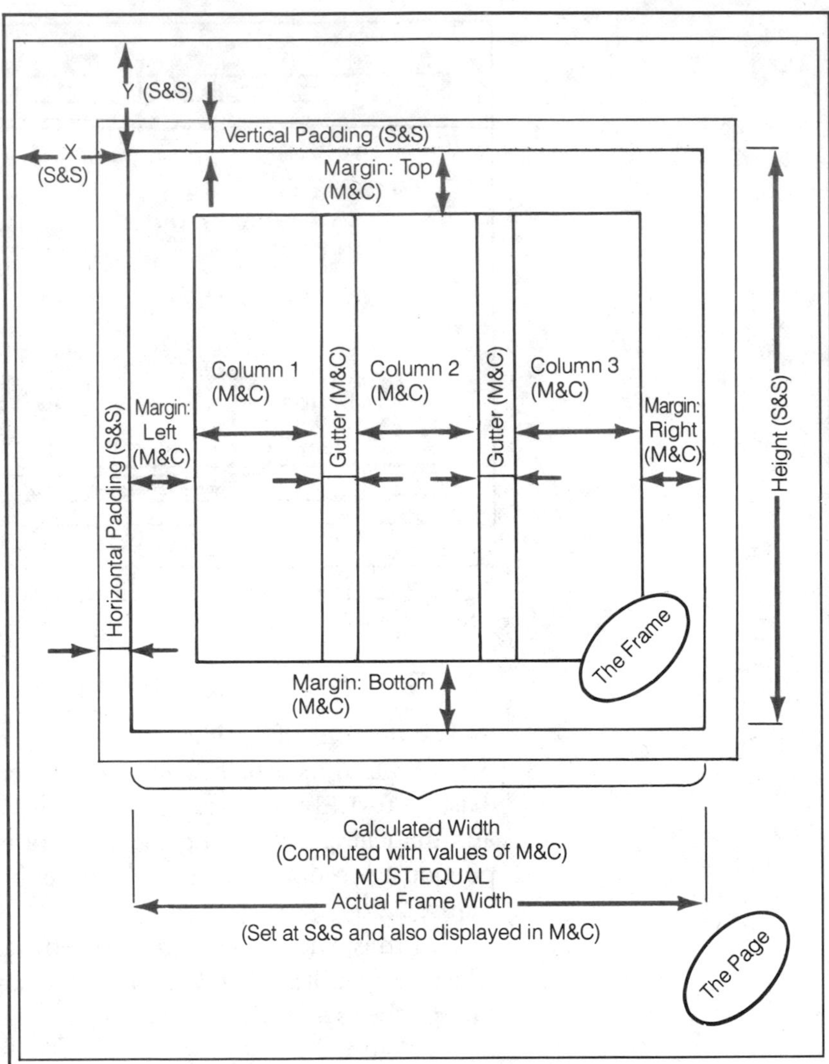

Note: Activate the appropriate frame to find its settings via the Frame pull-down menu.

M&C = Margins & Columns dialog box

S&S = Sizing & Scaling dialog box

If the frame is the same size as the page (i.e., you are working with the underlying-page frame), X and Y will be equal to 0, and Height and Width will match the page size.

Figure 2.23: Interaction of frame values

The Width and Height settings represent the dimensions of the frame. For the underlying-page frame, these values will match those set with the Chapter menu's Page Size & Layout dialog box.

FRAME PADDING

The Horiz Padding and Vert Padding settings control the border area just *outside* the frame. They prevent text in adjacent frames from touching the padded frame. Figure 2.24 shows how padding keeps text away from a frame. Notice how these settings contrast with the margin settings in the Frame menu's Margins & Columns dialog box (Figure 2.13). Margins regulate the border area *within* the frame.

- Click Cancel or press Ctrl-X to close the Sizing & Scaling dialog box.

SPECIFYING PAPER SIZE AND DOUBLE SIDES

The &NEWS-P2 sample we selected is already designed for letter-size paper. Your choice of paper size is stored as part of the style

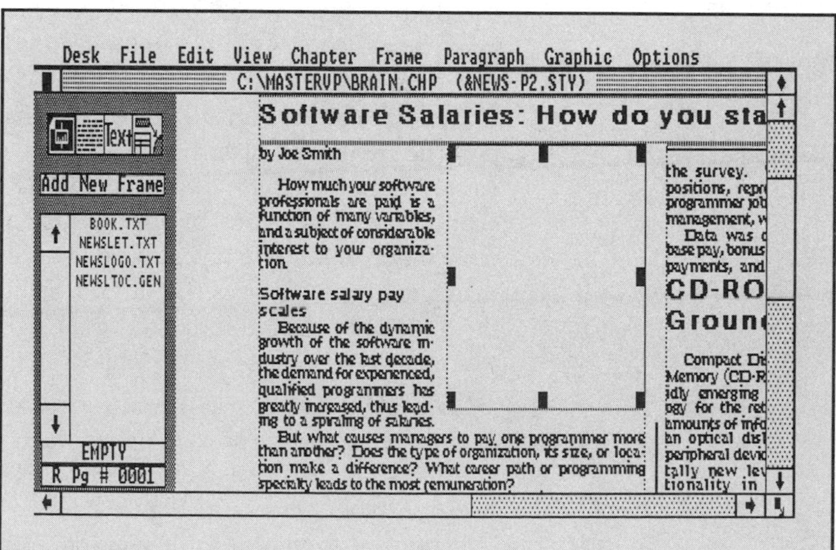

Figure 2.24: Frame padding

sheet. Seven standard sizes of paper are available with Ventura. They are illustrated in Figure 2.25. You're not, however, confined to these standard sizes. You can also create your own custom sizes, as we'll see.

Use the Chapter menu's Page Size & Layout command to check the size and shape of your pages, and change them when necessary. This is the same dialog box we examined in Chapter 1 in conjunction with pop-up menus.

- Drop the Chapter menu.
- Click Page Size & Layout.

The Page Layout dialog box, shown in Figure 2.26, appears.

! New for version 2.0

Kerning has been moved from the Chapter menu's Page Size Layout dialog box to the Chapter menu's Chapter Typography dialog box. We'll study kerning in Chapter 12.

SPECIFYING THE PAPER SIZE

Your two choices for Orientation are Portrait, for a vertical layout, and Landscape, for a horizontal one. Portrait orientation is considered easier to read and handle; hence, it's generally preferred. With some tables or pictures, however, you may find it necessary to use the landscape orientation. The sample should already be set to use portrait orientation.

Next look at the Paper Type & Dimension setting. When you position the mouse on it and press, the six types appear (Half, Letter, Legal, and so on), along with corresponding dimensions. You cannot change the dimensions by typing numbers in this field. You must choose one of the five types. Next, you'll see how you can use frame margins to specify sizes that aren't available here. In this example, the dialog box should indicate Letter size.

ODD-SIZE PAPER As mentioned earlier, Ventura accommodates seven standard sizes of paper, each in two orientations (portrait and landscape). These choices are found in the Chapter menu's Page Size & Layout, shown in Figure 2.26.

If none of these sizes suit you, choose one that is bigger than the size you need and adapt it. You do this by using the Frame menu's

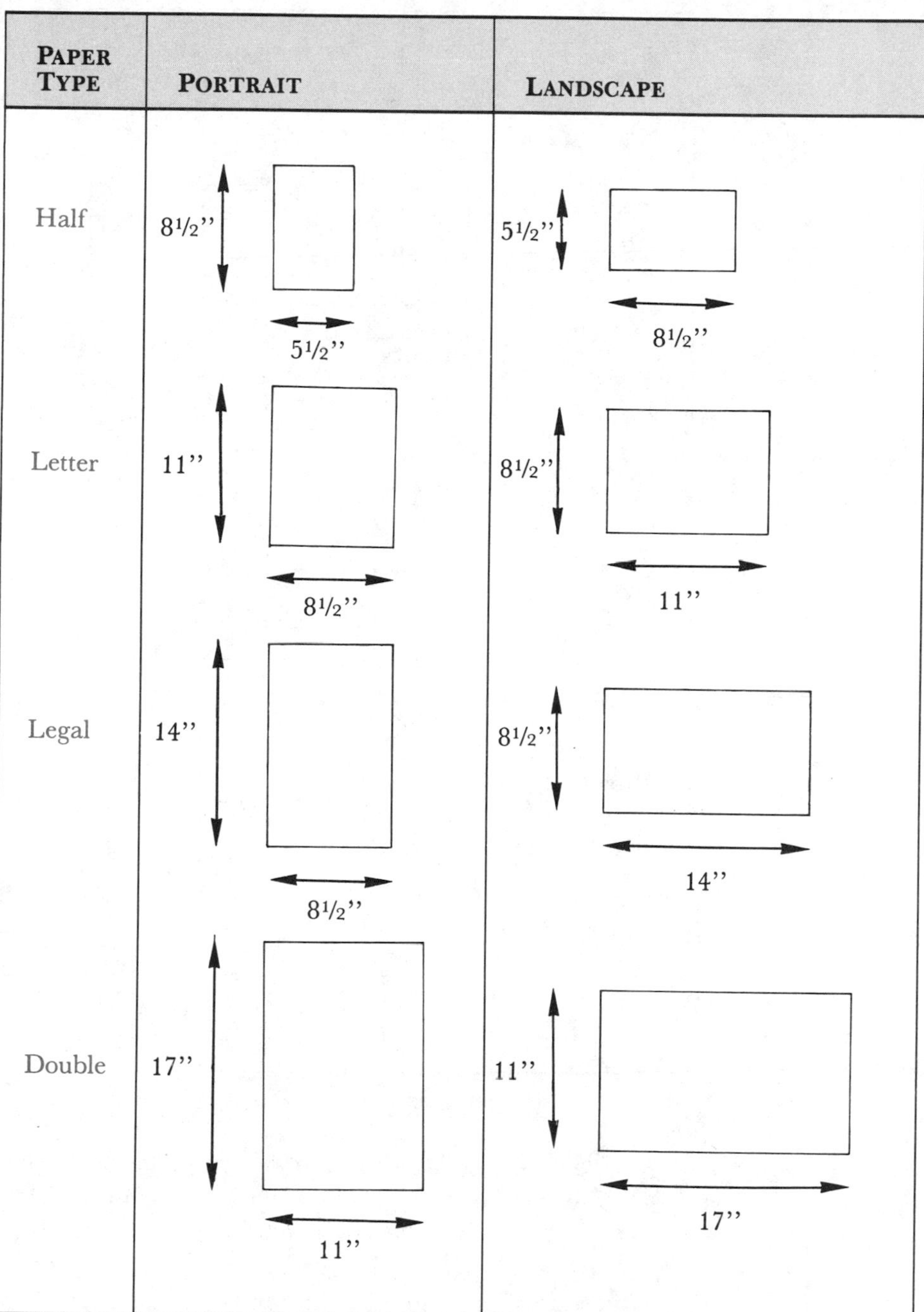

Figure 2.25: Standard paper sizes

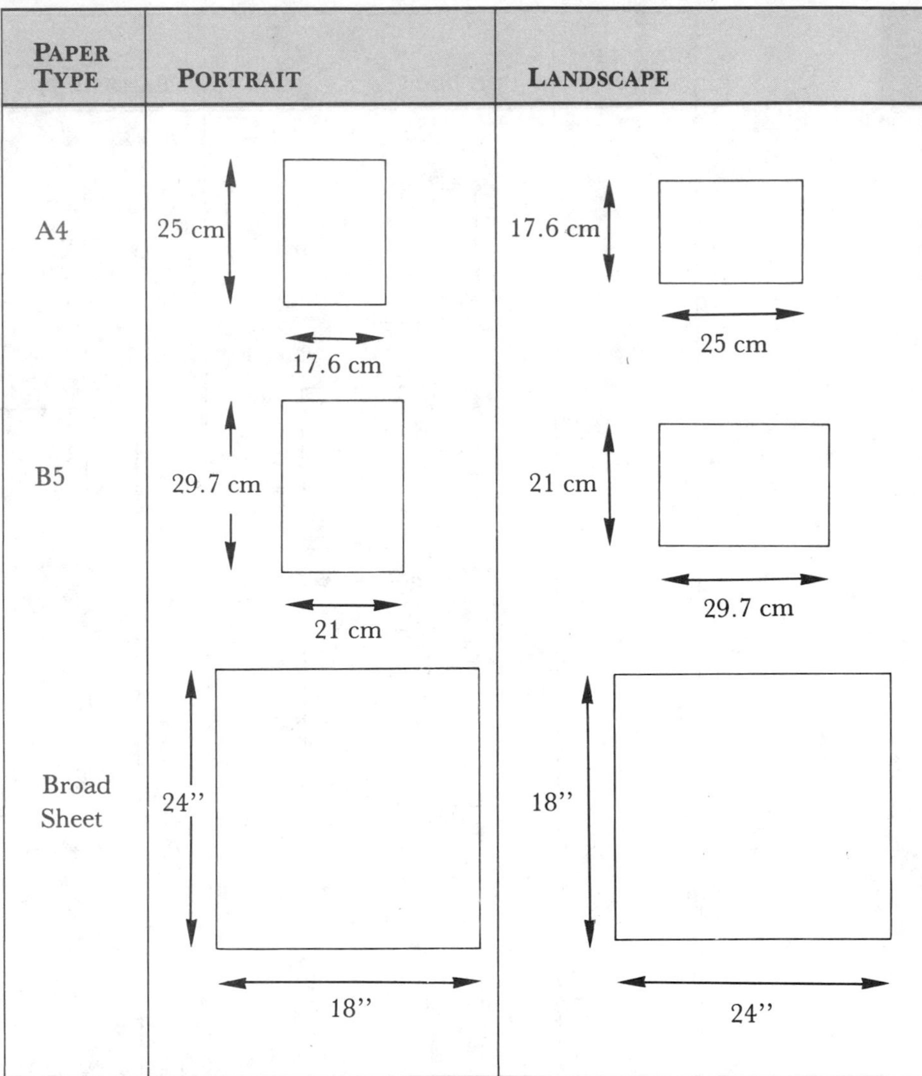

PAPER TYPE
PORTRAIT
LANDSCAPE
A4
25 cm
17.6 cm
17.6 cm
25 cm
B5
29.7 cm
21 cm
21 cm
29.7 cm
Broad Sheet
24''
18''
18''
24''

Figure 2.25: Standard paper sizes (continued)

Sizing & Scaling to change Frame Width and Frame Height. It may take some doing, so be prepared to experiment.

You can also increase the margins of the underlying-page frame (Frame menu, Margins & Columns), or use a repeating frame to reduce the printed area of a page. Repeating frames are discussed in Chapter 9.

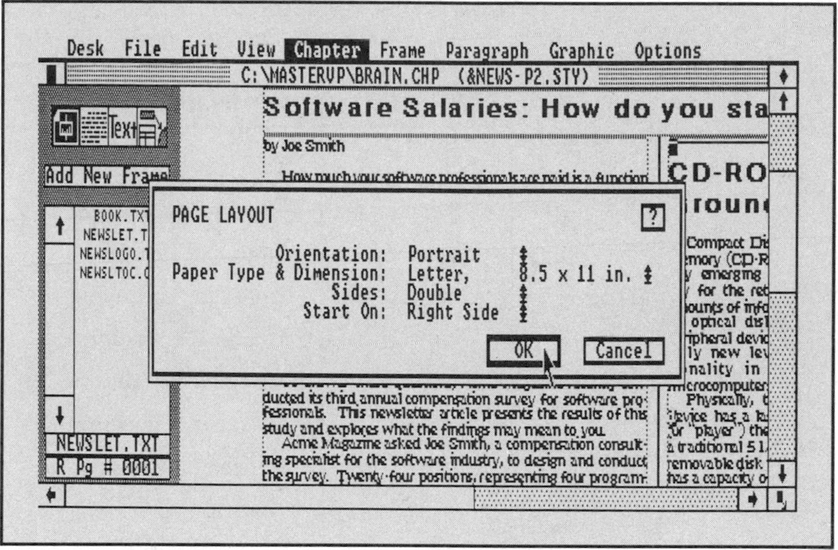

Figure 2.26: The Chapter menu's Page Layout dialog box

INDICATING SINGLE OR DOUBLE SIDES

With the Sides setting, you indicate whether you will be printing single-sided or double-sided. We won't be using double sides with our example, so:

- Change the Sides setting to Single.

Specifying double-sided allows you to treat special features, such as headers and footers, differently for left- and right-facing pages. That way, the features appear consistently on the inside or outside edges of the document. The features that you affect by specifying double-sided are listed in Table 2.1. Earlier, we saw how double-sided layout affects margins and columns.

With the Start On setting, you indicate whether the chapter should have its first page on the left or the right as you look at the document. This setting will take effect only if you've set the Sides setting to Double. Generally, a simple document that starts with page 1 should begin on the right side. This is because, by convention, odd-numbered pages are on the right.

Table 2.1: Settings Affected by Switching the Chapter Menu's Page Size & Layout to Double Sides

MENU	COMMAND	SETTING
File	To Print	Which Pages
View	Facing Pages View	(No Dialog Box)
Chapter	Page Size & Layout	Sides
Chapter	Page Size & Layout	Starts On
Chapter	Headers & Footers	Define
Frame	Margins & Columns	Settings For
Frame	Margins & Columns	Inserts
Frame	Repeating Frame	For All Pages
Frame	Vertical Rules	Settings For
Frame	Vertical Rules	Inserts
Paragraph	Spacing	Settings For
Paragraph	Spacing	Inserts
Paragraph	Breaks	Page Break

Once you change the settings to your satisfaction, give the OK with the mouse or the Enter key. (Note that you cannot double-click a choice to give the OK, as you could earlier with the file names in the Item Selector box. Double-clicking operates only with the Item Selector box, not dialog boxes.)

- Click OK or press the enter key to close the Page Layout dialog box and effect your settings.

HOW THE NEWSLETTER LOOKS NOW

So far, we have created a copy of the newsletter's chapter file and its style sheet, which shows on the Title line. We changed the right side from two columns to one column, and we set the chapter to single sides. Additionally, we added a frame beneath the byline (*by Joe Smith*); we'll use it to add a short biography about the author.

SAVING YOUR WORK

Though there remains quite a bit of work to do on our newsletter, you have already learned how to do most of the initial setting up.

* Save the work that you've done by dropping down the File menu and clicking Save.

As the menu indicates, there is a keyboard shortcut for saving: Ctrl-S. Either way, Ventura Publisher saves all elements of the displayed chapter that you've changed since you last saved. This includes the style sheet.

If you wish to save the chapter under a new name, use the Save As command instead.

* When you save your various Ventura Publisher files, consider whether you want the program to keep backup versions of the files. Normally, it does not. However, if you have the disk space, saving backups is a good precaution against accidental file losses. See Appendix A for information on how to keep backup files automatically.

NEW AND ABANDONED DOCUMENTS

You should become familiar with two other commands on the File menu. Use the New command when you want to clear the document that's displayed in order to commence work on a brand new (currently nonexisting) chapter. Use the Abandon command if you've loaded a chapter and then made changes to it that you don't want to keep. After getting verification from you, Ventura will discard the revisions you've made and reload the previous version of the chapter from the disk.

To use the Abandon command most effectively, think about using it before you need to. Just before you make a drastic change to a document, save the document. Then, if you don't like the results, simply use Abandon. Also save before you try a procedure with which you're unfamiliar, and certainly save regularly as a matter of course.

QUITTING

Let's finish up this Ventura Publisher work session.

* Use the File drop-down menu and click Quit.

Even though the Quit command allows you to save, don't rely on it. Sometimes, as in the case of a full disk, quitting will not allow you to save before quitting. Always use the File menu's Save command to save before quitting.

If you've made any changes in the chapter since you last saved, Ventura Publisher displays the message

> STOP
> Save or Abandon changes to this chapter?

Since you just saved your work, you shouldn't see this message. If you haven't saved and you want to keep the changes that you've made:

- Carefully click Save or Don't Quit. Use Abandon if you've made changes that you don't want to save.

In the next chapter, we'll see how to make changes in the material that we've been setting up.

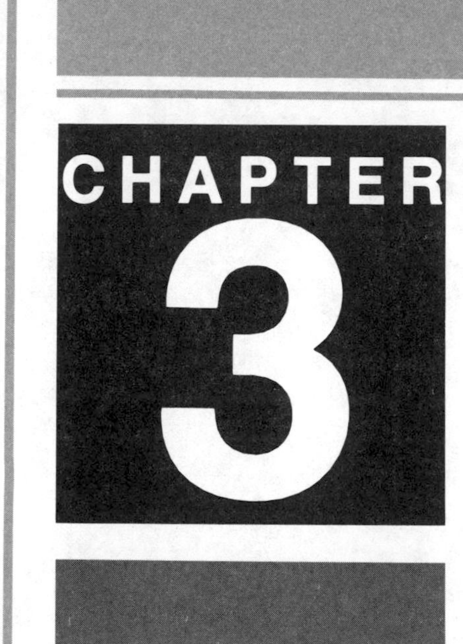
CHAPTER
3

Using Electronic Scissors and Glue

Fast Track

To use a file in a chapter 85

add it to the Assignment list. Use the File menu's Load Text/Picture dialog box. Click Format: Text and the type of format. Then use the Item Selector box to load the file.

To assign a file to a frame 87

in Frame mode, click the desired frame and then click the file's name on the Assignment list. If you want to assign the file to another frame as well, repeat the procedure; Ventura will pick up the text where it left off in the next frame.

To remove a file 88

from a frame or from the Assignment list in Frame mode, use the Edit menu's Remove Text/File. To remove a file from a frame, you must first click the frame.

To rename a file 90

or change its word-processed format, select the frame in Frame mode and use the Edit menu's File Type/Rename. Ventura makes changes to the file on disk when you save the chapter.

To move page by page within the document 91

press Ctrl-G or select the Chapter menu's Go To Page. By using Relative To, you can move relative to the document or relative to the file in the selected frame. Alternatively, use the keyboard shortcuts (Page Up, Page Down, Home, End).

To position the text cursor in text 94

activate Text mode and click the text with the mouse. You can then move the text cursor with the keypad arrows.

To type text directly into a frame 95

click the frame while in Text mode and start typing. Ventura 2.0 provides a name for new text in the first underlying-page frame (based on the chapter's name). Text you enter directly into other frames is called Frame text and is assigned to the chapter's CAP file.

To re-ink (refresh) the screen 97

press the Esc key. Various procedures will muddy the screen, necessitating this action.

To identify special characters 98

watch the Current box. The names of selected characters appear in this box when Text mode is active.

Edit text 99

with Delete, Backspace, and other keys, or by selecting the text with the mouse and using cut, copy, and paste procedures. Select text by dragging with the mouse or by Shift-clicking. Text that is cut (Delete key or Edit menu's Cut Text) or copied (Shift-Del or Edit menu's Copy Text) goes to the text clipboard. Paste the text (Ins key or Edit menu's Paste Text) to insert it elsewhere.

To cut, copy, and paste frames 100

follow procedures similar to those for text, but first activate Frame mode to select the frame. When you paste a frame on the page, Ventura locates it on the page in the same position from which you cut or copied it. First move an existing frame with the mouse to avoid placing a newly pasted frame on top of it.

CHAPTER 3

IN CHAPTER 2, YOU OPENED ONE OF THE SAMPLE chapters provided with Ventura, a newsletter named &NEWS-P2.CHP. You then created a new directory, MASTERVP, on your disk. In the MASTERVP directory, you made a copy of the &NEWS-P2.CHP chapter file, assigning it the name BRAIN.CHP. You also made a copy of its corresponding style sheet. You then used the frames and pages in BRAIN.CHP to practice positioning frames on the page.

Having mastered these tasks, you can now begin to develop your own documents by laying out frames and assigning material to them. You'll be using the same chapter, BRAIN.CHP, to create this ongoing example. Doing so will give you practice removing the sample material from the frames and replacing it with your own.

In general, when assigning material to frames, you'll find it necessary to play the role of editor. As you create layouts you'll need to make changes in the material that appears. For example, you may have to shorten an article or correct a misspelling. You might prepare a frame completely and then find that it would be better to locate it on a different page, perhaps next to a frame that contains similar material. You might even develop a complex set of formats for your document and then decide to reformat completely.

Before desktop publishing, such changes, small or large, called for scissors, glue, and a lot of effort. With Ventura, you use electronic equivalents of scissors and glue (and much less effort). For this reason, Ventura refers to editing work as *cut, copy,* and *paste* operations.

There are different ways to perform editing operations with Ventura. Roughly, they correspond to the operational modes of the program. In Frame mode, you cut, copy, and paste frames. In Text mode, you cut, copy, and paste text. In Graphics mode, you use these procedures on graphics. Paragraph mode, however, has no cut, copy, and paste procedure. Although you can duplicate and remove paragraph tags, that procedure is quite different from cut, copy, and paste operations. We'll see how that's handled in Chapter 4.

In this chapter, you'll learn how to cut, copy, and paste frames and text. (You'll perform these operations on graphics in Chapter 6.) We'll look at how you assign text files created with your word processor to frames in your document. You can use this procedure to replace the sample text files originally assigned by Ventura. Then we'll see how to make changes in your text, from minor line editing to moving whole blocks. Finally, we'll see how you can cut, copy, and paste frames themselves, along with the contents they hold.

ASSIGNING TEXT CREATED WITH A WORD PROCESSOR

Only one text file can be assigned to a frame. When a frame is active, the name of that text file appears above the page number in the Current box.

You can, however, assign the same file to several frames. If you do, Ventura will fill the first frame that you assign, and then go on to fill the next frame, with the remaining text picking up where it left off.

To practice working with text files in frames, start by opening the sample chapter you created:

1. If you quit Ventura at the end of Chapter 2, reload the program as explained in Chapter 1.
2. Drop the File menu and select Open Chapter.
3. In the MASTERVP directory, open the BRAIN.CHP chapter.

ADDING A FILE TO THE ASSIGNMENT LIST

The first step in assigning a text file to a frame is to use the File menu's Load Text/Picture command to add the file's name to the Assignment list on the Side-bar. Doing so makes it available for you to use. Once the name appears on the list, you can assign it to a frame. For practice, you'll replace the text of the article entitled

"CD-ROM Breaks New Ground" with the file BOOK.TXT provided with Ventura. Follow these steps:

1. Activate Frame mode. You do not have to do this to add a file to the Assignment list. This merely lets you see the list of the files that can be assigned to frames. Make sure you don't have an empty frame selected, or Ventura will assign the file you load to it.
2. Drop the File menu and click Load Text/Picture. The Load Text/Picture dialog box appears (Figure 3.1).
3. Click Text to specify the kind of file to load.
4. Click ASCII to specify that you want to load an ASCII text file.
5. Give the OK by pressing Enter or clicking the OK box.
6. Specify the TYPESET directory, if necessary, in the Item Selector box that appears.
7. Select BOOK.TXT and give the OK. The file name BOOK.TXT appears in the Assignment list.

You click ASCII because ASCII happens to be the file type of the sample file BOOK.TXT. If you wanted to load a file created with WordPerfect, you'd click WordPerfect (or WordPerfect 5) at this point. If you wanted to load a Microsoft WORD file, you'd click MS-Word, and so on.

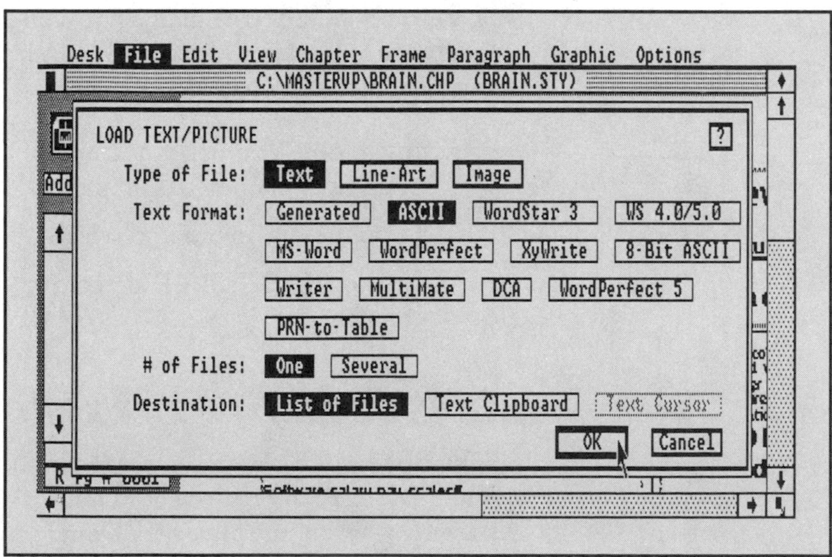

Figure 3.1: The Load Text/Picture dialog box

Ventura assumes that each type of file has a specific file extension. For example, a WP extension denotes a WordPerfect file. In some cases, the particular application you use to create the file assigns the extension, in some cases it does not. Either make sure that your application saves the file with the appropriate file extension, or when you use the File menu's Load Text/Picture, change the extension on the Item Selector box's Directory field. Make it match the file extension you're using (see Appendix C).

When you create text for Ventura with a word processor, you must keep the file simple. Do not press Enter except at the end of a paragraph. Don't indent paragraphs, center headings, or concern yourself with page layout; such features will be handled by Ventura. For more on entering text with a word processor, see Chapter 11.

ASSIGNING THE FILE TO A FRAME

Once a file is in the Assignment list, assigning it to a frame is a matter of simply clicking the desired frame, and then clicking the desired file:

1. With Frame mode operational, click the frame containing the headline "CD-ROM Breaks New Ground."
2. In the Assignment list, click BOOK.TXT. The file's contents appear in the frame, and the file's name (BOOK.TXT) appears in the Current box.

Ventura fills the selected frame with as much of the text file as the frame can accommodate.

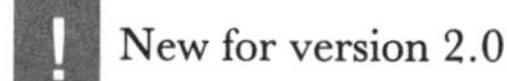

New for version 2.0

If you assign a file to the underlying-page frame of an untitled chapter, Ventura gives the chapter the same name as the text file when you save the chapter. The consistency in names reduces confusion. In addition, it expedites the first saving process, since Ventura 2.0 no longer pauses to request a name for the chapter.

If a file has more text than a frame can handle, you can make Ventura "pour" the leftover text into another frame. To assign a file to an additional frame on the same page, simply select the second frame and use the Assignment list to click the file's name again. Ventura will pick up the text where it left off when the first frame was full. In the example, the file NEWSLET.TXT is assigned to two frames: the one with "Software Salaries" and the one that begins "by Joe Smith." The program will always display text in frames in the same order that you create the frames (which is not necessarily the order that the frames appear on the page).

Be sure to look for the *End Of File marker* so that you know all of the file is showing in your frame (unless you deliberately want to cut an article short). The End Of File marker is a small square box (□), the size of other characters, that appears at the very end of the file when tabs and returns are showing (see Appendix A). If this code doesn't appear, there is additional text in the file. To display such additional text, enlarge the frame or assign the text file to an additional frame. We'll see how to edit text later in this chapter.

You can change the assigned order by cutting frames and repasting them, as discussed later in this chapter. Repasting is the same as creating the frame anew, and the text will be assigned accordingly.

Note, however, that Ventura always assigns text to pages in order. You cannot have text continue on a previous page, even by assigning it after you assign text to a later page.

If another file already occupies a frame when you assign a new file, the new assignment will take its place in the frame. The old file's name will still appear on the Assignment list. You can easily assign that file to another frame elsewhere in the chapter. Just select a new frame and click the file's name on the Assignment list.

REMOVING A FILE FROM THE ASSIGNMENT LIST OR FROM A FRAME

If you don't plan to use the file that you've eliminated from a frame, you can use the Edit menu's Remove Text/File command to remove the file from the Assignment list. Doing so may speed up operations while loading and allow you to create larger chapters. For practice, remove the file NEWSLET.TXT from a frame and from the Assignment list:

1. Activate Frame mode and click the frame whose file you wish to remove. Use the one containing the words "Software Salaries: How do you stack up?"
2. Drop the Edit menu and click Remove Text/File. The dialog box shown in Figure 3.2 appears. The name of the file contained in the selected frame, NEWSLET.TXT, appears in the File Name field.
3. Select Remove From: List Of Files and give the OK.

When you remove a file name from the Assignment list, it makes that file unavailable for use with the chapter. This action does not, however, erase the file from the disk. Thus, if you later wish to use the file, just add it to the Assignment list again, as described earlier. To remove a file from the disk, use the File menu's DOS File Ops command.

The file's contents disappear from the selected frame, and from the frame below it.

The Remove File dialog box has two choices for "Remove from": namely, List Of Files and Frame. There will be times when you want to remove a text file from a frame, even though you don't have another file ready with which to replace the text (as we replaced it earlier under "Assigning the File to a Frame"). You might want to do

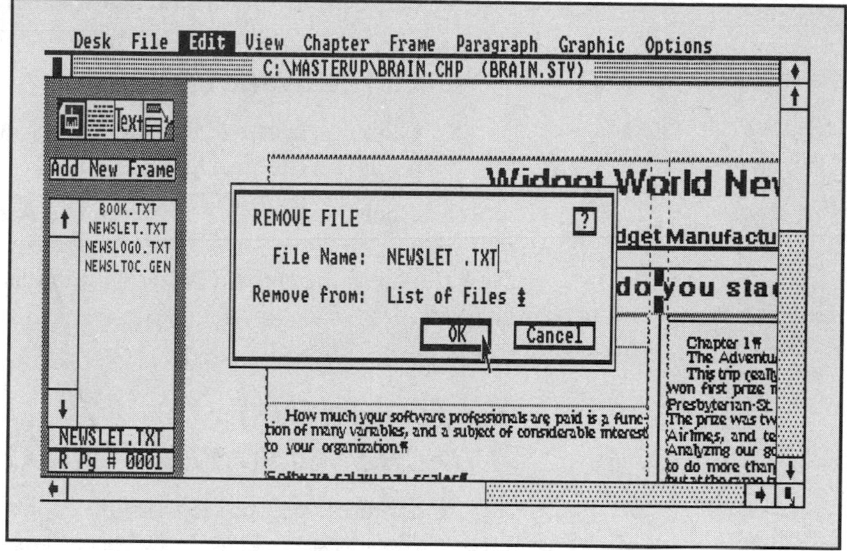

Figure 3.2: The Remove File dialog box

this, for instance, if someone working on an article for your newsletter has not yet finished it. To remove a text file in this manner, select the appropriate frame and select Remove From: Frame in this dialog box. This action removes all text from the chosen frame. You can later assign a text file to this frame.

Once a frame is empty, you can also type text, called *Frame text,* directly into it. We'll see how to do this shortly, using Edit mode. First, put the NEWSLET.TXT file back on the Assignment list and back into the frames from which it was just removed.

1. Activate Frame mode if necessary.
2. Click the empty frame under the frame containing "Widget World News."
3. Select the File menu's Load Text/Picture.
4. Click Text as the file type and ASCII as the text format, and then give the OK.
5. Use the Item Selector Box to select NEWSLET.TXT from the TYPESET directory. The file's contents fill the selected frame.

6. Click the empty frame below the frame that contains the text ''Software Salaries: How do you stack up?''
7. Click NEWSLET.TXT in the Assignment list.
8. Click the frame to the right of the current frame with ''Chapter 1'' as the first line of text.
9. Click NEWSLET.TXT in the Assignment list.

Now the file is the same as when you loaded it at the beginning of this chapter.

RENAMING FILES AND CHANGING THE FORMAT TYPE

In Chapter 2, you made working copies of the sample &NEWS-P2 chapter file and style sheet. Now you will use the Edit menu's File Type/Rename to make a working copy of the text file NEWSLET.TXT. File Type/Rename is useful if you wish to make changes in the contents of a text file but you want to keep the original intact.

1. Activate Frame mode if necessary.
2. Click the frame whose text file you wish to resume. In this case, use the frame containing the words ''CD-ROM Breaks New Ground.''
3. Select the Edit menu's File Type/Rename command.

This action displays the File Type/Rename dialog box, shown in Figure 3.3.

4. Change the New Name field to say

   C:\MASTERVP\NEWSLET.TXT

5. Give the OK.
6. Click the File menu's Save command. You must use Save or Save As to put the File Type/Rename changes into effect.

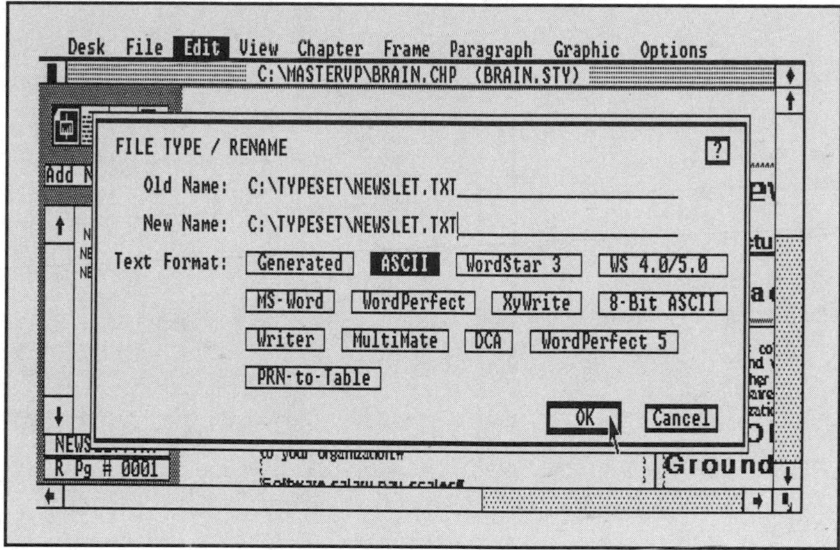

Figure 3.3: The File Type/Rename dialog box

MOVING WITHIN THE DOCUMENT

Shortly, we'll see how to perform a variety of editing procedures on files you've assigned to frames. To do so, however, you'll need to be able to display any page in your document that needs work.

With Ventura, you can easily move to any page. The two methods of doing this utilize the Go To Page dialog box, shown in Figure 3.4, and the shortcut keys associated with it.

The easiest way to display the Go To Page dialog box is to type Ctrl-G. You can also display it by dropping the Chapter menu and clicking Go To Page.

Usually, Relative To: Document appears, indicating that the settings you choose will operate relative to the document, as opposed to the filc. Let's examine moving relative to the document first.

MOVING RELATIVE TO THE DOCUMENT

The Which Page pop-up menu allows you to specify which page you want displayed on the screen. Choosing First displays the first

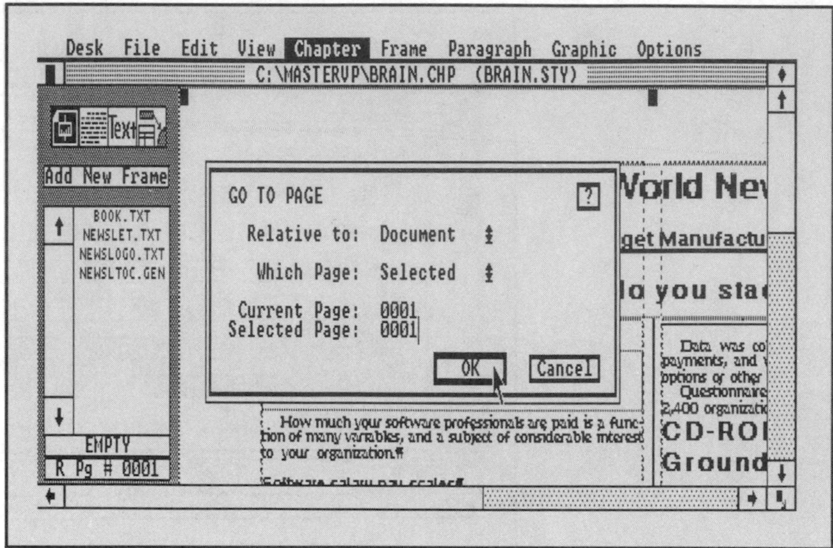

Figure 3.4: The Go To Page dialog box

page in the document (once you give the OK). Prev displays the previous page in the document; that is, the page before the one currently on the screen. Next and Last display the next page and the last page of the document, respectively.

Which Page: Selected initially appears. This setting operates in conjunction with the Selected Page field at the bottom of this dialog box. The Current Page field is an indicator that shows the page number of the page displayed on the screen. (You can also see the current page number at the bottom of the Side-bar.)

Initially, the Selected Page field displays the same number as the Current Page. Inserting a page number for Selected Page and giving the OK will display the page that you specify. You can wipe out the entire value that initially appears for Selected Page by pressing the Esc key.

Except for Selected, each of the Which Page settings has a shortcut key associated with its operation. Instead of displaying this dialog box and clicking one of the buttons, you can use a corresponding shortcut key, as follows:

First	Home key
Prev	Page Up key

Next Page Down key

Last End key

Thus, to go to the first page in your document you can simply press the Home key—the equivalent of displaying the dialog box, selecting Which Page: First, and giving the OK. As you can tell, these shortcut keys certainly warrant their name.

MOVING RELATIVE TO THE FILE

You can also use the settings in the Go To Page dialog box to move relative to the file. This ability of Ventura is designed for use with newsletter and magazine articles, for instance, that begin on one page and continue on another, many pages later.

As an example, assume that Frame mode is active and you have selected a frame with an article that leaves off at the bottom of the frame. The Go To Page dialog box will display the Relative To: File choice. By setting Which Page: Next and giving the OK, you will move to the page where the article picks up. Note that you must use the Which Page settings if you want to display a page relative to a file. The shortcut keys operate only with respect to the document.

If you go to a selected page relative to a file, and the file you've specified does not appear on the page you've indicated, Ventura will display the next page that does contain the file. If your selected page is after the last page containing the file, Ventura will display the last page on which the file appears.

PREPARING TO EDIT TEXT

Once you begin to move through your document and examine its contents, you may find that you need to make some changes in the text. You may even want to make a rough draft of your text and let another person proofread it for you. Because of Ventura's limitations, it's best to use a word processor for major edits. For example, with Ventura you can't edit text across pages, even when using the Facing Pages view. However, Ventura can handle minor and medium edits quite well. To make changes in text, you use Text mode.

ACTIVATING TEXT MODE

There are three ways to activate Text mode. You can drop the View menu and click Text Editing. More directly, you can click the third button of the Mode selector at the top of the Side-bar. Finally, you can press Ctrl-O on the keyboard. (Remember that the four mode keys, U, I, O, and P, are located on the keyboard in the same order as the four buttons of the Mode selector.)

- Activate Text mode using one of the methods described above.

The mouse I-beam appears.

THE MOUSE I-BEAM

Once you activate Text mode, the mouse cursor turns into an *I-beam* shape. It resembles an oversized capital *I,* as shown in Figure 3.5.

You use this mouse I-beam to accomplish two important tasks. First, with it you position the text cursor in the text. That is, clicking the mouse with the mouse I-beam at a certain spot causes the text cursor to appear in or move to that spot. If the text cursor is not on

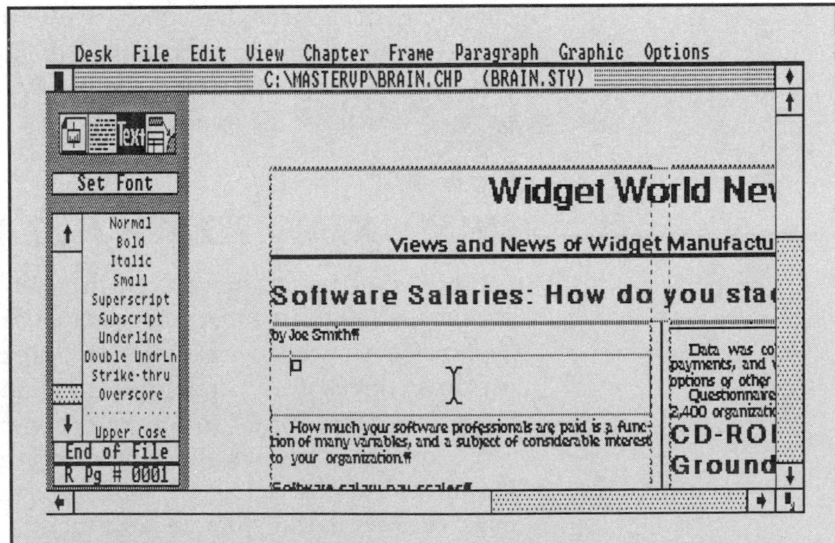

Figure 3.5: The mouse I-beam in Text mode

the screen (as is the case when you initially activate Text mode), this action causes it to appear where you click. If the text cursor is elsewhere on the page, this action relocates it to the new position. Either way, the two cursors then appear at the same location. With the text cursor in position, you can then edit.

The arrow keys on the keypad also maneuver the text cursor. Each arrow key moves the text cursor in its respective direction on the screen. As it does, the cursor passes over any text that appears, without disturbing it.

As you start to use the text cursor, the mouse cursor vanishes temporarily. However, it reappears as soon as you move the mouse.

! New for version 2.0

Version 2.0 lets you enter text on a blank underlying-page frame without first creating a text file. In Text mode you simply click the mouse in the blank working area. When you use the Save or Save As command, Ventura automatically saves the text to a text file. It uses the body of the chapter name (like *BRAIN* in *BRAIN.CHP*) as the body of the text-file name. The extension of the text file (like *TXT* in *NEWSLET.TXT*) is determined by the last type of text file you loaded with the File menu's Load Text/Picture command. (In earlier versions, if you were to click the I-beam cursor within a blank underlying-page frame, you'd see a message asking you to provide a name for a new file.)

You can also insert text into a standard frame, without assigning it to a file. Ventura calls it *Frame text;* when you use Frame mode to click the frame, this is the name that appears in the Current box toward the bottom of the side-bar. Ventura stores Frame text in the CAP file of the same name as the chapter file. In Chapter 2, you created a small frame to hold biographical information on the reporter Joe Smith.

- Practice creating Frame text by clicking this frame and typing in a make-believe bio. You can use the whimsical bio you see in Figure 3.6.

You can also use the mouse I-beam to designate text that you wish to change. This process is called *selecting* text. Ventura darkens the text to indicate that you've selected it. Then you can cut or copy that text. We'll examine the process later in this chapter, under "Selecting and Cutting Text." (In Chapter 4, we'll also see how you can change the attributes of the selected text. You can use this technique to italicize, for instance.)

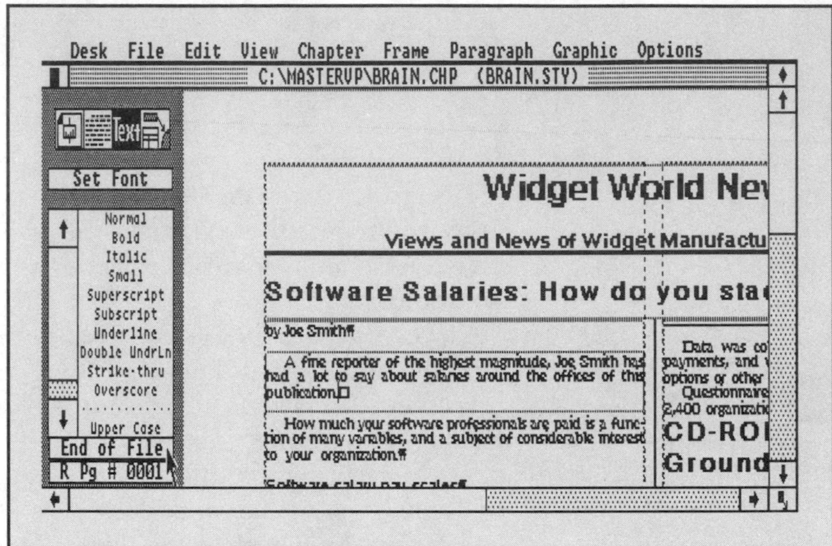

Figure 3.6: Frame text in a frame

Deactivating Text mode will undo your selection or cursor positions. For instance, if you switch to Frame mode, the text cursor disappears. When you reactivate Text mode, you will have to use the mouse cursor to reposition the keyboard cursor. Likewise, switching out of Text mode will cause any text you've selected (by darkening) to return to normal. Switching the page will also cause the text cursor to disappear and any selections you've made to return to normal.

KEEPING THE TEXT CURSOR IN SIGHT

There is another circumstance under which you may find the text cursor disappearing. If you move the cursor too far up, down, left, or right, it may go off the screen. This problem occurs especially when you use a standard-size screen.

Once off the screen, the text cursor may continue to operate as you type and thus affect unseen material in your document. So be careful. Make sure that you can always see the text cursor as you type in text.

If you lose the text cursor off the screen, use one of the following methods to get it back. (These techniques can also keep it from disappearing in the first place.)

- Use the mouse. Click and reposition the text cursor on some text that's displayed.
- Reverse the direction in which you were moving when the text cursor went off the screen. Often, such a turnabout will bring the cursor back into view.
- Change the view (Reduced, Normal, Enlarged). With a more general view, you may be able to display the portion of the page with the text cursor. Remember that with the keyboard shortcuts, Ventura uses the mouse cursor to determine the top-left corner of a more enlarged view.
- Change the displayed page with the Page Down or Page Up key if the text cursor has moved to the next or previous page. When you do, however, you will still not see the text cursor; as mentioned, switching pages causes the text cursor to disappear. To redisplay it, you will have to click the mouse on the new page.
- Remove the Side-bar to see more of the page and perhaps the text cursor. To do that, drop the Options menu and click Hide Side-Bar. You can also use the keyboard shortcut, Ctrl-W, to show or hide the Side-bar.
- Use the scroll bars to move the working area to another part of the page if the text cursor is on the same page but is not visible on the displayed portion. The scroll bar on the right of the screen moves the working area up and down the page. The scroll bar at the bottom moves the working area to the left and right.

RE-INKING IN TEXT MODE

As you edit your chapter, you may find it necessary to *re-ink* the page as you work. Due to its size, the text cursor often extends into text above and below the line that it's on. Thus, as you type, the text cursor will sometimes erase parts of such text as it passes. Various other procedures can cause text to disappear, too. To reset the text correctly, just press the Esc key when you have the working area displayed.

The kind of monitor you have may determine how often you need to re-ink. For instance, you'll find that a standard color/graphics monitor needs re-inking more often than a Genius monitor. This is apparently due to the lower resolution provided by the color/graphics monitor.

WATCHING FOR PARAGRAPH END SYMBOLS

* So that you don't erase Paragraph End symbols accidentally, it's best to keep them showing as you edit. Hide them only temporarily to check the appearance of your page; then redisplay them right away. To hide or display Paragraph End symbols, drop the Options menu and click Hide/Show Tabs & Returns or type Ctrl-T. (See Appendix A.)

As you edit, you'll also need to keep an eye out for Paragraph End symbols (¶). This mark shows where a paragraph ends—that is, where you pressed the Enter key. As we'll see in Chapter 4, this mark terminates the paragraph formatting. So be careful not to erase a Paragraph End symbol accidentally, or you may have to retag the following paragraph in order to regain its formatting.

USING THE CURRENT BOX TO WATCH FOR SPECIAL SYMBOLS

Besides the Paragraph End mark, there are several other special symbols that may appear on the screen, such as the End Of File, Line Break and Horizontal Tab symbols. If tabs and returns are hidden, you won't be able to see them. However, Ventura does provide you with a way to make their presence known, with or without displaying them. The Current box serves this function.

The Current box is located below the Assignment list in the Side-bar. (Look back at Figure 3.6, where the arrow is pointing.) The upper half of this box is often empty. However, when the working area has a special symbol to the *right* of the text cursor, the name of that symbol appears in the Current box. When a standard character that is always visible (such as a letter or number) appears to the right of the keyboard cursor, the upper half of the Current box is empty.

Use this flagging mechanism to judge your editing maneuvers, especially when you delete with the Del key. With the text cursor showing in the working area, pressing the Del key deletes the character to the right of the text cursor. By checking the Current box you can be certain not to accidentally remove a special symbol that's invisible. You should also check the Current box as you select text. That way, you'll be certain to darken only those special symbols that you want to affect, without unintentionally selecting or missing any.

CHANGING A TITLE

Now that you're aware of some pitfalls, you can practice editing with Ventura. Our first editing task will be to change the title of the sample newsletter. We'll replace *Widget World News* with *The Brainstorm.* Be aware, though, that the original title is still in the NEWSLOGO.TXT file. To keep the original file intact, be sure to rename the text file, as described earlier in this chapter.

1. Activate Text mode if it is not already operational.
2. Point the mouse I-beam to a spot somewhere in the middle of the title—say before the *W* in *World*—to observe differences in the way the Backspace and Del keys erase.
3. Click the mouse on that spot. The text cursor, a vertical bar, appears in the title (Figure 3.7).
4. Move the mouse cursor so that you can see what you're doing.
5. Remove all characters to the right of the text cursor except the Paragraph End symbol. To do so, simply press the Del key.

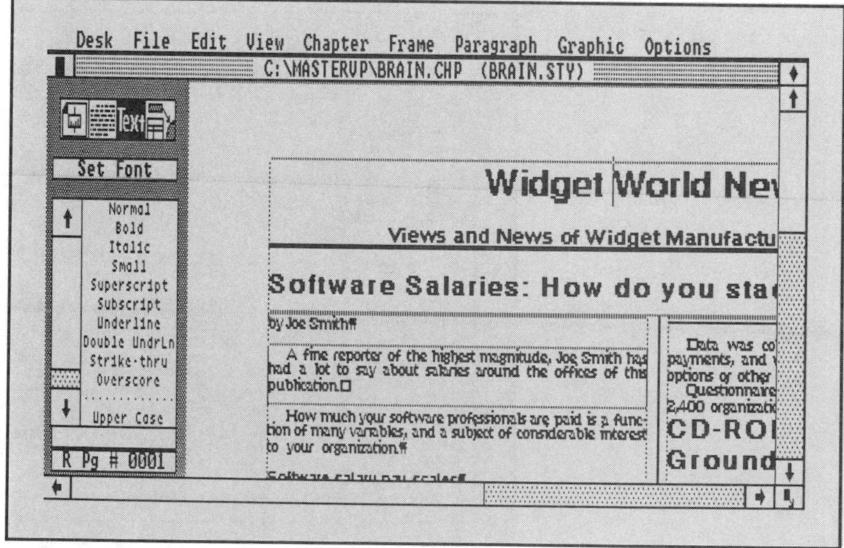

Figure 3.7: Text cursor in the newsletter title

Each repeated press removes one character; however, if you *hold* the Del key down, it removes characters one after another. Be careful that you don't hold the Del key down too long, or the text cursor may eat up more characters than you want.

6. Remove the text to the *left* of the text cursor. To do so, press the Backspace key. The same press-or-hold precaution just mentioned for the Del key also applies to the Backspace key.
7. Once you have removed all the characters except the Paragraph End symbol, as shown in Figure 3.8, type in the new title, **The Brainstorm**. As you do, you'll see that it appears in the same typeface as the previous title.

SELECTING AND CUTTING TEXT

Using the Backspace key or the Del key in conjunction with the text cursor works well for deletions of a single character or a few words. If you need to delete several words or more, however, it's best to use the mouse.

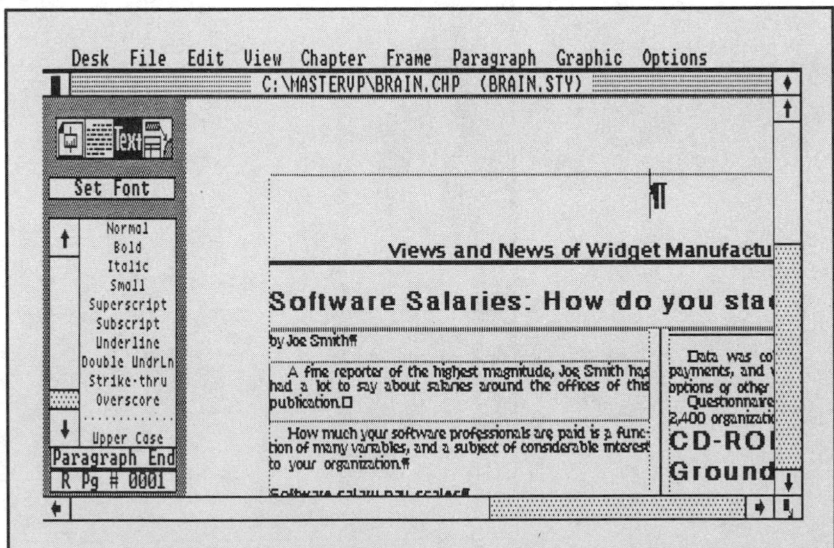

Figure 3.8: Paragraph End symbol

You can use the mouse in one of two ways to select the text that you want to delete. Once selected, the text appears darkened or in reverse video (see Figure 3.9). You can then perform a variety of operations on the selected text, such as copying or cutting it from its surroundings.

The two ways to select text with the mouse are dragging the mouse and Shift-clicking. For practice, follow these steps:

1. Bring the mouse I-beam to either the beginning or the end of the text you wish to select. For practice, use the darkened text in Figure 3.9.
2. Press the mouse button and hold it down.
3. Drag the mouse to the other end of the passage. As you move the mouse, the text that it passes over darkens.
4. Release the button. The text is now selected.

Now practice selecting text by Shift-clicking:

1. Click the mouse at the beginning or end of the text darkened in Figure 3.9. The text cursor appears in that spot.

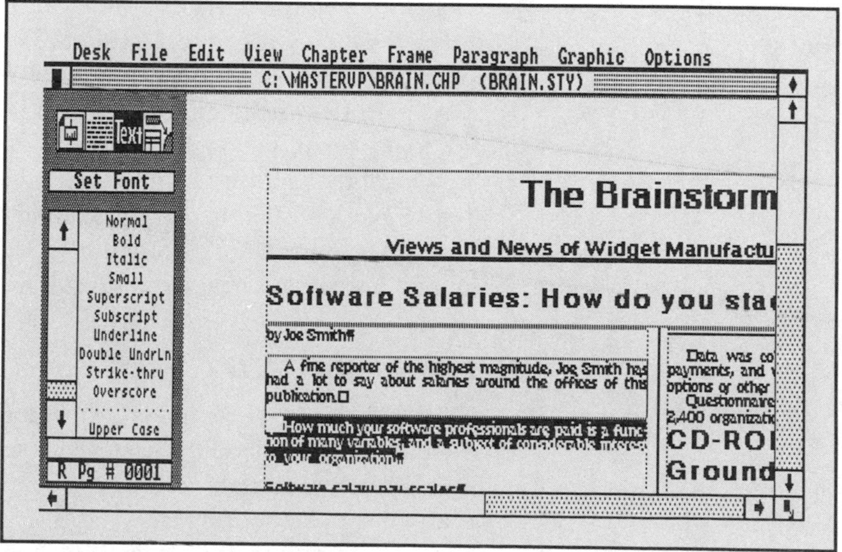

Figure 3.9: Selecting text

2. Move the mouse to the opposite end of the passage. (Do not hold the mouse button and drag.)
3. Press the Shift key and hold it down while you click the mouse at that spot. This action darkens the text between the two spots.

This second technique is especially handy when the text cursor already happens to be positioned correctly at one end of the desired text. All you need to do is Shift-click the mouse at the other end.

We could have used either of these techniques earlier to remove the old title, *Widget World News,* from the newsletter. Once the text is selected, you can cut it by pressing the Del key or by dropping the Edit menu and clicking Cut Text. The text is extracted from the screen and placed on an invisible clipboard (which we'll discuss shortly).

CORRECTING ERRORS IN A SELECTION OPERATION

You may make a mistake in the selection operation using either of the above methods. You may find that you have selected too little or too much. If so, you can use the Shift-click method of selection to shorten or extend the darkened area. Simply hold down the Shift key and click the mouse at the correct spot. The darkened area will adjust accordingly. If you shorten the darkened area by Shift-clicking, Ventura assumes that the beginning of the selected text (that is, the spot closest to the top of the page) is correct. The new darkened area covers text from that spot to the new spot you indicate.

If you make a mistake in cutting and find that you have cut the wrong material, stop. Don't touch anything! See "Pasting Text in a New Location" later in this chapter to learn how to restore the cut text.

THE CLIPBOARD

At any one time, you can cut any amount of text that's displayed on the page, as long as all the material you cut is initially on the same page. Once the material is on the clipboard, however, you can paste it on any page you desire.

The clipboard is an unseen area of Ventura. When you cut text, Ventura removes it from the page and places it on the clipboard.

From the clipboard, you can paste it into the chapter at another location. You can even insert the contents of the clipboard into a different chapter. The contents of the clipboard remain intact when you load another chapter. Ventura clears the clipboard only when you quit the program or replace its contents with new cut or copied text. That is, when you cut new text to the clipboard, the old text that was on the clipboard disappears forever. So if you plan to use text that's on the clipboard, be certain that you insert it somewhere in your document before you cut other text.

Unlike text selected on the screen, the contents of the clipboard remain there when you switch modes. In fact, Ventura has a total of three clipboards. One is used to store frames, one stores text, and one stores graphics. The content of each clipboard is separate. What you do to one does not affect the other two.

Thus, if we had selected the old title and then cut it with the Del key, the words *Widget World News* would have been deleted from the document and sent to the Text clipboard. They would remain there even as we changed modes or documents, until replaced by some other text.

COPYING TEXT

The procedure for copying text is similar to that for cutting text. Both procedures place the selected text on the clipboard. When you are cutting, you remove text from the page, and Ventura places it on the clipboard. Copying, however, places an exact copy of the selected text on the clipboard. The selected text remains on the page as well.

The procedure for copying text is very similar to the one used to cut. Follow these steps:

1. Activate Text mode if it's not already active.
2. Select the text shown in Figure 3.9 by darkening it with the mouse. Do so by dragging the mouse or Shift-clicking.
3. Copy the darkened text to the clipboard by dropping the Edit menu and clicking Copy Text, or by pressing Shift-Del.
4. To insert a copy of the text in a new location, follow the steps for pasting text outlined below.

PASTING TEXT IN A NEW LOCATION

Once you have cut or copied text to the clipboard, you can paste that text in a new location. (With version 2.0, you can also load text to the clipboard, as we'll see in the next section.) By cutting and pasting you effect a *move*; that is, you remove the text from one location and place it in another. This kind of operation is routinely performed when documents are revised for readability.

By copying and pasting, however, you place an exact copy of the text that's in one location into another location. This is handy when you're working with forms, for instance, or with other applications that involve repeating patterns.

To paste text, follow these steps:

1. You must, of course, have some text on the clipboard already. That is, you must have cut, copied, or loaded text to it, as described above. Text mode must be active.
2. Position the text cursor in the exact spot where you want the first character of the text to appear.
3. Press the Ins key. Alternatively, drop the Edit menu and click Paste Text.

When you paste, the first character of text on the clipboard appears right after (to the right of) the flashing text cursor. The remaining clipboard text follows. Text already on the page, originally following the text cursor, is pushed down the page and follows the newly pasted (inserted) text.

You can easily make multiple copies of the text that's on the clipboard. When you paste, you are pasting a *copy* of the text that's on the clipboard; after you paste, the same text remains on the clipboard. You can then relocate the text cursor and simply paste the same text again as many times as you like.

Use Text mode and these cut, copy, and paste operations when you want to edit the text file that appears in a frame. If you are editing a great deal of a file, however, it is better to use your word processor. That way you won't have to worry about difficulties like selecting text across pages. You can also take advantage of the word processor's search capability. Searching is necessary if the file is long and you have cross-references that you must check. See Chapter 11 for a discussion of word processors.

SENDING TEXT FROM DISK TO THE CURSOR OR THE CLIPBOARD

! New for version 2.0

Ventura now provides an extended method of inserting text into a chapter. You can take text directly from a word-processed file and place it in the chapter or on the clipboard. Simply use the File menu's Load Text/Picture.

After using the resulting dialog box to specify Type Of File: Text and to indicate the text format, use its Destination buttons. Normally, you select Destination: List Of Files, which adds the file's name to the Assignment list so you can assign it to a frame. However, you can click Destination: Text Clipboard; Ventura will place the file's contents on the clipboard for pasting in Text mode.

Alternatively, you can choose Destination: Text Cursor; Ventura will immediately insert the file's text into the document at the location of the text cursor, pushing down any existing text that follows the cursor. Give the OK and Ventura will display an Item Selector box that you use to indicate the file you wish to insert.

CUTTING, COPYING, AND PASTING FRAMES

You can perform cut, copy, and paste operations on frames as well as text. Many of the techniques used to manipulate frames are similar to those used for text. By applying these techniques, you can move or remove frames, or create duplicate frames with similar specifications.

Just as you must activate Text mode to cut, copy, and paste text, so you must activate Frame mode to manipulate frames. Also, just as you must indicate the text you want to change, so too you must indicate which frame is to change.

When you manipulate a frame in this manner, you manipulate the text file assigned to it. The frame is like a container, with text poured into it. If you've assigned a file to more than one frame on the page, and you cut one frame, Ventura will pour its text into the next frame the file is assigned to.

In Chapter 2, you saw how to move a frame using the mouse. Although moving frames with the mouse is easy to do, mouse moves will reposition a frame only on the same page. If you wish to move a frame to a new page, you must cut it from the first page and then paste it on the new page. You may also wish to cut a frame simply to delete it and its contents from the page.

CUTTING FRAMES

Cutting a frame that you no longer need or that you want to move to another location is quite similar to cutting unwanted text. Ventura places the cut frame on a *Frame clipboard*; you can paste it elsewhere from there. To cut a frame, follow these steps:

1. Activate Frame mode.
2. Select the frame that you wish to remove. The frame's black handles should appear at its edges. For practice, select the "By Joe Smith" frame.
3. Press the Del key or drop the Edit menu and click Cut Frame. The frame, and any file in it, disappears from the page. It is now on the Frame clipboard.

Notice that the "By Joe Smith" text has moved to the frame on the right, the next frame assigned the NEWSLET.TXT file (Figure 3.10).

If you inadvertently cut the wrong frame, reinsert it in the same spot before you do anything else. (See "Pasting Frames" just ahead.)

COPYING FRAMES

Often, you may wish to create several frames that are alike in some or all respects. In a newsletter, for instance, you may have an article that continues from page to page. To draw your readers to the continuing story, you may want to place it in sequential frames of the same size. To do that, you can create one version of the frame and then copy it.

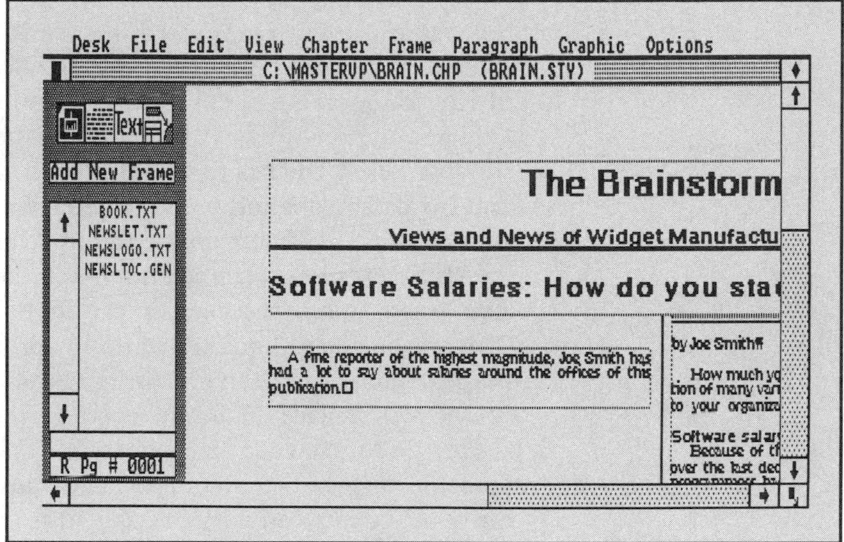

Figure 3.10: Text rearranged after cutting a frame

When you copy a frame, you leave it where it is on the page and make a copy of it on the Frame clipboard. You can then insert that copy elsewhere within the chapter or in other chapters. (Remember, the clipboards are not cleared when you change chapters.)

The steps for copying frames are similar to those for cutting. Make sure that Frame mode is active and that you've selected the appropriate frame. You press Shift-Del or choose the Edit menu's Copy Frame command to copy a frame.

PASTING FRAMES

Once you cut or copy a frame to the Frame clipboard, you can paste it on the same page or a different one. (It's tricky to paste a frame on the same page that you copied it from, as we'll see shortly.) To paste a frame on a page, follow these steps:

1. Activate Frame mode.
2. Go to the page where you want to paste the frame that's on the Frame clipboard.
3. Press the Ins key, or drop the Edit menu and click Paste Frame.

Try practicing by pressing the Ins key on the sample. You'll see the frame you cut reappear in the same position you cut it from. However, the order of NEWSLET.TXT is now switched. Ventura fills the frame on the right first, and then the frame you just pasted. In addition, the newly pasted frame covers the big frame. To correct the situation, use Ctrl-click to select the bio frame, and then press the Del and Ins keys to cut and paste the bio frame, placing it on top. Then cut and paste the frame on the right to change the order.

When you paste a frame on a new page, it initially appears *in the same position* that it occupied on the page you cut or copied it from. This arrangement shouldn't cause any problems. Once you paste the frame, simply use the mouse (or the Frame menu's Sizing & Scaling command) to place the frame where you want it on the page.

However, if you copy a frame to the clipboard and then insert it on the same page, you'll end up with *two* frames of the same size, one on top of the other. You won't be able to see the one that's underneath. To see and manipulate both frames under such circumstances, select the frame on top. Then use the mouse to move it off the one underneath. Alternatively, before you paste the copy of a frame from the clipboard, move the original frame to a different location.

- Save your file once you have the frame pasted properly.

As we mentioned, cut, copy, and paste operations also apply to graphics. We'll see how to perform these operations in Graphics mode when we study graphics in Chapter 7. Next, however, we will look at Ventura's Paragraph mode to see how to format text.

CHAPTER
4

Paragraph Tags and Text Attributes: Building Blocks for Formatting

Fast Track

To apply formatting 114

to text, use Text mode to assign text attributes. To apply formatting to paragraphs, use Paragraph mode to assign attributes to tags. Attributes assigned to tags extend to all paragraphs similarly tagged. A paragraph is any chunk of text ending with a return.

To apply a tag 115

activate Paragraph mode and click a paragraph. Then click the tag's name in the Assignment list. You can also assign a tag to one of the function keys and then apply it with that key. Activate Text mode and press Ctrl-K to reveal the Assign Function Keys dialog box.

To assign local formatting 119

(less than a paragraph) use Text mode. Select the text and apply the format. Ventura indicates the beginning and end of a format with Attribute Setting codes.

To set fonts 122

in Paragraph mode, select a paragraph and use the Paragraph menu's Font. In Text mode, select the text and use the Side-bar's Set Font button.

To set italics, boldface, and small type 129

in Paragraph mode, select a paragraph and use the Paragraph menu's Font. In Text mode, select the text and either use the Side-bar's Set Font button or click the format on the Assignment list. To undo text attributes, select the text and click Normal on the Assignment list.

To assign subscript or superscript 132

in Text mode, select the text. Then use the Set Font dialog box to assign Shift Up or Down, or click on the Assignment list.

To set alignment 136

activate Paragraph mode, select a paragraph, and use the Paragraph menu's Alignment dialog box. Use this dialog box to make text flush left, flush right, justified, centered, or decimal-aligned. Also use it to set vertical alignment to top, bottom, or middle.

To hyphenate text 140

Ventura provides a variety of tools. See Table 4.4.

To indent or outdent 152

the first line of a paragraph, use the Paragraph menu's Alignment dialog box. Specify Indent or Outdent and provide a distance for the indent. You can also specify more lines than the first one.

To determine how a paragraph begins and ends 158

use the Paragraph menu's Breaks dialog box. You can break for pages or columns, or create multitag paragraphs. You also use this dialog box to keep paragraphs together.

To add a new tag 163

in Paragraph mode, click a paragraph. Use the Side-bar's Add New Tag button to assign a name to the new tag. Then use the Paragraph menu to format the new tag.

To rename or remove a tag 166

from a style sheet, and to save and print the style sheet, type Ctrl-K in Paragraph mode or use the Paragraph menu's Update Tag List dialog box.

CHAPTER 4

FORMATTING IS THE PROCESS OF ASSIGNING FONTS and other typographical elements to text. The letter *A* is always the letter *A,* but a plain *A,* an italic one, a boldfaced one, and a boldfaced italic one each have a different impact.

Similarly, a paragraph that is single-spaced produces a different effect from one that is double-spaced, and text that is flush only along the left edge produces a different effect from text that is flush along both edges.

By formatting with Ventura, you can make the appearance of your documents help convey your thoughts. For instance, by using a certain type style consistently under similar circumstances, you make your ideas organized and clear. By using type sizes judiciously, you create a sense of relative importance for each use. In addition, you are sometimes required to format according to certain conventions, such as italicizing the title of a book.

METHODS OF FORMATTING

Ventura provides you with two means of formatting text. Because there is some overlap in the way they are used, we will present them together.

One method of formatting involves the use of *text attributes,* which are formatting characteristics that you apply by activating Text mode. Text attributes affect individual characters in reading order (that is, left to right, line by line). The effect has a beginning point and an ending point, and governs text in between. You apply text attributes only to text you specifically indicate; it can be as little as one character but should usually be less than a paragraph.

The second method uses *paragraph tags.* A tag is a collection of formatting specifications that you assign to a unit of text, called a *paragraph,* that ends with a return. You apply tags by activating Paragraph mode. With paragraph tags, the attributes you set influence the selected paragraph and all other paragraphs in the document that are similarly tagged. You can change a paragraph's attributes by changing those of the tag or by switching tags. The effect can even extend to other documents by way of a shared style sheet.

Before we begin to examine the formatting features themselves, we'll look at these two methods of formatting in more detail. First, though, load the sample chapter to make it available for practice:

1. If you quit Ventura at the end of Chapter 3, reload the program.
2. Use the File menu's Open Chapter to open the BRAIN-.CHP chapter in the MASTERVP directory.

PARAGRAPH TAGS

Paragraph tagging is the tool that Ventura uses to apply features to a self-contained cluster of text called a paragraph. This component is not necessarily a conventional paragraph. In fact, the paragraph is defined in Ventura simply as a unit of text that is tagged. A Ventura paragraph always ends with a return. Its size is not restricted by the program, though often it corresponds to the size of a traditional paragraph.

APPLYING TAGS Paragraphs with similar formatting share the same tag. Unless otherwise indicated, Ventura tags paragraphs as *Body Text.* This tag dictates the default or standard format for paragraphs in the chapter. Normally, when you pull word-processed text, such as the articles for your newsletter, into a chapter, all text—headlines, subheads, bylines, as well as the main body of the articles—has the tag of Body Text and therefore appears the same. You can change the characteristics of the body-text tag, but you cannot eliminate or rename this tag.

CHANGING TAGS WITH THE ASSIGNMENT LIST To change the formatting characteristics of a paragraph, you can use Ventura either to change the tag's format or to apply a different tag to the paragraph. (You can also pre-apply tags to text with your word processor; see Chapter 11.) To change the tag assigned to a paragraph—to change the text of a headline to an existing headline format, for example—proceed as follows:

1. Activate Paragraph mode.
2. Click the paragraph highlighted in Figure 4.1. The paragraph darkens, indicating that it is selected. The name of the tag currently assigned to the paragraph—here it is Subhead—appears in the Current box, toward the bottom of the Side-bar.
3. Move the mouse cursor to the Headline tag on the Assignment list. The tag name darkens when you point to it, as shown in Figure 4.1.
4. Click the mouse to apply the indicated tag. The paragraph takes on the new format, and the selected tag's name appears in the Current box, as shown in Figure 4.2.
5. Change the paragraph back to the original format by clicking the Subhead tag.

CHANGING TAGS WITH THE FUNCTION KEYS There's a tool you can use to speed up your application of tags to text. Ventura

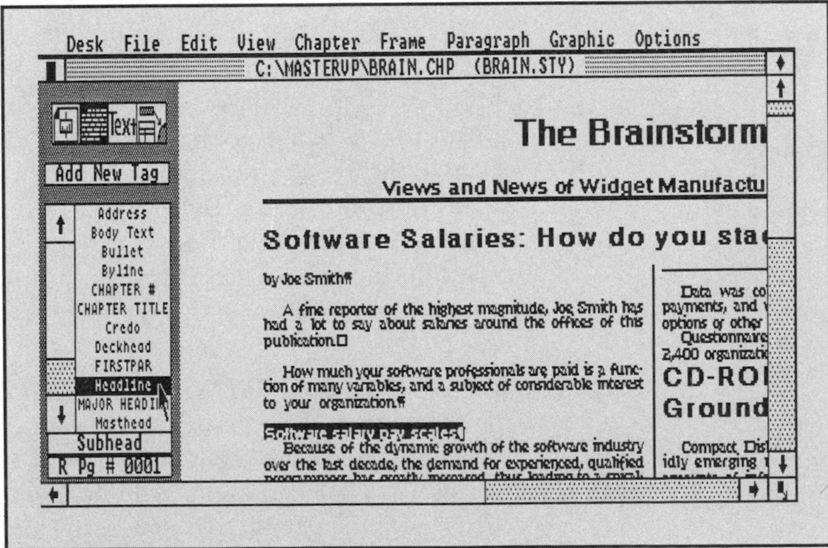

Figure 4.1: Selecting a tag to apply to a paragraph

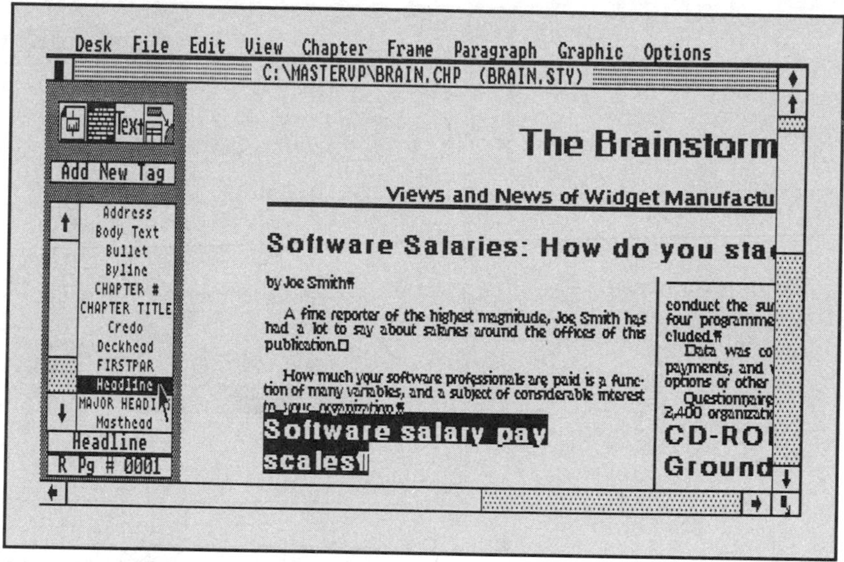

Figure 4.2: The selected tag applied

allows you to assign paragraph tags to the ten function keys (F1 to F10). The simplest way to do this is to activate Text mode and type Ctrl-K. You'll see the dialog box shown in Figure 4.3. Enter the names of the tags you plan to use on the lines corresponding to the function keys. F10 is automatically assigned to Body Text. (You can change this assignment if you like, but it's probably best to leave it for the sake of consistency.)

Once the tags are assigned, you can use the function keys to apply the tags in either Paragraph mode or Text mode. Just select the paragraph you want to format and press the appropriate function key. In Text mode, if you've selected the text of more than one paragraph, each will receive the tag assignment.

! New for version 2.0

The Update Tag List dialog box also provides access to the Assign Function Keys dialog box. You also use Update Tag List to rename and remove tags on the Assignment list and to save and print style sheets. We'll study these procedures at the end of this chapter.

CHANGING A TAG'S FORMAT When you change format specifications for a paragraph, as we'll be doing throughout this chapter, all the paragraphs that are similarly tagged change to the new settings

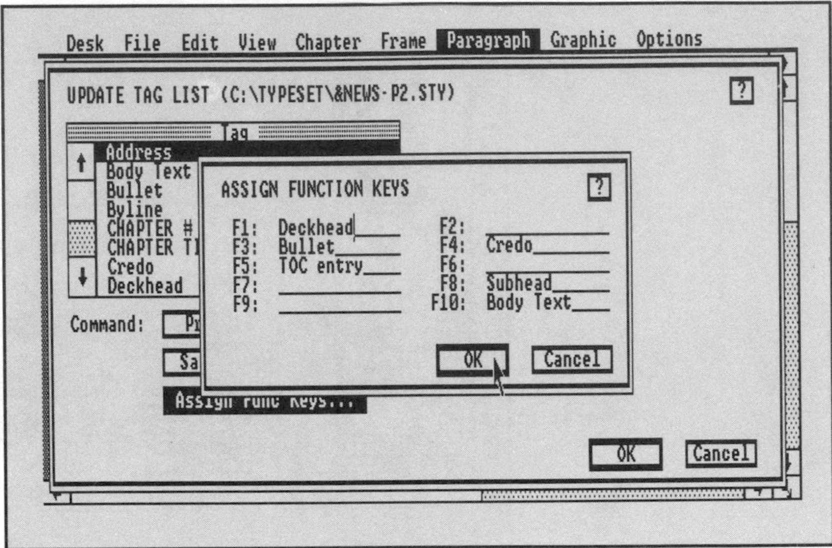

Figure 4.3: The Assign Function Keys dialog box

as well. It is therefore important to think of your chapter as a whole. Group your paragraphs mentally according to their purpose, and provide each group with a tag. For instance, you can use one tag for headings, another for subheadings, one for step-by-step instructions, another for callouts, and so on.

A *style sheet* is a collection of tags as well as other elements that are used with at least one chapter. Table 4.1 is a listing of the commands that control the elements of the style sheet. Every chapter has a style sheet associated with it.

As you work with a chapter and its style sheet, however, you must keep in mind that another document may reference the same style sheet. Changes you make in tags could affect paragraphs in the other document. So it's important to keep track of which documents reference the same style sheet, or you will find yourself changing the format of documents without realizing it. The positive side of this ability is that you can use it to achieve a consistent look in a group of similar documents. Just have them reference the same style sheet.

Appendix B shows a listing of the sample style sheets that come with Ventura, along with their paragraph tags. Be sure to consult this appendix for the tags that you can use, as well as some ideas for how to use them.

Table 4.1: Commands That Affect Style Sheets

PULL-DOWN MENU	**COMMAND**
File	Load Diff. Style
	Save As New Style
Chapter	Page Size & Layout
	Auto-Numbering
Frame (First underlying-page frame only)	Margins & Columns
	Sizing & Scaling
	Vertical Rules
	Ruling Line/Box
	Frame Background
Paragraph	All Commands
Options	Set Printer Info (width table only)

GENERATED TAGS There are some tags that Ventura manufactures automatically as you use certain features of the program. These tags are called *generated tags*. Table 4.2 lists the names Ventura assigns its generated tags, along with the kinds of paragraphs for which it creates them.

You can change formatting for these tags. In fact, you can do just about anything with them that you can do with a normal tag. You simply activate Paragraph mode and use the mouse cursor to select any paragraph with the generated tag you wish to modify. Then drop the Paragraph menu and make the changes you desire.

Normally, the names of generated tags do not appear with those of ordinary tags on Paragraph mode's Assignment list. However, you can have Ventura display generated tags. See Appendix A.

TEXT ATTRIBUTES

In Text mode, you format by selecting text and then applying *text attributes* to it. Text attributes include characteristics—such as italics, boldface, underlining, and fonts—that are more localized in nature

Table 4.2: Generated Tags

GENERATED TAG	FORMAT
Z_BOXTEXT	Box text
Z_CAPTION	Free-form captions (Text mode)
Z_FNOT #	Footnote numbers: reference numbers (or symbols such as *) at the bottom of the page
Z_FNOT ENTRY	Footnote entries: text at the bottom of the page
Z_FOOTER	Footers
Z_HEADER	Headers
Z_LABEL CAP	Caption labels without an automatic number
Z_LABEL TBL	Caption labels with a table number
Z_LABEL FIG	Caption labels with a figure number
Beginning with Z_SEC	Automatic section numbers
Beginning with Z_INDEX	Entries in the index
Beginning with Z_TOC	Entries in the table of contents

than formatting that you set in Paragraph mode. Usually, you use this technique for text units that are smaller than a paragraph.

As mentioned, formatting that you set by using text attributes affects only the text that you indicate; it has no effect on other documents by way of the style sheet. It doesn't even affect other parts of the same chapter. Such formatting is more or less ''cemented'' in place. It takes precedence over the tag settings and won't change even if you change tags or tag settings.

When you make such local formatting changes, how does Ventura keep track of which text differs from normal text? The system it uses is rather ingenious. Once you understand how it operates, you'll have a command of the program's formatting capabilities and will avoid a lot of undesirable surprises as you edit.

Begin by remembering that the settings in any paragraph tag are the standard or default values for all paragraphs formatted with that tag. At the place in text (in regular reading order) where nonstandard text begins, Ventura inserts an invisible *Attribute Setting* code. This code says that formatting changes take place at that spot. The code also contains a register that records the nature of the change.

Ventura also flags the spot where the text returns to the normal settings dictated by the paragraph tag. Again, it uses an invisible Attribute Setting code to accomplish this neutralization.

To examine how paragraph tags and text-attribute settings operate, let's examine the various formatting elements that utilize these building blocks. You can set some formatting features in more than one way. Table 4.3 lists the formatting features that you can control in several ways. We'll begin by looking at fonts.

Table 4.3: Text Formatting Features

FEATURE	METHODS OF SETTING
Font face, size, and color	Paragraph menu's Font command
	Text mode's Set Font button
	Text Mode's Assignment list and Paragraph menu's Attribute Overrides (Small size only)
	Shift-↑ and Shift-↓ (Interactive Size)
Italic and Bold	Paragraph menu's Font command
	Text mode's Set Font button
	Text mode's Assignment list
Superscript and Subscript	Paragraph menu's Font command (Shift setting)
	Text mode's Set Font button (Shift setting)
	Text mode's Assignment list
	Paragraph menu's Attribute Overrides

Table 4.3: Text Formatting Features (continued)

FEATURE	METHODS OF SETTING
Underline, Double Underline, Strike-Thru, Overscore	Text mode's Assignment list Text mode's Set Font button Paragraph menu's Attribute Overrides
Kerning	Text mode's Set Font button Paragraph menu's Paragraph Typography Frame menu's Frame Typography Options menu's Set Preferences Shift-← and Shift-→ (Interactive Kerning)

SETTING FONTS

One of the first formatting elements that you'll need to consider is the *font.* A font is a collection of letters of the alphabet, numbers, and other symbols with a particular design.

There are two ways that you can set fonts. The method you choose depends upon the amount of text you want to affect. You can go for a universal effect (using paragraph tags), or you can choose text selectively (using text attributes). When you want your choice of font to extend throughout a document, set the font in Paragraph mode. When your choice of font is local, use Text mode.

SETTING FONTS WITH PARAGRAPH TAGS

To set fonts in Paragraph mode, you change the paragraph tag for a sample paragraph. Once the change is set, Ventura will apply the font to all characters in the selected paragraph and to all paragraphs

Before you can use a command on the Paragraph menu, you must activate Paragraph mode and select a sample paragraph by clicking it. If you neglect to click a paragraph before dropping the Paragraph menu, the commands on the menu will ghost, showing that you can't use them.

with the same tag. This will also affect similarly tagged paragraphs in other chapters sharing the same style sheet.

To practice setting the font for a paragraph tag:

1. Activate Paragraph mode.
2. Click the sample paragraph shown earlier in Figure 4.1. The paragraph darkens and Subhead appears in the Current box.
3. Drop the Paragraph menu.
4. Click Font. The Font dialog box appears (Figure 4.4). The settings may differ due to your printer.
5. Click a different typeface in the Face box.
6. Give the OK. The typeface for the Subhead tag changes throughout the document.

The fonts that you actually see in the Font dialog box (Figure 4.4) may differ, depending on what's available for your printer. (Those shown in the figure are for the HP LaserJet.) Thus, having changed to a typeface for your printer, your document may differ from our

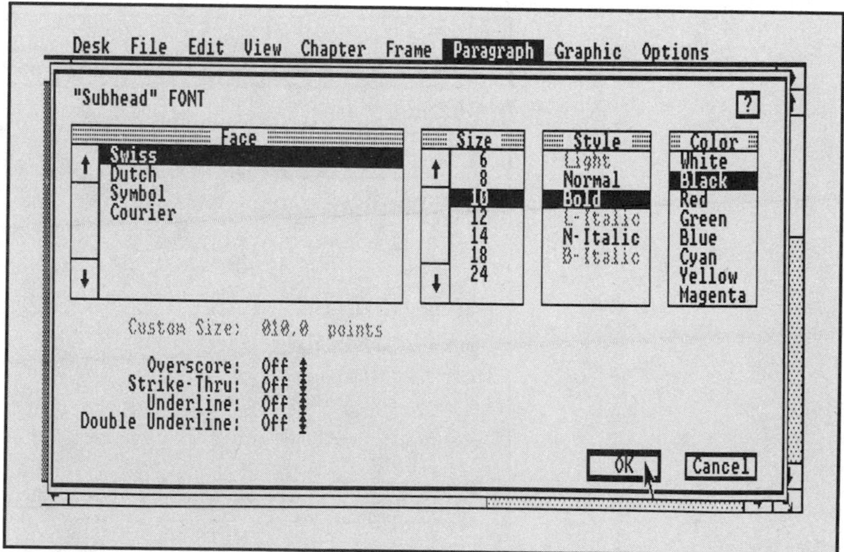

Figure 4.4: The Paragraph menu's Font dialog box

example, as we proceed. You can also add fonts to those initially available. We'll study more about fonts and printers in Chapter 5.

Note that this dialog box allows you to set a number of font features, not just the typeface and size. Ventura provides a great deal of flexibility for setting fonts.

Face refers to the actual design of the characters themselves. *Size* is the height of the font as measured in points. There are 72 points in one inch. The smaller the number that's listed for Size, the smaller the type. 10-point type is probably the most common type size and a good size for body text.

With PostScript printers, the word *CUSTOM* will appear in the Size column, as shown in Figure 4.5. For these printers, you simply enter a value between 1 and 254 points into the Custom Size field.

Figure 4.6 shows some sample typefaces that are available with Ventura on the HP LaserJet. Once you learn how to format, you may wish to create a sheet like this to list the fonts you have, and keep it near the computer as a handy reference.

As with other dialog boxes, the choices that you make in one category of the box may affect the choices that are available to you in other categories. For instance, the typeface that you choose may

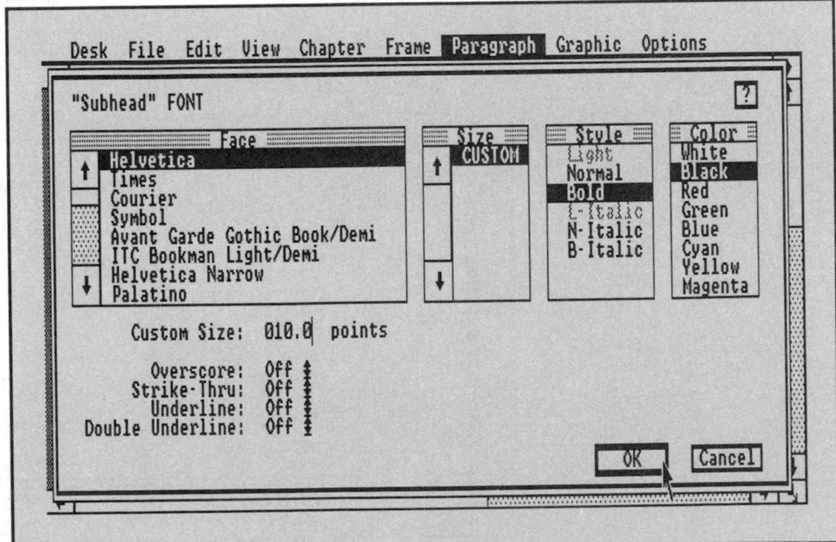

Figure 4.5: Custom Size fonts with PostScript printers

Face	Size	Style
Swiss	6	Normal
Swiss	8	Normal
Swiss	10	Normal, **Bold,** *Normal Italic*
Swiss	12	Normal, **Bold**, *Normal Italic*
Swiss	**14**	**Bold**
Swiss	**18**	**Bold**
Swiss	**24**	**Bold**
Dutch	8	Normal
Dutch	10	Normal, **Bold,** *Normal Italic*
Dutch	12	Normal, **Bold,** *Normal Italic*
Dutch	**14**	**Bold**
Dutch	**18**	**Bold**
Dutch	**24**	**Bold**
Σψμβολ (Symbol)	10	Νορμαλ (Normal)
Courier	12	Normal

Figure 4.6: Sample typefaces on the HP LaserJet

affect the sizes that are available. As usual, choices that are not available will ghost.

Before we look at the other settings that appear in the Font dialog box, let's consider an alternative way to gain access to the box, using Ventura in Text mode.

SETTING FONTS WITH THE SET FONT BUTTON

In Figure 4.7, the word *you* is an example of a font change within a paragraph. Such a change calls for formatting in Text mode.

Software Salaries: How do YOU stack up?

Figure 4.7: Font changes within a paragraph

For practice setting a font in this manner:

1. Activate Text mode. The Set Font button appears in the Side-bar.
2. Use the mouse to darken the "you" in the title "Software Salaries: How do you stack up?"
3. Click the Set Font button in the Side-bar, as shown in Figure 4.8. The Font dialog box appears. It looks as it does in Paragraph mode, except that its title appears as

   FONT SETTING FOR SELECTED TEXT
4. Change the font to a bigger size. Then give the OK.

> * If the Side-bar does not appear, it is turned off. Press Ctrl-W to display it. (See Appendix A.)

Ventura marks the spot where the new font takes effect (before the *y* in *you*) and stores the name of the typeface and the size of the font. We'll call such an initializing mark a *beginning attribute setting.* There's also an indicator where the text returns to normal. We'll call this code an *ending attribute setting.*

Even though you cannot see attribute settings on the screen, you can manipulate them (for instance, by cutting and pasting them) just as you can regular text. Therefore, you must be careful when you

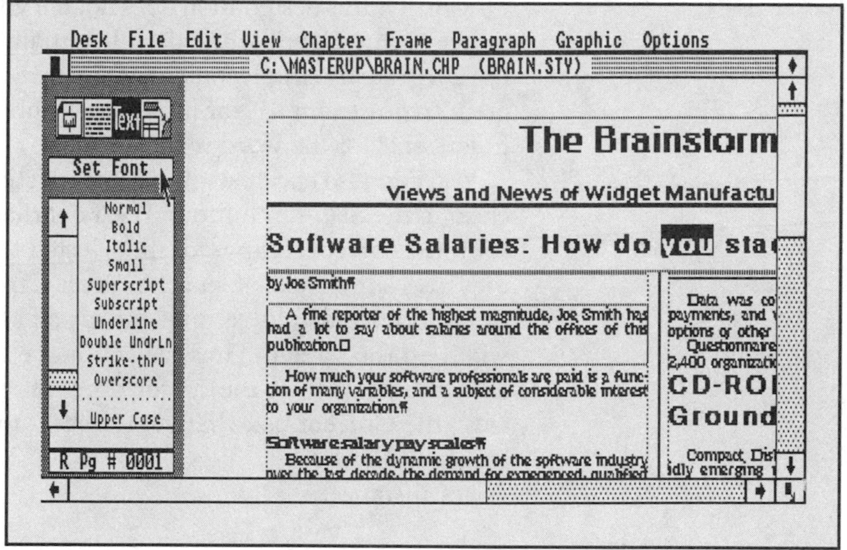

Figure 4.8: Clicking the Set Font button

edit. Inadvertently removing an attribute setting will usually affect the format of the text.

For instance, should you delete an ending attribute setting, Ventura would have no flag to tell it where the text should return to normal, and the nonstandard font would continue past the intended ending spot. Note, however, that Ventura will allow an unusual effect to continue only to the end of the paragraph. Thus, a Paragraph End symbol (¶) acts as an automatic ending attribute setting.

If the attribute settings are invisible, how can you watch out for them? The answer is by looking in the Current box at the bottom of the Side-bar. In Text mode, it indicates the *current character*—the character that is to the immediate right of the blinking text cursor in the working area. The Current box is often blank; nothing appears in it when the current character is a standard visible one, such as a letter of the alphabet or a number. (You don't need the box because you can see the character on the screen.)

If the character is an Attribute Setting code, however, the Current box will read

Attr. Setting

Obviously, this designation does not tell you which attribute setting is in place, but it's still quite useful. Usually you can tell the nature of the attribute by simply looking at the text that appears in the working area. In our example, for instance, it's obvious that there is a change in font size for the word *you.*

You can also check attributes by selecting the text in question and clicking the Set Font button. The Font dialog box thus displayed will show the current settings for the selected text. To leave the settings as they are, simply click Cancel or press Ctrl-X.

Although attribute settings occupy a place in the text, they have no width on the screen. Thus, as you move the keyboard cursor across an attribute setting, the cursor does not move on the screen. However, the Current box changes to reflect the presence of these nondimensional codes.

For instance:

1. Use the → key to move the text cursor across the sample headline

   How do you stack up?

2. Stop when you get to the spot before the *y* in *you,* which is set in a nonstandard font. Because the beginning attribute setting is just to the right of the cursor, the words

   Attr. Setting

   appear in the Current box.

3. Press the Del key. The setting is deleted, and the *you* reverts to normal type.

If, however, you had pressed the → key again at this point (instead of the Del key), the cursor would have moved past the setting. The *y* in *you* would have become the current character. As *y* is a standard character, nothing would have appeared in the Current box. Pressing Del at this point would delete the *y.* Pressing Backspace would delete the invisible attribute setting.

Attribute settings may indicate where other text formats, such as italics and boldface, begin and end. We've seen how to set font faces and sizes with either attribute settings or paragraph tags. You can use either approach to set italics and boldface, too.

SETTING THE FONT SIZE INTERACTIVELY

! New for version 2.0

Ventura now provides you with a quicker and more responsive method of setting the size of text fonts. Called *interactive setting,* this procedure works best with PostScript printers, which make use of the Custom Size settings described earlier.

Begin by activating Text mode and selecting the text whose font size you wish to adjust. Then, simply press Shift-↑ or Shift-↓. Each time you press these keys, Ventura adjusts the font size up or down, respectively, by 1 point. With custom sizes, the result appears immediately. With non-PostScript printers, as each press adjusts the size 1 point, you must press repeatedly if the next available size is greater than 1 point different. Thus, if the text is 14 points, and the next available size is 18 points, you must press Shift-↑ four times before you see the text increase in size.

This procedure creates Attribute Setting codes in the text, just as the Set Font button does. They are subject to the same rules, discussed above, as the codes created with the button.

- Practice changing the size of the word *you* by setting the font interactively. Be sure to consider the font sizes available as you look for results.

ITALICS, BOLDFACE, AND SMALL SIZE

To begin our examination of italics and boldface, let's consider the Font dialog box again. In the Style category, you have a choice of Light, Normal, and Bold. You can also choose italic versions of these three. Again, the styles you can use for a given font will vary; ghosting indicates those that are unavailable due to your printer or printing software. In Figure 4.4, Light, Light-Italic, and Bold-Italic versions of Swiss 10 are not available.

You can set italics and boldface in three ways. First, using Paragraph mode, you can select a sample paragraph, drop the Paragraph menu, and click Font. This displays the Font dialog box. Italic and bold settings you implement in this way affect all similarly tagged paragraphs in the chapter you're working on, as well as in all other chapters using the same style sheet.

Using Italics

Use italics for the titles of books, newspapers, periodicals, plays, motion pictures, musical compositions, and works of art. Also use italics for the names of boats and trains. Use quotes rather than italics to indicate short stories, short poems, and sections of a book. For example:

> Consult Chapter 10, "Tables, Columns, and Boxes" in *Mastering Microsoft WORD.*

Italicize foreign words, but not foreign words that have been accepted into the English language. Consult a dictionary if you're unsure about a word's status in this regard.

Italicize words, letters, and numbers referred to as such (for example, the word *the*). Italicize technical terms when you introduce them. This especially holds true when you follow the term with its definition.

Although italics can be used effectively to attract the reader's attention, use them sparingly in this manner. Generally, only a few words at a time should be italicized, and never as much as an entire passage. Since this use of italics is for providing emphasis, overdoing their use defeats the purpose.

The second way to set italics and boldface is to activate Text mode, use the mouse to darken your selected text, and click the Set Font button on the Side-bar. This also displays the Font dialog box, but only the selected text will change to italics or boldface. Attribute Setting codes mark the beginning and ending points.

The third method of assigning boldface and italics also uses Text mode and selected text. However, instead of displaying a dialog box, you use the Assignment list to apply formatting. This method is a little quicker to use. As with the second method, the resulting formats are local in nature, and Attribute Setting codes mark the beginning and ending points. The steps for assigning these text attributes are similar to those used for setting attributes with the Set Font button, except that you select them from the Assignment list rather than the Font dialog box. Here are the steps to follow:

1. Be sure that Text mode is active.
2. Use the mouse to darken the text that you will select for a special attribute.
3. Click the appropriate attribute name on the Assignment list, such as Bold or Italic.

You can set other formats besides italics and boldface with the Assignment list. For instance, you can quickly reduce the size of the font. The Small assignment reduces the font size from that specified by the tag, normally by 2 points. This feature is useful, for instance, in creating small capital letters. You just select the text, change it to uppercase (as we'll see shortly), and click Small.

If you later change the size of the tag's font, text formatted with the Small text attribute will adjust to 2 points smaller than that of the tag's new font size. Note that if you use the Set Font button to display the settings for text that you've formatted in this manner, you won't see the change reflected in the dialog box, which will still indicate the original font size. (Bold and Italic settings will be indicated correctly, however, and you may use the dialog box in Text mode to change them, even if you set them originally with the Assignment list.)

! New for version 2.0

You can now specify the exact size for Ventura to use when you assign the Small attribute to text. In Paragraph mode, click a paragraph whose tag you wish to adjust. Then use the Paragraph menu to display the Attribute Overrides dialog box. Adjust the value for Small Cap Size; thereafter, when you assign the Small text attribute inside paragraphs with that tag, Ventura will use the point size you specify. You can even specify a point size that's larger than that of the tag's font; then, assigning Small creates a larger font than usual!

You can use the Normal feature on the Assignment list to return selected text to the settings specified with the paragraph tag. (You can achieve the same effect by simply deleting Attribute Setting codes.)

In the next few sections, we'll discuss the remaining text attributes that appear on the Text mode Assignment list or in the Font dialog box. Note that not all settings in the Font dialog box are conveniently located on the Assignment list. For instance, the Color setting, which we'll study next, is not.

COLOR AND FONTS

* You can customize the colors that Ventura uses. See Chapter 5.

If your printer is capable of printing in color, the Color category of the Font dialog box allows you to utilize that capability. However, you can also use a regular printer to create originals for conventional color duplication, such as offset printing. Ventura 2.0 allows you to create *color separations* easily. We'll examine this ability in Chapter 5. And in Chapter 12, you'll see how you can use the White setting to create reverse type and other effects.

SUPERSCRIPT AND SUBSCRIPT

Two settings in the Font dialog box, Shift and Kern, do not appear when you invoke the dialog box while in Paragraph mode. You can only set them in Text mode. We'll examine kerning in Chapter 12.

The term *Shift* refers to the position of the text relative to the normal position, above or below the imaginary line on which the text sits. This line is called the *baseline.* Use Shift: Up in this dialog box or Superscript on the Assignment list to raise text above the baseline, as in $E = mc^2$. Use Shift: Down here or Subscript on the Assignment list to lower text below the baseline, as in H_2O. Notice that with the Font dialog box you can set the amount you wish the selected characters to be shifted up or down.

The reason why Ventura won't allow you to set the Shift feature in Paragraph mode is that formats you set with paragraph tags affect the entire tagged paragraph. Because Shift alters the placement of one piece of text relative to another on the same line, it would be meaningless to specify Shift for an entire paragraph.

! New for version 2.0

In Ventura 2.0 you can specify the font size and the amount of shift when you use the Assignment list to specify Subscript or Superscript. To do so, you click a paragraph in Paragraph mode and then use the Paragraph menu's Attribute Overrides dialog box. We'll examine this dialog box in the following section.

UNDERLINE, OVERSCORE, AND STRIKE-THRU

! New for version 2.0

Underline, Overscore, Double Underline (UndrLn), and Strike-thru are related text attributes that appear on the Assignment list.

With version 2.0, you can also use Text mode's Set Font button or the Paragraph menu's Font to assign these attributes.

Underline is self-explanatory: you use this setting to underline the text that you've selected. You might not use it much in desktop publishing, however, because underlining is usually a substitute for italics on a typewriter or word processor. With Ventura, italics are easily available.

The Professional Extension allows you to create extensive scientific formulas. See Chapter 13.

If you are engaging in accounting applications, however, you will probably use Underline, Double Underline, and Overscore. For instance, you can underline subtotals. Overscore draws a line *above* selected text. You can overscore or double-underline net amounts. You can also use Underline and Overscore to create a division line in a scientific formula.

Strike-thru draws a straight line through the center of a line of text. Typically, members of the legal profession make use of strike-thru when revising contracts and other documents to designate text that's being suggested for deletion.

As with the other attributes, you can undo these by using the Assignment list to set the text to Normal. Alternatively, you can simply delete the invisible Attribute Setting codes. Place the text cursor just to the right of the invisible code. The words

Attr. Setting

should appear in the Current box. Then press the Del key to delete the code.

! New for version 2.0

In version 2.0 you can apply Overscore, Strike-thru, Underline, and Double Underline to selected text by clicking the Side-bar's Set Font button. In the Font Setting dialog box that appears, there are four On/Off pop-up menus, one for each of these attributes. Use them to activate the effect you desire.

You can now also apply these four kinds of lines to entire paragraphs by means of the paragraph tag. In Paragraph mode, click a paragraph whose tag you wish to set for one of these effects. Then drop the Paragraph menu and click Attribute Overrides. You'll see the dialog box that appears in Figure 4.9.

You can set Line Width to either Text-Wide or Margin-Wide. Normally, you use Text-Wide, which makes the four kinds of lines

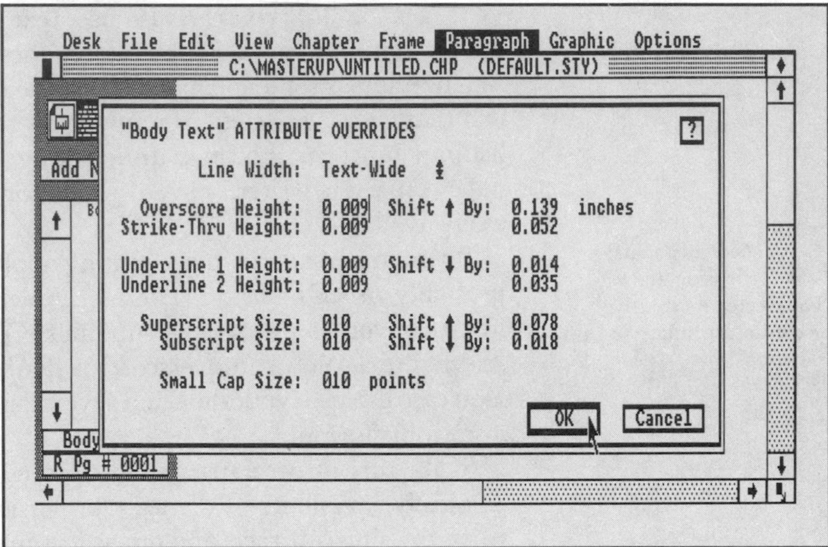

Figure 4.9: The Paragraph menu's Attribute Overrides dialog box

only as wide as the text you selected with the mouse. Choose Margin-Wide to extend the lines clear across the paragraph, from margin to margin, regardless of the amount of text you selected. This is handy for creating underlined headings at the top of a table (Chapter 7).

For each type of line, you can specify a Height setting. This refers to the thickness of the indicated line. Underline 1 regulates a single underline and the first line of a double underline. Underline 2 regulates the second line of a double underline. For Overscore and Strike-thru, you set the distance by which to shift the line up (Shift ↑ By). For Underline, you set the distance by which to shift the lines down (Shift ↓ By).

Notice that you can also use this dialog box to provide values to other attributes that you set with the Assignment list. Namely, you can set the size for the Assignment-list attributes of Superscript, Subscript, and Small (Small Cap Size). You can also specify the displacement distance for superscript (Shift ↑ By) and subscript (Shift ↓ By).

UPPER CASE, CAPITALIZE, AND LOWER CASE

Upper Case, Capitalize, and Lower Case operate on each other in a manner somewhat different from the other text attributes. They are grouped together below the dotted line on the bottom of the Text mode Assignment list. They are not available in a dialog box.

The same rules apply to setting these as apply to other text attributes. Text mode must be active, and you must have selected (darkened) some text. Although these attributes may be assigned when typing text at the keyboard, they are especially easy to implement when text is already selected for other formatting purposes. In our sample headline, for instance, after changing the font size, you might decide that it would be best to make *you* all uppercase.

When you click Upper Case on the Assignment list, all lowercase letters in the selected area change to uppercase.

- With *you* selected in the sample, click Upper Case on the Assignment list. The sample will then look like Figure 4.10.

Choosing Capitalize will capitalize the initial letter of each word in the darkened area. You can use this effect to assist you in capitalizing titles and headings. Remember, though, that by convention certain words are not capitalized in a title. Thus, you may need to adjust some letters individually when you use this feature. For instance, you shouldn't capitalize articles (*a, an, the*), conjunctions (*and, but, or*), or short prepositions (*with, into, by*) unless they occur at the beginning of the title.

- With *YOU* selected, click Capitalize. Now, only the *Y* is capitalized.

Choosing Lower Case changes all the capital letters in the selected area to lowercase. You can use this setting to undo text that you have capitalized in error. Be careful with it, too. It changes *all* characters to lowercase—even the first letter in a sentence if that letter appears in the darkened area.

- With *You* selected, click Lower Case. The *Y* changes to lowercase (*y*).

Software Salaries: How do YOU stack up?

Figure 4.10: Selected word changed to uppercase

The Normal setting at the top of the Assignment list will not reverse the effects of these items. Also, these features do not produce invisible Attribute Setting codes before and after selected text, as the other items on the list do. Instead, they change the characters themselves.

This completes our examination of the items that appear on the Assignment list in Text mode. We've seen how some choices appear only there, while others can also be set by clicking the Set Font button. In addition, we've looked at the Paragraph menu's Font dialog box. However, there are other paragraph commands below Font on the Paragraph menu. Each one contributes to the format that a tag provides to a paragraph. Let's examine some additional paragraph-formatting commands by proceeding to the next item on the Paragraph menu, Alignment.

HORIZONTAL ALIGNMENT

Ventura groups together a number of features that control the way in which elements in a paragraph line up with one another. Generally, these features determine where and how the edges of paragraphs appear. Chief among these features are justification (for text that's flush at the edges), centering, and automatic indenting of the first line in each paragraph. These features are collectively called *alignment.* Follow these steps to set them:

1. Activate Paragraph mode.
2. Click a sample paragraph whose alignment you wish to change. Remember, all paragraphs similarly tagged will change as well.
3. Drop the Paragraph menu.
4. Click Alignment. You'll see the Alignment dialog box, as shown in Figure 4.11.

The first category in the Alignment dialog box is Horz (Horizontal) Alignment.

ALIGNING TEXT FLUSH LEFT OR RIGHT

Horizontal alignment sets the placement of text with respect to the side edges of the paragraph. Figure 4.12 shows how the first column

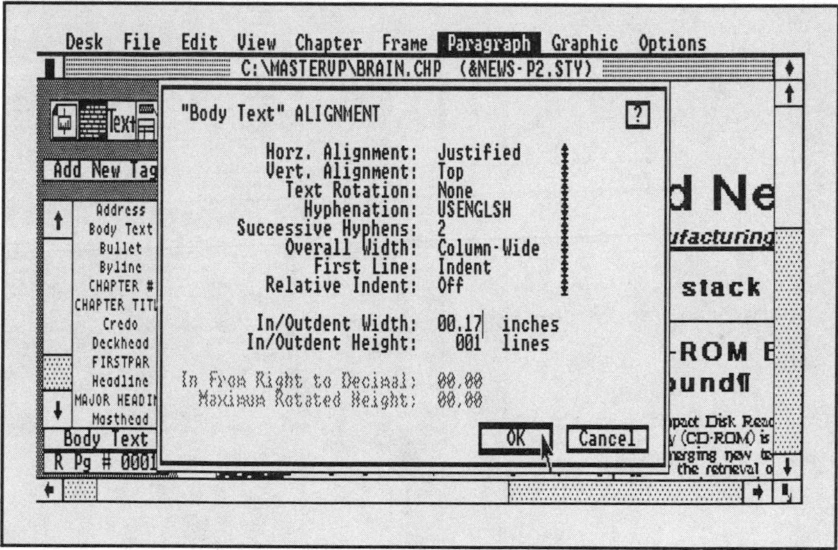

Figure 4.11: The Paragraph menu's Alignment dialog box

of the newsletter would look with left, right, centered, and justified alignment. (To emphasize the differences in alignment and make them more pronounced, we've eliminated the first-line indent, added spacing, and turned hyphenation off. We'll study each of these other paragraph features as we proceed in this chapter.)

Left alignment is rather like standard typewriter format. With left-aligned text, the left edge is flush; the right edge of the paragraph is *ragged.*

By setting Horz Alignment to Right, you get the opposite of left-aligned text; the right edge of the paragraph is flush and the left edge is ragged.

CENTERING TEXT

With centered alignment, each line of text in the paragraph is centered. You can have the text centered within the column in which it appears or, if the frame consists of more than one column, within the entire frame. It depends on the Line Width setting, which we'll see how to use shortly. Even when you have only one line to center, as is often the case with headings and titles, Ventura will center that one line. It considers the line to be a paragraph as long as it ends with a return.

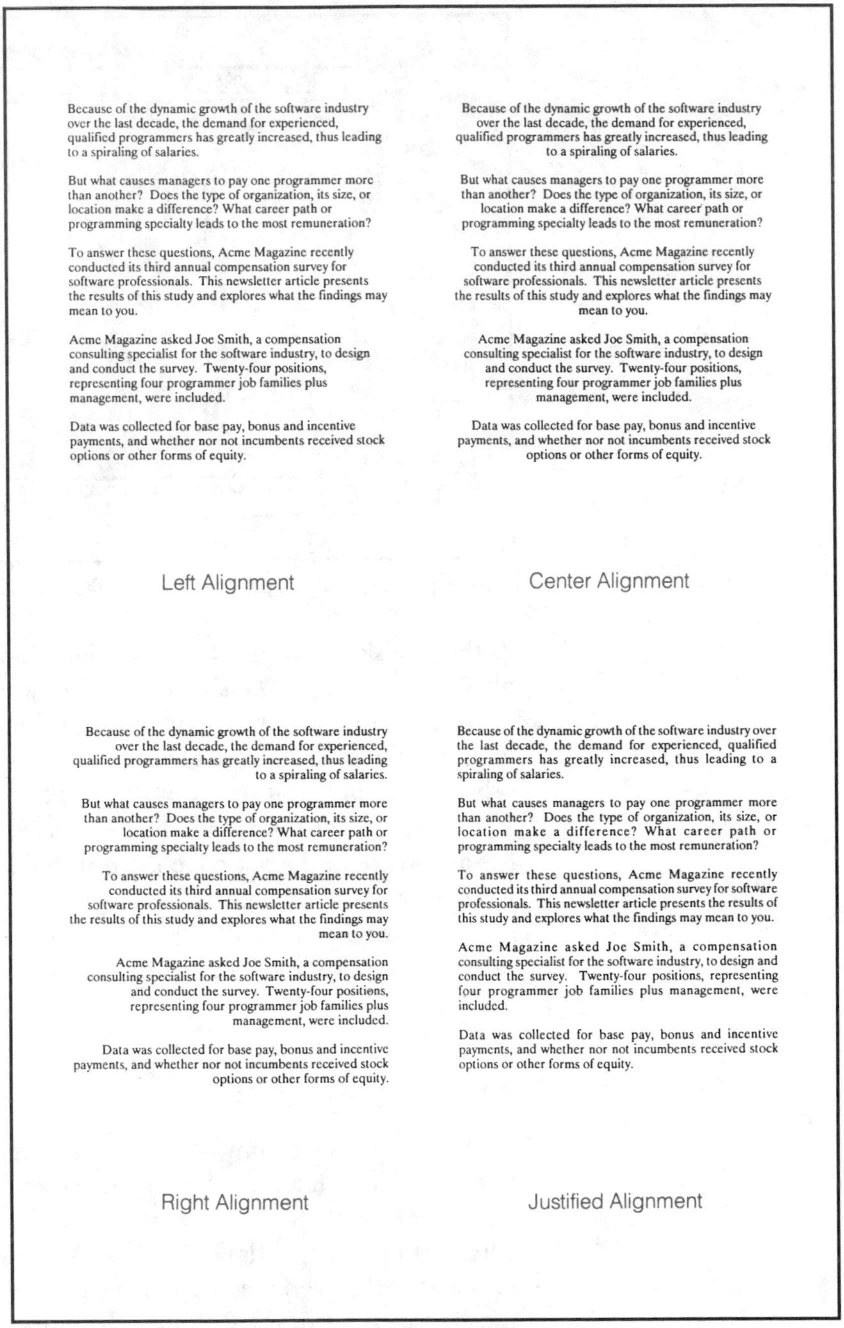

Because of the dynamic growth of the software industry over the last decade, the demand for experienced, qualified programmers has greatly increased, thus leading to a spiraling of salaries.

But what causes managers to pay one programmer more than another? Does the type of organization, its size, or location make a difference? What career path or programming specialty leads to the most remuneration?

To answer these questions, Acme Magazine recently conducted its third annual compensation survey for software professionals. This newsletter article presents the results of this study and explores what the findings may mean to you.

Acme Magazine asked Joe Smith, a compensation consulting specialist for the software industry, to design and conduct the survey. Twenty-four positions, representing four programmer job families plus management, were included.

Data was collected for base pay, bonus and incentive payments, and whether nor not incumbents received stock options or other forms of equity.

Left Alignment

Because of the dynamic growth of the software industry over the last decade, the demand for experienced, qualified programmers has greatly increased, thus leading to a spiraling of salaries.

But what causes managers to pay one programmer more than another? Does the type of organization, its size, or location make a difference? What career path or programming specialty leads to the most remuneration?

To answer these questions, Acme Magazine recently conducted its third annual compensation survey for software professionals. This newsletter article presents the results of this study and explores what the findings may mean to you.

Acme Magazine asked Joe Smith, a compensation consulting specialist for the software industry, to design and conduct the survey. Twenty-four positions, representing four programmer job families plus management, were included.

Data was collected for base pay, bonus and incentive payments, and whether nor not incumbents received stock options or other forms of equity.

Center Alignment

Because of the dynamic growth of the software industry over the last decade, the demand for experienced, qualified programmers has greatly increased, thus leading to a spiraling of salaries.

But what causes managers to pay one programmer more than another? Does the type of organization, its size, or location make a difference? What career path or programming specialty leads to the most remuneration?

To answer these questions, Acme Magazine recently conducted its third annual compensation survey for software professionals. This newsletter article presents the results of this study and explores what the findings may mean to you.

Acme Magazine asked Joe Smith, a compensation consulting specialist for the software industry, to design and conduct the survey. Twenty-four positions, representing four programmer job families plus management, were included.

Data was collected for base pay, bonus and incentive payments, and whether nor not incumbents received stock options or other forms of equity.

Right Alignment

Because of the dynamic growth of the software industry over the last decade, the demand for experienced, qualified programmers has greatly increased, thus leading to a spiraling of salaries.

But what causes managers to pay one programmer more than another? Does the type of organization, its size, or location make a difference? What career path or programming specialty leads to the most remuneration?

To answer these questions, Acme Magazine recently conducted its third annual compensation survey for software professionals. This newsletter article presents the results of this study and explores what the findings may mean to you.

Acme Magazine asked Joe Smith, a compensation consulting specialist for the software industry, to design and conduct the survey. Twenty-four positions, representing four programmer job families plus management, were included.

Data was collected for base pay, bonus and incentive payments, and whether nor not incumbents received stock options or other forms of equity.

Justified Alignment

Figure 4.12: Four types of horizontal alignment

JUSTIFYING TEXT

With *justified* text, both the left and right edges are flush. Ventura accomplishes justification by varying the amount of space that it inserts between letters and words (Chapter 12).

Use justification judiciously; it may look snazzy at first glance, but the additional space can make text more difficult to read. It's a good idea to print some sample text before committing to justification; compare the sample with left-aligned text for readability.

- In the sample document, use Paragraph mode to click the first paragraph in the first article.
- Use the Paragragh menu's Alignment dialog box and experiment with the four types of horizontal alignment in Figure 4.12.

DECIMAL-ALIGNED TEXT

New for version 2.0

A fifth kind of horizontal alignment is available with Ventura 2.0. When you set paragraphs for *decimal alignment,* Ventura lines up the first decimal point that appears in each line of the paragraph. Once you specify Horz Alignment: Decimal, provide a value for In From Right To Decimal. This setting determines the position of the aligned decimals. We'll examine this feature again when we study tables in Chapter 8.

VERTICAL ALIGNMENT

Ventura usually aligns a paragraph vertically with respect to the container holding the text. However, when a frame appears within a frame (including within the underlying-page frame), Ventura will also use the top and bottom

Another new feature Ventura 2.0 provides is the ability to specify alignment in a whole new dimension. You can now control the *vertical* placement of a paragraph with respect to its containing area. To do so, you use the Alignment dialog box's Vert Alignment settings.

You can set Vert Alignment to Top, Middle, or Bottom. Normally, paragraphs have a Top setting, and the paragraph appears at the top of its container—the page, frame, or box that contains it—with the next paragraph following right after it. Specifying Middle or Bottom vertical alignment makes the paragraph appear in the corresponding vertical position within the containing area. With these settings, Ventura bumps the paragraph that follows into the next area.

Try your hand at creating vertically aligned material. In Paragraph mode, click a paragraph that appears within a frame. Set Vert Alignment first to Middle and then to Bottom and observe the results.

TEXT ROTATION

! New for version 2.0

Another feature that's new with Ventura 2.0 is the ability to rotate text on the page. You can angle text in increments of 90 degrees. However, some printers, such as the LaserJet, cannot print more than one such orientation on a page.

In the Paragraph menu's Alignment dialog box, you can set Text Rotation to None, 90, 180, or 270. You can also use this dialog box to provide a value for Maximum Rotated Height. When rotating text, Ventura must have an area set aside into which it pours the text. The value you provide delineates the height of this area. The width Ventura uses is the normal width that would be available if the text were not rotated.

When you edit rotated text, use the cursor keys as you would if there were no rotation. Thus, with 90 degrees of rotation, you use the → and ← keys to move the text cursor up and down the text as it appears on the screen. If text is rotated 180 degrees (upside down), you move the cursor left with the → key and right with the ← key.

HYPHENATION

* The Professional Extension allows you to hyphenate documents more extensively and with more control than Ventura's base program. See Chapter 13.

With justified text, especially when it's set in narrow columns, standard practice is to hyphenate. Otherwise, you may end up with *loose lines*—lines that contain big gaps as a result of the justification process. These gaps can bring about the undesirable appearance of "rivers" of white space that flow down the length of the page. Wide columns that are not justified may not need hyphenation. You may also wish to turn hyphenation off for paragraphs in which it's not appropriate—for example, in a table of contents or in headline text.

Table 4.4 lists the tools that you can use to hyphenate text to exacting specifications.

Table 4.4: Tools for Hyphenating Text

TOOL	LOCATION	DESCRIPTION	COMMENTS
USENGLSH.HY1	File on the Loadable Filter disk (#3), copied into the VENTURA directory during installation	Standard hyphenation algorithm	This is the algorithm Ventura normally uses to hyphenate.
SPANISH.HY2 FRENCH.HY2 GERMAN.HY2 ITALIAN.HY2 UKENGLSH.HY2 USENGLS2.HY2	Files on the Loadable Filter disk (#3)	Second hyphenation algorithm	Copy one (and only one) of these into the VENTURA directory if you wish to have it available in addition to the standard algorithm.
Ctrl-hyphen	Keyboard	Discretionary hyphen	Type Ctrl-hyphen to add a hyphen to one particular word only. Ventura will not print the hyphen if subsequent editing causes it to fall within a line (rather than at the end).
Hyphen key	Keyboard	Standard hyphen	Avoid typing a standard hyphen in your documents except for words that should always be hyphenated, whether at the end of a line or within it.

Table 4.4: Tools for Hyphenating Text (continued)

TOOL	LOCATION	DESCRIPTION	COMMENTS
Hyphenation setting	Paragraph menu's Alignment dialog box	Off, or one of two algorithms	Turn this setting off if you don't want hyphenation for paragraphs formatted with the selected tag. Use one of the other settings if you want hyphenation performed using the indicated algorithm.
Successive Hyphens setting	Paragraph menu's Alignment dialog box	1 to 5 or Unlimited	Use this setting to limit the number of lines following one another that may be hyphenated.
HYPHEXPT.DIC	File on the Loadable Filter disk (#3), copied into the VENTURA directory during installation	Hyphenation Exception dictionary	This file contains a listing of hyphenated words that are exceptions to the algorithm rules. The listings override the algorithm on words for which the algorithm does not operate properly.
HYPHUSER.DIC	File on the Loadable Filter disk (#3), copied into the VENTURA directory during installation	Hyphenation User dictionary	Use this file to enter your own hyphenated words in ASCII. For a word you never want hyphenated, enter the word without a hyphen. The listings override both the algorithm and the Hyphenation Exception dictionary.

SETTING THE HYPHENATION STATUS FOR A PARAGRAPH TAG

You may not need to concern yourself with many of the tools listed in Table 4.4. For simple applications, it is sufficient to set hyphenation on or off in a given paragraph tag. You can do so by following these steps:

1. Activate Paragraph mode and select a sample paragraph, appropriately tagged. For practice, click the first paragraph in the first article which has the Body Text tag. You'll note it has a hyphenated line.
2. Drop the Paragraph menu and click Alignment. You'll see the dialog box that appeared in Figure 4.11.
3. Change Hyphenation from one of the USENGLSH settings (for Ventura's standard hyphenation) to Off for no hyphenation.
4. Click OK or press Enter.

To hyphenate text, Ventura uses computer *algorithms* (program procedures) to determine where to hyphenate. The standard algorithm by which Ventura hyphenates according to United States English usage is in the file USENGLSH.HY1. Ventura allows you to use a second algorithm for hyphenation as well. The second algorithm has an HY2 extension. However, when you install Ventura, USENGLSH is the only one available, so it appears in two positions of the pop-up menu for Hyphenation.

BILINGUAL HYPHENATION

If your documents contain text in two languages, you may wish to use a second hyphenation algorithm. If you do put a second hyphenation algorithm into operation, such as SPANISH, it will be available as the third Hyphenation setting. Once an algorithm is operational and its name is showing on the pop-up menu, using that setting will cause the selected paragraphs to use that algorithm for hyphenation.

To make a second algorithm available, copy the algorithm to your hard disk. Follow these steps to do this:

1. At the system prompt for your hard disk, insert the Loadable Filter disk (#3) into your floppy-disk drive.
2. Change to the VENTURA directory by typing

   ```
   cd \ventura
   ```

3. Type the word **copy**, a space, the letter **a**, a colon, and the name of the file as listed in Table 4.4. Thus, to copy the SPANISH.HY2 algorithm file, you'd enter

   ```
   copy a:spanish.hy2
   ```

You may have noticed that there is a second United States English file, USENGLS2.HY2. Although the original algorithm installed with Ventura hyphenates words correctly, it is not as thorough as some people would like. To speed hyphenation, it doesn't hyphenate some words at all, even when such hyphenation is permitted by standard usage. The algorithm seldom hyphenates incorrectly and works fine with most applications. When documents have very narrow columns, however, insufficient hyphenation can cause unacceptable gaps in justified text.

The second United States English algorithm, USENGLS2.HY2, is very thorough. It overlooks few opportunities for hyphenation, so it's better suited to use with narrow columns. However, it takes quite a bit longer to operate than the standard algorithm, so use it only when truly necessary. Chiefly, the delay occurs when you are loading a chapter.

SPECIFYING THE NUMBER OF SUCCESSIVE HYPHENATIONS

Regardless of the algorithm you use, you can instruct Ventura to restrict the number of lines it hyphenates in a row. Without this ability, hyphenating could cause *ladders*—line after line ending with a hyphen—which are distracting and undesirable. Just set Successive Hyphens to a number from 1 to 5. No more than 2 is ideal, but again the narrowness of the column is a key factor: the narrower the column, the more hyphenations you may need in order to avoid frequent gaps.

HYPHENATING INDIVIDUAL WORDS

You can also specify hyphenation in individual words that Ventura overlooks. The first line in the first example shown in Figure 4.13 is loose. This is because Ventura failed to hyphenate the word *keyboard* at the beginning of the second line. As the second version of the sentence shows, hyphenating that word causes its first syllable to move to the preceding line, tightening the line. To tighten a given line, hyphenate the first word on the line following it, using one of the techniques we'll examine shortly.

SHOWING LOOSE LINES Ventura can assist you in drawing your attention to such loose lines. Just drop the Options menu and click Show Loose Lines. Loose lines will appear darkened, in reverse video.

It's a good idea to turn off loose lines (by dropping the Options menu and clicking Hide Loose Lines) as soon as you're done. Loose lines that are shown look just like selected text and can be very confusing if left in view.

USING DISCRETIONARY HYPHENS There are two ways to hyphenate words that Ventura overlooks, such as *keyboard* in the previous example. Which method you use depends upon how often you expect to encounter a given word.

First, you can insert a *discretionary* hyphen directly into the overlooked word. You do this in Text mode by placing the text cursor at the point in the word where you want the hyphen to go and typing Ctrl-hyphen. You use a discretionary hyphen when the overlooked word is one that you don't expect to use often. For instance, if your newsletters are about corporate mergers and you usually don't write articles about keyboards, you would probably use this method to

Correct unacceptably loose lines by using the keyboard to insert a discretionary hyphen.

Correct unacceptably loose lines by using the key-board to insert a discretionary hyphen.

Figure 4.13: Hyphenating a word to tighten the previous line

hyphenate *keyboard.* If later editing or electronic paste-up should cause a word hyphenated with a discretionary hyphen to move to the center of the line, the hyphen would disappear in print.

A *standard hyphen,* obtained by hitting the hyphen key, is used only for *hyphenated compounds.* These are words that are always hyphenated, regardless of where they appear—words such as *double-cross, long-winded,* and *ill-fated.* This hyphen will always appear, regardless of the placement of the compound in the line. Thus, if you used a standard hyphen to hyphenate *keyboard* in the example, and later changed the margins, you might end up printing something like

by using the key-board to insert

> * You can display a discretionary hyphen on the screen, even when it falls in the middle of a line, if you use the Options menu and select Show Tabs & Returns (or type Ctrl-T). On the screen, a discretionary hyphen is slightly heftier than a standard hyphen. It's important to realize, however, that even though you may display discretionary hyphens on the screen, those appearing midline won't show up in the printed version of the document. Choose Hide Tabs & Returns to make midline discretionary hyphens disappear from the screen.

Typing Ctrl-hyphen to insert a discretionary hyphen allows you to avoid such an occurrence. If a discretionary hyphen falls in the middle of a line like this, Ventura will not print it. The discretionary hyphen appears only when the word straddles two lines.

As with Attribute Setting codes, which we discussed earlier in this chapter, you can use the Current box in Text mode to detect the presence of an invisible discretionary hyphen. When such a hyphen is located to the right of the keyboard cursor, the words

Discr. Hyphen

appear in the Current box. If desired, you can then delete the hyphen by pressing the Del key.

USING HYPHENATION DICTIONARIES There is another way you can have Ventura hyphenate a word that it would otherwise miss. You can add the word to the Hyphenation User dictionary. Ventura will then hyphenate such words as necessary, only at the ends of lines.

As mentioned, Ventura uses an algorithm as its chief means of determining where to hyphenate words. There are words, however, that do not adhere to the rules that the algorithm follows. To hyphenate these words properly, Ventura lists them in the Hyphenation Exception dictionary, which is contained in the HYPHEXPT.DIC file. These listings are checked automatically when hyphenation is on, and they take precedence over the algorithm.

In addition, Ventura consults the Hyphenation User dictionary, located in the HYPHUSER.DIC file in the VENTURA directory. This dictionary takes precedence over both the algorithm and the entries in the HYPHEXPT.DIC file. You can add entries to this dictionary yourself. (Ventura has some entries as samples in the file already.) Just use your word processor in ASCII mode to open this file (see Chapter 11). Type in your entries with standard hyphens in place. Enter each word on a separate line with a hard return at the end of the line. Save the file in ASCII format.

Use the Hyphenation User dictionary for words that you expect to use frequently in your desktop publishing. Thus, if you compose newsletters about pianos all the time, you may want to make the entry *key-board* a part of the HYPHUSER.DIC file.

Be aware, however, that each word you add will slow down the hyphenation process slightly. The effects are cumulative, so only add a word if you expect Ventura to encounter it in documents you later create. If you don't expect to use the word again, just load the document and insert a discretionary hyphen in the word as it appears in the working area.

KEEPING WORDS FROM BEING HYPHENATED There may be words that you do not ever want Ventura to hyphenate, such as proper names or regular words used as proper names. You can prevent Ventura from hyphenating a given word by using either a discretionary hyphen—for the rare word—or the Hyphenation User dictionary—for words that will be common in your documents. Again, the frequency with which you expect the program to encounter the word should be the factor that determines which method you use.

To use a discretionary hyphen for this purpose, press Ctrl-hyphen at the *beginning* of the word where it appears in the document. This will keep Ventura from hyphenating the particular word, no matter where it falls on the line.

To enter such a word into the HYPHUSER.DIC file, type the entire word *without* any hyphens. Ventura will never hyphenate a word that you designate in this manner.

HEADLINES THAT STRETCH ACROSS COLUMNS

Let's continue with our examination of the Paragraph menu's Alignment dialog box. Following the Successive Hyphens grouping, notice that the Overall Width of a tag can be set for Column-Wide or Frame-Wide.

If the frame you are working with is set for only one column, the Overall Width setting has no effect. However, if you are working with multiple columns in a frame, you have a choice: you can have your text occupy the width of one of the columns or have it as wide as the entire frame. Figures 4.14 and 4.15 show how the same headline can fill one column or stretch across two columns to fill the frame. In this way, you can make a headline appear above as many columns as the frame holds without creating a special frame just for the headline.

If the frame-wide heading is the first paragraph in the frame, Ventura will handle the entire procedure automatically. You need do nothing more than make the setting. There may be times, however, when you want to place such a heading in the middle of a frame. This would be the case, for instance, with two articles that follow each

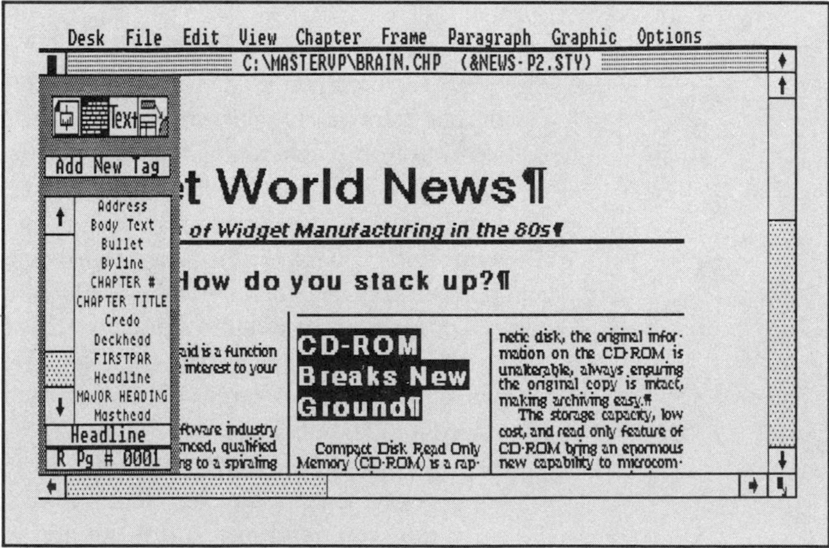

Figure 4.14: A column-wide headline

Figure 4.15: A frame-wide headline

other, each with its own heading, or one article with a frame-wide subheading.

In Figure 4.16 the subheading

Theory of Operation

has a column-wide format. We've numbered the text paragraphs in this article so you can easily follow along as we demonstrate. In Figure 4.17, we've given the same subheading a frame-wide format. Notice how the paragraphs rearrange themselves so that they still fall under the proper heading.

! New for version 2.0

To make paragraphs fall correctly under frame-wide headings, you must *balance* the columns. Balancing columns makes the text end evenly for each column in the frame. Ventura 2.0 provides you with two methods for balancing columns. First, you can turn Column Balance on for the entire chapter by using the Chapter menu's Chapter Typography dialog box and setting Column Balance: On. You can also adjust Column Balance for an individual frame. To do that, activate Frame mode, click the appropriate frame, and select the Frame menu's Frame Typography command. Normally, Column Balance is set for Default, and the frame takes its cues from the Chapter

CD-ROM Breaks New Ground

1) Compact Disk Read Only Memory (CD-ROM) is a rapidly emerging new technology for the retrieval of vast amounts of information from an optical disk. This new peripheral device allows a totally new level of functionality in the use of microcomputers.

2) Physically, the CD-ROM device has a laser disk drive (or "player") the same size as a traditional 5 1/4" drive. The removable disk is 4 3/4", and has a capacity of 550M bytes (equivalent to 1500 360K floppy disks).

Theory of Operation

3) Information stored on a CD-ROM can be loaded into memory (RAM), displayed and printed, as with other media. While that data in RAM may be altered and stored to a conventional magnetic disk, the original information on the CD-ROM is unalterable, always ensuring the original copy is intact, making archiving easy.

4) The storage capacity, low cost, and read only feature of CD-ROM bring an enormous new capability to microcomputer users – that is, information retrieval of very large reference publications. How people receive and use information in the immediate and long term future will be dramatically changed by CD-ROM.

5) In addition to the huge capacity of raw information storage, specialized software for the search of that information is currently being introduced. This software allows searching the information in areas, methods and speeds not previously feasible.

6) It now becomes possible to electronically publish reference material more economically than to print the same material in book form. That cost benefit, coupled with search and retrieval software, make an astonishing price/performance ratio.

Figure 4.16: A column-wide subheading

CD-ROM Breaks New Ground

1) Compact Disk Read Only Memory (CD-ROM) is a rapidly emerging new technology for the retrieval of vast amounts of information from an optical disk. This new peripheral device allows a totally new level of functionality in the use of microcomputers.

2) Physically, the CD-ROM device has a laser disk drive (or "player") the same size as a traditional 5 1/4" drive. The removable disk is 4 3/4", and has a capacity of 550M bytes (equivalent to 1500 360K floppy disks).

Theory of Operation

3) Information stored on a CD-ROM can be loaded into memory (RAM), displayed and printed, as with other media. While that data in RAM may be altered and stored to a conventional magnetic disk, the original information on the CD-ROM is unalterable, always ensuring the original copy is intact, making archiving easy.

4) The storage capacity, low cost, and read only feature of CD-ROM bring an enormous new capability to microcomputer users – that is, information retrieval of very large reference publications. How people receive and use information in the immediate and long term future will be dramatically changed by CD-ROM.

5) In addition to the huge capacity of raw information storage, specialized software for the search of that information is currently being introduced. This software allows searching the information in areas, methods and speeds not previously feasible.

6) It now becomes possible to electronically publish reference material more economically than to print the same material in book form. That cost benefit, coupled with search and retrieval software, make an astonishing price/performance ratio.

Figure 4.17: A frame-wide subheading

menu's Chapter Typography dialog box. Use On or Off to override the chapter's setting.

Failure to balance the columns can cause a variety of problems. You could end up with large empty columns, as shown in Figure 4.18; or with text for the first heading beneath the headline for the second article; or with text on top of text, as shown in Figure 4.19.

INDENTING AND OUTDENTING THE FIRST LINES OF PARAGRAPHS

Four settings in the Paragraph menu's Alignment dialog box (Figure 4.11) regulate the indentation of the first lines of all paragraphs that are tagged alike. Figure 4.20 shows two examples of indents and one example of an outdent.

With First Line in the dialog box, you can choose between Indent and Outdent as the examples indicate. A *first-line outdent* creates what is sometimes called a *hanging paragraph.* In this format, the first line of a paragraph protrudes beyond the main body of the paragraph, into the frame's left margin space.

When using outdents, you may need to increase the frame's left margin so the text doesn't spill out of the frame. To do that, activate Frame mode and click the appropriate frame. Then drop the Frame menu and click Margins & Columns. As an alternative, you can increase the paragraph's In From Left value. In Paragraph mode, select the paragraph with the outdent, and then use the Paragraph menu's Spacing command to increase the In From Left value.

To practice setting an indent or outdent for a paragraph, proceed as follows:

1. Activate Paragraph mode and click a Body Text paragraph.
2. Drop the Paragraph menu and click Alignment. (Remember what the settings are; you will restore them at the end of this exercise.)
3. In the Alignment dialog box, set First Line to Outdent.
4. Enter a value for In/Outdent Width. (If you wish, you can change the system of measurement by clicking the unit name, which is initially inches.)
5. Move the keyboard cursor (with Tab, ↓, or the mouse) to the In/Outdent Height field. Enter a value for the number of lines that should be affected.
6. Give the OK. The Body Text paragraphs are changed throughout the document.

CD-ROM Breaks New Ground

1) Compact Disk Read Only Memory (CD-ROM) is a rapidly emerging new technology for the retrieval of vast amounts of information from an optical disk. This new peripheral device allows a totally new level of functionality in the use of microcomputers.

2) Physically, the CD-ROM device has a laser disk drive (or "player") the same size as a traditional 5 1/4" drive. The removable disk is 4 3/4", and has a capacity of 550M bytes (equivalent to 1500 360K floppy disks).

Theory of Operation

3) Information stored on a CD-ROM can be loaded into memory (RAM), displayed and printed, as with other media. While that data in RAM may be altered and stored to a conventional magnetic disk, the original information on the CD-ROM is unalterable, always ensuring the original copy is intact, making archiving easy.

4) The storage capacity, low cost, and read only feature of CD-ROM bring an enormous new capability to microcomputer users – that is, information retrieval of very large reference publications. How people receive and use information in the immediate and long term future will be dramatically changed by CD-ROM.

5) In addition to the huge capacity of raw information storage, specialized software for the search of that information is currently being introduced. This software allows searching the information in areas, methods and speeds not previously feasible.

6) It now becomes possible to electronically publish reference material more economically than to print the same material in book form. That cost benefit, coupled with search and retrieval software, make an astonishing price/performance ratio.

Figure 4.18: An empty column due to columns not being balanced

CD-ROM Breaks New Ground

1) Compact Disk Read Only Memory (CD-ROM) is a rapidly emerging new technology for the retrieval of vast amounts of information from an optical disk. This new peripheral device allows a totally new level of functionality in the use of microcomputers.

2) Physically, the CD-ROM device has a laser disk drive (or "player") the same size as a traditional 5 1/4 drive. The removable disk is 4 3/4, and has a capacity of 550M bytes (equivalent to 1500 360K floppy disks).

3) Information stored on a CD-ROM can be loaded into memory (RAM), displayed and printed, as with other media. While that data in RAM may be altered and stored to a conventional magnetic disk, the original information on the CD-ROM is unalterable, always ensuring the original copy is intact, making archiving easy.

Theory of Operation

4) The storage capacity, low cost, and read only feature of CD-ROM bring an enormous new capability to microcomputer users—that is information retrieval of very large reference publications. How people receive and use information in the immediate and long term future will be dramatically changed by CD-ROM.

5) In addition to the huge capacity of raw information storage, specialized software for the search of that information is currently being introduced. This software allows searching the information in areas, methods and speeds not previously feasible.

6) It now becomes possible to electronically publish reference material more economically than to print the same material in book form. That cost benefit, coupled with search and retrieval software, make an astonishing price/performance ratio.

Figure 4.19: Text on top of text due to columns not being balanced

This paragraph has a first-line indent of 1/2 inch. Notice how the first line sinks into the main body of text. To achieve this effect, use the Paragraph menu's Alignment command. Set First Line to Indent. For In/Outdent Width, specify .5 inches.

This paragraph has the first three lines indented 1/2 inch. Notice how the first three lines sink into the main body of text. To achieve this effect, use the Paragraph menu's Alignment command. Set First Line to Indent. For In/Outdent Width, specify .5 inches. For In/Outdent Height, specify 3 lines.

This paragraph has a first-line outdent of 1/2 inch. Notice how the first line protrudes from the main body of text. To achieve this effect, use the Paragraph menu's Alignment command. Set First Line to Outdent. For In/Outdent Width, specify .5 inches.

Figure 4.20: Indenting and outdenting the first lines of paragraphs

7. Use the same dialog box to restore the Body Text tag to its original format.

Another indent setting in the Alignment dialog box is Relative Indent. This setting is used in conjunction with settings in other dialog boxes that you gain access to by way of the Paragraph menu. We'll study these later in this chapter under "Multitag Paragraphs".

We've seen how the Paragraph menu's Alignment dialog box controls the manner in which various elements of a paragraph line up. Next, we'll see how to control the amount of blank space a paragraph takes up.

LINE SPACING AND SET-IN PARAGRAPHS

The third item on the Paragraph menu is Spacing. Its dialog box controls the space between the lines of a paragraph, between paragraphs, and on either side of paragraphs. To set the spacing for a given paragraph tag:

1. Activate Paragraph mode and click a paragraph with the mouse.
2. Drop the Paragraph menu and click Spacing. This displays the Spacing dialog box, shown in Figure 4.21.

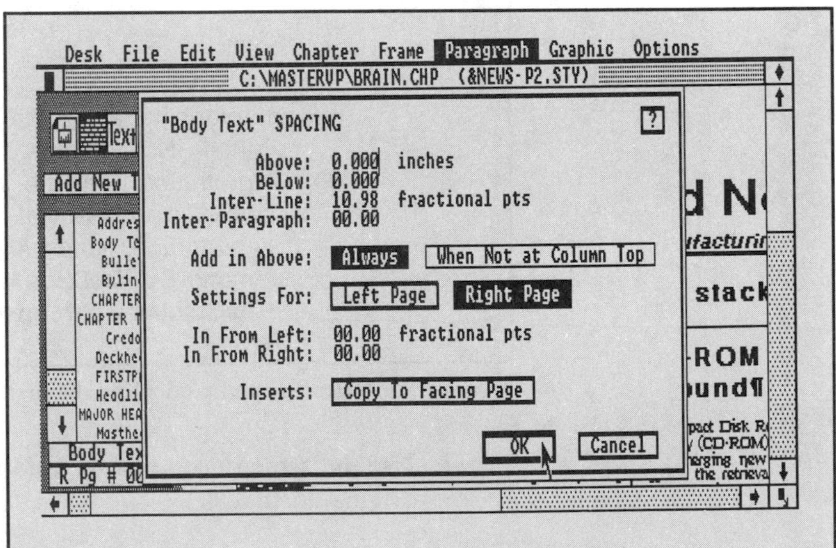

Figure 4.21: The Paragraph menu's Spacing dialog box

VERTICAL PARAGRAPH SPACING

The four values at the top of the Spacing dialog box control a paragraph's vertical spacing, while the two values toward the bottom of the box control the horizontal spacing.

Use the Above and Below settings to add space above and below paragraphs. By placing a value in either of these fields, you guarantee at least that amount of space above or below the paragraph.

The Inter-Line setting governs the amount of space between the lines of text. Typographers refer to this spacing as *leading*. The term is derived from the lead slugs that fill the space between lincs of manually set type. In Ventura, however, interline spacing is the distance from the top of a line of text, say the top of a capital letter, to the top of the same letter on the next line. Some recommend an interline spacing of 1.2 times the size of the font that composes the paragraph. However, this may be a bit much by other people's standards, especially with larger fonts. So others recommend 2 points more than the font size. Don't be afraid to experiment until you find spacing that makes the text seem most readable to you. We'll discuss spacing and Ventura's other typographic capabilities in greater detail in Chapter 12.

! New for version 2.0

With versions of Ventura prior to 2.0, you could have a lot of trouble with oversized fonts that appeared in just part of a paragraph. Without a great enough line spacing, enlarging a font would cause text to overlap lines above and below it. Now, when you increase the size of a local font, Ventura automatically adjusts the line spacing for the line that has the special font. This is handled by the paragraph tag with the Grow Inter-Line To Fit setting in the Paragraph menu's Paragraph Typography dialog box. Just set this to On and Ventura will specially handle the spacing of lines with large fonts.

The Inter-Paragraph setting adds additional space between identically-tagged paragraphs that follow one another. You can increase or decrease these values in order to fit the necessary amount of text on a page. Ventura also adds this space between differently tagged paragraphs when the value is identical for both tags. More on this in Chapter 12.

The Add In Above settings refer to the value you entered for the Above field. Click Always when you want the Above value to apply in every situation. The setting When Not At Column Top instructs Ventura not to add the Above value when a paragraph so tagged begins at the top of a column. Use this setting when you find that an inordinate amount of space occurs at the top of a column. We'll see an example of this in Chapter 12.

SETTING PARAGRAPHS IN FROM BOTH MARGINS

The In From Left and In From Right settings regulate the paragraph's horizontal spacing. You use them to set paragraphs farther in from the margins. For instance, a tag for extended quotations could cause the edges of paragraphs so tagged to be set in from those of regular text. Then those paragraphs will have wider margins than usual. These settings add the additional margin to any margin already set for the frame (with the Frame menu's Margins & Columns command).

The Settings For category, which has buttons for Left Page and Right Page, applies *only* to these horizontal measurements (In From Left and In From Right). It does not affect other items in this dialog box. Additionally, it only affects double-sided documents (set with the Chapter menu's Page Size & Layout). Clicking one button or the other allows you to see and set those measurements. If you adjust these settings for one page and then decide that you want the same settings for the opposite page, click Copy To Facing Page. Ventura registers the same horizontal values for the facing page. However, there will be no immediate feedback to let you know the transfer has occurred. You can make sure the values are registered by clicking the button for the opposite page.

CONTROLLING THE BREAKUP OF TEXT

The Paragraph menu's Breaks command displays a dialog box that deals with some sophisticated typographical concepts. Figure 4.22 shows the Breaks dialog box. The settings displayed in the figure are the default ones; if ever your paragraph breaks go awry, you can redisplay the dialog box, click the appropriate buttons to return to these settings, and try again.

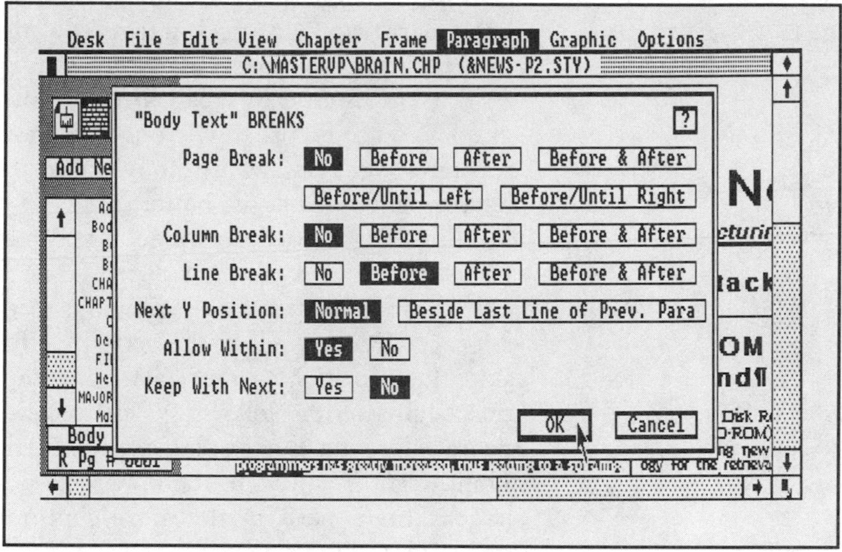

Figure 4.22: The Paragraph menu's Breaks dialog box

The categories in this dialog box are listed in order of priority; the effect each setting has on a paragraph so tagged nullifies the effect of any settings that follow.

Ventura describes a *break* as an "interruption in the flow of text at a paragraph boundary." That is, when a paragraph ends, you decide where the next paragraph begins. It can start on the next page, at the top of the next column, or on the next line.

For instance, when a standard paragraph ends, you indicate this with a return, and the text for the new paragraph begins on the next line. This arrangement constitutes a *line break.*

BREAKING FOR PAGES

You can cause a tag to create a page break. You might use such tags on titles of sections that should always begin on a new page. When you set Page Break to Before, Ventura will start the tagged text on a new page. It will cause a page break to occur *before* the tagged paragraph. If necessary, it will leave blank space at the bottom of the previous page to accomplish this.

If you set Page Break to After, the program will start the new page *after* a paragraph with such a tag. You might use this setting for the final paragraph of the section. This setup is rarely used.

You can also specify a page break before *and* after the tagged paragraph. You could use this arrangement for a table that you want on a separate page. Be aware, though, that the page before might have a large blank area at the bottom.

With double-sided documents, you may find it important that a new section begin on a left page. To accomplish this, click Before/Until Left. If the text for the previous section ends in the middle of a left page, Ventura allows the bottom of that page to be blank. It then skips the next (right) page, leaving it completely blank. The new section begins on the following (left) page. Thus, it leaves 1½ blank pages before starting the new section. Similarly, you can click Before/Until Right if you want the new section to always begin on a right page. This is perhaps the more common arrangement, although there are publications using both.

BREAKING FOR COLUMNS

The Column Break category is similar in operation to Page Break. The Before setting, which is frequently used for column headings, causes Ventura to place that heading in a new column along with the text that follows it. After and Before & After work the same way as their page-break counterparts, but with respect to columns.

MULTITAG PARAGRAPHS

Earlier, we examined how to apply text attributes in order to change fonts and other formatting attributes within a paragraph. Text attributes work fine for instances where a localized change is called for, within a specific paragraph only. Suppose, however, that you have a format you need to apply repeatedly and identically within several paragraphs. Magazine interviews, for instance, will often precede a series of quotes with the interviewee's name set in boldface. Using the text attributes to achieve this effect, you'd run the risk of accidentally applying the wrong effect to a few of the paragraphs. By creating multitag paragraphs with the Breaks dialog box, you can be sure that effects are applied consistently, and you can later change them as a group, rather than one by one.

As we discuss multitag paragraphs, it's again necessary to distinguish between two types of paragraphs. A *traditional* paragraph is a normal paragraph of text. A *Ventura* paragraph is any chunk of text that ends with a return. With multitag paragraphs, you combine two or more Ventura paragraphs into one traditional paragraph.

The Line Break setting for a given tag is usually set to Before. This causes a new Ventura paragraph to start on a new line, as a traditional paragraph does. If, however, you set Line Break to No, the new Ventura paragraph begins on the same line as the Ventura paragraph before it. When used in combination with other settings in this dialog box, the result is a traditional paragraph that actually contains more than one Ventura paragraph and hence possibly more than one tag. You may wish to use such multitag paragraphs to accommodate explanatory text that begins several paragraphs in succession. Such material is often called a *lead-in*.

Do not use multitag paragraphs in conjunction with justified text. If you do, Ventura will justify the second-tagged text, but not the first (the lead-in text). Thus, the first line of the second tag may well be unacceptably loose, while the lead-in text on the same line will be tight. For best results, use left-aligned text instead.

Figure 4.23 shows an example of a lead-in. The example is from the sample chapter and style sheet &PREL-P1. The text

LOS ANGELES, CA, July 17 —

ends with a return, making it a Ventura paragraph. It is formatted with one tag (the Dateline tag), while the rest of the traditional paragraph is formatted with another (the Firstpar tag).

To produce multitag paragraphs, be sure that the text meets the following conditions:

- The first tag must not have a line break set to occur after it. Thus, Line Break must not be set for After or Before & After.
- The second tag in the paragraph must not have a line break set to occur before it. Also, Next Y Position should be set to

LOS ANGELES, CA, July 17 – XYZ Corp., the leading manufacturer of widgets for the automated widget supply industry, announced that it has shipped its 1000th Model 123-X enhanced widget. The customer is ABC Inc. of Livonia Hills, MI.

Figure 4.23: A multitag paragraph

Beside Last Line of Prev Para. (We'll discuss this setting presently.)

- The second tag must also have a *relative indent.* To set this, select the paragraph, drop the Paragraph menu, and choose Alignment. Set Relative Indent: On. This will cause the first line of the second Ventura paragraph to be indented by the length of the lead-in; the text of the second tag will follow on the heels of the text for the first.
- If a third tag follows in the same paragraph, the second tag must not have a line break after it. The third tag must meet the same conditions as those listed for the second tag.

The Next Y Position setting is the distance for the tagged text down from the top of the previous paragraph. Setting it to Beside Last Line of Prev Para will cause text with the second tag to begin on the same line as the end of the text with the first tag. We'll study the Y position more when we work with tables in Chapter 8.

KEEPING PARAGRAPHS TOGETHER

The final two break settings regulate the cohesion of paragraphs. Ventura consults these settings as it is running out of room at the bottom of a page or a column.

When Allow Within is set for Yes, as it usually is, Ventura fills as much of the page as possible before starting to fill the next page. It's okay if part of one paragraph ends up at the bottom of the first page, with the rest on the next page. In other words, the setting instructs the program to allow a break to occur within the paragraph.

There may be times, however, when you want Ventura to keep an entire paragraph on the same page. For example, you'd want to keep a table all on the same page. To guarantee that this is the case, regardless of editing, set Allow Within to No. If the paragraph does not all fit at the bottom of one page, the entire paragraph will go to the top of the next page, leaving some blank space at the bottom of the first page.

There are some paragraphs, such as headings, that you want to keep with the paragraph that follows them. Otherwise, you could end up with a heading by itself at the bottom of a page. To keep this from occurring, set Keep With Next for the heading's tag to Yes.

There are other tasks that you use tags to accomplish. In Chapter 7, you'll see how to draw lines that are associated with paragraphs. In Chapter 8, you'll learn how to set tabs to create tables. For now, though, we need to consider how to manipulate the tags themselves.

ADDING, RENAMING, AND REMOVING TAGS

As you work with Ventura, you'll undoubtedly find that you want to customize the list of tags in your style sheets. Ventura allows you to add, rename, and remove tags. The procedures for these three operations are similar.

! New for version 2.0

Removal and renaming of tags in Ventura 2.0 is performed with the Paragraph menu's Update Tag List command. Assigning tags to function keys is performed here also. This new command also lets you print your style sheet, a capability not previously available (except with an outside, add-on utility program).

ADDING TAGS

You use a copy of an existing tag as the basis for a new tag. You can then format the new copy. For practice adding a tag:

Remember that names on the Assignment list appear in alphabetical order. To keep similar tags together, begin their names with the same general name rather than a specific one. Thus, names such as Column # 1, Column #2, and Column #3 are better than First Column, Second Column, and Third Column.

1. Activate Paragraph mode.
2. Click a Body Text paragraph.
3. Click the Add New Tag button in the Side-bar. The Add New Tag dialog box appears, as shown in Figure 4.24.
4. Type **BTEXT**.

The Tag Name To Copy From setting is initially the same as the original tag of the selected paragraph. Change it only if you want Ventura to copy the formatting from another tag. To do that, move to the field (using the Tab key, the ↓ key, or the mouse), press Esc to clear the field, and enter a different tag's name.

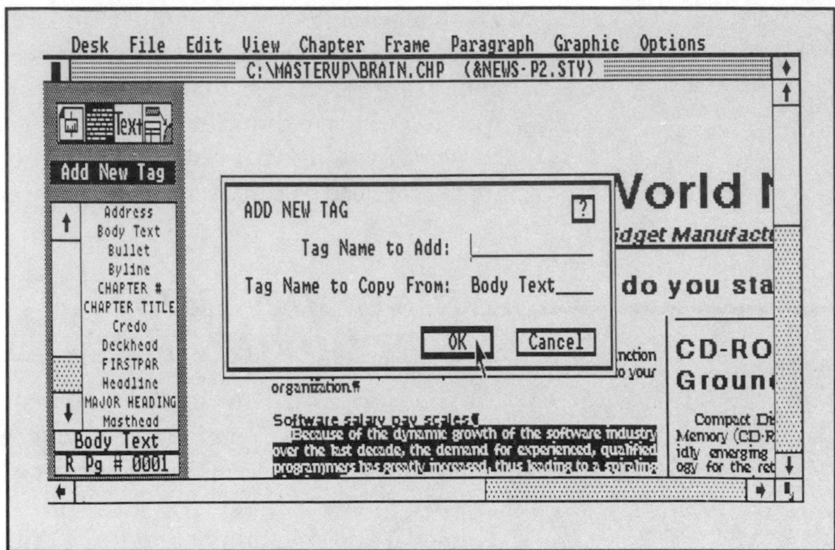

Figure 4.24: The Add New Tag dialog box

5. Give the OK by pressing Enter or clicking the mouse. Ventura adds the new tag name to the Assignment list.

Now you can change the formatting for the new tag using the tools we've covered in this chapter.

UPDATING TAGS AND STYLE SHEETS

New for version 2.0

Ventura 2.0 provides a centralized location for performing the tag-updating procedures. With the Update Tag List dialog box, you can rename and remove tags associated with a style sheet. You can also save and print the resulting style sheets and assign function keys to the tags.

To display this dialog box, proceed as follows:

1. Activate Paragraph mode.
2. Optionally, click a paragraph whose tag you wish to adjust.
3. Press Ctrl-K or click Update Tag List on the Paragraph menu.

4. If you have made edits in your document and not yet saved them, Ventura will prompt you to save. If it does, click Save or press the Enter key. The Update Tag List dialog box will appear (Figure 4.25).

At the top of the Update Tag List dialog box, you'll see the name of the style sheet the document is using, complete with the directory path. This is the style sheet you can now work on. Below that is the list of tags that the style sheet contains. (Tags appearing in a text file you loaded that are not on the current style sheet appear in all capital letters. More on this in Chapter 11.)

If you selected a tag before displaying this dialog box, that tag's name will be darkened, indicating it is selected for you to work on (that is, to remove or rename). If you wish to work on another tag, use the Tag list to select a different tag.

Use the five buttons to perform the indicated procedures. After you use any of these buttons, Ventura redisplays the Update Tag List dialog box. The sections that follow discuss Rename Tag, Remove Selected Tag, and Print Stylesheet.

You can use the Assign Func Keys button to display the Assign Function Keys dialog box, which we examined earlier. Note that

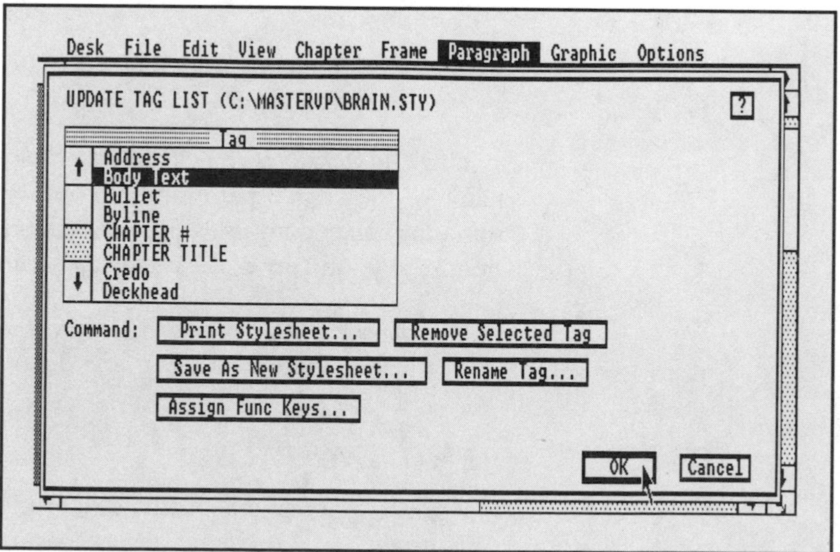

Figure 4.25: The Update Tag List dialog box

when Ventura is in Text mode, Ctrl-K displays the Assign Functions Keys dialog box directly. In Paragraph mode, Ctrl-K displays the Update Tag List dialog box; you can then click this button to assign the function keys.

If you want the changes you make to be separate from the existing style sheet, click Save As New Stylesheet. This procedure is the same as the File menu's Save As New Style, discussed in Chapter 2.

When the style sheet and its tags are as you desire, click OK or press the Enter key. Ventura will allow you to save the style sheet under the same name or a different name and then redisplay your document.

RENAMING TAGS

If you find that the names of your tags are unorganized or inappropriate, you can easily rename them. For practice renaming a tag:

1. Activate Paragraph mode and select the BTEXT paragraph created in the Adding Tags section above.
2. Drop the Paragraph menu and click Update Tag List. If you've made changes to the chapter, Ventura will ask if you want to save. Click Save, and the Update Tag List dialog box appears.
3. Click Rename Tag. The Rename Tag dialog box appears, as shown in Figure 4.26.

The Old Tag Name field in this dialog box initially displays the name of the tagged paragraph. If you want to change the name to some tag other than this one, erase the displayed name by pressing the Esc key, and enter the other tag's name.

4. Enter **BODTXT** in the New Tag Name field and give the OK. The Update Tag List dialog box reappears.

REMOVING TAGS

If you're not using a particular tag, it's wise to remove it from the Assignment list. Having fewer tags makes it easier to locate them. In

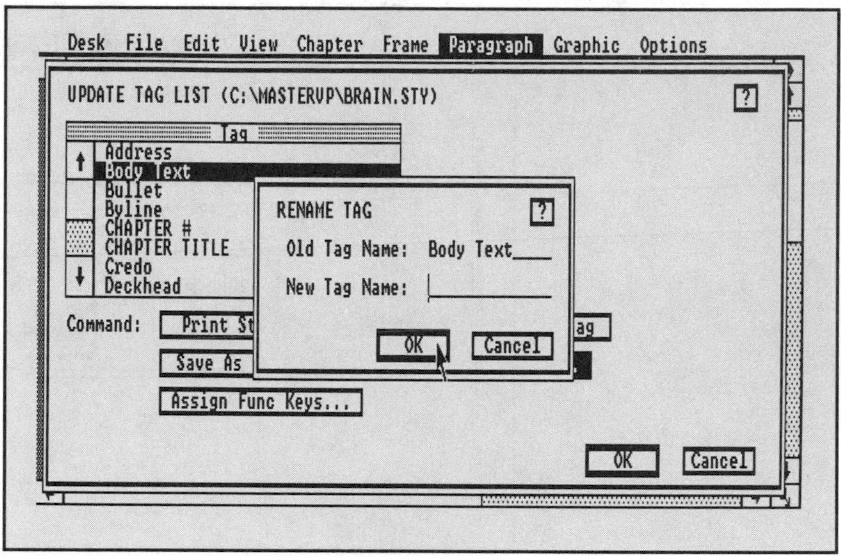

Figure 4.26: The Rename Tag dialog box

addition, fewer tags may improve the performance of the program and allow you to create larger chapters. Every tag takes up memory even if you don't use the tag. For practice removing a tag:

1. Activate Paragraph mode and select a BODTXT paragraph created in the Renaming Tags section above.
2. Drop the Paragraph menu and click Update Tag List. In the Update Tag List dialog box, click Remove Selected Tag. The Remove Tag dialog box, shown in Figure 4.27, appears.

The name indicated for Tag Name To Remove is initially the tag name of the selected paragraph. If you wish to remove the tag for a different kind of paragraph, press Esc and enter the appropriate name.

Tag Name To Convert To indicates how you want affected paragraphs to be retagged. The initial setting is Body Text, but you can change it if you wish.

3. Give the OK to remove the tag.

! New for version 2.0

You can use the Update Tag List dialog box as the first step toward obtaining a hard copy of the tags and other settings in place for your

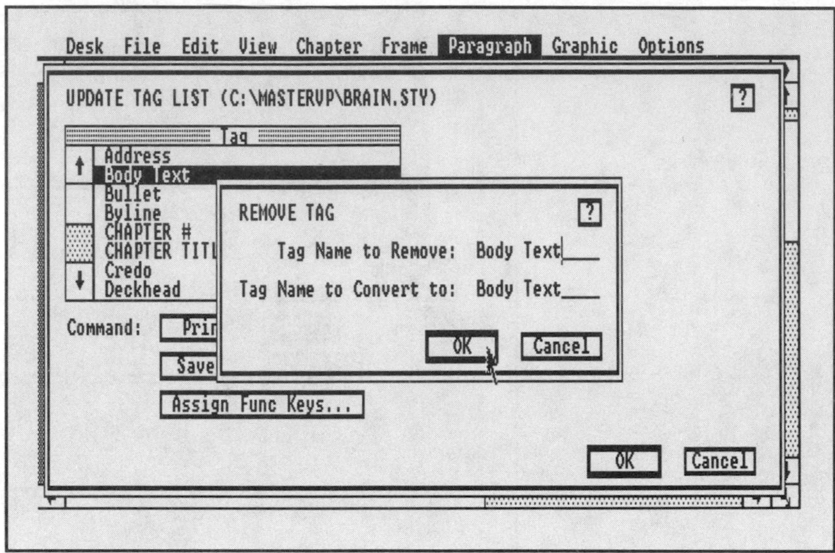

Figure 4.27: The Remove Tag dialog box

style sheet. Be aware, though, that printing the style sheet is not as immediate a process as you may suspect. Practice by following the steps to print the listing for the current style-sheet you're using.

1. Click the Print Stylesheet button. Ventura does not print the list immediately; rather, it displays an Item Selector box. Use it to assign a name to the generated text file (normally with the GEN extension) that Ventura then creates.
2. Once you've created the text file, give the OK to exit the Update Tag List dialog box.
3. Use the File menu's New to clear the working area.
4. Select the File menu's Load Diff Style. In the TYPESET directory, load the STYLOG.STY style sheet. This is a special style sheet formatted to accommodate the material in the generated text file you created.
5. Use the File menu's Load Text/Picture to load the text file you created. Specify Text Format as Generated.
6. Select the File menu's To Print option in order to print the style-sheet list.

This concludes our initial examination of formatting and of this document.

7. Save the document and quit Ventura.

Although we will be discussing formatting throughout the book, you should now know enough to create your own well-formatted publication. In the next chapter, you'll see how to deliver the end product of desktop publishing: printed matter.

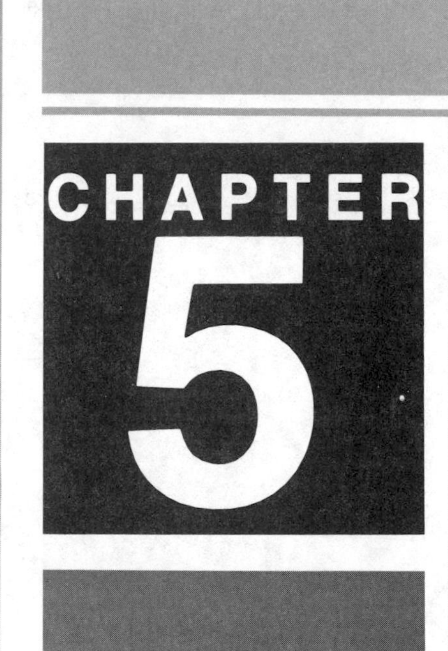
CHAPTER
5

Start the Presses: Printing and Other Output

Fast Track

To print a chapter 174

use the File menu's Open Chapter to display the chapter. For information about your printer and print configuration, select the Options menu's Printer Info. Use the File menu's To Print to indicate how much you wish to print and to begin printing.

To select a printer 177

use the Options menu's Set Printer Info dialog box. You can select among printers you've installed with the VPPREP program. Usually, when changing printers, you must change the width table as well.

To link fonts with your printer 180

select the appropriate width table. In the Options menu's Set Printer Info dialog box, click Load Different Width Table to change width tables. Generally, you use the width table that matches the printer you're using (ultimate quality). To create a draft version of output on a different printer, select the width table for that printer. The OUTPUT.WID width table matches the default (first listed) printer.

To print only certain pages 185

use Which Pages in the Print Information dialog box. Indicate All, Selected, Left, Right, or Current. With Selected, provide values for From Page and Through Page.

To print multiple copies 185

provide a value for Number Of Copies in the Print Information dialog box. Set Collated Copies On or Off to indicate whether you want Ventura to collate the multiple copies.

To begin printing 187

give the OK in the Print Information dialog box.

To add fonts to Ventura 191

use the Options menu's Add/Remove Fonts. Select Merge Width Tables to add them to the existing width table; use Save As New Width Table to save the combined fonts under a new name.

To change the download/resident status 194

of a font, change its setting in the Options menu's Add/Remove Fonts dialog box (under Style). You can expedite printing with resident (or previously downloaded) fonts if their status is correctly set. Each combination of Face, Size, and Style has its own download/resident status.

To print with typesetting equipment 195

construct the chapter, and all related files, on a floppy disk, or copy with the Multi-Chapter command (Chapter 10).

To print in color or in shades of gray 198

adjust color settings in the appropriate dialog box (Table 5.1). Use the Paragraph menu's Define Colors to customize colors for the chapter, and to define shades of gray. To print color separations, you first use this dialog box to enable and disable Color Settings. Then you select the File menu's To Print and set Spot Color Overlays: On.

To "print" to disk 200

click Filename in the Options menu's Set Printer Info. Then use the File menu's To Print, adjust the settings, and give the OK. Ventura will display an Item Selector box for you to specify the output file. You can then print the file with DOS's COPY command.

CHAPTER 5

WITH THE ADVENT OF DESKTOP PUBLISHING, typeset-quality printing is now available for many types of communications in the office. The move is on for paper communications of an increasingly high caliber. Gone are notions of the "paperless office" of the future. Gone is the once widely entertained idea that communication strictly by way of computer screens is a desirable goal.

While printing and other output operations are simple to perform with Ventura, the program nevertheless permits you to make numerous choices. Ventura wisely provides for a great deal of flexibility in printing, as it does in other areas. You can print plain or fancy, now or later, all or some, forward or backward.

While for most operations, output from a computer means printed output, Ventura can also create another form of output: output to a computer file. Doing so allows you to print the document at another time and place, even without Ventura.

These capabilities, though, are icing on the cake. Printing can also be simple and straightforward. In this chapter, we'll first examine simple printing procedures. Then we'll look at Ventura's flexibility in output.

LOADING A SAMPLE THAT TESTS YOUR PRINTER

To let you check the capabilities of your printer, Ventura provides you with a special chapter file called CAPABILI.CHP. It's located in the TYPESET directory.

1. Drop the File menu.
2. Click Open Chapter. The Item Selector box appears.
3. From the TYPESET directory, select the CAPABILI.CHP chapter.

A PRINTING OVERVIEW

As mentioned above, printing with Ventura is a simple process. In most circumstances, you'll probably find that you can just issue the printing command. Here is a summary of the procedures that we'll discuss in this chapter and that you'll utilize to print a document:

- Loading the chapter that you wish to print.
- Using the Options menu's Printer Info command to set up the appropriate printing configuration.
- Indicating how much you want to print and commencing the operation with the File menu's To print command.

These procedures are geared to printing a single chapter. We'll see how to print multichapter publications in Chapter 10.

We'll also examine printers and other hardware that you use in the printing process. If you don't have a printer yet, or you are considering the purchase of a new one, you'll be interested in reading "Which Printer Is Best for Me?" later in this chapter. If you already have one, you need to find out what it's capable of doing and not doing with Ventura. The next section describes the way to do this.

CHECKING YOUR PRINTER'S CAPABILITIES

Figure 5.1 shows two printouts of this test document you loaded at the beginning of this chapter. This document is used to test your printer's capabilities.

To print CAPABILI.CHP, or any document for that matter, follow the procedure we are about to describe. If all is working properly, you should get a printout like those in Figure 5.1.

The capabilities that this document tests are described in the document itself. Among other features, your printout will show you the point sizes that are available for your printer. It will also indicate the area around the edges of the paper on which the printer is unable to print. Notice how the capabilities of the two printers tested in Figure 5.1 differ.

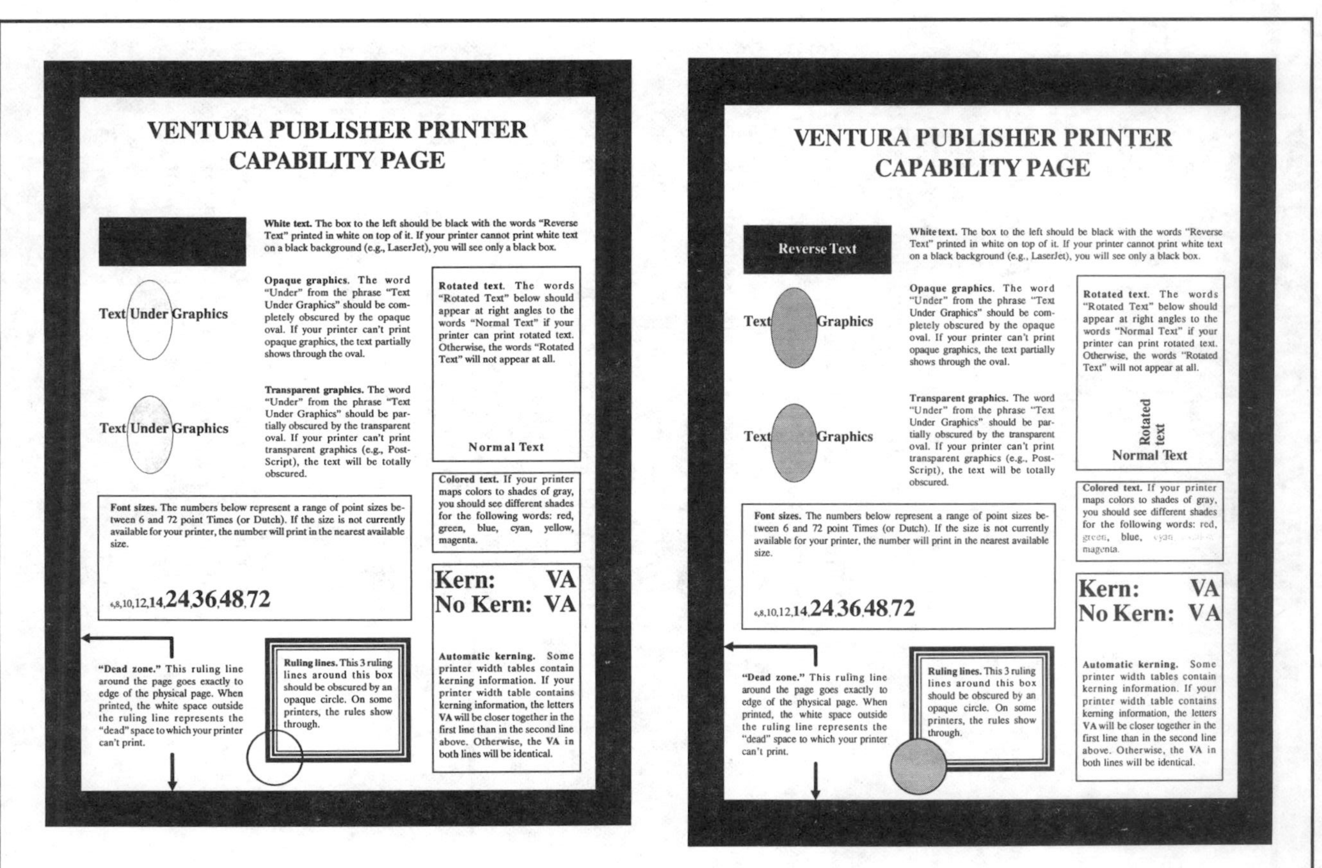

VENTURA PUBLISHER PRINTER CAPABILITY PAGE

White text. The box to the left should be black with the words "Reverse Text" printed in white on top of it. If your printer cannot print white text on a black background (e.g., LaserJet), you will see only a black box.

Text Under Graphics

Opaque graphics. The word "Under" from the phrase "Text Under Graphics" should be completely obscured by the opaque oval. If your printer can't print opaque graphics, the text partially shows through the oval.

Rotated text. The words "Rotated Text" below should appear at right angles to the words "Normal Text" if your printer can print rotated text. Otherwise, the words "Rotated Text" will not appear at all.

Normal Text

Text Under Graphics

Transparent graphics. The word "Under" from the phrase "Text Under Graphics" should be partially obscured by the transparent oval. If your printer can't print transparent graphics (e.g., PostScript), the text will be totally obscured.

Colored text. If your printer maps colors to shades of gray, you should see different shades for the following words: red, green, blue, cyan, yellow, magenta.

Font sizes. The numbers below represent a range of point sizes between 6 and 72 point Times (or Dutch). If the size is not currently available for your printer, the number will print in the nearest available size.

6,8,10,12,14,24,36,48,72

Kern: VA
No Kern: VA

"Dead zone." This ruling line around the page goes exactly to edge of the physical page. When printed, the white space outside the ruling line represents the "dead" space to which your printer can't print.

Ruling lines. This 3 ruling lines around this box should be obscured by an opaque circle. On some printers, the rules show through.

Automatic kerning. Some printer width tables contain kerning information. If your printer width table contains kerning information, the letters VA will be closer together in the first line than in the second line above. Otherwise, the VA in both lines will be identical.

VENTURA PUBLISHER PRINTER CAPABILITY PAGE

Reverse Text

White text. The box to the left should be black with the words "Reverse Text" printed in white on top of it. If your printer cannot print white text on a black background (e.g., LaserJet), you will see only a black box.

Text Graphics

Opaque graphics. The word "Under" from the phrase "Text Under Graphics" should be completely obscured by the opaque oval. If your printer can't print opaque graphics, the text partially shows through the oval.

Rotated text. The words "Rotated Text" below should appear at right angles to the words "Normal Text" if your printer can print rotated text. Otherwise, the words "Rotated Text" will not appear at all.

Rotated text
Normal Text

Text Graphics

Transparent graphics. The word "Under" from the phrase "Text Under Graphics" should be partially obscured by the transparent oval. If your printer can't print transparent graphics (e.g., PostScript), the text will be totally obscured.

Colored text. If your printer maps colors to shades of gray, you should see different shades for the following words: red, green, blue, cyan, magenta.

Font sizes. The numbers below represent a range of point sizes between 6 and 72 point Times (or Dutch). If the size is not currently available for your printer, the number will print in the nearest available size.

6,8,10,12,14,24,36,48,72

Kern: VA
No Kern: VA

"Dead zone." This ruling line around the page goes exactly to edge of the physical page. When printed, the white space outside the ruling line represents the "dead" space to which your printer can't print.

Ruling lines. This 3 ruling lines around this box should be obscured by an opaque circle. On some printers, the rules show through.

Automatic kerning. Some printer width tables contain kerning information. If your printer width table contains kerning information, the letters VA will be closer together in the first line than in the second line above. Otherwise, the VA in both lines will be identical.

Figure 5.1: The printer-capability page printed with different printers

SETTING UP PRINTER INFO

To prepare Ventura for printing, you need to provide the program with information about your printer and printing needs. With any of Ventura's four modes active, follow these steps:

1. Drop the Options menu.
2. Click Set Printer Info.

A dialog box for Set Printer Info, which looks something like Figure 5.2, appears. Its actual contents vary depending upon how you've set up Ventura (Appendix A). Examine the categories in this dialog box and decide on the setup that best meets your needs.

SELECTING THE PRINTER

In the Device Name category of the Set Printer Info dialog box, you'll see the printers that you can use. The names are those you specified with VPPREP, Ventura's installation program. The names that appear on your screen probably differ from those in the figure.

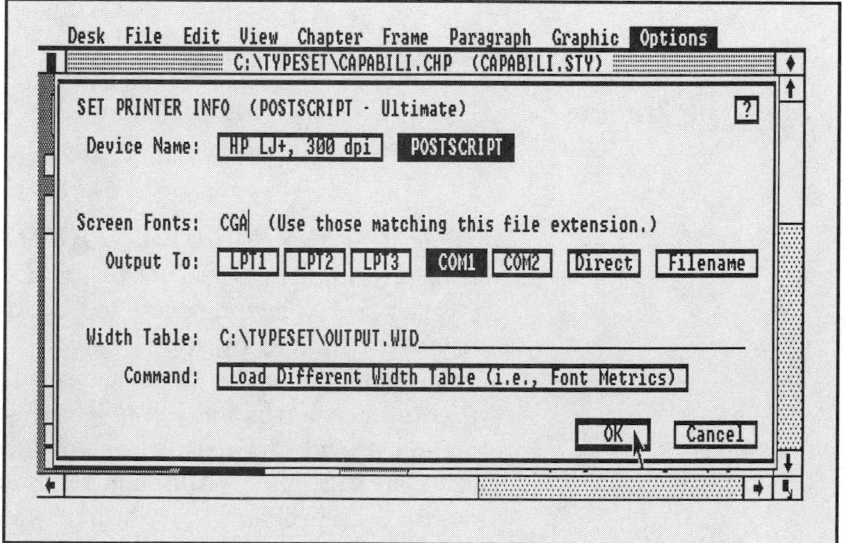

Figure 5.2: The Options menu's Set Printer Info dialog box

You may have installed only one printer. In that case, you would see only one printer listed for Device Name. Why install more than one? The answers usually have to do with quality and availability. You could use one printer to create rough drafts of your documents and another for the final versions. You could also install a color printer and a black-and-white one if you have access to both. However, you don't have to have a particular printer immediately available in order to use it later, as we'll see when we discuss the creation of output files.

When you change printers, be careful. There is more to changing printers than just clicking the button for Device Name. You also need to change the Width Table setting that is associated with the printer; we'll discuss this later in the chapter.

The printer that you installed first will appear first in the list. Initially, this first printer will be darkened, indicating that it is selected. If you wish to use this printer, you need do nothing. If you wish to use a different printer, click the button with that printer's name, which will then darken.

As mentioned, if you installed only one printer, only that printer will appear, and it will always be darkened. If you acquire a new printer, you can add its name by running the VPPREP program again.

By the way, the VPPREP program also sets the Screen Fonts field, which appears next in the dialog box. This setting is determined by the monitor you specify when you run the VPPREP program. We'll examine this setting later in this chapter when we look at how to add fonts.

CHOOSING AN OUTPUT

Next, take a look at the Output To setting. There are seven buttons associated with it.

SERIAL VERSUS PARALLEL PRINTERS The first five buttons begin with the letters *LPT* or *COM.* These five choices are usually called *ports.* They are provided by the operating system (DOS) and may be limited by your hardware. You may recognize these choices from other software packages with which you are familiar.

A computer port is simply one of the output connectors that your computer provides. Typically, one or more ports are located on the back of the computer. (Although DOS allows up to five ports on a computer, you probably have the hardware for only one or two.) You plug a cable from your printer into a port as you would a VCR or a cable-TV line into your television. Through this hookup, signals travel from the computer to the printer. The port does not provide electrical power to the printer; it only directs the signals.

The two kinds of ports, LPT and COM, reflect the two ways in which computers can send signals to a printer. You use LPT settings for *parallel* printers. COM settings are for *serial* printers. As you can see by the Output To grouping, DOS allows up to three parallel and two serial printers (or other devices).

Computers send serial signals "bit by bit": the computer fires out bits of information single file. With serial printers, there are no control signals to ensure that accurate data transmission occurs, so you must set up a variety of parameters. Computers send parallel signals in a "side-by-side" fashion, which keeps the signals aligned and organized.

Installation of parallel printers is simpler than serial printers. However, you must keep parallel printers within about ten feet of the computer, a restriction that doesn't apply to serial printers.

If you already have a printer, you must determine the signaling method it uses—parallel or serial. Usually, it's designated on the original box that the printer came in. Sometimes it's also specified in the printer's operating manual or even on the sales receipt.

You can also tell the signal method by examining the connectors on the back of the printer. Figure 5.3 shows the two connectors.

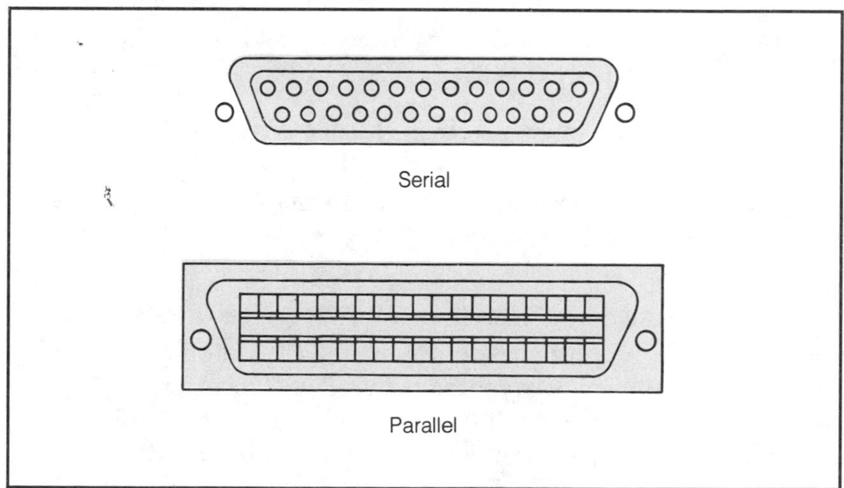

Figure 5.3: Parallel and serial connectors for printers

Many printers are available in either parallel or serial models. Because of their simplicity of installation and speed of printing, parallel printers are preferable. Some printers, like the Apple LaserWriter, are available only as serial. On the other hand, if you own an HP LaserJet, you can configure it to operate in either serial or parallel fashion.

DIRECT CONNECTIONS After the five LPT and COM settings is the Direct setting. You use the Direct setting in conjunction with printer configurations that do not use the ports. For instance, use this setting if your printer is operating with a JLaser card. The printer connects to the card, which plugs into a slot within the computer. This arrangement bypasses the ports altogether, and so the connection is direct.

PRINTING TO DISK The Filename button allows you to ''print'' the document to a file on the disk. Use this option to create output that you don't want to print just yet. Once you've created such a file, you no longer need Ventura to print it. The technique of printing to a file and the reasons for doing so are described in the section ''Printing from Output Files'' at the end of this chapter.

WIDTH TABLES

The next setting in the Set Printer Info dialog box is entitled Width Table. By its name, you can see that it's associated with the big button at the bottom labeled

Load Different Width Table (i.e., Font Metrics)

To understand these two settings, you need to know how Ventura works with fonts and printers.

HOW VENTURA LINKS FONTS AND PRINTERS In various files, Ventura has descriptions of the fonts it uses as well as particulars on the printers you have installed. However, it must associate these files in order to print your documents correctly. To link font and printer files meaningfully, Ventura uses *width tables.*

The names of the width tables match the names of the printers. There's also one we'll discuss shortly, called OUTPUT.WID, that's a copy of the default printer's width table. Let's say that you have installed Ventura for use with an Apple LaserWriter (a PostScript printer) and an HP LaserJet Plus. In this case, the installation program will copy the POSTSCPT and HPLJPLUS width tables from the original Ventura disks to your hard disk, making them available to print with.

ULTIMATE VERSUS DRAFT QUALITY You're probably wondering why Ventura doesn't simply keep the specifications for the font widths right along with the rest of the printer specifications. At first, such an arrangement seems to make sense. You wouldn't have to remember to change width tables whenever you change printers.

The reason is flexibility. Keeping the specifications in separate files allows you to mix printers and width tables. You do this, for instance, when you want to get a sample printout that approximates the final version, which you will print on a different printer. Just use the width table of the different printer.

Ventura uses the term *ultimate* quality to describe the final printout on the final printer. You achieve ultimate quality when you select a printer and a width table that match. When the width table doesn't match the printer in use, the resulting document is of *draft* quality.

Let's say that you want to create a company catalog on a LaserWriter. The problem is, however, that you have only a LaserJet printer at your desk. Now assume that a department elsewhere in the building does have a LaserWriter that they are willing to let you use. However, you want to do the bulk of your work at your desk, because all the information for the catalog is being channeled through you. Naturally, as you work, you'd like to get an idea of how the catalog will look when you print it.

If you were to set both Device Name and Width Table to LaserJet, you'd get a good printout at your desk. However, when you took the files to the LaserWriter station, you'd be in for some surprises. Different printers treat the same font differently; that is, the same font may be printed in different widths depending on the printer. If the widths of the letters differ, the number of words on a line will differ as well. This affects the length of the paragraphs as well as the amount of text on a page. The items in your LaserWriter catalog would be dislocated, and the catalog wouldn't look like the finely tuned document that it was at your desk.

To approximate the LaserWriter on the LaserJet, you wouldn't simply change Device Name to POSTSCRIPT. The signals Ventura sends to a LaserWriter would be meaningless to the LaserJet, and the resulting printout would be nonsense. Rather, you'd set Device Name to LaserJet and set Width Table for PostScript. The result would be a draft-quality document. This would be indicated by the word *Draft* at the top of the dialog box in place of the word *Ultimate* in Figure 5.2. Normally, you wouldn't use the draft version for duplication and distribution. Spacing could be odd and letters may overlap. You could, however, use it to get an idea of how the ultimate version will look. You could tell, for instance, where each line ends, how much of an article will fit on a page, and how many pages a chapter will run.

CHANGING WIDTH TABLES In the Set Printer Info dialog box, you cannot directly change the Width Table setting. It is only a display field that shows the system's current status. To change the width table, you must click the box that reads

Load Different Width Table (i.e., Font Metrics)

When you click this box, you see an Item Selector box like the one shown in Figure 5.4. This Item Selector box displays various width tables from which you may choose. Those displayed for you may differ from those in the figure; initially, the box shows the width tables that the VPPREP program copies onto your hard disk according to how you install Ventura. There will be one for each installed printer, each ending with a WID extension. There will also be a width table called OUTPUT.WID.

USING OUTPUT.WID OUTPUT.WID is identical to the width table for the default printer, the first printer listed on the Device Name line in the Set Printer Info dialog box. If LaserWriter is the default printer, as it is in our example, OUTPUT.WID will match POSTSCPT.WID. As a result, you could use either width table to achieve ultimate quality when you print with the LaserWriter printer.

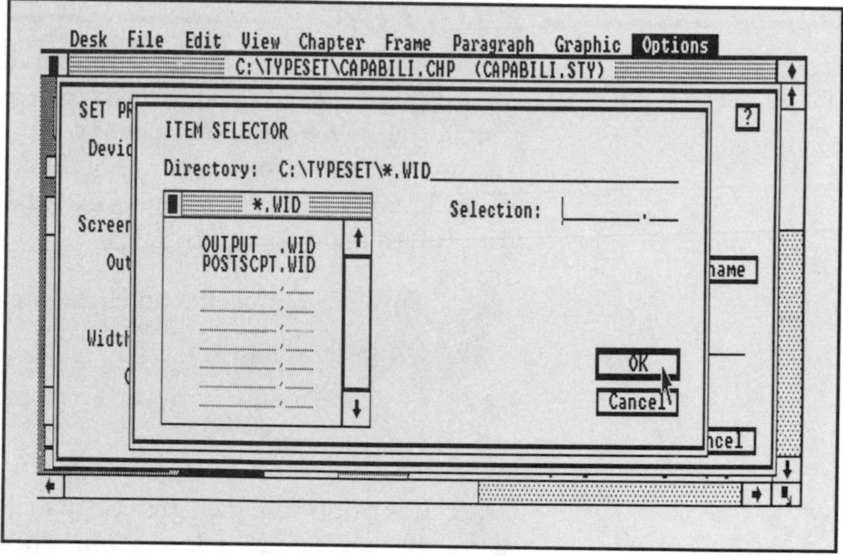

Figure 5.4: The Item Selector box for width tables

The style sheet stores your choice of width table. Those that Ventura initially provides are set to use the OUTPUT.WID width table. That way, you can print the samples with your default printer without having to change the width table.

Switch printers with care when you are concerned about exact line, paragraph, and page endings. Always check the results. Mixing printers works best in book-style publications—not newsletters, in which placement and line endings are important.

If you are designing a style sheet that people will use for printing at various stations with various printers, choose OUTPUT.WID for the width table. As long as only one printer (or the default printer) is in use, the document will be printed correctly; that is, the printout will be of ultimate quality.

If you'd like to use the width table for a printer you didn't originally install, you don't need to use the reinstallation procedure. Simply copy the width table from one of Ventura's original floppy disks into the Ventura directory on your hard disk. You may have to hunt for your width table, though, since they are stored on various disks; use the DOS asterisk wild card to search by typing

```
dir a:*.wid
```

at the DOS prompt.

PRINTING

Once you've selected all the settings in the Set Printer Info dialog box and given the OK, you're ready to begin printing. If you want to print the displayed document again, you don't need to use that dialog box unless you wish to change one of the settings. To print a chapter, which, in this case, is the sample CAPABILI.CHP chapter, use the Print Information dialog box (Figure 5.5). Display it as follows:

1. Turn on your printer and make sure it is properly connected.
2. Drop the File menu.
3. Point the mouse arrow at To Print and click.
4. Give the OK

Ventura prints out the printer-capability page, and you see the effects your printer can achieve. This document has only one page, but if it were longer, only one page would be printed. With Ventura 2.0, if you wish to print only the page displayed in the working area, you just give the OK without changing anything in the dialog box.

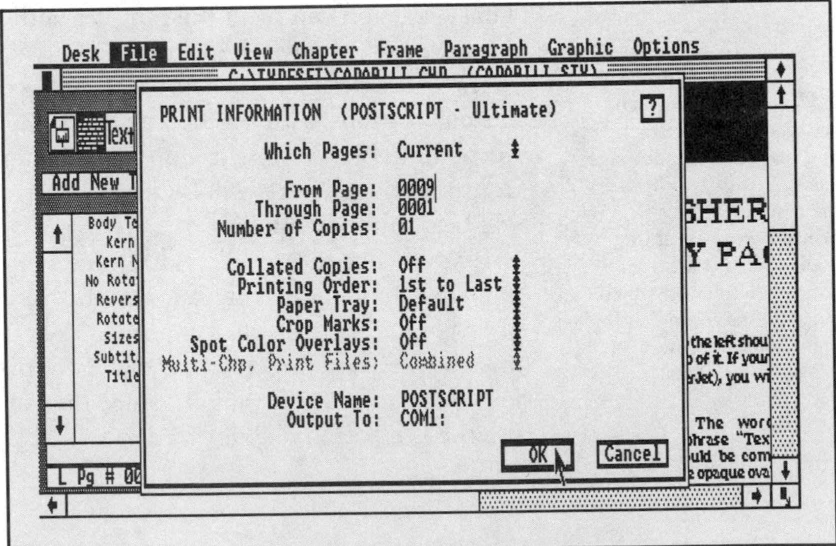

Figure 5.5: The Print Information dialog box

Ventura does, however, allow you to control much of the printing process. The following sections show you how to customize your printout choices, if you so desire.

SELECTING PAGES TO PRINT

The first setting in the Print Information dialog box, Which Pages, asks you to indicate how much of the chapter you'd like to print. The choices are All, Selected, Left, Right, and Current. Choose All for normal printing of the entire chapter or Selected if you wish to indicate a range of pages to print. Use Current (the default setting) if you want to print only the page that's on the screen.

You may wish to use Selected if, for instance, there are last-minute changes made after you've printed an entire document. If you do make changes after printing, though, be certain to reprint *all* affected pages, including those that follow the revised page. This will occur when text spills from one page to another as a result of edits on an earlier page. On the other hand, there's no need to waste time reprinting pages that remain the same despite a change elsewhere in the document. So use this setting to your advantage.

The Left and Right settings let you create double-sided printouts. First use Left and print all the left-hand pages in the document. Then, remove the stack from your printer's output tray, flip it over, reinsert it, and print the right-hand pages. (You may need to add a blank page if the document ends on a right-hand page.)

Now look at the next two settings, From Page and Through Page. When Which Pages is set for All, these two settings indicate that printing goes from page 1 to page 9999. (Of course, the printing actually stops with the final page of your document.)

If you choose Which Pages: Selected, use these two fields to indicate the pages you want to print. Type the number of the first page you desire into the From Page setting. Then use the mouse, Tab key, or ↓ key to move to the Through Page setting, and type the number of the last page you want to print. (Once the cursor is in this field, you can erase the entire set of four 9's by pressing the Esc key.)

MAKING MULTIPLE COPIES

If you want Ventura to print more than one copy automatically, enter the number of copies you desire at the Number of Copies setting. You can print up to 99 copies in a run. Of course, consider whether using Ventura is the most efficient way to make copies. Usually, it's faster to use some other conventional means, such as a photocopier or an offset printer. However, if you want exceptional quality for all copies, or if other means are not available, you may find this setting useful.

If you want to print multiple copies of a document that's more than one page long, consider the next setting. Usually, Collated Copies is set to Off. This way, Ventura prints all copies of page 1 first; only then does it go on to print all copies of page 2, then all page 3's, and so on. This means that once the chapter is printed, you must assemble the pages in proper sequence, which could be quite tedious with a long document.

If you turn this setting on, Ventura will print out one copy of the document in its entirety before proceeding to the next. So why shouldn't Ventura always collate as it prints? The reason is that when the pages you are printing have stringent memory requirements, such as pages with pictures, printing with Collated Copies set to On is much slower than it is with the normal Off setting. Because pictures require a large amount of memory, it takes a long time to load one. Once a page is loaded, it's more efficient to print as many copies as necessary, rather than load another page. However, if you're in no rush for the copies, and you don't need to free up the computer, it may be worth having Ventura collate for you. (Such a project may be a candidate for overnight printing.)

PRINTING FORWARD OR BACKWARD

When cut-sheet (individual page) printers eject a finished page, some scoot the new page behind or under those that are already printed, or stack the pages upside down. This set-up results in normal reading order, with page 1 followed by pages 2, 3, and so on. Other printers, however, lay the new page face up on top of pages already in the output tray; the resulting stack is in backward order.

Use the next setting, Printing Order, to compensate for such a backward printer. Usually, this setting should be on 1st to Last. With backward printers, such as the original LaserJet and LaserJet Plus, you need to make this setting Last to 1st for a normally ordered stack. However, Hewlett-Packard has corrected the problem with the LaserJet Series II, so with that printer you can use the lst to Last setting. With continuous-paper printers, there is no need to concern yourself with this setting.

OTHER PRINT INFORMATION

Use the Paper Tray pop-up menu to specify how Ventura should feed the printer paper. If your printer has multiple feeder trays, you can indicate which tray Ventura should use for paper. Each of the first three settings (Default, Alt #1, and Alt #2) could, for instance, correspond to a different size of paper. Use the fourth setting, Manual, for envelopes that you insert one at a time. Printers that have this capability pause after each envelope and restart printing once you've inserted a fresh one.

The Crop Marks setting works only when you use the Chapter menu's Page Size & Layout command to specify a paper type smaller than the size you're printing with. If that's the case, setting Crop Marks: On will cause Ventura to indicate the corners of the smaller page with *crop marks* (Figure 5.6). Layout photographers use crop marks to position material for accurate shooting.

Use Spot Color Overlays to create color separations. We'll examine color printing later in this chapter.

When you gain access to the Print Information dialog box, as we have, with the File menu's To Print command, the next setting ghosts. Mult-Chp Print Files is not adjustable here. We'll examine the use of this setting when we study multichapter publications in Chapter 10.

The Device Name and Output To settings are only indicators of the settings you've made with the Options menu's Set Printer Info dialog box, and cannot be changed directly. The Device Name field shows the name of the printer, and Output To shows the port or other output designation.

PRINTING AND INTERRUPTING

Once you've completed your settings in the Print Information dialog box, click the OK box or press Enter to commence printing. Normally, the printer will start to churn out the pages. Once printing

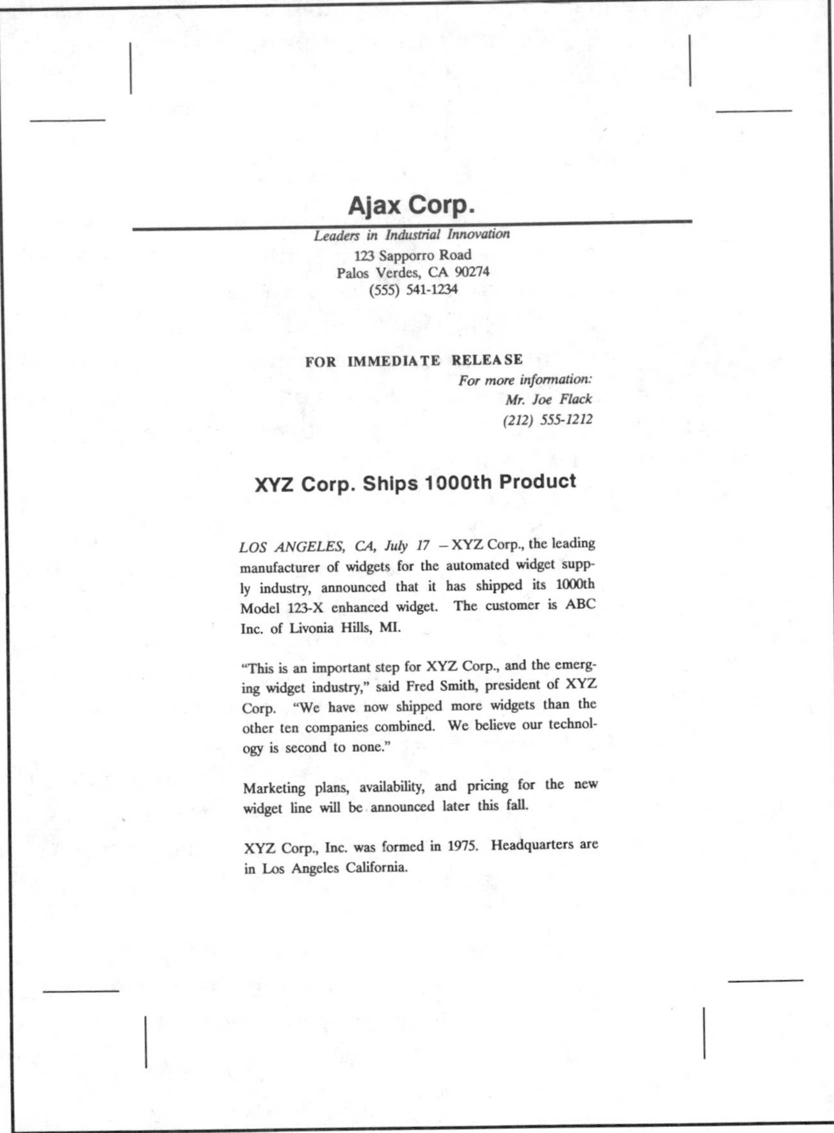

Ajax Corp.

Leaders in Industrial Innovation

123 Sapporro Road
Palos Verdes, CA 90274
(555) 541-1234

FOR IMMEDIATE RELEASE

For more information:
Mr. Joe Flack
(212) 555-1212

XYZ Corp. Ships 1000th Product

LOS ANGELES, CA, July 17 – XYZ Corp., the leading manufacturer of widgets for the automated widget supply industry, announced that it has shipped its 1000th Model 123-X enhanced widget. The customer is ABC Inc. of Livonia Hills, MI.

"This is an important step for XYZ Corp., and the emerging widget industry," said Fred Smith, president of XYZ Corp. "We have now shipped more widgets than the other ten companies combined. We believe our technology is second to none."

Marketing plans, availability, and pricing for the new widget line will be announced later this fall.

XYZ Corp., Inc. was formed in 1975. Headquarters are in Los Angeles California.

Figure 5.6: Crop marks

begins, you'll see a message that indicates the page number Ventura is printing (Figure 5.7). It also points out that you can stop the printing process by pressing the Esc key. If you press Esc (and confirm it), Ventura will finish printing the page it is working on and then stop, canceling the rest of the print job.

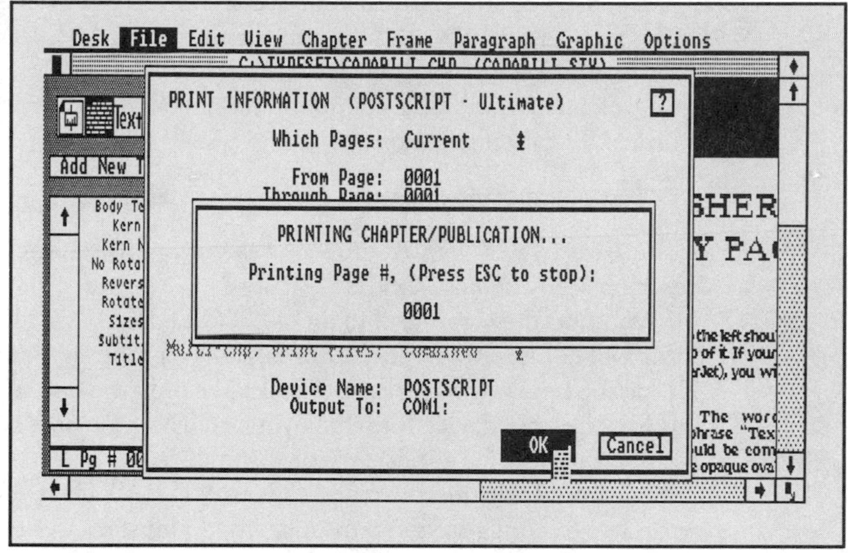

Figure 5.7: The screen during printing

New for version 2.0

When you begin printing, if your document contains pictures to which you've assigned "hidden" status (see Chapter 6), Ventura will ask whether you want to print the pictures. By not printing the pictures, you can obtain a quicker printout. This is useful if all you need is a rough draft. Keep an eye on the screen when you go to print. When Ventura asks whether to print pictures, it does nothing until you respond. If you're waiting for the printer to start, this could be the problem.

With what you know so far, you can do many print jobs; for instance, you've already printed the printer-capability page. The rest of this chapter contains an in-depth look at printing as well as a brief look at the state of printing in the world of desktop publishing. We begin with a discussion of serial printers.

SETTING UP A SERIAL PRINTER

When using a serial printer, you must configure the port prior to printing every time you turn on the computer. To save time and energy, it's wise to automate the procedure. Generally, you do this by using your word processor to add DOS's MODE command, which configures the port, to your AUTOEXEC.BAT file. Alternatively, you may wish to add the command to your VP.BAT file or to enter it in its own special batch file.

The exact syntax of this command differs from one serial printer to another. The configuration

```
mode com1: 96,n,8,l,p
```

is the one used by most popular laser printers, including the LaserWriter and the LaserJet.

If you add the command to the AUTOEXEC.BAT file, the computer will configure the port automatically as soon as you turn it on. This is the best way to proceed if you have only the one serial printer and it is the only device for which you are using the port. (You could also use the port for a modem, for instance.)

You should add the command to your VP.BAT file if you want the computer to configure the port only when you start Ventura. This is a good method if you are using the same port to accommodate more than one serial printer or another device. Assuming that you always use the same serial printer with Ventura, you can simply plug in the proper printer, and the port will be configured correctly when you start the program.

Lastly, if you use more than one serial printer with the same port and you plan to use either printer with Ventura, you'll need to set up a MODE command for each printer. Then, before you start Ventura, decide which printer to use, type in the command for the batch file corresponding to that printer, and then start the program. If you need to switch printers, you must exit from Ventura, run the new batch file, and start up the program again.

PAGE DESCRIPTION LANGUAGES

As our discussion of serial printers shows, printing can become a complicated process, depending upon the hardware. To standardize procedures and minimize the confusion caused by a variety of printers, programmers have begun developing *page description languages.*

Usually, when you install a piece of software, you must indicate the name of the specific printer you will be using. A page description language (PDL) standardizes the methods that computer systems use for printing. All printers that conform to a particular PDL's specifications will operate with that PDL. So instead of installing a specific printer, you simply install the PDL.

With good reason, interest in page description languages is on the increase. One reason is that PDLs are so useful with desktop-publishing applications. The ability to use more than one printer is important as you go from draft to finished product or from station to station. A PDL makes it easy to switch printers without producing unexpected results. Of course, such printers cost more, because you must pay for the PDL as well.

Various PDLs have been vying for top position in the marketplace, hoping to become the standard of the industry. PostScript, created by Adobe Systems, is a PDL that Ventura supports. The program also supports the Interpress PDL. IBM has announced the introduction of its own PostScript printer and endorsed PostScript as the only PDL that it plans to work with. With the Apple LaserWriter and numerous other printers already supporting this PDL, PostScript is likely to be the industry standard. As more printer manufacturers support PostScript, special installation of printers may become a thing of the past.

By using the Options menu's Set Printer Info box, you can specify a PostScript printer for Device Name (as long as you have installed PostScript with VPPREP). When you do, you can use any printer that adheres to the PostScript standard, and the output will be similar in design. In other words, lines of text will break at the same spot, the sizes of boxes will match, and so on. Depending upon the quality of the printer, the resolution on the printed page may differ, but that's about all. For example, you can use a less expensive printer for rough drafts and a higher quality printer for the final copy. You'll be certain of how the finished document will look, based on the appearance of the rough draft.

ADDING FONTS

Though a degree of page standardization is a real possibility due to the PDL, it's unlikely to happen in the area of fonts. Our appetite for typefaces seems to be insatiable. Fortunately, you are not confined to the fonts supplied with your printer, or even those provided by the printer's manufacturer. You can also use fonts that have been created by third-party vendors to work with Ventura and your particular printer (Appendix D).

To use a new font, you can simply add it to the fonts you already use for the printer. Existing fonts are in the width table for the printer, and you can create a new width table that combines both old and new fonts. You do this by following these steps:

1. For best results, acquire a font whose manufacturer provides a width table. More and more vendors are now providing these.
2. For safety, make a copy of the width tables for the fonts you are already using. Should something go wrong in the process of adding fonts (like erasing the fonts instead of adding to them), you can retrieve your old fonts.
3. Copy the new font along with its corresponding width table to the VENTURA directory, which is created when you install Ventura.
4. In Ventura, use the Options menu's Set Printer Info dialog box to load the width table for the printer you want to add fonts to.
5. Drop the Options menu and click Add/Remove Fonts. You'll see the dialog box shown in Figure 5.8. This dialog box displays the fonts whose specifications are currently stored in the width table you just loaded. Your new font will join this listing.
6. Click Merge Width Tables. In the resulting Item Selector box, choose the width table that corresponds to your new font. This action will combine the old fonts, already loaded, with the new one you specify.
7. Click the Save As New Width Table button and make up a new width-table name. Doing so will create a new table that contains the old fonts as well as the new one for the specified printer.

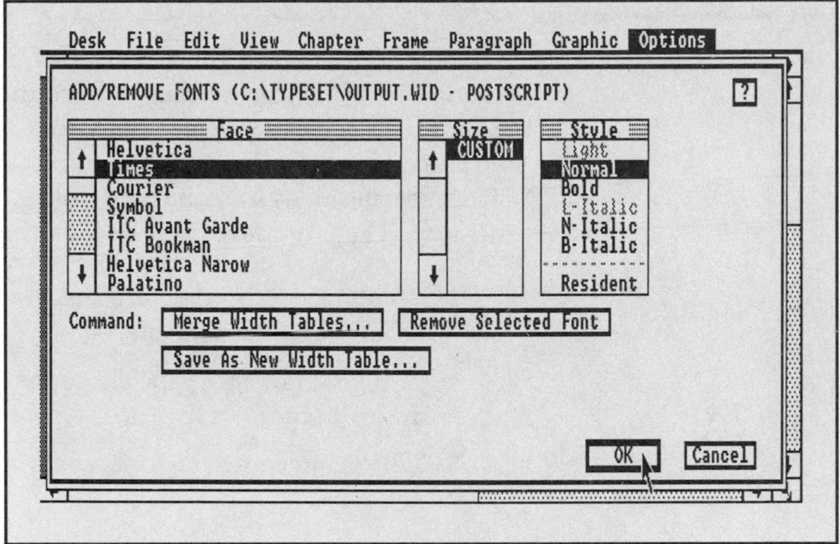

Figure 5.8: The Options menu's Add/Remove Fonts dialog box

From now on, you can use any of the fonts for a given printer just by loading this new width table (using the Options menu's Set Printer Info dialog box). If you want to use only the old fonts, load the old width table.

Be aware that Ventura will not always show added fonts on the screen; instead, it may replace them with standard fonts of the same size. However, it does show the new font names on the appropriate menus for selection.

Ventura can display the fonts exactly as they will appear when printed if the font manufacturer provides specifications for doing so. These specifications are contained in *screen-font* files. If the fonts you acquire have matching screen-font files, you need not use the Add New Fonts dialog box to add them to Ventura's fonts. Instead, you can simply use the Options menu's Set Printer Info dialog box. Click the Load Different Width Table button and select the new width table. Once you do, use the same dialog box's Screen Fonts field to enter the extension of the screen font you wish to use. The screen fonts will match their printed counterparts. If you need to change back to Ventura's screen fonts, be aware that Ventura uses the CGA extension for screens using the Color/Graphics Adapter, EGA for the Enhanced Graphics Adapter, PSF for PostScript, and VGA for full-page displays.

DOWNLOADING FONTS

In the Add/Remove Fonts dialog box, notice the unusually placed setting at the bottom of the Style column. This last item in the column will say either *Resident* or *Download.* Downloading refers to the process by which Ventura and some other programs make a copy of font specifications from the hard disk and load it into your printer's memory. The procedure uses the following steps:

1. Ventura goes to the hard disk to retrieve font specifications from the width-table file.
2. It then sends those specifications to the printer, where they reside in memory.
3. The printer uses the font specifications to place the fonts on the page.

The Download setting on the Add/Remove Fonts dialog box causes Ventura to perform the downloading procedure automatically when it comes time to use the particular font indicated. Some printers, however, have font specifications built into them. To indicate that Ventura does not need to copy these font specifications from the disk, the setting for such fonts is Resident. Printing is much faster when the fonts you need are resident.

The Download/Resident setting applies to the particular combination of Face, Size, and Style indicated by the darkened bars in the dialog box. Ventura considers each such combination to be a font, and hence each combination has its own Download/Resident setting that you can change. Figure 5.8, for instance, indicates only that the Times face, Normal style is set for Resident status. Other combinations may or may not be set for Resident. So, if you want to change all sizes and styles for a particular face, you must change each combination of face, size, and style.

Ventura's installation process sets the Download/Resident status for all fonts, and you usually don't have to make any changes. In fact, changing the status of a font without great care could cause problems if, for example, it causes Ventura to look for the font's specifications in the wrong location.

There may be times when it's desirable to change the setting—for instance, when using the Linotronic typesetter, which we'll examine in the next section. At those times, you may find it advantageous to use the printer's software to download fonts *before* using Ventura. For fonts that you download in this manner, change the setting to Resident. Doing so will save you the waiting time necessary to download the fonts a second time.

Note that the Add/Remove Fonts dialog box also allows you to remove font specifications from the width table you are using. You may wish to remove fonts you don't use in order to improve Ventura's performance. First, it's wise to make a copy of the width table's file. Then select the combination of face, size, and style you wish to remove and click the Remove Selected Font button. Note that if you have other fonts loaded that do not come with matching screen fonts, you must not remove the Swiss 10-point font. Ventura uses this font to create substitute screen fonts when necessary.

Now let's look at how you can use Ventura with a typesetter.

PRINTING WITH A TYPESETTER

Printing with a computer consists of using typefaces, images, graphics, and so on, that are composed of numerous tiny dots. The concentration of dots determines the resolution of the images on the printed page. Laser printers print with resolutions of up to 300 dots per inch (dpi). For truly snazzy output—for example, an annual report—you may want resolution better than 300 dpi. By using typesetting equipment, such as one of the Linotronic series of PostScript typesetters, you can print with resolution up to 2540 dpi.

Fortunately, you don't need to own such a typesetter to use one: You can rent time on one. For instance, you can use your PostScript laser printer for rough drafts. Once your document is assembled, you can create an output file and print it at a desktop-publishing service center.

If you initially create the document on a hard disk, use the Options menu's Multi-Chapter command to make a copy of a chapter file (see Chapter 10). Although the command is named Multi-Chapter, the copying procedure also works with individual chapters. Using Ventura to copy your chapter files is preferable to using DOS's COPY command. In addition to copying, Ventura automatically adjusts the location references for the files a chapter utilizes, so that they can be located on the appropriate disk drive and directory. Using DOS's COPY command leaves the old location references, which may no longer be correct, in place.

Alternatively, if the center has Ventura available at its stations, you can bring along the files that are associated with the document you want to print. If you anticipate that you will be going this route, you can create the document entirely on the floppy drive to begin with. That is, locate the style-sheet (STY), text and picture, chapter (CHP), and width-table (WID) files all on drive A. Then, all you have to do is insert the disk at the service center and you're ready to print.

Be aware, though, that using typesetting equipment in conjunction with personal computers is a new art. You may need to spend quite a bit of time working out the kinks. Be sure that you work with a knowledgeable typesetter who's enthusiastic about desktop publishing, not threatened by it.

You can limit the time you spend at the typesetter's with your strategy for downloading fonts. Often, fonts will already be downloaded when you start to use the equipment. If so, you can save time (and hence money) by setting your fonts to Resident, as described in the previous section.

WHICH PRINTER IS BEST FOR ME?

Although we've been discussing how to use more than one printer with the same document, it is possible that you don't even have your first printer yet. If you have one printer, though, Ventura's capabilities may be causing you to consider the acquisition of another. In either case, you're probably wondering which printer is best for you. The route you take depends upon the quality of output you desire and the budget that you have available. In this section, we'll discuss some popular types of printers.

DOT-MATRIX PRINTERS

If you're on a tight budget, you may be able to get by with a simple dot-matrix printer. With these printers, Ventura can create output of a surprisingly acceptable quality. However, you probably wouldn't want to use a dot-matrix printer for final output, except under limited circumstances. For instance, you could use such a printer to print a small newsletter for a hobby club. You could also use it to print simple intraoffice forms, handout fliers, errata sheets, and other publications where high quality is not a factor.

Another reason to use dot-matrix printers only for short applications is their slow speed. The print head moves from side to side, printing only a narrow strip on each pass. Also, it must move over the same area repeatedly.

Dot-matrix printers are also noisy. This is because they create printed copy by repeatedly firing tiny pins at the paper. This is an important factor to consider if your quarters are tight.

Some people use these printers to create rough drafts. People who don't have a laser printer available can use a dot-matrix printer to get an idea of how the output will ultimately appear.

LASER PRINTERS

The availability and increasingly low cost of laser printers makes them ideal for most desktop-publishing applications. For some people, in fact, printing with a laser printer is synonymous with desktop publishing. These printers are flexible in output, comparatively swift, and quiet as a whisper.

A laser printer is suited to the production of larger publications, such as well-circulated newsletters, technical manuals, catalogs, and booklets. You can also use them to print brochures, press kits, bulletins, and so forth.

You may wish to consider whether you should purchase a laser printer or do the work elsewhere. Some copying centers, for instance, will let you rent time on a laser printer.

COLOR PRINTING

Let's turn our attention now to one of Ventura's new printing features that is on the cutting edge of technology—namely, color printing. Although color printing with the computer is not widespread now, it's bound to be in the future.

With a color printer, you can add color in all four modes, by way of text or paragraph fonts, frame backgrounds, and graphics attributes. Table 5.1 lists the dialog boxes that have color settings.

Table 5.1: Features with Color Settings

MODE	MENU	ITEM TO CLICK	COLOR AFFECTS
Paragraph	Paragraph	Font	Font of all similarly tagged paragraphs
Text	Side-bar	Set Font button	Font of selected text
Frame	Frame	Frame Background	Space contained by a frame
Graphics	Graphic	Line Attributes	Line or outline of the graphic
Graphics	Graphic	Fill Attributes	Space contained by the graphic
Frame or Paragraph	Frame or Paragraph	Ruling Line or Box	Ruling line/box

In addition, you can actually adjust the colors that appear. Even without a color printer, you can use this capacity to set shades of gray. Also, you can easily create color separations for offset printing.

DEFINING COLORS AND SHADES OF GRAY

! New for version 2.0

By defining colors for a chapter, you specify the exact mixture of primary colors or the amount of black in a shade of gray. You can even provide a new name for the mixture.

To define colors (or shades of gray), follow these steps. If you like, you can practice on the printer-capability chapter. Just don't save the chapter when you're done, so it remains in its original condition.

Locating the Define Colors dialog box, which springs from the Paragraph menu, can be tricky. You'll find that it affects all colors Ventura uses, not just those associated with paragraphs. For example, when you use Frame mode and select the Frame menu's Frame Background dialog box, the colors you defined in this dialog box will appear there.

1. Activate Paragraph mode.
2. Drop the Paragraph menu and click Define Colors.

You'll see the Define Colors dialog box, shown in Figure 5.9.

DEFINING COLORS In the Define Colors dialog box, you can choose between Colors and Shades Of Gray. Set Screen Display to Colors if you are defining colors for use with a color printer.

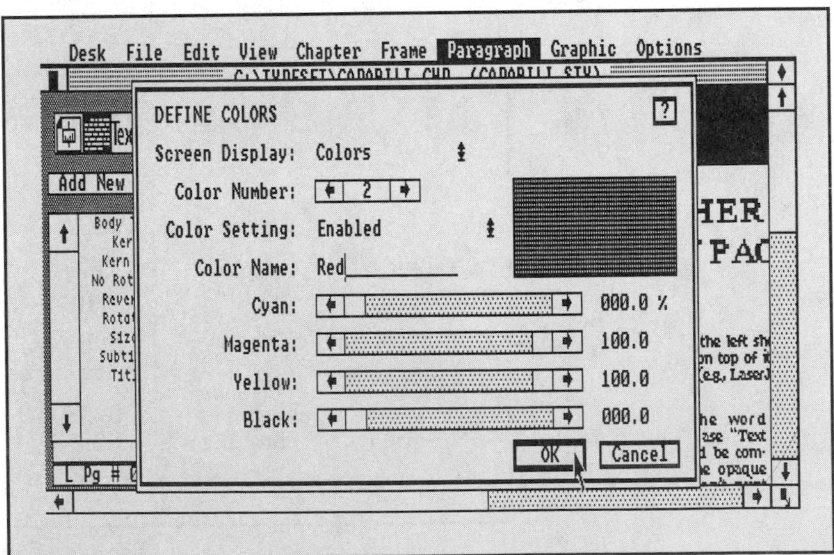

Figure 5.9: The Paragraph menu's Define Colors dialog box

The Color Number setting indicates the color number to which the remaining settings in the dialog box apply. Ventura allows you to redefine its six true colors, numbered 2 to 7. You cannot redefine white (0) or black (1).

By pressing the arrow buttons, you change the number displayed. As each number appears, the settings in the dialog box change to those that correspond to that number. Initially, the number 2 appears, along with its settings. When you click the → button, the number changes to 3 and you see the settings on file for color number 3. If you then click the ← button, the number 2 reappears and you see its settings again.

You use Color Setting in conjunction with creating color overlays. We'll discuss this subject shortly.

For color number 2, the name that appears in the field for Color Name is Red. To more accurately label a color that you custom-mix, you can provide an explicit name here.

Next there are four scroll bars that you use to mix your color. There is one bar for each of the primary colors, cyan, magenta, and yellow. There is also a scroll bar for black, which allows you to adjust the color's intensity.

You can set each scroll bar to a value between 0% and 100% in increments of 0.2%. Each time you click one of the arrow buttons on the scroll bar, the value changes by that increment. Each time you click the shadow area of the scroll bar, the value shifts by 10%. You can also slide the white box to adjust the values by rough amounts. Click OK or press the Enter key to register your choices.

DEFINING SHADES OF GRAY As mentioned, if you are using a black-and-white printer, you can define shades of gray for a chapter rather than true colors. In the Define Colors dialog box, set Screen Display to Shades of Gray. Set the scroll bars for the three colors to 0%. Then set Black to the level you desire. You can also change the color name.

For dialog boxes that include a Pattern setting (such as the Frame menu's Frame Background), set Pattern to Solid when you're using a custom shade of gray. The Pattern setting can set some shades of gray, but it's recommended that you not use these two features together.

PRINTING COLOR SEPARATIONS

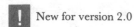

! New for version 2.0

If you have a color printer, however, it's important to take care when using it to create an original for color duplication. Check with a printing professional for the best way to prepare color text for printing at a print shop. It's usually best to create multiple versions of the original, all printed in black, each one separating various segments of the text according to the color that will be used. This printing technique is called *color separation.* The print shop runs the copies through the printer several times, once for each color. Each run uses a different version of the original. With version 2.0 of Ventura, you can easily create color separations.

Be sure to specify Color Setting: Disable for colors that you're not using. Otherwise, Ventura will "print" blank pages for those colors, wasting time and paper.

Display the Paragraph menu's Define Colors dialog box as we did in the previous section. For those colors you will be using to create color separations, set Color Setting to Enable. Set it to Disable for colors that you will not be using.

When you're ready to print the document, use the File menu and choose To Print as usual. In the Print Information dialog box that appears, set Spot Color Overlays to On. When you give the OK, Ventura will print each page with its color name and only the text that is set for that color. The ability to use this feature may vary depending upon your printer.

PRINTING FROM OUTPUT FILES

As we've discussed, you can use the Options menu's Set Printer dialog box to direct the output of a print operation to a disk file, rather than to a printer. Once you've created this file, you no longer need Ventura in order to print it. Printing from the disk is handy if a station has the printer you want but not the software (Ventura) you'd normally need for printing.

Before beginning, make sure you have enough disk space to create the output file. You will need at least the sum total of all the files that make up the document you want to print. This includes chapter files, text files, graphics files, and so on. Printing to disk combines them and creates one very long file (see Figure 5.10). Should Ventura run out of room, it provides no indication that the output was unsuccessful.

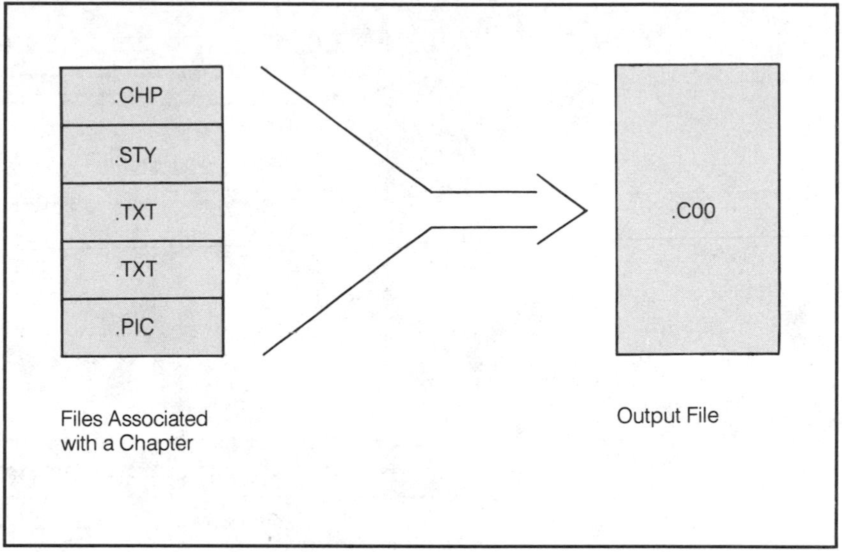

Figure 5.10: Using files associated with a chapter to create an output file

You aren't restricted to transporting an output file on a floppy disk. For instance, you can transmit the file over the phone lines with a modem. If you have a network setup, you can send the output file to another computer on the network. In any case, whatever you do with it, make sure that there's enough room for the file wherever it's expected to land.

Follow these steps to create an output file:

1. Use the Options menu's Set Printer Info dialog box and click the Filename button.
2. Drop the File menu and click To Print.
3. Choose the settings for the Print Information dialog box and give the OK, just as you would to print normally.
4. Instead of the printer beginning to print, an Item Selector box appears (Figure 5.11). Use this box to specify the disk, directory, and file name in which to store the output. If you plan to transport the output file on a floppy disk, you'll probably want to specify drive A.

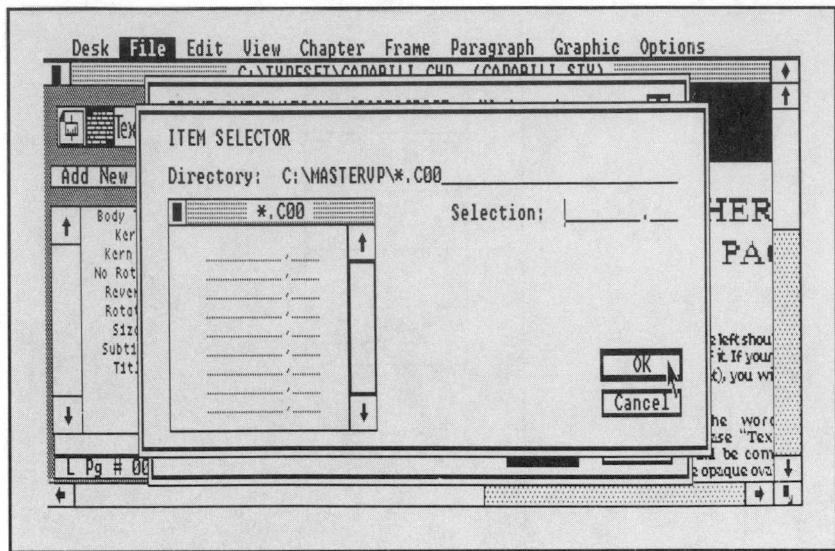

Figure 5.11: The Item Selector box used when printing to a disk file

5. When you give the output file a name without providing an extension, Ventura adds the letter *C* and two zeros (00) as an ending to the name you provide. Give the OK, and Ventura will begin to manufacture the output file.

Once you've created the output file, you can print the file from DOS. Of course, the printer you use must match the printer in effect when you created the output file.

If you have a serial printer, you must first perform the steps described in the next paragraph. (You can skip the next paragraph if you have a parallel printer.)

With a serial printer, of course, you must first issue DOS's MODE command, which specifies the baud rate, parity, and so on. Then, assuming the serial printer is connected to the COM1 port, type in the following command. (Be sure to type only one space after *mode,* and use colons, not semicolons, after the port numbers.)

```
mode lpt1:=com1:
```

Press Enter. If you've connected the serial printer to com2, substitute that port in place of com1.

Creating an Output File for a PostScript Printer

With a PostScript printer, you must perform an additional step when creating a disk file. Prior to printing, you must transmit the contents of a special file to your printer. The file's name is DTR.TXT, and it's located within the POSTSCPT directory on the Utilities disk (#5). To use this special file, perform these steps:

1. Make sure that your PostScript printer is on, connected, and online.
2. Insert disk #5 into drive A.
3. At the DOS prompt, type in the following (being certain to space correctly and to use the backslash and the colon as indicated):

```
copy  a:\postscpt\dtr.txt  lpt1:
```

4. If another program resets your printer, repeat these steps before you print again.

When you are ready to print from the output file, use DOS's COPY command. Remember to include the disk drive that has the file, a colon, the file's full name (including the extension), another space, the port that the printer is connected to (including the port number), a colon, and Enter.

Thus, let's say you have a newsletter that you've compiled in a disk file called BRAIN.C00 on a floppy disk in drive A. You want to print it on a printer that's connected to lpt1 on a second computer. At the DOS prompt, you'd type

```
copy a:brain.c00 lpt1:
```

and press Enter. If you're using the standard extension to the file name (as we have here), be sure to include zeros at the end of the extension, not the capital letter *O*.

If the file is contained in a directory, be sure to include that information. Thus, if you're printing the BRAIN.C00 file and it's located in the MASTERVP directory on drive C, you'd type

```
copy c:\mastervp\brain.c00 lpt1:
```

and press Enter to print at the lpt1 port.

In this chapter we've seen how printing with Ventura Publisher can be simple and straightforward or tailored to your needs. But suppose your needs include the printing of graphics. Printing of text has been a capability of personal computers for a long time, as has the printing of graphics. The integration, though, of both text and graphics on the same page is an innovation of desktop publishing. We'll see how to do that with Ventura in Chapter 6.

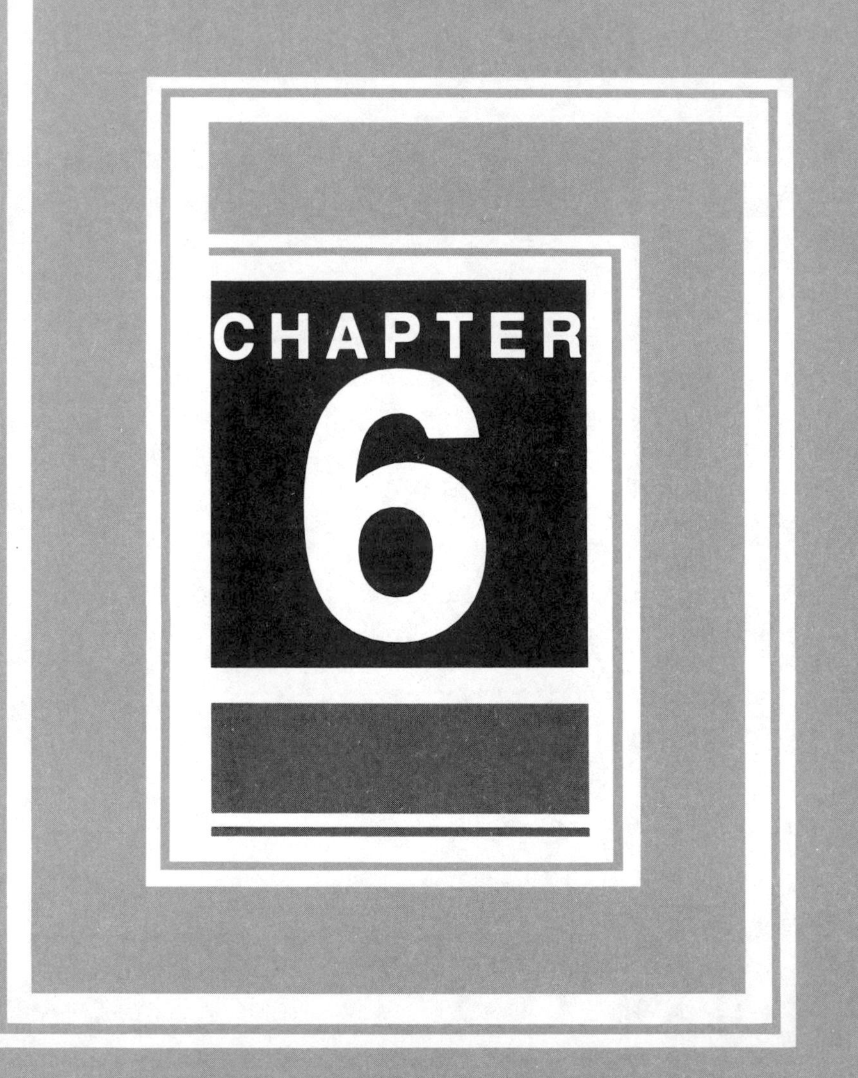
CHAPTER
6

Adding Pictures from Lotus 1-2-3 and Other Sources

Fast Track

To insert a picture into a Ventura document 210

load the picture, create a frame, and assign the picture to the frame. You can then crop or stretch the picture and assign it a caption if you wish.

To load a picture in a frame 217

select the frame and use the File menu's Load Text/Picture. You must specify the type of file you are loading, image or line art. This is generally determined by the software that creates the picture.

To hide all pictures 228

use the Options menu's Hide All Pictures. This expedites processing. You can also hide one or more individual pictures by selecting them before using the command.

To use rulers and cross hairs 229

choose the Options menu's Show Rulers to display the rulers. Use the Options menu's Set Ruler to adjust the increments on the rulers. Drag the mouse from the 0,0 box to use cross hairs and relocate the zero point.

To select multiple frames 231

Shift-click with the mouse. To select from among frames in a pile, use Ctrl-click.

To move frames and change their size 232

use the mouse or the Frame menu's Sizing & Scaling. In this dialog box, the aspect ratio is the ratio of a picture's height to its width; scale factors adjust a picture's size independently of its frame.

CHAPTER 6

THE ABILITY TO ADD PICTURES TO EXISTING TEXT and vice versa is one of the most exciting features of desktop publishing and, in a sense, defines how desktop publishing is different from both word processing and graphics programs. With Ventura, you can make text-graphics combinations that are truly striking, and you can do it easily.

Ventura provides you with lots of freedom in combining text and graphics. As we've mentioned, you can use text files from a variety of word processors. Likewise, you can use the graphics you create with a variety of graphics packages. With some graphics formats, you use the pictures as is; Ventura references the original file. With others, Ventura converts the original file to a format it utilizes quickly and automatically, whenever you load a chapter. Either method means that you can continue to work with the original file using the graphics software, if necessary. All updates are reflected automatically in your Ventura documents.

Once you've loaded pictures in Ventura, you can place them anywhere on the page: between paragraphs, within paragraphs, in one column, or straddling columns. Wherever you position them, text already in place automatically flows around the picture.

You can also manipulate pictures on the page. You can stretch them in one direction or another. You can use a certain area of a picture while ignoring the rest—a procedure called *cropping*.

As with text, Ventura uses frames to hold pictures. The steps you can perform to incorporate a picture are similar to those you use with word-processed text. Here is a summary of these familiar steps, along with a few that are new:

1. Create the picture with the appropriate graphics software.
2. Load the picture. This process adds the graphic file's name to Frame mode's Assignment list.

3. Create a frame, which demarcates the area for the picture on the page.
4. Use Frame mode's Assignment list to pull the picture into the frame.
5. Crop or stretch the picture as necessary.
6. Add a caption and other enhancements to the picture, if desired.

We'll use a variation of this method—one that reverses steps 2 and 3—for assigning a file to a frame. Using this method allows us to skip step 4, as you'll see.

Now for the picture itself. The spreadsheet program Lotus 1-2-3 is one of the most popular generators of business graphs. Business users take advantage of 1-2-3's ability to create graphs of all kinds instantly from its spreadsheets. In this chapter, we'll show how you can incorporate a 1-2-3 graph into an existing Ventura chapter. You'll also learn how to bring other kinds of pictures into your documents.

This chapter will describe in detail the two types of pictures with which Ventura operates: *images* and *line art.* You'll see the differences between them as well as the advantages and disadvantages of each. You'll also see how to move pictures around and change their size.

Our discussions of importing graphics will carry over into the next chapter. There, you'll see how to enhance imported pictures by adding various graphic elements that come with Ventura.

LOADING THE SAMPLE CHAPTER

In this chapter, you'll be using one of Ventura's sample tables, &TBL-P1.CHP, located in the TYPESET directory. The table is shown in Figure 6.1.

1. Load Ventura if you exited after Chapter 5.
2. Drop the File menu.
3. Select Open Chapter. The Item Selector box appears.
4. From the TYPESET subdirectory, select the sample chapter &TBL-P1.CHP.

	Year Ended December 31, 1992	Year Ended December 31, 1991
Income		
Sales	$1,234,567.00	$1,345,678.00
Other Income	12,678.00	24,677.00
Total Income	**$1,247,245.00**	**$1,370,355.00**
Cost of Sales		
Cost of Goods	$234,344.00	$456,765.00
Packaging	12,654.00	54,678.00
Other	12,232.00	56,567.00
Total Cost of Sales	**$259,230.00**	**$568,040.00**

Figure 6.1: Ventura's sample table

5. Use the File menu's Save As command to save a copy of &TBL-P1.CHP to the MASTERVP directory.
6. Use the File menu's Save as New Style command to save the style sheet, &TBL-P1.STY, to the MASTERVP directory.

If you intend to alter the text that makes up the document, rename those files with the Edit menu's File Type/Rename command, or use the Options menu's Multi-Chapter command to copy the chapter and its associated files (see Chapter 10).

INSERTING A 1-2-3 GRAPH

In this section, you'll see how easy it is to incorporate a graph created with Lotus 1-2-3 into a Ventura document. Once you've saved the chapter file under a new name, you can add the graph to it. In Chapter 2, you saw how to add a text file to a chapter. You can use the same technique to add a graphic file. Also, as mentioned earlier, you'll use an alternative technique to display our sample graph within the document. Instead of loading the file first, you begin by creating the frame. If you are unfamiliar with Lotus 1-2-3, you can use another spreadsheet program or a graphics package to create the chart we'll be working with. You can then load the file and automatically assign it to the new frame. Note that this method of assigning files to frames also works with text files.

Alternatively, you can practice with any chart or graphic, such as the nozzle graphic, NOZZLE.GEM, that comes with Ventura. It's in the TYPESET directory, which is created by Ventura during the installation process. The file is stored in GEM line-art format. This format is an important factor, as we'll see later on. Almost any figure will do for purposes of demonstration. However, when you create graphics for your own documents, the graphic and the accompanying text will of course be related, as they are in the example we will now develop.

CREATING A SAMPLE GRAPH WITH 1-2-3

We'll create a graph to illustrate the figures that appear in the working copy of Ventura's sample table, &TBL-P1.CHP, located in the MASTERVP directory. The table is shown in Figure 6.1. We'll add the graphic to the same sample page, just below the table.

To create the graph:

> You may notice that Total Cost of Sales shows an error in addition that the D10 cell formula in 1-2-3 caught. We'll ignore the error.

1. Enter the values in 1-2-3 as you see them in Ventura's sample table (see Figure 6.2).
2. Instead of the full titles at the top, just enter the year over each column.

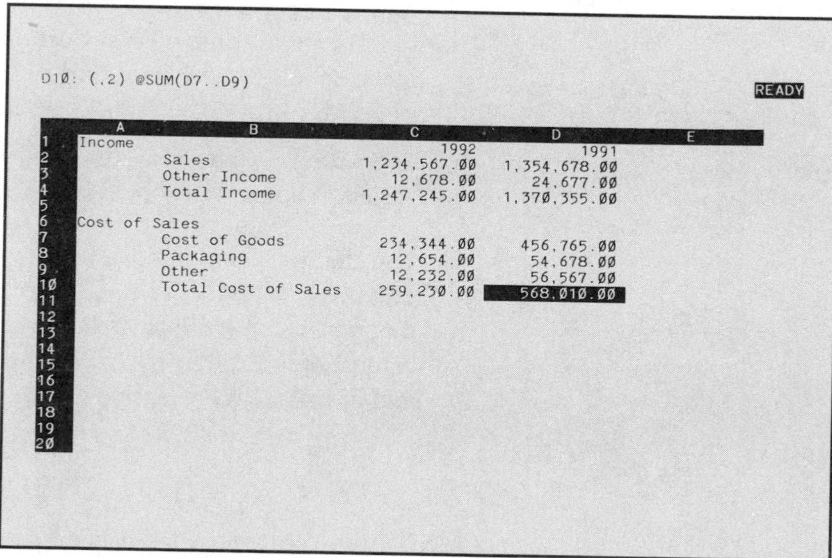

Figure 6.2: Creating a sample table in Lotus 1-2-3

3. Once you've entered the table in 1-2-3, use the / Graph command to display the / Graph menu.
4. Set the Type command to Bar. For the X value, use the year labels at the top of each column. For the A value, specify the two cells that contain the values for Total Income. For the B value, indicate the cells that contain the amounts for Total Cost of Sales.

Because Ventura is so flexible with text and formatting, you can avoid extra effort by not entering too many labels while still in 1-2-3. It's unnecessary to enter a title for the chart, for instance. Should you desire such a title, you can always add one after you import the graph into Ventura.

For the sake of organization, however, it is wise to insert some labels with 1-2-3. Later, you can cover the 1-2-3 text with Ventura text, as long as your printer has the capability of completely obscuring text under graphics. (See Chapter 5 for more on printers and their capabilities.) Inserting the labels with 1-2-3, though, will keep you from confusing the labels.

5. From the / Graph menu, choose the Options Legend command. For the A legend, enter the words **Total Income**. For the B legend, enter **Total Cost of Sales**. It's best to at least insert labels for the axes and indicate the legend while still in 1-2-3.
6. From the / Graph menu, use the View command to check your results. Your screen should look like the graph in Figure 6.3.
7. Use the Save command from the / Graph menu to save the graph in your MASTERVP directory. (This is the command that you usually use to create graph files you expect to print using Lotus PrintGraph.) Call the graph TABLE; 1-2-3 will add its usual PIC extension.

CREATING A FRAME FOR THE GRAPH

Once you've created the 1-2-3 graph, you can place it in a Ventura chapter. In this example, we'll insert our chart below the sample table that we used to create the chart.

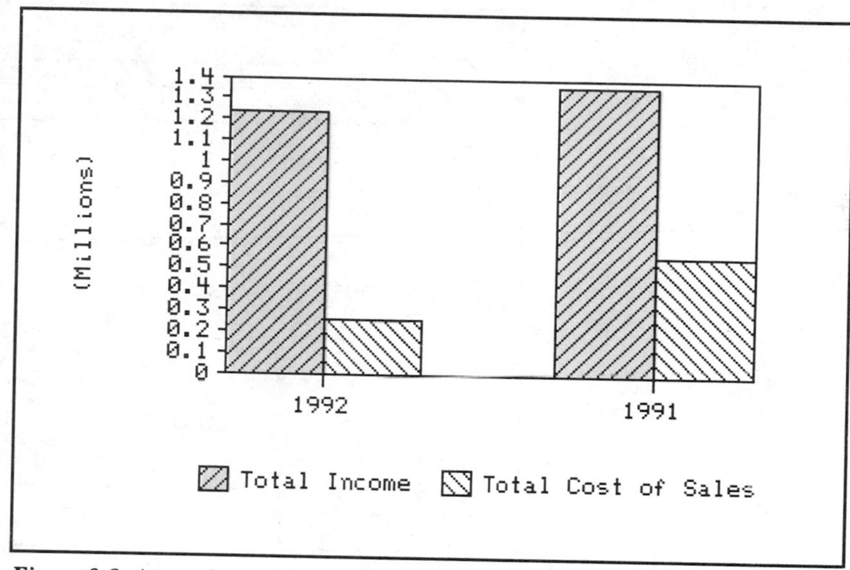

Figure 6.3: A graph created with Lotus 1-2-3

To create a frame that will hold our sample graph:

1. Scroll down the document (if you have a standard screen) to position the display so that only the bottom of the table appears, as shown in Figure 6.4.
2. Activate Frame mode, if it's not yet active.
3. Click the Add New Frame button in the Side-bar. (You can then turn off the Side-bar, if necessary, by pressing Ctrl-W.)
4. Position the mouse cursor for the upper-left corner of the frame that is to hold the picture. The mouse cursor changes to the letters *FR,* housed within a corner bracket.
5. Press the mouse button and hold. The mouse cursor changes to a pointing finger.
6. While holding its button, drag the mouse cursor to the lower-right corner of the frame (Figure 6.5).
7. Release the mouse button. This establishes the frame. The new frame is selected, as indicated by the eight black handles that appear along its periphery.

When you're working with large pictures, as we are, you may find it necessary to turn off the Side-bar in the process (as we have done in Figure 6.4), especially when using a standard-size display. Start the Add Frame procedure before turning the Side-bar off, however, since you'll need the Side-bar to add a frame (see Appendix A).

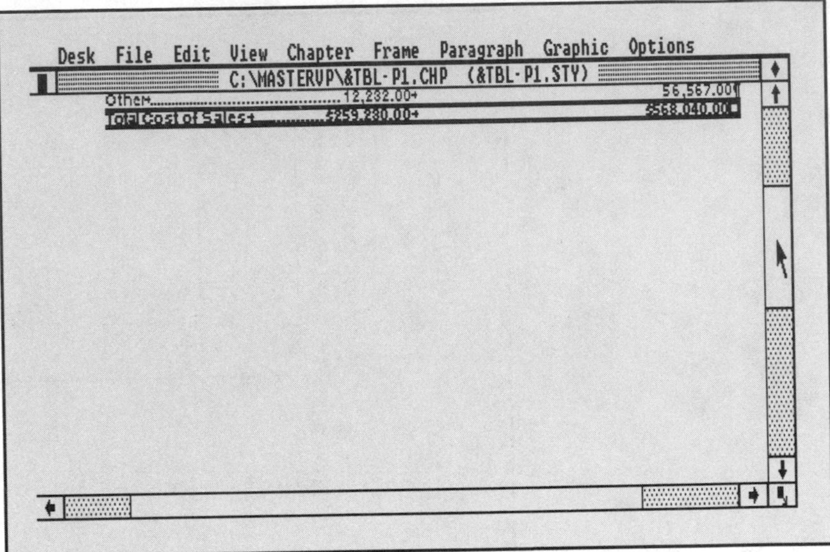

Figure 6.4: The sample table positioned to receive a graph

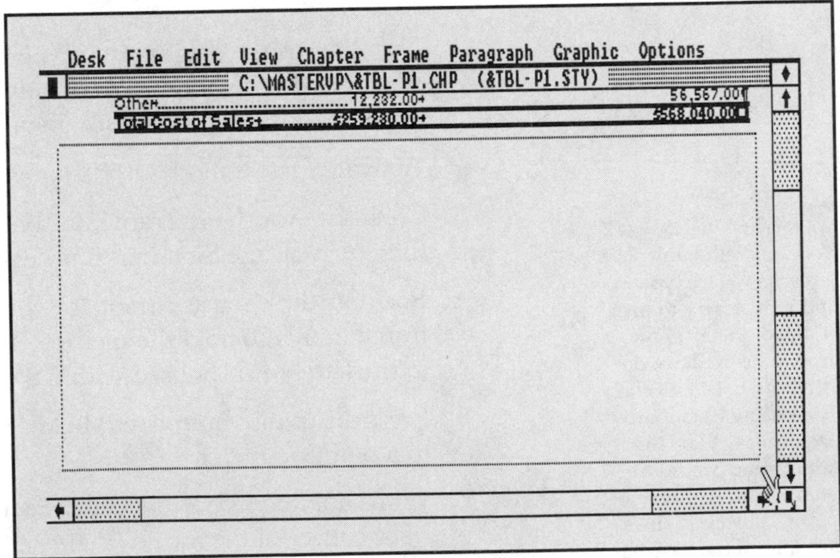

Figure 6.5: Creating the frame to hold the graph

LOADING AND ASSIGNING A 1-2-3 GRAPH

Next, you can load the graph, adding it to the Assignment list and assigning it to the frame in the same step. This will only work if your frame is selected and empty at the time you load the file. (The word *EMPTY* appears in the Current box when the Side-bar is showing and the frame is selected.)

Follow the steps below to add the 1-2-3 graph to the frame. (In step 3, you'll specify the type of picture that you're using. We'll examine the types of pictures Ventura accepts in the next section.)

1. Make sure that Frame mode is active and that an empty frame is selected.
2. Drop the File menu and select Load Text/Picture.
3. Click the Line-Art box. This makes the Line-Art Format group of buttons appear. The dialog box will look as it does in Figure 6.6.
4. Click the Lotus .PIC box.

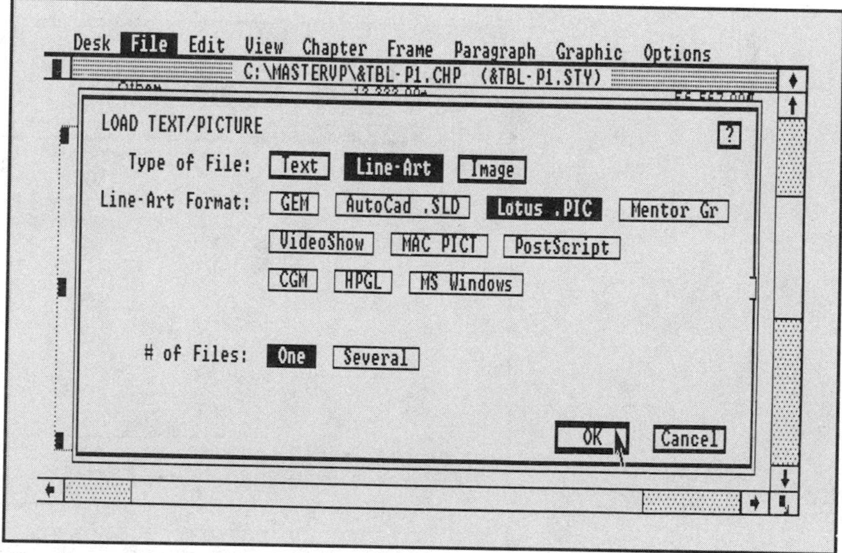

Figure 6.6: The File menu's Load Text/Picture dialog box

5. Give the OK.
6. Use the Item Selector box to indicate the PIC file you wish to use. (Our example is TABLE.PIC.) Don't forget that you can use the Backup button (right under the *D* in *Directory*) to back out of directories or to change drives.
7. Give the OK for the Item Selector box. Once you have, Ventura adds the name of the picture file to the Assignment list. (Of course, you'll only see it there when the Side-bar is showing.) It also assigns the file to the frame.

If you've followed these steps to add the graph to the sample table, your screen should look like Figure 6.7. Printed out, the page looks like Figure 6.8. Looking at these figures, you may notice that some aspects of the page could do with a little polishing; for instance, the positioning of the graph leaves a lot of space at the bottom of the page, and the text on the chart is rather small. Also, the LaserJet used to print Figure 6.8 was unable to print the sideways label *Millions*. We'll see how to fix these details as we proceed with this chapter and the next.

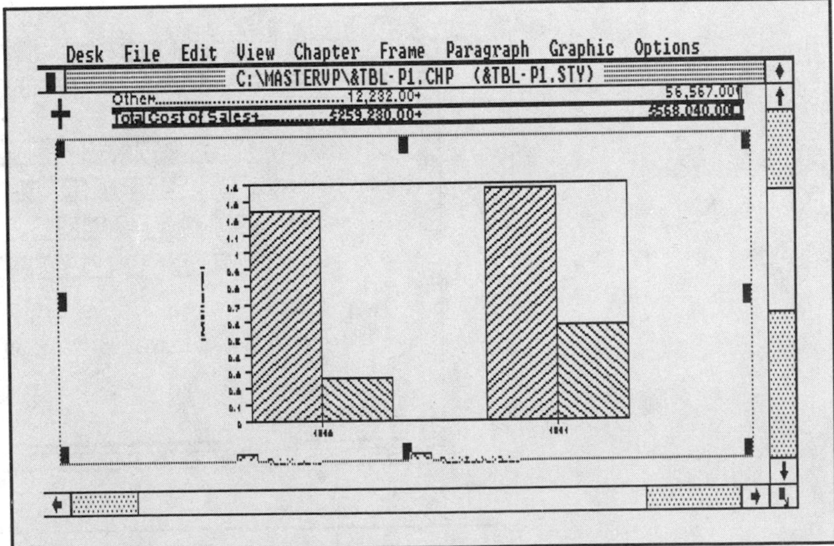

Figure 6.7: The graph file assigned to a frame

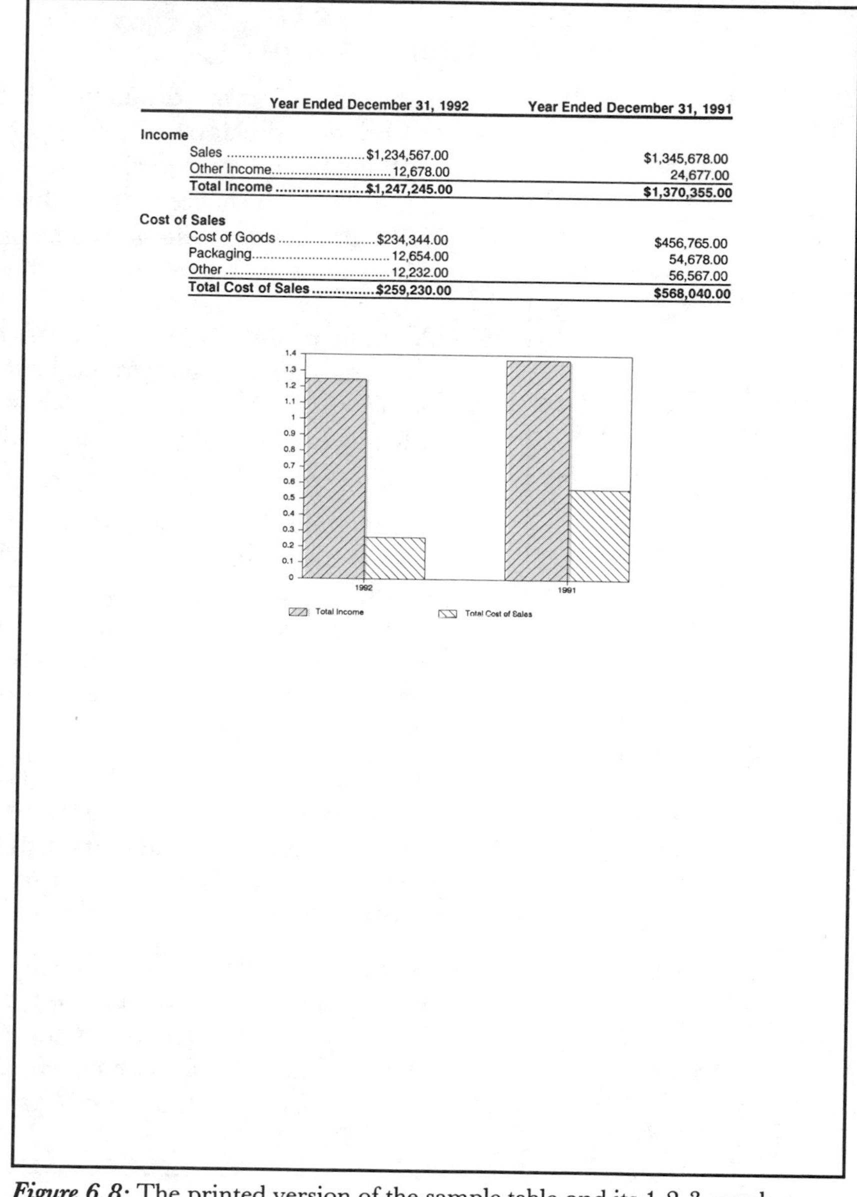

	Year Ended December 31, 1992	Year Ended December 31, 1991
Income		
Sales	$1,234,567.00	$1,345,678.00
Other Income	12,678.00	24,677.00
Total Income	**$1,247,245.00**	**$1,370,355.00**
Cost of Sales		
Cost of Goods	$234,344.00	$456,765.00
Packaging	12,654.00	54,678.00
Other	12,232.00	56,567.00
Total Cost of Sales	**$259,230.00**	**$568,040.00**

Figure 6.8: The printed version of the sample table and its 1-2-3 graph

Which Graph for the Job?

Graphs can add an important visual element to a variety of business-oriented desktop-publishing applications. Whatever the use, though, you must decide which kind of graph you should use. You can choose between bar graphs, line graphs, pie charts, and others. What are some of the factors that should be considered when you select the type of graph?

- Amount of data: If you're presenting a lot of data, you'll need to use a line graph. With less data, use a bar or pie chart. A lot of data makes bar and pie charts difficult to read, but can add to the impact of a line graph.
- Intervening data: Where data is continuous, such as with average rainfall, use a line graph. Where the data is individualized, such as with quarterly income for the year, use a bar chart with one bar for each quarter. You can't surmise the income of a given month from the quarterly income, so connecting quarters with a line chart would be misleading.
- Relationship to a whole: Pie charts are best for displaying a relationship of parts to the whole, such as a company's share of the total market. If critical pieces of the pie are missing, though, it's best to go with another kind of graph.
- Regularity of data: Where data occurs at regular intervals, such as with standard time periods, you can use bar or line charts. If events occur at irregular intervals, you'll want to avoid bar charts. A line chart would smooth the data out, and perhaps display a pattern.

VENTURA'S TWO PICTURE FORMATS

When you were loading the graph, you probably noticed that besides text, there are two categories listed on the File menu's Load Text/Picture dialog box (Figure 6.6). These are the types of pictures that Ventura can use. Table 6.1 summarizes the graphics terminology that Ventura uses, including these two formats. Refer to it as we examine the various graphics features.

HOW THE FORMATS ARE PRODUCED

As the Load Text/Picture dialog box shows, Ventura can use pictures classified as either *images* or *line art.* These names represent the different *formats* that computer programs use to create graphics. The

Table 6.1: Graphics Terminology in Ventura

TYPE OF GRAPHIC	DESCRIPTION
Picture	Any illustration used with Ventura, be it image or line art.
Line Art	Picture produced and stored as a collection of objects, also known as object-oriented art. Created with a ''draw'' program such as AutoCAD or with the Lotus 1-2-3 Graph Save command.
Image	Picture composed of individual dots, or *pixels.* Created with a ''paint'' program, such as Publisher's Paintbrush, or with a scanner.
Ventura Graphics	Line art that you create with Ventura by using the Graphics mode, as opposed to art you bring in from another program. Often, these graphic elements will supplement imported pictures.

format of a particular picture file depends upon the software with which it was created. Let's take a look at each of these formats now.

IMAGE FORMAT Programs that use the *image* format are sometimes called *paint programs* or *bit-mapped programs*. These programs create pictures by storing the settings for tiny dots (called *bits* or *pixels*) that the computer uses to display the picture on the screen or with the printer.

As an analogy, think of the big electric sign in New York's Times Square. It displays images in much the same manner as a paint program. Its many individual light bulbs turn on and off in various combinations, creating images you recognize to promote a product or service. Similarly, image programs store information about the screen's dots in image files. Displaying them on the screen switches the screen's dots on and off to create pictures that you recognize.

Typical uses for image format include reproducing photographs and simulating paintings and sketches. Image format works well with images in which objects tend to have soft edges, since arcs and diagonal lines are not always smoothly formed in image format. With these programs you can create brush-stroke, spray-paint, and air-brush effects.

Paint programs that Ventura supports include PC Paintbrush, GEM Paint, and MacPaint (imported from a Macintosh). Ventura also supports software that stores images in these formats. You should convert images obtained with a scanner into PC Paintbrush format if they're initially in some other format.

! New for version 2.0

Version 2.0 adds TIFF (Tagged Image File Format) to the list of image files that you can import into Ventura. When you print such images with a PostScript printer, Ventura converts the TIFF gray scale information to PostScript gray scale, and PostScript handles the halftoning. When you print with a non-PostScript printer, Ventura takes care of halftoning. We'll examine gray scaling and halftones more, later in this chapter.

LINE-ART FORMAT Line art is sometimes called *drawn* or *object-oriented* artwork. With line art, the computer stores information on the drawing in terms of geometric formulas. For example, rather than telling the computer that certain pixels giving the impression of a line should be dark, the specifications simply indicate the starting measurement, length, direction, ending measurement, and so on. The result is a cleaner looking line, especially in print. Lines and circles are sharp and smooth. Objects are layered one on top of another, allowing them to be manipulated individually.

Applications for line art include graphs such as the one that we created with Lotus 1-2-3. Ventura also supports graphs created with GEM Graph.

Other line-art applications are provided with drawing programs. You use drawing programs to create architectural diagrams, logos, and various other drawn objects. Supported programs include AutoCAD, the most popular design program available. Ventura also accommodates drawings created with GEM Draw, a simpler drawing package, and other programs you see in the Load Text/Picture dialog box.

Most line-art files can be used as is, but some you will have to adapt. With AutoCAD, for example, you must use the optional ADE-2 package to store artwork in slide-file format. (You use this format to create computer slide shows for quick viewing.) To create a slide, load your drawing and issue the MSLIDE (Make Slide) command. Doing so creates a new file with an SLD extension, which Ventura can then load. As with images, Ventura will support any software whose artwork you can convert to one of the listed formats.

! New for version 2.0

Version 2.0 adds Microsoft Windows files to the list of Line-Art files that you can import into Ventura. This means that Ventura can now use files from programs that save metafiles from the Windows clipboard. Version 2.0 will now display Encapsulated PostScript files (which have the EPS extension) on the screen if the EPS file contains TIFF image or Windows metafile instructions. If the EPS file does not contain these embedded instructions, then Ventura displays a large *X* in the picture's frame (which was the case for all EPS files before version 2.0). Ventura 2.0 allows you to use printers other than PostScript printers to print EPS files, as long as they contain embedded TIFF or Windows metafile instructions.

ADVANTAGES AND DISADVANTAGES OF EACH FORMAT

As you can see, the method Ventura uses depends upon the software with which you create your pictures. If you're committed to using pictures from one program or another, the method you use is determined for you. Suppose, however, you have yet to choose a graphics package, or you have access to several. Which technique should you use to create a picture? Let's look at the advantages each format has to offer.

With images, what you see on the computer screen is pretty much what you will get on the printer. That is, the resolution on the screen is the maximum you can expect to achieve with the printer. With many screens, the resolution is not so hot. Even though printer resolution is theoretically better, the printer merely copies images, dot for dot, from the screen. Thus, image files do not allow you to use printers to their fullest capacity.

With line art, since the program stores drawings in terms of computations, not dots, you always get the maximum amount of detail that the output device (printer or otherwise) has to offer. Thus, printed versions of pictures usually look better than their screen counterparts. If you use a Linotronic typesetter, pictures in line-art format will look better still. On the other hand, even on a Linotronic, pictures in image format look no better than they do on the screen.

With image programs, you can magnify an area of the picture and work on the pixels that make it up. This feature allows you to fine-tune the image, bit by bit. Figure 6.9 shows how part of a circle created with PC Paintbrush looks when you enlarge it with that program. Notice how jagged the edge is. Some line-art programs, such as AutoCAD, also allow you to zoom in on an area. With a drawing program, however, a curve remains sharp, even in close-up (Figure 6.10).

Because the dots that compose an image show up when you magnify it, it's important that you take care when constructing an image. Always consider the way in which your image will finally be put to use. Don't paint an image smaller than you intend to use it, expecting to magnify, or you'll lose resolution. Rather, always draw the image big, and reduce it later if necessary. Reducing will result in a cleaner image and fewer "jaggies" (jagged edges).

Image files also tend to take more disk space than do line-art files, because they must store information on every tiny dot that goes to make them up. This can be especially troublesome when you use a scanner to import an image, resulting in a very big file. Although

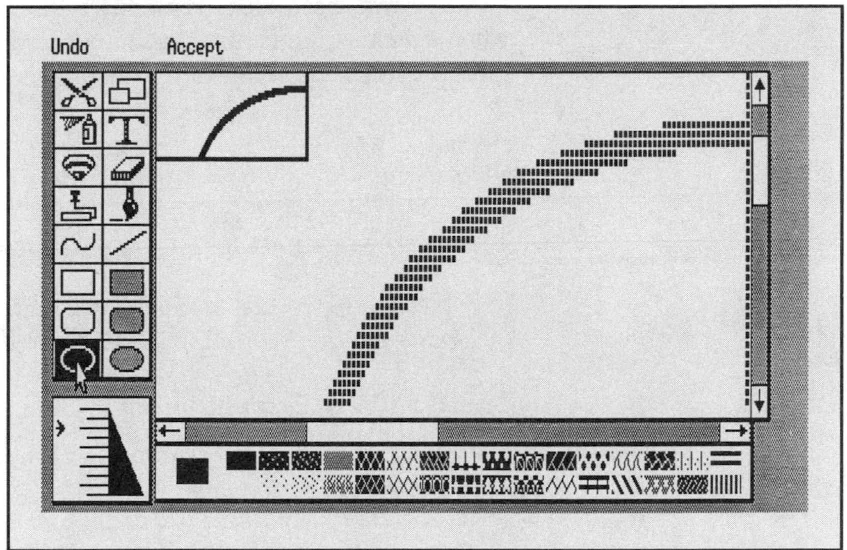

Figure 6.9: An enlarged portion of a circle created with PC Paintbrush

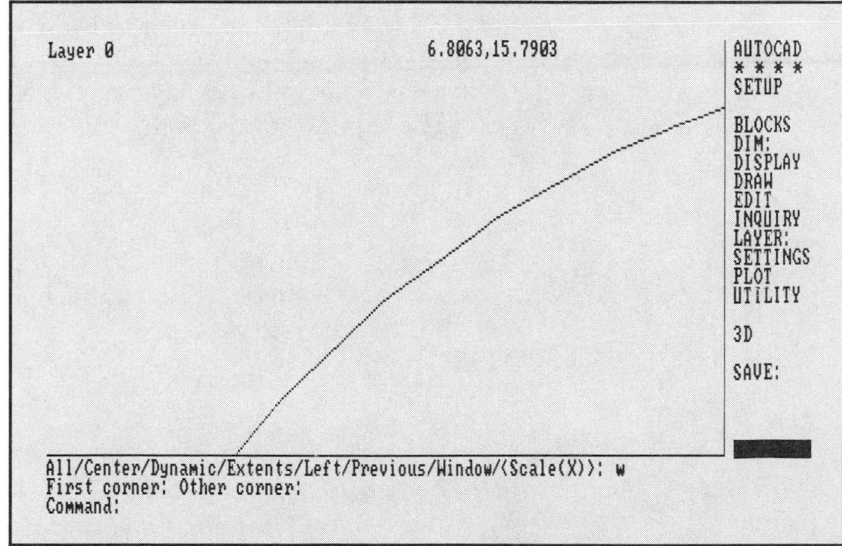

Figure 6.10: An enlarged portion of a circle created with AutoCAD

Ventura will crop very nicely, as we'll see, you should do some preliminary cropping yourself. To save disk space, only scan the portion of a picture that you are certain you will use.

To summarize, then, remember the effects you wish to achieve when selecting a graphics package, and consider storage requirements. Image programs, by their nature, create soft-edged, "painted" pictures. Line-art programs create sharp, drawn, exacting pictures.

GRAY SCALING AND HALFTONES

! New for version 2.0

For its best picture generation, Ventura will now create *halftones*—dots of varying density—for some kinds of pictures. The printed picture

- Must be a scanned image.
- Must be in PostScript or TIFF format.
- Must contain gray scaling.
- Must be printed on a PostScript printer.

The dots that make up the scanned image must consist of shades of gray; they cannot simply be all black. The halftone process converts the gray areas to small black dots of varying density. Thus, the printer—which can print only black dots—seems to print shades of gray. The varying density of the dots gives the impression of varying shades of gray.

To gain access to the dialog box that controls this process (Figure 6.11):

1. In Frame mode, click a frame holding a scanned image that meets the criteria above.
2. Drop the Frame menu.
3. Select Image Settings.

In the Image Settings dialog box, you can set Halftone Screen Type to Default, Dot, Line, Ellipse, or Custom. Default is the usual setting. However, if Default produces an undesirable pattern in the printed image, or if you want a special effect, you can use one of the others. If you change the Halftone Screen Type setting, you won't discern any difference on the screen, but the effect will be apparent when you print the image.

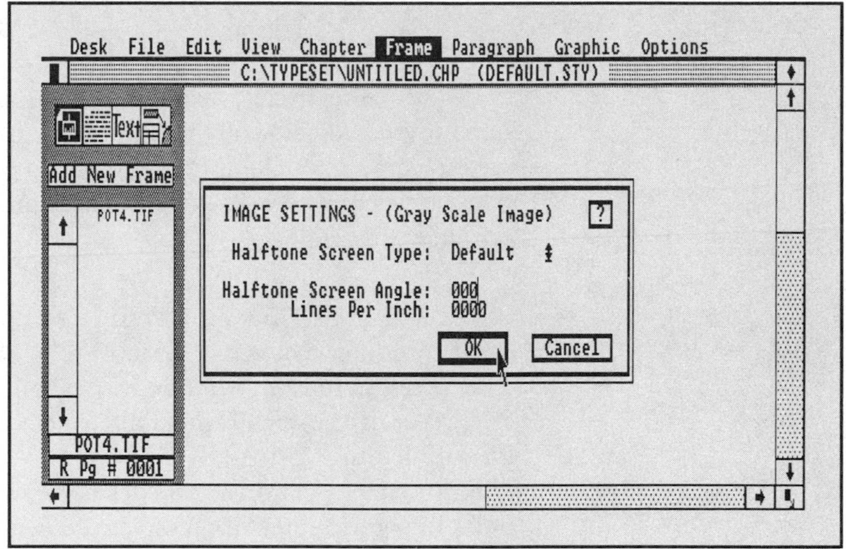

Figure 6.11: The Frame menu's Image Settings dialog box

Normally, you set Halftone Screen Angle to 45 (degrees). This setting rotates any such undesired pattern, ideally making it less noticeable. Experiment to determine the rotation that produces the best results.

Lines Per Inch relates the capabilities of your printer to Ventura. Set it to 60 for most laser printers, which are capable of 300 dots per inch (dpi). Set it to 90 for 1200-dpi typesetters, and to 150 for 2540-dpi typesetters.

MANIPULATING PICTURES

Regardless of which technique you use to create a picture, once you've imported it into a Ventura document, you can manipulate it in many ways. You can move the picture around on the page, change its size, delete it, or crop it. We'll study the techniques for performing these operations in this section.

Be aware, though, that you cannot use Ventura to rotate pictures. If you must rotate a picture (that is, change it to face horizontally or vertically), use your graphics software to do so.

TOOLS THAT SUPPLEMENT PICTURE MANIPULATION

Before we begin, let's examine some supplemental tools that Ventura provides to help you manipulate pictures. You'll need these tools as you work. These tools do not perform cut, copy, and paste operations per se, but they do expedite those procedures and make certain operations possible.

HIDING PICTURES TEMPORARILY Pictures consume a lot of the computer's memory, because a lot of data goes into composing them. For this reason, working with pictures can really slow down the operation of the program. This especially holds true for image-format pictures.

Fortunately, Ventura provides a way for you to hide pictures in order to speed things up. You can hide all pictures or only selected pictures. To hide all pictures:

1. Make sure no selected frame has a picture in it.
2. Drop the Options menu and select Hide All Pictures.

When you hide pictures, Ventura replaces each of them with a solid block on the screen. Usually, hiding pictures considerably improves the operation of the program.

To display hidden pictures, use the flip side of the same command—the Options menu's Show All Pictures command:

1. Again make sure that no picture frame is selected.
2. Drop the Options menu and select Show All Pictures.

Generally, you'll want to keep pictures hidden, except when you really need to look at them—to crop, for instance. When you're done, hide your pictures again right away.

! New for version 2.0

Version 2.0 lets you hide individual pictures as well as all pictures. To hide one or more individual pictures:

1. Use Frame mode and click the frame with the picture. Shift-click to select multiple frames.

2. Drop the Options menu and click Hide This Picture. This is the same option as with Hide All Pictures but the wording changes when you select a picture frame.

Also new with 2.0, when you print a document with hidden pictures, Ventura asks if you want to print the pictures. Not printing them can dramatically reduce the time it takes to print. To print drafts quickly, hide pictures before you print. Ventura stores each picture frame's hidden or displayed status when you save the chapter. The same status is again effective when you open the chapter.

USING RULERS You can also use rulers to help position frames. Rulers are measuring sticks that can appear at the top and left of the working area. These rulers each display a traveling marker that shows the position of the mouse cursor.

To display the rulers, pull down the Options menu and click Show Rulers. (If the option reads "Hide Rulers," the rulers are already showing, and clicking the command makes them disappear.)

You can change the system of measurement in which the rulers are calibrated and you can use different measuring systems for the top and left rulers. Drop the Options menu and click Set Ruler. You'll see the Set Ruler dialog box, as shown in Figure 6.12. This figure also shows the rulers.

Notice that you can also set the horizontal and vertical *zero point.* This is the distance that the beginning of the ruler is offset into the working area (that is, indented from the left or from the top). You might set the zero point to some value other than zero in order to measure from the center of the page rather than the left edge, for instance.

You can also use the mouse cursor to change the zero point and to display cross hairs. To do that, point to the 0,0 box in the top-left corner of the working area. Then drag (press and hold the left mouse button and move) the mouse into the working area. This allows you to see and use the cross hairs (Figure 6.13). When you release the mouse button, the zero point relocates to the position you've indicated. Releasing on one of the rulers affects only the zero point of that ruler. To make the ruler revert to normal, simply click the 0,0 box.

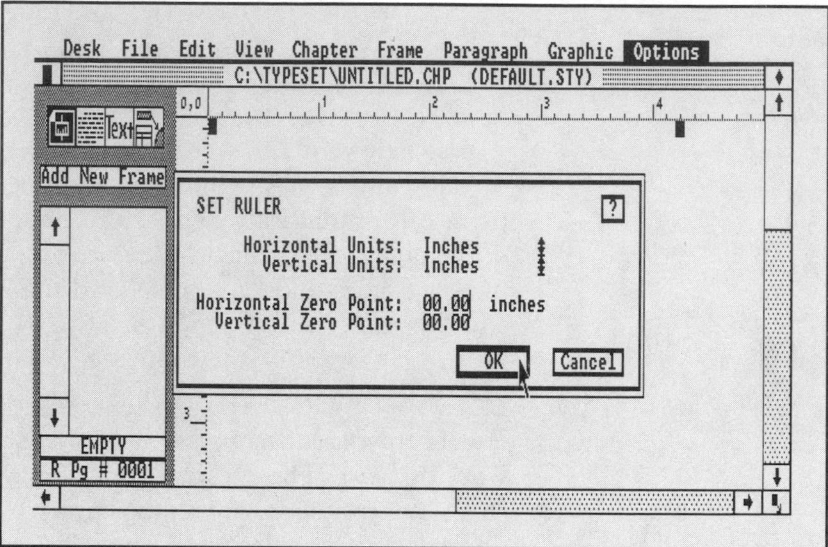

Figure 6.12: The Options menu's Set Ruler dialog box and the rulers it controls

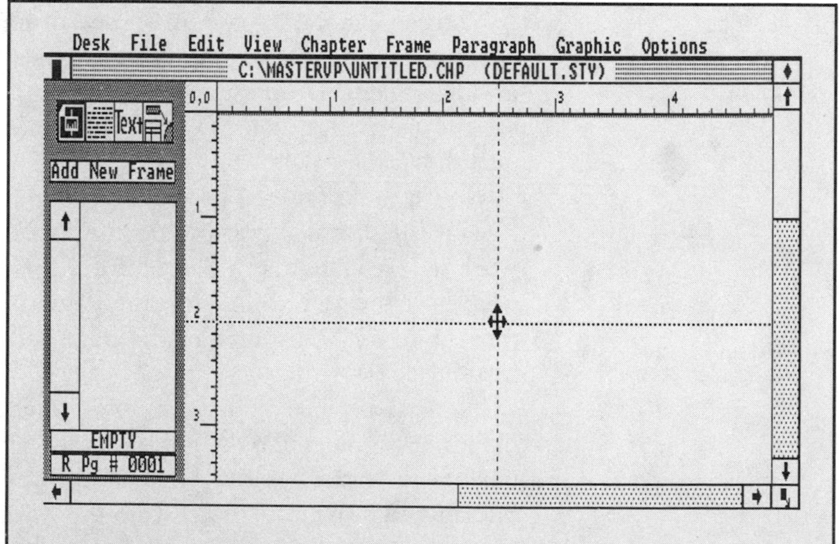

Figure 6.13: Cross hairs

Note that the exact position of the traveling markers on the rulers depends on the shape of the mouse cursor (Figure 6.14). When Ventura represents the mouse cursor with bracketed symbols (such as the bracketed *FR* for adding a new frame), the ruler hairlines correspond

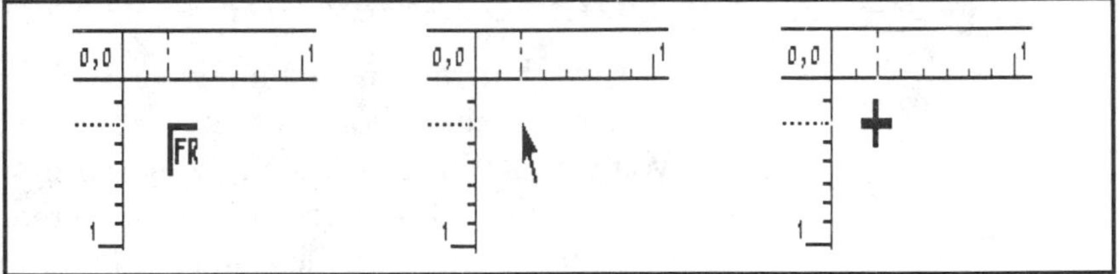

Figure 6.14: Ruler hairlines indicating the position of the mouse cursor

to the bracket's corner (top-left of the symbol). With pointing symbols (such as the arrow in Graphics mode), the hairlines correspond to the tip of the pointer. For the other kinds of symbols, the hairlines correspond to the center of the symbol.

CHANGING VIEWS When manipulating frames, don't forget to change to a more general view, as necessary. The larger the frame, the more likely that operations will be quickened by using Reduced or Facing Pages view. Be aware, though, that Facing Pages view has limitations. You cannot drag pictures across its page boundaries. However, you can use Facing Pages view in conjunction with cross hairs to check the alignment of frames on a two-page spread.

TECHNIQUES OF SELECTION To work with a picture frame, you must first select it with the mouse, just as you would a text frame. Selecting is discussed in Chapter 1. Remember, you can Shift-click to select multiple frames.

With the mouse, you can manipulate the frames as a group: moving, copying, stretching them, and so on. Be aware, however, that you cannot use the menus to change the characteristics of multiple frames simultaneously. For instance, once multiple frames are selected you cannot drop the Frame menu to set the margins for all selected frames. Only the settings for the first frame selected would be affected in this case.

Remember also that Ctrl-clicking allows you to select frames that are beneath other frames. For example, later in this chapter we'll see how to create a text run-around, which allows text to follow the contours of a picture. For this application, a picture frame must be on top of a frame that holds the text. You can Ctrl-click either frame as necessary to select the one that you need to work with.

MOVING A PICTURE

Now that you understand some basic tools, let's begin to examine picture manipulation. Some of the more straightforward operations you can perform include moving, cutting, and pasting frames. You move picture frames in the same way that you move other frames in Ventura. Just move the frame and you move the picture. The techniques are the same as those described in Chapter 2.

* You'll probably find it desirable to have the edges of your frames line up with columns and lines. To do that use the Options menu to turn Column Snap and Line Snap on. See Appendix A.

You can also use the menus to move a frame. Once you've selected the appropriate frame, drop the Frame menu and select Sizing & Scaling. In the resulting dialog box (Figure 6.15), adjust the Upper Left Y (top) and X (left) coordinates.

In addition, you can use the other cut-and-paste procedures to manipulate pictures. Just activate Frame mode and select the appropriate picture frame. Drop the Edit menu to cut, copy, and paste the frames, just as you do with frames of text. Alternatively, use the Del and Ins keys, as noted on the Edit menu.

! New for version 2.0

Now you can also use Graphics mode to perform many of the frame procedures. Thus as you work with Ventura Graphics (which we'll do in the next chapter), you don't have to switch to Frame mode as often.

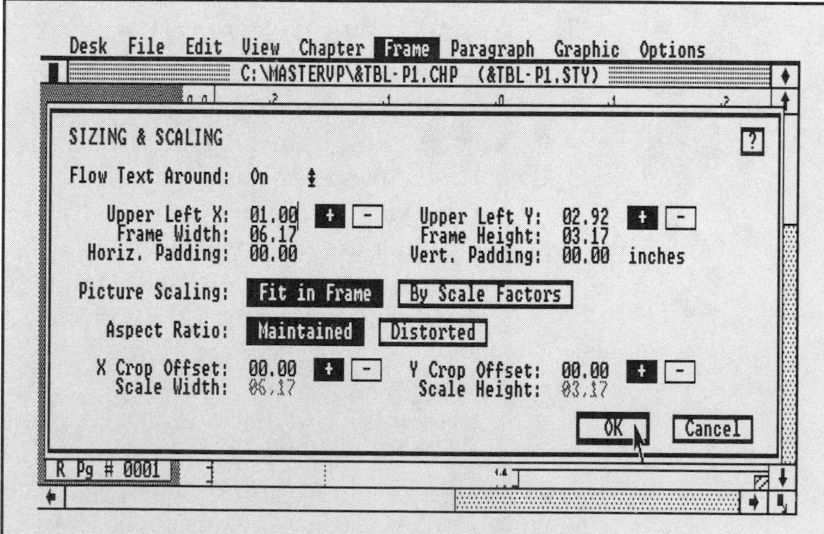

Figure 6.15: The Frame menu's Sizing & Scaling dialog box

RESIZING PICTURES

With Ventura you can change the size of pictures that you've imported. One way to resize a picture is simply to resize the frame that contains it. The picture enlarges or reduces to accommodate the frame. Again, the techniques are the same as those we've already studied. That is, once you've selected a frame, you use the mouse to grab one of the frame's handles and stretch the frame in one direction or another. Alternatively, you can use the Frame menu's Sizing & Scaling dialog box (Figure 6.15).

- Drop the Frame menu and select Sizing & Scaling.

The Sizing & Scaling dialog box lets you adjust the frame's settings for Upper Left Y and X, and for Frame Width, Frame Height, and Padding. As the frame changes size, the picture will too. For instance, Figure 6.16 shows how you could stretch the graph we worked with earlier in order to fill the remainder of an 8.5-by-11-inch page.

There may be times, though, when you want to resize a picture without changing the size of its frame. This dialog box also allows you to accomplish that. A picture will resize as you adjust the frame, as long as Picture Scaling is set to Fit in Frame. If you set Picture Scaling to By Scale Factors, Ventura will instead scale the picture according to the values you provide for settings in the bottom part of the dialog box. These settings scale with respect to the original size of the picture, independent of the size of the frame. We'll examine these settings in a moment.

CHANGING THE ASPECT RATIO When resizing pictures in Ventura, we can make use of Ventura's ability to maintain or distort the *aspect ratio* of a picture. The aspect ratio is the ratio of a picture's height to its width. A picture that's 8 by 10 inches, reduced without distortion to 4 by 5, maintains the same aspect ratio, since these measurements have the same ratio.

Stretching pictures can produce some odd results, but it can also prove a useful tool in putting together your pages. To stretch the bar chart in order to fill the page, we had to allow its aspect ratio to be distorted. However, you probably wouldn't want to stretch a pie chart; because of the distortion in the aspect ratio, the pie would come out looking egg-shaped.

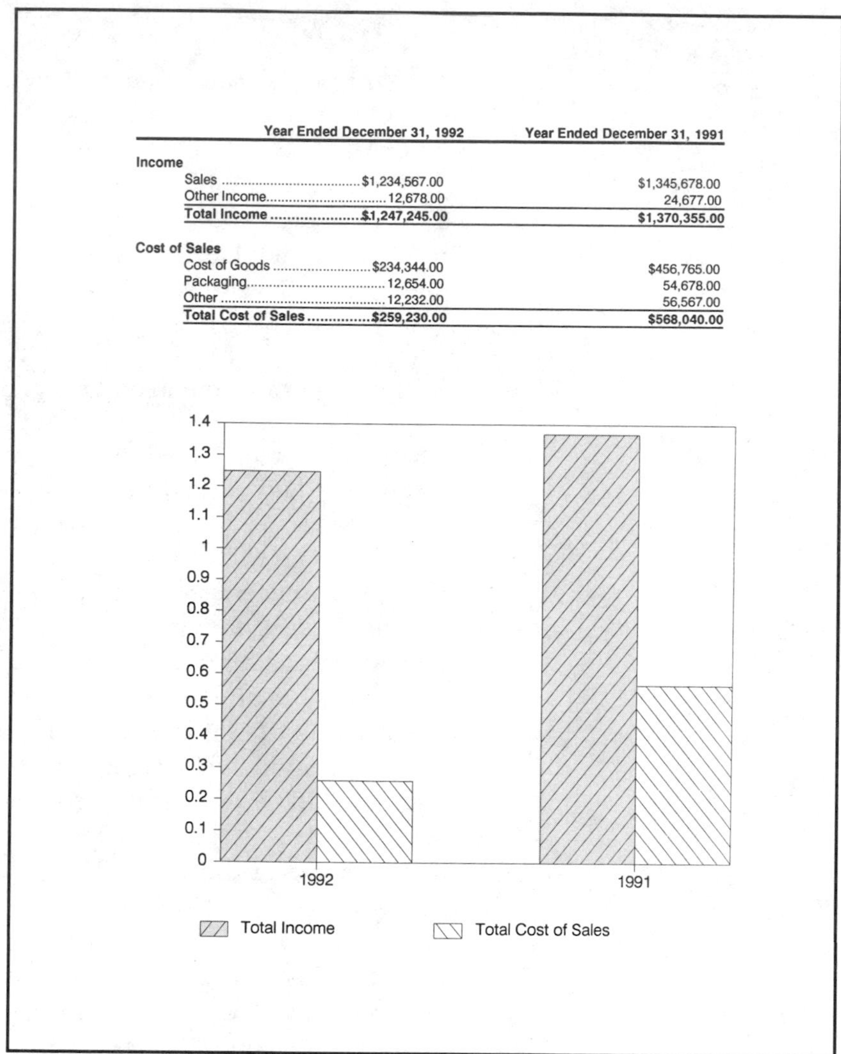

	Year Ended December 31, 1992	Year Ended December 31, 1991
Income		
Sales	$1,234,567.00	$1,345,678.00
Other Income	12,678.00	24,677.00
Total Income	**$1,247,245.00**	**$1,370,355.00**
Cost of Sales		
Cost of Goods	$234,344.00	$456,765.00
Packaging	12,654.00	54,678.00
Other	12,232.00	56,567.00
Total Cost of Sales	**$259,230.00**	**$568,040.00**

Figure 6.16: The chart stretched to fill the page

Now consider Figure 6.17. This is an image-type picture. It was created from a photo that was scanned using a Princeton scanner with Publisher's Paintbrush, and then placed in a Ventura document. In the image on the left, the aspect ratio is normal. If you keep Aspect Ratio set on Maintained, the picture will continue to resemble the original as you enlarge or reduce. Ventura will crop the picture or add white space, if necessary, so as not to distort the picture.

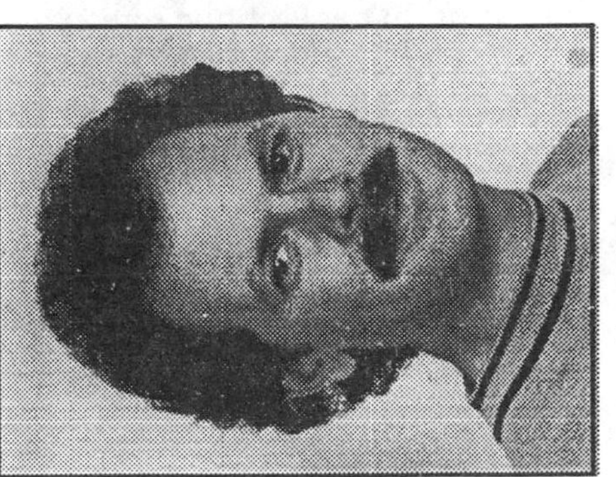

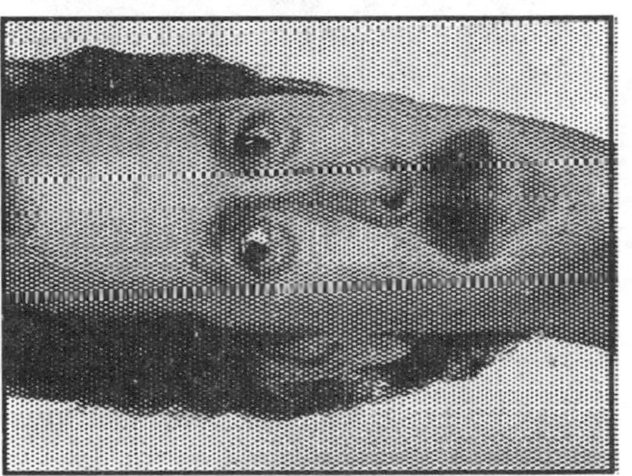

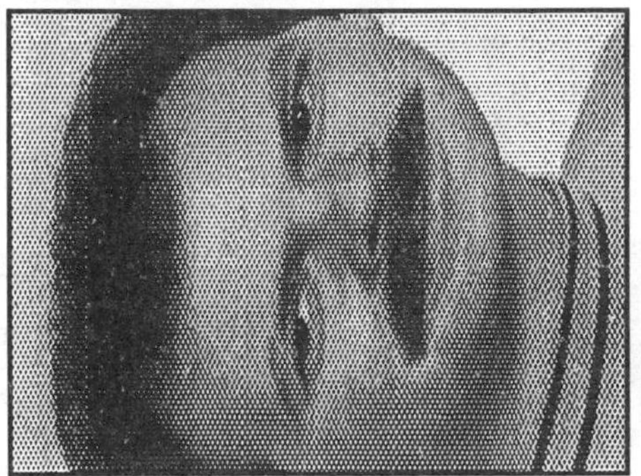

Figure 6.17: Distorting the aspect ratio

In the same figure, the two images on the right have been scaled by scale factors, with Aspect Ratio set to Distorted. To practice such image distortion, you can use your own file or the CHANEL.IMG file that's located in the TYPESET directory. CHANEL.IMG is in GEM image format.

SETTING SCALE FACTORS As mentioned, you can click the By Scale Factors button in order to adjust a picture's size independently of its frame. When Fit in Frame is selected, values will ghost for Scale Width and Scale Height toward the bottom of the dialog box. When By Scale Factors is selected, one or both of these Scale dimensions become available. The ghosting of Scale Height will change as you change the Aspect Ratio setting.

If Aspect Ratio is set to Distorted, both Scale Width and Scale Height become available. The values you see will change from the ghosting (frame size) values to the actual size of the picture, independent of its frame. You can then adjust these settings to increase or decrease the size of the picture. Adjusting the settings stretches the picture accordingly, as in Figure 6.17.

The original size of the picture appears just after you click By Scale Factors. You may wish to bear this value in mind as you adjust picture size. Thus, for instance, if you want to double a picture that's initially 1.02 inches wide, change the scale width to 2.04 inches.

As you resize scanned images, you may see unexpected bars across the face of the picture. However, they will not be present in the printed version of the document. They're caused by differences in resolution between the screen and the image as it was scanned.

If you've selected By Scale Factors and have Aspect Ratio set to Maintained, the Scale Height setting will ghost. You will only be able to set Scale Width. Scale Height will adjust automatically in order to maintain the correct aspect ratio.

Above the Scale Width and Height settings you can see settings for Crop Offset. Let's discuss cropping and see how Ventura accomplishes it.

CROPPING

Cropping is the technique of cutting away parts of a picture or matting it so that only the desired portion appears. By displaying only what you want shown, Ventura allows you to edit your pictures. Cropping only affects the picture as it's displayed by your chapter file. The original picture always remains intact, so you can crop again later to show a different portion.

USING ALT-MOUSE As with other features we've studied, there is both a fast, easy way to crop, and a more exacting method. The easy way to crop is by using the Alt key in conjunction with the mouse, as follows:

1. Set Picture Scaling to By Scale Factors. Fit-in-Frame pictures cannot be cropped; they always adjust to the frame.
2. Point the mouse cursor anywhere on the picture in the frame. You will see only that portion of the original picture that can fit in the frame.
3. Press the Alt key and hold it down.
4. While holding the Alt key, press the mouse button and hold it down. The mouse cursor will change to the shape of a flattened hand (Figure 6.18). Once you're holding the mouse button down, you may release the Alt key, if you wish.
5. While still pressing the mouse button, drag the picture as desired. You'll see the picture move beneath the frame.
6. When the picture is cropped to your liking, release the mouse button.

Watching Ventura crop for the first time is thrilling. It looks as though the flattened hand of the mouse cursor is moving a picture beneath a cutout in the page. It's a great visual example of the ingeniousness that went into the design of this program. You can also crop in a less dramatic fashion by using settings in the Frame menu's Sizing & Scaling dialog box.

USING OFFSET SETTINGS To use the Sizing & Scaling dialog box for cropping, adjust the values for X and Y Crop Offset and their accompanying Plus and Minus buttons. Use X Crop Offset to adjust the picture left (+) and right (–) with respect to the frame. Use Y Crop Offset to adjust the picture up (+) and down (–). For example,

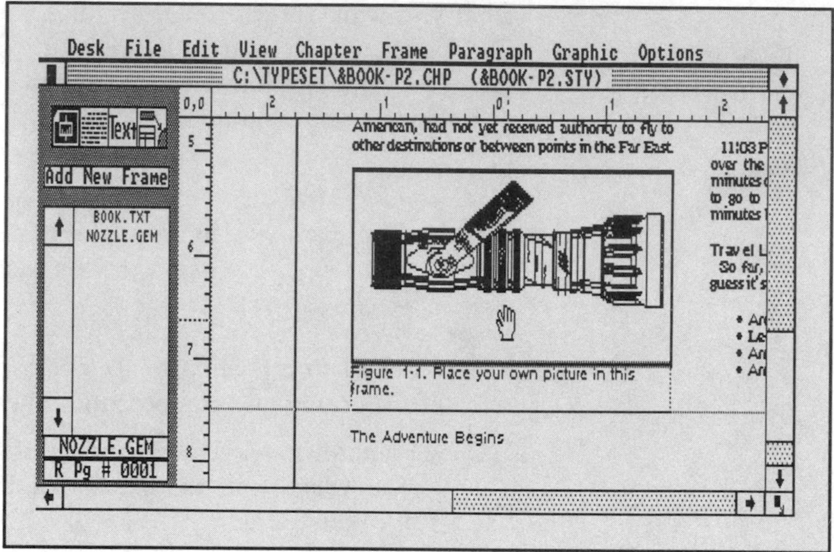

Figure 6.18: The mouse cursor in the shape of a flattened hand for cropping

let's say you have a picture that's originally 3 inches high, with the middle third showing in the frame. You want to show the top third of it in a frame that's 1 inch high. To do this, you'd set Y Crop Offset to 1 inch and click the Minus button. This would adjust the picture down the frame, thus showing the top third.

CHANGING FRAME MARGINS

We've seen how you can change the size of a picture and crop to control the portion of the picture that's seen. You can also limit the area within a frame that's available for the picture. When pictures are used with densely written material, for instance, you can use this technique to create white space for clearly setting off the image from the text. Do so by following these steps to increase the frame's margins:

1. Activate Frame mode and select the frame with the image.
2. Drop the Frame menu and select Margins & Columns.
3. Set the margins as desired and give the OK.

Once the display area is reduced, you can then crop to display the portion of the image you wish to show.

- Click Cancel to put away the Sizing & Scaling dialog box.

CREATING TEXT RUN-AROUNDS

So far, we've been manipulating frames to influence the display of pictures they contain. Now let's turn our attention to using frames in order to influence the text that surrounds a picture.

A *text run-around* is text that follows the contours of a graphic, such as a company logo. See Figure 6.19 for an example. Normally, Ventura diverts text around frames that you create for holding pictures. However, you can allow the text to flow beneath the frame that holds a picture. Then, by using a series of stepped frames, you can cause text to conform to the outline of the picture. Here are the steps for creating a text run-around with Ventura:

When creating a text run-around, placement off to one side (Figure 6.19) is the easiest to accommodate. If you position your picture in the middle of a column, with text on either side of it, you must create a separate small frame for each line of text. If the logo in the example were placed within a column, for instance, the single frame around the word *SYBEX* would have to be replaced with several smaller frames, one for each line of text. Otherwise, the text would first flow down the left side of the single frame and then down the right side, disrupting the reading pattern at that point.

1. In Frame mode, use the Add New Frame button to create a frame on top of the text. Then load the picture into it. The text will flow around the frame as usual.

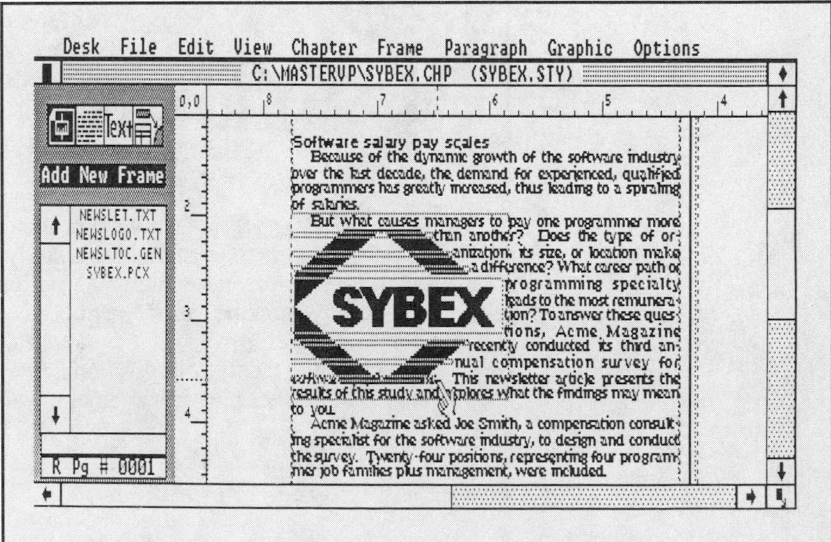

Figure 6.19: Using small frames to create a text run-around

2. With this picture frame selected, use the Frame menu's Sizing & Scaling dialog box and set Flow Text Around to Off. Text will then flow beneath the frame and you'll see your picture superimposed on the text.
3. Within the picture's frame, create a series of small frames that cover those areas of the picture you want protected from text. Hold down the Shift key while you position these frames and the Add New Frame button will remain operational, relieving you of the need to click repeatedly. Line by line, these small frames will nudge the text out from protected portions of the picture's frame, creating the type of text run-around shown in Figure 6.19. Figure 6.20 shows the completed text run-around in print.

Software salary pay scales

Because of the dynamic growth of the software industry over the last decade, the demand for experienced, qualified programmers has greatly increased, thus leading to a spiraling of salaries.

But what causes managers to pay one programmer more

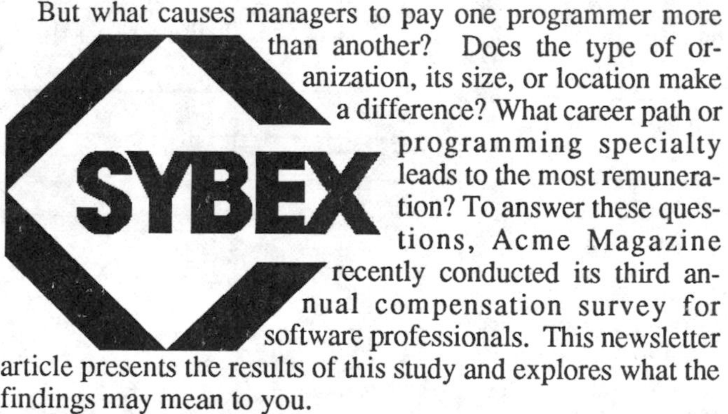

than another? Does the type of or-anization, its size, or location make a difference? What career path or programming specialty leads to the most remuneration? To answer these questions, Acme Magazine recently conducted its third annual compensation survey for software professionals. This newsletter article presents the results of this study and explores what the findings may mean to you.

Acme Magazine asked Joe Smith, a compensation consulting specialist for the software industry, to design and conduct the survey. Twenty-four positions, representing four programmer job families plus management, were included.

Figure 6.20: Text run-around in print

ADDING CAPTIONS WITH AUTOMATIC FIGURE NUMBERS

Many applications that use pictures require captions to accompany the pictures. From short newsletters to book-length documents, captions allow the reader to associate the picture with related material in text. In addition, some documents require a figure number in the caption for text that directly references a picture. Ventura allows you to accomplish captioning with ease and dispatch. It also provides you with the means of automatically numbering the captions in a variety of styles.

CREATING CAPTION LABELS

To create a caption for a figure, you begin by creating a *caption frame.* A caption frame is a special frame that is associated with a particular standard frame—namely, the one holding the picture you wish to caption. The caption frame piggybacks onto the standard frame, and the two stay together wherever you move either. To create a caption frame for the Lotus graph you loaded earlier, display the dialog box for setting captions, as follows:

1. Activate Frame mode and select the frame containing the Lotus graph (or NOZZLE.GEM if you did not use Lotus).
2. Drop the Frame menu.
3. Select Anchors & Captions.

This action displays the dialog box in Figure 6.21.

4. Change Caption to the Below setting.
5. In the Label line, type **Figure**. Leave a space after the word *Figure.*
6. Click the button labeled Figure #. Ventura adds a special bracketed code, [F#], to the Label line.

In doing this, you are using Ventura's automatic figure-numbering system. This code indicates that the automatic figure number should

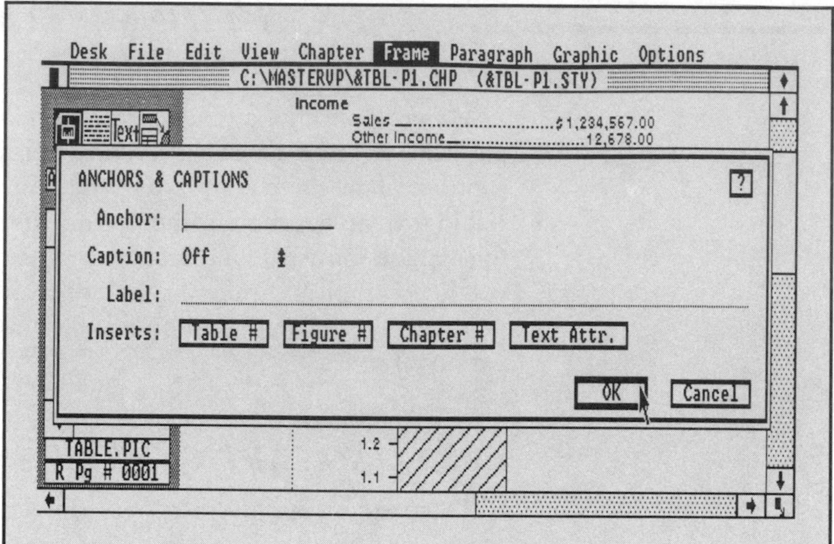

Figure 6.21: The dialog box for the Frame menu's Anchors & Captions

appear in that position. Thus, the finished label line will look like this:

Figure [F#]

When printed, this caption label would appear like this for the first figure:

Figure 1

You have created a *caption label.* Note that there is only one line provided for you to type the label in. This does not mean, however, that your captions can be only one line long. Rather, this line in the dialog box is for earmarking the caption. The standard style for such earmarking uses the word *Figure,* a space, and then the figure number. This text becomes the caption label. Material that you enter as a caption label can only be edited in this dialog box. However, you can add (and edit) additional explanatory material, if necessary, directly within the caption frame in Text mode. We'll see how to do this in the next section.

Ventura inserts bracketed codes like this for your convenience, so that you can use automatic numbering without having to remember the exact syntax for the codes. If you wish, though, you can simply type in the entire label line, including the bracketed code.

- Give the OK.

You should see the label appear on the screen, along with the appropriate number. If you can't see it all, you may need to enlarge the caption frame. Do so as you would with any frame: Use the frame's handles or the Frame menu's Sizing & Scaling command. Alternatively, you may wish to shorten the wording in the caption label.

As you may have noticed, Ventura also provides boxes for the automatic numbering of tables and chapters. These are each separate counters. You can use them separately or in conjunction with each other. Thus, let's say that you'd like tables to be numbered using the chapter number and the table number. For example, if you want the third table in Chapter 1 to be captioned

```
Table 1–3
```

here's what you'd enter on the label line:

```
Table [C#]–[T#]
```

Again, you can simply type it all in just as it appears above, or you can click boxes as appropriate. Here you would type the word **Table** followed by a space, then click the Chapter # box, type the hyphen, and finish by clicking the Table # box. Either method of entering the label is acceptable.

There is even a code that doesn't have a box counterpart. By typing

```
[P#]
```

you insert the page number into the caption label automatically. You can use this undocumented feature to position the page number in captions. We'll see more about pages in Chapter 9.

The Text Attr insert allows you to assign text attributes such as font sizes, underlining, and boldface to the caption labels. This box inserts the <D> codes, which you can then edit to provide codes as you would with a word processor in a text file. We'll study these codes in Chapter 11 and Appendix E.

FREE-FORM CAPTIONS

If the one line allowed for captions in the dialog box isn't sufficient, you can add a *free-form* caption. A free-form caption consists of one or more paragraphs that follow the caption label in the caption frame.

You create and edit a free-form caption just as you do normal text: directly in the caption frame, rather than in a dialog box. In Text mode, place the text cursor directly in front of the square-shaped end box (□) that terminates the caption and type in the additional text. Remember that you cannot use Text mode to edit the caption label that precedes the free-form caption. To change a caption label, you must activate Frame mode and use the Frame menu's Anchors & Captions dialog box.

TAGGING CAPTIONS

* You can display a list of the generated tags that Ventura has created for the document. Use the Options menu's Set Preferences dialog box and change Generated Tags to the Shown setting. See Appendix A.

As soon as you create caption labels and free-form captions, Ventura automatically creates special tags that it assigns to them. These are part of the set of generated tags that we discussed in Chapter 4.

Remember also that you can alter the format of generated tags just as you would any other tag. Figure 6.22 shows how you can change these tags to achieve a variety of captioning effects.

CAPTIONS AND YOUR WORD PROCESSOR

When you save your chapter, Ventura creates a file that holds free-form captions. The caption file has the same name as its chapter file, except that Ventura assigns a CAP extension to it.

If you're careful, you can use your word processor to edit this file. For precautions to use when doing so, see Chapter 11.

AUTOMATIC COUNTERS FOR CAPTIONS

! New for version 2.0

Finally, let's look at how you can adjust the numbers that appear with your captions. With version 2.0, Ventura provides one dialog box that allows you to change numbers for both tables and figures.

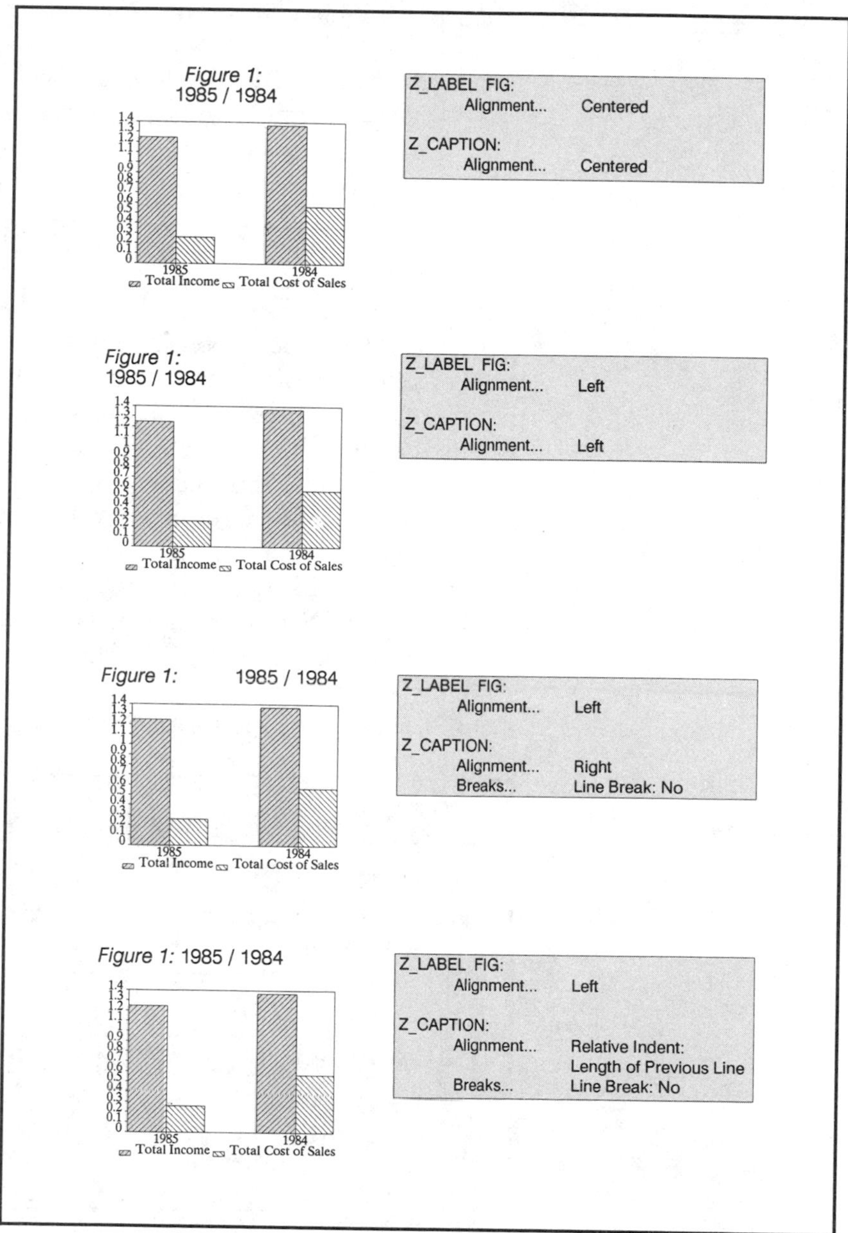

Figure 6.22: Formatting caption labels and free-form captions

To display it, follow these steps:

1. Activate Frame mode and select the caption frame (or its hosting frame) that has the figure or table reference you wish to adjust.
2. Drop the Chapter menu.
3. Click Update Counters. The dialog box shown in Figure 6.23 appears.

Use this dialog box to set the number for the caption should you need to adjust it. Click Restart Number and provide the new starting number. The indicated caption will adjust, and all those that follow it will increment automatically.

You can also use this dialog box to set the numbering format for your captions. You can number with Arabic and Roman numerals (indicated with *1*, *2*; *I*, *II*; *i*, *ii*), with capital or lowercase letters (*A*, *B*; *a*, *b*), or even with numbers that are spelled out (*One*, *Two*; *ONE*, *TWO*; *one*, *two*). Set Number Format to the setting that corresponds to your choice and give the OK when your settings are complete.

So far we haven't looked at the Anchors portion of the Anchors & Captions dialog box. Let's turn to these settings now.

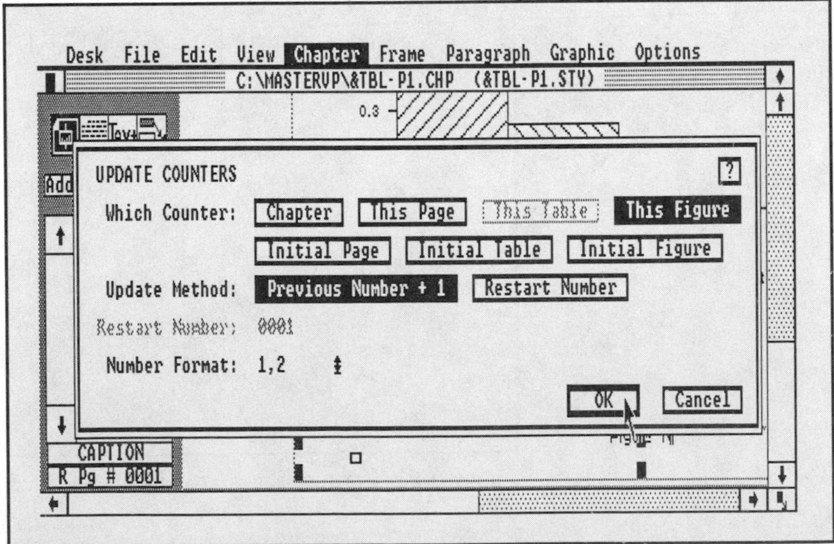

Figure 6.23: The Chapter menu's Update Counters dialog box

ANCHORING PICTURES TO TEXT

People in the publishing world who work with figures know that during edits, figure placement requires constant attention. As editors revise material, there's always the possibility that pictures will become too far removed from the text they complement. Fortunately, Ventura provides the means to keep pictures with their associated text. By using an *anchor,* a specially coded flag at a critical spot in the text, you can have a picture frame (or any frame, for that matter) stay with related material. However, for most frames, the process is not fully automatic, so you must still remain vigilant.

Anchor operations make use of three commands and the dialog boxes these commands give rise to:

- The Frame menu's Anchors & Captions command.
- The Edit menu's Insert/Edit Special item command.
- The Chapter menu's Re-Anchor Frames command.

Using anchors is a three-step procedure that corresponds to these three commands. First, you choose a frame you wish to anchor and give the frame an *anchor name* for reference. Then you pick out a spot in text and link it with the frame by way of the frame's anchor name. You repeat these two steps for all frames that you wish to anchor.

You can then proceed to work with your document as usual; this is where you must remain alert. As you edit, some pictures may still drift from their anchors in the text. So before printing, you perform the third step, re-anchoring, which reunites wayward frames with their appropriate anchors in text. Let's examine these three procedures.

CREATING THE ANCHOR NAME FOR A FRAME

The first procedure in anchoring a frame is to assign an anchor name to the frame, using the following steps:

1. Activate Frame mode and select the frame you wish to anchor.
2. Drop the Frame menu and select Anchors & Captions. The dialog box we looked at in Figure 6.21 appears.
3. Enter an anchor name in the Anchor field and give the OK.

Although you can click the Inserts buttons and enter bracketed codes, like the figure number used with captions, it's best not to. Relocating pictures could change the reference number of the frame. If so, the figure number of the anchor in text would no longer agree with that of the figure.

Use anchor names that are short yet unique. They should be descriptive and pertain to the contents of the frame. Be sure to take note of the name that you assign; you'll need it later to reference the frame.

INSERTING ANCHORS

Once you've created an anchor name for your frame, you next create an anchor in text that's linked to the frame. (You can reverse the order of these first two procedures if you wish.)

When you create the anchor, you use a dialog box to specify where the anchored frame should be placed with respect to its corresponding anchor in text. You can have the frame placed in one of three relative locations: below or above the line of text with the anchor, or with version 2.0, automatically at the anchor itself. Or you can have it placed in a fixed location: always in the same position that it occupies on the page, as long as it's on the same page as the anchor in text.

! New for version 2.0

You can now anchor frames automatically at the anchor itself, and such frames will stay with the text even as you edit. You do not have to use the re-anchoring procedure with such frames. You may wish to use small frames like this to hold symbols or characters, specially created and imported with the File menu's Load Text & Picture.

Here, then, are the steps for creating an anchor in text and specifying the frame's location with respect to it:

1. Activate Text mode and click the spot in text where you wish to place the anchor. Usually this would be immediately after a reference made to the picture, such as *See Figure 1.*
2. Drop the Edit menu and select Insert Special Item. Or use the keyboard shortcut, Ctrl-C.
3. From the Special Item dialog box, click Frame Anchor or press F5. The dialog box in Figure 6.24 appears.
4. Enter the reference name of the frame you wish to anchor. Make sure that you spell the name exactly as the one you assigned to the frame.
5. Select one of the buttons to specify the frame's location and give the OK.

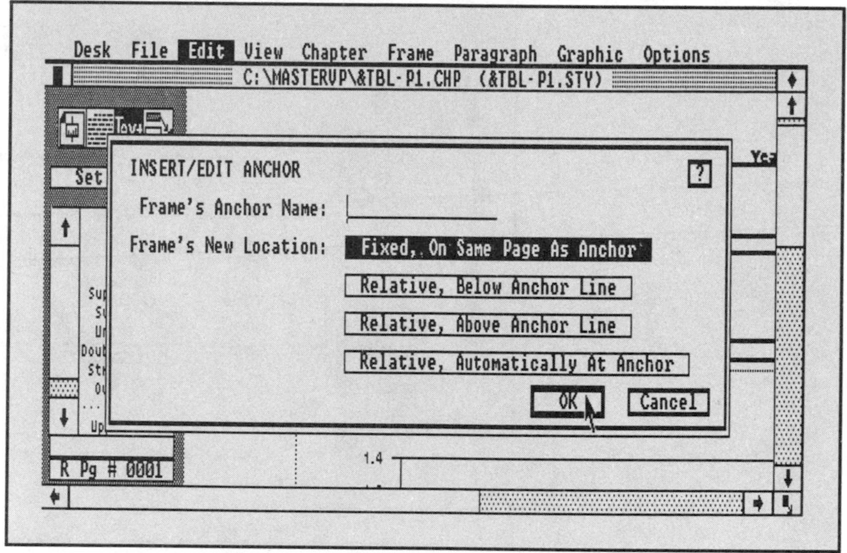

Figure 6.24: The Edit menu's Insert/Edit Anchor dialog box

> * You won't be able to see anchors in text if the Options menu is set to Hide Tabs & Returns. However, the anchors will still operate as they do when showing. See Appendix A.

To indicate an anchor in text, Ventura uses a small circle, like the degree symbol (°). These symbols will not appear in the printed version of your documents.

If you move the text cursor so that this symbol is immediately to its right, the symbol is selected, and the word *Anchor* appears in the Current box. Pressing the Del key at this point would delete the anchor.

The command you use to edit anchors is similar to the one you use to create them. Just select the anchor in text, and issue the Edit menu's Edit Special Item command. Or use the keyboard shortcut, Ctrl-D. Then make adjustments in the dialog box that appears.

RE-ANCHORING FRAMES

Once you've given anchor names to frames and placed their corresponding anchors in text, you can properly reposition the frames whenever it's necessary. This process, called *re-anchoring,* is not necessary for anchors with the Relative, Automatically At Anchor setting.

Use the Chapter menu and select Re-Anchor Frames. The atypical dialog box shown in Figure 6.25 appears. Respond by indicating whether you want to re-anchor all the frames or just those on the page you're working with, and the re-anchoring process will begin.

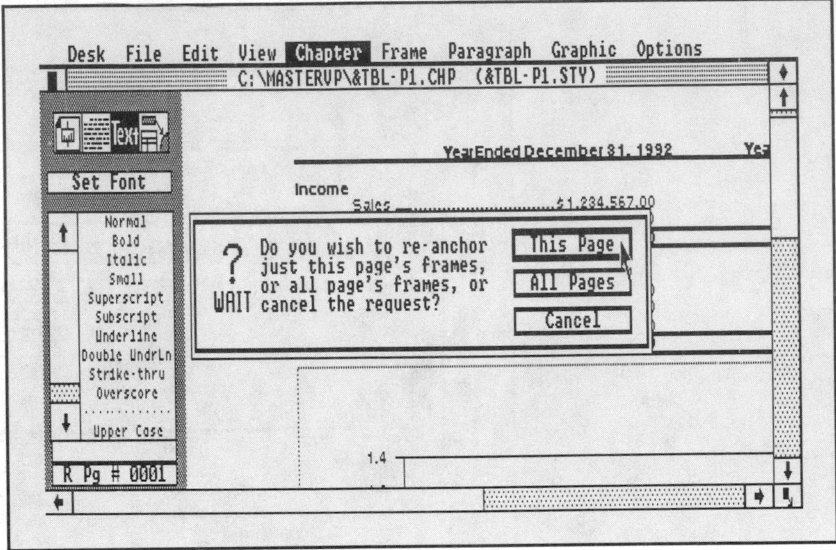

Figure 6.25: The dialog box displayed by the Chapter menu's Re-Anchor Frames command

Once Ventura finishes re-anchoring, you should check the results. Frames will be placed on the correct page, but you may need to do some manual fine-tuning of the positioning. For instance, re-anchored frames may overlap each other, or Ventura may place a frame in a margin. So be sure to check the entire document after re-anchoring and before printing.

SAVING THE SAMPLE CHAPTER

- Use the File menu's Save command, or press Ctrl-S to save your working copy of the table chapter, &TBL-P1.CHP.

Ventura Publisher has a variety of graphics capabilities you can use to enhance pictures you import from other programs. For instance, we can improve the legends that appear with our sample graph by assigning them better fonts. We can also add arrows to point at salient features, along with accompanying descriptions. In the next chapter, we'll put these graphics tools to work by using them to improve the look of our chart. We'll also see how you can use Ventura to draw circles, lines, and rounded boxes.

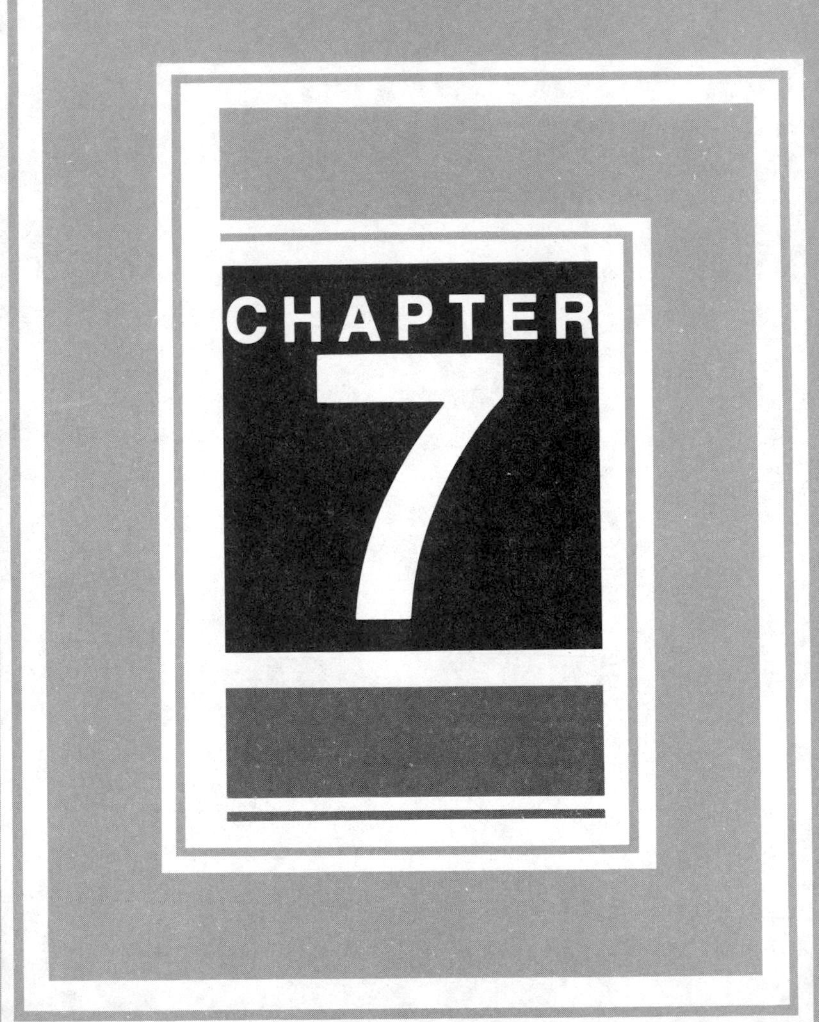
CHAPTER
7

Lines, Circles, and Boxes

Fast Track

To create lines, circles, and boxes 257

you can use paragraph tags, frames, or Graphics mode.

To create column rules and other vertical lines 259

select the Frame menu's Vertical Rules. Use Inter-Col Rules to create rules between columns. Use Rule 1 and Rule 2 to create rules measured for the left edge of the page.

To create horizontal lines for frames 263

in Frame mode, select the frame and use the Frame menu. Choose Ruling Line Above or Below. Select a width setting and provide a height (thickness). Frame rules appear within the frame. You can have up to three rules above or below. You can also have dashed lines.

To create horizontal rules for paragraph tags 268

in Paragraph mode, select the paragraph and drop the Paragraph menu. Click Ruling Line Above or Below. The available lines are like those for frames, but with a greater variety of widths. All similarly tagged paragraphs will receive the same treatment.

To extend underline 272

and other types of text lines when they appear in a paragraph, select a sample paragraph in Paragraph mode. Then use the Paragraph menu's Attribute Overrides. Set Line Width to Margin-Wide.

To create boxes for frames and paragraphs 272

activate their respective mode and menu, and select Ruling Box Around. The settings are similar to those for lines. You can use the Box feature to create a vertical line for paragraphs.

To create a box character in text 274

position the text cursor and use the Edit menu's Ins Special Item (or press Ctrl-C). Then click Box Char (or press F1). You can specify hollow or filled box characters.

To turn on the graphics grid 276

use the Graphic menu's Grid Settings. Graphics you create or move will snap to the grid.

To draw a Ventura graphic 277

activate Graphics mode and click the appropriate icon on the Side-bar. Then position the mouse at one corner for the graphic, drag the mouse to the opposite corner, and release.

To constrain graphics 277

hold the Alt key as you draw. This creates only squares, circles, and lines in increments of 45 degrees.

To change a graphics line or outline 281

use the Graphic menu's Line Attributes or press Ctrl-L. To change the interior space of a graphic, use the Graphic menu's Fill Attributes or press Ctrl-F.

To create Box text 285

use the Box-text icon to draw. Then you can enter text into the box. Ventura stores the text in the chapter's CAP file. You can use Box text to add labels to an imported picture.

To select multiple graphics 287

hold down the Shift key as you select. To select all graphics, use the Graphic menu's Select All (or Ctrl-Q). To reorder a pile of graphics, use the Graphic menu's Send To Back (or Ctrl-Z) or the Graphic menu's Bring To Front (or Ctrl-A).

CHAPTER 7

LOOK AT ALMOST ANY PROFESSIONALLY PUBLISHED document and you're bound to see that it uses straight lines in some fashion. Such lines, also called *rules* or *ruling lines,* are a vital layout tool. For instance, the judicious use of lines can group related newspaper articles so they appear to be associated. Conversely, lines can separate items so that they are distinct on the page. You may see lines below or above titles, or between columns. In addition, the thickness, length, and placement of lines can contribute to the style of a document. Lines can also communicate ideas, indicating a flow of information, as they do with some diagrams. Certain publishing applications call for lines connected to form boxes, or curved to form circles.

As we've seen, Ventura can import line art created with a variety of software. Graphics software is one way for you to create the lines you need. Sometimes, however, the imported graphic appears unfinished or stylistically ill-suited to your document; it needs to be touched up. In addition, it would be impractical to import lines for every need, such as when you want to associate lines with specific tagged paragraphs.

Fortunately, Ventura has the capability of creating its own graphics. Thus you can add lines, circles, and boxes to a document without using an external graphics package. The graphics you create with Ventura can stand on their own, or you can use them to enhance graphics that you import into your documents.

Ventura is very clever in the way it combines imported graphics and its own graphics. To display a graphic, it utilizes the original graphics file directly. Any enhancements you provide stay with the Ventura document and, although they affect the look of the file in the Ventura document, they do not alter the graphics file. Thus, the original remains fully functional; you can then use the original in a different application altogether, or you can use your graphics software to make changes in it as necessary. Any changes you make will be automatically reflected in your Ventura file.

By combining graphics files with the lines, circles, and boxes that Ventura draws, you can achieve just the right graphic look for your document. With the right fonts, the result is a document that's visually inviting and cohesive.

In Chapter 6, you created a working copy of Ventura's sample table, &TBL-P1.CHP, in the MASTERVP directory. To load this chapter now so you can try your hand at making the suggested enhancements as you study the techniques in this chapter:

1. Load Ventura.
2. Drop the File menu and select Open Chapter.
3. Change to the MASTERVP subdirectory and select the &TBL-P1.CHP chapter. (If you renamed it in Chapter 6, then select the name you assigned.)

FOUR METHODS OF CREATING GRAPHIC ELEMENTS

When we worked with fonts, you saw that Ventura provides several ways to set font attributes. Similarly, it provides you with four basic methods of drawing its graphic elements:

- In conjunction with paragraph tags, you can draw straight lines horizontally and you can create boxes.
- In conjunction with a frame, you can draw straight lines horizontally or vertically and create boxes.
- You can extend text lines (such as underline and overscore) and you can create box characters in conjunction with text.
- You can use Graphics mode to draw in a more free-form manner. You can draw lines horizontally or vertically, at any angle, boxed or curved.

The first two techniques are similar in operation. Therefore, we'll study them together. Then we'll examine how to extend lines and create box characters in Text mode. Later in the chapter, we'll see how you can use the fourth method, Ventura's Graphics mode, to create free-form graphics.

Your choice of method is important, as it affects the subsequent line. Your choice can affect the line's relationship to elements on the page, the ease with which you create the line, and the speed with which the line adapts to changes you make in the document.

The paragraph tagging method works with paragraphs—that is, any unit of text ending with a return. The paragraph tagging method is useful for adding lines to callouts or headlines, for instance. If you use the paragraph method, all paragraphs that you've tagged similarly will receive the same lines. Thus, if you use this method to add lines to chapter headings, all of your chapter headings will automatically have similar lines. Note that Ventura is not designed to create vertical lines with the paragraph method. However, you can trick the program into creating such lines, as we'll see when we study boxes.

With Frame mode, you can create horizontal or vertical lines. The resulting lines are associated with the frame you've selected. For this reason, Frame mode is useful with elements that are larger than paragraph size. Frames can, in fact, hold several paragraphs, and, of course, when you import graphics, Ventura assigns them to frames as well. As you use this technique, though, remember that the underlying-page frame is also a type of frame, and you can assign graphics to it as well. We will examine the underlying-page frame more closely in Chapter 9.

! New for version 2.0

With the third method, Ventura now allows you to extend horizontal lines that are tied to your text. This ability makes it easier to underline table headings, for instance. You can now also embed a box character in text, which is useful for check boxes.

The fourth technique, which uses Graphics mode, provides more flexibility with the shape of graphic elements than either of the other two methods.

! New for version 2.0

Version 2.0 makes Ventura's graphics capabilities easier to use. Version 2.0 lets you select a graphic without first selecting its associated frame, reducing time spent switching from mode to mode. Also, when you now tie a graphic to the underlying-page frame, it appears only on the current page, unless you use the new Graphic menu command, Show On All Pages. Version 2.0 also lets you add, move, and resize frames, and access the Frame menu when in Graphics mode.

Let's begin our look at lines by studying vertical lines. As mentioned, Frame mode is the primary means of creating vertical lines.

COLUMN RULES AND OTHER VERTICAL LINES

In Frame mode, you can create vertical lines that are associated with any frame. This includes the underlying-page frame. When you create lines for the underlying-page frame, the settings you specify appear repeatedly on similar pages.

Ventura provides two methods of creating vertical lines directly associated with a frame. First, you can create *intercolumn rules.* These are lines that appear between columns of text. This application is perhaps the most common use for vertical lines. Adding lines between columns can give a more structured, formal feeling to a document. Sometimes it makes the text more readable as well.

Second, Ventura allows you to insert one or two freely placed vertical lines anywhere on the page. Regardless of the frame you use, you position these lines with respect to the underlying page. You might use these to create a wide line along the left edge of letterhead stationery.

LINES BETWEEN COLUMNS

To create lines between columns, first decide which frame you want to use for the rules. Then follow these steps to display the dialog box that appears in Figure 7.1:

1. Activate Frame mode and select the appropriate frame.
2. Establish columns for the frame using the Frame menu's Margins & Columns command (see Chapter 2).
3. Drop the Frame menu.
4. Click Vertical Rules.

Once you have selected the appropriate frame and displayed the dialog box for Vertical Rules, you can create your lines. If you've used the Chapter menu's Page Size & Layout command to set up double-sided pages for the document, first consider Settings For. Click Left Page or Right Page to display the settings for these respective pages. Once you've established the settings for one side, you can

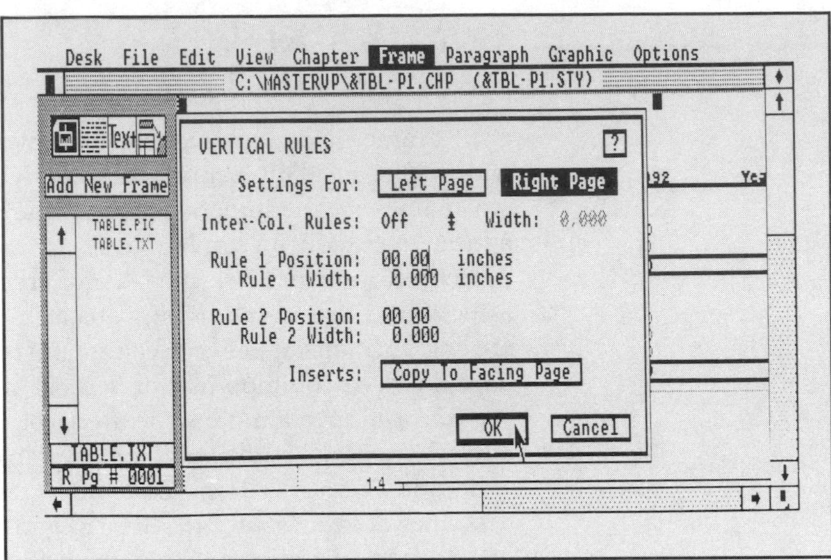

Figure 7.1: The dialog box for the Frame menu's Vertical Rules command

Be careful which frame you select for the column rule. Suppose, for example, that you set up a two-column format for the underlying-page frame of a newsletter. Next, you create two long frames in each column, because you want each to hold a different text file. To add intercolumn rules between the two articles, select the underlying-page frame, since that's the frame with the two-column format. Don't make the mistake of using one of the two smaller frames.

duplicate them for the other side, if desired. Just click the button labeled

Copy To Facing Page

at the bottom of the dialog box, and Ventura transfers your settings to the opposite page.

Next, look at the Inter-Col Rules line. Here you indicate that you want vertical lines to appear between columns within the selected frame. Select the appropriate setting, On or Off, to turn the column lines on or off. If you click On, indicate the width you'd like for the line. (If Off is selected, the Width setting has no effect, whether or not a value appears within it.) Ventura shows the values that appear here in terms of the units used for Rule 1 Width. To change the system of measurement for the width of intercolumn rules (from inches to fractional points, for instance) click the unit name that appears for Rule 1 Width. For greatest precision, you may want to use fractional points.

Note that the width of your gutters, as specified with the Frame menu's Margins & Columns command, will restrict the width of the intercolumn rule. Thus to widen an intercolumn rule, you may need to widen the gutter.

VERTICAL PAGE BARS

Use the Rule 1 and Rule 2 settings to create what we'll call *vertical page bars*. Note that the values you enter into these settings have no effect whatsoever on intercolumn rules.

Vertical page bars are rather odd creatures. It's hard to know why for sure, but Ventura makes these lines operate in an unusual manner. Here are the points to bear in mind when you work with vertical page bars.

- You can create only one or two vertical page bars.
- The measurements you provide always position the bar from the left edge of the page. This is true even when you create the bar by using a frame smaller than the full page. Thus, as you move such a frame around on the page, the bar remains stationary relative to the page as it shows through the frame.
- Column-wide text does not automatically flow around these bars. To make the text do so, you must use the Frame menu's Margins & Columns command and provide a text-free margin for the bar. Otherwise, the bar will cover any text it encounters, hiding the text from the reader's view.
- There is no way to directly indicate the length of the bars themselves. They extend all the way from the top margin of the selected frame to its bottom margin.

Because of the peculiar way in which these lines operate with regard to smaller frames, it is wise to confine their use to the underlying-page frame.

Figure 7.2 shows a vertical page bar in use. This figure is an enhanced version of the table we worked with in the last chapter.

The vertical page bar shows along the left edge of the page. This enhancement serves to tie elements of the page together. As a result, the table and its accompanying chart seem to belong together and appear less disjointed. Notice that we used the same width for the vertical rule as that of the existing horizontal rule along the top. This choice serves to further unify the elements on the page.

As mentioned, sometimes a vertical page bar will cover existing text. Specifically, the bar will cover column-wide paragraphs, but not frame-wide ones. To change this setting for a given tag, activate

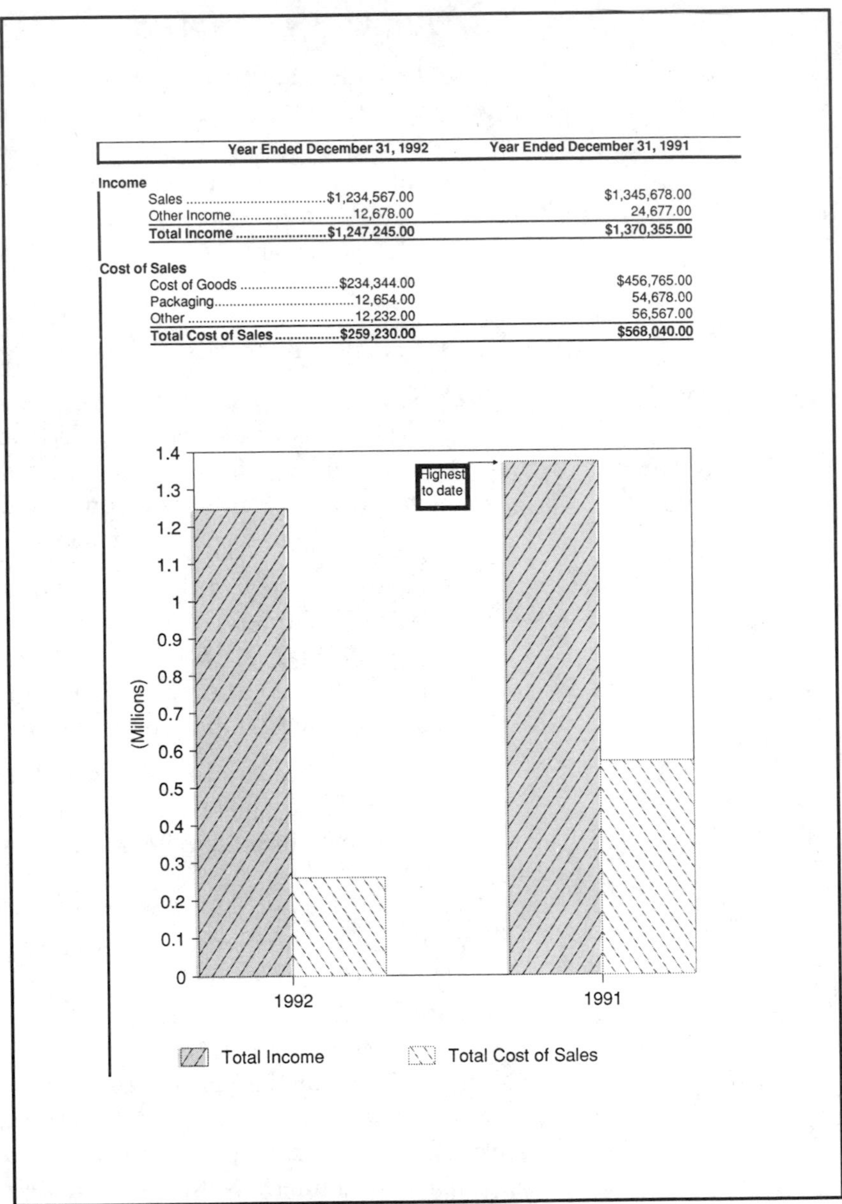

	Year Ended December 31, 1992	Year Ended December 31, 1991
Income		
Sales	$1,234,567.00	$1,345,678.00
Other Income	12,678.00	24,677.00
Total Income	**$1,247,245.00**	**$1,370,355.00**
Cost of Sales		
Cost of Goods	$234,344.00	$456,765.00
Packaging	12,654.00	54,678.00
Other	12,232.00	56,567.00
Total Cost of Sales	**$259,230.00**	**$568,040.00**

Figure 7.2: A chart enhanced with line graphics

Paragraph mode, select a sample paragraph, drop the Paragraph menu, and click Alignment. Use the Overall Width setting to make the adjustment.

Don't forget that the vertical lines you create are associated with the frame that's selected when you use the Frame menu's Vertical Rules command. Thus, they'll always be associated with that frame, no matter where you position it. You can also create horizontal lines that stay with the frame they're a part of; we'll look at these next.

HORIZONTAL LINES

Ventura allows you to create horizontal rules that are positioned with respect to either frames or paragraphs. When you do, the lines stay with the frame or paragraph to which you've assigned them, regardless of where you move the frame or paragraph. In addition, should you widen or narrow the frame or paragraph, associated horizontal lines can be made to adjust automatically.

You can also extend horizontal lines in text, such as underline and strike-thru. The effect is assigned by the tag.

First let's see how horizontal ruling lines work with frames.

HORIZONTAL LINES FOR FRAMES

When you create horizontal lines in conjunction with frames, you can position them at the top or bottom of the frame. One typical use is in creating lines that set off pictures from text. You could also use horizontal lines to separate one newspaper article, contained within a frame, from the articles above or below it.

RULES AT THE TOP OF A FRAME To study horizontal frame lines, let's begin at the top. You can make rules appear at the top of any given frame by using the dialog box shown in Figure 7.3. Follow these steps to display the dialog box:

1. Activate Frame mode and select the frame or frames for which you want lines at the top.
2. Drop the Frame menu.
3. Click Ruling Line Above.

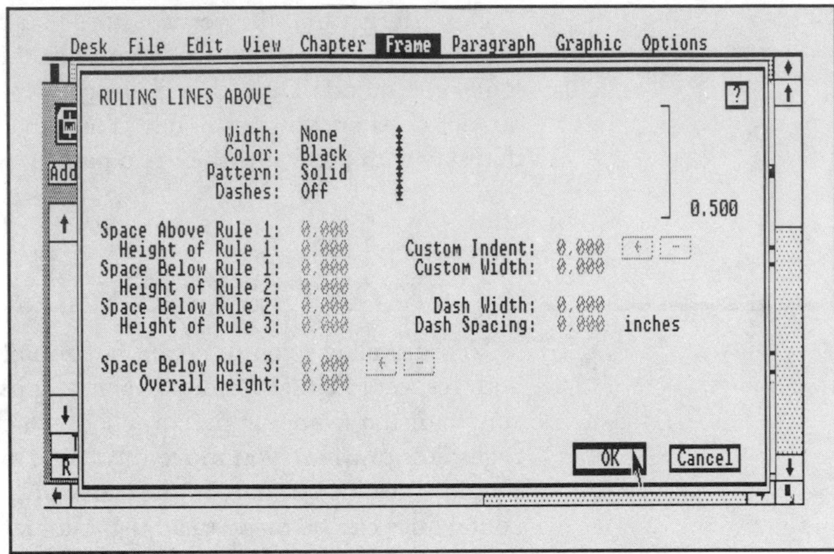

Figure 7.3: The dialog box for creating rules at the top of a frame

The name for this dialog box, Ruling Lines Above, is actually misleading. The name implies that ruling lines will appear above the frame in question. This is not the case. A frame's ruling lines actually appear *within* the frame. Thus, a more appropriate name for this dialog box might instead be Ruling Lines At Top. When we look at paragraphs shortly, you'll see that ruling lines for paragraphs can be made to appear above the selected paragraph using Paragraph mode. Since this latter procedure uses this same dialog box, the box's name is appropriate for paragraph tagging.

To create a ruling line at the top of a frame, set the first category of the dialog box, Width, to Frame. To remove existing ruling lines, use None. Notice that these two settings are the only ones available for Width. The other four choices are not used for frames; they are used only for horizontal lines you create in Paragraph mode.

> * You can change the colors that Ventura has available for your use. See Chapter 5.

Next, look at the Color category. Normally, Black is selected. If you have a color printer, or if you plan to create color separations, you can make use of the other boxes to color your ruling lines. With some printers, you can use the White setting. For white to appear, though, it must be against a dark background, usually black. You create such a background for the same frame using the Frame menu's Frame Background command.

Next, you can choose a pattern for the ruling line. The chart we've created in Figure 7.4 shows the patterns that Ventura provides. Once you've indicated the height (that is, the thickness) of the ruling line, the pattern you've selected will appear in the dialog box. Thus you can try out various patterns to see which you like. Ventura makes these patterns available for a variety of lines and boxes, including frame backgrounds.

Use the next group of settings to specify the thickness of your ruling lines and the amount of space between them. Figure 7.5 shows how these settings determine the spacing for ruling lines. (This figure also contains an example of spacing for boxes, which we'll look at in more detail later in the chapter.) Note that with the dialog box for Ruling Lines Above, the last setting, Space Below Rule 3, does not apply. (This setting does apply when the dialog box is used elsewhere, such as with Ruling Lines Below.) Don't make the mistake of thinking that this space will be the distance before the text in the frame appears. Text and pictures in a frame are completely independent of the ruling lines. To keep collisions from occurring, you must use the Frame menu's Margins & Columns command and create adequate text margins to hold the rules. The ruling lines will then rest within those margins and not interfere with the text.

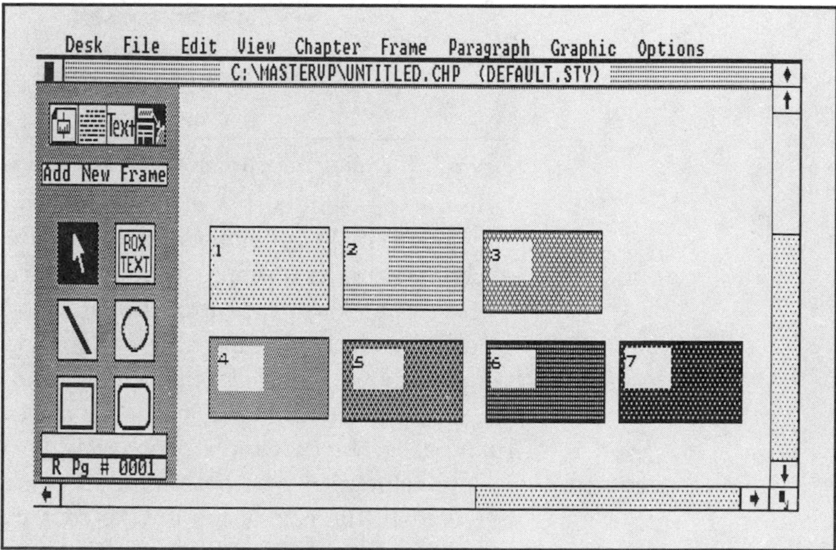

Figure 7.4: Patterns available for ruling lines and other formats

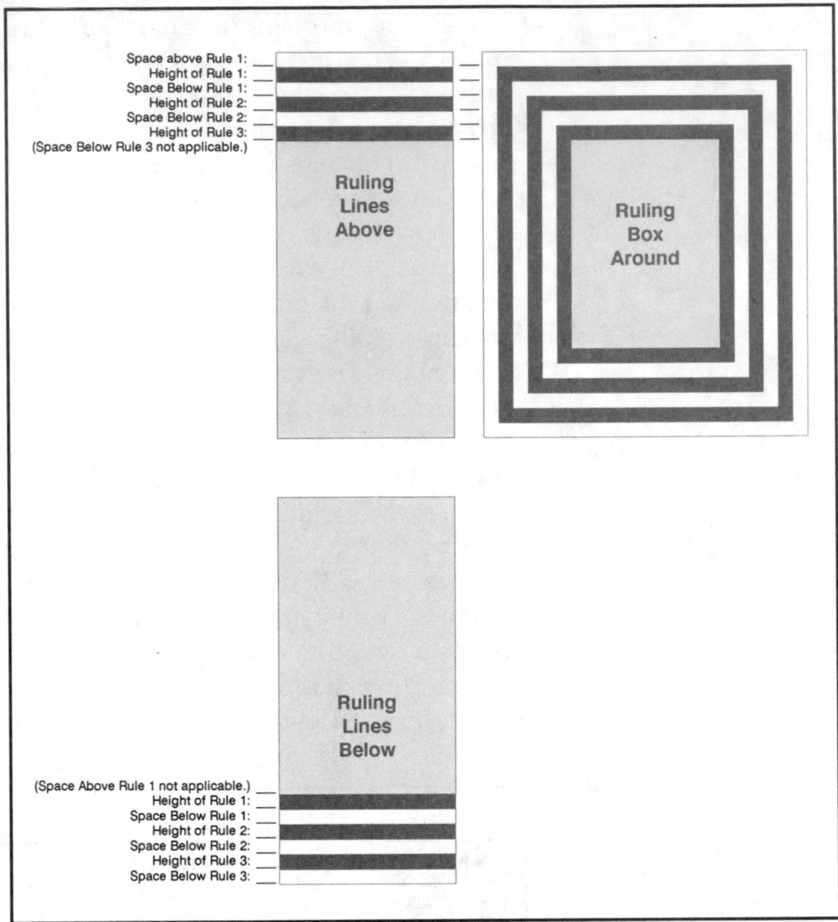

Figure 7.5: Ruling measurements for frames

In the top-right corner of the dialog box there is a bracketed area. As you specify heights (thicknesses) for the rules, you'll see blown-up thickness samples of the first 0.5 inch of ruling lines within this area. These samples will appear in the same color and pattern that you've specified with the settings above them. Be aware, however, that the samples shown are *double* the thickness of their true counterparts in the actual frame. That is, although the bracket displays 0.5 inch of ruling area, the bracket is 1 inch long.

The value displayed before the measurement unit is always equal to 0.5 inch, the size of the bracketed area. You cannot change this value. You can, however, change the measurement units in which it is expressed, as we'll see shortly.

Be careful with regard to the 0.5-inch limit of this display. If you've specified heights and spacing totaling more than 0.5 inch, you won't see samples for the area beyond the 0.5-inch bracket. However, your settings will still take effect and display the rules you've specified in the frame.

If you're uncertain about the amount of space your rules occupy, you can see a measurement of their total area by checking the Overall Height setting at the bottom of the dialog box. Note that you cannot enter a value directly into this setting. It is simply a display that provides you with a sum of the values above it.

Farther down the right side of the dialog box, we see settings concerned with dashes. Ruling lines are normally unbroken. However, you can create rules made up of dashes (often called "dotted lines"). Broken lines are useful for such applications as lines around coupons. To create dashes, change Dashes to On. You can then enter values into the two Dash settings. Use them to specify the width of a dash and the amount of space between it and the next dash.

The notation for picas and points can be confusing if you are used to working with different units. For example, in centimeters or inches, 5.1 is very close to 5.0—just one-tenth of a unit greater. 5,1 picas & points, however, is interpreted by Ventura as 5 picas, 10 points. Since there are 12 picas to a point, this is closer to 6 picas than to 5. To specify 5 picas and 1 point, you would use 5,01 picas and points. Be sure you understand the picas-and-points system before working with these units, or be willing to experiment.

On the right, opposite Dash Spacing, is a unit indicating the system of measurement that Ventura is using to display values in this dialog box. Initially, it uses inches. If you wish to change the system of measurement (to centimeters, picas and points, or fractional points), successively click this name until the desired units appears. If you want to use picas and points as your system of measurement, remember that 12 points make up 1 pica and that approximately 6 picas make up 1 inch. Thus, 5 picas and 12 points (written as *5,12*, with a comma between the pica and point quantities) is the same as 6 picas (6,00), which is the same as 1 inch.

This completes our look at the dialog box for Ruling Lines Above. As we turn to the box for Ruling Lines Below, you'll see that it's quite similar to this box.

RULES AT THE BOTTOM OF A FRAME Creating ruling lines at the bottom of a frame is similar to the process for creating them at the top. To specify rules for the bottom of a frame, display the dialog box for Ruling Lines Below with these steps:

1. Activate Frame mode and select the appropriate frame(s).
2. Drop the Frame menu and click Ruling Line Below.

When you do this, a dialog box very similar to the one for Ruling Lines Above will appear. The only difference, in fact, lies in the name at the top of the box, with *Below* replacing *Above.*

Note that, just like the Above box, this dialog box is misnamed. The ruling lines do not appear below the frame; rather, they appear within the frame, but at the bottom of it.

Here are some additional points to remember with regard to ruling lines at the bottom of a frame. In the dialog box for Ruling Lines Below, the setting for Space Above Rule 1 has no effect. Remember, text or graphics that appear within the box (and hence above these rules) are not controlled by the rules. These elements are controlled by the Frame menu's Margins & Columns command. Thus, there is nothing regulated above Rule 1 from which the rule can be spaced.

On the other hand, Space Below Rule 3 does have an effect. As you can see in Figure 7.5, it governs the distance between the third rule and the bottom edge of the frame. Be aware that if the frame does not have three rules, this value controls whichever rule is last in the frame. In other words, it controls rule 2 if there are 2 rules, rule 1 if there's only 1 rule.

In addition, you can use the small Plus (+) and Minus (–) buttons that appear to the right of the value for Space Below Rule 3. These buttons regulate the vertical placement of the last rule with regard to the frame. Normally, the Plus button is selected, resulting in ruling lines placed within the frame. By using the Minus button, the ruling lines can be made to appear below the frame. This feature is put to best use by creating reverse text in Paragraph mode, as you'll see in Chapter 12.

Otherwise, the regulations for ruling lines at the bottom of a frame follow those for rules at the top. Use the earlier discussion of the dialog box to set rules at the bottom of a frame.

HORIZONTAL PARAGRAPH RULES

The same dialog box that appears for the Frame menu's Ruling Line Above and Ruling Line Below commands also appears when you set the ruling lines for a paragraph tag. In many ways, it operates in the same fashion. There are, however, some key ways in which paragraph rules differ from frame rules:

- Paragraph rules work with paragraphs. As such they are usually best used when your application contains a small amount of text, or even none at all.
- You set paragraph rules with tags. Thus, they affect all paragraphs tagged with the same tag. By contrast, what you do to one frame will not affect other frames, except when you're working with the underlying-page frame.
- Unlike frames, paragraph rules above and below are, indeed, above and below the paragraph. They do not normally cover the text. With paragraph rules, there is no need to set aside margins for text as you must with frames.
- You can set paragraph rules for a variety of horizontal widths, independent of the paragraph. The widths of frame rules are controlled by the width of the frame.

The sample style sheets provided with Ventura use horizontal paragraph rules for many effects. Table 7.1 shows some of the style sheets that include tags with horizontal ruling lines. You can compare them by loading a sample chapter or checking Appendix B.

Notice that this table lists a variety of widths for the sample tags. To set a ruling-line tag, begin by following these steps to display the dialog box for Ruling Lines Above or Below (Figure 7.6).

1. Activate Paragraph mode and select a sample paragraph.
2. Drop the Paragraph menu.
3. Click Ruling Line Above or Below, as appropriate.

Although the dialog box that appears looks almost identical to the box Frame mode uses, there is an important difference. The Width category for the Paragraph version has four additional settings available for your use: Text, Margin, Column, and Custom. These four buttons ghost in the Frame version.

Table 7.1: Sample Style Sheets with Ruling Line Tags

STYLE (.STY) AND CHAPTER (.CHP)	TAG	RULING LINE	WIDTH
&BOOK-P1	Chapter #	Above	Margin
		Below	Margin
&BOOK-P2	Major heading	Below	Column
&BRO-L2	Title	Above	Column
		Below	Column
	Setting	Below	Text
&BRO-P3*	Table header	Below	Margin
&INV-P1	Address	Above	Margin
	Invoice**	Above	Margin
	Column heads	Below	Margin
	Total	Above	Margin
&LSTG-P2	Category	Below	Column
<R1-P1	Name	Below	Frame
&MAG-P3	Lift	Above	Frame
		Below	Frame

* Table item heading was made with the Underline text attribute.
** This tag uses Pattern 1. It has a negative value for Space Below Rule 3 that's equal to the height of Rule 1. More on this in Chapter 12.

Select Text if you want the ruling line to be the same width as the text in the paragraph. If lines of the tagged paragraph are of varying lengths, Ventura uses the length of the line closest to the rule to determine its length. That is, if you're using Ruling Lines Above, the program will use the paragraph's first line of text to determine the width of the rule. If you're using Ruling Lines Below, it uses the last line of

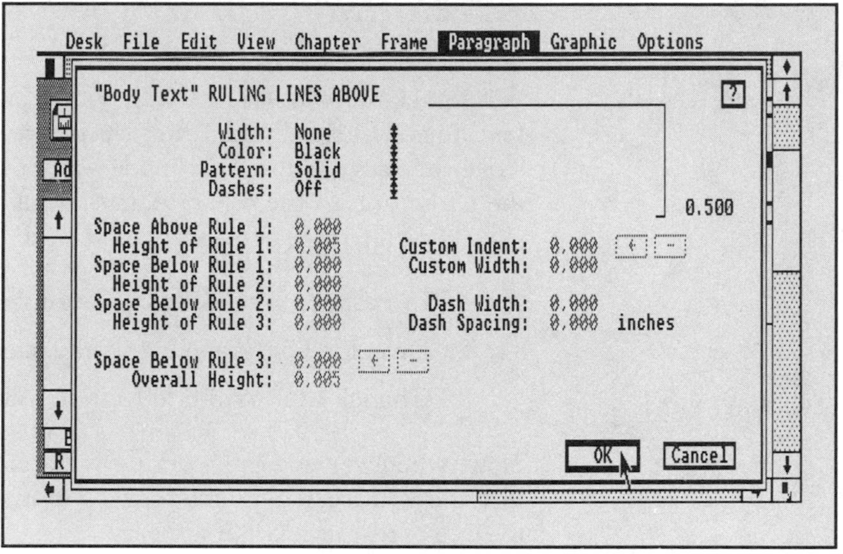

Figure 7.6: The Paragraph menu's Ruling Lines Above dialog box

text. For an example of how this looks, observe the Setting tag in the &BRO-L2 sample chapter and style sheet.

Set Width to Margin if you want the program to set the rule according to the paragraph's In From Left and In From Right settings. (These settings appear in the Paragraph menu's Spacing dialog box.) The rule will begin at the paragraph's In From Left position and end at its In From Right position.

The next two settings, Column and Frame, seem to indicate that the makers of Ventura originally hoped to provide flexibility with regard to placement of ruling lines when such placement differs from the paragraph's alignment. However, at this writing a little experimentation reveals that the program ignores these settings. Instead, it takes its cues for the width of ruling lines from the Paragraph menu's Alignment dialog box, using the Overall Width setting as the determining factor.

The last button, Custom, allows you to create paragraph rules with a great deal of flexibility. Once you choose Custom, you must provide a Custom Width in order for the line to appear. Optionally, you can provide a Custom Indent, which determines how far from the left edge of the paragraph the left end of the line begins. By clicking the Minus button to the right of Custom Indent, you create an outdented line—one that protrudes beyond the left edge of the paragraph.

EXTENDING UNDERLINE AND OTHER TEXT LINES

New for version 2.0

A final kind of line is new with Ventura 2.0. You can now extend text lines—that is, underline, overscore, double underline, and strike-thru assigned in Text mode—automatically from one edge of the paragraph to the other. A tag setting stores this attribute. To assign this attribute to a paragraph tag, follow these steps:

1. In Paragraph mode, click a sample paragraph.
2. Drop the Paragraph menu and click Attribute Overrides.
3. Change Line Width to Margin-Wide and give the OK.

Now, whenever you are working with text in that paragraph, any text line you create—no matter how short—will extend clear across the line of text in which it appears.

This new feature is handy to use when you create headings for tables. Previously, you had to create a separate tag just for the headings, or you had to carefully underline the headings in Text mode. Now, once you assign this tag attribute, just underline any heading; the entire row of headings will become underlined.

CREATING BOXES

In much the same way that you create ruling lines, you can create ruling boxes. Except for the name—Ruling Box Around—the dialog box you use is identical to the one used for ruling lines.

BOXES FOR FRAMES AND PARAGRAPHS

You can make ruling boxes for frames or for paragraphs. Typically, you might place frame boxes around pictures to set them off from text. You might use a paragraph box around a *liftout* in a magazine article. (A liftout is an important paragraph or sentence that's copied from the text and set in a larger type. Its purpose is usually to draw readers' attention and to interest them in the article.) The sample document &MAG-P3 uses a liftout (the Lift tag) but sets it off with ruling lines above and below, an alternative method.

Ruling boxes follow the same regulations as Ruling Lines Above. Look back at Figure 7.5 and notice how ruling boxes for frames use the same settings as Ruling Lines Above.

Ruling boxes around paragraphs are generally used for short amounts of text only, such as a heading. If you use them for long paragraphs, be careful with paragraphs that start in one column and continue in the next. Ventura will only place a box around the first part of the paragraph. It will ignore the second half of the paragraph at the top of the next column. To prevent a boxed paragraph from straddling columns in this fashion, drop the Paragraph menu and click Breaks. Set Allow Within to No, causing the entire paragraph to move to the next column rather than allowing it to break within.

For the same reason, ruling boxes around paragraphs must not be interrupted with an overlaid frame—one containing a picture, for example. However, not allowing a break within will not prevent this from happening. If a frame interrupts such a paragraph box, you must reposition the frame manually.

CREATING VERTICAL RULES WITH THE BOX FEATURE

As we mentioned, you can use the Ruling Box Around feature to create a vertical line that's associated with a paragraph. A typical use for such a line is in creating a *change bar.* Some editors use change bars to flag material that they have altered in some way. The change bar is placed to the left of any paragraph that's been revised since the previous version of a document. The sample chapter and style sheet &BOOK-P1 has a tag labeled Change Bar with this feature in place (see Appendix B).

To create a change bar, proceed as follows:

1. In Paragraph mode, select a paragraph for which you want to create a change bar.
2. Click Add New Tag on the Side-bar. Make up a name for the new tag (Change Bar, for example) and give the OK.
3. Drop the Paragraph menu and click Ruling Box Around. Specify a Custom Width for the rule and give *the same value* for Height of Rule 1.

Thus, the sample change bar has a custom width of 1.98 fractional points, and a height of 1.98 as well. Since the width of the box is the same as the thickness of its rules, all you see is the box's left and right rules, superimposed. Any paragraph you format with such a Change Bar tag will have a line along its left edge that extends the length of the paragraph.

Be aware that the same restrictions that apply to boxes apply to change bars. For the tag, use the Paragraph menu's Breaks and set Allow Within to No.

CREATING A BOX CHARACTER

! New for version 2.0

A final kind of box is new with Ventura 2.0. You can now create two kinds of box characters, hollow (□) or solid (■), directly in your text. Hollow boxes are handy for creating checklists. Some people use solid boxes as a kind of bullet to set off items in a list.

To create a box character:

When you select a solid box character, it will turn white and seem to disappear. However, it is still present and selected. Perform any procedure you want on it as usual.

1. In Text mode, position the text cursor at the spot where you want the box character to appear.
2. Use the Edit menu to select Ins Special Item, or use the keyboard shortcut, Ctrl-C.
3. Click Box Char or press F1.
4. In the dialog box that appears, click Hollow (or press the Enter key), or click Filled to indicate the kind of box character you desire.

Ventura will enter your box character into the text. These characters perform just like other characters. That is, they move as you edit text, they can be cut, copied, and pasted in Text mode, and so on.

USING BUILT-IN GRAPHICS

So far, you've seen how to create lines and boxes in a structured format that relates directly to frames and paragraphs. With Ventura, you can also create lines and boxes, as well as other shapes, in a more free-form fashion. You gain this additional flexibility by using Graphics mode.

With Graphics mode you can create boxes, lines, circles, ovals, and arrows. You can even create round-edged boxes.

The shapes you create can come in a variety of sizes. You can vary thicknesses and fill patterns, too. What's more, by combining these shapes and masking parts of them, you can create a greater variety of forms.

Don't overestimate these graphics capabilities, though. Ventura's graphics are not a substitute for a complete graphics package, any more than its ability to edit text is a substitute for a full-fledged word processor. However, Graphics mode may allow you to create just the shapes that your documents need.

You can also use Graphics mode to spruce up graphics that you import into Ventura. That way, your text and graphics may blend better on the page. They'll look like they belong together, rather than having a patchwork-quilt appearance of input from various sources.

ACTIVATING GRAPHICS MODE

The process of drawing a graphic is fairly straightforward:

1. Activate Graphics mode.
2. Draw the graphic and set its characteristics.

Activate Graphics mode using one of these three methods. All three methods are equivalent; use the one with which you feel most comfortable.

- Drop the View menu and click Graphic Drawing; or
- click the rightmost button in the Mode Selector of the Side-bar; or
- type Ctrl-P.

Once you've activated Graphics mode, you see the Side-bar change to the format shown in Figure 7.7. The standard Assignment list that is usually on the Side-bar disappears, and six icons replace it.

The first icon, with the arrow, is different from the other five. This is the graphics-selection icon. You use it to select a shape you've previously created with one of the other five icons. Like frames, selected graphics are indicated with handles. Don't make the mistake of

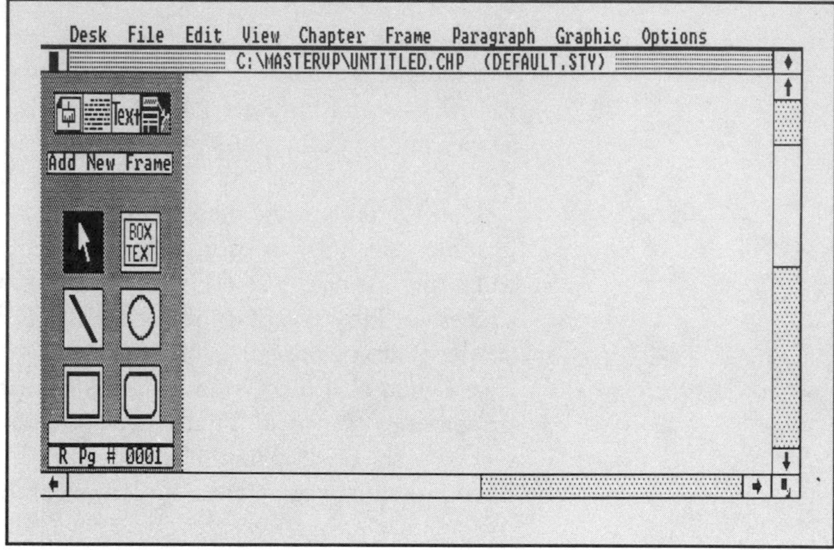

Figure 7.7: The Side-bar in Graphics mode

thinking that you use this arrow icon to create arrows. In fact, to create an arrow you use the icon right below it containing the diagonal line, which also creates lines.

USING THE GRAPHICS GRID

Regardless of the icon, you should first decide if you wish to use Ventura's graphics grid. With this invisible grid, the points of your graphics snap to meet and line up at predetermined intervals. Generally, this arrangement results in cleaner, more precise graphics. It also makes it possible to align graphics with other elements on the page, such as frames. Set up the graphics grid as follows:

1. Activate Graphics mode.
2. Drop the Graphic menu.
3. Click Grid Settings. The dialog box shown in Figure 7.8 appears.

In the dialog box, set Grid Snap to On to make the graphics grid operational. Then insert values for the horizontal and vertical spacing of the grid and give the OK.

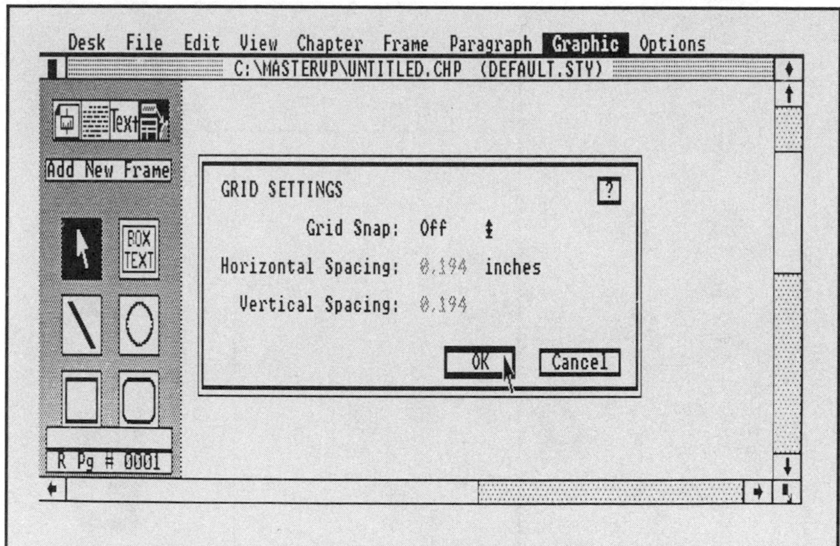

Figure 7.8: The dialog box for the Graphic menu's Grid Settings command

DRAWING WITH GRAPHICS ICONS

Once you've set the graphics grid as you desire, you can draw with Ventura. To draw with one of the graphics icons, follow these steps:

1. Click the icon that represents the shape you wish to use.
2. Move the mouse cursor into the working area. The cursor changes into a shape representing the graphic shape you've chosen. Figure 7.9 shows how the mouse-cursor shapes correspond to the various graphic shapes.
3. Position the mouse cursor at the spot for one corner of the graphic. Press the mouse button and hold it down.
4. Still pressing the mouse button, drag the mouse to the other corner for the graphic.
5. Release the mouse button when the mouse cursor is at the spot you desire for the bottom-right corner. The graphic corresponding to the icon appears.

! New for version 2.0

You can use version 2.0's new Constraint feature when drawing graphics to ensure perfect horizontal and vertical lines, squares, and

GRAPHIC NAME	SIDE-BAR MENU	MOUSE CURSOR SHAPE
Box Text	BOX TEXT	Te
Line		
Circle		
Rectangle		
Rounded Rectangle		

Figure 7.9: Graphic icons and their corresponding mouse-cursor shapes

circles. To use the Constraint feature, hold down the Alt key when you draw. Drawing constrained lines creates them in increments of 45 degrees.

Once the graphic is created, it is also selected, as indicated by handles that appear around it. Its name appears in the Current box. With the graphics-selection icon—the one with the arrow on it—active, you can grab one of the handles and stretch or shrink the graphic, just as you do with frames.

Figure 7.10 shows some graphic shapes that you can create in Graphics mode. For each shape, the figure indicates the icon(s) that you use to create the shape. As the bottom row shows, you can create additional shapes by combining two or more of the standard shapes. You can create the shape in the lower-right corner, for instance, by first drawing a circle, then drawing (or moving) two opaque boxes over it to cover three-fourths of it. On top of those boxes, draw lines that connect with each end of the remaining arc.

Figure 7.11 outlines this process. For display purposes, the boxes at the top have edges so you can see them. In actual use, they would be simply opaque white blocks whose presence you could tell only by the handles that would appear if you should select them.

Up to eight handles can appear to stake out a selected graphic. There can be fewer than eight, depending upon the size and orientation of the graphic. Figure 7.12 shows examples of selection handles as they appear in conjunction with various graphics.

Although moving graphics is generally straightforward, moving a horizontal or vertical line (or arrow) can be tricky because of the placement of its selection handles. Figure 7.13 gives some tips for moving a horizontal or vertical line.

Unfortunately, you cannot save graphics independent of your document. However, you can cut and paste them, just as you do frames. Press Del, Shift-Del, or Ins to cut, copy, or paste, respectively; or use the Edit menu to perform these procedures. Graphics that you cut or copy are placed on a graphics clipboard for subsequent pasting, separate from material on the clipboards for frames and text. The clipboard is not cleared when you load a new chapter, so you can use it to move graphics from one chapter to another.

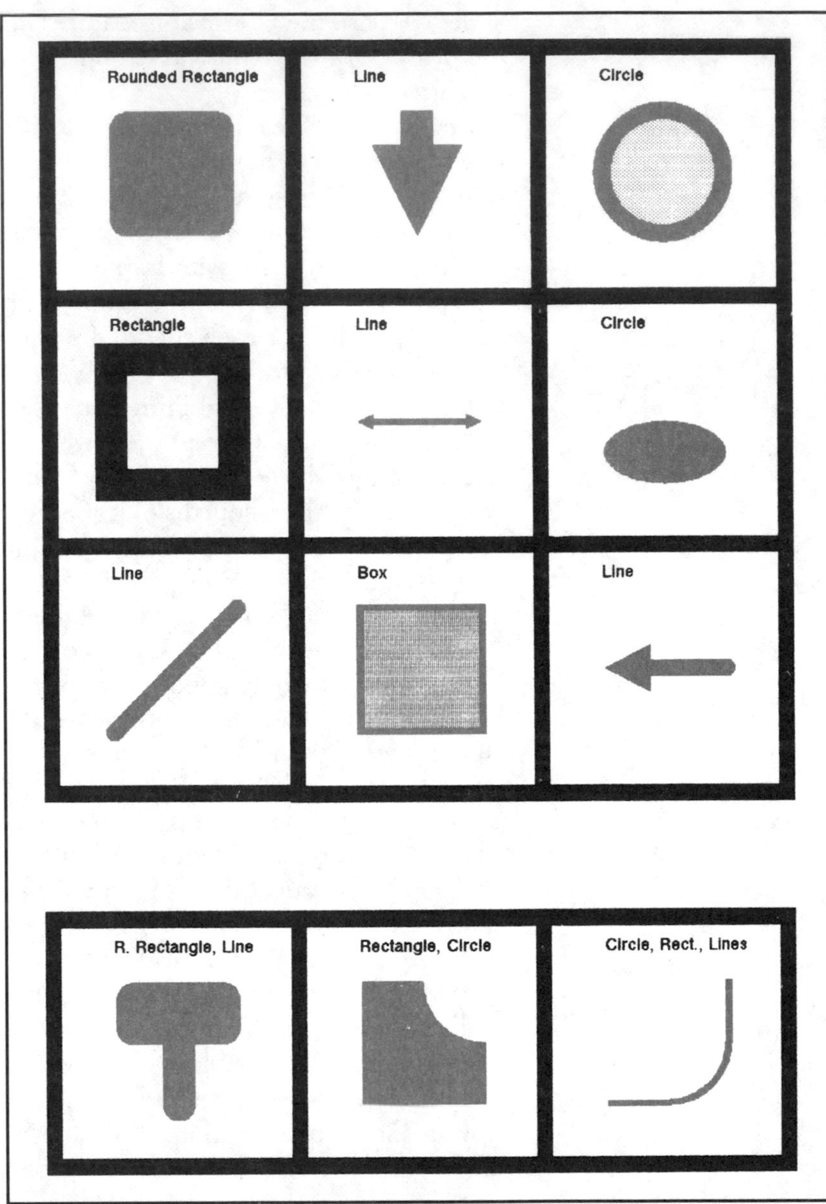

Figure 7.10: Shapes created in Graphics mode

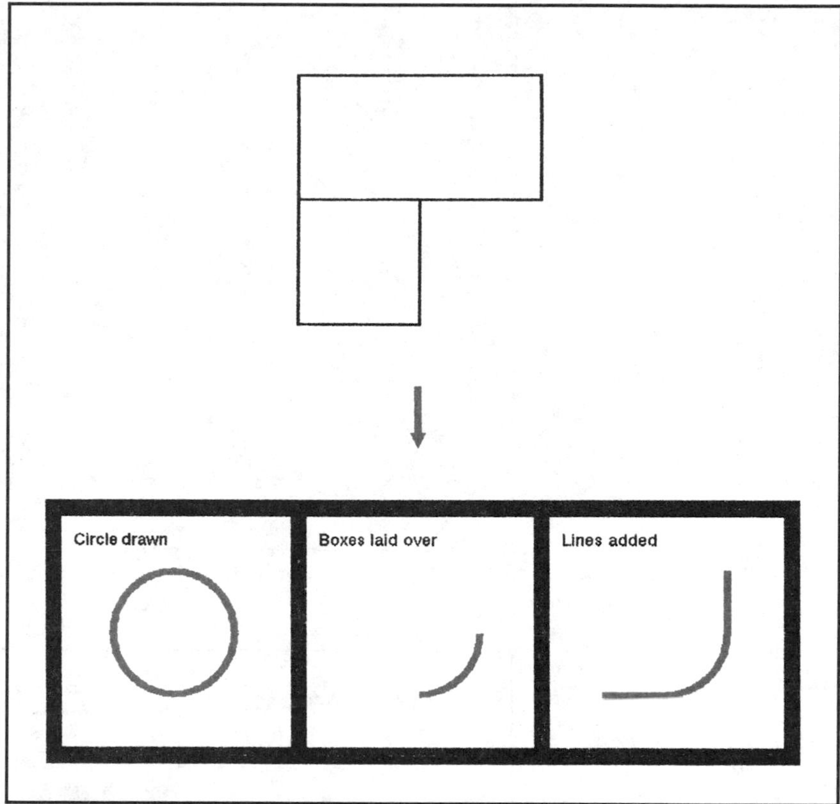

Figure 7.11: Creating an arc in Graphics mode

CHANGING LINE ATTRIBUTES

As we've discussed, graphics can vary in size and shape. In addition, you can control two other characteristics of graphics: *line attributes* and *fill attributes.*

Line attributes control lines that you create with the line icon. They also control lines that make up the outline of other graphic shapes. To set line attributes for a given graphic, you must display the Line Attributes dialog box as follows:

1. Activate Graphics mode and select the graphic you wish to change; that is, click the graphic you've created in the working area.

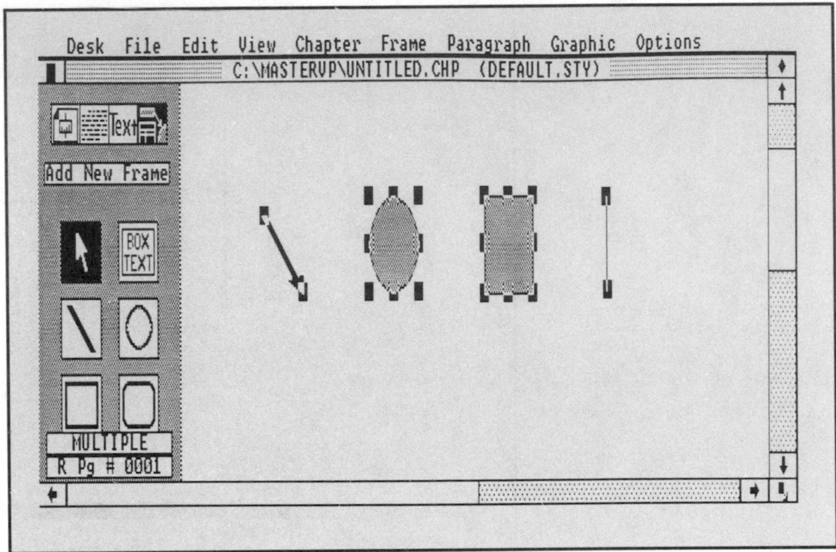

Figure 7.12: Selection handles for graphics

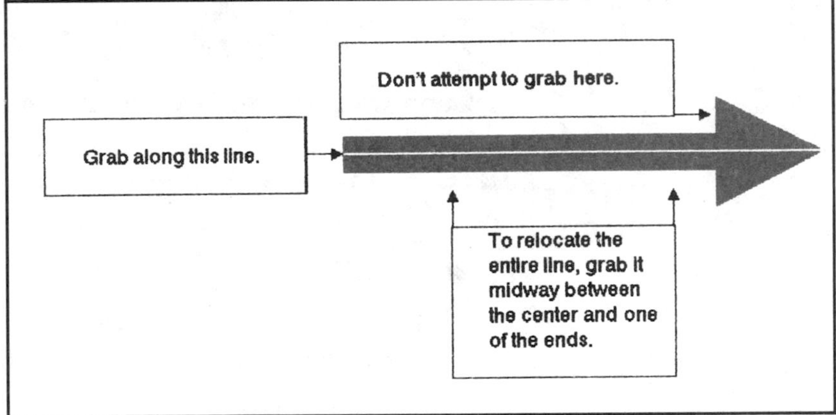

Figure 7.13: Moving a line or arrow

2. Drop the Graphic menu and click Line Attributes, or type Ctrl-L.

This procedure displays the dialog box shown in Figure 7.14.

With the Thickness category, you can set the selected line to one of the standard thicknesses (None, Thin, 2, 3, 4, Thick). When you do,

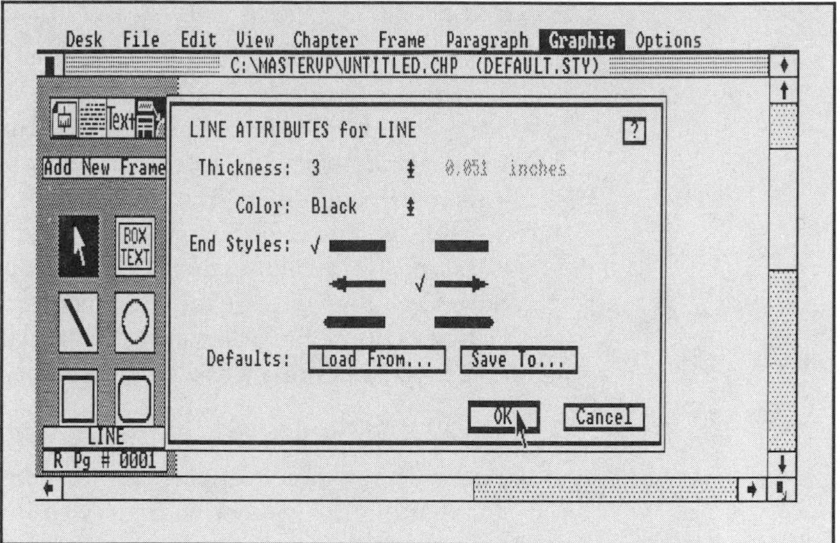

Figure 7.14: The dialog box for the Graphic menu's Line Attributes command

its dimension appears, ranging between 0.06 points and 18 points. Select Custom Width to create your own specification, and enter the appropriate value. Select none and the line becomes invisible (though this does not delete it; you can still select the line).

Set the color you desire by clicking the appropriate box. With some printers, you can use the White setting to create a white arrow against a black background. As you adjust the colors, the End Styles grouping reflects your choice. White causes the grouping to disappear.

The End Styles settings dictate the manner in which a line terminates. Click these settings to create arrowhead and rounded endings, as well as the standard flat ends. The current settings have a check mark next to them. The left column corresponds to whichever end you created first; the right column corresponds to the other end. Note that they do not necessarily correlate with the left and right ends of the line.

Once you've created the settings you desire, you can set them aside for use with a similar graphic. Do this by clicking the Save To button. This copies the settings to a kind of holding area, similar to the clipboard. To duplicate the settings with another graphic of the same icon, display its Line Attributes dialog box and click Load From. These values also become the default settings for newly created graphics.

SPECIFYING FILL ATTRIBUTES

The other graphic attribute you can control is the fill attribute. This setting controls the manner in which Ventura treats the interior space of the graphic, including the color and pattern. Note that you cannot set fill attributes for the graphics lines themselves; they're always solid. This differs from the way you can set interior line patterns with the Frame or Paragraph menu's Ruling Line commands.

To specify fill attributes for a selected graphic, follow the same procedure as that of line attributes, but use the Graphic menu's Fill Attributes command. Alternatively, after selecting the appropriate graphic, you can press Ctrl-F. You see the dialog box shown in Figure 7.15.

Use this dialog box to specify the graphics color and pattern. A preview of your choices appears in the Result box.

One setting that cannot be previewed is the choice of Opaque or Transparent. This setting is meaningful only when a graphic is to be placed on top of text or other graphics. It governs the manner in which that graphic treats the underlying material. If opaque, the graphic will hide all material beneath it from view (Pattern must not be set to Hollow). If transparent, it will allow the material to bleed through the graphic (Pattern must not be set to Solid). The printer

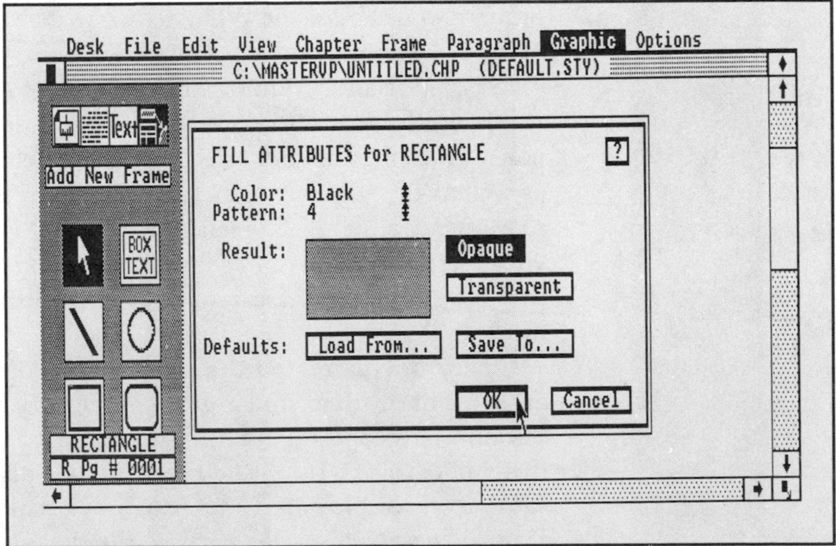

Figure 7.15: The dialog box for the Graphic menu's Fill Attributes command

capability page that we created in Chapter 5 has examples of both opaque and transparent circles. Check your printout to see if your printer has the capacity to create transparent graphics.

The Load From and Save To buttons operate the same way they do for the Graphic menu's Line Attributes command. Use them to transfer fill attributes easily from one graphic to another and to set the default values.

USING BOX TEXT

One important use of opaque graphics is covering portions of an imported picture, such as the labels in our Lotus 1-2-3 graph from Chapter 6. Once you've hidden the imported labels, you can add Ventura labels that use fonts similar to those you're using elsewhere on the page. Doing so lets you make the new graphic conform to the rest of the document.

The graphic feature called *Box text* provides the means to accomplish both of these operations simultaneously. Use the Box-text icon to create a box just as you would use the other icons to create other graphic elements. Click the icon, position the mouse cursor, and then drag and release.

! New for version 2.0

In Version 2.0, the words *Box Text* no longer appear with Box text. Instead, an end-of-file marker appears—a small empty box (□). This saves you the task of deleting the words *Box Text* every time you use this feature. Simply place the text cursor before this marker and type your text.

At first, Box text may seem quite similar to a standard frame filled with a text file. There are, however, several ways in which the two differ:

- With Box text you can't store the text in a text file as you can with a standard frame. All Box text is stored in the chapter's CAP file.
- You can use Box text as you would other Ventura graphics. For example, you can move other graphics above or beneath it, selecting with Ctrl-click.

In Figure 7.16, a Box-text box covers the label on the Y-axis of the graph from Figure 7.2 and replaces it with a better font. Box text

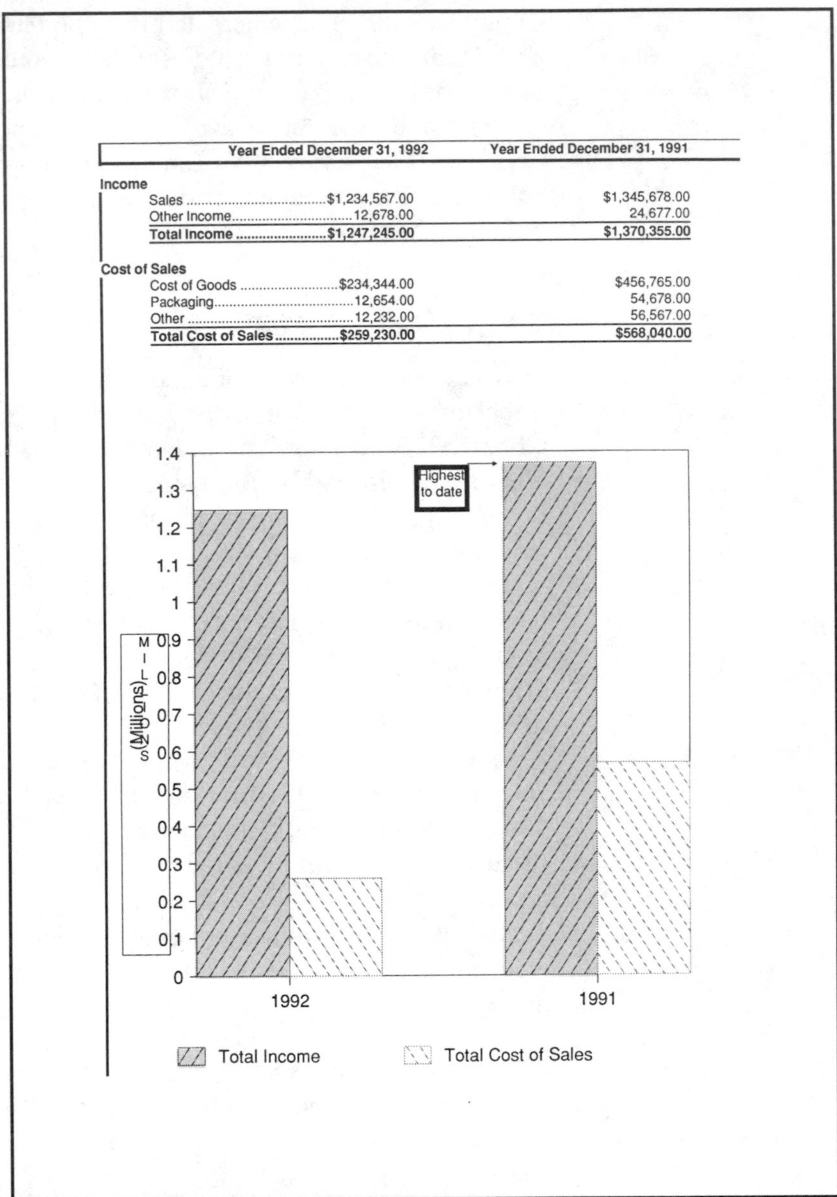

	Year Ended December 31, 1992	Year Ended December 31, 1991
Income		
Sales	$1,234,567.00	$1,345,678.00
Other Income	12,678.00	24,677.00
Total Income	**$1,247,245.00**	**$1,370,355.00**
Cost of Sales		
Cost of Goods	$234,344.00	$456,765.00
Packaging	12,654.00	54,678.00
Other	12,232.00	56,567.00
Total Cost of Sales	**$259,230.00**	**$568,040.00**

Figure 7.16: Using Box text to enhance the 1-2-3 graph

covers the sideways label *Millions* and replaces it with a vertical label. The same box also covers the unnecessary and distracting zeros that appear in the scale. Figure 7.16 shows the underpinnings of the reformatted graph. (For the purpose of demonstration, we have changed this box to transparent and given it a thin outline.) Each letter in the word *MILLIONS* has a return following it and is thus a separate paragraph. The alignment for these paragraph/letters, specified with the Paragraph menu's Alignment command, is Centered.

MANIPULATING MULTIPLE GRAPHICS

As you create graphics that are more sophisticated, you will find it necessary to place graphics on top of one another more often. When you do this, you will need to reorder the various layers. To do so, select a graphic and use the Graphic menu's Send To Back (Ctrl-Z) or Bring To Front (Ctrl-A) command. To select a graphic that's behind another, hold down the Ctrl key when clicking the graphic with the mouse. The procedure is the same as that used to select piled frames (Chapter 2). Figure 7.17 shows how the circle, at the back of the custom graphic we created in Figure 7.11, changes the graphic when brought forward with Ctrl-click and then Ctrl-A. One use of these commands is to display a graphic that has been inadvertently obscured by another.

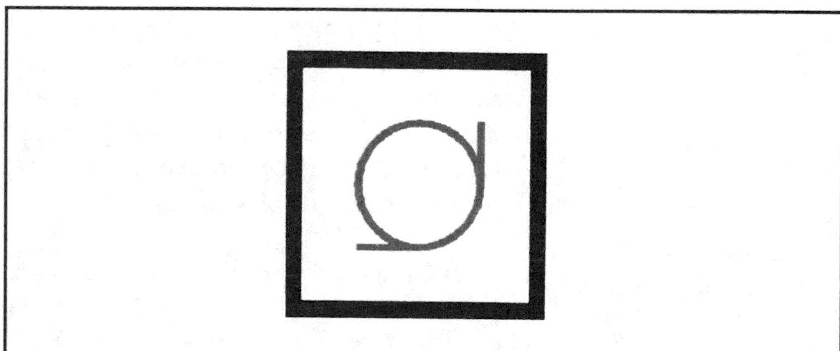

Figure 7.17: A circle brought forward to change a graphic

Sophisticated graphics may also require that you select several elements at once. Doing so allows you to move all selected graphics as a unit. To select several graphics in succession, hold down the Shift key as you click each one with the mouse.

To select all the graphics in one step, drop the Graphic menu and click Select All (or use Ctrl-Q). You can use this technique to move graphics around on a page while keeping them equidistant with respect to each other. You can also use this technique to cut or copy the graphics all at once. The Select All command allows you to relocate the graphics that are tied to the underlying-page frame, which of course can't be moved. For example, once we created the boxes of shadings that you saw in Figure 7.4, we were able to position them within the screen by first selecting them as a unit.

REPEATING GRAPHICS

! New for version 2.0

As we mentioned, with version 2.0 Ventura no longer repeats graphics tied to the underlying-page frame on every page. So Ventura provides a means of making the graphic repeat on the pages if you so desire.

1. In Graphics mode, select the graphic.
2. Drop the Graphic menu and click Show On All Pages

The graphic will then appear on all pages of the document. Of course, this procedure will also work on multiple-selected graphics.

To change a repeating graphic back to a standard graphic, follow the same procedure. When a repeating graphic is selected, the Graphic menu's Show On All Pages changes to Show On This Page. Clicking this choice removes the graphic from pages other than the page currently displayed.

In Chapter 8, you'll see how you can use the box-text techniques you've learned to create tables. We'll also look at other methods of creating tables in Ventura.

CHAPTER
8

Creating Tables

Fast Track

To create tables by setting tabs 296

in Paragraph mode, select a paragraph and use the Paragraph menu's Tab Settings. Click the Tab Number arrows to display and change up to 16 tab settings.

The Tab Type setting for each tab number 298

can be Off, Left, Center, Right, or Decimal. You can have the tab turned off or use one of the alignments to turn it on.

Make sure that tabs you set are in the right order. 301

Make each tab setting far enough from the previous one to accommodate existing text. Do not justify the text. Use distances from the left edge of the paragraph.

Leader characters 305

automatically fill in the space occupied by the tab. With the Paragraph menu's Tab Setting dialog box, you can specify the leader character to use, generally the period. You can also use an automatic leader to fill in the space from the last character in the paragraph to the right edge of the paragraph.

Column tags, vertical tabs, or side-by-side paragraphs 306

set up columns by assigning a different tag to paragraphs in each column. For each tag, you use the Paragraph menu's Spacing to set the In From Left and In From Right values so the columns don't overlap. In the Paragraph menu's Breaks dialog box, you use Line Break to make paragraphs that follow one another line up side by side.

To create new entries in the same column 311

with column tags, use a line-break character (Ctrl-Enter) or add a new row of entries.

To add a new row of entries 312

with column tags, copy an existing row and delete inappropriate material. Alternatively, you can press the Enter key the required number of times (one for each column) and format the new paragraphs with the appropriate tags.

You can also use Box text 317

to create tables. Activate Graphics mode, click the Box-text icon, and draw the boxes. Then enter text in each box. Box text is good to use when the form of the table is important and not expected to change. Box text is a graphic, and you can format it and perform other procedures on it as you do any graphic.

Avoid creating tables with spaces. 319

However, some material you import may use this method. You may wish to change such material in order to follow another method.

CHAPTER 8

AS WITH SO MANY OTHER FEATURES OF VENTURA, there are several approaches you can follow to make tables. Naturally, you'll want to examine all the methods that are available. Then you'll be able to decide which technique is the best to use under the circumstances.

We'll begin one examination of tables with a sample document that has a small table in it. You'll be using a copy of Ventura's sample brochure, &BRO-P3.CHP, located in the TYPESET directory.

1. Load Ventura.
2. Drop the File menu and select Open Chapter.
3. From the TYPESET directory, select the &BRO-P3.CHP chapter.
4. Save a copy of &BRO-P3.CHP in the MASTERVP directory using the File menu's Save As command.
5. Save the stylesheet &BRO-P3.STY in the MASTERVP directory using the File menu's Save As New Style command.
6. Because you'll be altering the text that makes up the document, use the Edit menu's File Type/Rename command to copy the chapter's text files to the MASTERVP directory.

METHODS OF TABLE CONSTRUCTION

There are four basic ways to construct tables. The method you choose will dictate what you can enter into the table, how you enter it, and how your printed table will look. Let's examine the four methods, see how they differ, and discuss the circumstances under which each is appropriate.

Table 8.1 summarizes the methods of creating tables. Although the methods are listed separately, be aware that one table can mix several techniques. For instance, Box text can contain paragraphs that are formatted with tab settings.

To examine these methods, let's agree on some terminology. *Table entries* are the individual items that collectively create the table. Table entries combine to create *rows* and *columns* and so make up a table. Rows of table entries go across the table horizontally; columns span

Table 8.1: Techniques for Creating Tables

METHOD	COMMENTS
Tabs	Requires that table entries be no more than one line each.
	Provides decimal tabs.
	Can use leader characters.
	Resetting can be difficult.
Column Tags	Accommodates descriptive text of varying lengths automatically.
	Tricky to set up.
	Makes changing column widths an involved process. Usually necessitates changing other columns as well.
Box Text	Very visual. Easy to set up.
	Each item requires a separate box.
	Useful when the shape of table is important, such as with invoices.
	Does not use imported word-processed text.
	Easy to surround table items with outlines and backgrounds.
	Easy to make changes because of visual orientation.
	Must adjust format manually if text length is too great.
Space Characters	Should generally be avoided due to lack of flexibility.
	May be used with nonproportional fonts only.

table entries that line up vertically. A row or column can consist of a single entry.

Regardless of which of the four techniques you use, creating a table consists of two fundamental operations: setting up the structure of the table and making entries into it. Usually, you set up the structure of the table before making the entries, but some methods allow you to perform either operation first.

With some methods, you can use your word processor or other programs, such as an electronic spreadsheet, to input entries. Under most circumstances, however, you'll probably find that it's easiest to use Ventura to make the entries into tables you create. This is because it's difficult, and in fact unnecessary, to get your word processor's settings to match those you create with Ventura. Thus, the word-processed version of the table file generally bears little resemblance to the final Ventura version. However, if you want to use your word processor to make entries, you should check the procedures discussed in Chapter 11.

Let's begin by studying the method that is closest to using the typewriter and to word processing.

SETTING TABS TO CREATE TABLES

Each method of creating tables has advantages and limitations, and each is best suited to a particular kind of task. One advantage of using tabs is that each tab setting offers you a variety of alignments. Depending on which you choose, you can have the columns of your table line up in various ways, including along decimal points. The limitation, however, is that it's only practical to use tabs when each entry in the table is no longer than one line.

Setting up a table consists of assigning *tab settings* by using paragraph tags. Tab settings affect only that paragraph (or those paragraphs) that you format with this same tag. Thus, to assign tabs to a paragraph, you assign the tab settings for a paragraph tag, and assign that tag to the paragraph. Remember, though, that paragraph tagging is stored with the style sheet. Thus, any Ventura chapter that references the same style sheet can use tags with the same tab settings. That way, you can use your tab settings in various documents.

Tabs you set for a tag operate very much like tabs that you set when you use a typewriter. With a typewriter, you set a tab stop.

When you press the typewriter's Tab key, the carriage jumps to the tab stop. Then you continue typing from the new position.

Ventura's tab settings operate like the tab stops of a typewriter, but in a more sophisticated fashion. When you type in your entries, you press the Tab key after each entry. Doing so inserts a *tab character* into the text. The tab character extends from the end of one entry to the next tab setting to the right. Ventura aligns the text that follows the tab character with respect to the tab setting.

You can work with tabs in Ventura using one of two approaches: Type in your text first and then set up the structure of the table (by setting tabs), or set the tabs first and then type in the table entries. If you press the Tab key before you set the tabs, Ventura will insert a tab character into the text nonetheless. However, the tab character will not affect positioning of the text until you set the tab, at which time the tab effect will take place retroactively.

Usually it's best to set the tabs first, even if you have only a vague idea of their actual positions. That way, as you make the entries, you'll be able to see the table take some shape. If, when you add text, your entries don't fit between the tab settings, you can fine-tune the tab settings as necessary. Ventura automatically adjusts the table entries to conform to the new settings.

To display the dialog box that allows you to set tabs:

1. With Paragraph mode active, select the paragraph within the table at the top of the brochure that looks something like this on your screen:

   Graphic Yes Yes Yes

2. Drop the Paragraph menu and select Tab Settings. The dialog box you see in Figure 8.1 appears.

A paragraph tag can contain up to 16 tabs, identified by a Tab Number setting. When you click the Arrow buttons associated with Tab Number, the Tab Number setting increases (→) or decreases (←). As you display each Tab Number, the dialog box displays the settings that are in place for the corresponding tab. In this way, the Tab Number setting regulates all of the other settings in the dialog box.

Let's say that your paragraph tag has three tab settings associated with it. They would probably be numbered with Tab Numbers 1, 2,

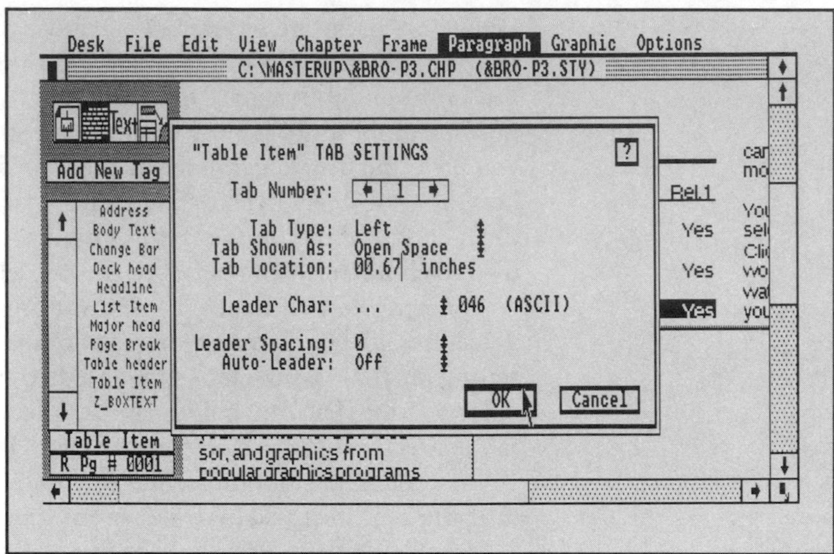

Figure 8.1: The Paragraph menu's Tab Settings dialog box

and 3. With 1 appearing for Tab Number, you'd see the characteristics of Tab Number 1 displayed in the dialog box, and you could adjust these characteristics as necessary. By displaying Tab Number 2, you could see and adjust its characteristics. Likewise, displaying 3 would allow you to work with Tab Number 3's settings.

TURNING TABS ON AND OFF

The Tab Type category has five settings. You can choose Off or one of the tab alignments: Left, Center, Right, or Decimal.

Once you've selected a tab setting by number, click Off if you want to make the indicated Tab setting nonoperational. If you click Off, none of the other settings in the dialog box will affect that tab setting. To turn a tab on, choose one of the four alignments available.

Left alignment is the standard type of alignment. When a tab setting is left-aligned, the table entries associated with the tab setting (that is, text that follows the corresponding tab character) will begin at the tab location. Tab Location is a field setting that appears midway in the dialog box. It shows the distance from the left edge of the table to the tab setting in question. When they are left-aligned, table entries have their left edge even with the tab location. The location of the right edge of such entries will vary, depending upon the amount of text in the entry, similar to the "ragged right" text format we saw in Chapter 4.

Figure 8.2 shows part of the sample chapter you loaded at the beginning of this chapter. (You may notice some differences between the document shown in Figure 8.2 and the document on your screen.) To more fully examine tabs, you'll make the changes that appear in Figure 8.2.

- Click Cancel (or press Ctrl-X) to put away the Tab Settings dialog box.

Look at the small table in the center of the screen. To demonstrate the types of alignment used in these columns:

- Activate Text mode and change the last entries in the columns to *Maybe* as shown in Figure 8.2.

Now examine Figure 8.3. In it you'll see the same table, but in this figure you can see the tab characters between each table entry, in the

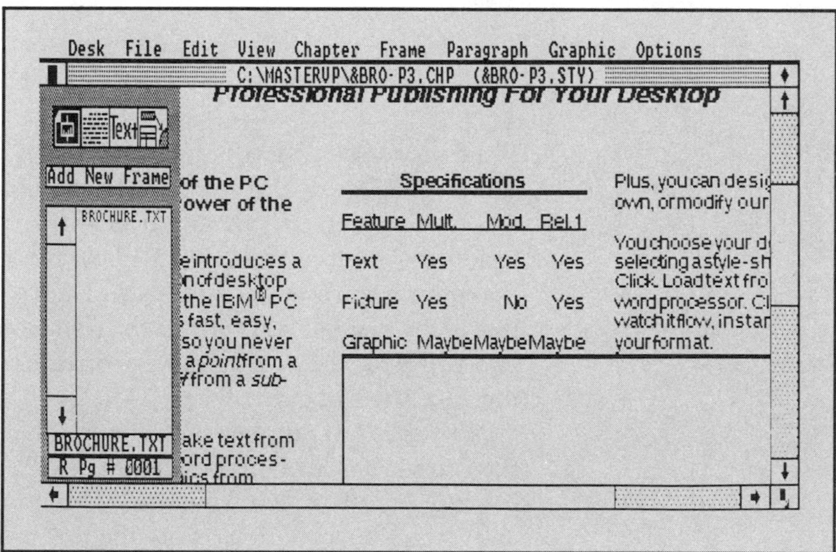

Figure 8.2: A small table in a document

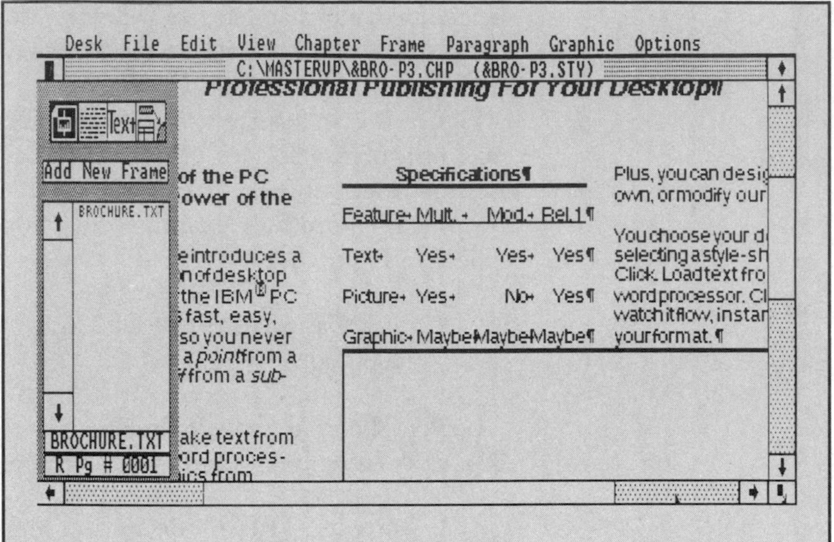

Figure 8.3: The table with tab characters displayed

form of → characters. In the Current box, these characters are referred to as Horizontal Tab codes when their presence is detected by the text cursor.

- If these characters are not present, press Ctrl-T or drop the Options menu and select Show Tabs and Returns.

If the menu says Hide Tabs and Returns, then the tabs are already showing. Selecting this command or typing Ctrl-T will turn them off.

The first tab in this example—the one set up for the *Mult.* heading—is left-aligned. Notice how the first letter of each word in the column starts at the same spot. Each word begins at the tab location of the first tab and ends on the right according to the length of the entry. Thus, the word *Maybe* protrudes farther to the right than the *Yes* entries above it.

Note that tab numbers usually do not correspond to the columns they control: Tab Number 1 governs the alignment of the second column, Tab Number 2 governs the alignment of the third column, and so on. This occurs because the first column of a table is not usually offset by a tab. Generally, the first column is aligned with the left edge of the table, as it is in the example.

You may find this arrangement confusing. If so, you can remedy the situation with any table by simply setting Tab Location for Tab Number 1 to zero. If you do that, Tab Number 2 will control column 2, Tab Number 3 will control column 3, and so on. However, we'll leave our example as it has been set by the makers of Ventura.

The second Tab setting in the example controls the column under *Mod.* This column is right-aligned. Notice how the last letter of each entry in this column ends at the same spot, causing the column to be even on the right. The tab position is the spot where the last letter in these entries ends.

Now you'll change the setting of the third tab, which controls the fourth column, to center alignment.

1. Activate Paragraph mode and select the paragraph that says:

    Graphic Maybe Maybe Maybe

2. Drop the Paragraph menu and select Tab Settings. The Tab Settings dialog box appears (Figure 8.1).
3. For Tab Numbers, click the → button until *3* is displayed. This stands for the third tab setting.
4. Use the Tab Type pop-up menu to select Center.
5. Give the OK.

Notice how each entry in this column (*Rel. 1*) is now centered on either side of a common invisible vertical line. The position of this line corresponds to the Tab Location setting of the third tab.

This example shows only three of the four types of tab settings. In a moment, we'll look at the last type of tab, Decimal.

PRECAUTIONS FOR SETTING TABS

Besides taking care that Tab Numbers correspond to column numbers, as mentioned above, there are other traps you should watch out for in creating tables. First, when you use tabs, always assign your tab settings by Tab Number in the same order they occur on the page, from left to right. Ventura ignores any tab settings that are out of order.

> You can display or remove the Side-bar with the Options menu or Ctrl-W (see Appendix A).

If you wish to use the same tab setting with a different tag, you can add a tag that initially has the same tab settings. In Paragraph mode, select the paragraph with the original tab settings and click the Side-bar's Add New Tag button. You can add or remove the tab settings of the new tag. They cannot be rearranged, however; you can only adjust existing tabs.

Be sure each tab setting is wide enough. It must accommodate the widest entry in any column that precedes it in this or any other table using the same tag. In the case of right-aligned tabs, the tab must accommodate the widest entry in the column it controls. Any text from a previous column that extends past the position of a tab will move to the right—to the next Tab setting—when you insert a tab character after the entry. In the example, if you were to replace the word *Picture* with a longer entry, such as *Reproduction*, that extended beyond the tab setting for the *Mult.* column, the *Yes* under *Mult.* would be bumped into the *Mod.* column. The *No* under *Mod.,* in turn, would be repositioned under *Rel. 1.* The results appear in Figure 8.4.

Notice that the final *Yes* in the line has been moved out of the column. A line with tab characters in it still accepts as much text as it would without the tab characters. This holds true even if it means

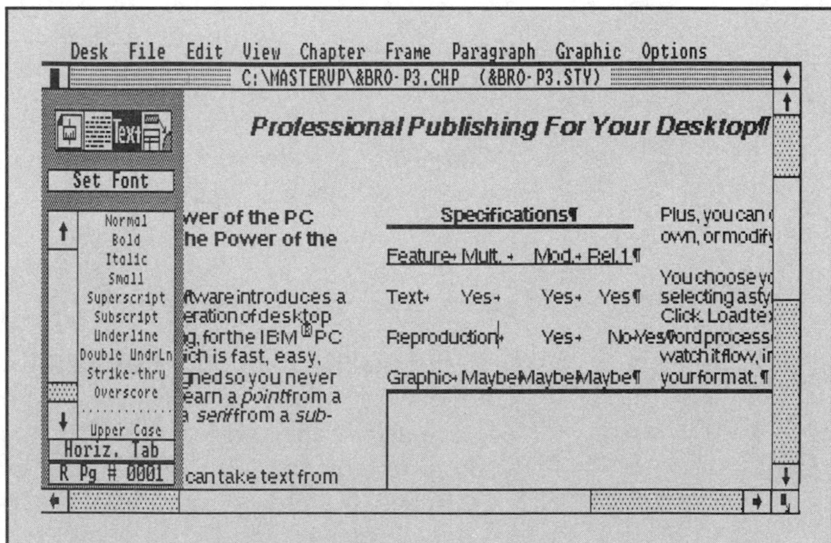

Figure 8.4: Displaced table entries

that text may be pushed past the edge of the column, or even past the edge of the page, causing some text to disappear. If you're working with a left-aligned tab setting, Ventura could push text past the right edge of the page. If the Tab setting is right-aligned, additional text will be pushed to the left, past the left edge of the column or off the page to the left.

Note also that the paragraph tag for a table entry must not be set for Justified in order for tabs to show up. To check and change the alignment setting for a tag, drop the Paragraph menu and select Alignment.

Finally, note that when you insert values into the Tab Location setting, Ventura does not consider a tag's In From Left value, as specified with the Paragraph menu's Spacing dialog box. For the tab position, Ventura always measures from the left edge of the paragraph, as if the paragraph has no In From Left indent.

SETTING DECIMAL TABS

Let's turn to another example for our look at decimal tabs. The sample Lotus 1-2-3 table that we've been working with in the past couple of chapters contains examples of decimal alignment. Figure 8.5 shows these examples.

1. Drop the File menu and select Open Chapter. A dialog box appears asking you to Save, Abandon, or Cancel.
2. Click Save to save the changes you've made. The Item Selector box appears.
3. Select &TBL-P1.CHP from the MASTERVP directory. (If you renamed the chapter when you saved it in previous chapters, then select the new name you assigned.)

Notice that the decimal points in each column are lined up one under another. The location of the decimal tab determines where the decimal points line up.

In the figure, it appears that the last table entry in the bottom right does not line up. This is due to the End Of File mark (□), which is wider than the Paragraph End symbols (¶) above it. Even though this value does not look aligned, it will be lined up in the printed version, or if you choose Hide Tabs & Return.

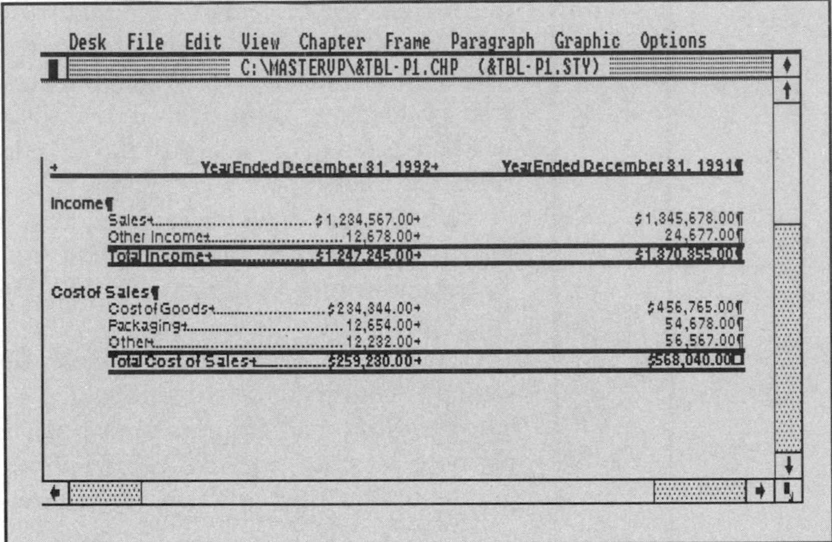

Figure 8.5: Decimal-aligned tabs

Normally, Ventura recognizes the period character as a decimal point when determining the placement of numbers associated with a decimal tab. However, you can direct Ventura to recognize any character of your choosing. Use the Options menu's Set Preferences dialog box and provide the ASCII value in the Decimal Tab Char field (see Appendices A and E).

When typing currency amounts with decimal-aligned tab settings, begin with the cursor to the left of the tab location. When you press the Tab key, the cursor moves to the decimal tab location. Then type in your dollar sign, if desired, and the whole-dollar values.

As you type, the characters are pushed backwards, to the left. When you press the period, the decimal point freezes at the tab location. Then, as you enter the cents, typing proceeds normally, moving to the right.

For example, let's say that you wanted to type in *$125.35*. Here's how the screen would look at each successive keystroke, as you entered this value:

```
(press Tab)
     $
    $1
   $12
  $125
  $125.
  $125.3
  $125.35
```

The result is that the decimal point remains at the location of the decimal tab, and other characters adjust accordingly.

Alignment by decimal point operates regardless of the number of digits that a table entry contains. Even if you were using five or more decimal places for scientific work, the decimal points would always line up.

! New for version 2.0

Version 2.0 of Ventura offers two enhancements to decimal alignment. The first enhancement causes Ventura to automatically align each line in a paragraph at its first decimal point. To do that in Paragraph mode, select a sample paragraph. In the Paragraph menu's Alignment dialog box, set Horz Alignment to Decimal. In the same dialog box, provide a value for In From Right To Decimal, the distance from the right edge of the paragraph to the decimal. Using this method, you can create a column of decimal-aligned figures without setting a tab.

! New for version 2.0

The second enhancement is a great help to those who import spreadsheet data. It addresses the problem of negative values, which people in finance often indicate with parentheses. In earlier versions when such numbers did not contain decimal points, Ventura would align them with the right parenthesis. In Version 2.0, these numbers align according to the digit farthest to the right.

USING LEADER CHARACTERS

Besides decimal tabs, the table shown in Figure 8.5 also provides us with an example of *leader characters.* By using Tab Shown As: Leader Char, you can have leader (pronounced (''LEED-er'') characters automatically fill in the space occupied by a tab character. Such characters lead up to the entry controlled by the next tab setting using a specified leader character. (The other setting in the Tab Shown As pop-up menu is to have the tab character displayed as open space.) Figure 8.5 shows periods used as leader characters for Tab Number 1 (the 1992 column). There is a tab character following the word *Sales* and leading up to the decimal-aligned value $1,234,567.00. The space occupied by that tab character is automatically filled in with periods.

Periods are the most common type of leader character. For this reason, Ventura provides a setting for periods, as well as one each for spaces and underlines, in the Leader Char pop-up menu of the Tab Settings dialog box. However, you can choose any character you'd like as a leader by selecting Custom and then entering the ASCII value for the character of your choosing (see Appendix E).

The Leader Char setting applies to all Tab Numbers set for Tab Shown As: Leader Char, not just the Tab Number displayed. Closing Leader Char: Spaces has the same effect as choosing Tab Shown As: Open Space for each tab setting, but applies to all tab settings in the paragraph.

Leader Spacing controls the number of character spaces Ventura inserts between each leader character. You can set it from 0 to 8 spaces. For short tab distances, you'll want to insert fewer spaces. Figure 8.5 has leader spacing set for zero. If the tab is traveling across greater expanses of the page, you may wish to spread out the leader characters by using a larger number. This value also applies to all Tab numbers set for Tab Shown As: Leader Char.

! New for version 2.0

The Tab Settings dialog box now offers an Auto-Leader option. When you turn it on, Ventura automatically creates leader characters from the last character in the paragraph to the right edge of the paragraph. This feature is great for places where you want a leader to fill empty space in a table. Try it also in catalog entries, where a leader often fills the empty space at the end of the last line of a paragraph.

COLUMN TAGS

Now that you've seen how to set tabs to create tables, let's look at Ventura's second method for making tables: *column tags.* The column-tag method is sometimes called *vertical tabs* or *side-by-side paragraphs.* Be aware, however, that this method does not have anything to do with columns as specified in the Frame menu's Margins & Columns dialog box. When you use column tags, each column in the table has a corresponding paragraph tag. Thus, if your table has four columns in it, you would create four tags with indicative names, such as Col 1, Col 2, Col 3, and Col 4.

1. Drop the File menu and click Open Chapter. A dialog box appears, asking you to Save, Abandon, or Cancel.
2. Select &TBL2-L1.CHP from the TYPESET directory.

3. Use the File menu's Save As command to save a copy of &TBL2-L1.CHP to the MASTERVP directory.
4. Use the File menu's Save As New Style command to save the style sheet, &TBL2-L1.STY, to the MASTERVP directory.
5. Because you may be altering the text that makes up the document, use the Edit menu's File Type/Rename command to copy the &TBL2-L1.CHP text files to the MASTERVP directory.

Figure 8.6 shows this sample chapter. Note that you could not create this table by using tabs. Tabs only operate with table entries that are no more than one line; most of the entries shown in the second and third columns are several lines long.

Instead, you set up tags for each column. Each table entry is a separate paragraph, tagged with the appropriate column tag. Thus, the table entries in the first column—*First Entry, Second model., Entry #3*—are each separate paragraphs and each tagged with the Col 1 format. The paragraphs in the next column are each tagged with Col 2. Likewise, each entry in the third column is a separate paragraph, tagged with Col 3, and each price in the last column is tagged with the Col 4 format.

FORMATTING COLUMN TAGS

For these four paragraph tags to operate, they must receive some special, unusual formats. First, in order to position each paragraph correctly, you must use the Paragraph menu's Spacing command. In the dialog box that this command displays, you set the In From Left and In From Right values so that each column entry is positioned properly from left to right. Figure 8.6 shows the values that are set for Col 2 and Col 3.

There are also some adjustments you must make in the Breaks dialog box, shown in Figure 8.7. To display this dialog box:

1. Activate Paragraph mode and click a sample paragraph.
2. Drop the Paragraph menu and click Breaks.

Figure 8.8 summarizes the settings in the Spacing and Breaks dialog boxes that affect column tags.

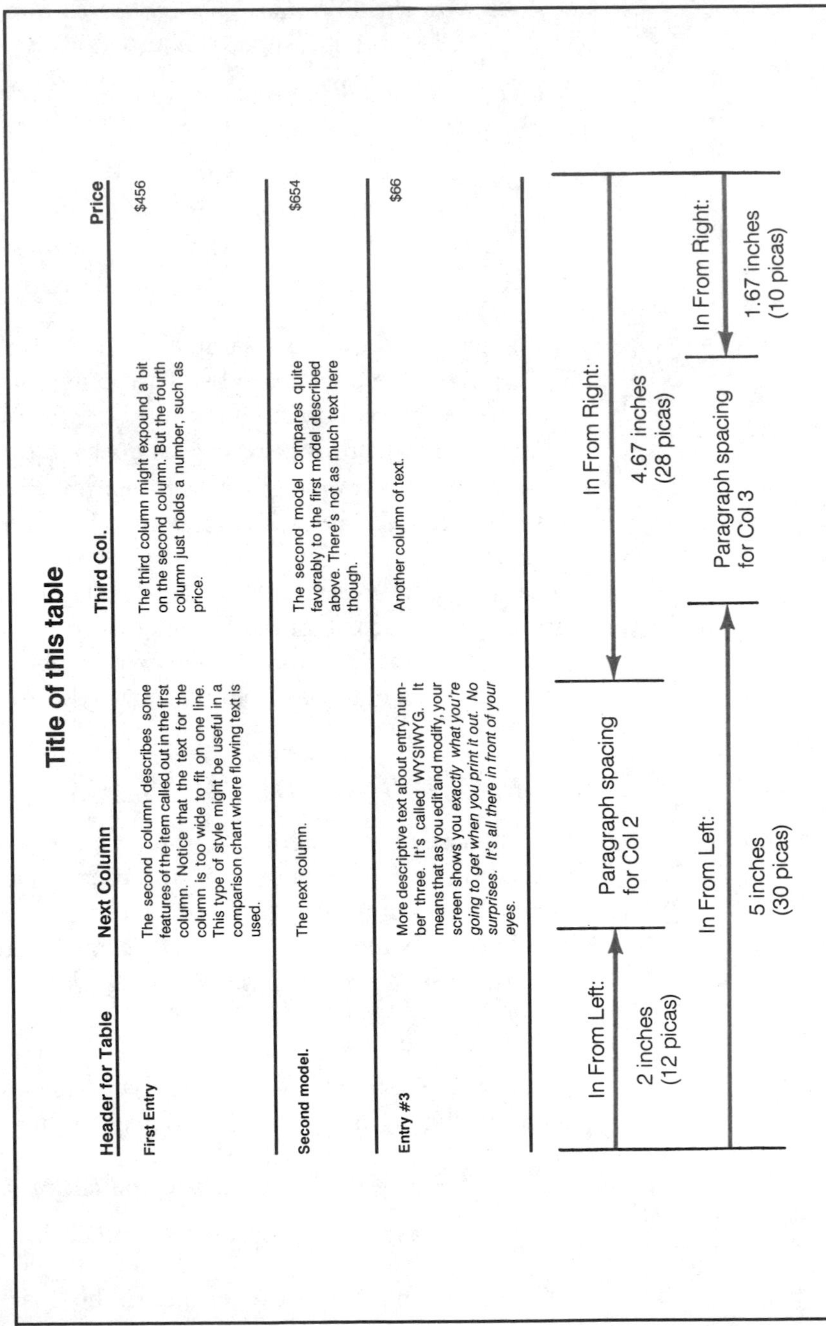

Title of this table

Header for Table	Next Column	Third Col.	Price
First Entry	The second column describes some features of the item called out in the first column. Notice that the text for the column is too wide to fit on one line. This type of style might be useful in a comparison chart where flowing text is used.	The third column might expound a bit on the second column. But the fourth column just holds a number, such as price.	$456
Second model.	The next column.	The second model compares quite favorably to the first model described above. There's not as much text here though.	$654
Entry #3	More descriptive text about entry number three. It's called WYSIWYG. It means that as you edit and modify, your screen shows you *exactly what you're going to get when you print it out. No surprises. It's all there in front of your eyes.*	Another column of text.	$66

Figure 8.6: A table created with column tags

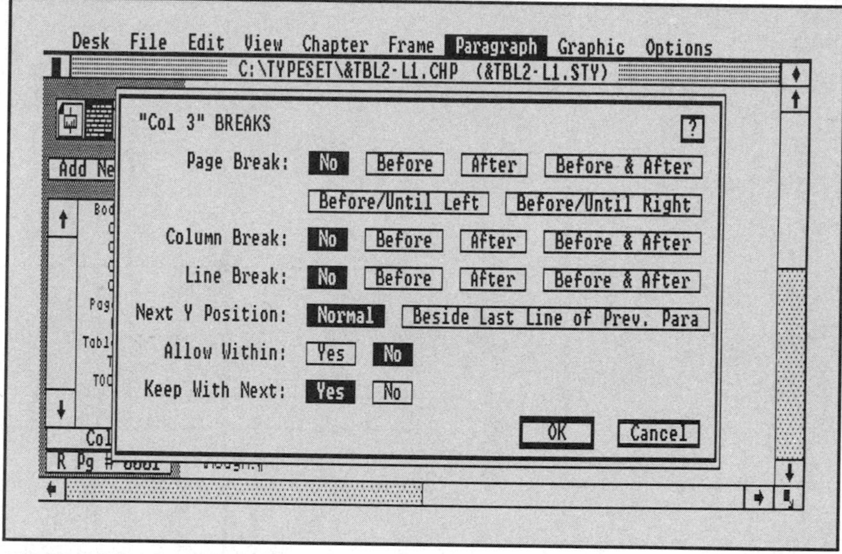

Figure 8.7: The Paragraph menu's Breaks dialog box, with tag settings for columns 2 and 3

In order to understand the Paragraph Breaks settings, let's first consider the standard paragraph. When you finish typing a regular paragraph into a document and press Enter, the cursor moves down to the line below the paragraph you've just completed. This action constitutes a *line break.* You then type in your text, beginning at the new spot.

For the Col 1 tag, Line Break is set to Before. This will cause the Column 1 entries—the first table entries in each row of entries—to begin on a new line, just as a standard paragraph does.

For the intermediate tags, Col 2 and Col 3, paragraphs must appear to the *right* of the previous paragraph, rather than below it. The second entry in a table is the paragraph that should be placed to the *right* of the first entry, not below the first entry. Thus, rather than breaking to the next line, you want the text to move back up to the *same* line that the previous paragraph began on. This arrangement allows paragraphs to line up horizontally on the page. By adjusting the Line Break setting, you control placement of the new paragraph.

For Col 2 and Col 3, click the No button for Line Break. This will make these table entries begin on the same line as the table entry before them. Normally, because this setting controls only vertical placement, returning to the same line as the previous paragraph

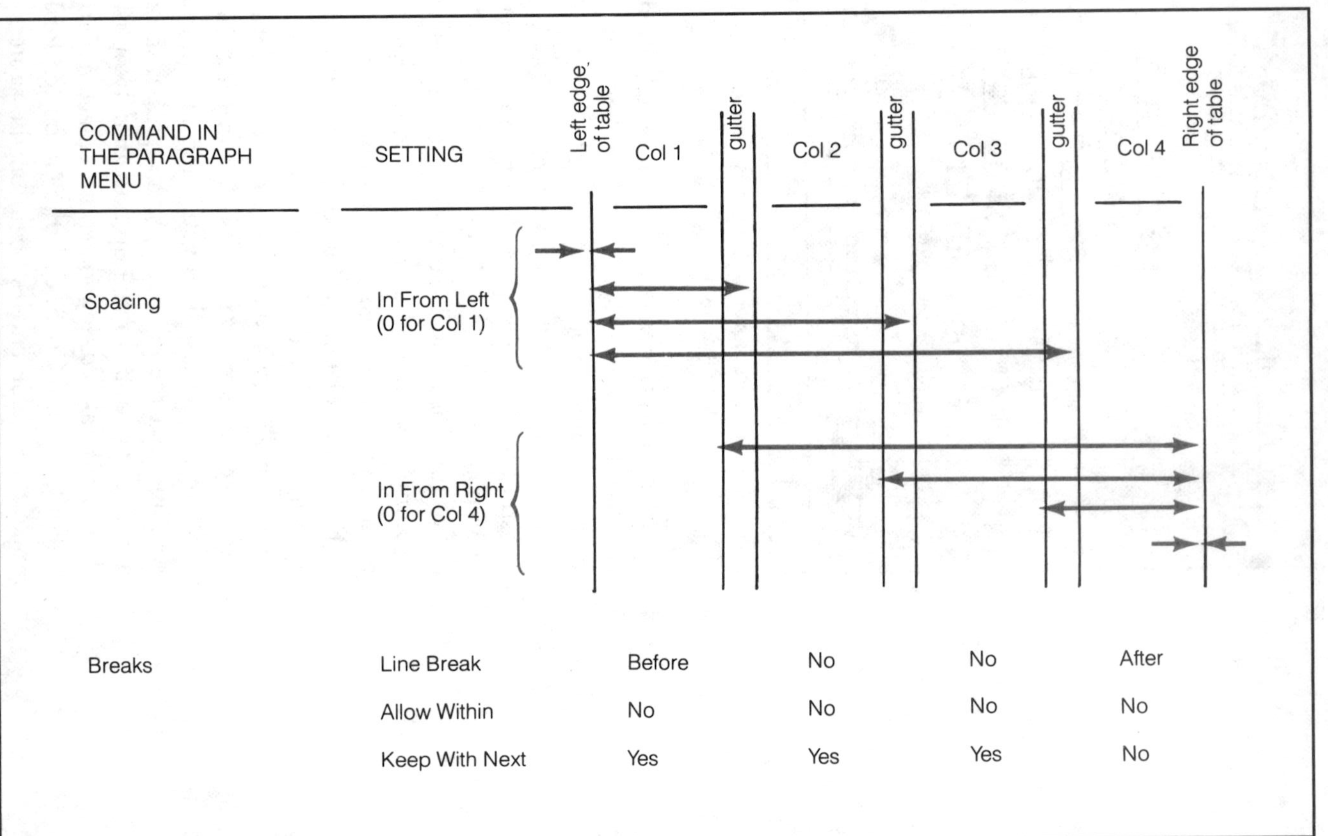

Figure 8.8: Settings that affect column tags

would cause a new paragraph to be superimposed on the previous one. However, the new paragraphs in this case have In From Left and In From Right values different from those of the preceding paragraph. The new paragraph will be offset to the right of the previous paragraph, rather than placed squarely on top of it.

Once you affix column tags to your text, you must never press Enter to begin a new paragraph within interior columns (that is, Col 2 and Col 3). Doing so will start a new paragraph, to be sure, but the new paragraph will be tagged the same as the previous paragraph. Because there would be no break between the paragraphs, the new paragraph would begin *at the same spot* as the previous paragraph. Ventura would superimpose the text of the new paragraph on that of the previous paragraph. If you should accidentally press Enter like this, immediately press the Backspace key to delete the return.

SINGLE COLUMN ENTRIES

There are two ways to create a single entry for a row. First, you can insert a Line Break code in the paragraph above the prospective entry by pressing Ctrl-Enter. This character looks like a broken arrow pointing to the left (Figure 8.9). The text will start on a new line, giving the appearance of a new paragraph.

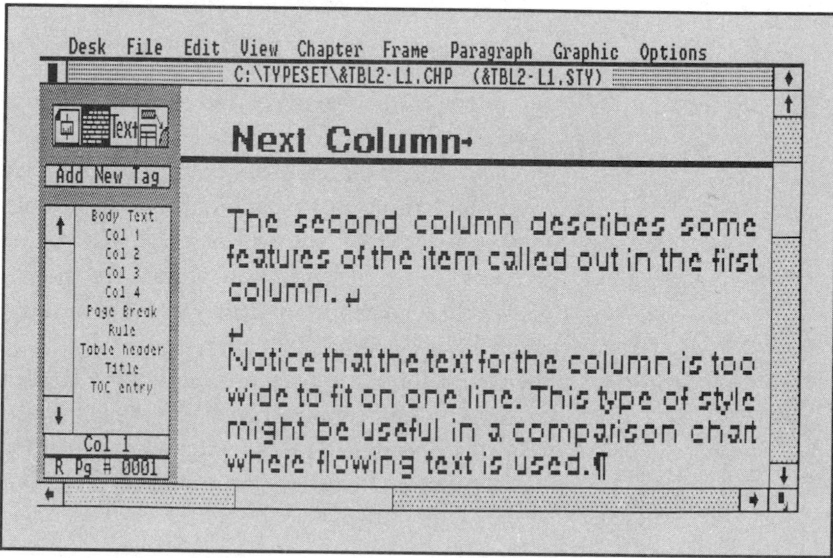

Figure 8.9: Creating a new paragraph with Line Break codes (Ctrl-Enter)

In Figure 8.10, the paragraph beginning with *Notice that the text* has received this treatment. Since it isn't a new paragraph as Ventura defines it (one created with a return), the Line Break settings in the Paragraph menu's Break dialog box do not take effect.

Unfortunately, other characteristics of the various Paragraph commands won't take effect either. For instance, if you're using the Paragraph menu's Spacing command to set Inter-Paragraph space, it won't apply to the space between paragraphs created with Ctrl-Enter. However, you can add space between such paragraphs by pressing Ctrl-Enter repeatedly to insert additional Line Break codes, as was done in this example.

The other way to create a single entry is to enter it after the last entry of the previous row of entries. After making the entry, tag it with the appropriate column format.

Note that this method in fact creates a new row. As such, the entry in the new row will begin after the entry of the previous row with the most lines. When used with our example, the result of this technique is identical to Figure 8.10. You can insert one or more individual entries like this as long as the entry at the end of the previous row is set to have a line break after it. If you can't use either of these techniques—if, for instance, the lines aren't breaking correctly—you can create an entirely new row of blank table entries.

ADDING A NEW ROW OF ENTRIES

If you need to add a new row of table entries, copying is probably the easiest way to accomplish it. Just copy the text of an existing row using the cut-and-paste techniques we discussed in Chapter 4. Then replace the text for each entry with the new text as required.

Figure 8.11 shows the table we've been studying, in Reduced view. Here the third row of the table has been copied, creating a new fourth row that's identical to the third. The new fourth row is darkened, since it has just been pasted in position. Text in the fourth row, except for the return characters (or Paragraph End codes) would be deleted and replaced with appropriate entries for the fourth row.

Although this technique is easy to understand and perform, it usually results in a lot of unnecessary text that you must delete. If you'd

Title of this table

Header for Table	Next Column	Third Col.	Price
First Entry	The second column describes some features of the item called out in the first column. Notice that the text for the column is too wide to fit on one line. This type of style might be useful in a comparison chart where flowing text is used.	The third column might expound a bit on the second column. But the fourth column just holds a number, such as price.	$456
Second model.	The next column.	The second model compares quite favorably to the first model described above. There's not as much text here though.	$654
Entry #3	More descriptive text about entry number three. It's called WYSIWYG. It means that as you edit and modify, your screen shows you *exactly what you're going to get when you print it out. No surprises. It's all there in front of your eyes.*	Another column of text.	$66

Figure 8.10: Creating a row containing a single entry

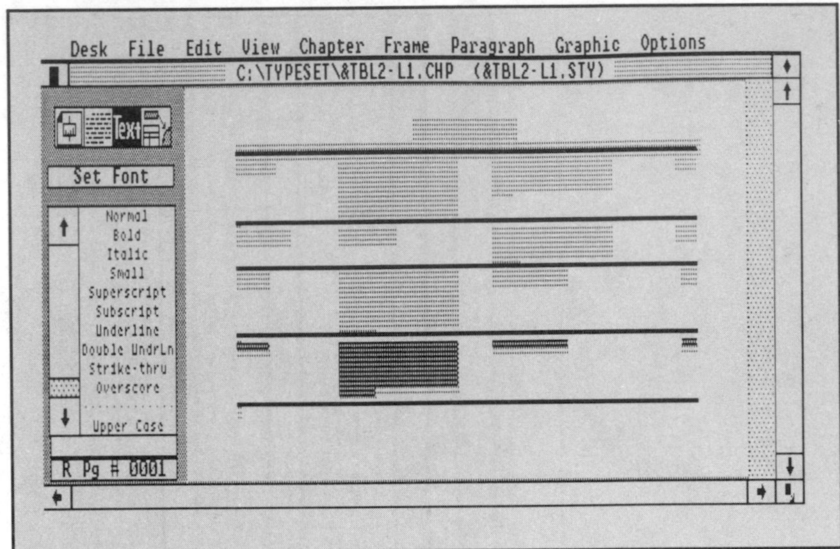

Figure 8.11: Copying to create a new row

prefer to begin with a clean slate, follow this method:

1. Start in Text mode. Position the text cursor at the beginning of the row of table entries that you wish to place the new row *above.* Press Enter the required number of times to create the appropriate number of Paragraph End codes (one for each column plus others to format intervening paragraphs, such as rule paragraphs).
2. Change to Paragraph mode. Tag each Paragraph End code appropriately (for example, Rule, Col 1, Col 2, and so on). The Paragraph End code will in turn position itself in the appropriate column.
3. Change back to Text mode. Position the cursor before each Paragraph End code in turn and type in your text.

In our example, let us assume that we wish to create an empty row before the row that begins with *Second model.* Consider that a row of table entries consists first of the Paragraph End code formatted with the Rule tag. There's no text in this "paragraph," only the code.

The sole purpose of this tag is to create the horizontal line that separates each row of entries. So for the first step:

- Activate Text mode, position the cursor just before the code formatted with the Rule tag, and press Enter five times.

Because all the Paragraph End codes will initially have the Rule tag, this action creates five additional horizontal lines (Figure 8.12).

1. Activate paragraph mode and tag the codes appropriately. Leave the first code tagged with the Rule format. Tag the code right below it as Col 1. When you do, the horizontal line above that code disappears as it takes on its new format, that of Col 1.
2. Tag the code below Col 1 as Col 2, causing this code to lose its rule and move up and over to column 2 (Figure 8.13).
3. Repeat the process for the last two Paragraph End codes and your four columns are formatted and ready for text.

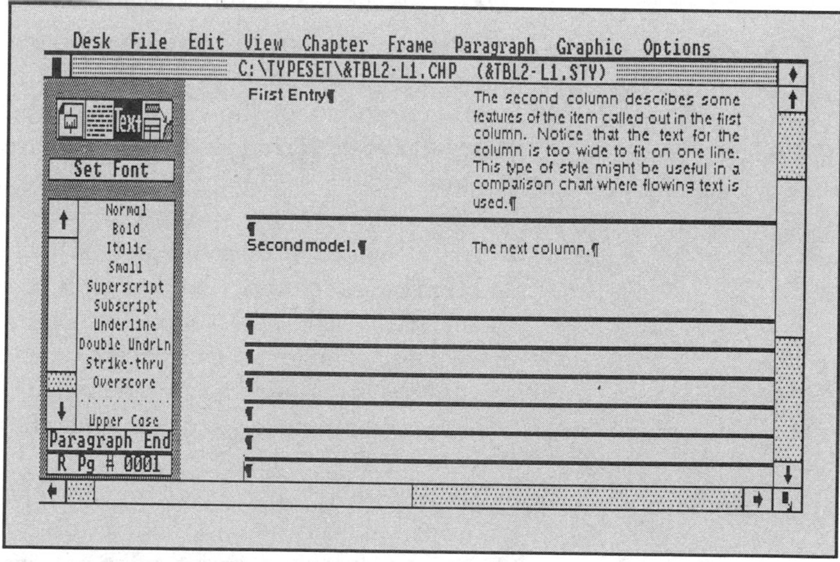

Figure 8.12: Creating Paragraph End codes to be formatted as columns

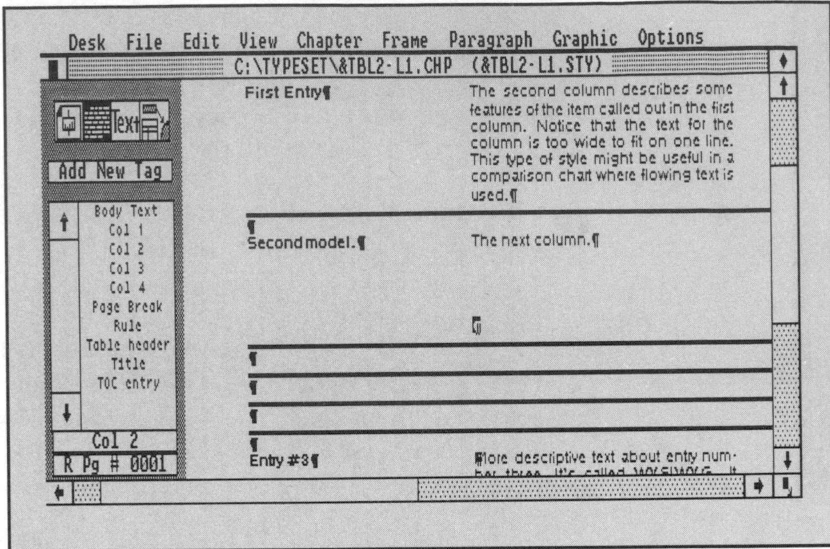

Figure 8.13: Tagging a Paragraph End code to position it in the second column

ADJUSTING THE SAMPLE FOR USE

Before we finish with our discussion of column tags and our work with the sample table shown in Figure 8.5, there is one last point we need to make about the sample. The discussion that follows is for those who wish to change the text and use the sample for their own purposes.

Notice that column 1 and column 4 each have very short table entries in them. Specifically, there is a short "header" in column 1 and a price in column 4. If you wish to use these two columns for longer entries like those you see in columns 2 and 3, you'll have to make some changes in paragraph spacing. Apparently, columns 1 and 4 weren't designed for long entries. If you start to type into these columns without making adjustments, the text you enter will overlap parts of columns 2 and 3.

To properly space these columns so that the distance between each column matches the space currently between columns 2 and 3, change the Paragraph menu's Spacing dialog box as follows. For the Col 1 tag, change In From Right to 7.67 inches (or 46 picas). For the Col 4 tag, change In From Left to 8 inches (or 48 picas).

As you can see, using column tags can become quite complex as the various properties of the tags interact with each other. However, once you set up a format, you can use it with any document that references the same style sheet. Column tags are especially helpful when you have long columns, with lots of descriptive or narrative text. Because the table length (that is, the number of lines the table occupies) adjusts automatically, the form of the table is dictated by its contents. If, on the other hand, the form of your document should control the length of its contents, you may want to use the third method of creating tables: Box text.

BOX TEXT

With Box text, you decide the shape of the table in a way that's independent of its contents. If the shape of your table must conform to a predetermined, highly structured format, such as that of an invoice, Box text may be the most appropriate way to produce it. Figure 8.14 shows a sample table using this method. The shape of a Box-text table does not adjust automatically as its contents change. If it becomes necessary to change the shape of such a table, you must do so as a separate operation.

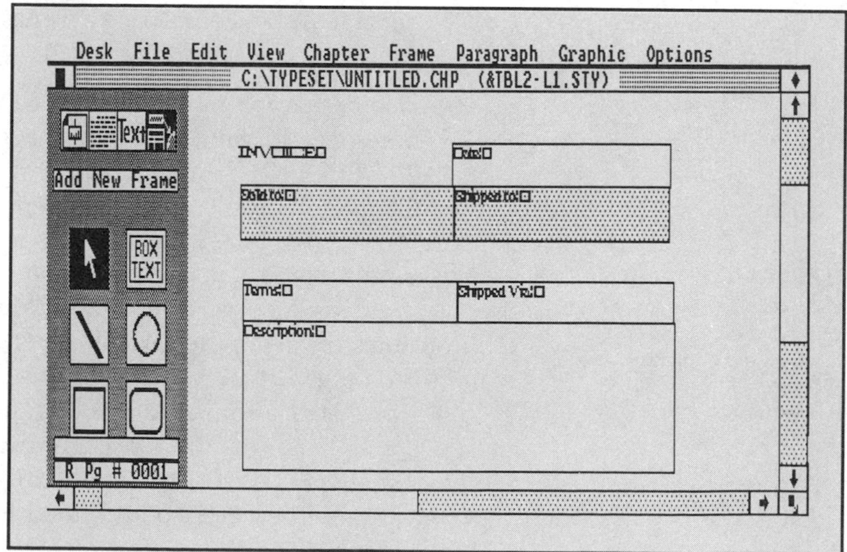

Figure 8.14: Creating a table with Box text

We examined Box text in the previous chapter, using it to create labels for a graph. Remember that the contents of Box text are stored in the chapter's CAP file; that is, the file with the same name as the chapter, except with a CAP extension. This means that you do not bring in word-processed files to use with Box text.

This also means that when you use Box text, you must set up the structure of the table before you can make any entries in it. You cannot create the table entries first and then shape those entries into a table, as you can with the previous methods.

Here are the steps to create a table, such as the invoice shown in Figure 8.14, using Box text:

1. Activate Graphics mode. If you want your boxes positioned at regular intervals, use the Graphic menu's Grid Settings command to indicate Grid Snap.
2. To create Box text, click the Box-text icon. Position and stretch each box into place. If you wish to create multiple boxes, hold down the Shift key as you create and size each one. That way, you won't have to click the Box-text icon for each box.
3. Add the appropriate text to each box. Use Text mode to create and edit this text.
4. Format the boxes as desired, using the various Graphic menu commands.
5. Use Paragraph mode to format the Box-text paragraphs as necessary. Initially, Box text is tagged with the generated tag Z_BOXTEXT, which you can change as desired. (See Chapter 4 for a discussion of Ventura's generated tags.)

With the Options menu, you can make generated tags show or not show on the Paragraph mode Assignment list. See Appendix A.

When first created, each Box-text entry usually has a thin outline around it. As we have seen, however, you can eliminate or modify such outlines by using the Graphic menu's Line Attributes command (or typing Ctrl-L).

You can add backgrounds to Box text, too. This makes special formats possible, like the address backgrounds in Figure 8.14. Use the Graphic menu's Fill Attributes command (or type Ctrl-F). Don't forget, you can use the Save To and Load From buttons to share line and fill attributes.

With Box text, you can change formatting attributes for more than one box at a time. Once you select one box, pressing the Shift key as you click allows you to select additional boxes simultaneously. Multiple selected boxes can then be formatted together; moved, stretched, and shrunk with the mouse; and cut or copied with the Del key. For instance, you may wish to move the bottom three boxes in Figure 8.14 away from the others. Select these three as a group and move any one of them; the other two will move with it. (Note that this capability differs from that available to multiple frames. You can cut, copy, and move frames as a unit, but you cannot incorporate formatting changes to multiple frames at one time.)

We've now examined the three most common and effective ways to create tables. There is a fourth way, however, that you may need to consider.

USING SPACES TO CREATE TABLES

You can also use spaces, created by pressing the space bar, to separate the entries in a table. It's undesirable to do so, however, because of the limitations imposed by using spaces.

First, you can only print tables created with spaces if you use a nonproportional font. With proportional fonts, characters vary in width, making it hard—often impossible—to line up columns containing different characters.

In addition, it's difficult to make changes to a table created with spaces. To move columns, you have to add or remove spaces for each line of text involved.

Unfortunately, tables you import will often have spaces between entries. For instance, if you use the Lotus 1-2-3 / Print File command to export a table, the resulting table has spaces between entries. In addition, people preparing tables with a word processor often make the mistake of using spaces to separate entries. In a word processor, where proportional fonts are not displayed, columns separated by spaces may line up very nicely—not so once the text is transferred to Ventura.

If you should acquire a table that uses spaces, you have two options for dealing with it. You can use it as is and print the table with a nonproportional font, if your printer has one. (Of course, only the table needs the nonproportional font. Text above or below the table can use proportional fonts.)

Alternatively, you can go through the table—with Ventura or with your word processor—strip away the spaces between entries, and replace them with tabs. Then you could use tab settings to align the columns properly. There are programs that perform the substitution automatically; one of the most effective is available with Microsoft WORD 4.0. (see Chapter 11).

Placement of the items in a table is important in determining how the table looks and communicates its subject matter. In Chapter 9, we'll see how placement of items on the page is just as important in determining how the page looks and communicates.

CHAPTER
9

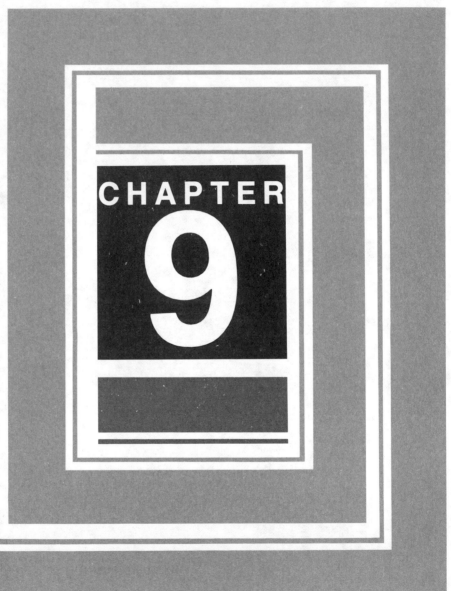

Working with Pages: Formats and Page Headings

Fast Track

To create a book-style document, 326

assign a word-processed file to the underlying-page frame. To create a layout-intensive document, divide up the page by filling it with frames.

To add a page to a document 328

use the Chapter menu's Insert/Remove Page. When you insert a page like this, it has a new underlying-page frame. Pages that Ventura generates from it share this underlying-page frame. Use the same command to remove a page from the document.

To have Ventura automatically generate pages 329

assign a text file to the underlying-page frame. Ventura generates as many pages as necessary to accommodate the text in the file. Alternatively, insert the text cursor in the underlying-page frame and then fill the page with frames. This pushes the text cursor to the next page, automatically generating a new page.

To combine text files 330

place the text cursor at the end of one loaded file and use the Edit menu's Load Text/Picture dialog box. Specify Destination: Text Cursor to load the second file. You can also assign the file you're loading to a newly inserted page and to a frame following the first file.

To make a frame repeat on each page 334

begin by creating a standard frame. Then, with the frame selected, use the Frame menu's Repeating Frame to change it into a repeating frame. Use the same procedure to change a repeating frame back into a standard frame. You cannot cut, copy, or paste a repeating frame, and it cannot have a caption.

To hide individual repeating frames 337

on any given page, use the Frame menu's Repeating Frame. Use the same dialog box to redisplay hidden frames.

To create more columns on a page 337

than Ventura's standard eight columns, add one or more repeating frames to the page. Assign to it the same file as that of the underlying-page frame.

To regulate the number of isolated lines 339

at the top (*widows*) or bottom (*orphans*) of a page or column, use the Chapter menu's Chapter Typography. You can also override the chapter's widow and orphan settings by activating Frame mode to select a frame and then using the Frame menu's Frame Typography.

To match the ending positions of text 341

in columns, insert a thin frame within a short column of text to move text down. The thin frame is often no bigger than one line of text.

To create headers and footers 341

use the Chapter Menu's Headers & Footers. You can create one- or two-line headers and footers at the left, center and right positions on the page. You can create such setups independently for left- and right-hand pages. Use the 1st Match and Last Match settings to create catch phrases that pick up text (such as headings) from the page and place them in the page's header or footer.

To turn a header or footer off for a page 349

use the Chapter menu and select Turn Header Off or Turn Footer Off.

CHAPTER 9

GENERALLY, A DESKTOP-PUBLISHED DOCUMENT falls into one of two categories. The first type of document emphasizes elements on the page. You create it with the computer equivalent of a layout artist's pasteup board. Individual pages are important in this type of document. Each page is carefully composed, and the elements on the page are strategically positioned. This kind of document is often deemed *layout-intensive,* or *pasteup-oriented.* Sometimes it is called a *complex document.* Most newsletters and magazines are layout-intensive documents.

The second type of document emphasizes one long section of text. Books and manuals both fall within this category. The strategy for creating these documents lies in setting up general parameters for pages. Pages are not individually crafted (although they are usually fine-tuned). Instead, the computer constructs the document more or less automatically, guided by the parameters you set. Sometimes the resulting document is called a *batch-processed document* or a *simple document.* Perhaps *book-style document* is the most direct term.

Fortunately, Ventura has the ability to create and handle both types of documents. With Ventura, it's as easy to paste up individual pages as it is to set up the parameters for a book. And regardless of the method, Ventura allows you to see on the screen what you'll get when you print (which is not the case with other programs, especially those that create book-style documents).

To create book-style publications with Ventura, you assign a word-processed file to the underlying-page frame. The amount of material in the file initially determines the number of pages in the document. This is because Ventura automatically creates as many pages as necessary to accommodate all the text in the assigned file. To create layout-intensive documents, on the other hand, you generally use numerous standard frames that are placed on top of the underlying-page frame. Sometimes, the underlying-page frame holds little or no material.

You use a variety of Ventura commands to set up the respective formats for both types of documents. Be aware, however, that most formatting commands do not apply strictly to one type of document or the other; most are used with either type. Also be aware that not all documents fall neatly into one of these two categories. Many documents possess properties of both types.

Bearing this in mind, in this chapter we'll examine Ventura commands chiefly as they apply to layout-intensive documents. Even so, we must examine the underlying-page frame, as it forms the substratum of both kinds of documents in Ventura. In Chapter 10, we'll focus on commands that are more generally utilized with book-style documents.

The newsletter we studied earlier in this book is an example of a layout-intensive document. As constructed, it has numerous standard frames that hold text and pictures. However, there is no material in its underlying-page frame; all its material is in the various standard frames that sit on top of the underlying-page frame.

You can store the text for standard frames in either of two ways. You can use word-processed text in files that you assign to the frame with the Assignment list. Or, in Text mode, you can click the frame and simply type your text directly into the standard frame. Such directly entered text is called *Frame text.* When you select such a frame in Frame mode, this is the designation that appears in the Current box. Ventura stores Frame text in the chapter's CAP file. (Note that you cannot store text directly in the underlying-page frame; such text must be stored in a file. However, with version 2.0, Ventura will automatically assign a file name, based on the chapter name, to text you enter in the underlying-page frame.)

You do not have to load Ventura to understand this chapter. However, you can do so if you would like to view the various menus and dialog boxes being discussed.

ADDING AND REMOVING PAGES

With layout-intensive documents, you carefully construct each page. Initially, a Ventura document has only one page. So working with layout-intensive documents usually means crafting the first page and adding additional pages, laying out each one as you go.

CUSTOM PAGES

The usual way to add pages is with the Chapter menu's Insert/Remove Page dialog box (Figure 9.1). As indicated by the darkened button in this dialog box, the default choice inserts a new page after the page that is current when you invoke the dialog box. You can also insert a page before the current page by using the first button in the dialog box.

When using this dialog box, however, be aware that the page you insert differs from other pages that Ventura may have generated automatically to accommodate text in the underlying-page frame. With pages that are generated automatically, underlying-page attributes that you set for one page—such as margins and columns, ruling lines and boxes, and frame background—affect all the pages. However, when you insert a page using the Chapter menu, these frame attributes are handled separately for the new page. Likewise, graphic elements that you subsequently cause to repeat on the underlying-page frame will not appear on the inserted page. (In fact, inserting a page creates a second underlying-page frame. As we'll see shortly, this new underlying-page frame can generate additional pages that share its attributes.)

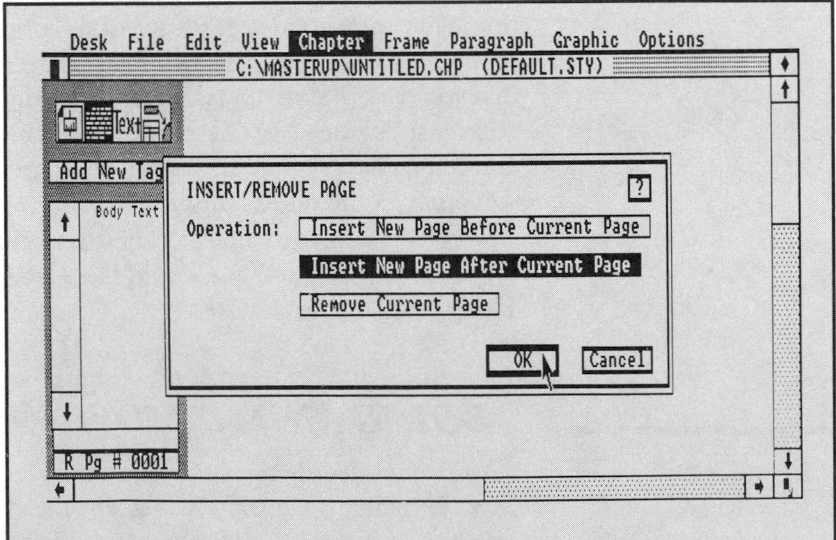

Figure 9.1: The Chapter menu's Insert/Remove Page dialog box

You can snap frames to the columns in the underlying-page frame and display the edges of the columns with the Options menu. See Appendix A.

The fact that an inserted page can have margins, columns, and other attributes different from those of other pages makes inserted pages useful in layout-intensive documents. With such documents, it's often necessary to set up each page differently. Using inserted pages you can have, for instance, page 1 set up for 2 columns, and page 2 set up for 3 columns. Even if you do not use the columns to hold text directly, you can then use them to snap standard frames into place.

The underlying-page frame of a newly created page has the same initial format as the page that comes before it in the chapter. This holds true whether the previous page was generated automatically or custom-created by inserting. It also holds true whether you created the page by inserting it before or after the current page. You can change this format, as we'll see in a moment.

In addition to creating pages, you use the Chapter menu's Insert/Remove Page dialog box to remove the currently displayed page. Be very careful when you remove a page. Once you do, it cannot be retrieved. There is no clipboard that stores the removed page. However, if you wish to save the contents of the current page for later use, you can effectively move the page items as a group by moving multiple frames. In Frame mode, select all the frames (by Shift-clicking each one) and delete them as a group (with the Del key or the Edit menu's Cut Frame command). Once you've created a new page, you can use the Ins key (or the Edit menu's Paste Frame command) to place the group of frames in their same relative positions on the new page.

AUTOMATICALLY GENERATED PAGES

As mentioned, when you assign a file to the underlying-page frame, Ventura automatically generates as many pages as necessary to accommodate the text in that file. In addition, you can trick Ventura into generating additional pages even when you don't use the underlying-page frame to accommodate a file. To do so, you fill each page with standard frames; as you do, Ventura automatically generates additional pages. Place your text into these standard frames, rather than in the underlying-page frame. The resulting pages, because they are automatically generated, all share the same underlying-page frame and hence the same format. This holds true even if you later change the format of any page. Use this technique when you want features of the underlying-page frame to be similar throughout the document and to remain similar, even though the standard frames on top may differ. Here's how you get Ventura to automatically create pages without text:

* To show tabs and returns (and the End Of File marker) use the Options menu or Ctrl-T. See Appendix A.

1. In Text mode, click the underlying-page frame as if you were placing the Text cursor into position. The End Of File marker (□) appears (if tabs and returns are showing).
2. Place your frames on the underlying-page frame as usual.
3. When you fill up an entire page with frames, these frames will push the End Of File marker off the page, causing it to create a new page. The new page shares the same underlying-page frame as the page from which it was generated.

Once created, new pages will be formatted similarly and will adjust as you make changes to the underlying-page frame on any page. Use this method if, for instance, you expect to have three columns of frames and constant margins throughout. If you want to be able to mix formats on the underlying-page frame, use the method outlined earlier to create additional pages.

Even with layout-intensive documents, you may wish to use the underlying-page frame if your document addresses one main text file at a time and you want to use the entirety of that file in sequence. Thus, a magazine that uses a lot of frames would usually be considered a layout-intensive document. If there is one main article at a time, however, you would probably want to assign that article to the underlying-page frame. Because Ventura creates as many pages as necessary to hold the contents of the underlying-page frame, all the material in the assigned file will always be displayed. Removing a page that is automatically generated will not decrease the number of pages; Ventura will immediately recreate the page to accommodate the text.

COMBINING TEXT FILES

When, in the course of the magazine, a new article becomes the main article, there are two ways you can accommodate the new article. Obviously, you can place the second article in the same word-processed file as the first article. With Ventura 2.0 you can add the second article to the first by using the File menu's Load Text/Picture dialog box, specifying Destination: Text Cursor. Once the articles are in the same file, the second article will naturally follow right on the heels of the first. Of course, you'll want to tag the article's title to set it off from body text and separate the articles. If you want the second article to begin on a new page, create a title tag that has the Paragraph menu's Breaks dialog box set for Page Break Before. Follow a similar strategy with Column Break Before if you want the second article to start at the top of a new column.

Another way to deal with the second article is to keep it in a separate file. You won't be able to assign it to the same underlying-page frame as the first article; doing so would cause the second article to replace the first on all pages the first article appears on. Instead, use the Chapter menu's Insert/Remove Page command to insert a new page. The newly inserted page will initially be blank. Assign the second article to the inserted page. This creates a new underlying-page frame. As such, Ventura will generate as many additional pages as necessary to accommodate the second article.

You can insert the additional page at the beginning, middle, or end of existing pages. Ventura will cause newly generated pages to immediately follow the page you originally inserted. For example, assume you insert a page in the middle of the first article. When you assign the second article to it, Ventura will generate as many pages as necessary to accommodate the second article and push the last half of the first article back. The first article will continue on its pages after the second article is complete (Figure 9.2).

If you want the second article (in a separate file) to appear on the page where the first article ends, create a standard frame on the page, after the end of the first article. Assign the second article to that frame. Figure 9.3 shows such a frame, indicated by the selection handles. The frame holds the beginning of the second article. The left-hand page has the first article, which ends just above the standard frame, assigned to it. The right-hand page, created with the Chapter menu's Insert/Remove Page, has the second article assigned to it. Because of how it's created, this page has a new underlying-page frame, and it generates as many pages as necessary to accommodate the second article. The article picks up at the top of the right-hand

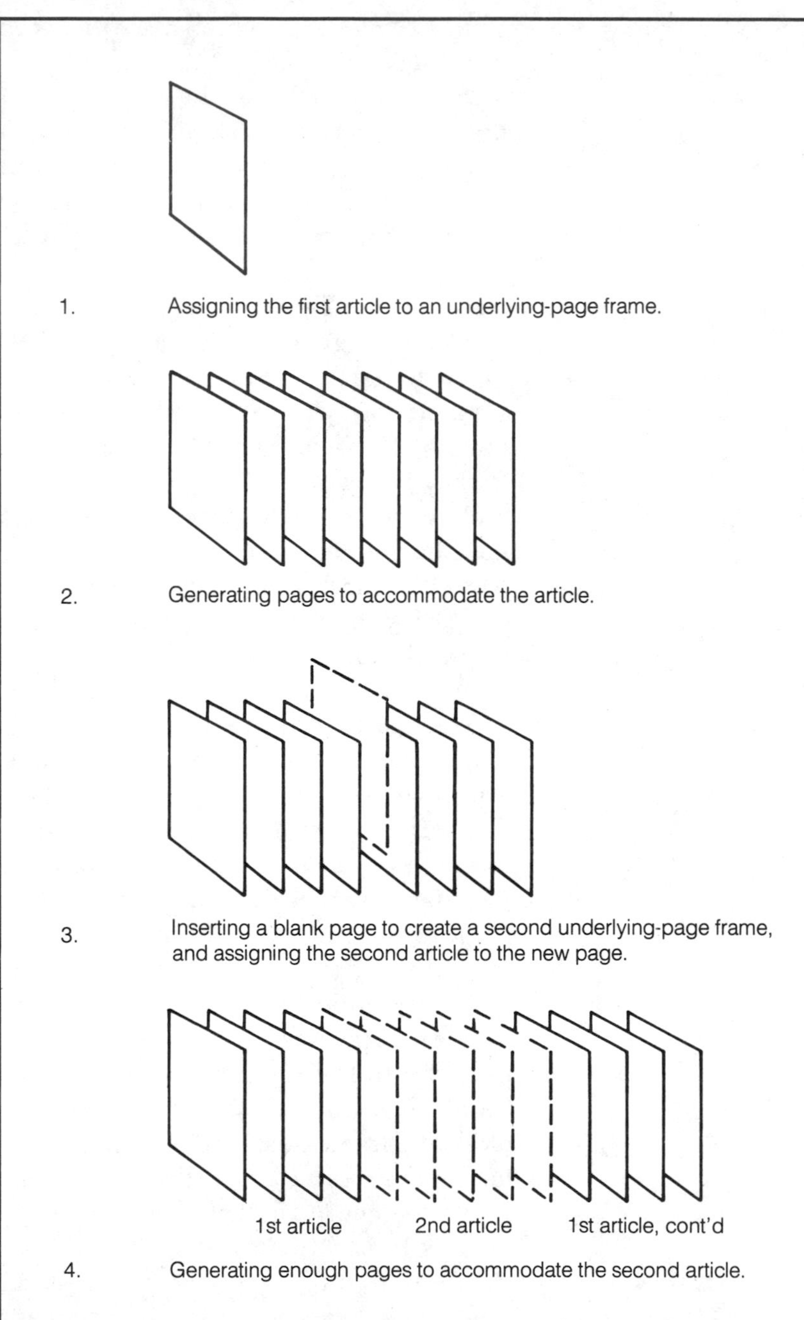

1.
Assigning the first article to an underlying-page frame.
2.
Generating pages to accommodate the article.
3.
Inserting a blank page to create a second underlying-page frame, and assigning the second article to the new page.
1st article
2nd article
1st article, cont'd
4.
Generating enough pages to accommodate the second article.

Figure 9.2: Inserting a page to create a second underlying-page frame

page where it left off at the bottom of the standard frame on the left-hand page.

Now that you have an understanding of underlying-page frames, let's look at another feature of page layouts: frames that repeat on every page.

REPEATING FRAMES

Ventura's repeating-frame feature allows you to create a frame that Ventura duplicates on every page in the chapter. With this feature, you can make any frame and its contents, such as your company logo and slogan, appear on every page. Ventura will repeat the entire frame in the same size and position on every page, whether automatically generated or custom-inserted. Other attributes assigned to the frame, including vertical rules, ruling lines, and frame background, also repeat. There are some restrictions, however. You cannot cut, copy, or paste repeating frames, and they cannot have captions. You would have to change a repeating frame back to a standard frame to perform these operations.

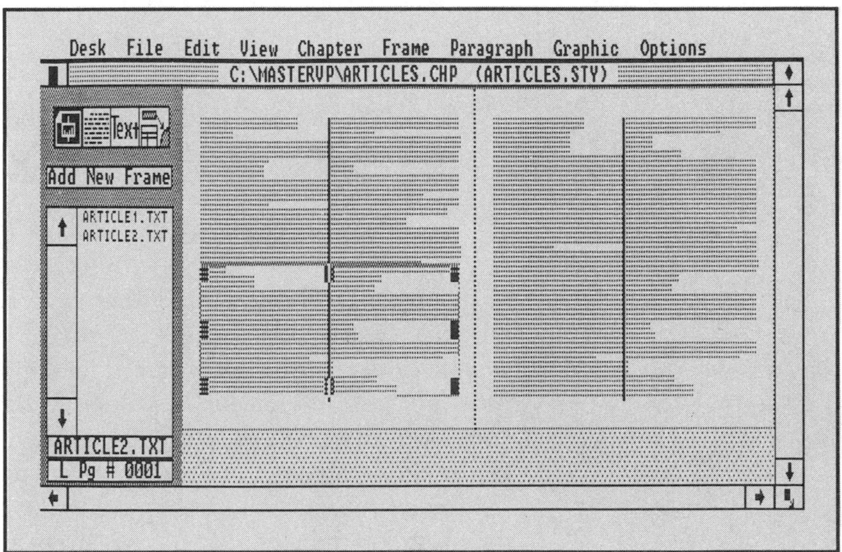

Figure 9.3: A second file's article beginning on the same page as the first

CREATING REPEATING FRAMES

To make a repeating frame, begin by creating a standard frame on any page of the document.

If you are using double-sided pages (as specified with the Chapter menu's Page Size & Layout command), you can create a repeating frame on the left- or right-hand pages or both. If you plan to create a frame that repeats on the left-hand pages only, create the initial standard frame on a left-hand page for the most predictable results. Likewise, create a standard frame on a right-hand page if you want it to repeat on right-hand pages only.

Once the standard frame is created, select it in Frame mode to assign a text or picture file to it. Or place the Text cursor in the frame and type in Frame text. Add any decorating attributes, such as ruling lines and frame background, that you desire. Use Graphics mode to create graphics tied to the frame if you wish. (You can also change or add to frame attributes or graphics after the repeating frame is created.) Once you've fashioned the standard frame to your satisfaction, proceed as follows to change the standard frame into a repeating frame:

1. Activate Frame mode and select the standard frame you wish to change into a repeating frame.
2. Drop the Frame menu and select Repeating Frame. You'll see the dialog box shown in Figure 9.4.
3. In the For All Pages grouping, click the Left, Right, or Left & Right button to indicate where you want the repeating frame to appear.
4. Give the OK to create the repeating frame.

If you designate the frame to repeat on both left- and right-hand pages, Ventura will reflect placement of the frame on the page opposite the one on which you created it (Figure 9.5). If you want placement of the frame on the opposite page not to reflect but rather to copy *exactly* the original, copy the original to one of the facing pages before changing the standard frame into a repeating frame. Make the version on the left-hand page a repeating frame for left pages. Make the frame on the right-hand page a repeating frame for right pages. (Of course, this procedure isn't necessary for repeating frames that span the page.)

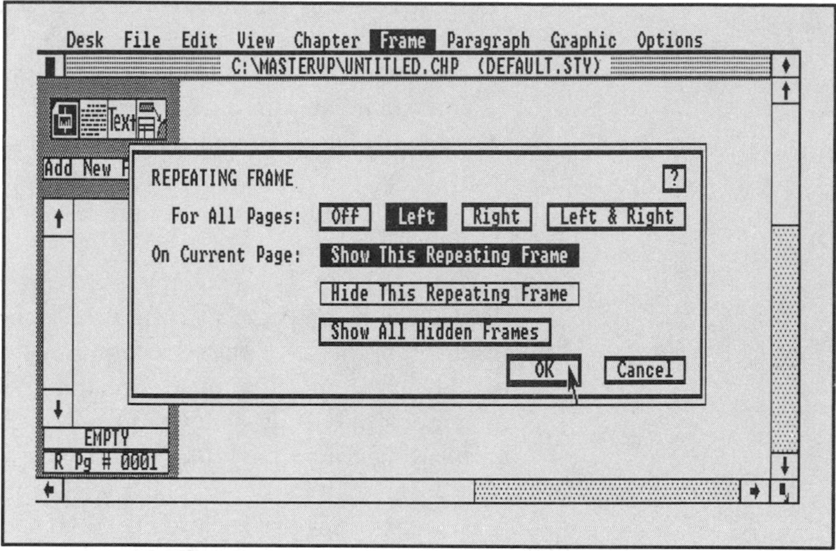

Figure 9.4: The Frame menu's Repeating Frame dialog box

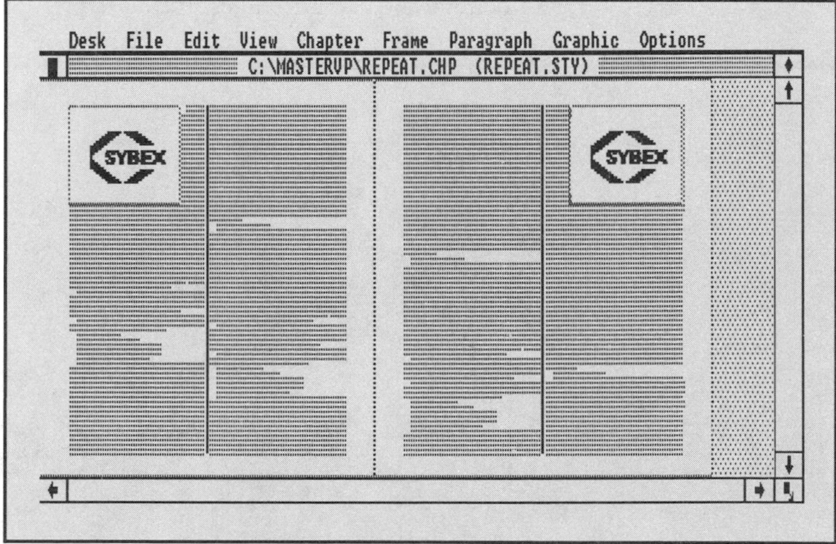

Figure 9.5: A repeating frame reflected on the facing page

You click a repeating frame in the working area to select it. You can then change its various characteristics and move or resize it. Changes that you make to a repeating frame on any page affect its clones on all other pages. When you select a frame, handles appear along the frame's edges, just as they do when you select a standard frame. However, the handles for repeating frames are shaded instead of black, indicating they're attached to a repeating frame (Figure 9.6).

You can create up to six repeating frames in a chapter. However, you cannot change standard frames into repeating frames simultaneously by selecting them as multiple frames. Likewise, you cannot change repeating frames that are selected as multiple back to standard frames simultaneously.

If you need to change a repeating frame back to a standard frame, display the page where you want the standard frame to appear. For instance, if you have placed a company logo on each page of a document using a repeating frame, and then decide that you want the logo on the first page only, you would call up this page. Once you change a repeating frame back to a standard frame, it will appear on this page and no others. If you plan to delete the frame, choose any page. (You must change a repeating frame back to a standard frame before you can delete it.) Activate Frame mode and select the repeating frame. Then use the Frame menu's Repeating Frame dialog box and change the For All Pages setting to Off. When you give the OK, the frame will become a standard frame, which you can cut or copy as you wish.

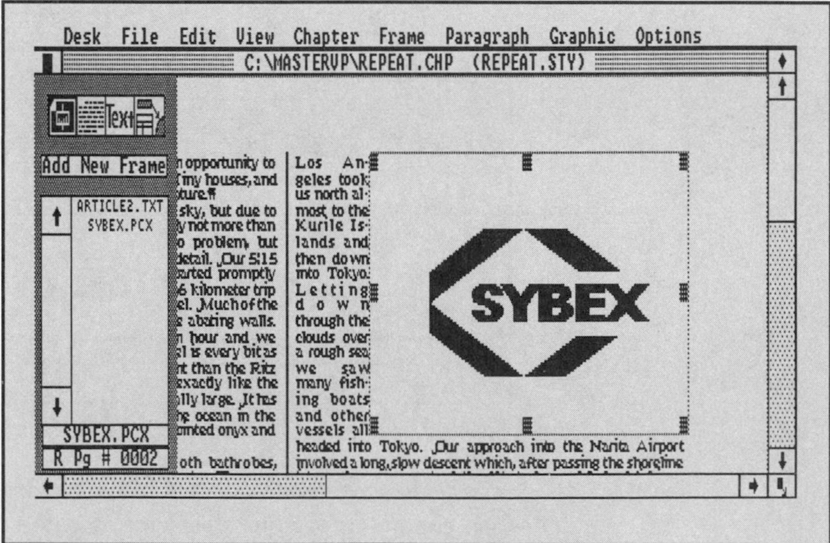

Figure 9.6: Shaded handles indicating a repeating frame

HIDING AND SHOWING INDIVIDUAL REPEATING FRAMES

You can use the Repeating Frame dialog box to keep a repeating frame from being displayed on any given page. You may wish to do this if the repeating frame would disrupt the contents of a given page, such as a table occupying an entire page. To hide a repeating frame, display the page with the repeating frame that you wish to remove. Select the repeating frame on that page. Then use the Frame menu's Repeating Frame dialog box and click Hide This Repeating Frame.

Once you hide a repeating frame, you can redisplay it in one of two ways, depending upon when you decide to do so. Right after you hide a frame, it remains selected and continues to appear on the page, though ghosting. If you change your mind at this point and decide to display the repeating frame, use the Repeating Frame dialog box and click Show This Repeating Frame. If, after hiding a repeating frame, you should choose some other frame or change operating modes, the hidden repeating frame will disappear. To redisplay it, you must click the button labeled Show All Hidden Frames. When you give the OK, the hidden repeating frame will appear. At the same time, any other repeating frames you've hidden on that page will appear as well. You must again hide those repeating frames that you don't want shown.

CREATING ADDITIONAL COLUMNS

* Using the Professional Extension in conjunction with expanded memory helps eliminate messages saying that the frame is too complex. See Chapter 13.

As you know, all frames can accommodate up to eight columns. Since this includes the underlying-page frame, this means that you should normally be able to get eight columns of text per page as well. Yet when you attempt to use eight columns, Ventura may display an error message saying that the frame is too complex to format. By utilizing repeating frames on top of the underlying-page frame, you can eliminate the error message and still use eight or more columns. To make the text flow unnoticeably from frame to frame, you assign to the repeating frames the same text file as the one assigned to the underlying-page frame.

Be aware, however, that applying these techniques can be tricky. Creating columns of equal width, keeping underlying text from appearing between frames, and avoiding frames that are too complex in the process all require a considerable understanding of how Ventura operates.

Consider the nine columns we have created in Figure 9.7 on a letter-size page. All displayed columns are .63 inch wide, and all gutters are .17 inch wide. (In addition, the underlying-page frame has margins of .75 inch all around.) The selection handles indicate the positions of two repeating frames placed over the underlying-page frame. Each of these repeating frames contains three columns. Although the underlying-page frame appears to have three columns as well (the first three on the left), it actually has five columns. The two additional columns are under each of the two repeating frames. They are each 2.22 inches wide. No text, however, flows into these two additional columns, because they are fully covered by the two repeating frames. Note that we had to create two additional columns rather than one; with only one additional column, underlying text would show between the two repeating frames.

So far we've looked at commands that control the layout of frames on the page. Now let's look at how Ventura's widow and orphan control affects where lines of text are placed.

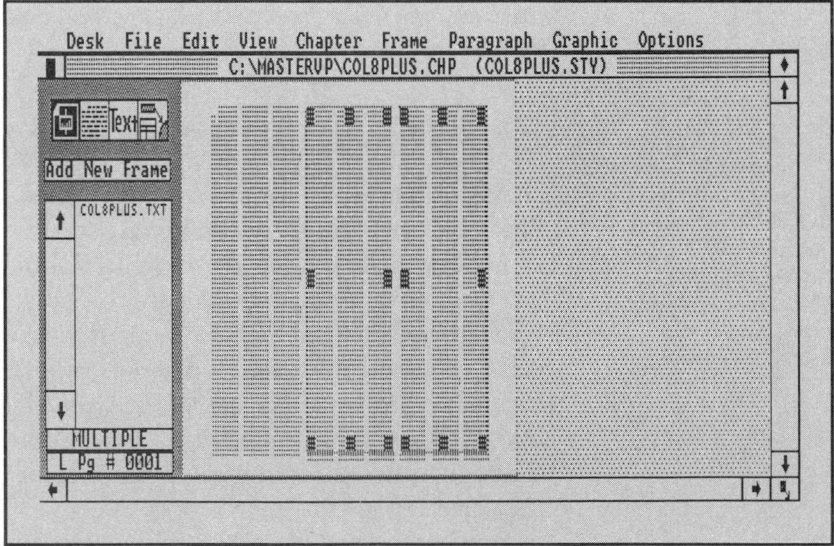

Figure 9.7: Repeating frames used to create additional columns

WIDOWS AND ORPHANS

When filling a page with text, Ventura encounters situations where it is necessary to split a paragraph between the bottom of one page and the top of the next. Ventura allows you to specify how many lines may be separated from the bulk of the paragraph by such a split. In Ventura *widows* are lines separated from a paragraph and placed at the top of the new page. *Orphans* are lines at the bottom of a page that begin a paragraph but are separated from the bulk of the paragraph, which is placed at the top of the next page. (Be aware that these definitions are specific to Ventura. They may differ from those of other software packages, such as WordPerfect, or from a standard typographic definition.)

A single such isolated line is generally thought undesirable. Consider that as you read text, you usually have an idea of where a paragraph is going to end. You sense the size of a paragraph in order to judge the amount of thought in it. So when you turn the page on a split paragraph, a single line can be jolting when you suddenly realize that the paragraph is ending. This draws your mind to the mechanics of the document and away from the subject matter.

Normally, widow control is set for two lines. This setting means that a minimum of two lines must be carried over to the next page when a paragraph runs out of room. So, when necessary, instead of filling in the first page with all but one line, Ventura will fill it in with all but two lines and then place those two lines at the top of the next page. Orphan control is usually set for two lines as well.

Figure 9.8 shows the dialog box that regulates widows and orphans with regard to chapters. To display this dialog box, drop the Chapter menu and select Chapter Typography. Notice that it doesn't matter which mode is active.

For the Widow grouping, you can have between 1 and 5 isolated lines. Clicking 1 essentially turns widow control off. It allows single lines to be isolated at the top of the page should that condition arise. When the dialog box is set at 2, the default setting, one-line widows will not be allowed. A single line at the top of a page will always be joined by another line pulled from the bottom of the previous page. This, of course, adds a blank line to the bottom of the previous page. Such an additional blank line is generally acceptable, unless you are creating a

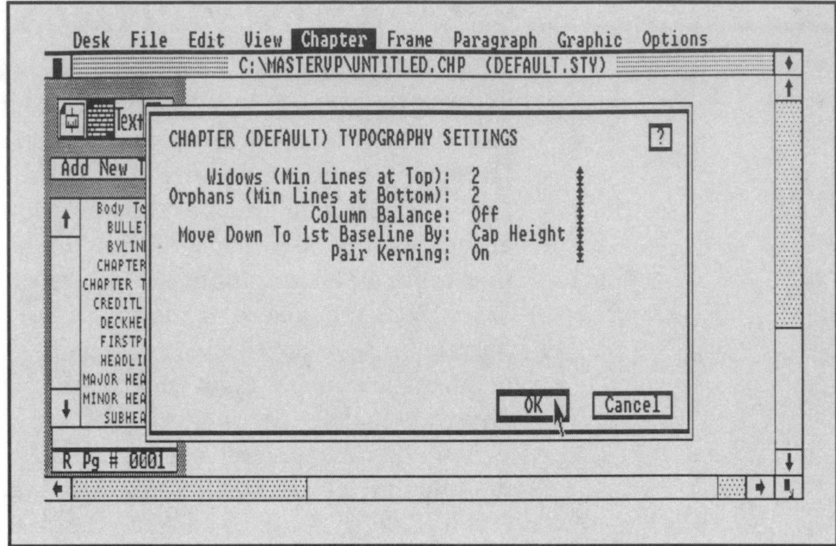

Figure 9.8: The Chapter menu's Chapter Typography Settings dialog box

document with facing pages, in which case text on the facing pages should end at the same place. You can adjust page depth by using a thin frame, as we'll see in the next section.

By providing numbers larger than 2 for Minimum Isolated Lines, Ventura provides additional flexibility. If you change the setting to 3, the program will not allow two lines to be widowed. Assume, for instance, that you're creating a catalog and each paragraph describes a product. Let's say that the last two lines of each paragraph list the prices of the item described in the paragraph. It would confuse the reader to allow these prices to be removed from at least some of the description. By changing the At Top setting to 3 you would guarantee that at least one line of descriptive text would precede the two lines of prices.

However, the one line of descriptive text could itself be considered undesirable. By changing the A-1 Top setting to 4, you would ensure that at least two lines of description would always precede the two lines of prices.

Now let's consider orphans. By changing the Orphan setting in the dialog box, you can control the minimum number of lines required at the bottom of the page. Setting At Bottom to 1 eliminates control of orphan lines. The default setting is 2.

! New for version 2.0

In any given frame, you can now override the chapter's widow/orphan settings. In Frame mode with the frame selected, use the Frame menu's Frame Typography command. As with chapter typography, you can set widows and orphans from 1 to 5 lines each. You can also use the Default setting, which causes the frame to take its setting from the chapter setting.

Although widow and orphan control is usually considered with regard to pages, Ventura's controls operate with respect to columns as well. The settings in this dialog box control the amount of text that can be separated from a paragraph at the top or bottom of a column. Of course, they only take effect when you're using multiple columns.

ENDING COLUMNS EVENLY

As we mentioned, widow and orphan control can sometimes cause pages or columns to end in slightly different places. It's best if facing pages and especially columns on the same page end evenly. To correct such a problem, judiciously place a thin frame into short columns. The thin frame, often the equivalent depth of one line, will push material down so that text at the bottom of the page is flush with text on a facing page or in a matching column.

Ventura's sample document &MAG-P3 has this problem when printed with the HP LaserJet and some other printers. Examine the document in Figure B.8 in Appendix B. Figure 9.9 shows this document with thin frames added to correct the problem by pushing down text in the second and third columns. Selection handles indicate the thin frames. We've shown this document with a full-page display so that you can see the thin frames and their effect at the same time.

Now let's look at another design element that affects the tops and bottoms of pages, headers and footers.

HEADERS AND FOOTERS

A *header* is textual material that appears at the top of each page in a document. Typically, it consists of information about the chapter or about material on the page where it appears. Headers are also called *running heads*. A *footer* is similar material that appears at the bottom of the page.

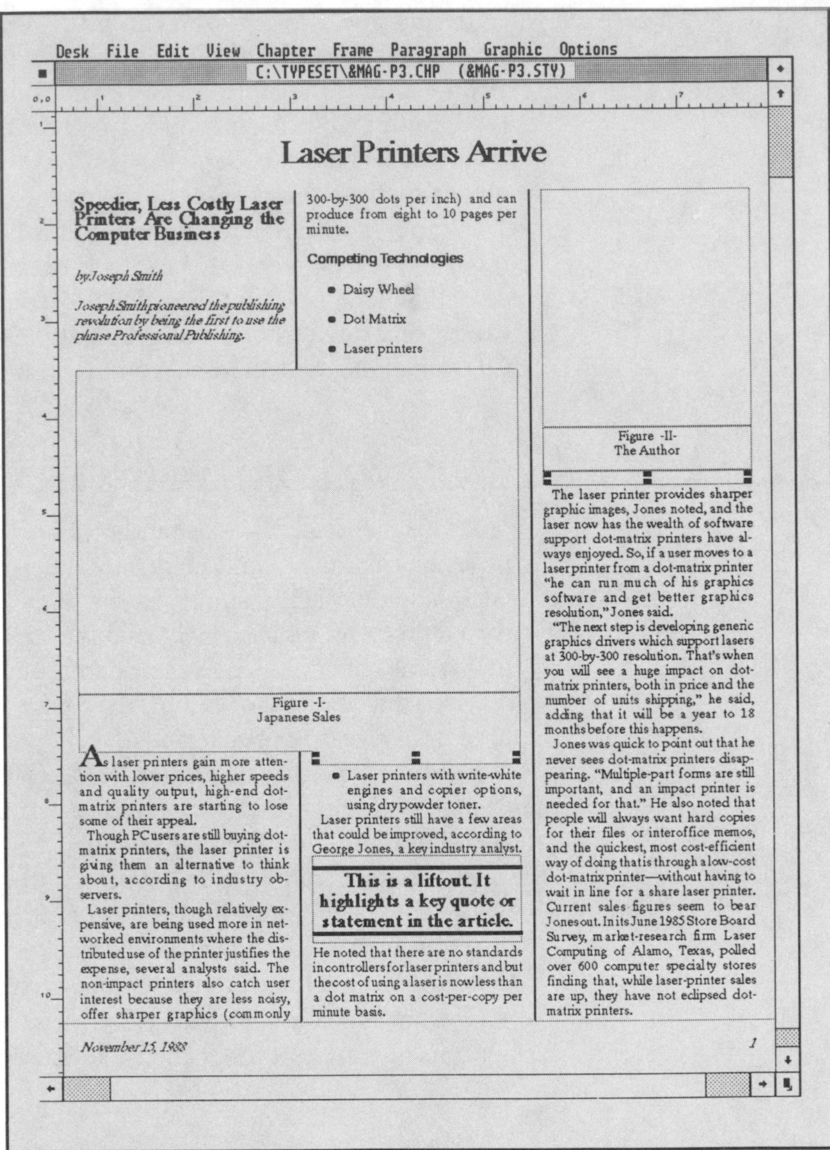

Desk File Edit View Chapter Frame Paragraph Graphic Options

C:\TYPESET\&MAG-P3.CHP (&MAG-P3.STY)

Laser Printers Arrive

Speedier, Less Costly Laser Printers Are Changing the Computer Business

by Joseph Smith

Joseph Smith pioneered the publishing revolution by being the first to use the phrase Professional Publishing.

Figure -I-
Japanese Sales

As laser printers gain more attention with lower prices, higher speeds and quality output, high-end dot-matrix printers are starting to lose some of their appeal.

Though PC users are still buying dot-matrix printers, the laser printer is giving them an alternative to think about, according to industry observers.

Laser printers, though relatively expensive, are being used more in networked environments where the distributed use of the printer justifies the expense, several analysts said. The non-impact printers also catch user interest because they are less noisy, offer sharper graphics (commonly 300-by-300 dots per inch) and can produce from eight to 10 pages per minute.

Competing Technologies

- Daisy Wheel
- Dot Matrix
- Laser printers
- Laser printers with write-white engines and copier options, using dry powder toner.

Laser printers still have a few areas that could be improved, according to George Jones, a key industry analyst.

This is a liftout. It highlights a key quote or statement in the article.

He noted that there are no standards in controllers for laser printers and but the cost of using a laser is now less than a dot matrix on a cost-per-copy per minute basis.

Figure -II-
The Author

The laser printer provides sharper graphic images, Jones noted, and the laser now has the wealth of software support dot-matrix printers have always enjoyed. So, if a user moves to a laser printer from a dot-matrix printer "he can run much of his graphics software and get better graphics resolution," Jones said.

"The next step is developing generic graphics drivers which support lasers at 300-by-300 resolution. That's when you will see a huge impact on dot-matrix printers, both in price and the number of units shipping," he said, adding that it will be a year to 18 months before this happens.

Jones was quick to point out that he never sees dot-matrix printers disappearing. "Multiple-part forms are still important, and an impact printer is needed for that." He also noted that people will always want hard copies for their files or interoffice memos, and the quickest, most cost-efficient way of doing that is through a low-cost dot-matrix printer—without having to wait in line for a share laser printer. Current sales figures seem to bear Jones out. In its June 1985 Store Board Survey, market-research firm Laser Computing of Alamo, Texas, polled over 600 computer specialty stores finding that, while laser-printer sales are up, they have not eclipsed dot-matrix printers.

November 15, 1988 1

Figure 9.9: Thin frames

Using Ventura's standard header and footer mechanisms, you can create headers and footers of one or two lines. Each header and footer makes material appear at the left, center, or right of the page. Unless you indicate otherwise, headers and footers appear on all pages in a document, whether custom-inserted or automatically generated.

If necessary, Ventura moves standard text out of the way in order to accommodate headers and footers. Of course, Ventura won't need to move text if you've set top or bottom margins large enough to accommodate the extra text of the header or footer. If the margin is greater than necessary, Ventura will center the header or footer vertically between the top or bottom edge of the page and the top or bottom of the text (Figure 9.10). Headers and footers appear above or below the text area only—never above or below the left or right margins.

Besides standard text, you can have the chapter number or page number appear automatically, and you can even have the header or footer display text that's on the page. By displaying text from the page, you can create *catch phrases*: indicative entries similar to the first and final names that appear atop pages in a phone directory. The results usually change with each page; for this reason they are sometimes called *live* headers or footers.

You can also use repeating frames to supplement Ventura's standard header and footer capabilities. With repeating frames you can provide more material, so your headers and footers can be more than two lines long and can even contain pictures. Likewise you can use Ventura graphics to enhance headers and footers, and you can use the Graphics

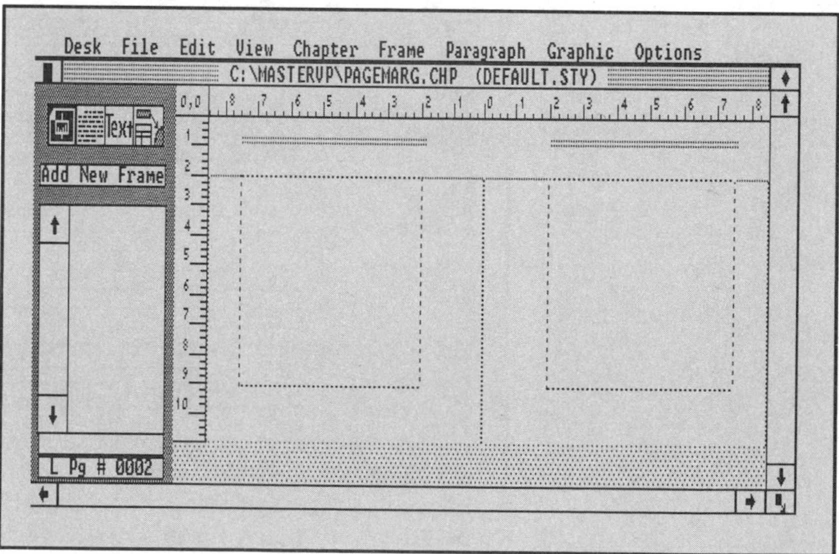

Figure 9.10: A header centered vertically within the top margin

menu's Show On All Pages to make graphics repeat on all pages formatted with the same underlying-page frame.

To create a header or footer for any chapter, drop the Chapter menu and select Headers & Footers. You can have any page in the chapter displayed when you do. The dialog box you see in Figure 9.11 appears.

DEFINING USAGE

To set up a header or footer, begin by clicking a button in the Define grouping to indicate its position on the page. Left Page and Right Page distinctions will only operate if you've used the Chapter menu's Page Size & Layout command to specify Double Sides.

Once you select a Define button, the current settings that apply to that button will appear within the dialog box. (For new documents, of course, there will be nothing on the lines.) You can change the settings as you wish. Then, if desired, click another button in the Define grouping. The settings that define that button will then appear, and you can adjust them as well.

Next, you'll want to consider the Usage setting. Click On or Off as appropriate to indicate whether you want the selected header or

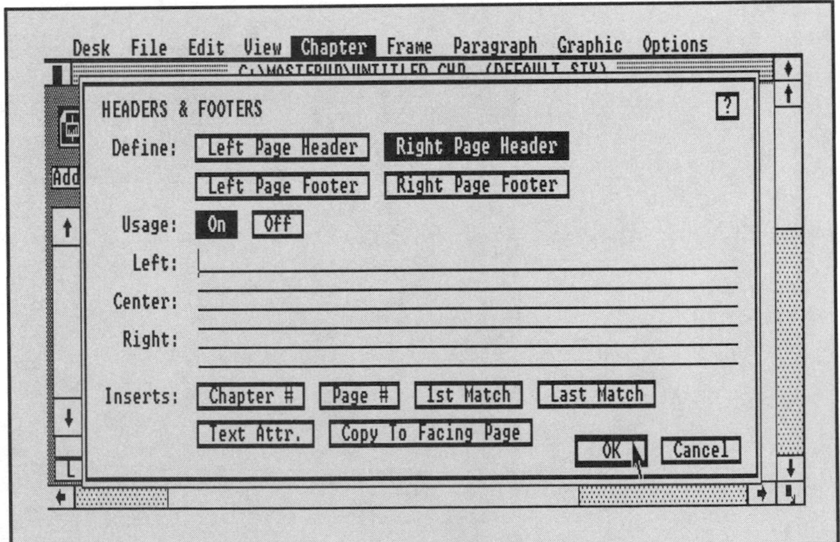

Figure 9.11: The Chapter menu's Headers & Footers dialog box

footer in the Define grouping to appear. When Usage is On, the entries you make into the field lines below (labeled Left, Center, and Right) will appear aligned with the left edge, center, or right edge of pages in the Define location. Each position has two lines available. Unless you make an entry, Ventura does not set aside space for the header or footer, even though Usage is On. Be aware that if you enter excessive amounts of text into the field lines, your entries could compete for the same space on the page and therefore overlap.

When you click Usage Off, any text entered on the field lines will ghost. However, the entries remain available. Should you later turn Usage On, the entries will fully reappear.

ADDING INSERTS

At the bottom of the dialog box, notice the Inserts buttons. The buttons operate similarly to those we examined in the Frame menu's Anchors & Captions dialog box (Chapter 6), but there are two additional buttons, 1st Match and Last Match. These buttons allow you to specify catch phrases and thus create live headers and footers. We'll examine these buttons in a moment.

The Copy To Facing Page button allows you to make the settings for the facing page automatically reflect the settings that are displayed in the dialog box. Because this button creates a mirror image, entries you make on the Right field lines will appear on the Left lines for the facing page, and vice versa. To create headers and footers on the left-hand page and copy them to the right, proceed as follows:

1. Click Left Page Header. If Usage is set to Off, the Left, Center, and Right entries (if any) will ghost.
2. Click Usage On. The Left, Center, and Right entries will appear in normal intensity.
3. Enter material for Left, Center, and Right to appear in those locations at the top of the left-hand page. Use the mouse, the Tab key, or the ↓ key to move between the fields. Use the Esc key to delete an entire entry. Use the Inserts buttons as necessary. (Don't use the Copy To Facing Page button just yet.)
4. When your settings for Left Page Header are complete, click the Copy To Facing Page button. The left-hand page settings

you provided for the header will be mirrored on the right-hand page. You won't get any immediate feedback that the transfer has taken place, but you can see that the settings are in place by clicking the Right Page Header button.

5. Click Left Page Footer, set Usage On for the footer, and make entries into the Left, Center, and Right fields for the bottom of the left-hand page. Click the Copy To Facing Page button to mirror the footer entries on the right-hand page.
6. Give the OK to register the settings.

Let's say that you want to place the newsletter title *The Brainstorm* in the top center of each page in a newsletter. In addition, on the outside edges at the top, you want the word *Page* followed by the page number.

To set this up, begin by clicking Left Page Header. (Of course, you could begin with the right and just reverse the instructions.) Position the text cursor in the Center field. Enter the newsletter's title, **The Brainstorm**, next to the word *Center:*

```
Center: The Brainstorm
```

Then, to have the page number displayed on the outside edge of the left page, position the Text cursor next to the Left setting. Type in the word **Page** and then click the Page # button. The code for page numbers appears, so the completed setting should look like this:

```
Left: Page [P#]
```

Finally, click the Copy To Facing Page button. This causes the settings to be reflected on the facing page. You can check by clicking the Right Page Header button. When you do, you'll see

```
Center: The Brainstorm
 Right: Page [P#]
```

Figure 9.12 shows the results of these maneuvers. It's a Facing Pages view of pages 2 and 3 of the document.

By default, Ventura numbers the pages with Arabic numbers, beginning with the number 1. In Chapter 10 we'll see how you can adjust the page-numbering system.

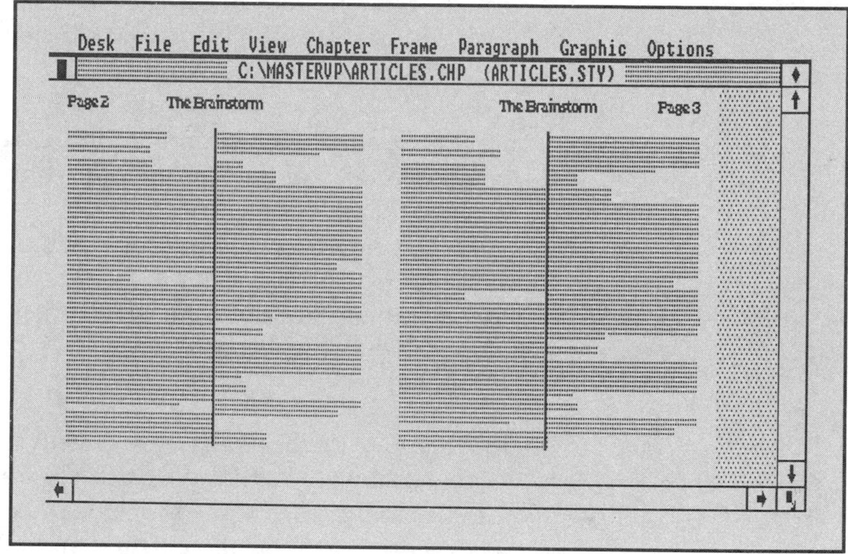

Figure 9.12: A Facing Pages view of headers and footers

FORMATTING HEADERS AND FOOTERS

You can format headers and footers just as you do any paragraphs in the document. Activate Paragraph mode and click the header or footer as it appears in the working area of the screen. For headers, you'll then see the tag name

Z_HEADER

The names of the generated tags will not appear on the Assignment list unless you use the Options menu's Set Preferences dialog box to set Generated Tags to Shown. See Appendix A.

appear in the Current box. This is a generated tag that Ventura automatically assigns to headers (see Chapter 4). You can format this tag by dropping the Paragraph menu and selecting commands of your choice. For footers, you'll see the tag name

Z_FOOTER

which you can format as well.

CREATING CATCH PHRASES

As we mentioned, there are two buttons, 1st Match and Last Match, that allow you to create catch phrases in your headers and footers. You may wish to use catch phrases in a catalog to show item numbers, or in a technical manual to show the name of the section that appears on the page.

As with the other inserts, you can either type in the entire entry that you desire or click the applicable insert button. Clicking the button guarantees that the appropriate syntax appears, but you'll have to adjust the resulting entry.

If you want Ventura to use the first paragraph on the page tagged with a particular tag, click the 1st Match button. You'll see the following text appear on the line where the text cursor is positioned:

```
[<tag name]
```

You then replace the words *tag name* with the name of the tag used for the material you want for the catch phrase.

Let's assume that at the top-left corner of the left-hand page you want Ventura to show the heading of the first subsection appearing on the page. You select Left Page Header, click Usage On, and then click 1st Match. The entry shown above will appear on the field line, with the text cursor positioned just to the right of this entry. You then use the ← key to float the text cursor over the bracket on the right and the Backspace key to delete the words *tag name.* In their place, type the tag name you use for subsection headings. Assuming that this tag name is Head Subsect, here is how the entry would look, next to the Left setting:

```
[<Head Subsect]
```

If you wish, you can simply type in the entire entry just like this, rather than clicking the 1st Match button and replacing the words.

If you want to display the last paragraph tagged with a certain tag, click the Last Match button. This displays the entry

```
[>tag name]
```

where the text cursor is positioned. Again, you replace the words *tag name* with the name of the tag. You can use the Last Match button to have Ventura display the last subsection on a page. As a counterpart to the earlier catch phrase, you might want to do this on the top right of the right-hand page, as is often done in dictionaries.

You may wonder what happens if a tag that's used to designate a catch phrase does not appear on a given page. In that case, Ventura uses the previous occurrence of the tag. Let's say, for instance, that you set a header for Ventura's sample technical document &TDOC-P1. Within that header you set up a 1st Match that uses the Major Heading tag, like so:

[<Major Heading]

On page 1 of the document, there are two headings that use this tag: WYSIWYG and ITEM SELECTOR. As such, the header on the page would display WYSIWYG because it is the first match of the tag. On page 2, though, no paragraphs are tagged with the Major Heading tag. The header for page 2 would therefore display ITEM SELECTOR, the most recent use of this tag, appropriately describing the material on the page. (With Last Match inserts, Ventura also displays the text most recently used.)

TURNING HEADERS AND FOOTERS OFF AND ON PAGE BY PAGE

When you establish headers or footers for a chapter, the header or footer you indicate initially appears on every page of the document. However, you can turn headers and footers off for any given page, if you choose. Doing so does not affect the headers and footers on the other pages. Many applications require that you suppress headers and footers on the first page, for instance. Some magazines suppress headers and footers on those pages that contain full-page ads.

To suppress the header or footer on a given page, follow these steps:

1. Display the chosen page on the screen.
2. Drop the Chapter menu.
3. Select Turn Header Off or Turn Footer Off as appropriate.

Do not use these commands to turn headers or footers off for the entire document. To do that, use the Chapter menu's Headers & Footers command.

Once you turn the header or footer off for a given page, you can turn it back on should you change your mind. If the page you've displayed on the screen has the header or footer turned off, dropping the Chapter menu displays the command

Turn Header On

or

Turn Footer On

as applicable. Selecting one of these commands turns the header or footer for the page back on.

CREATING OVERSIZED HEADERS AND FOOTERS

You can create headers and footers larger than the two lines allowed by the Chapter menu's Headers & Footers dialog box by using repeating frames. Just place a standard frame with the contents you desire in position near the top or bottom of the page and use the Frame menu's Repeating Frame command.

! New for version 2.0

Version 2.0 lets you insert the current page or chapter number in Box text, frames, and underlying-frame text. Now you can use the Frame menu's Repeating Frame command to create headers and footers that are many lines long and still have page and chapter numbers appear. You can also place such numbers in unusual locations, such as along the edge of the pages. To use this capability, create the repeating frame. Then use Text mode to position the text cursor where you want the reference. Then press Ctrl-C or use the Edit menu's Insert Special Item dialog box. Select Cross Ref or press F6 and Ventura will present a dialog box in which to click Page # or Chapter #.

Ventura will not allow the contents within a repeating frame to cover a standard header or footer. However, frame attributes (such as ruling lines and frame background) are not affected. Thus you can enhance standard headers and footers by framing them with repeating frames. The same holds true for a standard (nonrepeating) frame, but of course it would appear on only one page.

SPEED TECHNIQUES FOR LAYOUT-INTENSIVE DOCUMENTS

Now let's look at some techniques that will help you to work with Ventura quickly and efficiently. These techniques are especially useful when working with layout-intensive documents. Such documents can have numerous frames and files; efficient use of the mouse and the keyboard allows you to combine these elements quickly. We've discussed most of these techniques previously, so we'll just mention each one briefly.

- Load several files of the same type in succession. When you use the File menu's Load Text/Picture dialog box, specify Several for the # Of Files setting. As you load files, Ventura will repeatedly display the Item Selector box, so you can easily choose successive files. When you're done, click the Cancel button (or press Ctrl-X).
- Add several frames in succession. When you click the Add New Frame button in Frame mode, hold down the Shift key as you add successive frames. The Add New Frame button will remain selected. Release the Shift key before you add the last frame.
- Format all applicable paragraphs on a page with the same tag simultaneously. To do that, select multiple paragraphs. Hold down the Shift key as you click paragraphs in succession. With the paragraphs selected, click the proper tag name in the Assignment list to assign that tag's attributes to all selected paragraphs. To deselect the paragraphs, simply click some other paragraph without the Shift key, or change operating modes. Remember, you can only use this technique to assign tags. You can't use it to simultaneously change the attributes of paragraphs formatted with a variety of tags.
- Select multiple frames or graphics to cut, copy, move, or size them as a group. Shift-click frames or graphics in succession. You can then perform all these operations with the mouse. Cutting all the frames on one page and pasting them on

another allows you to rearrange layout-intensive pages. And although you can't change attributes such as frame background and ruling lines for a selected group of frames, you can change attributes for graphics, such as line attributes and fill attributes. Once the multiple graphics are selected, just use the Graphic menu's various commands.

- Copy frames or graphics with similar characteristics, even if some characteristics differ. Even if you are creating frames or graphics that don't share all characteristics, it's usually helpful to copy rather than create each one from scratch. For example, it's a good idea to copy frames with similar ruling lines and frame backgrounds, even if you intend them to have different sizes. Likewise, it's beneficial to copy frames that are to have the same size even if you intend to provide them with other attributes that differ.
- Hide pictures to speed screen and print processing. Use the Options command to do this. Display pictures only when you truly need to work with them. When you're about to begin working with one picture, you may find it helpful to move a neighboring picture off the screen temporarily before selecting Show Pictures. That way, Ventura won't have to redraw the additional picture unnecessarily. Hide pictures as soon as you're finished working with them. Hide before, not after saving, loading, setting options, and scrolling, as Ventura redraws pictures after each of these procedures. When printing with version 2.0, don't forget to watch for Ventura's prompt that asks whether to print the hidden pictures.
- Greek larger-sized text to speed screen processing in Reduced or Facing Pages view. Use the Options menu's Set Preferences dialog box. Greeking all text makes for a turbo-charged screen—a great improvement over the sluggish performance these views sometimes create.
- Keep the names of your directories low in alphabetical order. Doing so minimizes scrolling of Item Selector lists, and you'll be able to select Ventura directories more quickly. You may wish to reverse the trick that Ventura uses with names of its generated tags and begin your Ventura-related directories with A_, as in A_BRAIN.

- Preassign tags and other attributes in word-processed files so you don't have to tag paragraphs in Ventura. The techniques for doing this are discussed in Chapter 11.

- Create a template for documents that are repeatedly laid out in a similar fashion. Once you finish with the first volume of a document, such as a monthly newsletter, use the Edit menu's Remove Text/File command and remove most of the files that appear on the Assignment list. Keep only those that you plan to reuse in the next issue, such as the masthead. (Initially, you could instead place such material within a frame without assigning it to a file.) Save the resulting empty *template* or *shell* under a name designating it as such. Next month, load the template and save it under a name designating that month's issue. Then load it with that issue's files and otherwise alter it as necessary.

- Use the Chapter menu's Go To Page command when you need to follow a selected frame's text from page to page. In this command's dialog box, select Relative To: File. Then select Which Page: Next and give the OK. Ventura quickly displays the next page in which the selected frame's material continues, even when the next frame is on a far-flung page.

- To reformat quickly, standardize the tag names in all your style sheets. For instance, if you use Heading 1 for major headings in a style sheet, use the same name for major headings in all style sheets. With standardized tag names, you can quickly apply any style sheet to any document. New attributes will be automatically applied to all appropriately tagged paragraphs. Without identical tag names, Ventura will not apply the new tag's format automatically.

You cannot use this technique to reassign Body Text paragraphs to a different tag, because Ventura will not allow you to remove the Body Text tag.

- To change all similarly tagged paragraphs to a different tag, remove the tag they're assigned to. When you're switching style sheets as just described, and tag names do not agree, you do not need to retag the paragraphs one by one. Instead, use the Paragraph menu's Update Tag List command to remove the tag name carried over from the old style sheet. When you do, the command's dialog box will allow you to specify a tag name to convert to. Specify the appropriate tag name as it appears on the newly assigned style sheet. The paragraphs will convert, and all formats will be applied automatically.

- Assign and use the function keys for tagging. Here, too, it's a good idea to standardize. As much as possible, you should use the same function key for the same tag. Always assign F10 to Body Text, following Ventura's convention. You could use F1, F2, and F3 for Headings 1, 2, and 3, respectively. If you forget which tags are assigned to the keys, the quickest way to check is to use Text mode and type Ctrl-K.

In this chapter, we've focused on Ventura features chiefly as they work with layout-intensive documents. In the next chapter, we'll examine features that are often used with book-style documents, including Ventura's ability to print multichapter documents.

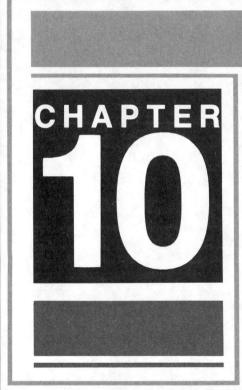

CHAPTER
10

Multichapter Features: Tables of Contents, Indexes, Footnotes, and Numbering

Fast Track

should use. This creates a generated text file which you can load into a chapter, format with a style sheet, and print.

To make an index entry with Ventura *376*

use Text mode and place the text cursor where you want to insert the index entry. Use the Edit menu's Ins Special Item (or Ctrl-C). Then click Index Entry (or press F3). You can specify primary and secondary entries.

To delete and move index entries *380*

use the Del and Ins keys to move the index-entry code. Associated settings move as well.

To generate an index *381*

use Make TOC on the Multi-Chapter Operations dialog box. Then load the generated index file and apply a style sheet to it.

To create numbering of section headings automatically *386*

use the Chapter menu's Auto-Numbering. Ventura will place numbers and text you specify before paragraphs assigned the tag you indicate. To renumber such headings, use the Chapter menu's Renumber Chapter (or Ctrl-B).

To use footnotes *397*

you must turn on footnote operations and provide specifications for it with the Chapter menu's Footnote Settings. Then insert the footnote: Use Text mode to position the text cursor, use the Edit menu to select Ins Special Item (or press Ctrl-C), and then click Footnote (or press F2). Replace "Text of Footnote" with the actual text of the footnote. You can also adjust the settings of the footnote's generated frame.

To print a publication *402*

open the publication and use Multi-Chapter's Print.

CHAPTER 10

JUST AS CHAPTER FILES COORDINATE PICTURES, text files, and other elements, Ventura provides you with the means to coordinate various chapter files to create multichapter documents. A *publication* file is simply a listing of one or more chapters that you want treated as a unit. Ventura can use this listing to prepare an index and a table of contents for the entire multichapter publication and to print material in succession. With version 2.0, Ventura will number pages, chapters, figures, and tables from one chapter to the next. Little else, however, is carried over from chapter to chapter; page formats, such as margins and columns, are not coordinated on a publication-wide basis. Also, you can't successively page through an entire publication on the screen.

THE MULTI-CHAPTER COMMAND

To create a publication and manipulate it, you use the Options menu's Multi-Chapter command. This command also performs some operations for single chapters, including:

- Displaying a listing of the files that are associated with a chapter. This is the easiest way to see which files the chapter references.
- Copying a chapter from one disk or directory to another. This procedure copies the chapter file and all files that are associated with it, including width tables but not including hyphenation dictionaries.

Similarly, you can display a listing of the files associated with a multi-chapter publication or make a copy of a publication file and all files associated with it.

To work with publications or individual chapters in this fashion, proceed as follows:

1. Drop the Options menu.
2. Select Multi-Chapter.
3. If you didn't save your chapter just prior to selecting this command, Ventura will ask you if you wish to save it. Ventura makes this request because some of its multichapter operations make and save changes in files that are referenced by the displayed chapter. Normally, of course, you should specify Save. Ventura then displays the Multi-Chapter Operations dialog box shown in Figure 10.1. As you work with this dialog box, Ventura redisplays it after each operation.
4. When you're finished with the Multi-Chapter Operations dialog box, click the Done button or press Enter.

When you first display this dialog box, Ventura lists the chapter that's showing in the working area. The chapter name is selected, as indicated by the darkened bar that surrounds the name.

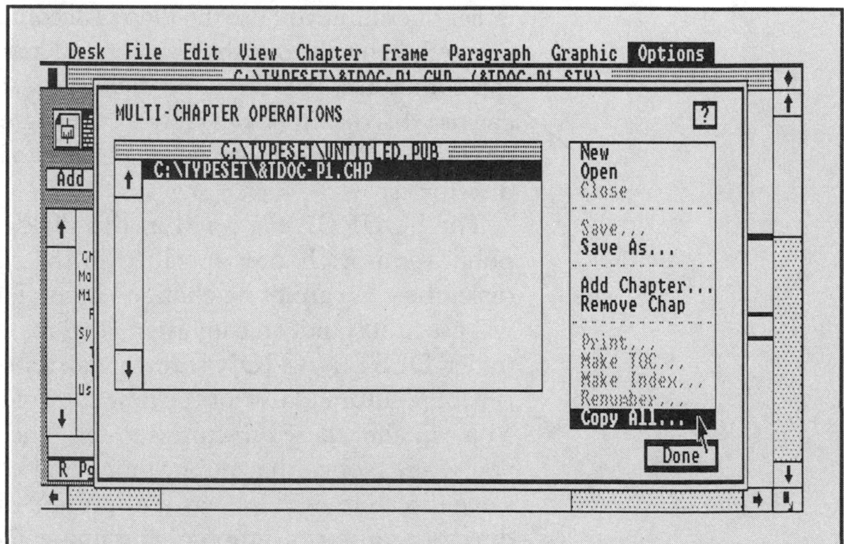

Figure 10.1: The dialog box displayed with the Options menu's Multi-Chapter command

Work in the Multi-Chapter Operations dialog box is directed at the selected file. For example, if you've been working with the chapter C:\TYPESET\&TDOC-P1.CHP, Ventura lists that chapter and displays it as selected. The program is assuming you would like to construct a publication that includes this chapter or to use the file for a single-chapter operation.

However, if the dialog box has been used before, the name of the publication last used may be displayed instead of the current chapter. If so, you can click New (which clears the publication) and Done (which redisplays the current document). If you use the Options menu's Multi-Chapter command again (immediately or later), the current document's name will then appear and will be selected.

COPYING CHAPTERS AND PUBLICATIONS

You can use the Multi-Chapter Operations dialog box to make a copy (or *archive* as Ventura calls it) of a document. Doing so allows you to copy all material associated with a publication or with just one chapter, even if it's not part of a larger publication. To perform either operation you use the Copy All command. If a single chapter is selected, you will copy the chapter and its related files. When you use this command, you'll see the dialog box shown in Figure 10.2. You can use this dialog box to copy all the material to the same directory, or you can split the material, according to type of file, among several directories.

The SOURCE file listed in this dialog box merely indicates the publication or chapter specified in the Multi-Chapter Operations dialog box; it cannot be changed here. This is the file that Ventura will use as its guide to copying related material from the disk. Below, under DESTINATION, are categories specifying various directories for Ventura to use for the new copy of the publication or chapter. You can alter these directories to send the files to various locations if you wish. Notice that publications and chapters go together in the same directory, style sheets and printer width tables go to the same directory, and text, graphic, and image files can each go to separate directories.

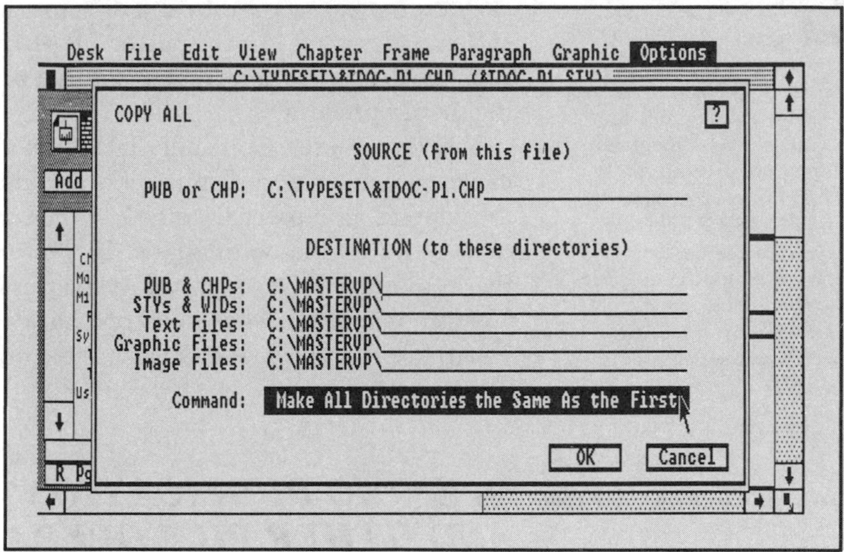

Figure 10.2: The Copy All dialog box

If you wish to copy all material for a chapter to the same directory, simply adjust the directory name for the first field (PUB & CHPs). Then click the box labeled

> Make All Directories the Same As the First

Ventura will immediately duplicate the name of that directory in the other four fields.

- If you'd like to work through the process as we create the material in this chapter, make a copy of the sample file &TDOC-P1.CHP in the MASTERVP directory.

To trigger the copying process, you must click the OK button. With this dialog box, and others that spring from the Multi-Chapter dialog box, you cannot hit the Enter key to give the OK. This is to keep you from beginning the procedure accidentally, which could copy over existing files (although you would be warned before it did so).

Ventura will display messages that show which files are being copied. At the same time, it adjusts all the unseen pointers within the

As we'll see, it's a good idea to use file names of five letters or fewer if you plan to create an index and a table of contents. To demonstrate this as we proceed, once copying was complete, we used DOS's REN command to change file names. Since the first title appearing on this sample is *USER INTERFACE,* we chose the name USER.

chapter, indicating the disk and directory location of each related file. If Ventura can't find a referenced file—if, for example, it was erased from the disk—you'll see a message that notifies you and asks if copying should proceed.

You can use the Copy All dialog box to copy a chapter or publication to one or more floppy disks and then copy the material from the floppies to another hard disk. When copying to floppies, specify drive A for all the destinations. If Ventura fills up one disk, it will pause, giving you the opportunity to insert a different disk. Likewise, Ventura will pause when you copy back from the floppies, allowing you to insert additional disks as necessary.

OPENING PUBLICATIONS AND OTHER FILE OPERATIONS

Once you have copied your publication files and are ready to work with them, Ventura offers a series of commands for adding, moving, and generally reorganizing chapters in your publication. As with the Copy All command, these procedures spring from and return to the Multi-Chapter Operations dialog box. Perhaps the most important of these is the Open command, which we'll look at next.

OPENING PUBLICATIONS AND CHAPTERS

Just as the Copy All command can make copies of either publications or individual chapters, the Open command provides two services for publications or chapters. With the Open command, you can open a publication and list the chapter files that the publication coordinates, or you can open a chapter and see a listing of the various files the chapter orchestrates.

OPENING A PUBLICATION To open a publication, you must first have no chapter selected. That is, there should be no chapter in the publication listing with a darkened bar on it. If there is, you can deselect the chapter by clicking some area of the dialog box other than a chapter's name.

Ventura includes one sample publication file in the TYPESET directory. When you select the Open command for a publication, you'll see the Item Selector box screened for PUB files, so that only files ending with PUB appear.

1. Make sure no chapter name is selected.
2. Use the Open command to open the sample file called &EXAMPLE.PUB. You'll see the listing in Figure 10.3.

As you may be able to tell, this publication file is a compilation of all the samples provided with Ventura. Printing it would simply print each sample document, one after another, in the order listed.

Such a hodgepodge of chapters is not how you'll usually use a publication file. Figure 10.4 shows a chapter listing for a more typical publication. As you can see, the files are all in the same directory, MASTERVP. In addition, they each begin with the same four letters, which in turn serve as the name of the publication (indicated at the top of the listing). The next three letters in each chapter name designate the specific contents of the chapter. Thus, TOC indicates

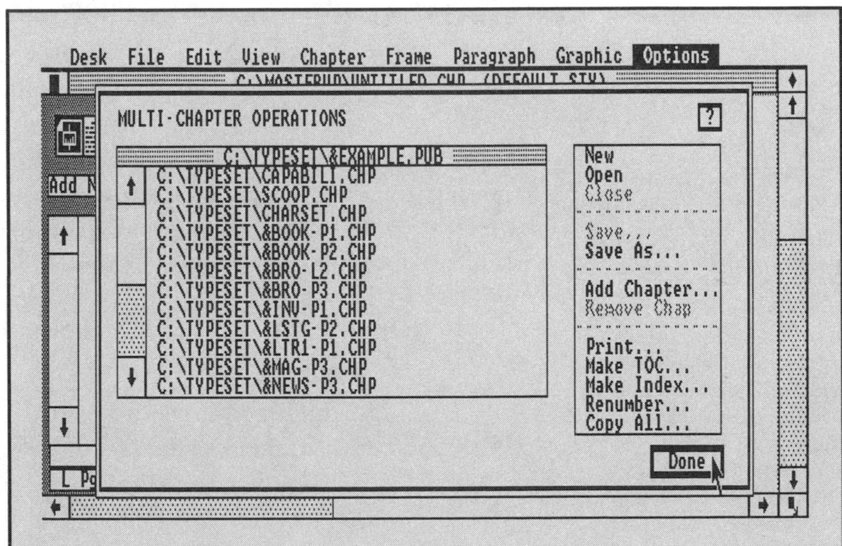

Figure 10.3: Listing of chapters referenced with &EXAMPLE.PUB publication file

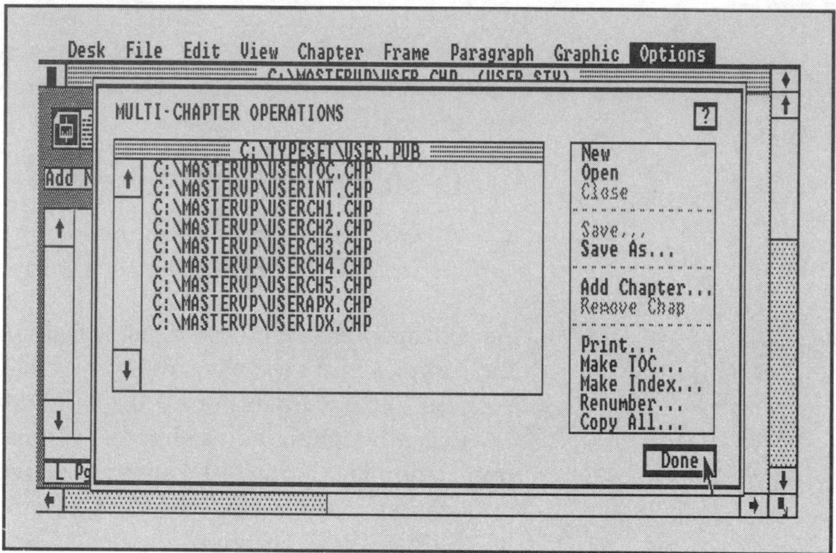

Figure 10.4: A typical publication listing

the table-of-contents file, followed by the introduction (INT). Each of the publication's (conventional) chapters is then listed in order (CH1 to CH5). At the end of the chapter listing is the appendix (APX) followed by the index (IDX). We'll see how you can generate the material for an index and a table of contents later in this chapter.

OPENING A CHAPTER LISTING Once you have Ventura list the chapter files for a publication with the Open command, you can open one of the listed chapters to see the names of the files that are associated with it. To open a chapter, follow these steps:

Be aware that the dialog box that appears in Figure 10.6 will not show important additional files that may be associated with a chapter file automatically. These are the CAP (caption) file, the CIF (chapter information) file, and the VGR (Ventura graphics) files.

1. Select the chapter of your choice by clicking it, as shown in Figure 10.5.
2. Click Open. You see a list of the files that compose the selected chapter (Figure 10.6).

Once a chapter is opened, only one command is available: Close. (You can also click the Done button.) This command is only available when you are examining a chapter (not a publication). When

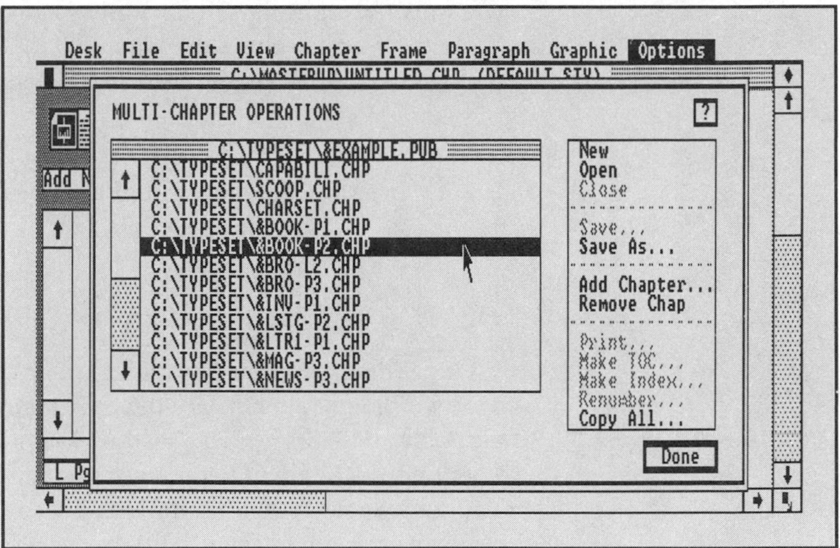

Figure 10.5: Selecting a chapter in a publication

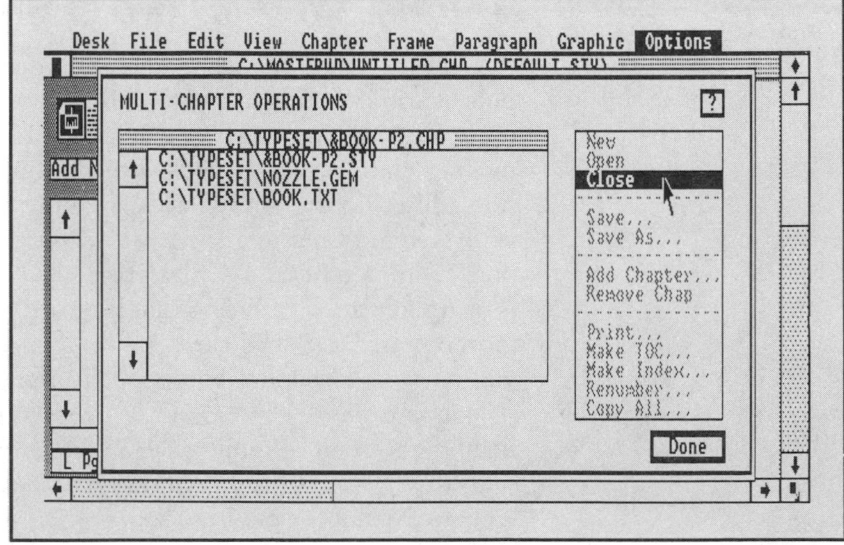

Figure 10.6: An open chapter

you finish examining the file names associated with a chapter, click Close to redisplay the publication listing, or Done to complete your multichapter work and go back to the document in the working area.

1. Follow the steps above to open the chapter in Figure 10.5.
2. Use the Close command to close the chapter listing.

OTHER FILE COMMANDS

Other filing commands work for publications just as they do for chapters with the File menu. Use the Save command to save your work on the publication file. Use the Save As command to save your publication work under a different name or to assign a name to a new publication. You must save a publication file at least once before making a table of contents or an index for it. Use the New command when you want to begin work on an entirely new publication.

ADDING, MOVING, AND REMOVING CHAPTERS

With the Add Chapter command you can add a chapter to the publication. When you use this command, the resulting Item Selector box allows you to add the chapter. If you've been consistent in naming chapters associated with a publication, you can use Ventura's filtering capability to display only chapter names that match your system of naming. Figure 10.7 shows the technique in operation. By means of the DOS asterisk wild card (*), the Directory field is set up to display only files that begin with *USER*. (See Appendix C for more on DOS wild cards.) This approach is not so important if you store the files for only one publication in each directory.

You can move chapters from one position in the publication to another. Remember, the order in which the chapters are listed dictates their order in the publication. Ventura will follow this order when you print the publication, or when you renumber its elements, such as page numbers. To rearrange chapters within a publication,

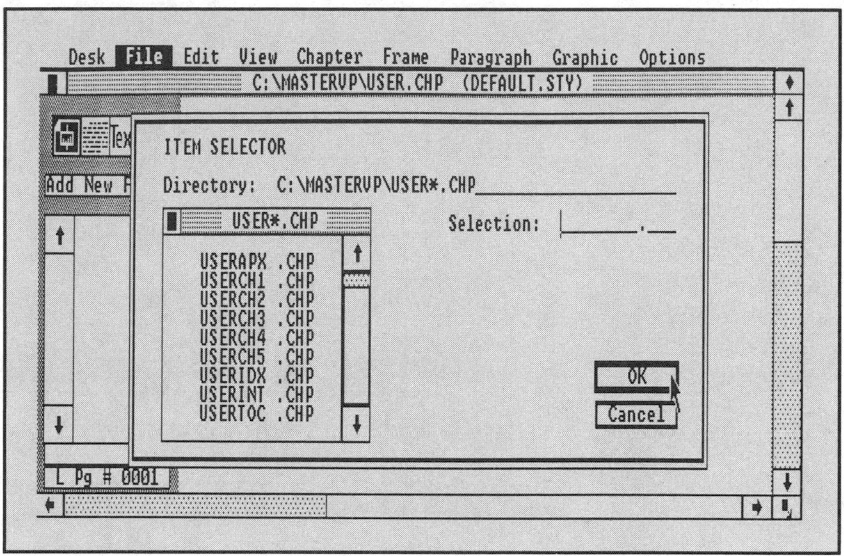

Figure 10.7: A DOS wild card used to filter chapter names

follow these steps:

1. Place the mouse cursor on the name of the chapter that you wish to relocate.
2. Hold down the mouse button and drag the file name to a different location. As you do, the mouse cursor will turn into the shape of a flattened hand (like the shape we saw in conjunction with cropping pictures), and the bar indicating your selection will ghost (Figure 10.8).
3. Position the selection bar so it straddles the files that you want to place the chapter between (or is on the one you want the chapter to precede), and release the mouse button.

If the displayed list represents only a portion of the chapter names for the publication, you might not be able to reposition the chapter with one drag. In that case, drag the chapter name as far down or up the list as possible. When you release the mouse button, Ventura will obligingly scroll the list of file names in the direction you are headed. You can then drag the chapter name again and repeat the procedure if necessary.

Chapters that you need to dissociate from the displayed publication may be removed with the Remove Chap command. Use this command if you mistakenly add a chapter to the publication, if circumstances have made the chapter obsolete, or if you decide to use the chapter in a different publication. Removal is immediate upon selecting the command. Ventura does not ask for verification before

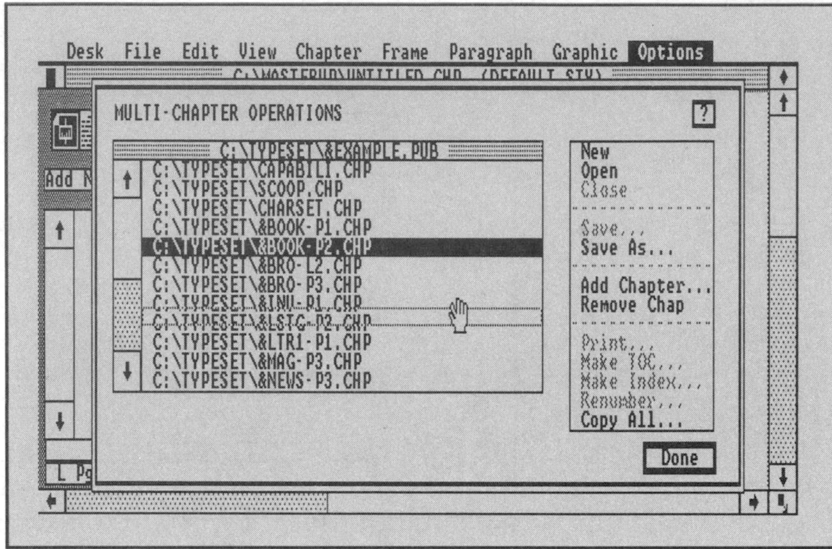

Figure 10.8: Moving a chapter within a publication

removing a chapter because removed files are not erased from the disk and can easily be added again.

CREATING A TABLE OF CONTENTS

Once your chapters are properly organized, you can create a table of contents. Ventura makes it quite easy to assemble a table of contents for a multichapter publication. If you want one for a single chapter, however, you must save the single-chapter "publication."

1. Make a publication for USER.CHP and call it USER.PUB.
2. Once you have a publication, click the Make TOC command. You'll see the Generate Table of Contents dialog box (Figure 10.9).

With the buttons in the Inserts grouping at the bottom of the dialog box, you insert various codes into the field lines that you see above them. Clicking them ensures the correct syntax for codes representing page numbers, tags, and other inserts. Their operation here is similar to the Insert buttons we examined in the Frame menu's Anchors & Captions dialog box (see Chapter 6).

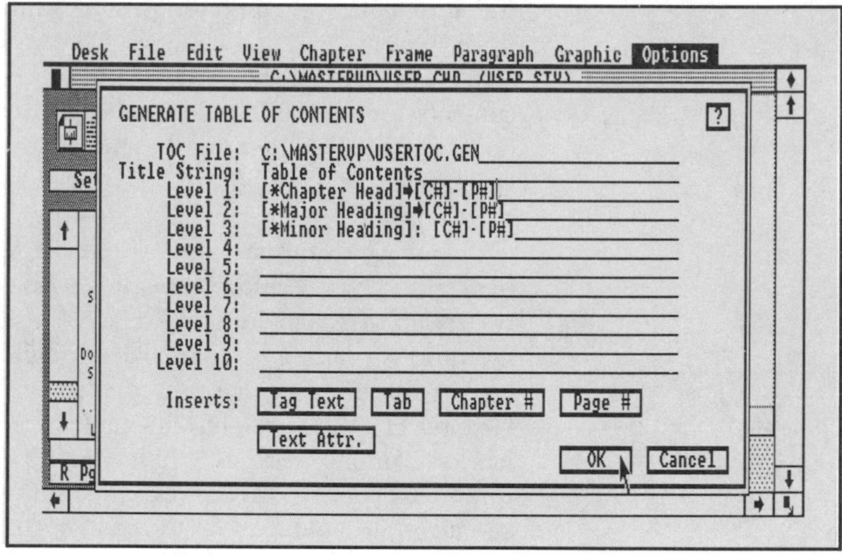

Figure 10.9: The Generate Table of Contents dialog box

At the top of the dialog box is a field labeled TOC File. When Ventura creates the table of contents, it places the output into a text file, which is much like the word-processed files you create for documents. You can assign this *generated file,* as Ventura calls it, to any document just as you do other text files.

The name that Ventura inserts into the TOC File field line consists of the first five letters of the publication and the letters TOC, indicating a table-of-contents file. The GEN extension identifies the file as a generated file. Although you can change the name, it's best to use it as is. When loading generated files, Ventura automatically filters for this extension.

The next line in the dialog box is the Title String. This is simply the name that appears at the top of the table of contents. By default, this consists of the words *Table of Contents*. You can change the string; for example, you can shorten it to simply *Contents.*

Next are the ten levels to be displayed in the table of contents. These are simply the categories and categories within categories that will be included. Level 1 is the broadest category. Ventura's ten levels provide more levels of organization than you will ever use, except perhaps in extremely technical and highly organized material. For the most part, you probably won't want to use more than two or three levels.

We have created the entries shown in order to generate the table of contents for the USER document (Figure 10.10). Notice that the document uses chapter numbers and a letter of the alphabet to number pages. We'll see how to set up page-numbering formats later in this chapter.

Before we examine the exact entries we used, it's important to understand how Ventura generates a table of contents. Ventura uses two sets of tags to make a table of contents. The first set is made up of the various headings that appear throughout your document. In the case of the sample style sheet, the Level 1 heading is the tag named Chapter Head, Level 2 has the name Major Heading, and Level 3 is labeled Minor Heading. When creating the table of contents, Ventura scans your document, examining it for text formatted with the specified tags, and extracts the contents of the paragraphs so tagged, along with the corresponding page numbers. This information is placed in the TOC file specified at the top of the dialog box.

Table of Contents

USER INTERFACE 1-A

WYSIWYG 1-A

Keyboard Keys: 1-A

ITEM SELECTOR 1-A

Description: 1-A

Application: 1-B

Figure 10.10: The generated table of contents

The second set of tags is applied to text in the table of contents as it is generated. The tags include Z_TOC TITLE for the title, Z_TOC LVL 1 for Level 1 text, Z_TOC LVL 2 for Level 2 text, and so on. Once the table of contents is generated, you can create a Ventura chapter file and load the generated TOC file. You can then format these generated tags just as you would any tags. If you make changes in the document and need to regenerate the table of contents, all entry placement and formatting is handled automatically when you give the OK in the Generate Table of Contents dialog box. When you look at the table of contents, the new material is fully incorporated.

Rather than creating the entire format for elements in the table of contents, you can simply apply one of Ventura's sample style sheets that includes tags for generated table-of-contents text. Of course, you can then modify that style sheet if desired. If you have the table-of-contents chapter referencing the USER.STY style sheet, the table of contents will not come out formatted, since this style sheet (originally named &TDOC-P1.STY) does not have tags for a table of contents; all the generated tags were formatted as Body Text. However, if you apply &TCHD-P1.STY, which does contain the properly formatted tags, you will obtain the results shown in Figure 10.10.

In summary, then, here are the steps for creating a fully formatted table of contents, such as you see in Figure 10.10:

1. Using the Generate Table of Contents dialog box, specify the format and tags for each level in the table of contents.
2. Give the OK to initiate the generating process.
3. Open a chapter file for the table of contents.
4. Within the chapter, use the File menu's Load Text/Picture command, indicate Generated for Text Format, and load the table-of-contents text file.
5. Format the table-of-contents chapter file or apply a sample style sheet to format it for you.

Now let's examine the various field lines that allow Ventura to create this format. To indicate that Ventura should use a certain tag for a given level, click the Tag Text button in the Inserts grouping. Ventura will display the code

    [*tag name]

on the line where the text cursor is positioned. You then remove the words *tag name* and replace them with the actual name of the tag. For instance, on Level 1 you can see that the tag name *Chapter Head* is inserted. As with other inserts, you can type in the insert rather than clicking its button.

After Chapter Head, we want Ventura to insert a tab character. To get a tab, you must click the Tab button on the screen. You cannot insert a tab by pressing the Tab key, because that moves the cursor to the next line. The presence of a tab is indicated by the left-pointing arrow following Chapter Head.

After the tab character, we needed to have Ventura insert Chapter # (indicated with [C#]), a dash, and Page # (indicated with [P#]). This format is required by the unusual manner in which the document is numbered. The result is the words *USER INTERFACE,* followed by a tab, and then the page number. (The Z_TOC LVL 1 tag is formatted with a ruling line below, which creates the line below this entry.)

The titles WYSIWYG and ITEM SELECTOR are both tagged as Major Heading in the main document and as Z_TOC LVL 2 in the table of contents. This tag has leader dots that fill in the space where the tab character occurs.

Once Ventura generates the table-of-contents file and you load it into a document, the document is just like any other; you can edit it as you wish. Thus, although Ventura does not provide the means of making multiple entries on the same line, once the file is generated you could edit it to provide that. Be aware, though, that if you make changes in your document and have to regenerate the table of contents, you'll have to repeat each individual enhancement.

If possible, leave the table of contents as Ventura creates it. This is especially true if you expect to make changes to your document later on, thus necessitating a regeneration of the table of contents. The beauty of following Ventura's lead is that the table of contents is fully recreated and formatted automatically at your command. Just redisplay the Generate Table of Contents dialog box and give the OK.

With no additional effort on your part, any changes you make in the document are reflected in the table of contents, including page numbers and headings. Ventura creates the text file, applies the tags, and formats the text accordingly, all automatically.

1. Use the Generate Table of Contents dialog box to create a TOC file for the USER.CHP chapter.
2. Format the text file by loading it in a new chapter and applying the sample &TCHD-PI.STY style sheet.

MAKING AN INDEX

Some of the processes involved in creating an index are similar to those used for a table of contents. Be aware, however, that the process is not so straightforward and automatic. As it does when generating a table of contents, Ventura scans your document to make the entries for an index. Unlike the process involved in creating a table of contents, though, Ventura's indexing process doesn't make use of tags and text that are already in place as a result of standard editing and formatting. Instead, you must perform these initial steps before generating the index. You must insert index entries into the document and provide the text for those entries as well.

The simplest method available for creating an index is unfortunately quite time-consuming. It involves using a dialog box to type in index entries one by one for every page an entry should indicate.

However, there are two main ways you can speed up the indexing process, and you will probably want to use them for any extensive indexing. One is by using a word processor (Chapter 11). The other is by incorporating index entries into headers or footers. Using headers and footers, Ventura can be made to list a range of pages that a section of text covers.

The simplest method should be used only for short documents with simple indexing requirements, or to add overlooked entries. Let's look at how this method works, though, since doing so will provide an understanding of the indexing process.

MAKING INDEX ENTRIES

The first step to creating an index with Ventura is to insert index entries in the document. These are positioned at those points where you want Ventura to check the page number and generate entries for the index accordingly.

You can provide two levels of entries within the index—primary and secondary—but no more than that. *Primary* entries are the major alphabetized entries in the index, representing the general topics covered in text. *Secondary* entries are generally indented below primary entries, representing topics subordinate to a broader general topic.

Often, entries can be both primary and secondary within the same index. For example, once we create the sample index you'll be able to see how the entry *Cursor keys* is used alone as a primary entry. There is also an entry that has *Text editing* as a primary entry and *Cursor keys* as a secondary entry under that. There are a few other operations, such as making cross-references, that add greater flexibility to your indexing. Here, however, are the steps for making most simple entries:

1. Activate Text mode and insert the text cursor at the spot in text where you wish to place the index reference. This is the spot Ventura will use to determine the page number for the entry. (If you want your index entry associated with a particular word, you can place it within, at the beginning, or at the end of the word.)
2. Drop the Edit menu and select Ins Special Item. The click Index Entry. You'll see the dialog box displayed in Figure 10.11. (You can also reach this dialog box with the shortcut keys Ctrl-C and then F3.)
3. With Type Of Entry set to Index, enter a primary entry and a secondary entry if desired.
4. Give the OK. Ventura inserts an Index Entry mark into the document at the position of the text cursor.

The Index Entry mark is only visible if you've set the Options command to Show Tabs & Returns. The mark looks like a temperature degree symbol (°). When it's to the right of the text cursor, the words *Index Entry* appear in the Current box.

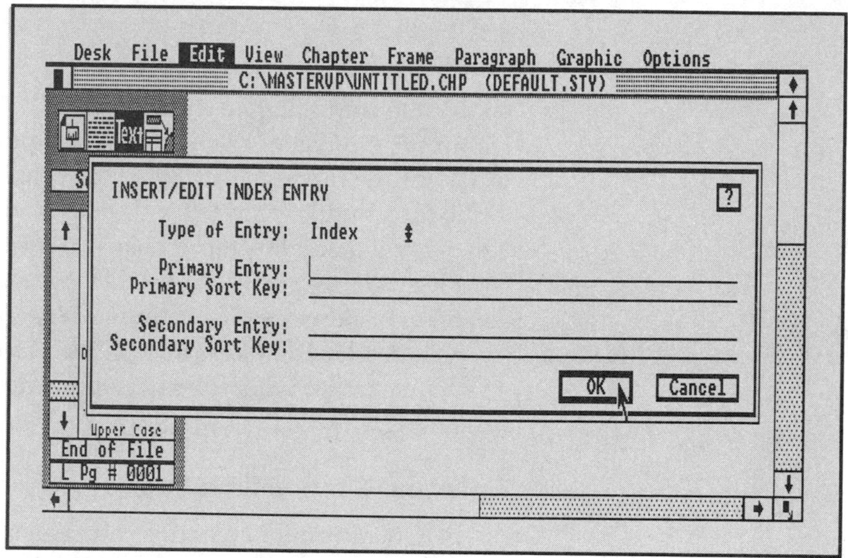

Figure 10.11: The Insert/Edit Index Entry dialog box

The USER sample document has various index entries. Figure 10.12, in Enlarged view, shows several of the entries in place. Notice how one of the entries is to the right of the text cursor; hence, *Index Entry* appears in the Current box.

- Position the text cursor as shown in Figure 10.12. Note the contents of the Current box.

If you want Ventura to indicate a range of page numbers in the index for any given entry, you must insert identical index entries on each page of the range. For such consecutive page entries, Ventura will show only the beginning and ending entries according to a format you specify, as we'll see shortly.

If you create more than one reference for the same index entry, be certain to spell the index entry exactly the same each time. Different singular and plural usage, for instance, will result in multiple entries. On the screen sample, there is an index reference for the PgUp key. In the dialog box that created this reference, the primary entry specifies *Page Up key*. Therefore, even though *PgUp* appears in the text of the document, if you use *Page Up* as the entry in the dialog box, you would have to be certain to spell out all such entries, or you would

Compiling Index Entries

When compiling an index, look at the individual entries from the intelligent reader's point of view. The reader will look for the more general entry first, and then for more specific topics under that entry. If readers cannot find the topic they are looking for, they consider synonymous terms. Make the index as extensive as possible, but do not include items that no reader would ever think of searching for.

When selecting terms and phrases in your document from which to create index entries, follow these basic rules of indexing:

- Index by significant words or phrases.
- Choose concrete nouns rather than general descriptive nouns as entries—use *Printers, types of,* not *Types of printers.*
- List entries under the key word of a phrase—*Commands, miscellaneous,* not *Miscellaneous commands.*
- Never use an adjective alone as an entry.
- Entries should be alphabetized by their major words, disregarding prepositions and conjunctions.

have some entries listed under *PgUp* and some under *Page Up.* Be sure to proof your index printout for inconsistencies like this. Correct erroneous entries and regenerate the index as necessary.

To correct an entry, place the Text cursor to the left of the Index Entry mark whose settings you wish to adjust. Then drop the Edit menu and select Edit Special Item. You can also use the keyboard shortcut, Ctrl-D. You'll see the dialog box with the current settings for the selected mark. Adjust them as necessary and give the OK to register the new settings.

- Use the Edit menu or Ctrl-D to examine the index entry. Then close the dialog box.

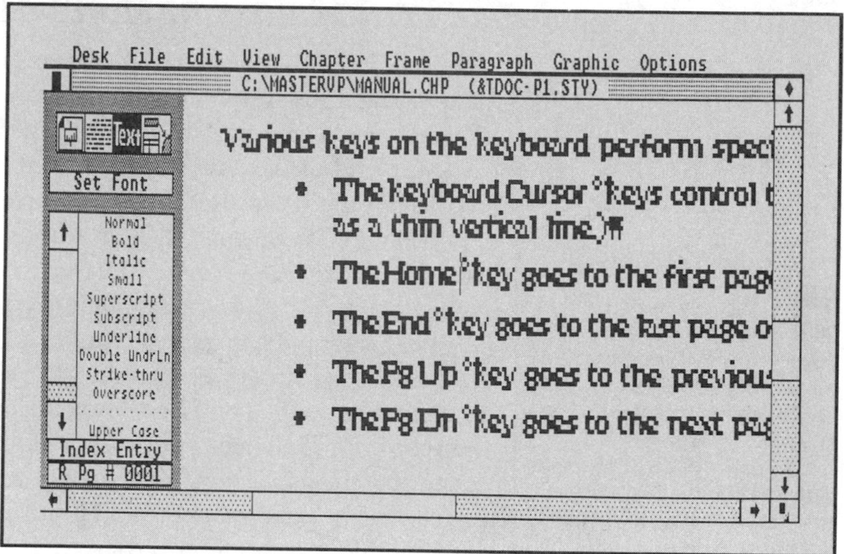

Figure 10.12: Index Entry marks in a document

SPECIFYING SORTING EXCEPTIONS

To alphabetize your index, Ventura normally uses the Primary Entry and Secondary Entry fields. Some entries, however, may need to be spelled one way and alphabetized another. If so, you can use the Primary Sort Key and Secondary Sort Key fields to indicate how Ventura should sort the entry. Thus, for example, since an index should be alphabetized without regard to prepositions, a primary entry such as *Home key* that has a secondary entry *with Ctrl key* should have *Ctrl key* specified for Secondary Sort Key. Otherwise, the secondary entry would be sorted under the word *with.* Other common applications for sort keys include titles that begin with *The* or *An* (although it's probably best to form the entry using the main title followed by a comma and then the article). In Ventura, numbers are grouped together separately from letters of the alphabet. To alphabetize a number, spell the number out in the appropriate Sort Key field.

For the majority of your work, however, you won't need to make any entries into the fields for Primary Sort Key and Secondary Sort Key.

CREATING CROSS-REFERENCES

As you can probably surmise, you use the See and See Also buttons to create cross-references for your index. These entries do not indicate page numbers, so you may wish to group them in one place—the end of the chapter, for instance. That way you can find and consider them together, and so be sure that all appropriate cross-references have been made. This works especially well when you create the index with a word processor.

In the generated index, See Also references should come at the end of a list of secondary entries. Normally, however, Ventura will simply insert them alphabetically into the list. To ensure that Ventura places See Also entries at the end, provide them with a Secondary Sort Key that is low in alphabetical priority, such as Zzzz.

When you use these buttons, the text you enter into the Secondary Entry field will not be used as a regular subordinate entry. Rather, it will be another primary entry that you wish to point the reader to. You cannot make See and See Also entries for secondary entries.

Suppose, for instance, you want the reader who's looking under *Revising* to consult *Editing*. You'd click the See button and specify Revising for the primary entry and Editing (which is actually another primary entry, cross-referenced) as the secondary entry.

Use the See button when there are no secondary entries elsewhere in the document for the primary entry specified. Use the See Also button when the primary entry does have secondary entries elsewhere. Since you may have a difficult time keeping track of which ones do and which do not, be certain to proof your index carefully, make corrections, and regenerate it as necessary.

DELETING AND MOVING INDEX ENTRIES

To delete an index entry, select it by positioning the text cursor to the left of the reference mark. The words *Index Entry* should appear in the Current box. Then press the Del key.

Once you delete the Index Entry mark in this fashion, it's placed on the text clipboard along with its entries, sort keys, See button status, and so on. You can insert the mark in a different location to effect a move. Simply place the text cursor where you want the mark to go, and press the Ins key. (Note that this method of moving works only for special text-entry characters, like Index Entry, Footnote, and Frame Anchor marks. Ventura will not move standard characters, such as letters and numbers, in this way. Standard characters individually deleted by placing the text cursor before them are not sent to the clipboard.)

If you use the Insert/Edit Index Entry dialog box and remove the entries from the field lines (with the Esc key, for instance), Ventura will remove the corresponding index mark when you give the OK. Therefore, when you first use this dialog box to insert an entry, you must provide some entry in the field, or Ventura will not create the reference mark.

GENERATING THE INDEX

To generate the index, use the Options menu to display the Multi-Chapter Operations dialog box. Open the appropriate publication and use the Make Index command. If you wish to index a single chapter, you must make and save a publication file for it.

When you commence generation of the index, the dialog box shown in Figure 10.13 appears. As we saw when creating a table of contents, you use this dialog box to create a text file of entries. You can then incorporate this generated text file into any Ventura chapter file.

The settings displayed are Ventura's defaults, except for the Index File name, which will vary to correspond with the associated publication file. This field indicates the name given to the text file that will store the generated index. As with the table-of-contents generator,

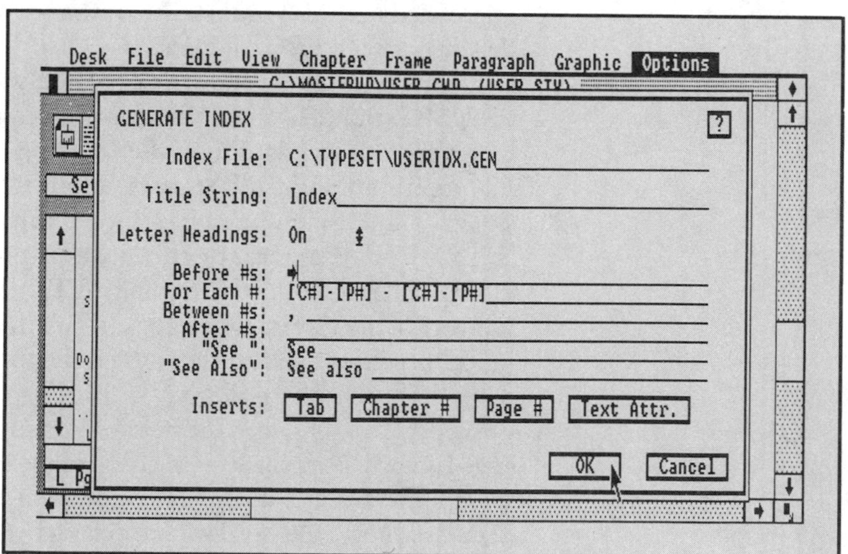

Figure 10.13: The Generate Index dialog box

this setting displays the first five characters in the name of the publication file. It adds the letters IDX to those five, indicating that it is an index file, and the extension GEN to indicate that the file is automatically generated by Ventura.

Title String sets the title that Ventura places at the top of the index. The title is formatted with the tag Z_INDEX TITLE. The Letter Headings setting, when turned on, inserts the appropriate letter of the alphabet before each group of entries beginning with the same letter. Letter headings receive the tag Z_INDEX LTR.

The main grouping of field lines in the dialog box sets up the format for the index entries. Index entries are formatted with the tag Z_INDEX MAIN. The Before #s setting shows that a tab insert is the default before numbers in the index. The For Each # setting shows how numbers that indicate a range will be displayed. The default shows numbers as the chapter number, a hyphen, and the page number. The beginning and ending page numbers are separated by a space, a hyphen, and another space. The Between #s setting shows that a comma and a space will separate successive page numbers when more than one page number appears for the same entry. After #s shows that nothing special will be added after the page numbers. (You could specify a period here.)

The See and See Also settings change the wording for cross-referenced entries. For instance, rather than *See Editing* you may want the entry to read *Refer to Editing*.

Figure 10.14 shows an index created with the entries provided in the USER sample. Once Ventura created the index text file, we did, however, enhance it. First, after loading the index file we used the File menu's Load Diff Style to apply the &TCHD-P1.STY style sheet. This style sheet has index tags (those beginning with Z_INDEX) that create the paragraph formats you see. The USER.STY style sheet (originally &TDOC-P1.STY) does not contain any of the special index tags. When this style sheet is used in conjunction with the index, all of the index comes out looking like body text.

We have also changed the Before #s and For Each # fields in the Generate Index dialog box. We've changed the default tab for Before #s to a space, and changed the hyphen indicating a number range in the For Each # setting to the word *to*. The default hyphen in the range proves too

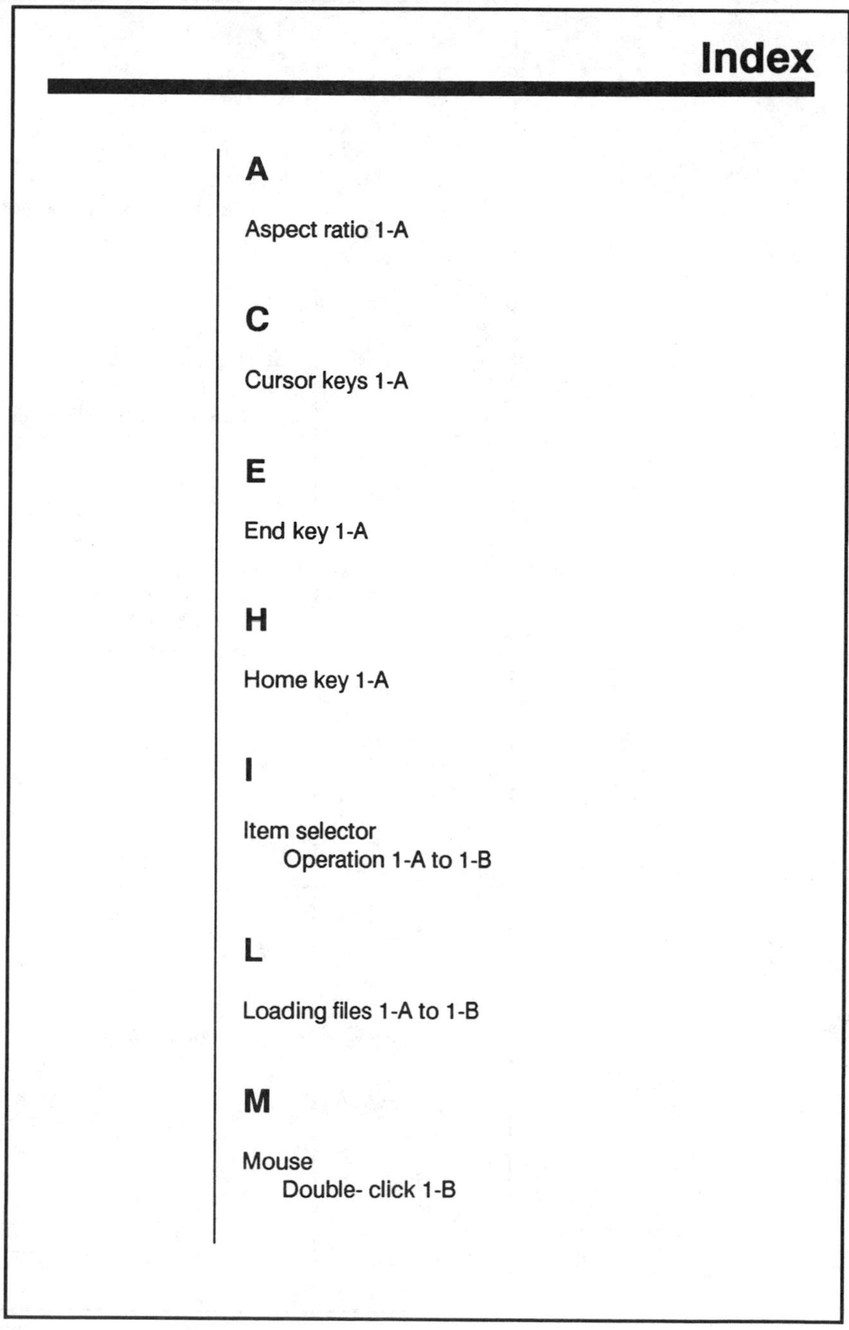

Figure 10.14: A generated index

Figure 10.14: A generated index (continued)

confusing when used in conjunction with hyphens between chapter and page numbers as well.

1. For the USER.PUB publication, display the Generate Index dialog box.
2. Revise the settings as discussed above.
3. Generate the index.
4. Use the &TCHD-P1.STY style sheet to format the index.

EXPEDITING INDEXING

As we mentioned at the start of the chapter, there are two ways to expedite the creation of index entries; you'll probably want to use one of them for extensive index creation. The first method is to make the entries with your word processor in the text files. When used in conjunction with a keyboard enhancer or a macro generating feature, the work is quite a bit less arduous. We'll examine the codes you enter into word-processed text in Chapter 11.

The other technique uses the section headings of text in your document in conjunction with headers or footers. This is a very useful feature for creating references to page numbers in succession. What you do is create the index entry in a section title, which is referenced by a header or footer (using the 1st Match or Last Match insert). The header or footer repeats, showing index entries on every page until the next section title. When Ventura compiles the index, it sees references on each page, and so creates a range of page numbers.

For instance, if the words *Item Selector* are the title of a section, and you want Ventura to index the entire section as a range, you could insert an index entry into that title. For Primary Entry, you'd type in the words *Item Selector.* In the header or footer, you'd make a match reference to the tag with which *Item Selector* is formatted.

You don't even have to insert section titles into the headers and footers (or even use headers and footers that actually appear) to apply this technique. The section title can consist of nothing other than the index reference, and the header and footer can contain just the match reference. The operation consists of these steps:

1. In Text mode, create text for the section title (if any) and insert the index reference into it. This material must be in a

paragraph separate from any others. It must also be in the underlying-page frame; standard Frame text does not work.

2. In Paragraph mode, format the paragraph with the tag for section titles. This will create a starting point for the index entry, which will continue until the next paragraph formatted with the same tag.
3. Use the Chapter menu's Headers & Footers command and reference the section-title tag. Use the 1st Match or Last Match button.

Later, be sure to provide a paragraph with the same tag in order to provide an ending page for the index entry.

AUTOMATIC NUMBERING OF SECTIONS

Another feature that is useful in organizing long documents is Ventura's ability to number the sections of your documents automatically. It can number sections, and sections within sections, up to ten levels deep. The key to numbering lies in two paragraph tags for each level. One tag is the standard one for a specific type of text in the document (usually headings), while the other tag is one of Ventura's generated tags.

The process of section numbering is quite similar to the one Ventura uses for captioning pictures. You may recall that to caption pictures, you work with two tags as well. You create a label tag for the caption text, such as *Figure 1.1:*, and then you can create a free-form caption that follows the caption label.

There are two parts to section numbering. For all items that are numbered, there is a label, such as *Section 1.1:*, that contains the automatic number. Other than the number, which increments automatically, labels can contain only text that is identical for all items with the same level of importance. This label precedes the free-form paragraph (in this case, the heading), which contains information that varies for each section. Paragraph tags are used to combine these two elements. Once you indicate which tag you wish to use for each level, all heading paragraphs formatted with that tag receive the same numbering label. The numbers for similarly tagged paragraphs increment automatically.

To set up automatic numbering, use the Auto-Numbering dialog box. Proceed as follows with USER.CAP:

1. Drop the Chapter menu.
2. Select Auto-Numbering. You now see the dialog box shown in Figure 10.15.

With the Auto-Numbering dialog box, you create and control section numbering. Because numbering is operational, the On button in the Usage category appears as selected.

CREATING SECTION LABELS

The Auto-Numbering dialog box works in a way similar to the box we studied when creating captions. On each line, you indicate the label with which you wish to precede paragraphs tagged with the specified tag. This label consists of a combination of standard text, which is the same from paragraph to paragraph, and variable inserts, set using the Inserts grouping at the bottom of the screen. In order to click any of these buttons, you must first set Usage to On.

LABELS WITH NUMBERS ONLY The USER sample chapter and style sheet that we have been working with contain an example of

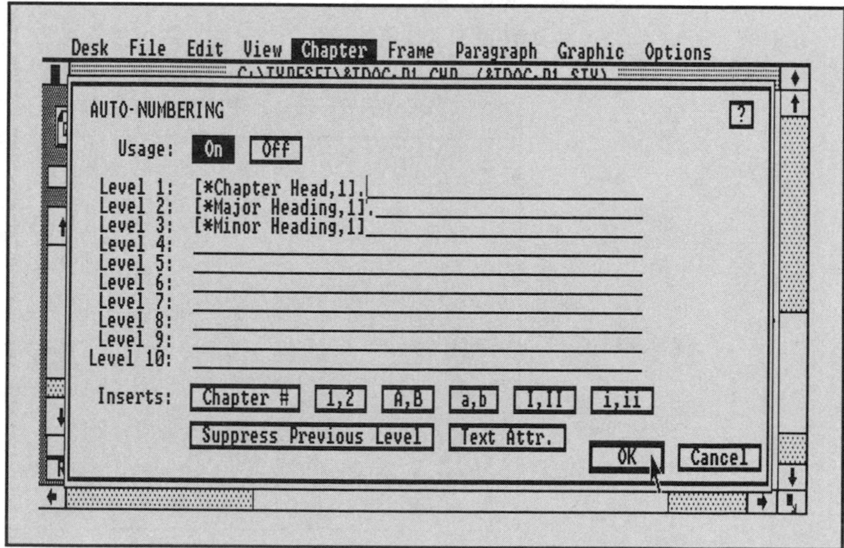

Figure 10.15: The Chapter menu's Auto-Numbering dialog box

auto-numbering, using variable inserts only. In Figure 10.15, the dialog box indicates the auto-numbering settings that are in place for the USER.STY style sheet (originally &TDOC-PI.STY). With these settings in place, Ventura numbers all paragraphs that are tagged as Chapter Head, Major Heading, and Minor Heading. The Chapter Head tag receives Level 1 format, Major Heading receives Level 2, and Minor Heading is formatted according to Level 3. Figure 10.16 shows the printed chapter with the numbered headings set in place.

In the sample, the heading *USER INTERFACE,* tagged as Chapter Head, is numbered for Level 1. The headings *WYSIWYG* and *ITEM SELECTOR,* tagged as Major Heading, are numbered for Level 2. The headings *Keyboard Keys* and *Description,* tagged as Minor Headings, are both numbered as Level 3.

To create the settings for each of these levels, you can insert variable codes in the relevant field by clicking the button in the Inserts grouping that displays the style of numbering (or lettering) that you want to use. A corresponding code will appear for the level field that contains the text cursor. Table 10.1 lists the insert buttons along with the matching codes that each creates.

Notice that many of the Insert codes contain the words *tag name.* As with previous features we've examined, you substitute the names of the tags that you want Ventura to use in place of these words. Thus,

Table 10.1: Insert Buttons and Codes for Auto-Numbering

INSERT BUTTON	INSERT CODE
Chapter #	[C#]
1,2	[*tag name,1]
A,B	[*tag name,A]
a,b	[*tag name,a]
I,II	[*tag name,I]
i,ii	[*tag name,i]
Suppress Previous Level	[-]
Text Attr.	<D>

1. USER INTERFACE

1.1. WYSIWYG

Figure 1-1
This is the caption for the figure. It is anchored below **WYSIWYG**

Ventura Publisher is designed to provide What You See (on the screen) Is What You Get printed (WYSIWYG). This means that the computer display should match as closely as possible, at all times, what you will see on the final printed page. Of course, the difference between the technology used to display a page on a CRT screen, and the technologies used to print a page on a laser printer or typesetter, do create some unavoidable differences. In particular, because the computer CRT screen cannot produce anywhere near the same resolution of a printer or typesetter, and because what is displayed is shown in a different aspect ratio (height to width ratio), the space between words and between lines may appear to be bigger or smaller than the printed page under certain circumstances. Several thin ruling lines, with little space between, may show on the screen as one thick line.

1.1.1 Keyboard Keys

Various keys on the keyboard perform special functions:

- The keyboard Cursor keys control the Text Cursor (The text cursor is displayed as a thin vertical line.)
- The Home key goes to the first page of the document.
- The End key goes to the last page of the document.
- The Pg Up key goes to the previous page.
- The Pg Dn key goes to the next page.

1.2. ITEM SELECTOR

1.2.1 Description

The display shown in Figure 10-2 is called an Item Selector. The Item Selector is used for saving and retrieving files.

1-A WYSIWYG

Figure 10.16: A sample chapter using auto-numbering

to create the setting shown in the Level 1 field, follow these steps:

1. Place the text cursor in the Level 1 field.
2. Click the 1,2 button in the Inserts grouping.
3. Replace the words *tag name* by typing in **Chapter Head**.

ADDING TEXT TO LABELS As mentioned, you can use constant text in a numbering label. To use constant text, you simply type it into the field that corresponds to the level you wish to use. You can also use the keypad in conjunction with the Alt key to create characters from the international font to be used in the text portion of the label (Appendix E).

For example, let's say that you want to create a label that has a bullet, the word *Part* followed by a space, the chapter number, a comma, and a space. Then you want the word *Section* followed by a space and the section letter. After the section letter you want a colon. To create this format, proceed as follows:

1. Press Alt-195 for the bullet; type a space, the word **Part**, and another space; click the Chapter # insert; and type a comma and a space.
2. Type the word **Section** and a space, and then click the A,B button.
3. Type a colon.

The result would be an entry that looks like this:

• Part [C#], Section [*tag name, A]:

Let's say that you want to put this effect into place for every paragraph formatted with the Chapter Head tag. You would substitute *Chapter Head* for the tag name as follows:

• Part [C#], Section [*Chapter Head, A]:

SUPPRESSING SECTION NUMBERING

When numbering sections and subsections, Ventura usually includes the section number as part of the subsection number. Ventura does, however, provide you with the means of showing only the subsection number. Use the Suppress Previous Level button with any given level to keep the previous level's number from appearing.

When you click this button, a minus sign within brackets ([–]) appears at the location of the Text cursor. Usually, it's kept at the end of the field for easy editing. Thus, in the USER document, to suppress the previous level for Level 2, you'd use this entry:

```
[*Major Heading,1].[–]
```

To suppress for Level 3, you'd use this entry:

```
[*Minor Heading,1][–]
```

Figure 10.17 shows the results of suppressing these levels. Notice how the headings WYSIWYG and ITEM SELECTOR no longer carry the number 1 of the previous level, USER INTERFACE.

- Suppress previous-level numbering so the sample looks like Figure 10.17.

RENUMBERING SECTIONS

When you finish using this dialog box, Ventura automatically renumbers the tagged material appropriately. If, however, you make changes in the free-form text as it appears in the working area, such as deleting a heading, Ventura will not renumber immediately. Instead, you must instruct it specifically to do so. Drop the Chapter menu and select Renumber Chapter, or type Ctrl-B. The numbers will be adjusted correctly.

For instance, let's say that upon examining the document, we wish to adjust the Keyboard Keys heading. The heading really has nothing to do with WYSIWYG, so it should receive the Level 2 tag, Major Heading.

1. Apply the Major Heading tag to the heading. This makes the document look like Figure 10.18.
2. Renumber the document and use the Text mode Assignment list to change the heading to uppercase letters. This makes the document look like Figure 10.19.

1. USER INTERFACE

1. WYSIWYG

Figure 1-1
This is the caption for the figure. It is anchored below **WYSIWYG**

Ventura Publisher is designed to provide What You See (on the screen) Is What You Get printed (WYSIWYG). This means that the computer display should match as closely as possible, at all times, what you will see on the final printed page. Of course, the difference between the technology used to display a page on a CRT screen, and the technologies used to print a page on a laser printer or typesetter, do create some unavoidable differences. In particular, because the computer CRT screen cannot produce anywhere near the same resolution of a printer or typesetter, and because what is displayed is shown in a different aspect ratio (height to width ratio), the space between words and between lines may appear to be bigger or smaller than the printed page under certain circumstances. Several thin ruling lines, with little space between, may show on the screen as one thick line.

1 Keyboard Keys

Various keys on the keyboard perform special functions:

- The keyboard Cursor keys control the Text Cursor (The text cursor is displayed as a thin vertical line.)
- The Home key goes to the first page of the document.
- The End key goes to the last page of the document.
- The Pg Up key goes to the previous page.
- The Pg Dn key goes to the next page.

2. ITEM SELECTOR

1 Description

The display shown in Figure 10-2 is called an Item Selector. The Item Selector is used for saving and retrieving files.

Figure 10.17: Suppressing the previous level of numbering

1. USER INTERFACE

1.1. WYSIWYG

Figure 1-1
This is the caption for the figure. It is anchored below **WYSIWYG**

Ventura Publisher is designed to provide What You See (on the screen) Is What You Get printed (WYSIWYG). This means that the computer display should match as closely as possible, at all times, what you will see on the final printed page. Of course, the difference between the technology used to display a page on a CRT screen, and the technologies used to print a page on a laser printer or typesetter, do create some unavoidable differences. In particular, because the computer CRT screen cannot produce anywhere near the same resolution of a printer or typesetter, and because what is displayed is shown in a different aspect ratio (height to width ratio), the space between words and between lines may appear to be bigger or smaller than the printed page under certain circumstances. Several thin ruling lines, with little space between, may show on the screen as one thick line.

1.1.1 Keyboard Keys

Various keys on the keyboard perform special functions:

- The keyboard Cursor keys control the Text Cursor (The text cursor is displayed as a thin vertical line.)
- The Home key goes to the first page of the document.
- The End key goes to the last page of the document.
- The Pg Up key goes to the previous page.
- The Pg Dn key goes to the next page.

1.2. ITEM SELECTOR

1.2.1 Description

The display shown in Figure 10-2 is called an Item Selector. The Item Selector is used for saving and retrieving files.

Figure 10.18: The document with a new heading tag before renumbering

1. USER INTERFACE

1.1. WYSIWYG

Figure 1-1
This is the caption for the figure. It is anchored below **WYSIWYG**

Ventura Publisher is designed to provide What You See (on the screen) Is What You Get printed (WYSIWYG). This means that the computer display should match as closely as possible, at all times, what you will see on the final printed page. Of course, the difference between the technology used to display a page on a CRT screen, and the technologies used to print a page on a laser printer or typesetter, do create some unavoidable differences. In particular, because the computer CRT screen cannot produce anywhere near the same resolution of a printer or typesetter, and because what is displayed is shown in a different aspect ratio (height to width ratio), the space between words and between lines may appear to be bigger or smaller than the printed page under certain circumstances. Several thin ruling lines, with little space between, may show on the screen as one thick line.

1.2. KEYBOARD KEYS

Various keys on the keyboard perform special functions:

- The keyboard Cursor keys control the Text Cursor (The text cursor is displayed as a thin vertical line.)
- The Home key goes to the first page of the document.
- The End key goes to the last page of the document.
- The Pg Up key goes to the previous page.
- The Pg Dn key goes to the next page.

1.3. ITEM SELECTOR

1.3.1 Description

The display shown in Figure 10-2 is called an Item Selector. The Item Selector is used for saving and retrieving files.

Figure 10.19: The document after renumbering

CHANGING PAGE AND CHAPTER NUMBERS

In several of the dialog boxes we've examined in this chapter, we've seen the use of chapter-number and page-number inserts. In Chapter 9 we used such numbers in headers and footers. You can adjust Ventura page numbers and chapter numbers through the use of *counters*.

! New for version 2.0

Ventura 2.0 controls page, chapter, figure, and table counters all from the Update Counters dialog box (Figure 10.20). To display this dialog box, drop the Chapter menu and select Update Counters. Let's look at how these counters operate, and then we'll examine some strategies for their use.

THE PAGE COUNTER

When you use the Chapter menu's Go To Page command, Ventura always uses the page number displayed in the Side-bar as its reference. This number may not agree with those appearing on the page if you have adjusted them with the page counter. Similarly, when printing a document, should you print only selected pages, Ventura will use the Side-bar when calculating the pages to print.

You can use the Update Counters dialog box to start numbering the pages with some number other than one. This counter affects numbering as it appears within the document, as set by [#P] Insert codes in headers, footers, captions, and section headings. Be aware,

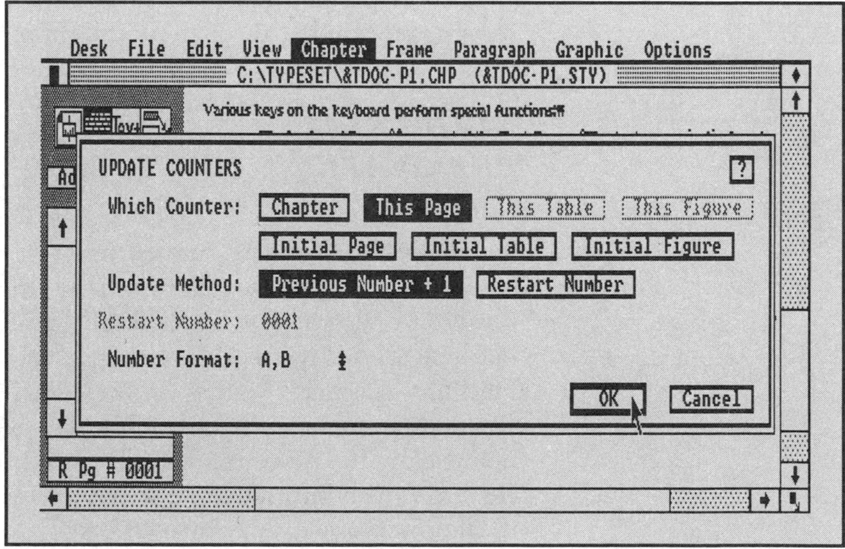

Figure 10.20: The Chapter menu's Update Counters dialog box

however, that it will not renumber the page numbers that appear in the Current box at the bottom of the Side-bar.

Click the This Page button to change the number of the currently displayed page. There is one page counter for each page of the chapter. By changing the page counter for any given page, you change the number of that page and of all pages that follow it. To change from standard numbering, click the Restart Number button and provide a number to restart with.

By using the Number Format settings, you can also adjust the style of the page numbers. Normally, the format is Arabic numerals, as indicated with the 1,2 button. You may wish to apply different numbering formats to different parts of a publication, such as lowercase Roman numerals for the front matter.

! New for version 2.0

From any page in the chapter, you can change the number of the first page. Click the Initial Page button to do this.

THE CHAPTER COUNTER

The chapter counter operates like the page counter, with two exceptions. First, it regulates chapter-number inserts, indicated by the [C#] Insert code. Second, there is only one chapter counter to a chapter. Adjusting that counter on any page in the chapter changes the chapter number throughout the chapter.

NUMBERING PUBLICATIONS ACROSS CHAPTERS

! New for version 2.0

The Multi-Chapter dialog box's new Renumber command allows you to number chapters, figures, and tables for an entire publication across chapters. To use this command, the Chapter menu's Update Counters dialog box for each counter should be set to Previous Number + 1. This is the default setting, so unless you've changed it, you need not consider it. Then, in the Multi-Chapter dialog box, click Renumber. After verification, Ventura will renumber the publication, saving the new number within each chapter involved on disk. Be sure you go through these steps before you print a publication, or the numbering will be incorrect.

USING FOOTNOTES

Just as Ventura's new handling of page numbering is elegant and straightforward, so too is its handling of footnotes. There are three steps to creating footnotes. First you turn the footnote system on and indicate how you want the footnotes to appear. Then you must insert *footnote references* into the text of your document. Finally, for each footnote, you provide the text of the footnote as it will appear at the bottom of the page. Ventura places the footnote text below the standard text and above any footer that you specify.

SETTING FOOTNOTES ON

To turn on footnote operations:

- Display the Chapter menu's Footnote Settings dialog box (Figure 10.21).

With the Usage & Format grouping, you indicate whether you want Ventura to number the footnotes from the start of each page—using numbers or user-defined strings—or from the start of each

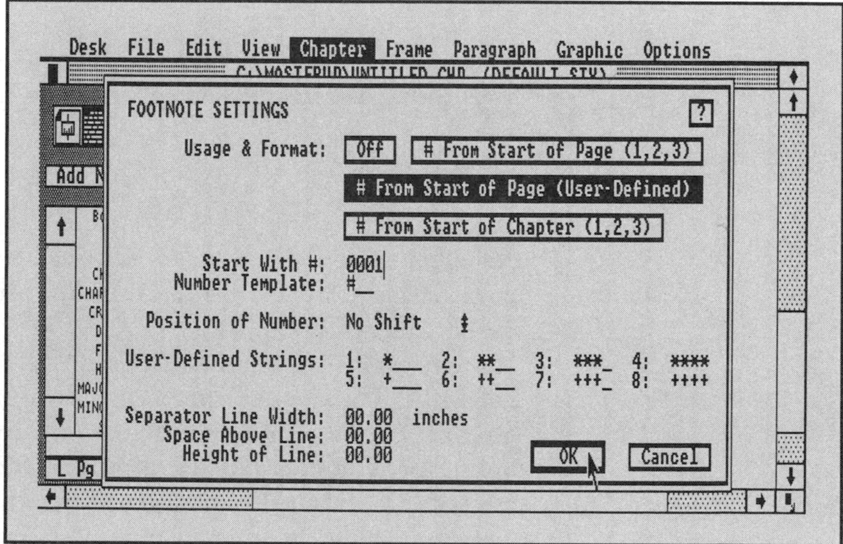

Figure 10.21: The Chapter menu's Footnote Settings dialog box

chapter. *User-defined strings* are symbols that you provide for indicating footnotes. In the User-Defined Strings grouping, you specify the symbols you want Ventura to use. Defaults are the asterisks and plus signs indicated in Figure 10.21.

From the Start With # setting, you can regulate the number with which Ventura should start footnotes. Normally, you would use 1. Even if you link chapters into a publication, footnote numbering usually begins with 1 for each chapter, so there would be no need to adjust this setting.

The Number Template field indicates how Ventura should display the number at the bottom of the page. You can type in three characters, using the number symbol (#) to represent the footnote number (or other reference mark). For instance, if you enter

```
#.
```

for Number Template, Ventura will print the number at the bottom followed by a period. Thus the first footnote number would appear as

```
1.
```

If you enter

```
(#)
```

for Number Template, Ventura will print the first number at the bottom as

```
(1)
```

Note that this template only affects the number at the bottom of the page. It has no effect on the number as it appears in the text of the document.

Position Of Number has three settings: No Shift, Superscript, and Subscript. The settings control only the number in the text and have no effect on the number at the bottom. By selecting Superscript or Subscript, you can shift the number above or below other text, respectively. Doing so normally decreases the size of the font, and you can regulate the size and amount of shift by activating Paragraph mode, clicking the paragraph that the footnote appears in, and using the Paragraph menu's Attribute Overrides dialog box.

A *separator line* is a horizontal rule that separates the text of footnotes at the bottom of the page from the rest of the text on the page. By inserting values, you create the line. Separator Line Width specifies the length of the line from left to right. Space Above Line is the distance from the text area to the line. Height of Line represents the line's thickness from top to bottom.

1. We'll use a number for a footnote, so click the # From Start Of Page button.
2. Provide the following values to create and position a separator line: Separator Line Width: 3 inches; Height of Line: 00, 02 picas & points (the same thickness as that of the rule below the Item Selector heading).

INSERTING FOOTNOTES

Once you've provided the footnote settings, you can insert footnotes into the text. To do that, activate Text mode and position the text cursor at the proper spot in the text. Then use the Edit menu to select Ins Special Item (or press Ctrl-C). In the Special Item dialog box, click Footnote (or press F2). When you do, no dialog box appears. Instead, Ventura immediately inserts the footnote number or other reference mark into position. At the same time, the corresponding reference mark appears at the bottom of the page, as does any separator line that you've specified, along with the words

Text of Footnote

Simply delete these words just as you would any normal text, and replace them with the text you want for your footnote. (Be certain you only attempt to delete those words, not the reference mark, or you'll receive an error message.)

To practice inserting a footnote:

1. Position the screen as you see in Figure 10.22.
2. Place the text cursor after the heading *ITEM SELECTOR*.
3. Insert a footnote at this spot.

At this point, Ventura inserts a footnote, but text at the bottom of the page disappears, leaving a large gap. This is because Ventura has moved the footnote and the text holding its corresponding reference mark to the next page. There wasn't enough room at the bottom of the first page.

4. Display the next page. You'll see that the words *Text of Footnote* appear at the bottom of the page in conjunction with a separator line.

The text of the footnote receives the Z_FNOT ENTRY tag automatically. The reference number at the bottom receives the Z_FNOT # tag. These are both generated tags. To change their settings, activate Paragraph mode and select their paragraphs at the bottom of the page. For instance, to lessen the distance that the text of the footnote is displaced from the number, click the Text Of Footnote paragraph. Then use the Paragraph menu's Spacing command and decrease the In From Left setting. To change the size of the numbers at the bottom, click one of the numbers and use the Paragraph menu's Font dialog box.

Shifting a footnote number at the bottom is trickier. it seems Ventura is not designed to allow this; apparently Ventura's designers feel

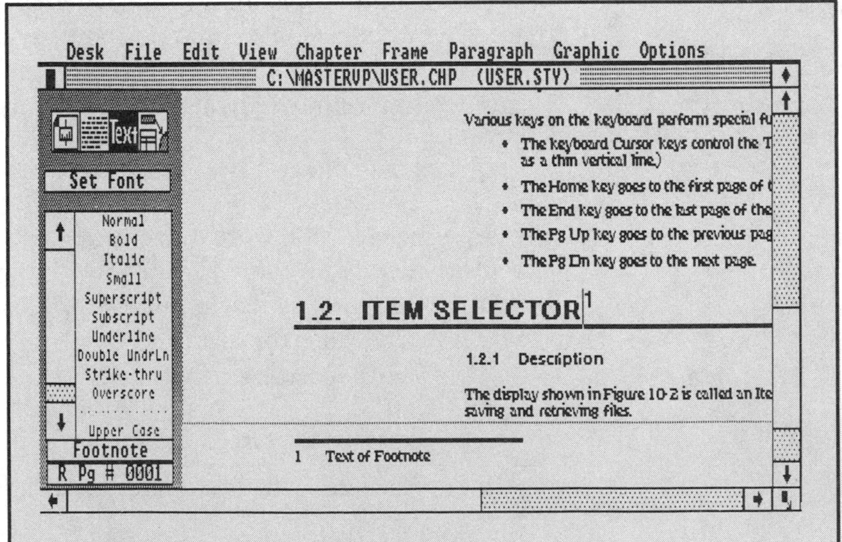

Figure 10.22: A footnote inserted in text

Because this trick utilizes the Big First Character setting, it only works on the first character of the number. Once you have more than nine footnotes on a page, only the first digit will be raised. With footnote number 10 for instance, the 1 would be raised but not the 0, resulting in [1]0 at the bottom of the page.

it's best to keep the baseline of numbers and notes even at the bottom of the page. However, you can do it by adjusting the number as a Big First Character. As before, in Paragraph mode click the number at the bottom to make Z_FNOT # appear in the Current box. Then drop the Paragraph menu and select Special Effects. In the resulting dialog box, click the Big First Char button. Then click Set Font Properties and provide a value by which to shift the font up. Press Enter twice to register the settings in the two dialog boxes.

THE FOOTNOTE FRAME

When you insert a footnote, Ventura creates a frame to hold the footnote text at the bottom. You can adjust some of the attributes of this generated frame. For example, you can adjust the frame's margins to make it smaller.

As we saw, a footnote frame that's too big may move to the next page and create a large gap at the bottom of the first page. This is especially possible with a multiline footnote. Ventura does not allow you to break footnote text from one page to the next. However, you can decrease the size of the footnote frame, and doing so may allow the footnote in its entirety to be accommodated on the first page.

Let's do this, so that we fill in the bottom of the first page by bringing the footnote and its reference mark in text to the first page.

1. In Frame mode, click the footnote frame.
2. Drop the Frame menu and select Margins & Columns.
3. Click the Top value and change it to 0.1 inches. Then do the same for Bottom and press Enter. With smaller top and bottom margins, the frame decreases in size. The frame and its footnote text move to the first page.

The bottom of the first page should look like Figure 10.22. In this figure, the text cursor is to the left of the footnote reference. Hence, the word

Footnote

appears in the Current box on the Side-bar.

Of course you should replace the words *Text of Footnote* with actual footnote text, such as *Also known as the File Selector.* To do this, follow these steps:

1. Drag the mouse across *Text of Footnote,* thus darkening it.
2. Press the Del key.
3. Type in the actual footnote text.

PRINTING A PUBLICATION

Once you've created a publication, you can print it. The printing procedure for publications is very similar to that used for printing an individual chapter. Be careful if your publication has special needs such as page numbers, an index, or a table of contents. Before you print, be sure to check the sections in this chapter that cover those features.

To print a publication, follow these steps:

1. Bring up the Multi-Chapter Operations dialog box.
2. Open the appropriate publication file.
3. Click Print. You'll see the Print Information dialog box (Figure 10.23), which looks just like it does when displayed with the File menu's To Print command.
4. Set the print information you desire and click OK to print the publication.

If you plan to output to disk with each chapter going to a separate file, it would be wise to place all your publication's front matter into one chapter. This material would continue to become the C00 file. Then chapter numbers will agree with output-file numbers; Chapter 1 would become the C01 file, Chapter 2 would become the C02 file, and so on.

The Multi-Chp Print Files pop-up menu in this dialog box will usually ghost with multiple chapters, just as it does with a single chapter. It will only become available when you've used the Options menu's Set Printer Info and specified Output To: Filename. (Chapter 5 examines this procedure.)

When outputting to a file, you use this menu's Combined setting to combine all chapters into one output file. Use the Separate setting to locate each chapter in a separate output file. Once you give the OK, Ventura will ask you to provide a name for the output. If you are using the Separate setting, Ventura will add sequential extensions to the

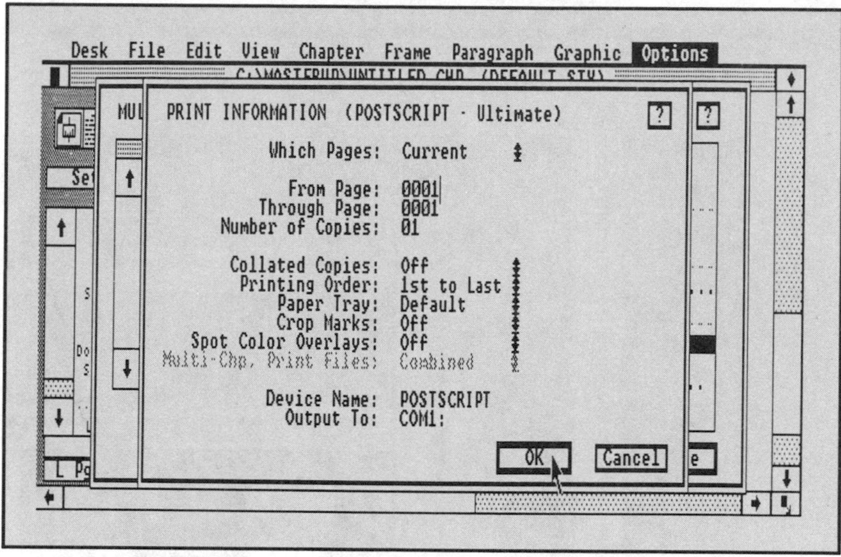

Figure 10.23: The dialog box displayed by the Multi-Chapter Print command

name you specify for the output. The first file is labeled with C00 and the others in turn with C01, C02, C03, and so on.

- Try printing a publication by printing USER.PUB.

Effective use of other programs with Ventura can expedite the work you perform on extensive projects. In the next chapter we'll look at how other programs work with Ventura.

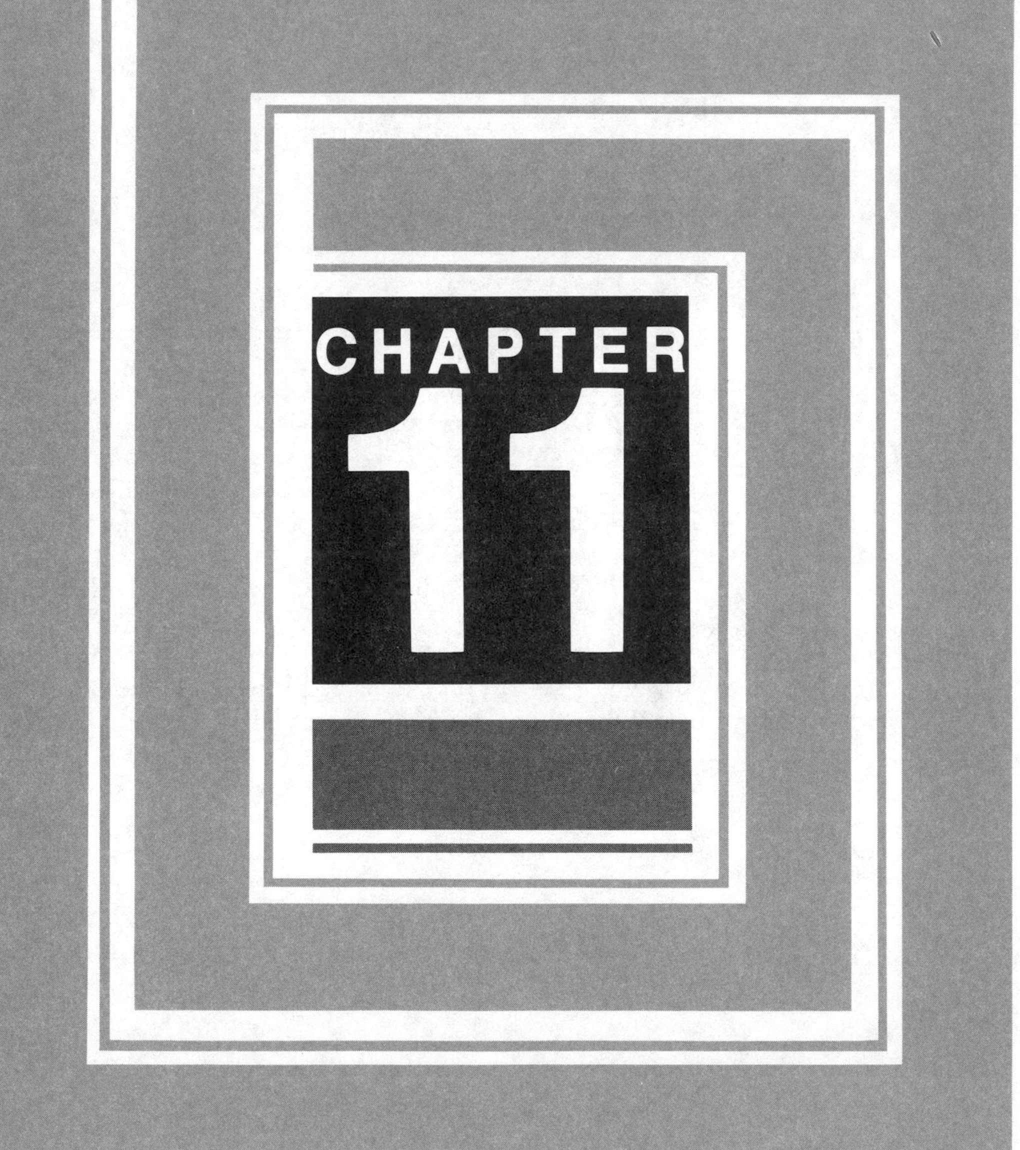
CHAPTER
11

Using Other Programs with Ventura

Fast Track

To preformat text with a supported word processor 409

you can insert some text attributes with the word processor's equivalent means of creating the effect. Use text attributes for local formatting, generally no longer than a paragraph. Alternatively, you can enter Ventura's code words and symbols to insert text attributes. You can also use a word processor to tag paragraphs and to insert special text items.

Follow these rules when entering text with a word processor: 410

- Do not assign margins or other page formats.
- Do not indent paragraphs.
- Do not justify or center text.
- Press the space bar only once after a sentence.
- Place the return that ends a paragraph immediately after the final visible character in the paragraph.
- Enter only one return at the end of each paragraph, or place @PARAFILTR ON = at the beginning of the file.

To apply a paragraph tag with the word processor 412

enter an At symbol (@) followed by the name of the tag, a space, an equal sign (=), and another space at the beginning of the paragraph. Paragraphs without specially assigned tags receive the Body Text tag.

To insert codes equivalent to the Edit menu's Ins Special Item 414

type **<$** followed by a code letter for the effect, the text, and the > symbol. Table 11.1 list the codes and the syntax for special items.

To assign text attributes 417

that appear on the Text mode Assignment list, use the equivalent means of creating it with the word processor, or enter the codes that begin and end the effect. You can also enter equivalents for codes you create with the keyboard in Ventura. All these codes appear in Table 11.2 and Appendix E.

To strip a text file 419

of excessive space characters, or to insert an extra return after using @PARAFILTR ON =, use search and replace in your word processor. You can also use the Options menu's Set Preferences to automatically convert inch marks to true quotation marks and double hyphens to em dashes.

To insert codes, 420

especially tag names, quickly and accurately, use your word processor's macro capability. You can also use a macro generator with small Ventura chapters.

To work with unsupported word processors 421

use ASCII format, which requires two returns at the end of each paragraph. You may also wish to import such files in WordStar 3 format, which uses only one return.

To create a table with tabs 428

insert tab characters when entering the text in the word processor. The columns in the word processor do not need to line up accurately. Be sure to insert a true tab character, not a series of space characters. When you use column tags, each item for the table should end with a return.

CHAPTER 11

ONE OF THE KEY FEATURES OF VENTURA IS ITS ability to work with a wide variety of software—especially word processors—for entering text. Rather than attempting to do all things for all people with the text editor, Ventura's creators instead chose to coordinate many word-processing standards. That way, you can choose the best word-processing package for your job or continue to use the software that you are accustomed to. Ventura's support is so extensive that most users find themselves immediately comfortable using their own familiar software.

Ventura's support of the major word processors means that it is possible to have the power of a full-featured word processor of your choice as you enter and revise the material. At the same time, you can have the material carry immediately over to Ventura. Much of the current desktop-publishing software can use text that has been saved in various word-processed formats; once it enters the desktop-publishing system, however, there's no going back. You can no longer use the original word-processing package to examine the text or to edit it.

Ventura, however, is quite a pioneer in creating a system that not only recognizes a variety of formats, but *saves* edits you make in the original file in the same word-processing format with which it was created. What's more, if you don't like that format, you can change it to another.

Even if Ventura does not fully support your word processor, you can still enter and edit text using ASCII format. The rules for this format differ from the rules for standard text in supported word processors. We'll look first at using supported word processors, and then we'll examine the ASCII method.

USING SUPPORTED WORD PROCESSORS

Traditional publishing involves the talents of at least three types of persons: writers, editors, and typographers. With Ventura, you can perform all three of these jobs yourself. On the other hand, you may find it helpful to separate all three tasks or combine one or two. As we examine the work you do with text in this chapter, we'll see how people working in these different roles can use Ventura and supported programs.

As you compose your document, or use the work a writer composes, there are two ways to format it. As an editor and typographer, you can use the various Ventura commands to specify text attributes, apply paragraph tags, lay out pages, create frames, and so on. Although page layout and frame manipulation must be handled with Ventura, there is another way to format text and paragraphs: you can use your word processor to provide the format information. This technique is known as *preformatting*; it allows writers to specify formats as they compose the text.

METHODS OF PREFORMATTING

When you or your writers enter the text for a document, there are two ways to preformat it. First, if Ventura supports your word processor, you can preformat some text attributes with the formatting operations that are built into your word processor. For italics, boldface, underlining, and some other straightforward text attributes, this means you can use the same system that you've already mastered.

When you alter your word-processed files in Ventura, Ventura uses the word processor's own codes to enter the formats into the text. This means that when you look again at the text file with the word processor, you'll see incorporated into the text those attributes that you set in place with Ventura.

Be aware, however, that you should only follow this approach with effects that are to be local in nature; that is, on short passages, no more than a paragraph long. For more lasting effects, or for effects that are to be repeated regularly, enter codes for paragraph tags.

This point brings us to the other way you can specify formatting in the word processor: You can enter Ventura code words and symbols directly into the word-processed text. Once these codes are entered, Ventura will recognize them and understand the information they contain. You can use these codes for local effects just as you do your word processor's commands.

More importantly, though, you can use codes to tag paragraphs as you do in Ventura. Assign a tag name with the word processor and, once the paragraph is in a Ventura chapter, it will receive the attributes that you set up for the corresponding tag on the style sheet. In addition, you can use codes to enter special text items, such as index references and footnote text.

Note that you can use the File Type/Rename dialog box to change the word-processor format that any file uses. Just click the button that's labeled with the word processor you want. The next time you save the chapter (with the File menu's Save or Save As command), Ventura will convert the file to the new format.

ENTERING TEXT WITH A WORD PROCESSOR

When using your word processor to create Ventura files, you may find it helpful to think of your word processor in a different way. Rather than the formatting and layout software that it usually is, consider it simply a data-entry device. You will use it primarily to indicate the text for a document. You don't lay out and format displayed material except as helpful for display on the screen or for rough drafts. The formatting that you do indicate is in the form of directions and codes that Ventura translates into the real thing.

Keep your text as simple as possible. For example, do not press the Tab key to indent the first line of your paragraphs. Let Ventura shape the paragraph by providing a first-line indent for the paragraph's tag. Likewise, don't use the word processor to create indented paragraphs, as is the practice for extended quotations. Handle that format within Ventura.

Do not attempt to right-justify text. Depending on the word processor, doing so could waste your time or wreak havoc on the Ventura document that contains the file. The same is true for centering. Don't center text; let a Ventura tag accomplish that.

* Remember, the Professional Extension provides the easiest means of creating and editing tables. See Chapter 13.

If you will be entering tables, don't attempt to format them with your word processor. Be certain that you understand the different kinds of tables you can create with Ventura (Chapter 8), and read the section on tables later in this chapter.

When entering text, you need only press the space bar once after a period or colon. In most typing and word-processing applications, there are usually two spaces after a sentence or a colon. In typesetting, however, two spaces create too much space, making for loose lines of text. When Ventura imports text with two spaces like this, it will display the second space as a nonstandard space. This is indicated by a lazy (upward-pointing) bracket (␣). This conversion also takes place when you save and retrieve a document with Ventura. When you see this symbol after the end of a sentence, it's wise to delete it.

With text at the end of a paragraph, place the return that ends the paragraph immediately after the period or other visible character that ends the sentence. Do not place a space after the period and then enter the return. Doing so sometimes causes Ventura to create an unnecessary additional line in the paragraph.

Press the Enter key only one time between paragraphs. Once you provide a tag for the paragraph, you will be able to indicate the amount of space between paragraphs. Suppose, however, that as an editor you receive material from a writer that has two returns between paragraphs. Fortunately, you don't have to go through the file and remove the extra returns one by one. Ventura has a special code that will perform that tedious job for you. At the very beginning of the file, type

```
@PARAFILTR ON =
```

which stands for Paragraph Filter On. This instruction will cause Ventura to remove the extra return when two follow in succession. Be aware, however, that when you save your document in Ventura, it will be saved without the extra return; that is, it will be saved with only one return between each paragraph. If you then view the file with your word processor, you may have trouble telling one paragraph from the next.

This brings us to another important point about text files. Once you create a text file for use with Ventura, you turn it over to Ventura. When you save Ventura documents, the program may perform all sorts of unusual acts to the related text file. The margins may change, character attributes may disappear, and new code words may show up. Therefore, if you want to use the material that's in your document for some other application, don't assign the original file to Ventura. Instead, use a copy of the file.

To recap, here are the important points to bear in mind when you use a word processor to enter text for Ventura:

- Do not set up margins and other page formats.
- Do not indent paragraphs.
- Do not center or justify text.
- Do not format tables completely.
- Insert only one space after a period or colon.
- Press Enter only once after each paragraph.
- Enter only local formatting, no longer than a paragraph.

Figure 11.1 shows how you would enter the initial text for the USER.CHP document (originally called &TDOC-P1.CHP) that we've been examining in the last few chapters. (Of course, the text for this document has already been entered.) Each paragraph symbol (¶) indicates where you would press the Enter key.

ENTERING CODES FOR PARAGRAPH TAGS AND SPECIAL ITEMS

As you can see from Figure 11.1, all the text is the same. How does Ventura know which text is a headline, subheading, and so on? The answer is that, as the text file stands, Ventura wouldn't. If you were to load the file into Ventura in this condition, you'd see it all formatted as body text. You could then apply other tags to format the paragraphs. Doing so would insert special codes into the text file, which is how Ventura keeps track of which tags have been assigned to which paragraphs. However, you can assign the same codes with your word processor.

```
USER INTERFACE¶
WYSIWYG¶
Ventura Publisher is designed to provide What You See (on
the screen) Is What You Get printed (WYSIWYG).  This means
that the computer display should match as closely as
possible, at all times, what you will see on the final
printed page.  Of course, the difference between the
technology used to display a page on a CRT screen, and the
technologies used to print a page on a laser printer or
typesetter, do create some unavoidable differences.  In
particular, because the computer CRT screen cannot produce
anywhere near the same resolution of a printer or
typesetter, and because what is displayed is shown in a
different aspect ratio (height to width ratio), the space
between words and between lines may appear to be bigger or
smaller than the printed page under certain circumstances.
Several thin ruling lines, with little space between, may
show on the screen as one thick line.¶
Keyboard Keys¶
Various keys on the keyboard perform special functions:¶
The keyboard Cursor keys control the Text Cursor (The text
cursor is displayed as a thin vertical line.)¶
The Home key goes to the first page of the document.¶
The End key goes to the last page of the document.¶
The Pg Up key goes to the previous page.¶
The Pg Dn key goes to the next page.¶
ITEM SELECTOR ¶
Description¶
The display shown in Figure 10-2 is called an Item Selector.
The Item Selector is used for saving and retrieving files.¶
Application¶
The Item Selector allows you to save and retrieve files by
pointing to the file name, or by typing the file name.¶
The Item Selector also provides a simple way to move between
various DOS subdirectories (sometimes called folders) where
text, Line Art, Image, chapter, and publication files may be
stored.¶
Finally, the Item Selector automatically filters the files
displayed so that you need only search for files which match
specified criteria.  For instance, only chapter files (which
are stored with a file extension CHP) are displayed when
loading or saving chapters.  The method for filtering the
files to be displayed follows standard DOS conventions,
including wildcard characters (e.g. * and ?).  These filters
can be changed by placing the text cursor on the Directory
line and typing a new filter name.  Figure 10-2 shows the
filter set to only display chapter (CHP) files that are
contained in the subdirectory called TYPESET.¶
Pointing to the desired file name, holding the mouse
stationary, and pressing the mouse button twice, with little
hesitation between each depression double-click, is
equivalent to selecting the file name and then selecting
OK.¶

If you only need one or two symbols within a paragraph, then
Tag the paragraph with a non-symbol typeface, and select the
one or two characters you wish to change to a symbol, and
change them using the Font Settings button.  For instance,
to put a p in the formula¶
pr2¶
type the letter p, then select this letter and use the Font
Settings button to change this one letter to a symbol font.¶
Function  Key¶
Bring to Front         ^A¶
Copy           Shift Del¶
Cut            Del¶
Enlarged View          ^E¶
Fill Attributes            ^F¶
Frame Setting Function     ^U ¶
```

Figure 11.1: An unformatted document entered with a word processor

Paragraph-tagging codes are placed at the beginning of the paragraph that they apply to. They begin with the At symbol (@), followed by the name of the tag, a space, an equal sign (=), and another space. The name of the tag is usually in uppercase, but this is not required by Ventura.

When you enter a tag name to preformat, the At symbol (@) must be the first character in the paragraph. Do not place anything, including space or tab characters, before the At symbol. Since the At symbol is a special flag to Ventura, you must follow a special approach if you ever need to literally use an At symbol at the beginning of a paragraph. To have one At symbol actually appear in text, you must type *two* At symbols together (@@).

Thus, for instance, the first paragraph in our example consists of the heading USER INTERFACE. It should be tagged with Chapter Head. To apply this tag, you'd type

```
@CHAPTER HEAD = USER INTERFACE
```

If you then looked at the file in Ventura, you'd see *USER INTERFACE* formatted with the Chapter Head tag. Any paragraph attributes you set up for that tag would be applied to the heading.

Now consider what happens when you don't insert tag codes with a word processor. If you simply left the paragraph alone in the word processor and then applied the tag within the Ventura document, the effect on the text file would be the same as preformatting. Upon opening the file with your word processor, you would see the same code in place, just as though you had typed it in yourself.

If you insert a tag name with your word processor but it doesn't appear on the style sheet, Ventura will display the tag name in all capital letters on the Assignment list.

If you look at Figure 11.2, you can see how the file is coded on your disk. Look at the first line and you see the tag code and then the text that appears in that paragraph: USER INTERFACE. Other tag names appear along the left edge: MAJOR HEADING, MINOR HEADING, BULLET, WARNING, and so on. These are the same tag names that you would see in the Assignment list with Paragraph mode activated.

Be aware that, because of Ventura's special use of the < and > characters, the same "two-for-one" rule mentioned for the At symbol applies to them. That is, if you want one < to appear, you must type << when entering the symbol with your word processor.

After the text for the first heading, there is another code. This is a code for an index entry. The less-than symbol (<) indicates the beginning of the code. This is followed by $I, the code that flags index entries. The words that follow, *User interface,* are the entry for the index, as discussed in Chapter 10. These are the words you would enter in the Primary Key field with the Edit menu's Ins Special Item command. The greater-than symbol (>) marks the end of the coded entry.

Table 11.1 shows the codes you can use with your word processor to insert special text into your text file. These inserts are equivalent to those you'd insert in Ventura with the Edit menu's Ins Special Item.

```
@CHAPTER HEAD = USER INTERFACE<$IUser interface>
@MAJOR HEADING = <$&WYSIWYG[v]>WYSIWYG
<$IProblem;Can't print what's on
screen><$IWYSIWYG;Defined>Ventura Publisher is designed to
provide What You See (on the screen) Is What You Get printed
(WYSIWYG).  This means that the computer display should
match as closely as possible, at all times, what you will
see on the final printed page.  Of course, the difference
between the technology used to display a page on a CRT
screen, and the technologies used to print a page on a laser
printer or typesetter, do create some unavoidable
differences.  In particular, because the computer CRT screen
cannot produce anywhere near the same resolution of a
printer or typesetter, and because what is displayed is
shown in a different <$IAspect ratio>aspect ratio (height to
width ratio), the space between words and between lines may
appear to be bigger or smaller than the printed page under
certain circumstances.  Several thin ruling lines, with
little space between, may show on the screen as one thick
line.
@MINOR HEADING = Keyboard Keys
Various keys on the keyboard perform special functions:
@BULLET = The keyboard Cursor <$ICursor keys><$IText
editing;Cursor keys>keys control the Text Cursor (The text
cursor is displayed as a thin vertical line.)
@BULLET = The Home <$IHome key><$IText editing;Home key>key
goes to the first page of the document.
@BULLET = The End <$IEnd key><$IText editing;End key>key
goes to the last page of the document.
@BULLET = The Pg Up <$IPage up key><$IText editing;Page up
key>key goes to the previous page.
@BULLET = The Pg Dn <$IPage down key><$IText editing;Page
down key>key goes to the next page.
@MAJOR HEADING = ITEM SELECTOR <$IItem
selector;Operation><$ISaving files><$ILoading files>
@MINOR HEADING = Description
The display shown in Figure 10-2 is called an Item Selector.
The Item Selector is used for saving and retrieving files.
@MINOR HEADING = Application
The Item Selector allows you to save and retrieve files by
pointing to the file name, or by typing the file name.
The Item Selector also provides a simple way to move between
various DOS subdirectories (sometimes called folders) where
text, Line Art, Image, chapter, and publication files may be
stored.
Finally, the Item Selector automatically <169>filters<170>
the files displayed so that you need only search for files
which match specified criteria.  For instance, only chapter
files (which are stored with a file extension CHP) are
displayed when loading or saving chapters.  The method for
filtering the files to be displayed follows standard DOS
conventions, including wildcard characters (e.g. * and ?).
These filters can be changed by placing the text cursor on
the Directory line and typing a new filter name.  Figure 10-
2 shows the filter set to only display chapter (CHP) files
that are contained in the subdirectory called TYPESET.
@WARNING = <$IShortcut;Mouse double-click><$IMouse;Double-
click>Pointing to the desired file name, holding the mouse
stationary, and pressing the mouse button twice, with little
hesitation between each depression <169>double-click<170>,
is equivalent to selecting the file name and then selecting
OK.
If you only need one or two symbols within a paragraph, then
Tag the paragraph with a non-symbol typeface, and select the
one or two characters you wish to change to a symbol, and
change them using the Font Settings button.  For instance,
to put a <F128M>p<F255D> in the formula
@SYSTEM PROMPT = <F128M>p<F255D>r2
type the letter p, then select this letter and use the Font
Settings button to change this one letter to a symbol font.
@TABLE HEAD = Function   Key
@TABLE ITEM = Bring to Front        ^A
@TABLE ITEM = Copy           Shift Del
@TABLE ITEM = Cut            Del
@TABLE ITEM = Enlarged View         ^E
@TABLE ITEM = Fill Attributes       ^F
@TABLE ITEM = Frame Setting Function     ^U
```

Figure 11.2: The text file with paragraph tags

Table 11.1: Word-Processor Codes for the Edit Menu's Ins Special Item

FORMAT	SPECIAL ITEM	TEXT INSERT
Anchor for Frame—Fixed, On Same Page As Anchor	Frame Anchor (F5)	<$&*Anchor name*>
Anchor for Frame—Relative, Below Anchor Line	"	<$&*Anchor name*[v]>
Anchor for Frame—Relative, Above Anchor Line	"	<$&*Anchor name*[^]>
Anchor for Frame—Relative, Automatically At Anchor	"	<$&*Anchor name*[-]>
Box Character: Hollow	Box Char (F1)	<$B0>
Box Character: Filled	"	<$B1>
Equation with value over value	Fraction (F4)	<$E*Numerator* over *Denominator*>
Equation with values separated by slash	"	<$E*Numerator / Denominator*>
Footnote	Footnote (F2)	<$F *Text of footnote*>
Index Entry with Primary Entry only	Index Entry (F2)	<$I*Primary entry*>
Index Entry with Secondary Entry too	"	<$I*Primary entry*;*Secondary entry*>
Index Entry with Sort Keys specified	"	<$I*Primary entry*[*Primary sort key*]; *Secondary entry*[*Secondary sort key*]>

Table 11.1: Word-Processor Codes for the Edit Menu's Ins Special Item (continued)

FORMAT	SPECIAL ITEM	TEXT INSERT
Index Entry with See	"	<$S*Primary entry;cross-reference*>
Index Entry with See Also	"	<$A*Primary entry;cross-reference*>
Reference mark for chapter number	Cross Ref (F6)	<$R[C#]>
Reference mark for page number	"	<$R[P#]>
Hidden Text (for display in the word processor but not in Ventura)	(N/A)	<$!*Hidden text*>

Likewise, these are the codes that are inserted in your word-processed text file when you use their equivalent commands in Ventura.

Note that there is a code for hidden text, which has no equivalent on the Special item menu. Use this code for text that you want to see with the word processor but that you don't want to appear in the Ventura document. Such text is used primarily by writers to leave themselves notes. It can also be used to send notes back and forth between writers and editors.

* You can show or hide tabs and returns with the Options menu or Ctrl-T. See Appendix A.

When tabs and returns are showing, Ventura marks the location of hidden text by displaying a small temperature degree symbol (°), as it does with index entries and footnotes. This mark does not show in the printed version of a document. When the text cursor is positioned to the left of this marker, Ventura displays the words *Hidden Text* in the Current box.

ENTERING TEXT ATTRIBUTES

You can also enter and see codes for text attributes. In fact, all text attributes that appear on the Side-bar in Text mode have equivalent corresponding codes (except, of course, Upper Case, Capitalize, and Lower Case.) Even attributes that you assign with the Set Font button can be duplicated. There are other codes inserted with the keyboard in Ventura that you can duplicate with the word processor.

Table 11.2 shows the codes for the various items on the Text mode Assignment list or in the Current box. It also shows how to insert the codes using the three word processors we'll examine in this chapter.

Table 11.2: Code Equivalents of Text Attributes and Inserts

CODE	NAME ON ASSIGNMENT LIST OR CURRENT BOX	MICROSOFT WORD	WORDSTAR	WORDPERFECT
<D>	Normal	Alt-Spacebar		
<B>	Bold	Alt-B	Ctrl-PB	F6 or Ctrl-F8 2 1
<I>	Italic	Alt-I		Ctrl-F8 2 4
<S>	Small	Format Character		Ctrl-F8 2 7
<^>	Superscript	Alt-Plus	Ctrl-PT	Ctrl-F8 1 1
<v>	Subscript	Alt-Minus	Ctrl-PV	Ctrl-F8 1 2
<U>	Underline	Alt-U	Ctrl-PS	F8 or Ctrl-F8 2 2
< = >	Double Underline			
<X>	Strike-thru	Alt-S	Ctrl-PX	Ctrl-F8 2 9
<O>	Overscore			
<->	Discretionary Hypen (Ctrl-Hyphen)	Ctrl-Hyphen	Ctrl-OE	Ctrl-Hyphen
<N>	NoBreak Space (Ctrl-Spacebar)	Ctrl-Spacebar	Ctrl-PO	Home Spacebar
<R>	Line Break (Ctrl-Enter)	Shift-Enter		

Note that you can insert the Ventura codes in the first column with your word processor even if the effect you desire is not supported by the word processor you're using.

If you create one of these effects in Ventura and you're using a supported word processor, the codes won't appear in the word-processed document. Instead, Ventura will convert them into the word processor's version of the effect. Thus if your supported word processor shows underlining, text you underline with the Text mode Assignment list will appear underlined when you look at it with your word processor. You will only see the <U> code, beginning the underlining, if your word processor can't produce the effect.

The code you enter has two purposes: It indicates what the effect is, and it starts the effect. Text-attribute effects continue in the text until the end of the paragraph or until they encounter the Normal code, <D>, or a code that begins a different effect, whichever comes first.

There are other codes that you can enter and store in text files, affecting the specialized typographical features available in Edit mode. We'll examine typography and these codes in Chapter 12 and Appendix F.

USING SEARCH AND REPLACE

You can use your word processor's search and replace capabilities to correct a variety of problems you may encounter with text files. Using these commands can be especially helpful to an editor who is receiving text from other sources. Consider the problem cited earlier in which a writer inserts two spaces at the end of a sentence instead of one. You could have your word processor find all occurrences of two spaces and replace them with one. You can also use search and replace to recreate some spacing in order to make the text more readable in the word processor, after Ventura's @PARAFILTR ON = code has stripped away the second return between paragraphs. Use your word processor to search for one return and replace it with two returns.

! New for version 2.0

The Options menu's Set Preferences command now offers an Auto-Adjustment option that automatically converts inch marks to true quotation marks, and double hyphens to em dashes. Set Auto-Adjustments to "And -- for Ventura to make this conversion when it loads and saves the text file. This means it is no longer necessary to search for and replace inch marks and double hyphens. Set Auto-Adjustments to Both and Ventura will also automatically adjust line spacing to accomodate a large text font (Chapter 4).

MACRO GENERATORS

If you're inserting a lot of coding in a word-processed file, you will undoubtedly wish to use some kind of macro-generating capability to enter the codes. When using such a facility, you simply issue some quick keystrokes (defined by you), and the macro program enters the entire code in its place. The result is increased efficiency and accuracy.

Macros are especially helpful in tagging paragraphs. Thus, assume that you have a tag for Chapter Head. Rather than typing in **@CHAPTER HEAD** = each time you need to tag a paragraph, you might set up a macro to insert it by typing Alt-CH, or Esc C, or Ctrl-C, depending on the system.

Most popular word processors now possess some ability to create macros. Besides "macro generator," this feature goes by a wide variety of names: keyboard enhancer, glossary, key code, or shorthand.

* Using the Professional Extension in conjuction with expanded memory makes the use of a keyboard enhancer with Ventura more practical, becuase you can create larger chapters. See Chapter 13.

There are also resident programs like SmartKey that perform the same function but with greater ability. Even if your word processor does have a macro generator, you may wish to consider a keyboard utility. Because the program is resident, you can use it with Ventura as well as your word processor. Of course, you wouldn't use it to insert tag names in Ventura, where you simply use the mouse or function keys to tag. However, such programs can be handy for inserting repeated text, such as a company letterhead.

Be aware that resident programs use computer memory, which can decrease the size of Ventura chapters. As such, they're handiest with small chapters. It's important to use one that goes easy on the memory; SmartKey is good in this regard. (Keep SmartKey's Definition Table's size small.) You may also need to adjust Ventura's /A = parameter in the VP.BAT file (see Appendix A).

USING ASCII TEXT FOR UNSUPPORTED WORD PROCESSORS

Even if your word processor isn't supported by Ventura, you can use it by creating ASCII text. ASCII stands for American Standard Code for Information Interchange. It's a standard that is supported not only by almost all word processors, but also by database management systems, electronic spreadsheets, and other programs. ASCII text is sometimes known as unformatted text, print-to-disk files, nondocuments, and DOS text files.

Usually, entering text in ASCII format requires that you press the Enter key at the end of each line. This being the case, how does Ventura differentiate between the end of an ASCII line and the end of an ASCII paragraph? The answer is that Ventura looks for and expects two returns between paragraphs. It only does this with ASCII text. Therefore, if you want to use ASCII format, you must place two returns between paragraphs.

Unlike supported word processors, though, ASCII is generally a one-way operation. If your text doesn't have a return at the end of each line, once you start to edit and save it with Ventura, Ventura will go ahead and add the format. The resulting text is hard to work with in the word processor.

WordStar 3 format is closely akin to ASCII. However, when importing files in this format, Ventura doesn't look for two returns to signal the end of a paragraph and doesn't insert returns at the end of each line. Therefore, you may be able to import text to Ventura in WordStar 3 format when it's in ASCII style except for the two returns at the ends of paragraphs. Doing so would keep Ventura from adding the unwanted returns at the ends of lines.

POPULAR WORD PROCESSORS

Now let's examine some of the most popular word-processing systems and see how they operate with Ventura. We won't look at all of those that operate with Ventura, but by examining these few, you should get an idea of the various ways that word processors work with Ventura text files.

MICROSOFT WORD

Among popular word processors, Microsoft WORD may be the one best suited for use with Ventura. WORD's approach to formatting text is similar to that used by Ventura, allowing you to prepare text efficiently. You can enter text into WORD in ways that allow you to work easily with the text as you're preparing it. Additionally, WORD has a Glossary feature that you can use to insert paragraph tags.

Some of WORD's formatting is applied to text by the paragraph, similar to the way tags operate in Ventura. In addition, WORD has its own style sheets that operate like Ventura's to coordinate documents and apply formatting consistently. Although you cannot convert WORD's style sheets to Ventura format, they make it easier to enter and format text in WORD.

For instance, we mentioned how conforming to Ventura's formatting can make your word-processed text difficult to read. First, Ventura prefers text paragraphs formatted without a tab character in the first line. Second, although you can put two returns after a paragraph in your original text file and then place the @ PARAFILTR ON = code at the beginning of the file, when you save the document with Ventura, the extra return will be gone. Without a first-line indent or an extra blank line between paragraphs, the paragraphs appear to run together.

How, then, can you keep paragraphs visually distinct in the word-processing file? WORD provides an answer with its style sheet. You can create a style sheet called NORMAL.STY that's applied to documents in the same directory automatically. After inserting a Standard Paragraph style (the default style for paragraphs) into the style sheet, you can specify the format, and it will be applied to paragraphs in WORD automatically, just as Body Text is applied in Ventura documents. You can thus make the format add a first-line indent or additional space between paragraphs.

WORD also has a feature called *hidden text.* Text formatted as hidden can be either seen or made temporarily invisible. As you prepare text files in WORD, you can format Ventura commands as hidden text. That way you can see the text with or without the embedded Ventura commands. Unfortunately, once Ventura starts to work with the hidden text, it strips away the hidden format, so that if you use WORD to examine the text later, you won't be able to hide the codes unless you format them as hidden again.

Figure 11.3 shows the sample file in WORD, with Ventura commands formatted as hidden text. Notice how you can distinguish standard text, in bold, from the Ventura codes. Also notice, as the paragraph marks indicate, there is only one return after each paragraph. Nonetheless, there is still space between the paragraphs, making them readable. In addition, each paragraph has the first line indented. Since this indent is created with a WORD style sheet, and not the Tab key, there will be no surprises when you load the text file in Ventura.

Figure 11.4 shows the same file, but with the command codes hidden. The small double-headed arrow indicates the location of the hidden text. Displaying these arrows, as well as the paragraph marks, is optional.

You can use WORD's Glossary feature—a version of the macro generators discussed earlier—to enter the codes for tagging paragraphs and making special text entries. The glossary entries can be formatted as well, allowing you to apply hidden text automatically. Another advantage of WORD is that the Glossary abbreviation you use to represent the Ventura code can be short or very long (up to 31 characters). Thus you can use abbreviations that make sense to you;

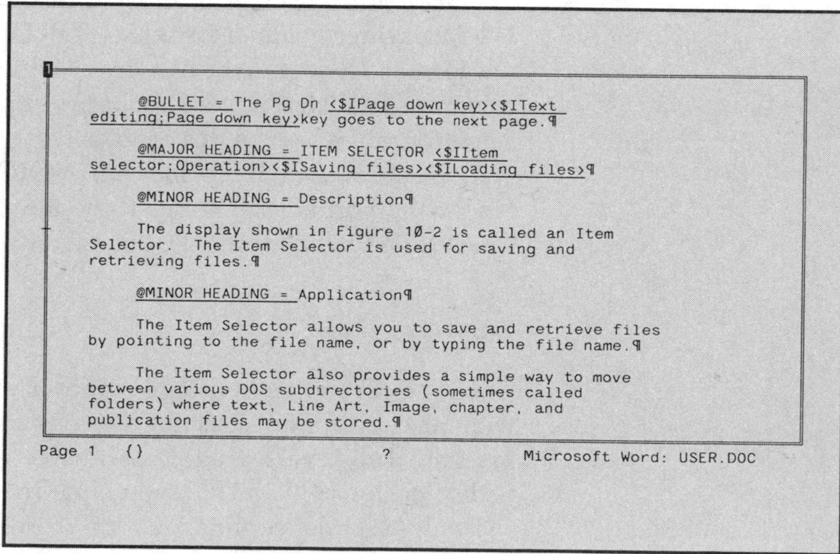

Figure 11.3: Ventura codes in a WORD text file

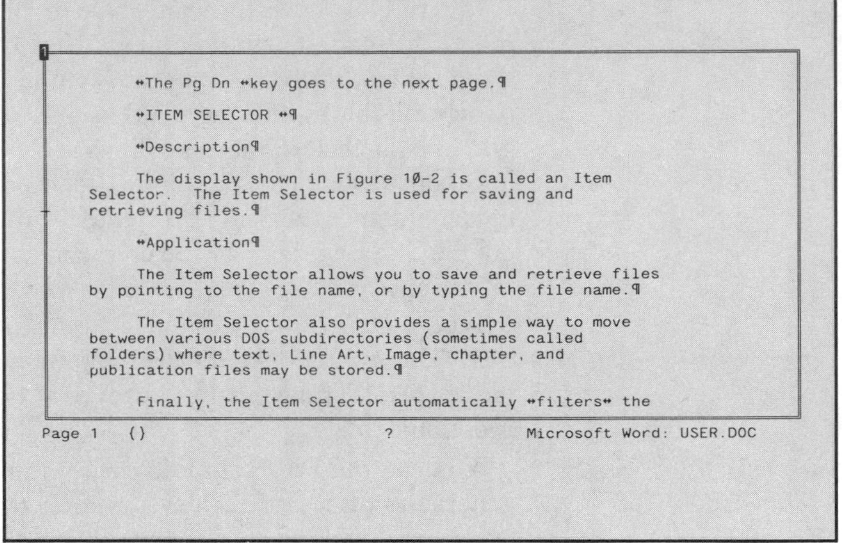

••The Pg Dn ••key goes to the next page.¶

••ITEM SELECTOR ••¶

••Description¶

The display shown in Figure 10-2 is called an Item Selector. The Item Selector is used for saving and retrieving files.¶

••Application¶

The Item Selector allows you to save and retrieve files by pointing to the file name, or by typing the file name.¶

The Item Selector also provides a simple way to move between various DOS subdirectories (sometimes called folders) where text, Line Art, Image, chapter, and publication files may be stored.¶

Finally, the Item Selector automatically ••filters•• the

Page 1 {} ? Microsoft Word: USER.DOC

Figure 11.4: A WORD file with Ventura codes hidden

for instance, you can use H1 for main headings, H2 for secondary headings, and so on. Or, if you prefer codes that spell it out more, you can use HEAD1, HEAD2, and HEAD3.

In addition, WORD's Library Link command allows you to load 1-2-3 files directly into a text file. WORD converts the 1-2-3 file into the format Ventura can use, by placing tab characters between columns. You'll learn more about the importance of using tab characters for tables later in this chapter.

To create an ASCII text file with WORD, save the file, indicating No for the Formatted setting. If the file was originally created as a standard WORD document, this action will convert it to ASCII.

WORDSTAR

The chief concern in using WordStar with Ventura is taking care with tabs. WordStar does not insert a true tab character when you press the Tab key. Instead, it inserts five spaces. To insert a true tab with WordStar 4.0 and 5.0, you type Ctrl-PI or Ctrl-P Tab.

Don't enter dot commands with WordStar. Ventura doesn't recognize them, so they'll appear "as is" in your document, just like any other text.

WordStar also has a macro capability, called *Shorthand,* which works quickly and efficiently. You gain access to it by pressing the Esc key within a document.

To create ASCII text in WordStar, open a new file by typing **N** for Nondocument at the opening menu. Be aware that opening an existing WordStar document in this manner will not convert it to ASCII format. To do that, you must "print" the output to a disk file. You do this when printing by entering the word **ASCII** as the name of the printer. This creates a file called ASCII.WS, which is the ASCII version of the file you specified.

WORDPERFECT

WordPerfect is straightforward in its use with Ventura. The general principles we discussed with regard to word processors apply to work you do with WordPerfect. WordPerfect has a macro feature; you define macros with Ctrl-F10, and you invoke them with Alt-F10 or with an Alt-letter combination. To create an ASCII file, use Text In/Out (Ctrl-F5) and save the file in DOS text-file format.

DATABASE PROGRAMS

You can use Ventura's ability to work with ASCII text in conjunction with a database. Database-management programs, such as dBASE III PLUS, can store large amounts of information in a highly structured fashion. A common desktop-publishing operation is to use the records stored in such a system to publish a directory, such as a listing of names and phone numbers. Ventura's ability to use codes embedded in ASCII text makes its use with a database program a natural, since most database programs can create ASCII text files, inserting the codes automatically.

To use an existing database with Ventura, proceed as follows:

1. Create and run a *report,* a database feature that processes information and creates output. The report should be designed to send its output into a text file.
2. Create a Ventura chapter.

3. Load and use the text file in the Ventura chapter just as you do any text file.

4. Print the Ventura chapter to obtain the final directory.

When you load the file, specify either ASCII or WordStar format, depending on how you want the returns formatted (as discussed earlier in the section "Using ASCII Text for Unsupported Word Processors").

In the report design, specify codes for tags and other kinds of formatting as *constant* or *background* text within the layout of the report. This is text that doesn't change as the data is processed. Place *variables,* which indicate material that may change from one use to the next, where appropriate amidst the codes and other text.

Let's say that you are using the dBASE label generator to create a client directory (Figure 11.5). On the first line of each listing you want to have the client's first name (which you've assigned to the fname field), followed by the last name (assigned to lname). You want this line formatted with the tag called CLIENT NAME. In addition, you want the last name to appear in bold.

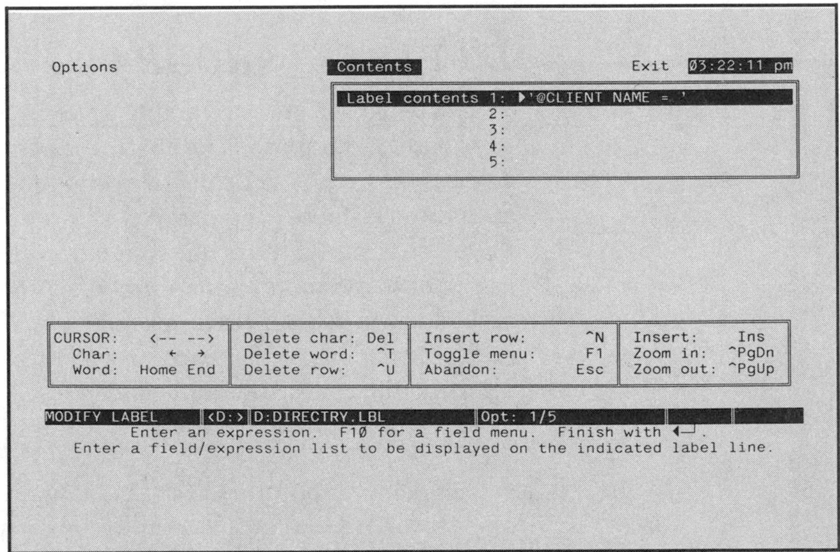

Figure 11.5: Using the dBASE label generator to enter a Ventura tag

For the contents of this line in the label, you'd enter

```
'@CLIENT NAME = '+trim(fname)+' <B>', trim(lname)+'<D>'
```

The Trim command keeps unwanted spaces from appearing when the names don't fill the field. The <B> starts the bold effect for the last name, and the <D> discontinues it.

Eliminate blank lines between records on the report and set the left margin at zero. Remember, however, that you're only using the report to create a text file. Formatting effects such as spacing between paragraphs and indents from the left are created in tags with the Ventura chapter file.

When dealing with a large database, you may find it beneficial to restrict the number of paragraphs contained in the text file in order to speed operations. Ventura can accommodate approximately 48,000 paragraphs. Still, the fewer paragraphs you use, the better Ventura's performance will be and the larger your text file can be.

To decrease the number of lines, insert a line break between information that you want on separate lines in the Ventura document but that is to receive the same paragraph tag. Then combine the information on the same line in your report. A line break is indicated by the code

```
<R>
```

Thus, let's say that you want a person's name, street address, and city on separate lines but similarly formatted. You want Ventura to consider these three items as a unit so you can change the spacing between one person's information and the next. To do that, you'd first enter the tag code for the paragraph (unless you want the paragraph treated as body text, in which case no code is necessary). Then you'd place the field for the first name, the Line Break code, the street-address field, another Line Break code, and the city field on the same line, with a return only at the end.

You can also use Ventura with a database for some mail-merge applications, such as personalized form letters. The general procedure for this involves making each page of a chapter hold a copy of an identical letter addressed to different people. To make the identical material appear on each page, create repeating frames to hold the constant text, such as the body of the letter. For the personalized material, create a text file containing alternating names and addresses, with each line separated by a return. Use the file-output techniques discussed earlier to create this file from the database. Then assign this file to the underlying-page frame. To cause each form letter to appear on a separate page, format the last paragraph of each person's information with a tag that has the Paragraph menu's Breaks command set for Page Break After. By using the techniques discussed earlier, you can automatically apply this tag to each person's last paragraph as the output file is being created.

Now let's examine another type of data application: entering the text for a Ventura table.

ENTERING TEXT FOR TABLES WITH A WORD PROCESSOR

Entering table text with a word processor is very tricky, regardless of the technique you use to set up the table's format. If you must use the word processor, be very careful. Allow yourself enough time to proceed with care. Chapter 8 contains a detailed discussion of formatting tables.

Entering text for tables is easiest and surest if you simply use Ventura to do so. However, you can enter the text for your tables by using your word processor. The technique you follow varies depending upon which method you use to create the table (Chapter 8).

USING TABS FOR TABLES

When you use the tab method for creating tables, each item in the table has a tab character between it and the next item on the same line. When you use the word processor to make table entries, you must insert tabs between each item in the table and the next item on the same line. Do not insert spaces and attempt to line up columns in the word processor that way. The distance a tab is set to travel in Ventura will undoubtedly be different from that set in your word processor, and the width of the spaces will probably be different as well. So these blank spaces will come back to haunt you when you work on tables in Ventura.

You don't need to adjust tab settings in your word processor at all. Just be certain to type in a tab character between each table item. Most likely, the text in your word processor won't even line up in columns. This doesn't matter. As long as you insert the tab characters correctly, you will be able to line up the columns in Ventura. For example, notice how the table at the end of Figures 11.1 and 11.2

appears, as shown in a text file. Compare these with how the table looks in the Ventura sample chapter, &TDOC-P1, shown in Appendix B.

Similarly, if you want to use leaders, do not enter leader characters, such as periods, between the items in the table; just enter the tab character. As long as you properly specify the leader in the paragraph's tag, leaders will appear in the Ventura document even though they don't show in the word processor.

When you insert a tab, you must be certain that your word processor is truly inserting a tab character. Some, as we saw with WordStar, do not normally insert a tab character, but instead simulate a tab character by inserting multiple spaces. Spaces won't do for tab characters in Ventura.

You can test your word processor on the creation of tab characters. To do this, enter the questionable tab character with the word processor. Make the tab setting long enough so that it covers the distance of several spaces. Then, using the keys that move the cursor (probably the ← and → keys), move the cursor over the area covered by the tab. As you do so, if the cursor jumps from one side of the tab area to the other with one keystroke, it means the word processor is inserting one character, the tab character. On the other hand, if each keystroke moves the cursor the distance of only one space, the word processor is inserting space characters to simulate a tab character.

If you cannot get tab characters into the word-processed version of your text file, you must perform major surgery once the file is in Ventura. To make use of Ventura's ability to work with tabs, you must delete all the inappropriate space characters and replace them with tab characters by pressing the Tab key.

Some other programs that "print" to disk, such as Lotus 1-2-3 (the / Print File command), insert spaces as well. If you want to use the output in a Ventura tab table, you must replace the space characters as discussed. The only way you can use spaces as they are is by printing the table with a nonproportional font. In this case, you can't use Ventura to change various characteristics of the table, such as the width of columns, other than by inserting and removing space characters up and down the table. (Alternatively, as mentioned earlier, use Microsoft WORD to import a 1-2-3 file directly into a text file. This allows you to avoid use of the / Print File command and space characters altogether.)

USING COLUMN TAGS

If you enter the text for column tags in your word processor, don't attempt to create anything that resembles a table. Instead, just enter one standard paragraph after another, following the order of the table entries. Remember, table entries go left to right across the first row of entries, then down to the first item in the next row, then across that row from left to right, and so on.

Figure 11.6 shows the order of the paragraphs in the sample table we examined in Chapter 8. Remember, this table also has a paragraph-end character (that is, a return character) tagged to create the horizontal lines. As indicated by the numbering in the figure, you must press Enter for each return your file needs. Let's take a closer look at the sample's text file, shown in Figure 11.7.

Once you have entered your text for the table, you can use Ventura to tag it and so create a table by way of column tags. If, however, you use your word processor to assign tags to the paragraphs, the tag names must follow the same strict order as they do in the table. Thus, in the example, the first column entry is tagged as Col 1. So if you were to enter the first entry with your word processor, you'd begin by entering the tag code

```
@ COL 1 =
```

Then, you'd follow this code with the text for the first column. Press Enter only at the very end of the entire entry for the first row of the first column.

Note that this table is created in ASCII format. As such, you would enter a blank line between the paragraphs. In word-processor format, the paragraph would have one return only at the end, unless you used the @PARAFILTR ON = feature at the beginning of the file.

Continuing with the demonstration, once you complete the first entry, on the next line you'd insert the tag code

```
@ COL 2 =
```

followed by text for the second entry in the first row of the table. In ASCII, the paragraph would again have two returns at the end. You'd then continue in kind for the remaining columns.

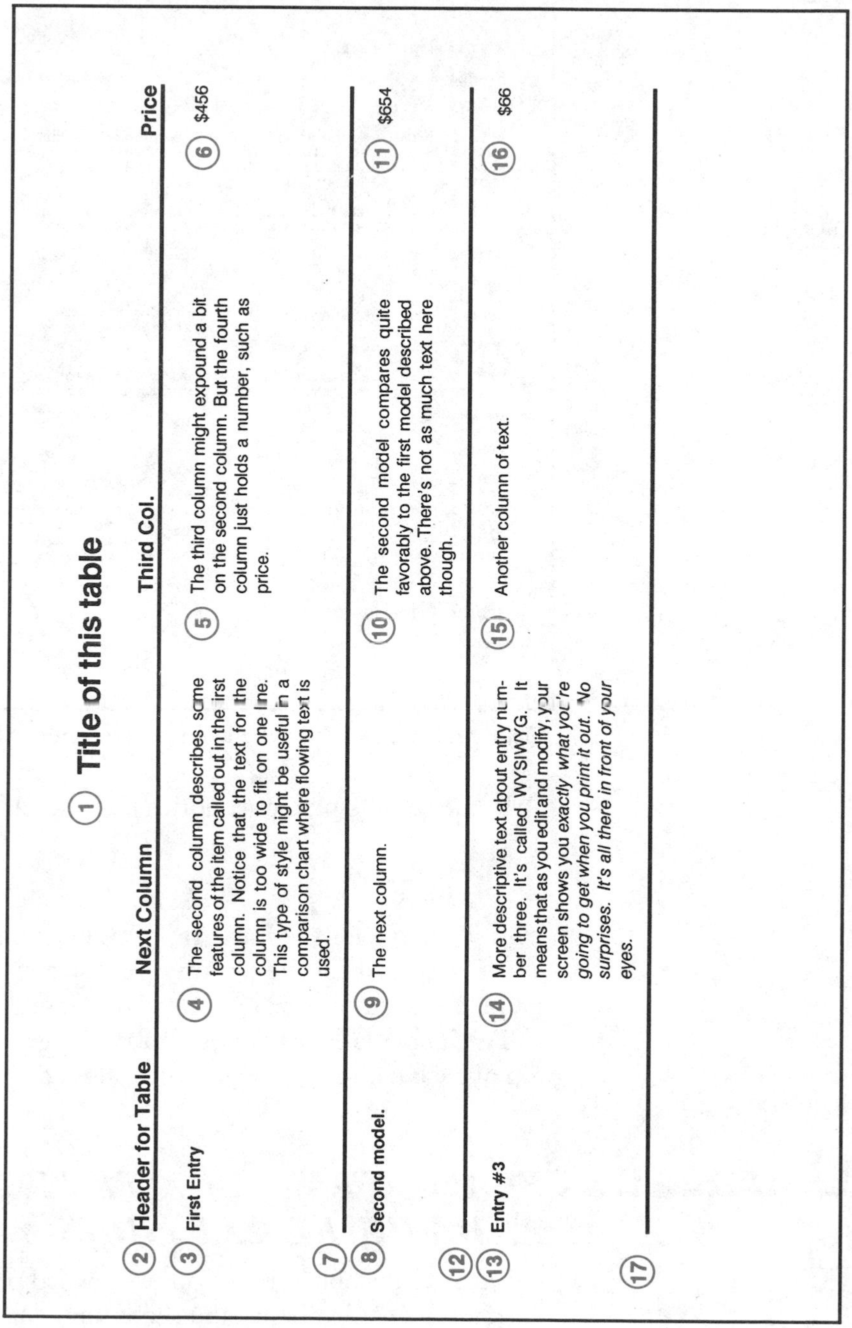

(1) **Title of this table**

(2) Header for Table	Next Column	Third Col.	Price
(3) First Entry	(4) The second column describes some features of the item called out in the first column. Notice that the text for the column is too wide to fit on one line. This type of style might be useful in a comparison chart where flowing text is used.	(5) The third column might expound a bit on the second column. But the fourth column just holds a number, such as price.	(6) $456
(7)			
(8) Second model.	(9) The next column.	(10) The second model compares quite favorably to the first model described above. There's not as much text here though.	(11) $654
(12)			
(13) Entry #3	(14) More descriptive text about entry number three. It's called WYSIWYG. It means that as you edit and modify, your screen shows you *exactly what you're going to get when you print it out. No surprises. It's all there in front of your eyes.*	(15) Another column of text.	(16) $66
(17)			

Figure 11.6: The order of paragraphs using column tags

```
@TITLE = Title of this table

@TABLE HEADER = Header for Table        Next Column     Third Col.      Price

@COL 1 = First Entry

@COL 2 = The second column describes some features of the item called
out in the first column. Notice that the text for the column is too
wide to fit on one line. This type of style might be useful in a comparison
chart where flowing text is used.

@COL 3 = The third column might expound a bit on the second column.
But the fourth column just holds a number, such as price.

@COL 4 = $456

@RULE =

@COL 1 = Second model.

@COL 2 = The next column.

@COL 3 = The second model compares quite favorably to the first model
described above. There's not as much text here though.

@COL 4 = $654

@RULE =

@COL 1 = Entry #3

@COL 2 = More descriptive text about entry number three. It's called
WYSIWYG.  It means that as you edit and modify, your screen shows
you <MI>exactly<N> what you're going to get when you print it out.  No
surprises.  It's all there in front of your eyes.

@COL 3 = Another column of text.

@COL 4 = $66

@RULE =
```

Figure 11.7: An ASCII text file for a table using column tags

In the sample printout, notice that the file has the code

```
@RULE =
```

This is the tag for the Paragraph End symbol with the Rule format. There's no text for the paragraph, but by itself the formatted Paragraph End symbol will create the horizontal line.

The Table Header tag uses tab settings to place a heading at the top of each column. One tab separates each of these items.

FRAME TEXT, BOX TEXT, AND FIGURE CAPTIONS

Lastly, let's look at how you use a word processor with CAP files. A chapter's CAP file has the same name as the chapter, but with a

CAP extension. Ventura creates this file to hold all entries you make for the chapter's Frame text, Box text, and free-form captions. As you may recall, Frame text is text that you enter into an empty standard frame with Text mode active. Frame text, however, is not assigned to a standard file and displayed on the Assignment list when Frame mode is active. Box text is also entered in Text mode. Boxes for the Box text are created in Graphics mode.

You can work with a chapter's CAP file in your word processor, with two stipulations. First, always save it in ASCII format. For instance, you could use a spelling checker to check the CAP file and make corrections as long as the file is ASCII text when you are done. Ventura does not deal with other formats for the CAP file.

Second, when working with the CAP file, it's important not to tamper with the returns. Ventura uses the returns it inserts to keep track of which entries go where in the document. So don't add any returns and don't delete any. Changing them in the CAP file will cause incorrect placement of your entries in the chapter.

In the next chapter, we'll see how you can use advanced features of Ventura to work with typographical elements in your documents.

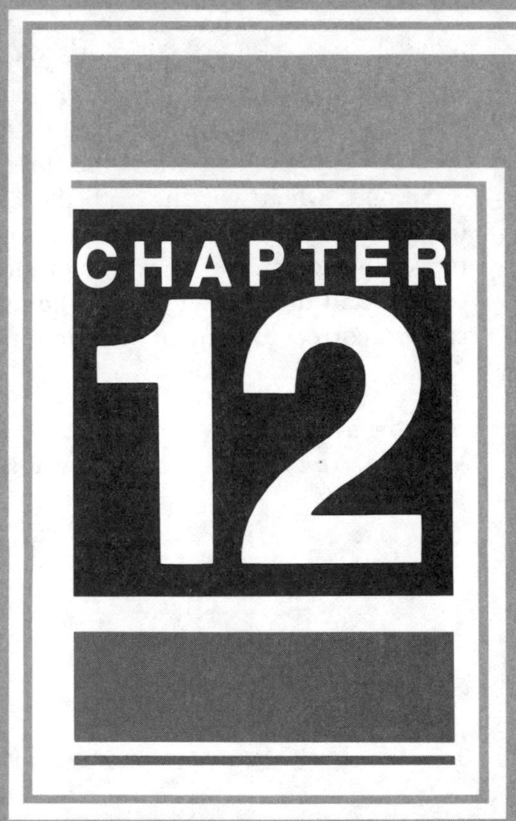
CHAPTER
12

Typographical Elements and Effects

Fast Track

To begin paragraphs with a special effect 441
in Paragraph mode select a paragraph and use the Paragraph menu's Special Effects dialog box. You can use this dialog box to create dropped capitals and bullets.

To create a dropped capital 442
use the Special Effects dialog box and click Big First Char. Click Set Font Properties to increase the size of the first letter in the paragraph. You can also use Custom to specify the number of lines that the character displaces.

To create bullets 445
use the Special Effects dialog box and click Bullet. Choose the character for the bullet and set other font properties for it as desired.

To create reverse type and related effects 452
you can change a frame's background or Box text's fill attributes. To create reverse type that's associated with a paragraph tag, use a ruling line above that's displaced downward behind white text.

To move specific characters in text closer together 455
kern the text. You can kern by the following methods:

- Kern one or more individually selected characters, either with the Set Font button, or interactively by pressing Shift-← and Shift-→.
- Have Ventura kern pairs of letters for all paragraphs with a particular tag by using the Paragraph menu's Paragraph Typography dialog box to set Automatic Pair Kerning: On.
- Set kerning for the chapter by using the Chapter menu's Chapter Typography to set Automatic Pair Kerning: On or Off. This setting must be on for tag kerning to operate.

- Override the chapter's kern setting on a frame-by-frame basis by selecting the frame in Frame mode and using the Frame menu's Frame Typography dialog box.

To adjust the overall spacing between words and letters 459

adjust letter spacing, tracking, or the width of a space character. Settings that control these features are in the Paragraph menu's Paragraph Typography dialog box. Turning on letter spacing justifies text by adding space within words as well as between words. Tracking increases or decreases the spacing between all letters and words with the selected tag. Adjusting the width of a space character affects the amount of leeway Ventura has in stretching or compressing the spaces in order to justify text.

To create space characters that don't change size 467

in justified text, insert the following solid spaces in Ventura or with your word processor:

- Em space (Ctrl-Shift-M or <_>): the size of the @ symbol
- En space (Ctrl-Shift-N or <~>): half the width of the em space
- Figure space (Ctrl-Shift-F or < + >): the width of a digit in the font
- Thin space (Ctrl-Shift-T or < | >): the width of a period

To create typographically correct fractions 472

position the text cursor and use the Edit menu's Ins Special Item (or Ctrl-C). Click Fraction (or press F4) and enter the fraction. To create the division mark, select the Edit menu's Choose Fraction Text (or press Ctrl-C). Then click Fraction (or press F1) for a slash (/) or Over (F2) for an over bar (–). Exit fraction creation with the Edit menu's Exit Fraction Editing or Ctrl-D.

CHAPTER 12

TYPOGRAPHY IS THE CRAFT AND ART OF PLACING type and its equally important counterpart, space, on the printed page. As a craft, typography is utilitarian. You use it to disseminate information. Correct use of typography clues the reader in on the organization of the reading matter. It allows the reader to perceive the hierarchy of various subjects that are covered and the relation of text to pictures. As an art, typography makes the page aesthetically appealing and hence inviting. When typography is properly used, the reader learns with pleasure and ease.

Space is as much an element in a page's design as type. Insufficient or poorly placed spacing may make the reader feel that the material is too dense to penetrate, and hence not worth the effort of reading. An inordinate amount of space, on the other hand, can cause text to appear to be lost on the page. As such, the material may seem without substance, causing the reader to question it even before reading, or to assume the document is geared toward youngsters.

To disseminate information effectively, text on a page must remain readable. Do not allow design choices to counteract this end. Lines of text should be of an appropriate length, so that the eye does not lose its place when scanning the line. Text should not contain an inordinate amount of boldface or italics, making the page look heavy and defeating the purpose of these emphasizing elements.

IMPROVING A SAMPLE DOCUMENT

Ventura has some extraordinary typographic capabilities, but even a simple document can be enhanced with properly used typographical elements. Consider the sample document and style sheet &NEWS-P3. The printed version of the document, as printed with the HP LaserJet, appears in Appendix B. It also appears as a full-page display in Figure 12.1. In this chapter, we'll see how we can

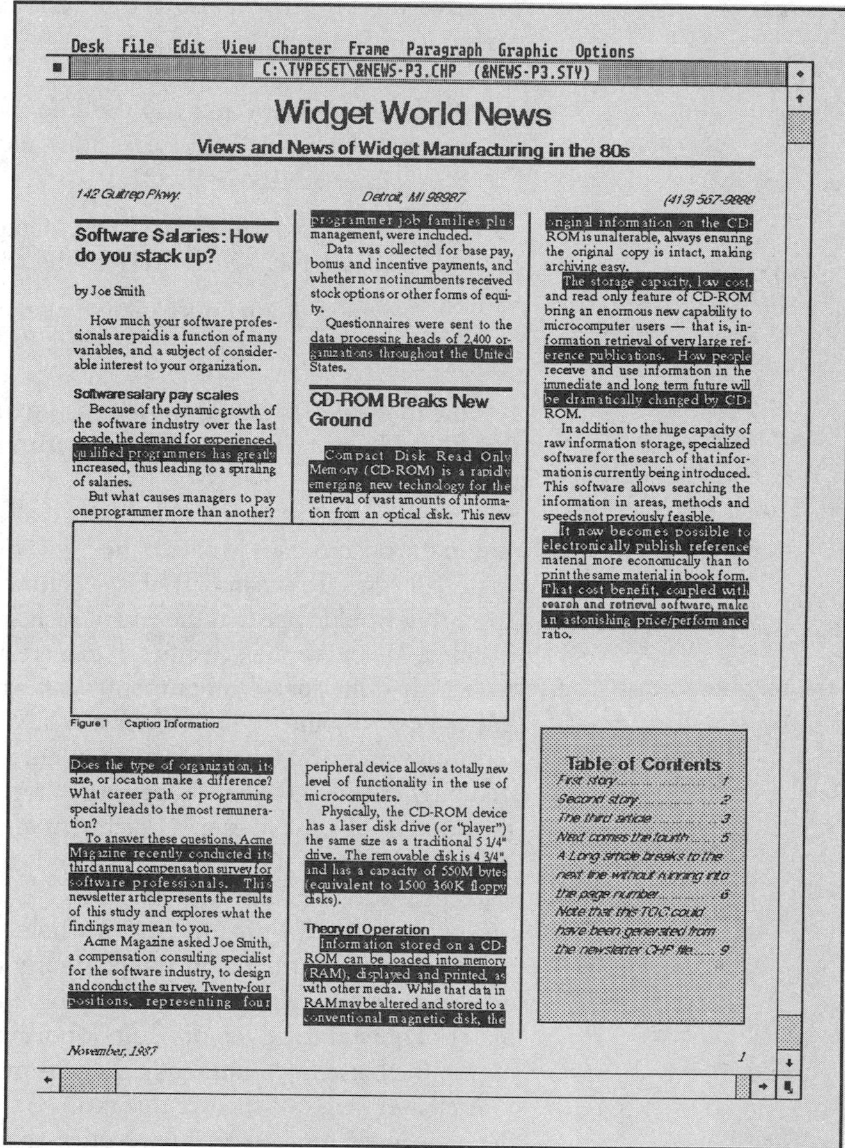

Desk File Edit View Chapter Frame Paragraph Graphic Options

C:\TYPESET\&NEWS-P3.CHP (&NEWS-P3.STY)

Widget World News

Views and News of Widget Manufacturing in the 80s

142 Guitrep Pkwy. Detroit, MI 98987 (413) 567-9888

Software Salaries: How do you stack up?

by Joe Smith

How much your software professionals are paid is a function of many variables, and a subject of considerable interest to your organization.

Software salary pay scales

Because of the dynamic growth of the software industry over the last decade, the demand for experienced, qualified programmers has greatly increased, thus leading to a spiraling of salaries.

But what causes managers to pay one programmer more than another?

Figure 1 Caption Information

Does the type of organization, its size, or location make a difference? What career path or programming specialty leads to the most remuneration?

To answer these questions, Acme Magazine recently conducted its third annual compensation survey for software professionals. This newsletter article presents the results of this study and explores what the findings may mean to you.

Acme Magazine asked Joe Smith, a compensation consulting specialist for the software industry, to design and conduct the survey. Twenty-four positions, representing four programmer job families plus management, were included.

Data was collected for base pay, bonus and incentive payments, and whether nor not incumbents received stock options or other forms of equity.

Questionnaires were sent to the data processing heads of 2,400 organizations throughout the United States.

CD-ROM Breaks New Ground

Compact Disk Read Only Memory (CD-ROM) is a rapidly emerging new technology for the retrieval of vast amounts of information from an optical disk. This new peripheral device allows a totally new level of functionality in the use of microcomputers.

Physically, the CD-ROM device has a laser disk drive (or "player") the same size as a traditional 5 1/4" drive. The removable disk is 4 3/4", and has a capacity of 550M bytes (equivalent to 1500 360K floppy disks).

Theory of Operation

Information stored on a CD-ROM can be loaded into memory (RAM), displayed and printed, as with other media. While that data in RAM may be altered and stored to a conventional magnetic disk, the original information on the CD-ROM is unalterable, always ensuring the original copy is intact, making archiving easy.

The storage capacity, low cost, and read only feature of CD-ROM bring an enormous new capability to microcomputer users — that is, information retrieval of very large reference publications. How people receive and use information in the immediate and long term future will be dramatically changed by CD-ROM.

In addition to the huge capacity of raw information storage, specialized software for the search of that information is currently being introduced. This software allows searching the information in areas, methods and speeds not previously feasible.

It now becomes possible to electronically publish reference material more economically than to print the same material in book form. That cost benefit, coupled with search and retrieval software, make an astonishing price/performance ratio.

Table of Contents

November, 1987 1

Figure 12.1: The &NEWS-P3 sample document as it appears on a full-page display

improve this document using the various typographical elements available in Ventura.

1. Load Ventura and use the File menu's Open command to access the TYPESET directory and load the sample Ventura chapter &NEWS-P3.CHP.
2. In the Options menu's Multi-Chapter dialog box, use Copy All to copy &NEWS-P3.CHP to the MASTERVP directory.
3. Use the File menu's Open to open the new copy of the newsletter.

Note that as we proceed, we'll be using the LaserJet to work on this file. Should you be using a different printer, your results may differ from ours.

First, let's look at the darkened text that appears on the screen. The text in the document is justified: the right edge of the text is flush as well as the left edge. To accomplish this, Ventura inserts space within lines—space that would appear at the end of each line if the document were not justified. When Ventura justifies, it can create *loose lines.* Such lines have too much white space within them, making the letters or words in the line appear disjointed. The reader can have difficulty stringing the letters into words and the words into sentences, making the writer's train of thought hard to follow. Proper use of typography can help minimize the number of loose lines in a document and make the text more readable. The Options menu's Show Loose Lines indicates loose lines with darkened text (see Appendix A).

Now consider the document as a whole. Is it inviting? If you saw a stack of such documents in the company cafeteria, would you pick one up even though you were carrying a tray of food? Or does the material appear to be too difficult or boring to bother with? Tightening up the loose lines can make the text more inviting.

A clearer sense of the organization of the material can also make the document more readable. Notice that the page obviously contains two articles; the two headlines clearly indicate this. Further organization, though, is not immediately apparent. Subheads appear in bold, but this alone doesn't strongly differentiate them from other text, so they become lost on the page.

Also notice that the table of contents has a great deal of space at the bottom, but not enough at the top (below its title and the first story listing). Also in the table of contents, multiline listings (such as the entry beginning with *A Long article*) at first seem to be several separate listings.

> * The Professional Extension allows you to use vertical justification to fill a page with text. See Chapter 13.

Finally, notice that the text of the newsletter does not fill the page. The second article ends with the words *astonishing price/performance ratio.* After that, there's just leftover space on the page. Proper use of typography allows you to enlarge and reduce text in order to fit it within a given space.

Let's see how to adjust these typographical elements and thus enhance this newsletter. We'll correct these problems and others, starting with broad stokes and progressing toward more detailed kinds of work.

PARAGRAPHS BEGINNING WITH SPECIAL EFFECTS

Let's start with paragraph beginnings. By changing the way a paragraph begins, you can draw attention to it. One use of unusual paragraph beginnings is to signal the onset of a new idea. As such, special effects at the beginning of paragraphs can help to organize material visually.

Ventura provides two explicit effects for paragraph beginnings. (It also provides the means to create others.) These two *special effects,* as Ventura calls them, are the *bullet* and the *big first character* or *dropped capital.* Both are features that typesetters use frequently and that you've no doubt seen in print. To set either effect for a particular paragraph tag, display the Special Effects dialog box shown in Figure 12.2:

1. Activate Paragraph mode and select the paragraph that begins "How much your software professionals are paid . . ."
2. Use the Side-bar's Add New Tag button to create a new tag (see Chapter 4). You'll apply this tag to paragraphs to create a dropped capital.
3. Drop the Paragraph menu and select Special Effects.

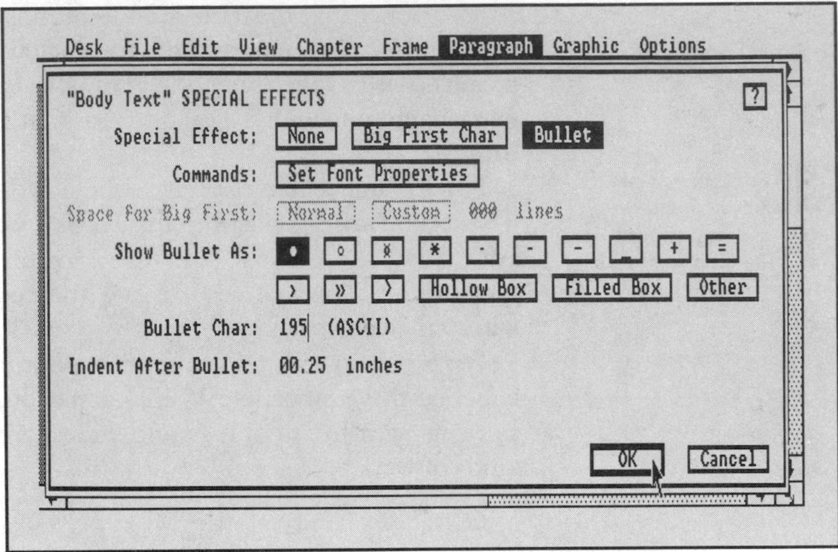

Figure 12.2: The Paragraph menu's Special Effects dialog box

DROPPED CAPITALS

The first special-effect button is labeled Big First Char.

- Click the Big First Char button to create a dropped capital.

A *dropped capital*—a large letter, at the beginning of a line, that drops below the regular base of the line—often appears in the first paragraph of a chapter or a magazine article. If you choose this effect, Ventura will automatically convert the first character in each appropriately tagged paragraph.

Dropped capitals aren't confined to the paragraphs that begin an article, however. Often, they can be used in the middle of an article to show a slight shift in thought—one not strong enough to warrant a new heading.

Figure 12.3 shows dropped capitals placed in our newsletter. This simple change makes the material more inviting. (For these paragraphs, we also used the Paragraph menu's Alignment dialog box to delete the In/Outdent Width. This eliminates their first-line indent.)

Widget World News

Views and News of Widget Manufacturing in the 80s

142 Guitrep Pkwy. *Detroit, MI 98987* *(413) 567-9888*

Software Salaries: How do you stack up?

by Joe Smith

How much your software professionals are paid is a function of many variables, and a subject of considerable interest to your organization.

Software salary pay scales

Because of the dynamic growth of the software industry over the last decade, the demand for experienced, qualified programmers has greatly increased, thus leading to a spiraling of salaries.

But what causes managers to pay one programmer more than another? Does the type of organization, its size, or location make a difference? What career path or programming specialty leads to the most remuneration?

To answer these questions, Acme Magazine recently conducted its third annual compensation survey for software professionals. This newsletter article presents the results of this study and explores what the findings may mean to you.

Acme Magazine asked Joe Smith, a compensation consulting specialist for the software industry, to design and conduct the survey. Twenty-four positions, representing four programmer job families plus management, were included.

Data was collected for base pay, bonus and incentive payments, and whether nor not incumbents received stock options or other forms of equity.

Questionnaires were sent to the data processing heads of 2,400 organizations throughout the United States.

CD-ROM Breaks New Ground

Compact Disk Read Only Memory (CD-ROM) is a rapidly emerging new technology for the retrieval of vast amounts of information from an optical disk. This new peripheral device allows a totally new level of functionality in the use of microcomputers.

Physically, the CD-ROM device has a laser disk drive (or "player") the same size as a traditional 5 1/4" drive. The removable disk is 4 3/4", and has a capacity of 550M bytes (equivalent to 1500 360K floppy disks).

Theory of Operation

Information stored on a CD-ROM can be loaded into memory (RAM), displayed and printed, as with other media. While that data in RAM may be altered and stored to a conventional magnetic disk, the original information on the CD-ROM is unalterable, always ensuring the original copy is intact, making archiving easy.

The storage capacity, low cost, and read only feature of CD-ROM bring an enormous new capability to microcomputer users — that is, information retrieval of very large reference publications. How people receive and use information in the immediate and long term future will be dramatically changed by CD-ROM.

In addition to the huge capacity of raw information storage, specialized software for the search of that information is currently being introduced. This software allows searching the information in areas, methods and speeds not previously feasible.

It now becomes possible to electronically publish reference material more economically than to print the same material in book form. That cost benefit, coupled with search and retrieval software, make an astonishing price/performance ratio.

Figure 1 Caption Information

Table of Contents

November, 1987 1

Figure 12.3: Dropped capitals

You must specify the format that the dropped capital takes. This includes all font features, especially Size and including Face, Style, and so on.

1. Click Set Font Properties in the dialog box. You'll see the Font Setting dialog box, like the dialog boxes we examined in conjunction with paragraph tags and text attributes in Chapter 4. You must use this dialog box to set the size of the dropped capital. If you don't, the character will remain the same size as standard characters in the paragraph.
2. Set the size—we use 24 point with the LaserJet—and other characteristics, and give the OK. Ventura then redisplays the Special Effects dialog box.

You can also use the Special Effects dialog box to set the number of lines that this effect occupies. Do so to create a *stickup initial*: a character that rises above the first line of the paragraph (Figure 12.4). In the Space For Big First setting, click Custom, and then enter the number of lines you desire. (These settings ghost in the dialog box shown in Figure 12.2 because the Big First Char button is not selected.) With the Normal setting, Ventura automatically displaces just enough lines to fully sink the character in the paragraph. In order to raise the character up so it's level with the base of the line, use a number smaller than the amount Ventura allocates. For the example shown in Figure 12.4, the big first character that displaced two lines as a dropped capital has been converted to a stickup initial by setting Custom to 1 line.

- Give the OK again. Tag the appropriate paragraphs and you'll see dropped capitals appear.

Software Salaries: How do you stack up?

by Joe Smith

How much your software professionals are paid is a function of many variables, and a subject of considerable interest to your organization.

Figure 12.4: A stickup initial

Should you change your mind, you can neutralize the effect. Use the Paragraph menu's Special Effects dialog box and click the None button. Give the OK, and the effect will be undone.

When using Ventura's special effects, you may need to make adjustments if you switch printers. For example, when printed with the Hewlett-Packard LaserJet, the sample document and style sheet &BOOK-P1 sinks the dropped capital too far into the first paragraph. The result appears in Figure 12.5. Dropped capitals in another sample, &BOOK-P2, have the same problem. Apparently, this occurs because Ventura's samples were prepared initially with a PostScript printer.

However, we can fix the effect. By clicking the Set Font Properties button, we can change the settings to shift the dropped capital up. In Figure 12.6, we've raised the dropped capital to an acceptable level by shifting it up 6 points. This is the paragraph display we have used in the document as it appears in Appendix B.

BULLETS

The second special effect Ventura provides is bulleted paragraphs. A *bullet* is a character that sets off items in a list, usually appearing to the left of each item that's listed as a separate paragraph. Generally, a bullet is displayed as a dot.

1. Click one of the paragraphs under the words *Table of Contents*.
2. Drop the Paragraph menu and select Special Effects. The Special Effects dialog box appears (Figure 12.2).

> This trip really began in September last year when Gerry won first prize in a raffle at the fashion show which Rush-Presbyterian-St. Luke's Medical Center holds every year. The prize was two round trip tickets to Hong Kong on United Airlines, and ten nights in the Hong Kong Hyatt Hotel. Analyzing our good fortune, we concluded that we wanted to do more than spend ten days in Hong Kong and return, but at the same time, United, having just gotten its routes and equipment from Pan American, had not yet received authority to fly to other destinations or between points in the Far East.

Figure 12.5: A dropped capital set too low

This trip really began in September last year when Gerry won first prize in a raffle at the fashion show which Rush-Presbyterian-St. Luke's Medical Center holds every year. The prize was two round trip tickets to Hong Kong on United Airlines, and ten nights in the Hong Kong Hyatt Hotel. Analyzing our good fortune, we concluded that we wanted to do more than spend ten days in Hong Kong and return, but at the same time, United, having just gotten its routes and equipment from Pan American, had not yet received authority to fly to other destinations or between points in the Far East.

Figure 12.6: A dropped capital shifted up

3. Click Bullet and give the OK. Bullets appear in the table of contents.

In Figure 12.7, you can see how bullets clear up the confusion within items in the table of contents.

Ventura allows you to display bullets as a variety of other shapes. Once you click the Bullet button, 13 choices appear in the Show Bullet As grouping. If these choices aren't enough, click Other. This will allow you to type the ASCII code for any character into the Bullet Char field. (See Appendix E for a listing of the ASCII codes.)

Regardless of the character you choose for your bullet, you can set its formatting characteristics—such as font size, color, and so on—with a great deal of flexibility, just as you can with dropped capitals. You need change the settings only if you want the bullet to be formatted differently from the rest of the paragraph. Just as you do when working with Big First Char, click Set Font Properties and proceed.

When you apply the bullet special effect, there must be a value for Indent After Bullet. This value controls the amount of indent for the left edge of the entire bulleted paragraph. This indent is in addition to any other margin or indent you may set. Figure 12.8 diagrams the values you must consider in determining the placement of the left edge of a bulleted paragraph from the left edge of the page. Note that the first paragraph in the figure has the same indent settings as the second, except that the first has no bullet specified. (We've increased some of the values from those of the &NEWS-P3 sample document to make the relationships clear.)

Widget World News

Views and News of Widget Manufacturing in the 80s

142 Guitrep Pkwy. *Detroit, MI 98987* *(413) 567-9888*

Software Salaries: How do you stack up?

by Joe Smith

How much your software professionals are paid is a function of many variables, and a subject of considerable interest to your organization.

Software salary pay scales

Because of the dynamic growth of the software industry over the last decade, the demand for experienced, qualified programmers has greatly increased, thus leading to a spiraling of salaries.

But what causes managers to pay one programmer more than another? Does the type of organization, its size, or location make a difference? What career path or programming specialty leads to the most remuneration?

To answer these questions, Acme Magazine recently conducted its third annual compensation survey for software professionals. This newsletter article presents the results of this study and explores what the findings may mean to you.

Acme Magazine asked Joe Smith, a compensation consulting specialist for the software industry, to design and conduct the survey. Twenty-four positions, representing four programmer job families plus management, were included.

Data was collected for base pay, bonus and incentive payments, and whether nor not incumbents received stock options or other forms of equity.

Questionnaires were sent to the data processing heads of 2,400 organizations throughout the United States.

CD-ROM Breaks New Ground

Compact Disk Read Only Memory (CD-ROM) is a rapidly emerging new technology for the retrieval of vast amounts of information from an optical disk. This new peripheral device allows a totally new level of functionality in the use of microcomputers.

Physically, the CD-ROM device has a laser disk drive (or "player") the same size as a traditional 5 1/4" drive. The removable disk is 4 3/4", and has a capacity of 550M bytes (equivalent to 1500 360K floppy disks).

Theory of Operation

Information stored on a CD-ROM can be loaded into memory (RAM), displayed and printed, as with other media. While that data in RAM may be altered and stored to a conventional magnetic disk, the original information on the CD-ROM is unalterable, always ensuring the original copy is intact, making archiving easy.

The storage capacity, low cost, and read only feature of CD-ROM bring an enormous new capability to microcomputer users – that is, information retrieval of very large reference publications. How people receive and use information in the immediate and long term future will be dramatically changed by CD-ROM.

In addition to the huge capacity of raw information storage, specialized software for the search of that information is currently being introduced. This software allows searching the information in areas, methods and speeds not previously feasible.

It now becomes possible to electronically publish reference material more economically than to print the same material in book form. That cost benefit, coupled with search and retrieval software, make an astonishing price/performance ratio.

Figure 1 Caption Information

Table of Contents

November, 1987 1

Figure 12.7: Bullets used to differentiate list items

As with dropped capitals, should you switch printers, you may need to make adjustments. For example, Figure 12.9 shows how the bulleted material in the &BOOK-P1 sample document appears when printed with the HP LaserJet. In Figure 12.10 we have increased the Indent After Bullet value to compensate for the change

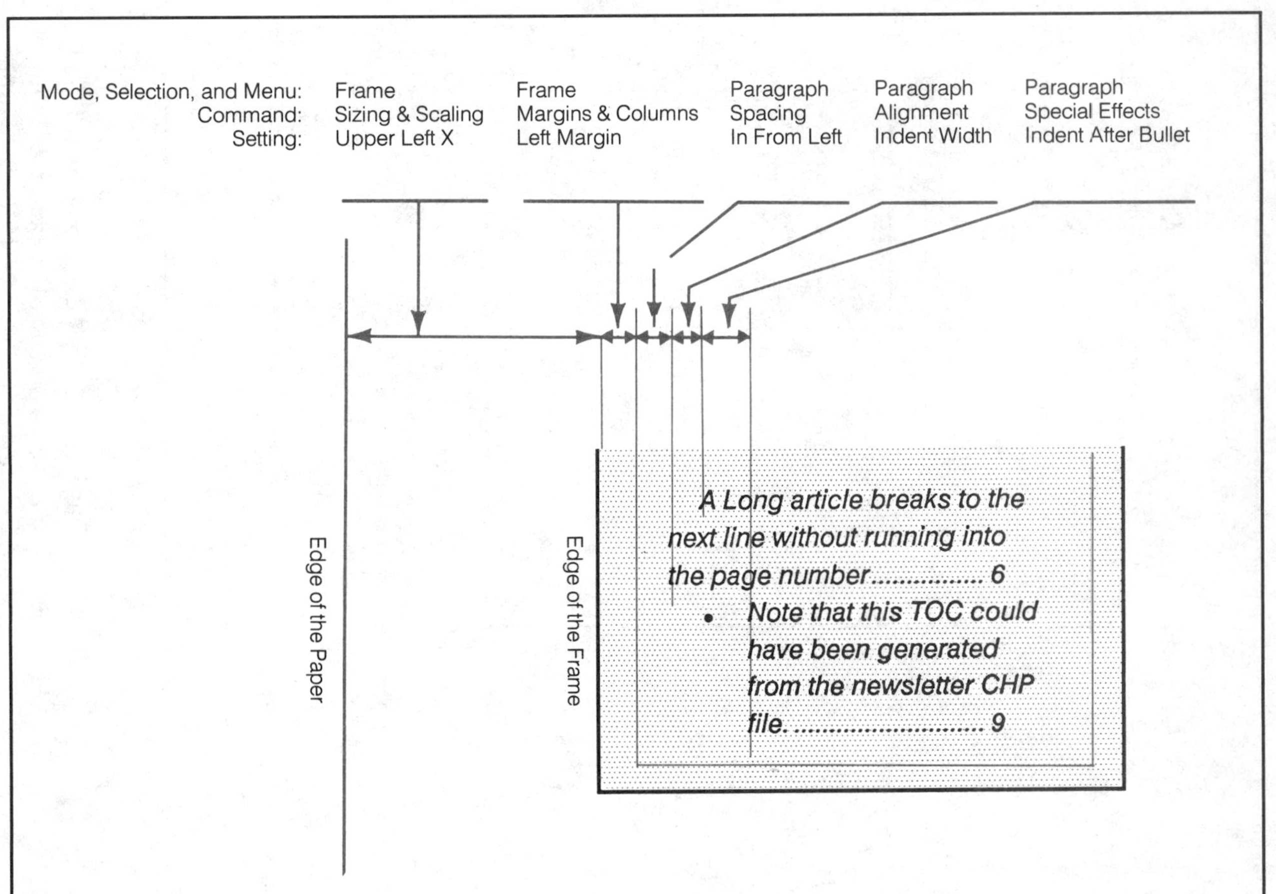

Figure 12.8: Indent settings for a bulleted paragraph

•Arose at 5:30 A.M.
•Left the house at 7:00 A.M.
•Arrived in Los Angeles at 12:35 P.M.
•Arrived in Tokyo at 11:46 P.M.

Figure 12.9: An insufficient indent after bullets

• Arose at 5:30 A.M.
• Left the house at 7:00 A.M.
• Arrived in Los Angeles at 12:35 P.M.
• Arrived in Tokyo at 11:46 P.M.

Figure 12.10: Increasing the indent after bullets

in printers. These results have been used to print the sample in Appendix B.

OTHER EFFECTS

You can create effects for paragraph beginnings besides those shown in the Paragraph menu's Special Effects dialog box. Figure 12.11 shows paragraphs formatted with a beginning black box. The box appears at the start of paragraphs that occur right after subheads. (With Ventura 2.0 you could insert a box character at the beginning of each paragraph, but the following procedure creates the box automatically before *all* similarly tagged paragraphs.) To create a box like this, follow these steps:

1. Select the paragraph under the heading "Software salary pay scales" and add a new tag for the beginning box effect.
2. Using the Paragraph menu's Alignment command, indent the first line or lines enough to accommodate the beginning box. (In the example, the first line was already indented, so we actually skipped this step.)

3. With the Paragraph menu's Ruling Lines Above dialog box, set Width to Custom.

4. In the same dialog box, enter a value for the thickness of the rule in Height Of Rule 1. We used **00,06** (in picas & points).

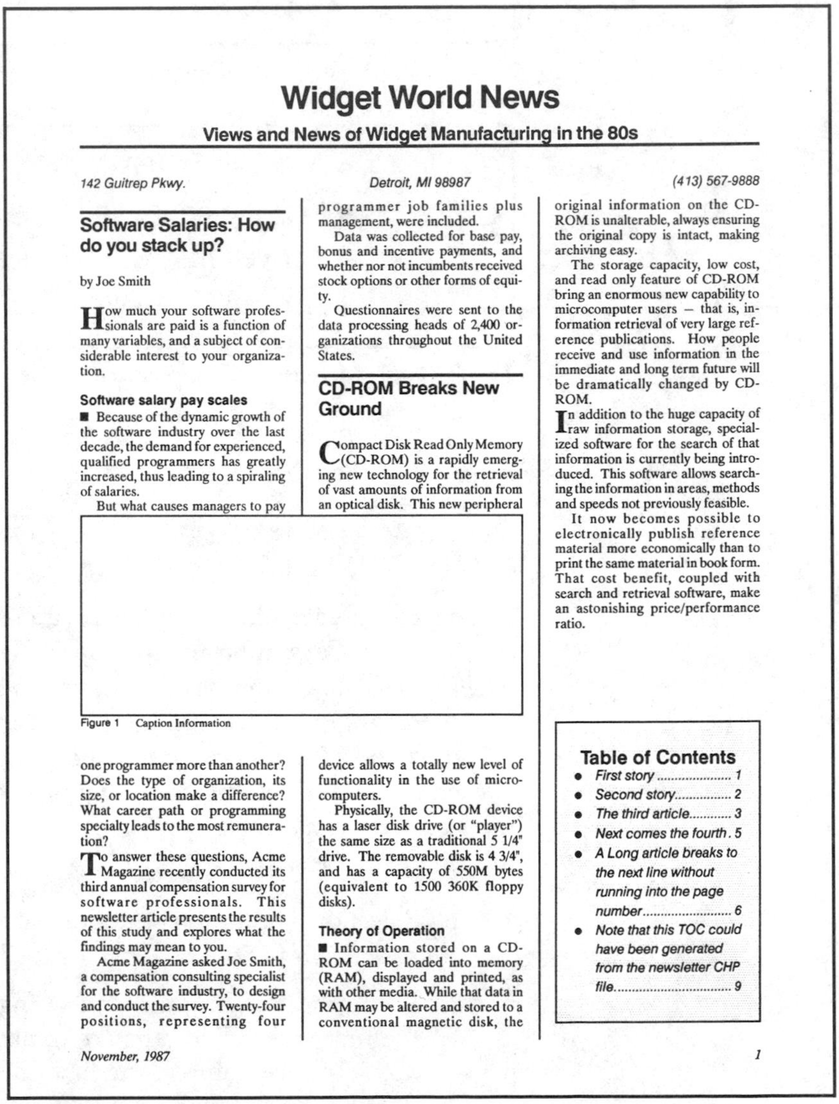

Widget World News

Views and News of Widget Manufacturing in the 80s

142 Guitrep Pkwy. *Detroit, MI 98987* *(413) 567-9888*

Software Salaries: How do you stack up?

by Joe Smith

How much your software professionals are paid is a function of many variables, and a subject of considerable interest to your organization.

Software salary pay scales

■ Because of the dynamic growth of the software industry over the last decade, the demand for experienced, qualified programmers has greatly increased, thus leading to a spiraling of salaries.

But what causes managers to pay one programmer more than another? Does the type of organization, its size, or location make a difference? What career path or programming specialty leads to the most remuneration?

To answer these questions, Acme Magazine recently conducted its third annual compensation survey for software professionals. This newsletter article presents the results of this study and explores what the findings may mean to you.

Acme Magazine asked Joe Smith, a compensation consulting specialist for the software industry, to design and conduct the survey. Twenty-four positions, representing four programmer job families plus management, were included.

Data was collected for base pay, bonus and incentive payments, and whether nor not incumbents received stock options or other forms of equity.

Questionnaires were sent to the data processing heads of 2,400 organizations throughout the United States.

CD-ROM Breaks New Ground

Compact Disk Read Only Memory (CD-ROM) is a rapidly emerging new technology for the retrieval of vast amounts of information from an optical disk. This new peripheral device allows a totally new level of functionality in the use of microcomputers.

Physically, the CD-ROM device has a laser disk drive (or "player") the same size as a traditional 5 1/4" drive. The removable disk is 4 3/4", and has a capacity of 550M bytes (equivalent to 1500 360K floppy disks).

Theory of Operation

■ Information stored on a CD-ROM can be loaded into memory (RAM), displayed and printed, as with other media. While that data in RAM may be altered and stored to a conventional magnetic disk, the original information on the CD-ROM is unalterable, always ensuring the original copy is intact, making archiving easy.

The storage capacity, low cost, and read only feature of CD-ROM bring an enormous new capability to microcomputer users — that is, information retrieval of very large reference publications. How people receive and use information in the immediate and long term future will be dramatically changed by CD-ROM.

In addition to the huge capacity of raw information storage, specialized software for the search of that information is currently being introduced. This software allows searching the information in areas, methods and speeds not previously feasible.

It now becomes possible to electronically publish reference material more economically than to print the same material in book form. That cost benefit, coupled with search and retrieval software, make an astonishing price/performance ratio.

Figure 1 Caption Information

Table of Contents

November, 1987 1

Figure 12.11: Paragraphs with beginning black boxes

5. Also set Custom Width to the same value (00,06). The value you use determines the size of the box.
6. Lastly in this dialog box, insert a negative value—greater than this amount—for Space Below Rule 3 (try **00,09 –**). The negative value will lower the rule, which normally appears above the paragraph, into the body of the paragraph.
7. Using the Paragraph menu's Spacing command, increase the Above setting (try **00,04**). Creating the rule upsets the paragraph's spacing above; this setting restores the original spacing. (We'll examine such spacing later in this chapter.)

Another effect used at the beginning of paragraphs is the hanging indent, or *outdent.* We examined this effect in Chapter 4. To create it, you use the Paragraph menu's Alignment command. Figure 12.12 shows the table of contents with the outdent treatment.

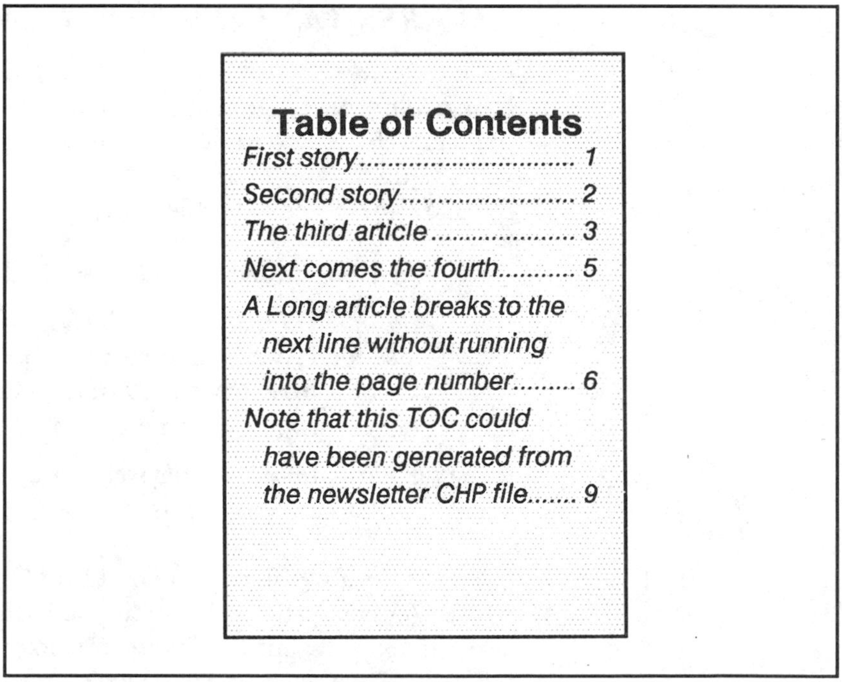

Table of Contents

First story............................. 1
Second story........................ 2
The third article..................... 3
Next comes the fourth........... 5
A Long article breaks to the next line without running into the page number......... 6
Note that this TOC could have been generated from the newsletter CHP file....... 9

Figure 12.12: Outdent (or hanging indent)

Now let's examine another effect that makes text distinctive: reverse type.

REVERSE TYPE AND RELATED EFFECTS

Reverse type is a technique that typographers sometimes use to gain the reader's attention. It is created by placing white letters on a black background. You may want to use this effect to draw attention to a page element like a table of contents.

To use reverse type, your printer must be capable of creating white letters on a black background. The HP LaserJet, for example, does not have this capability. To determine if your printer can produce reverse text, check your printout of the printer-capability page, as discussed in Chapter 5.

REVERSE TEXT IN FRAMES AND BOXES

One way to create reverse text is with frames. You can change the background of the frame to black; when you do, all text inside the frame changes to white automatically. This treatment even works with the underlying-page frame.

Follow these steps to achieve the effect:

1. Activate Frame mode and select the frame holding the table of contents.
2. Use the Frame menu's Frame Background command to set Color to Black and Pattern to Solid. Figure 12.13 shows the table-of-contents frame presented in reverse type.
3. Follow the preceding steps to change the table of contents back to the way it was.

If you use this effect, remember that various screen effects with which Ventura catches your attention will also be reversed. Thus, selected text will appear in white instead of black, and the handles on a frame you've selected will be white, too.

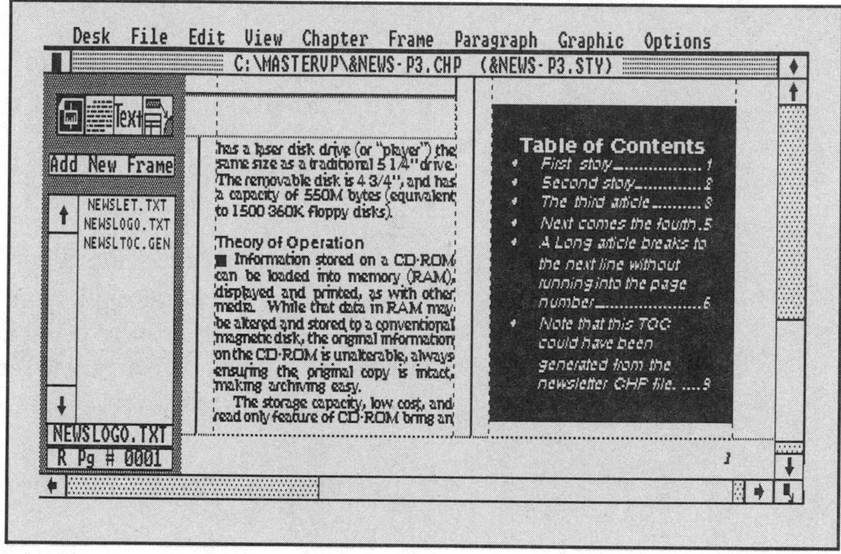

Figure 12.13: Reverse type

A variation on the black background is achieved with one of the patterns in the Frame Background dialog box. The table-of-contents frame shown in Figure 12.1 has a shaded background.

When you use a pattern, the text will not change to white automatically. With the Paragraph menu's Font command, however, you can change the font color for paragraphs appearing within the frame.

You can also create reverse and shaded text with Box text. Use the Graphic menu's Fill Attributes command. Box text produces the same effects as frames: Ventura changes text to white, but only when you indicate solid black.

If you change back and forth from one effect to another, you may find it necessary to re-ink the screen in order to see the effect take place. To do so, press the Esc key.

USING RULES TO CREATE REVERSE TEXT

Creating reverse text with frames is easy and quick. However, if you plan to repeat the effect regularly throughout your document, you may prefer to associate reverse text with a tag. Be aware, though, that these steps (as they stand) will only create reverse text for paragraphs that contain no more than one line.

This technique uses the Space Below Rule 3 setting to achieve reverse type with titles or headings. The process involves changing the font to white, and then creating a black ruling line above with a negative space below it. This negative space moves the ruling line down into line with the text. The result is a black bar with white text across it. Here are the steps for creating reverse text with a tag:

1. Activate Paragraph mode and select the paragraph that says "Table of Contents."
2. Drop the Paragraph menu and select Font.
3. Set Color for the paragraph's font to White. Make a mental note of the font size you're using and give the OK. Against a white background, the text will seem to disappear, but don't be alarmed. It's still there, but its font is the same color as the background.
4. Drop the Paragraph menu again and this time select Ruling Line Above.
5. Set Width as you desire for the darkened bar against which the type will appear.
6. Set Color to Black and Pattern to Solid. (You can vary these choices.)
7. Set the units of measurement to Fractional Points or Picas & Points.
8. For Height Of Rule 1, specify an amount equal to the font size or larger. This value determines the thickness of the bar. If you're using fractional points, insert the point value to the left of the period. If you use picas and points, insert it to the right of the comma.
9. For Space Below Rule 3, insert a value determined with the following formula: Add the point size of the font to the value you've specified for Height of Rule 1; divide the result by 2; then insert a value that is slightly more than this amount—2 points more seems to work well.
10. Click the Minus (−) box, so that the value is a negative one. Then give the OK.

If you vary the settings for the ruling line's color and pattern, be careful to consider the paragraph font's color. For the sake of readability, always use a font that will provide your readers with a sharp contrast to the background.

Figure 12.14 shows the "Table of Contents" heading in reverse against a frame-wide band. Notice in this case that no characters

You can customize the colors that are available. See Chapter 5.

descend below the line of text and thus out of the reverse band. If your heading contains descending characters, such as *g* or *y*, you will have to add extra points to the Space Below Rule 3, to lower the reverse band further. This, in turn, may require that you thicken the band so it reaches higher, by increasing the value for Height Of Rule 1.

If you set the Width of the rule to Text, you may find that it's a good idea to add space before and after the text. Doing so increases the ends of the frame that the rule creates, ensuring that the white text doesn't bleed into the white background. You may wish to use one of the solid spaces that we'll examine shortly, such as an en space, to do this.

Now that we've examined some type effects, let's examine spacing effects. Ventura has several ways to handle spacing.

KERNING TEXT

Kerning refers to the technique of moving a character closer to the previous character on the same line. Normally, as with a typewriter, when Ventura places characters side by side, the leftmost part of a character is positioned after the rightmost part of the character before

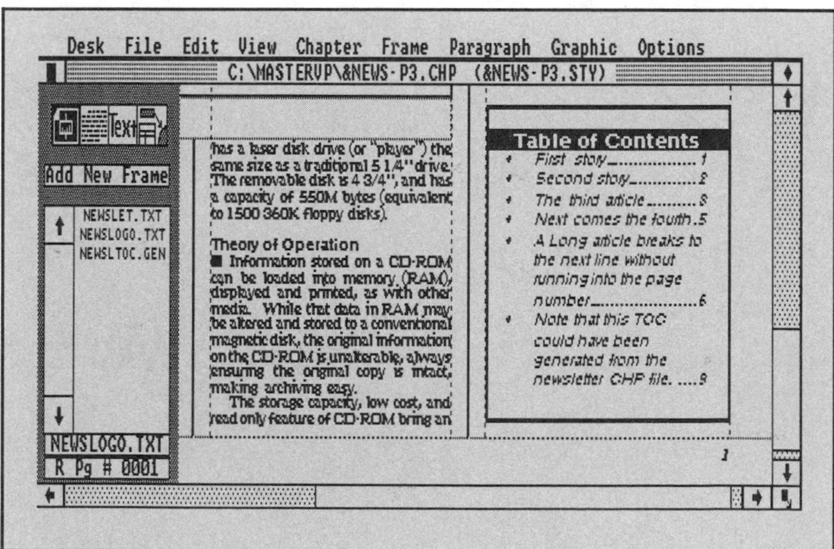

Figure 12.14: Reverse text created with a paragraph tag

it. With certain combinations of characters, such as when a *V* follows an *A,* there may be an inappropriate amount of space between the letters. This can make the text loose and difficult to read. By kerning, you draw characters closer to one another; hence the text becomes more readable.

When you kern with Ventura 2.0, the letter you kern pulls the character on its right slightly to the left, and thus closer to it. You can also kern strictly for effect—to join two characters together, for instance.

KERNING INDIVIDUAL LETTERS

There are several ways to kern. First of all, you can kern individual letters. When you kern individual characters, you usually do so only with large characters, such as those that make up headlines or mastheads. It would be impractical to individually kern large amounts of small text such as body text.

Figure 12.15 shows an example of text before and after kerning. Notice the difference in space between the characters in the kerned text, especially between *W* and *A* and between *A* and *V.* The *W, A,* and *V* are kerned closer together, while *N* and *E* are kerned together for effect.

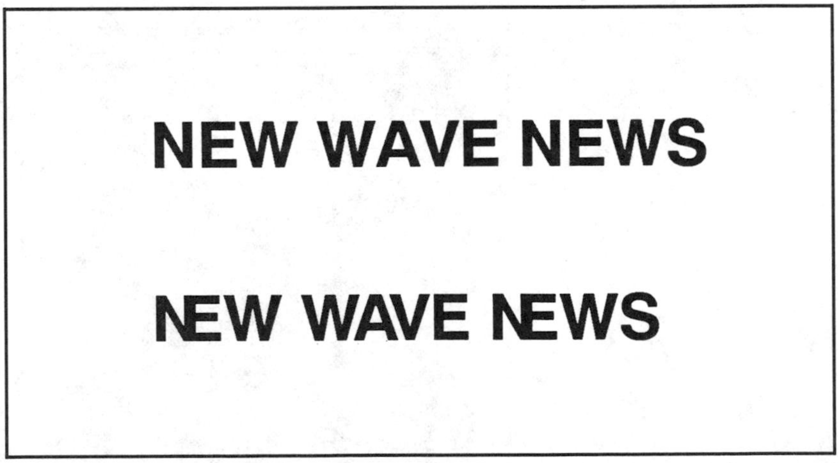

NEW WAVE NEWS

NEW WAVE NEWS

Figure 12.15: Kerning text

To kern an individual letter, use Text mode and select the letter by darkening it with the mouse. The letter you select will pull the letter to its right closer. Then click the Set Font button in the Side-bar.

! New for version 2.0

In the Set Font Properties dialog box you can set Kern to Tighter (which moves letters closer) or Looser.

Also new with Ventura 2.0, you provide a value in ems by which to kern. The *em* is an important measurement in typography. An *em* is an amount of horizontal space equal to the size of the font you're using. Thus, with a 10-point font, an em is equal to 10 points. (Usually you kern with only a fraction of an em.) Should you later change the size of your font, Ventura will adjust the kerning automatically because the size of an em changes.

Be aware that when you kern, there may be more or less kerning in the printed version of your document than in what you see on the screen. This is due to the difference in resolution between printed text and text on the screen. Allow yourself enough time to perform a few trial printouts of kerned material.

Figure 12.16 shows the results of kerning the masthead in the sample document. The distances between *W* and *o* in *World* and between *N* and *e* in *News* are kerned.

! New for version 2.0

You can kern interactively with Ventura 2.0. Select a letter to kern, and hold down the Shift key while you press the ← or → key. Ventura will move the letter following the one selected in the direction of the arrow.

Widget World News

Views and News of Widget Manufacturing in the 90s

142 Guitrep Pkwy.	*Detroit, MI 98987*	*(413) 567-9888*

Figure 12.16: The masthead from the sample document after kerning

If you select more than one letter, you can kern the entire range of letters using either kerning technique. That is, you can use the Set Font button or kern interactively. Ventura changes the distance between all selected letters. This ability is great for fine-tuning text to fit within a certain amount of space.

AUTOMATIC KERNING WITH TAGS

In addition to kerning character by character, Ventura can kern *globally* with some fonts. That is, you can kern throughout all paragraphs that are similarly tagged, moving every *V* closer to a preceding or subsequent *A,* and so on for other letter combinations. However, the program can only do this if the font already contains the kerning information; that is, information about which pairs of characters should be kerned, and how much. Ventura 2.0 provides pair-kerning information for almost all printers.

1. Activate Paragraph mode and select a paragraph.
2. Drop the Paragraph menu and select Paragraph Typography. You'll see the dialog box shown in Figure 12.17. You use the Paragraph Typography command to kern globally by setting Automatic Pair Kerning to On and giving the OK.

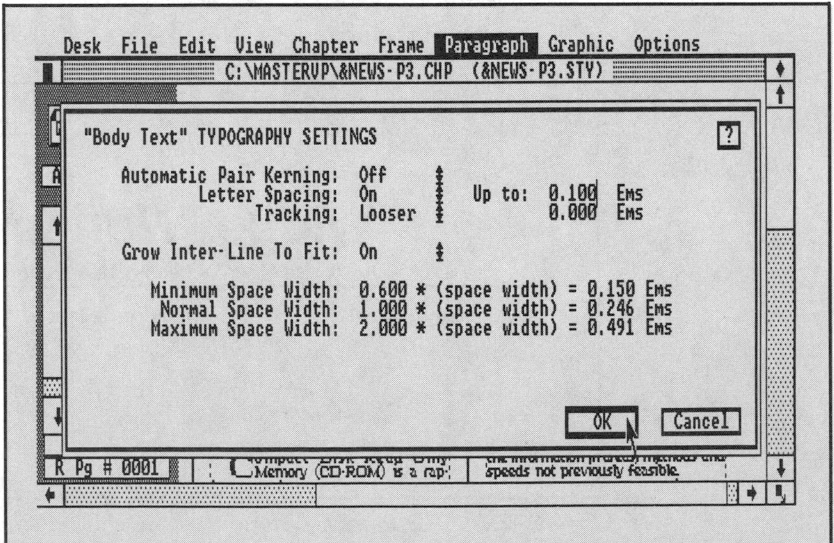

Figure 12.17: The Paragraph menu's Paragraph Typography dialog box

Several other commands can affect kerning that you perform in this manner. First, you can use the Chapter menu's Chapter Typography dialog box. In this dialog box, you can set Pair Kerning On or Off. When you set Automatic Pair Kerning On for any paragraph tag, the setting will only take effect as long as the chapter's kerning is on. If you switch the chapter's kerning off, automatic kerning is temporarily suspended. Automatic kerning can slow down processing, so you may want to turn the chapter's kerning off as you work with a document. Even so, the automatic kerning status stays with a paragraph tag. When you turn the chapter's kerning back on, all appropriately tagged paragraphs receive kerning treatment once again. This command does not affect kerning of individual characters, the first method of kerning we discussed.

! New for version 2.0

You can override the setting for chapter kerning on a frame-by-frame basis in Ventura 2.0. In Frame or Graphics mode, select the frame and use the Frame menu's Frame Typography dialog box. In this dialog box, Pair Kerning is normally set to Default, and the frame takes its cue for kerning from that for the chapter. Change it to On or Off to override the chapter's setting.

A final setting to consider appears in the Options menu's Set Preferences dialog box. Here you can indicate whether you want Ventura to display automatic kerning on the screen, and if so, for what size font. Displaying kerning on the screen can slow down operations because of the additional computations Ventura must perform. Set On-Screen Kerning to None and Ventura will only kern when you print the document. Set it to All and all appropriately tagged material will be kerned on the screen. Set it to one of the point sizes listed (between 10 and 36) and on the screen Ventura will only kern fonts as large as or larger than the size you indicate. Again, this setting does not affect kerning you set with Text mode's Set Font button.

SPACING BETWEEN WORDS AND LETTERS

Let's continue to look at the dialog box for Paragraph Typography and see how we can use its settings to improve the sample document. Whether you use many of the settings discussed in the next few sections depends on whether the document you are working with is justified.

Justifying a document can cause a host of problems. Deciding how Ventura should insert spacing between words and letters is an exacting chore. Many problems can therefore be avoided by simply not justifying. Use the Paragraph menu's Alignment command to accomplish this. Results can be quite acceptable, especially with vertical rules between columns, as Figure 12.18 shows. Additional improvements can be obtained by using the slower, but more thorough, algorithm for hyphenating (see Chapter 4). If you do justify the text, however, the first setting you may wish to consider is Letter Spacing.

LETTER SPACING

In the Paragraph Typography dialog box, Letter Spacing can be set On or Off. When Letter Spacing is Off, Ventura will justify by adding space between words only. When Letter Spacing is On, Ventura justifies by adding space between words and within words as well—that is, between the letters that make up the word. It will add spacing up to the amount indicated in ems after the Letter Spacing setting. As mentioned previously, an em is equal to the size of the font you're using.

Consider the justified version of the sample document (Figure 12.11). The way it stands, Letter Spacing is on and set to operate up to one-tenth of an em (.1 Ems). Look at the two lines at the top of the second column. The lines are loose and appear to be stretched out.

Figure 12.19 shows how adjustments to spacing affect this paragraph. In the first treatment, we've turned Letter Spacing off. Notice how Ventura achieves justification by adding additional spacing between words only. Spacing within words is the same as it is for left-aligned text.

The second treatment shows the paragraph as it appears in Figure 12.11. Words in the loose lines are stretched out.

In the third treatment, Letter Spacing is on, but we've decreased the Up To amount by half. Although the lines are still loose, the words are stretched less and are more clearly separated. This is probably the best arrangement, although it's a matter of personal taste. In Figure 12.20 we've applied this treatment to the sample.

Widget World News

Views and News of Widget Manufacturing in the 80s

142 Guitrep Pkwy. *Detroit, MI 98987* *(413) 567-9888*

Software Salaries: How do you stack up?

by Joe Smith

How much your software professionals are paid is a function of many variables, and a subject of considerable interest to your organization.

Software salary pay scales

■ Because of the dynamic growth of the software industry over the last decade, the demand for experienced, qualified programmers has greatly increased, thus leading to a spiraling of salaries.

But what causes managers to pay one programmer more than another? Does the type of organization, its size, or location make a difference? What career path or programming specialty leads to the most remuneration?

To answer these questions, Acme Magazine recently conducted its third annual compensation survey for software professionals. This newsletter article presents the results of this study and explores what the findings may mean to you.

Acme Magazine asked Joe Smith, a compensation consulting specialist for the software industry, to design and conduct the survey. Twenty-four positions, representing four programmer job families plus management, were included.

Data was collected for base pay, bonus and incentive payments, and whether nor not incumbents received stock options or other forms of equity.

Questionnaires were sent to the data processing heads of 2,400 organizations throughout the United States.

CD-ROM Breaks New Ground

Compact Disk Read Only Memory (CD-ROM) is a rapidly emerging new technology for the retrieval of vast amounts of information from an optical disk. This new peripheral device allows a totally new level of functionality in the use of microcomputers.

Physically, the CD-ROM device has a laser disk drive (or "player") the same size as a traditional 5 1/4" drive. The removable disk is 4 3/4", and has a capacity of 550M bytes (equivalent to 1500 360K floppy disks).

Theory of Operation

■ Information stored on a CD-ROM can be loaded into memory (RAM), displayed and printed, as with other media. While that data in RAM may be altered and stored to a conventional magnetic disk, the original information on the CD-ROM is unalterable, always ensuring the original copy is intact, making archiving easy.

The storage capacity, low cost, and read only feature of CD-ROM bring an enormous new capability to microcomputer users — that is, information retrieval of very large reference publications. How people receive and use information in the immediate and long term future will be dramatically changed by CD-ROM.

In addition to the huge capacity of raw information storage, specialized software for the search of that information is currently being introduced. This software allows searching the information in areas, methods and speeds not previously feasible.

It now becomes possible to electronically publish reference material more economically than to print the same material in book form. That cost benefit, coupled with search and retrieval software, make an astonishing price/performance ratio.

Figure 1 Caption Information

Table of Contents

November, 1987 *1*

Figure 12.18: Left-aligned text

Whichever way you go, the lines are still loose. Better hyphenation would be in order, and we'll do this later in the chapter. In fact, better hyphenation may obviate the need for letter spacing.

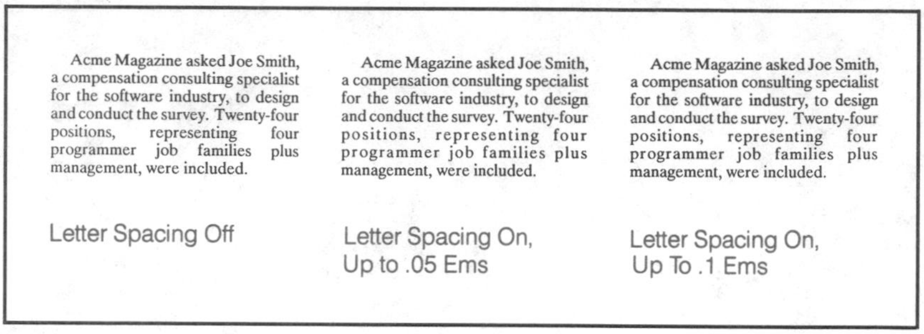

Acme Magazine asked Joe Smith, a compensation consulting specialist for the software industry, to design and conduct the survey. Twenty-four positions, representing four programmer job families plus management, were included.	Acme Magazine asked Joe Smith, a compensation consulting specialist for the software industry, to design and conduct the survey. Twenty-four positions, representing four programmer job families plus management, were included.	Acme Magazine asked Joe Smith, a compensation consulting specialist for the software industry, to design and conduct the survey. Twenty-four positions, representing four programmer job families plus management, were included.
Letter Spacing Off	Letter Spacing On, Up to .05 Ems	Letter Spacing On, Up To .1 Ems

Figure 12.19: Various letter-spacing treatments

TRACKING

Tracking is another spacing feature in the Paragraph Typography dialog box. However, tracking controls *all* spacing. It decreases or increases the spacing between letters and the spacing between words. It operates whether the text is justified or not.

With tracking, you can make paragraphs looser or tighter. With a value of 0 in the Tracking field, tracking is not operational. To use tracking, enter a value and then choose either Looser or Tighter as appropriate.

Tracking serves two useful purposes. First of all, you can use tracking to adjust text to fit into a fixed amount of space. Figure 12.21 shows the same sample paragraph, left-aligned in this case, first with no tracking, and then with tracking set tighter and looser. Notice how the length of the paragraph varies with each treatment, allowing it to occupy varying amounts of space.

To assist in lining up the right edge of multiple lines of text, remember that you can drag the ruler line's cross hairs from the 0,0 mark. You use the Options command to show rulers. See Appendix A.

Another popular tracking application involves headlines, titles, and logos. You can use tracking to match the lengths of lines of text that would otherwise not match. For example, in Figure 12.22, tracking for the word *Universe* is tighter than normal, while tracking for the first two lines is looser, allowing all three lines of the title to match in length.

In the sample document, we could use looser tracking to fill in the page with text. However, since many lines are already too loose, we won't change this setting. We'll use another technique to fill out the page.

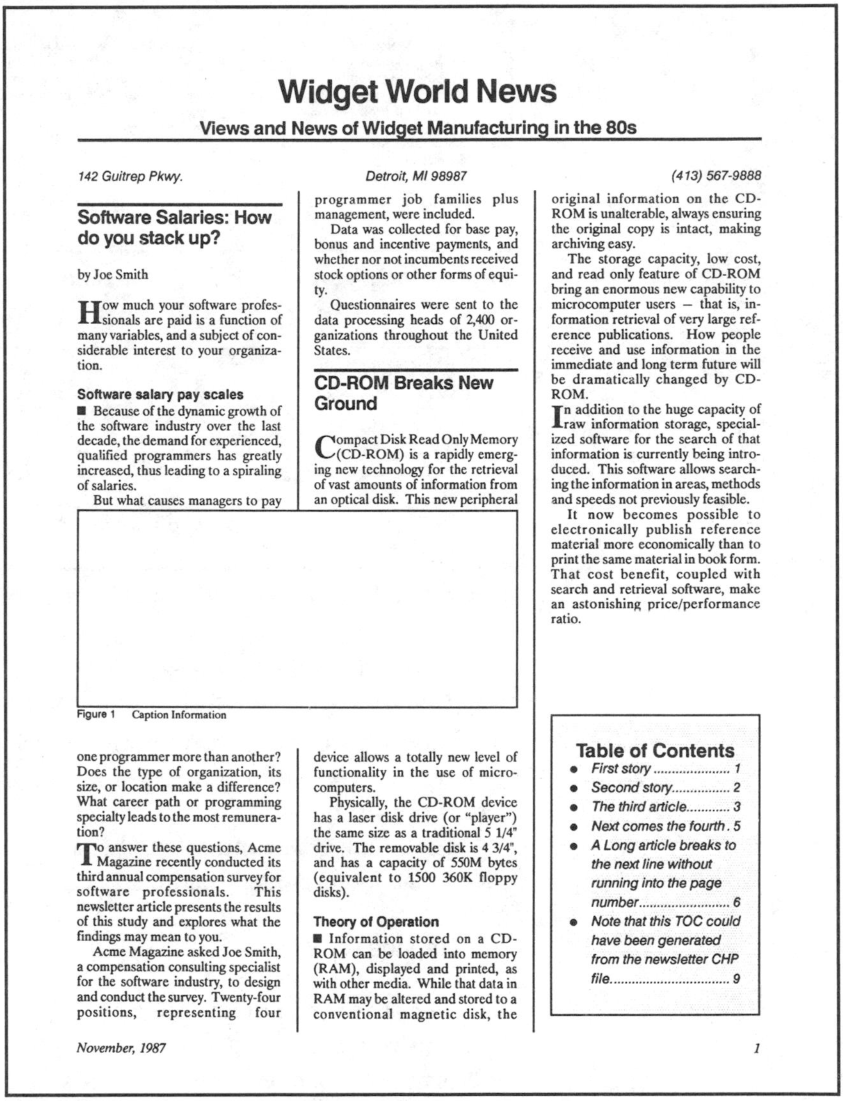

Widget World News

Views and News of Widget Manufacturing in the 80s

142 Guitrep Pkwy. *Detroit, MI 98987* *(413) 567-9888*

Software Salaries: How do you stack up?

by Joe Smith

How much your software professionals are paid is a function of many variables, and a subject of considerable interest to your organization.

Software salary pay scales

■ Because of the dynamic growth of the software industry over the last decade, the demand for experienced, qualified programmers has greatly increased, thus leading to a spiraling of salaries.

But what causes managers to pay one programmer more than another? Does the type of organization, its size, or location make a difference? What career path or programming specialty leads to the most remuneration?

To answer these questions, Acme Magazine recently conducted its third annual compensation survey for software professionals. This newsletter article presents the results of this study and explores what the findings may mean to you.

Acme Magazine asked Joe Smith, a compensation consulting specialist for the software industry, to design and conduct the survey. Twenty-four positions, representing four programmer job families plus management, were included.

Data was collected for base pay, bonus and incentive payments, and whether nor not incumbents received stock options or other forms of equity.

Questionnaires were sent to the data processing heads of 2,400 organizations throughout the United States.

CD-ROM Breaks New Ground

Compact Disk Read Only Memory (CD-ROM) is a rapidly emerging new technology for the retrieval of vast amounts of information from an optical disk. This new peripheral device allows a totally new level of functionality in the use of microcomputers.

Physically, the CD-ROM device has a laser disk drive (or "player") the same size as a traditional 5 1/4" drive. The removable disk is 4 3/4", and has a capacity of 550M bytes (equivalent to 1500 360K floppy disks).

Theory of Operation

■ Information stored on a CD-ROM can be loaded into memory (RAM), displayed and printed, as with other media. While that data in RAM may be altered and stored to a conventional magnetic disk, the original information on the CD-ROM is unalterable, always ensuring the original copy is intact, making archiving easy.

The storage capacity, low cost, and read only feature of CD-ROM bring an enormous new capability to microcomputer users — that is, information retrieval of very large reference publications. How people receive and use information in the immediate and long term future will be dramatically changed by CD-ROM.

In addition to the huge capacity of raw information storage, specialized software for the search of that information is currently being introduced. This software allows searching the information in areas, methods and speeds not previously feasible.

It now becomes possible to electronically publish reference material more economically than to print the same material in book form. That cost benefit, coupled with search and retrieval software, make an astonishing price/performance ratio.

Figure 1 Caption Information

Table of Contents

November, 1987 *1*

Figure 12.20: The sample with letter spacing decreased

ADJUSTING THE WIDTH OF A SPACE

Lastly, let's consider the Space Width settings. These settings allow you to control the width of a space—that is, the amount of spacing that Ventura inserts between words. Be aware, though, that it is usually unnecessary to adjust these settings.

Acme Magazine asked Joe Smith, a compensation consulting specialist for the software industry, to design and conduct the survey. Twenty-four positions, representing four programmer job families plus management, were included.	Acme Magazine asked Joe Smith, a compensation consulting specialist for the software industry, to design and conduct the survey. Twenty-four positions, representing four programmer job families plus management, were included.	Acme Magazine asked Joe Smith, a compensation consulting specialist for the software industry, to design and conduct the survey. Twenty-four positions, representing four programmer job families plus management, were included.
Tracking 0	Tracking .01 Ems Tighter	Tracking .01 Ems Looser

Figure 12.21: Various tracking treatments

History
of the
Universe

Figure 12.22: Using tracking to match line lengths

Note that the three settings—Minimum Space Width, Normal Space Width, and Maximum Space Width—apply only to the spacing between words. These settings operate whether letter spacing is functional or not; they have no effect on the amount of space between letters within the same word.

As the dialog box indicates, the space widths are determined by a value that you provide, multiplied by the actual space width. The words

(space width)

represent the width of a space as contained in the width table for the font you're using.

Normally, spacing between words is the same amount as that of the standard width of a space. Thus, the value specified for Normal Space Width is usually 1. When 1 is used, the number of ems that appear is the amount given for space width in the font's width table. Ventura will use this value as the average space between words when justifying text. As necessary, Ventura will decrease the space between words, but no less than the amount you indicate for Minimum Space Width.

The Maximum Space Width setting is deceptively named. The indicated value does not limit the maximum width of a space in the way that the value for Minimum Space Width does. Regardless of what you specify as a maximum, Ventura will add as much space between words as necessary to achieve justification. However, Ventura will flag as loose lines any lines where the amount of space between words exceeds the value you've indicated for Maximum Space Width. These are the lines that will darken when you use the Options menu to show loose lines (see Appendix A).

Use of these settings can change the overall appearance of your document. In Figure 12.23 you can see how changing the Normal Space Width setting affects the distribution of space between words. The first treatment shows the text as it initially stands (although we've turned Letter Spacing off in order to isolate the effects of changing the space width). Although the second and third treatments are different, their impact is about the same. Both represent an improvement over the first treatment; spacing is more evenly distributed in the two treatments on the right.

These settings can sometimes cause undesirable results. Although the sample paragraph looks better with a smaller width, we won't change the setting on our sample. If we did, other paragraphs, similarly tagged, would actually become looser when this treatment was applied.

- Click Cancel (or press Ctrl-X) to put away the Paragraph Typography dialog box.

There is another dialog box with fine-tune settings that you may find unnecessary to adjust.

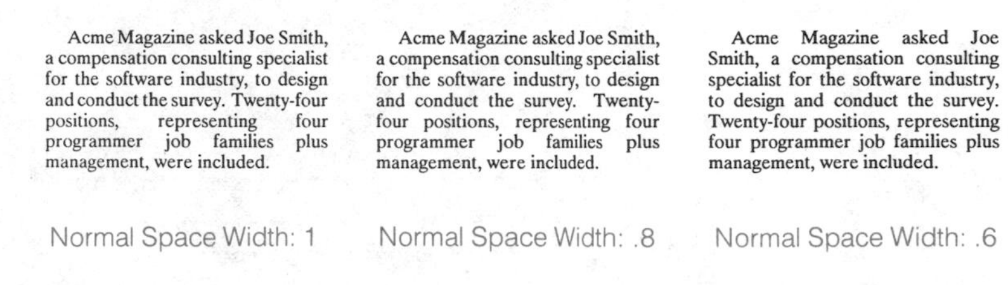

Figure 12.23: Changing the Normal Space Width setting

TEXT ATTRIBUTE LINES

You can use the Paragraph menu's Attribute Overrides dialog box to control placement of text attribute lines: underline, overscore, and strike-thru (Figure 12.24). In Chapter 8 we discussed how you can use Line Width: Margin-Wide to extend these text lines to the width of the paragraph. The Height and Shift settings regulate the location and size of lines created as part of the text attributes indicated. These are attributes you set by clicking them on Text mode's Assignment list.

If, however, you wish to change the thickness of your underline (from top to bottom), for instance, you could adjust the Underline 1 Height. Underline 2 Height comes into play only with double underlining. You can also change the thickness of the Overscore and Strike-thru attributes, and you can adjust the vertical position of any of these lines by changing the corresponding Shift settings.

SETTING SOLID SPACES AND OTHER CHARACTERS

We've been examining typographic effects created with dialog boxes, but there are other means for creating some unusual characters with

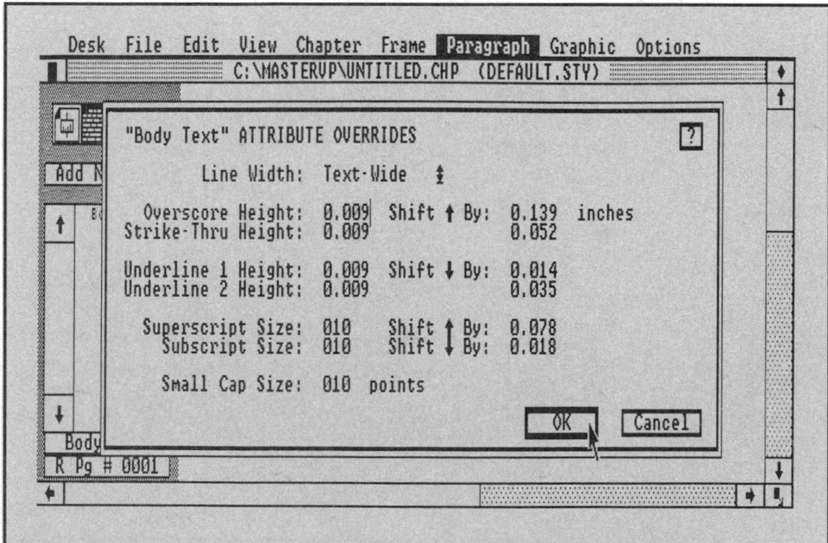

Figure 12.24: The Paragraph menu's Attribute Overrides dialog box

Ventura. For instance, you can create a variety of characters that do not appear on the keyboard. This includes such symbols as the trademark symbol, the copyright symbol, the registered symbol, and others. You create these using an Alt code in conjunction with the keypad, or using a word processor to enter a code into a text file. These special characters appear in Appendix E.

In addition, you can create even more nonkeyboard characters by using the Symbol font. To use it, simply assign Symbol as the face of the font (see Chapter 4). With this font, an entire set of characters, completely different from those on the keyboard, appears on the screen and in print. For instance, if you're using the Symbol font and you type the letter **p**, the Greek letter π appears. The Symbol font makes a new set of Alt codes available as well. Appendix E also lists the characters in the Symbol font.

You can also enter four types of *solid spaces* or *fixed spaces*. These spaces are always the same width. They will not shrink and grow in order to justify text as standard spaces do. You may find them useful with part numbers, numeric tables, and lines of computer code, for instance. You can enter these spaces in Ventura with the keyboard, or you can type in a code with your word processor. Here is a list of the four types of solid spaces, along with the two ways to enter them:

- Em space (Ctrl-Shift-M or <_>). In Ventura 2.0 an em space is the same width as the @ symbol of the font you're using.

- En space (Ctrl-Shift-N or <~>). An en space is half the width of an em space.

- Figure space (Ctrl-Shift-F or <+>). The figure space is the same width as any one of the font's numeric digits (0 to 9). This space is useful when you need to line numbers up in columns without using tabs.

- Thin space (Ctrl-Shift-T or <|>). The thin space is the same width as a period. We'll use a thin space in our sample document shortly.

SPACING BETWEEN PARAGRAPHS THAT FOLLOW ONE ANOTHER

In Chapter 4 we examined interline and interparagraph spacing. These properties, set with the Paragraph menu's Spacing dialog box, are also typographical elements (see Figure 12.25). Let's examine them more closely and consider their application with regard to our sample.

1. Activate Paragraph mode and select a paragraph.
2. Drop the Paragraph menu and select Spacing. The Spacing dialog box appears (Figure 12.25).

Ventura computes the spacing between paragraphs that follow each other according to the formula shown in Figure 12.26. The first value it uses is the Inter-Line setting of the first paragraph. Added to this value is either the Below setting of the first paragraph and its lower ruling lines, or the Above setting of the second paragraph and its upper ruling lines, whichever combined value is greater.

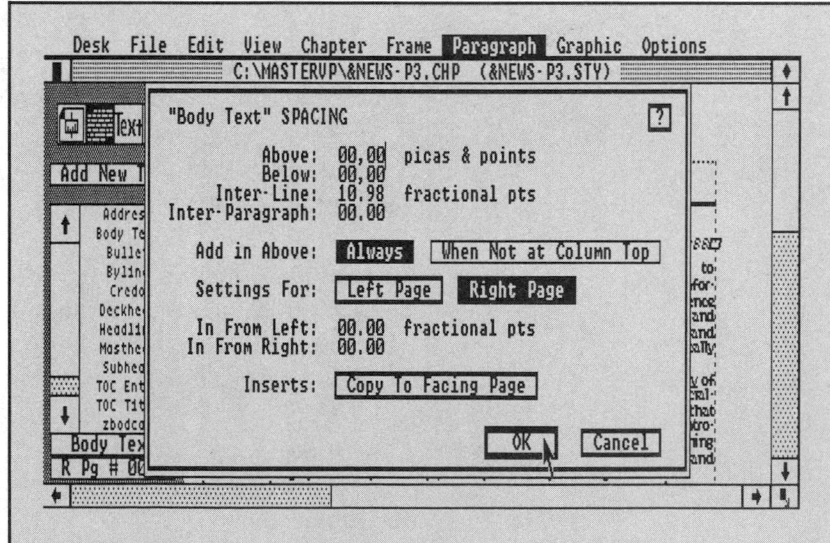

Figure 12.25: The Paragraph menu's Spacing dialog box

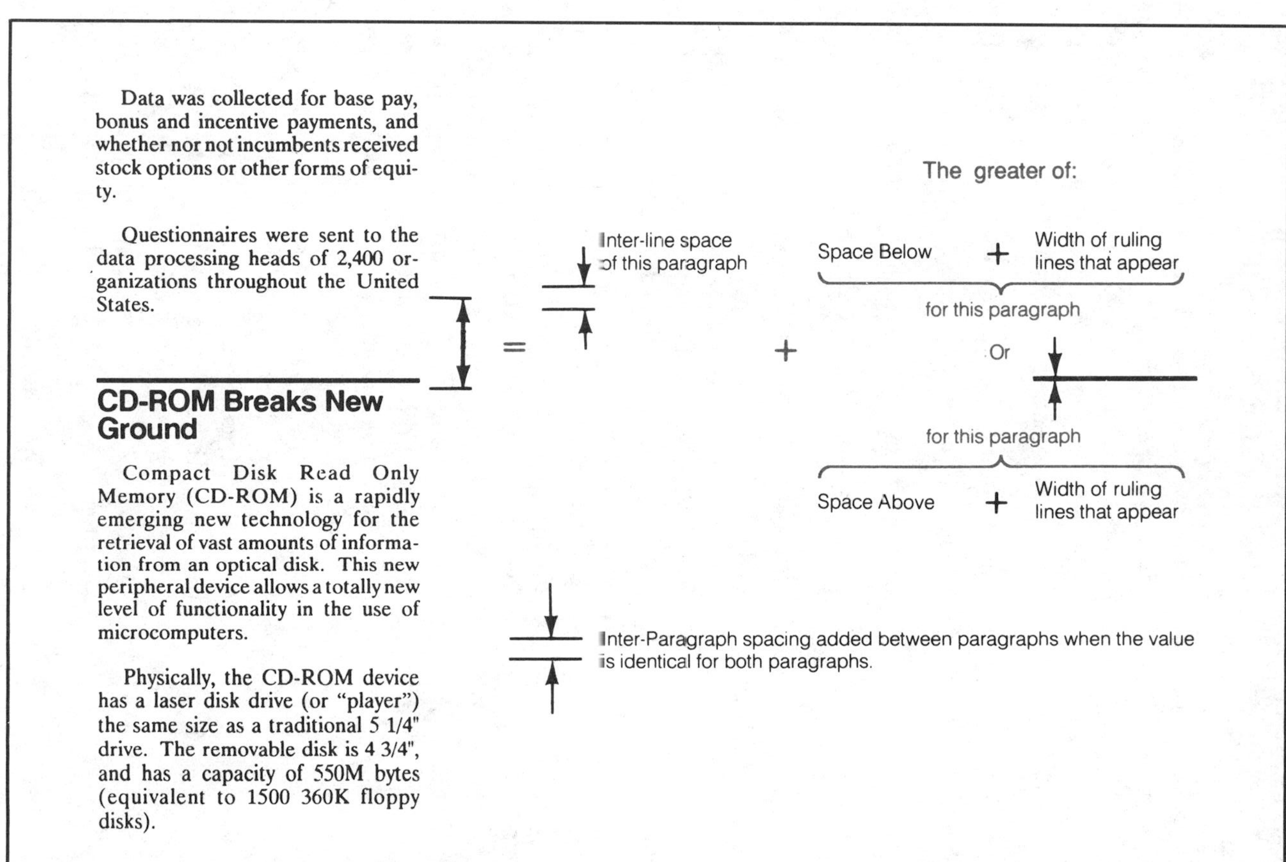

Figure 12.26: How Ventura determines the space between paragraphs

If you're not comfortable converting points to picas, Ventura will do it for you. You can simply enter 20 points and when you give the OK, Ventura will convert the measurement. There may be some inconsequential rounding differences.

For settings that affect spacing between paragraphs, it's generally a good idea to enter values that are multiples of the interline spacing. For that reason, set picas and points as the system of measurement. That way, lines of text in neighboring columns and on facing pages will line up. So if interline spacing is 10 points, you can create two lines of space by entering 20 points (or 1 pica, 8 points).

To modify the sample document as shown in Figure 12.27, make the following changes to the indicated tags:

1. Change Headline Above to 40 points (converted to 03,04).
2. Change Headline Below to 10 points.
3. Change Subhead Above to 20 points (converted to 1,08).
4. Change TOC Title Below to 10 points.

These changes aid in setting off sections of the text and in filling out the page.

We've made another change to the Headline tag. The way this tag was initially set up, both paragraphs that use it would always have some space above. This is desirable in the second instance (*CD-ROM Breaks . . .*) but it means that the first use (*Software Salaries . . .*) would be displaced inappropriately down the first column. Use the Paragraph menu's Spacing dialog box to keep such displacement from occurring; for Add In Above, click When Not At Column Top.

One other numeric setting in this dialog box is a special case. Ventura will only add in the Inter-Paragraph value when that value is identical for both paragraphs involved. Most often, this occurs when the paragraphs have the same tag, as in the case of body text.

Thus, we can add some space between body-text paragraphs. In addition, paragraphs in the sample with a dropped capital and the small square block should receive the same treatment. Except for their special features, these paragraphs are essentially the same as body text. To have them similarly spaced, provide their tags with the same Inter-Paragraph value as that of body text.

! New for version 2.0

Ventura 2.0 provides a new spacing tool in the Chapter menu's Chapter Typography dialog box. There is a pop-up menu for

Move Down To 1st Baseline By:

that you can set to Cap Height or Inter-Line. The setting you choose determines the placement of the first line of text in the frames on the

Widget World News

Views and News of Widget Manufacturing in the 80s

142 Guitrep Pkwy. *Detroit, MI 98987* *(413) 567-9888*

Software Salaries: How do you stack up?

by Joe Smith

How much your software professionals are paid is a function of many variables, and a subject of considerable interest to your organization.

Software salary pay scales

■ Because of the dynamic growth of the software industry over the last decade, the demand for experienced, qualified programmers has greatly increased, thus leading to a spiraling of salaries.

But what causes managers to pay one programmer more than another? Does the type of organization, its size, or location make a difference? What career path or programming specialty leads to the most remuneration?

To answer these questions, Acme Magazine recently conducted its third annual compensation survey for software professionals. This newsletter article presents the results of this study and explores what the findings may mean to you.

Acme Magazine asked Joe Smith, a compensation consulting specialist for the software industry, to design and conduct the survey. Twenty-four positions, representing four programmer job families plus management, were included.

Data was collected for base pay, bonus and incentive payments, and whether nor not incumbents received stock options or other forms of equity.

Questionnaires were sent to the data processing heads of 2,400 organizations throughout the United States.

CD-ROM Breaks New Ground

Compact Disk Read Only Memory (CD-ROM) is a rapidly emerging new technology for the retrieval of vast amounts of information from an optical disk. This new peripheral device allows a totally new level of functionality in the use of microcomputers.

Physically, the CD-ROM device has a laser disk drive (or "player") the same size as a traditional 5 ¼" drive. The removable disk is 4 ¾", and has a capacity of 550M bytes (equivalent to 1500 360K floppy disks).

Theory of Operation

■ Information stored on a CD-ROM can be loaded into memory (RAM), displayed and printed, as with other media. While that data in RAM may be altered and stored to a conventional magnetic disk, the original information on the CD-ROM is unalterable, always ensuring the original copy is intact, making archiving easy.

The storage capacity, low cost, and read only feature of CD-ROM bring an enormous new capability to microcomputer users — that is, information retrieval of very large reference publications. How people receive and use information in the immediate and long term future will be dramatically changed by CD-ROM.

In addition to the huge capacity of raw information storage, specialized software for the search of that information is currently being introduced. This software allows searching the information in areas, methods and speeds not previously feasible.

It now becomes possible to electronically publish reference material more economically than to print the same material in book form. That cost benefit, coupled with search and retrieval software, make an astonishing price/performance ratio

Figure 1 Caption Information

Table of Contents

November, 1987 *1*

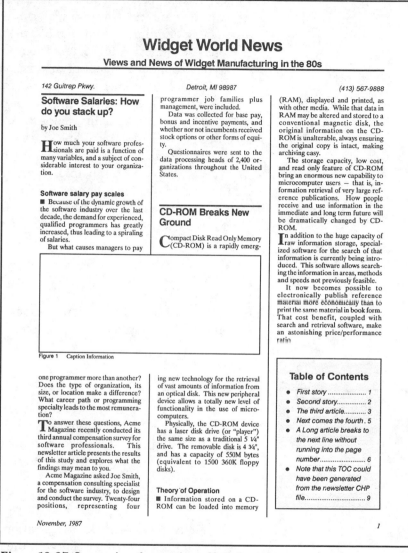

Figure 12.27: Improving the spacing of headings

page. This includes the underlying-page frame. (If your page has more than one column, it affects the first line of text in each column.)

Normally, you would use Cap Height, which sets the baseline of the text down the distance of a capital letter. Basically, this means that the top edge of the text appears flush inside the top edge of the frame. (This assumes that there is no top margin, as set by the Frame menu's Margins & Columns dialog box. If there is, the distance would be in addition to the top margin.) If you are using more than one font size in the first line of text, Ventura uses the size of the largest font to determine placement of the first baseline of text.

Specifying Inter-Line causes Ventura to displace the baseline of the first line of text downward by the value specified for its tag (with the Paragraph menu's Spacing dialog box for Inter-Line). Basically, what this does is insert any blank spacing that appears (between lines of text) above the first line, between the first line of text and the top edge of the frame. This is helpful in instances where you don't want the text directly against the inside edge of the frame—for instance, when you have a ruling box around the frame.

You can override the Move Down setting on a frame-by-frame basis. In Frame mode, select the frame that will be an exception to the chapter's setting. Then use the Frame menu's Frame Typography dialog box. Here, Move Down To 1st Baseline By is usually set for Default, and the frame takes its setting from the chapter. Set it to Cap Height or Inter-Line and text appearing in the frame will adhere to that setting, regardless of the chapter's setting.

INSERTING FRACTIONS

! New for version 2.0

Another new feature of Ventura 2.0 allows you to insert typographically improved fractions into your text. You can create fractions that use a slash (such as 1/2) or those that use an "over" bar ($\frac{1}{2}$). In either case, Ventura automatically reduces the size of the font for the fraction.

To create a fraction, follow these steps:

1. Activate Text mode and position the text cursor where you want to create the fraction in the text.
2. Use the Edit menu to select Ins Special Item, or press Ctrl-C as a keyboard shortcut.
3. On the Special Item menu, click Fraction or press F4. You'll see the screen go blank, with a horizontal bar dividing it into

two parts. (The view Ventura initially uses corresponds to the view you were using before inserting the fraction. However, even as you edit the fraction, you can change the view with the Edit menu or the equivalent keyboard shortcuts.)

Remember, press Ctrl-C—for Create—to create a division mark. When you do, a menu courteously appears. It prompts you that F1 creates a slash (/) and F2 creates an over bar (–). When you've finished with the fraction, press Ctrl-D for Done.

4. Use the text cursor (which appears in the top portion of the screen) to type the fraction. As you do, the fraction will appear in the lower portion. When you're ready to enter the division mark, use the Edit menu's Choose Fraction Text command (or press Ctrl-C). Then click Fraction (or press F1) for a slash (/) or Over (F2) for an over bar (–).
5. When you're done, use the Edit menu's Exit Fraction Editing or press Ctrl-D.

Ventura will insert your fraction into the text.

To edit an existing fraction, position the text cursor before (to the left of) the fraction. The word *Fraction* should appear in the Current box. Press Ctrl-D or use the Edit menu to select Edit Special Item. This causes the split screen to appear with the fraction, which you can then edit.

Use this feature to improve the fractions in the sample.

1. Delete the fractions that appear toward the bottom of the second column ($^1/_4$ and $^3/_4$).
2. Use the Special Item menu to insert fractions in their place.

In Figure 12.27, these fractions have been so replaced.

FINISHING TOUCHES

In Figure 12.28 you can see how 6-point spacing between paragraphs takes effect on body text and these other paragraphs. This figure also shows other final touches, applied as follows:

- The figure and its caption have been added.
- The font for the caption has been changed. It's wise to limit the number of fonts you use. The italic font, used elsewhere

on the page, serves nicely as a caption font. There is no need for it to have a separate font that's used nowhere else.

- The figure in its frame has been repositioned. Initially, the line art extended clear to the top edge of its frame. To make the spacing similar to that between column rules and text in the columns, we added a top margin of 1 pica to the frame. The amount is half that of the gutter of the underlying-page frame.
- The frame with the picture has been relocated. With the frame moved up, it doesn't interrupt the first paragraph of the second article.
- The slower, but surer, hyphenation algorithm has been implemented. It's wise to do this for text that appears within narrow columns like this. However, this caused too many lines to be hyphenated one after another, so we used the Paragraphs menu's Alignment dialog box to reduce Successive Hyphens to 2.
- Line breaks have been added to the headlines. By inserting a line break (Ctrl-Enter) after *Software Salaries* and *CD-ROM Breaks,* we improved the readability of the headlines considerably.
- The ruling line below the Credo ("Views and News . . .") was lowered by providing a Space Above Rule 1 setting of 1 point. This keeps the descending letters from touching the line.
- A thin space has been inserted between numbers and letters—specifically *550 M* and *360 K*.
- Second spaces that follow the ends of sentences have been eliminated. You can do this with Ventura in Text mode, or you can use your word processor's search-and-replace capability.
- Except in headlines, the Small attribute has been applied to acronyms appearing in all capital letters (CD-ROM, RAM).

Finishing touches such as these can truly enhance your documents. These capabilities show once again how sophisticated Ventura is. Even so, as you progress, you may find that you have "industrial-strength"

Widget World News

Views and News of Widget Manufacturing in the 80s

142 Guitrep Pkwy. *Detroit, MI 98987* *(413) 567-9888*

Software Salaries: How do you stack up?

by Joe Smith

How much your software professionals are paid is a function of many variables, and a subject of considerable interest to your organization.

Software salary pay scales

■ Because of the dynamic growth of the software industry over the last decade, the demand for experienced, qualified programmers has greatly increased, thus leading to a spiraling of salaries.

But what causes managers to pay one programmer more than another? Does the type of organization, its size, or location make a difference? What career path or programming specialty leads to the most remuneration?

To answer these questions, Acme Magazine recently conducted its third annual compensation survey for software professionals. This newsletter article presents the results of this study and explores what the findings may mean to you.

Acme Magazine asked Joe Smith, a compensation consulting specialist for the software industry, to design and conduct the survey. Twenty-four positions, representing four programmer job families plus management, were included.

Data was collected for base pay, bonus and incentive payments, and whether nor not incumbents received stock options or other forms of equity.

Questionnaires were sent to the data processing heads of 2,400 organizations throughout the United States.

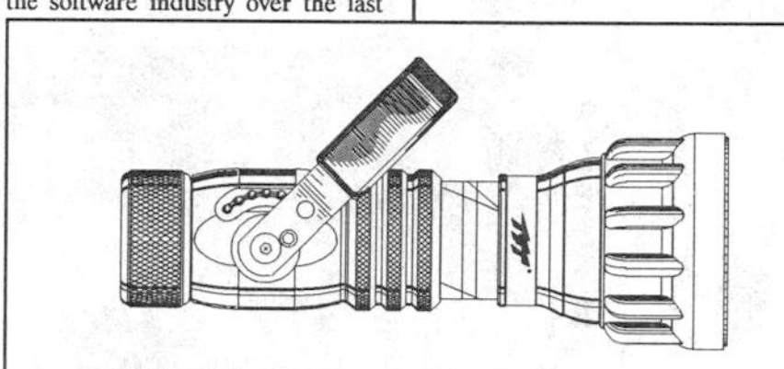

Clever CD-ROM connector that doubles as a garden hose nozzle

CD-ROM Breaks New Ground

Compact Disk Read Only Memory (CD-ROM) is a rapidly emerging new technology for the retrieval of vast amounts of information from an optical disk. This new peripheral device allows a totally new level of functionality in the use of microcomputers.

Physically, the CD-ROM device has a laser disk drive (or "player") the same size as a traditional 5 ¼" drive. The removable disk is 4 ¾", and has a capacity of 550 M bytes (equivalent to 1500 360 K floppy disks).

Theory of Operation

■ Information stored on a CD-ROM can be loaded into memory (RAM), displayed and printed, as with other media. While that data in RAM may be altered and stored to a conventional magnetic disk, the original information on the CD-ROM is unalterable, always ensuring the original copy is intact, making archiving easy.

The storage capacity, low cost, and read only feature of CD-ROM bring an enormous new capability to microcomputer users — that is, information retrieval of very large reference publications. How people receive and use information in the immediate and long term future will be dramatically changed by CD-ROM.

In addition to the huge capacity of raw information storage, specialized software for the search of that information is currently being introduced. This software allows searching the information in areas, methods and speeds not previously feasible.

It now becomes possible to electronically publish reference material more economically than to print the same material in book form. That cost benefit, coupled with search and retrieval software, make an astonishing price/performance ratio.

Table of Contents

November, 1987 1

Figure 12.28: Finishing touches applied

applications that the standard Ventura package is unable to handle. If that's the case, you may wish to upgrade—to Ventura's Professional Extension, the subject of the next chapter.

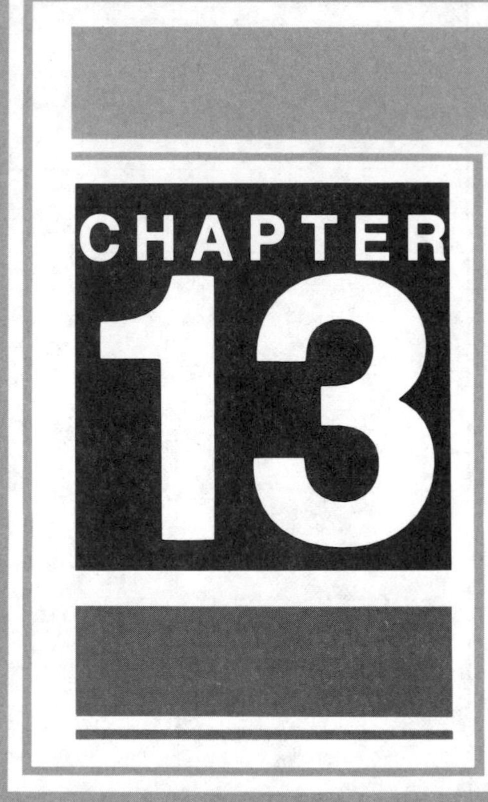
CHAPTER
13

Enhancing Ventura with the Professional Extension

Fast Track

To activate Table mode 481

with the Professional Extension, click the Table Edit button or use the Edit menu's Table Editing.

To insert a new table 481

activate Table mode, select a paragraph, and click the Ins New Table button. You can also insert a new table by choosing Table from the Edit menu's Ins Special Item (or Ctrl-C F9).

To edit an existing table 482

activate Table mode, click the table, and use the Edit menu's Edit Table Settings (or Ctrl-D).

To manipulate rows and columns 483

select by dragging with the mouse, and either use the Assignment list or cut, copy, and paste.

To change a table's column width 483

select a cell in the column, and then use either the Edit menu's Set Column Width or press Ctrl-C.

To join, split, or tint cells 483

select the cells and use Table mode's Assignment list.

To mark for cross-referencing 484

use the Edit menu's Ins Special Item (Ctrl-C) and click Marker Name (F7). You can also use a frame's anchor name as a marker.

To insert cross-references 485

place the text cursor in position, use the Edit menu's Ins Special Item (Ctrl-C), and click Cross Ref (F6). For At The Name provide the marker to which you wish to direct the reader.

To use variables 487

insert a cross-reference at each position in text, with the variable and the Refer To V* setting. Then place a variable definition at the beginning of the publication by using the Edit menu's Ins Special Item (Ctrl-C) and clicking Variable Def (F8).

To insert equations into text 488

activate Text mode and position the text cursor. Then use the Edit menu's Ins Special Item (Ctrl-C) and click Equation (F4). Enter the equation or use the Edit menu's Choose Equation Text to select with the Function keys. When done, use the Edit menu's Exit Equation Editing (Ctrl-D).

CHAPTER 13

VENTURA'S PROFESSIONAL EXTENSION PROVIDES professional typesetting features that enhance Ventura's performance. Much of Ventura looks and operates the same with the Professional Extension installed as without. However, when you purchase the Professional Extension and add it to your Ventura package, you can do all you can with Ventura's base program and more.

You will be quite aware of some special features as you use the Professional Extension. You'll detect their presence on menus and in dialog boxes throughout Ventura. These features include the Professional Extension's ability to create equations for scientific and mathematical purposes, an ability to insert ''live'' cross-references into your documents, a sophisticated module for generating tables much more easily than you can with the base program, and the capacity to justify text vertically so it reaches the bottom of every page.

However, the Professional Extension also works behind the scenes, enhancing operations in ways that may not be immediately apparent. If you have the hardware, it provides support for expanded memory (EMS). It also provides hyphenation according to the EDCO hyphenation dictionary, an industry standard. This makes for hyphenation that's as efficient as you probably would ever want. You must have EMS to use the EDCO dictionary.

In this chapter we'll examine those features of the Professional Extension that have wide appeal. We'll also discuss its other features. If you don't have the Professional Extension, you can use this chapter to help determine whether you need it. If you do have the Professional Extension, this chapter will introduce you to its operations. You can get ideas for using it by following along on your screen. Let's begin by seeing how you can create tables.

CREATING TABLES

Perhaps the first difference you'll notice when you use the Professional Extension is the appearance of an additional mode button on the Side-bar. The Professional Extension affords you a fifth mode, Table Edit mode (or simply Table mode). The button that activates this mode, labeled *Table Edit,* appears in the Side-bar below the other four mode buttons.

ACTIVATING TABLE MODE

Click the Table Edit button to activate Table mode (see Figure 13.1). You can also use the View menu's Table Editing command to activate Table mode. In Table mode, the mouse cursor in the working area appears as a small plus sign.

INSERTING A TABLE

To insert a new table, you use the Insert/Edit Table dialog box (Figure 13.2). To display this dialog box:

1. Activate Table mode.
2. Click the paragraph before which you want to insert the table. The *table cursor,* a thin, gray horizontal line the width of text in the column, appears above the paragraph.

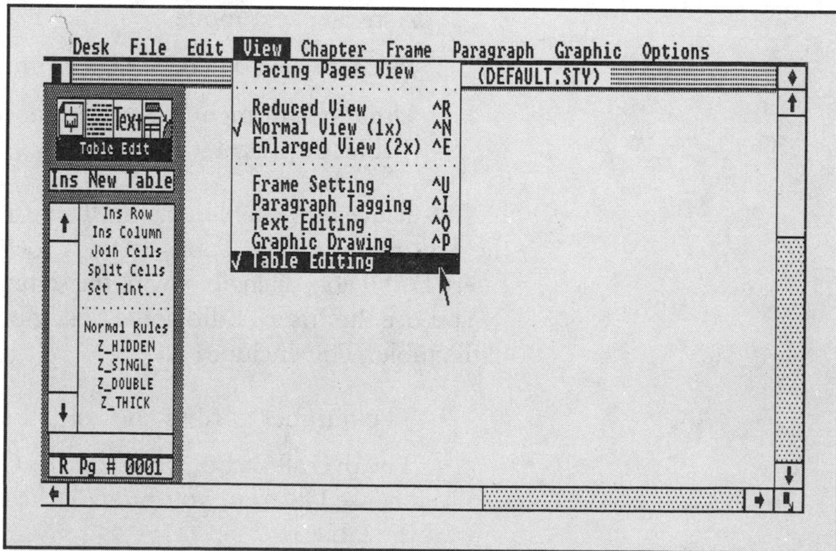

Figure 13.1: Ventura in Table mode

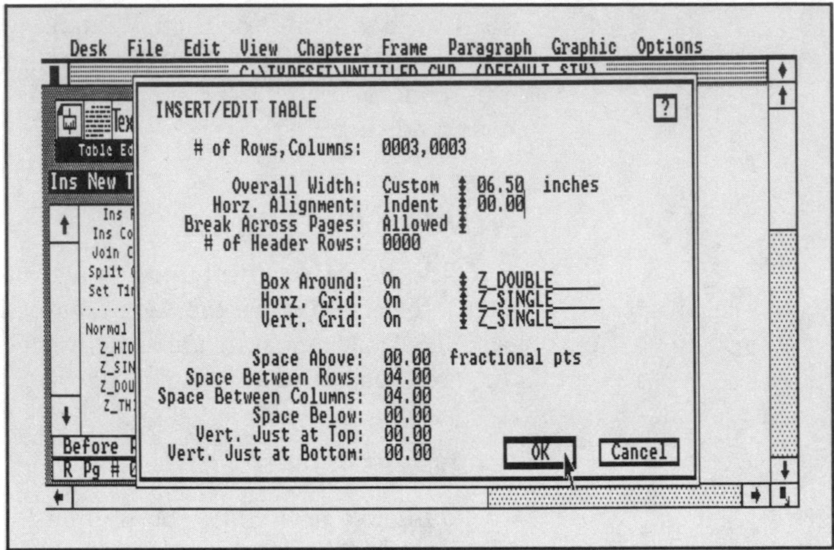

Figure 13.2: The Insert/Edit Table dialog box

3. Click the Side-bar's Ins New Table button.

You can also display the Insert/Edit Table dialog box to insert a table from Text mode:

1. Activate Text mode.
2. Place the text cursor at the beginning or end of a paragraph.
3. Use the Edit menu's Ins Special Item (or Ctrl-C) and select Table (or press F9).

To edit an existing table, activate Table mode and click the table. Use the Edit menu's Edit Table Settings (or Ctrl-D). This displays the Insert/Edit Table dialog box with the settings of the selected table.

You use the Insert/Edit Table dialog box to set the characteristics of the table. This includes

- The number of rows and columns.
- The overall width, which can be Column or Custom. (If you choose Custom, you provide the Horz Alignment setting of the table.)

- Whether Ventura can break the table across pages.
- Header rows, which repeat at the top of pages or columns.
- Boxes and lines around and within the table (which you can override on a cell-by-cell basis with the Assignment list).
- Space above, below, and within the table.

Once you create the table, you can enter text into the table cells. You enter one paragraph of text per cell. As you add text to a cell, Ventura increases the height of its row when necessary to accommodate the text.

SELECTING AND MANIPULATING ROWS AND COLUMNS

To manipulate cells in the table, you activate Table mode and select the cells with the mouse. You can drag the mouse to select multiple adjacent cells. Ventura indicates selected cells with a gray dotted line.

To insert a new row or column, select any cell before which you want to place the new row or column. Then click the appropriate assignment on the Side-bar: Ins Row or Ins Column.

You can also cut, copy, and paste rows and columns. Use the usual cut/copy/paste procedures: the Edit menu or the Delete and Insert keys.

CHANGING COLUMN WIDTHS IN TABLES

To change the width of a column, click a cell in the column. Then use the Edit menu's Set Column Width (or Ctrl-C). This displays the Table Column Widths dialog box. You can provide a measurement for the size of the column (the Fixed setting), or indicate a proportional value based on other columns (the Variable setting).

You can also change column widths interactively. In Table mode, hold the Alt key as you drag with the mouse.

JOINING, SPLITTING, AND TINTING CELLS

You can join multiple adjacent cells to create a larger cell. Select the cells by dragging with the mouse, and click Join Cells on the

Assignment list. You can split such joined cells by clicking the Split Cells assignment. There is also a Set Tint assignment. This allows you to specify the background color of selected cells.

TAGS FOR TABLE PARAGRAPHS

You can apply tags to the cells of a table just as you apply them to paragraphs. This means you can apply formats consistently to multiple cells. Use this ability to set fonts for the cell, specify alignment and spacing, create ruling lines within the cell, and apply other Paragraph menu commands.

CROSS-REFERENCING

Automatic cross-referencing is invaluable in a long document that has material examined from a variety of viewpoints. The Professional Extension's cross-referencing abilities are quite comprehensive. They can precisely direct the reader to related material elsewhere in the document, and Ventura will adjust the cross-references after you edit. Even so, the cross-reference tools are not difficult to learn, because they operate in ways that you'll probably find familiar if you've used other Ventura features, such as anchoring frames and compiling an index.

ESTABLISHING MARKER NAMES

One way to use cross-references is to begin by inserting a marker name in the text. Follow these steps to do so:

1. Activate Text mode and place the text cursor in the spot to which you wish to refer the reader.
2. Drop the Edit menu and select Ins Special Item (or use the keyboard shortcut, Ctrl-C).
3. On the Special Item menu, click Marker Name (or press F7). The resulting dialog box is quite simple, with only one field for you to fill in:

   Marker Name:

4. Provide a marker name—a unique name that you assign to this spot in the text.
5. Click OK or press the Enter key.

If you later wish to change the marker name, place the text cursor before the marker in the text. The words *Marker Name* should appear in the Current box. Then use the Edit menu and select Edit Special Item (or press Ctrl-D). Note too that you can use cut, copy, and paste procedures to manipulate the marker as you do other special items.

You can also use the anchor name of a frame as a marker name. Do this if you wish to refer the reader to a frame—one that contains a picture, for instance. To assign an anchor name to a frame, activate Frame mode to select the frame, and use the Frame menu's Anchors & Captions dialog box (see Chapter 6).

INSERTING CROSS-REFERENCES

Once you've inserted a marker name in text or assigned an anchor name to a frame, you can refer the reader to that location by inserting a cross-reference for it. You create the default setup, which references the page number, as follows:

1. In Text mode, position the text cursor at the spot where you want to alert the reader to related material. For example, you might type in the following text:

   (For more information, see page

   and then type a space after the word *page* and leave the text cursor there.
2. Use the Edit menu's Ins Special Item (or Ctrl-C) and click Cross Ref (or press F6). You'll see the Insert/Edit Reference dialog box (Figure 13.3).
3. In the At The Name field, provide the marker name in text or the frame anchor to which you wish to refer the reader.
4. To insert the page number as the cross-reference, leave the other settings as they are and click OK or press Enter.

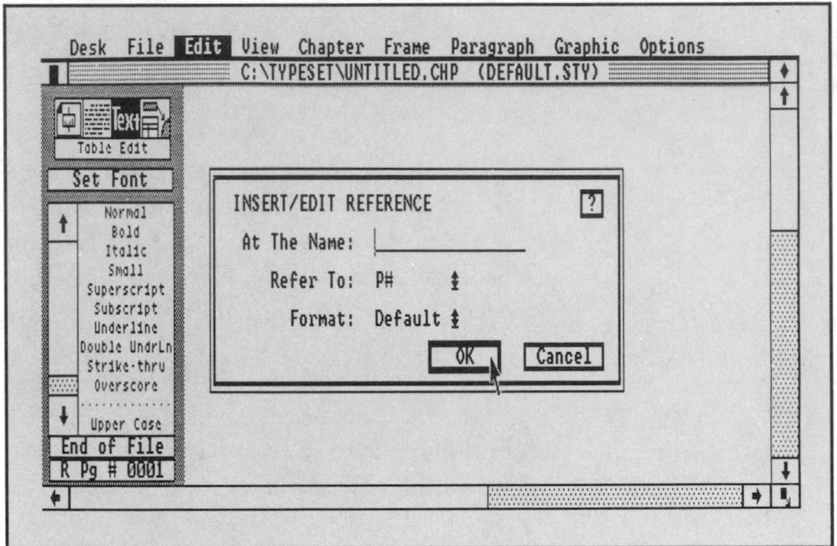

Figure 13.3: The Insert/Edit Reference dialog box

You won't see the reference page number appear immediately. However, if tabs and returns are showing, you'll see a degree symbol (°) indicating the cross-reference position, as it always does for special items. (When this indicator is to the right of the text cursor, the word *Reference* appears in the Current box.) To make the actual page number appear, you must use the Options menu's Multi-Chapter dialog box and select Renumber (see Chapter 10).

You can edit an existing cross-reference like other special items. Position the text cursor and use the Edit menu's Edit Special Item (or Ctrl-D).

To make cross-references to elements other than page numbers, begin, of course, by making the text of your document reflect the nature of the reference. For example, it could read

See Chapter

if you want to refer the reader to the chapter number of a marker. Position the text cursor, and use the Refer To pop-up menu in the Insert/Edit reference dialog box to specify the nature of the reference you wish to provide. This menu is initially set for P#, providing the page number of the text marker or the frame anchor. To make a reference to the chapter number, choose C#. Other numbered items are the figure number (F#) or table number (T#). You can also refer the reader to the section text (S*) that precedes what you're referencing, to the caption label (C*) of a frame anchor, or to variable text (V*), which we'll discuss shortly.

For number references (such as P#), you can use the Format pop-up menu to specify the numbering format you want for the spot where the cross-reference appears. Choices include Default and the usual numbering formats (1, A, a, I, and so on). Specifying Default causes Ventura to use whatever numbering format is set up for that particular counter (see Chapter 10).

USING VARIABLES

With the cross-referencing mechanism, you can insert variables into text and assign text to them. This gives Ventura a kind of global search-and-replace capability. However, you must anticipate your needs by inserting the variable in advance for text you expect to change, such as a client whose name you don't yet know, or the working title of a script.

1. In each text location where you want to insert a variable, use the Edit menu's Ins Special Item (or Ctrl-C) and click Cross Ref (or press F6). In the At The Name field, enter the variable, such as **Client**. Set the Refer To pop-up menu to V*.
2. To assign text to the variable, open the first chapter in the publication. Activate Text mode and insert the text cursor before the first piece of text on the first page. (You can actually use any spot before the location of the first variable; this is the conventional position because it makes the assignment easy to find.)
3. Use the Edit menu's Ins Special Item (or Ctrl-C) and click Variable Def (or press F8). In the Variable Name field of the resulting dialog box, indicate the variable you've used throughout the document. In the Substitute Text field, provide the text you want Ventura to insert in its place. An example appears in Figure 13.4.

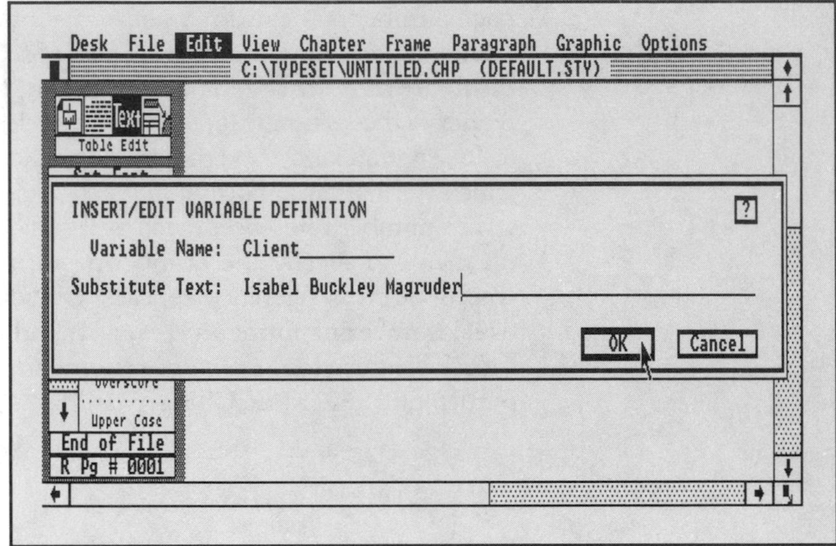

Figure 13.4: The Insert/Edit Variable Definition dialog box

4. Use the Options menu's Multi-Chapter to renumber. This causes Ventura to make the substitutions.

EQUATIONS

The Professional Extension enables you to insert sophisticated and typographically attractive equations into your documents. You can even provide special formatting within the equations.

The procedure for inserting equations is quite similar to that for inserting fractions with the Ventura base package.

1. Activate Text mode and position the text cursor.
2. Use the Edit menu's Ins Special Item (or Ctrl-C) and click Equation (or press F4).
3. A blank screen appears with a horizontal equation line. Enter the equation text above the line. As you do, the properly formatted result appears below the line.
4. When you're done, use the Edit menu's Exit Equation Editing or Ctrl-D. Ventura inserts the equation into the document.

Ventura provides some shortcuts for entering equations. Select the Edit menu's Choose Equation Text or press Ctrl-C and Ventura displays a list with ten types of equations along with their associated function keys. You can select from these by clicking one with the mouse or by pressing its function key. Ventura inserts the equation above the equation line and the result appears below the line. Figure 13.5 summarizes the steps involved.

Selection	Ventura's entry (above the line)	Result
F1: fraction (/)	1/2	½
F2: over (–)	1 over 2	$\frac{1}{2}$
F3: sub/sup	x sub {i^ + ^1} sup {n^ + ^1}	x_{i+1}^{n+1}
F4: square root	sqrt x	$\sqrt{x}$
F5: summation	sum from 0 to inf i	$\sum_{0}^{\infty} i$
F6: integral	int sub 0 sup 1 {x^dx}	$\int_0^1 x\,dx$
F7: matrix	matrix{ccol{a above b}~ccol{c above d}}	$\begin{matrix} a & c \\ b & d \end{matrix}$
F8: center col	ccol{a above b}	$\begin{matrix} a \\ b \end{matrix}$
F9: center pile	cpile{a above b above c}	$\begin{matrix} a \\ b \\ c \end{matrix}$
F10: left/right ()	left ({x} right)	$\left(x \right)$

Figure 13.5: Equation text assigned to function keys

These are the ten most popular types of equation text. The documentation for the Professional Extension lists over 100 kinds of equation text that you can enter. Included are all Greek characters, a wide variety of mathematical symbols, and commands that change font sizes.

HYPHENATION

If you choose to install the EDCO hyphenation dictionary, you can obtain extremely thorough hyphenation, with a great deal of control. Chiefly, you can stipulate the shortest word Ventura may hyphenate and the minimum number of characters allowed before or after a hyphen.

There are also utilities provided that allow you to check how a word is hyphenated, and to add and delete words or change their hyphenation points.

MEMORY ENHANCEMENT

The Professional Extension automatically makes use of expanded memory (EMS) if your system has it. This allows you to create very large documents, and makes the program operate more quickly and efficiently. It also makes the use of resident programs more practical. The EDCO hyphenation dictionary requires at least 1.2 megabytes of EMS.

VERTICAL JUSTIFICATION

With vertical justification, Ventura automatically adds spacing to fill out the material on the page or within the frame. This means that undesirable gaps at the end of a column of text are avoided.

With Chapter Typography, Frame Typography, Paragraph Typography, and Insert/Edit Table, you can specify the maximum amount of space Ventura may insert before and after various components that make up the document. Ventura then follows a strict order in adding such space, as it inserts up to the maximum amount you allow for each component. First it adds space above and below frames. Then it adds space above and below paragraphs and tables.

Finally, it adds space above and below individual lines in the paragraphs.

You can have Ventura justify vertically by inserting space only in interline increments (as specified for Body Text). Called *carding,* this feature assures that text in adjacent columns or pages will maintain baseline alignment.

The Professional Extension makes Ventura extremely comprehensive and a remarkable piece of software. And despite all that the program can do, Xerox will undoubtedly continue to create updated versions. As they do, look for corresponding future editions of this book.

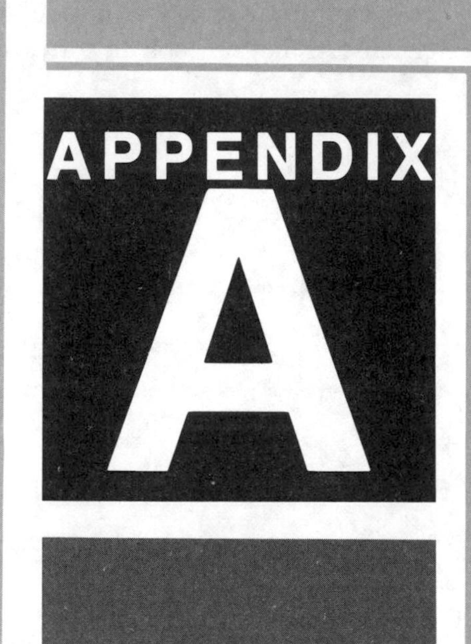
APPENDIX
A

Installation and Alternative Setups

APPENDIX A

THE VENTURA PROGRAM CONSISTS OF 15 DISKS, which are labeled with various names and numbered 1 through 15. (The Professional Extension version consists of 19 disks.) They contain the program itself as well as specifications for various printers that Ventura supports. When you install Ventura, a process we'll look at in a moment, the specifications for your printer or printers are automatically copied onto your hard disk.

The disks for Ventura 2.0 come packaged in convenient plastic pouches that allow you to view the name and number of each disk. When you install the program, don't obstruct the names and numbers of the disks. The installation program will prompt you for which disks you need to insert according to number and name.

The disks also contain examples of various documents. In conjunction with these examples, there are 25 style sheets.

INSTALLING VENTURA

As with most software, you must install Ventura before you can use it on your computer. When you install the program, you provide it with the specifications for your computer system, telling it what your monitor is like, what printer you will be using, and so forth. Ventura transfers the appropriate information from its disks onto your hard disk. Ventura will need 1.5 to 3.5 megabytes of memory on the hard disk to store this information and the program, depending on your printer. (The LaserJet Series II requires the most.) Be sure you have sufficient space on the disk before you begin installation; if Ventura should run out of room as it's being installed, it will terminate the installation, and you'll have to start over.

USING THE INSTALLATION PROGRAM

The installation program (VPPREP) can take a half hour or more to complete its work. If you should later decide to change some aspect of the installation, you can easily do so. (You can change some parameters by editing the VP.BAT file; see below. To install new fonts, see Chapter 5.)

The installation program will ask you for the following information. It is a good idea to know the answers before you run the installation, so the process proceeds smoothly.

- The type of graphics board that's installed in your computer and the display you are using.
- What brand of printer you are using.
- The printer port that connects your printer. If you're unfamiliar with ports or printers, you may wish to consult Chapter 5, where we discuss them in detail.
- Which brand of mouse you are using.
- How that mouse connects to your computer. It may connect via a serial port or it may be using a board.

To install Ventura, insert disk #1, the Application disk, into drive A. Then type

```
a:vpprep
```

and press the Enter key.

To follow the exercises in this book, be certain to install the sample files that come with Ventura. VPPREP provides you with the opportunity to do this.

The installation program will proceed to ask you about your equipment (see Figure A.1) and then prompt you to insert the appropriate disks. As you install Ventura, you will probably find that there are some disks you use more than once and some you don't use at all; this is normal. Just follow the instructions on the screen. If you decide that it's necessary to terminate the installation at any time, you can do so by pressing the Ctrl key and holding it down while you push the key labeled Scroll Lock Break.

If you are going to install more than one printer, decide which one you will install first. The one that you specify first will be the default printer—the first one that Ventura displays when you print your documents.

Though lengthy, the installation process is simple because its questions are straightforward; Ventura creates its own directories

```
Which graphics card and display do you have?

A   IBM CGA or compatible / Color Display (640x200).
B   IBM EGA or compatible / Color Display (640x200) 2 colors.
C   IBM EGA or compatible / Enhanced Display (640x350) 2 colors.
D   IBM EGA or compatible / Monochrome PC Display (640x350).
E   IBM VGA or compatible (640x480) 2 colors.
F   IBM PS/2 Model 30 MCGA or compatible (640x480).
G   Hercules Card or compatible / Monochrome PC Display (720x348).
H   Xerox 6065 / AT&T 6300 (640x400).
I   MDS Genius Full Page Display (720 x 1000).
J   Xerox Full Page Display (720 x 992).
K   Wyse WY-700 Display (1280 x 800).
L   THESE DRIVERS SHOULD BE USED FOR COLOR OR GREY SCALE (EMS RECOMENDED)
M   IBM EGA or compatible / Color Display (640x200) 16 colors.
N   IBM EGA or compatible / Enhanced Display (640x350) 16 colors.

Press PgDn for additional options or
Type the letter of the graphics card you have:
```

Figure A.1: Installing Ventura

(VENTURA, which contains the program, and TYPESET, which contains the examples) and copies the appropriate information into the directories automatically.

COMPLETING THE INSTALLATION PROCESS

When VPPREP is finished, there are a couple of other steps you should perform to complete the installation process. You'll need to use your word processor to create or modify certain files on disk, including VP.BAT, which is created with the installation process and loads Ventura, and AUTOEXEC.BAT (you create this file if you like), which runs programs when you turn the computer on. You'll also work with the CONFIG.SYS file, which configures the operating system to your specifications.

Use your word processor in ASCII mode to modify these files. If you're unsure how to do this, check Chapter 11. It describes the methods of creating ASCII text with some of the more popular word-processing systems. If your word processor is not listed, check the documentation that came with it.

When you create these files, be certain that you spell their names correctly. Also be sure to type the commands exactly as shown, with no extra spaces. Each line must end with a return.

First, you'll need to add the following line to the CONFIG.SYS file on your hard disk or another disk from which you boot your computer:

```
BUFFERS=20
FILES=20
```

These numbers control the amount of data (number of buffers) read from the disk at one time and the number of files that can be opened at one time. You can use numbers greater than 20 if another program you're using demands that you do. If you see these lines already in the file, and if they're set for 20 or greater, leave them. If not, change them to 20.

If you have a bus mouse (one that uses its own board instead of plugging into a serial port), the software that runs it must be installed before each work session. You'll probably want to automate this installation of your mouse. That way, you won't have to reload it each time you use Ventura Publisher. To do this, add the line

```
c:\mouse
```

to the VP.BAT file (described below) or the AUTOEXEC.BAT file. Be sure to specify the path, if any, where you have the mouse software located. Thus, if your Microsoft Mouse software is stored in the MSMOUSE directory on drive C, you'd enter

```
c:\msmouse\mouse
```

PREPARING A POSTSCRIPT PRINTER FOR PRINTING AN OUTPUT FILE

With a PostScript printer, you must prepare the printer if you intend to use it for printing a disk file. Prior to printing, you must transmit the contents of a special file to your printer. The file's name is DTR.TXT, and it's located within the POSTSCPT directory on the Utilities disk (#5). To use this special file, perform these steps:

1. Make sure that your PostScript printer is on, connected, and on-line.
2. Insert disk #5 into drive A.
3. At the DOS prompt, type in the following (being certain to space correctly and use the backslash and the colon as indicated):

   ```
   copy a:\postscpt\dtr.txt lpt1:
   ```

4. If another program resets your printer, repeat these steps before you print again.

You need peform this process only once. The settings remain with the printer even when you turn it off (unless another program resets it).

EDITING THE VP.BAT FILE

As mentioned, Ventura creates the VP.BAT file as part of the installation process. This is the file that runs when you type **VP** at the DOS prompt. It, in turn, loads Ventura. Normally, this file is installed in the C:\ directory (the root of drive C).

You can edit this file with your word processor in ASCII mode (see Chapter 11). The DRVRMRGR line is the command line that invokes Ventura. You can edit the parameters that make up this line and hence affect the parameters that Ventura installs when it boots itself.

A typical DRVRMRGR line (labeled with the parameters you can edit) might look something like this:

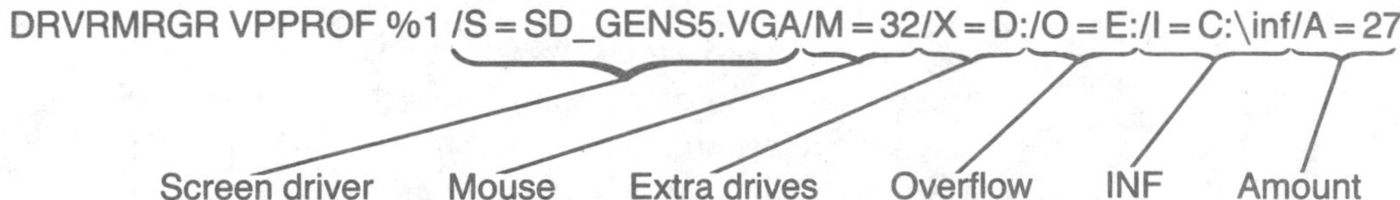

The %1 parameter allows you to load a chapter file at the same time you load Ventura. Thus, to load the BRAIN chapter when loading Ventura, you would enter

```
VP BRAIN
```

This parameter should not be changed.

However, you can edit the remaining parameters as follows:

/S = Indicates the screen driver Ventura uses. The extension (for example, VGA) dictates the extension Ventura initially uses in the Options menu's Set Printer Info dialog box for the Screen Fonts setting (see Chapter 5).

/M = Indicates the port and the type of mouse you're using. The first digit is for the port (0 = COM1, 1 = COM2, 2 or 3 = all others); the second digit is the for the type of mouse (0 = no mouse, 1 = Mouse Systems or PC Mouse, 2 = mouse using MOUSE.COM or MOUSE.SYS, 3 = Microsoft serial mouse, 4 = IBM PS/2 mouse).

/X = Indicates additional disk drives for the Item Selector boxes. You can specify as many drives as you wish by repeating the parameter. For example, you'd set up drives D, F, and K by entering **/X = D:/X = F:/X = K:**. One handy use of this ability is for establishing directories that you set up as drives with the DOS SUBST command.

/O = Indicates the disk drive to contain Ventura's overflow files. Under Alternative Setups below, you'll see how you can use this parameter to direct such files to a RAM drive.

/I = Indicates the directory where Ventura should store the INF files (for example, the C:\INF directory). These files store the Options menu's Hide/Show toggles (see below) and others that are in place when you quit Ventura. This includes the final operating mode

(Frame, Paragraph, Text, Graphics), the view (Normal, Enlarged, Reduced, or Facing Pages) and the system of measurement in the dialog boxes. You can copy the VP.BAT file to create one for each user of the program. Then, by using this parameter to specify different directories, you can ensure that users keep their settings separate.

/A = Indicates the amount of memory to be subtracted from the graphics buffer (for images) and font buffer, and added to the text area. Specify an integer between 1 and 32. Your needs in one regard or the other determine the most advantageous value. If you are unable to load Ventura, you may see a prompt instructing you to change this parameter.

CUSTOMIZING WITH THE OPTIONS MENU

One of the chief uses for the Options menu is to customize Ventura's *user interface*. The user interface refers to the manner in which Ventura presents itself to you. The settings that control these features appear on the Options menu or spring from it. There are four sections to the Options menu, and our discussion is grouped accordingly.

The options operate in conjunction with features that appear elsewhere in this book. Cross-references refer you to those features.

FIRST SECTION: OPTIONS-SETTING DIALOG BOXES

To use one of these dialog boxes:

1. Drop the Options menu.
2. Click Set Preferences, Set Ruler, Set Printer Info, or Add/Remove Fonts.

The first section of the Options menu leads to four dialog boxes that allow you to set options: Set Preferences, Set Ruler, Set Printer Info, and Add/Remove Fonts.

SET PREFERENCES DIALOG BOX The Set Preferences dialog box consists of several menus. Following is a discussion of those menus along with the settings you can use for them.

Generated Tags Set to Hidden, the names of generated tags do not appear with those of standard tags on the Paragraph mode Assignment list. Set to Shown, the names of tags that have been generated for the displayed document appear in the Assignment list. All generated tags begin with the letter *Z*. This is so that if they appear on the Assignment list, where tags are listed in alphabetical order, generated tags will be placed at the bottom of the list. Besides keeping the generated tags together, this positioning gives them lowest priority in terms of scrolling the Assignment list. As generated tags are assigned automatically, you shouldn't need to reference them as often as regular tags; hence the low priority.

Text to Greek When you use Reduced or Facing Pages view, Ventura may *greek* some of the text; that is, substitute plain straight lines for some or all lines of text. Greeking allows Ventura to operate more quickly as you edit.

Set to None, no greeking takes place. The sizes (2 through 10) represent the number of screen dots (pixels). Set to one of the sizes, Ventura will greek all text that size and smaller. Thus, the larger the size you choose, the more text that will be greeked. Set to all, Ventura will greek all text in these views, making for very efficient processing.

Keep Backup Files Set to Yes, Ventura will retain the previous version of its files each time it saves. Ventura does this by keeping the same file name for the backup but replacing the first character in the extension with a dollar sign. Thus, the backup file for the chapter BRAIN.CHP would be named BRAIN.$HP. Set to No, Ventura will not keep back-up versions of its files.

Double Click Speed This pop-up menu allows you to vary the amount of time that's required between successive clicks. There are five settings, from slow to fast. Experiment to determine the setting that's most comfortable for you.

On-Screen Kerning The setting you choose affects kerning as set by the paragraph tag. Set to None, Ventura will not kern text on the screen. Set to one of the font sizes, Ventura will only kern for fonts of the size you indicate or larger. Set to All, Ventura will kern all text. Kerning is discussed in Chapter 12.

Auto-Adjustments Set to none, Ventura makes neither of the auto-adjustments to be described.

Set to Style, when you adjust the font size for a paragraph tag, Ventura automatically adjusts various other attributes associated with the tag. This includes the tag's Line Attributes setting; Superscript, Subscript, and Small font sizes; and Above, Below, Inter-Line, and Inter-Paragraph values. Thus, if you had a paragraph with a 10-point font and a 12-point interline spacing, changing the font to 20 points would change interline spacing to 24 points.

Set to " And --, when Ventura loads a text file, it makes text that follows typewriter conventions more correct typographically. It automatically converts inch marks (") to true quotes (“ and ”). At the same time, it also converts two hyphens together (--) to an em dash (—).

Set to Both, Ventura both adjusts styles and makes quote/hyphen conversions.

Pop-Up Menu Symbol Set to Hidden, Ventura does not display the pop-up symbol (↕) in dialog boxes. Set to Shown, the pop-up symbol appears. This symbol indicates the availability of a pop-up menu.

Menu Type Set to Drop-Down, menus appear at the top of the Ventura screen when you position the mouse cursor on the name of the menu. You then select from the menu by clicking one of the choices.

Set to Pull-Down, the menu appears when you position the mouse cursor on the name of the menu, press the mouse button, and hold it down. While holding the mouse button, you select from the menu by dragging the mouse to the menu item and releasing.

Decimal Tab Character Normally Ventura recognizes the period character as a decimal point when determining the placement of numbers associated with a decimal tab. With this field you can direct Ventura to use any character by providing the ASCII value for the character you prefer. Appendix E lists the ASCII characters, along with their code-number equivalents. Those who wish to follow European style and set the comma character as the decimal point should specify a value of 44.

OTHER DIALOG BOXES For a discussion of the other dialog boxes that spring from the first section of the Options menu, see the chapters indicated:

OPTION	*SEE*
Set Ruler	Chapter 6
Set Printer Info	Chapter 5
Add/Remove Fonts	Chapter 5

SECOND SECTION: HIDE/SHOW TOGGLES

Use the options in this section to show (display) or hide (take away) features and codes from the Ventura screen. When you choose one of these settings, it toggles (changes) to its opposite. For instance, if the Side-bar is showing and you choose Hide Side-Bar, the Side-bar disappears and this option changes to Show Side-bar (which would be evident next time you looked at the Options menu).

These settings carry over from one Ventura session to the next. They are stored in files with an INF extension, which is initially in the VENTURA directory. (You can change where Ventura stores these settings by editing the VP.BAT file, as discussed earlier.) To regain Ventura's default settings, erase the INF files. If they are on drive C in the VENTURA directory, then you can delete them by typing

```
DEL C:\VENTURA\*.INF
```

Two of these toggles have Ctrl-key shortcuts, as indicated below and on the Options menu. You can use the shortcuts instead of the Options menu.

Hide/Show Side-Bar (Ctrl-W) Hide removes the Side-bar on the left side of the screen to provide more room for editing. Show displays the Side-bar to make the selections on the Side-bar available for viewing and use.

Hide/Show Rulers Hide removes the rulers from the top and left edges of the screen, providing more room for editing. Show displays the rulers, allowing you to use them.

Hide/Show Column Guides Removes and displays light dashes that indicate the positions of columns as set for the underlying-page frame.

Hide/Show All/This Picture(s) Hide removes pictures to increase the speed of editing operations. Show displays pictures so you can see them. This option operates on This Picture for the last selected picture, or on All Pictures when the underlying-page frame (or no frame) is selected in Frame mode.

Hide/Show Tabs & Returns (Ctrl-T) Hide removes various screen codes (which don't appear in the printed version of your document) so you can see an accurate representation of the printed document. Codes include those for the horizontal tab, paragraph end (return), line break, and special items and spacing. Show displays these symbols so you can be aware of the codes' positions.

Hide/Show Loose Lines Hide removes the reverse-video indication of loose lines (which doesn't show when printed) to accurately represent the printed version. Show displays loose lines to aid in tightening them.

THIRD SECTION: TURN SNAPS ON/OFF

When you move a frame with the mouse, you have the option of using *Column Snap.* Column Snap allows the left and right edges of the frame to favor landing on the edges of columns specified for the underlying-page frame. This ensures that columns will line up where they should and won't end up too close together. It also aids in keeping the distance between frames similar, or in regular multiples.

You turn Column Snap on by pulling down the Options menu and clicking Turn Column Snap On. If, when you pull down the menu, the command says "Turn Column Snap Off" then Column Snap is already on. (You can then turn it off by clicking that command.)

You can also use the Options menu to turn *Line Snap* on or off. Line Snap operates like Column Snap, but it regulates the upper and lower edges of standard frames. It forces the edges to line up according to spacing set for standard text (*body text*) that makes up the underlying-page frame.

FOURTH SECTION: MULTI-CHAPTER

This option leads you to the Multi-Chapter Operations dialog box. You use this dialog box to create publications. These features are discussed in Chapter 10.

ALTERNATIVE SETUPS FOR VENTURA

Most people use Ventura with a mouse, standard RAM up to 640K, and a standard graphics monitor. However, other setups are possible. The program is designed so that you can use it, if necessary, without a mouse; you can also use Ventura with extended RAM and with large (full-page) displays. We look at these alternative setups in this section.

OPERATING VENTURA WITHOUT A MOUSE

Although most people use Ventura with a mouse, it is possible to operate the program without one. You may find that you need this option if you have a mouse that isn't working or if you've removed it for use with a different computer.

There are also some users who aren't aware of Ventura's hardware needs and who acquire the program without buying a mouse. Even though you can learn Ventura without using a mouse, it's not really advisable. It's easier to use the program without a mouse once you've become conversant with using Ventura with a mouse.

When installing Ventura, you have the option of specifying No Mouse. However, you are not required to use this installation option in order to use Ventura without a mouse. The techniques discussed here will work if you've installed Ventura for a particular brand of mouse as well.

Ventura's strategy for operation without a mouse makes the keypad perform double duty. Normally, the directional arrows on the keypad control the text cursor on the screen. When using Ventura without a mouse, you can toggle the operation of some of the keypad keys. As you do, these keys change between Normal mode, where the arrow keys control the keyboard cursor, and Mouse mode, where the arrow keys control the mouse cursor. To switch between modes, you press the Ctrl key and the Shift key on the right. When you do, you'll hear a beep tone, indicating that the change has taken place. Pressing this key combination again causes the operating mode to switch back.

When the keypad keys are in Mouse mode, the Home key (which normally displays the first page in the document) duplicates clicking the mouse button. Pressing and releasing it is the same as if you click the mouse. The End key (which normally displays the last page in the document) simulates a press-and-hold or drag operation with the mouse button. Pressing the End key is the same as pressing the mouse button and holding it down. You release the theoretical mouse button by pressing the Home key. The other keys on the keypad—PgUp, PgDn, Del, and Ins—are not affected, and operate the same in both keypad modes.

With the keypad in Mouse mode, it is sometimes necessary to move the mouse cursor a smaller amount than the arrow keys allow. By pressing and holding the Shift key as you use the keypad arrows, you move the mouse cursor in smaller increments, allowing you to fine-tune its position.

Other keys pressed in combination with the Home and End keys sometimes work as they do when used with the mouse button. For example, you can use the Shift key with Home and End to select text. You can also use Shift-Home to select multiple paragraphs that you wish to tag similarly, or to select multiple frames or graphics. However, you cannot use the Alt key to crop pictures or the Shift key to add multiple frames, as you can when using Alt and Shift with the mouse. You cannot use the Ctrl key to select frames in sequence that are stacked on top of one another as Ctrl-mouse does.

Moving the mouse cursor with the keypad arrows is quite a bit slower than using a mouse. Therefore, be sure to learn and use the keyboard shortcuts extensively when using Ventura without a mouse. For instance, press Ctrl-U, -I, -O, and -P to change operating modes rather than the Mode buttons. Use Ctrl-2 instead of clicking the Addition button and Ctrl-X to redisplay the last dialog box with which you worked or to cancel a displayed dialog box.

Switching the operation of the keypad can be especially confusing as you work with dialog boxes. For that reason, keep the switching to a minimum. Generally, keep the keypad in Mouse mode. Instead of using the mouse cursor or the keypad arrows to move the keyboard cursor from field to field, use the Tab key. Press Shift-Tab to move the keyboard cursor back to a previous field. Press the Enter key to give the OK rather than clicking the OK button.

In the Item Selector box, you'll probably find that it's faster to type in drives, directories, and file names than to click them on the Item Selector list or use the Backup button. Again, press Tab and Shift-Tab to change fields. Use the Esc key to clear out previous names that are no longer applicable.

A keyboard enhancer, such as SmartKey, can assist you in using Ventura without a mouse, by creating macros that speed up the keypad arrows. For instance, you could make pressing Alt-→ the same as pressing the → key six times. This speeds moving the mouse cursor around the screen with the keypad arrows. Remember, though, that using resident programs, such as a keyboard enhancer, can limit the size of your Ventura chapters and slow down operations. If you have a keyboard enhancer and not a mouse, though, the trade-off may be worth it.

You can also create macros that trigger the various pull-down menus. To program the keyboard enhancer to do this, start with the mouse cursor in the bottom-right corner. This will allow the macro to control the most extreme situation, and all others as well. Start recording with the keyboard enhancer, and then use the arrow keys to move the mouse cursor all the way to the left, then up the left edge of the screen to the menu line, and finally across the menu line to the menu name of your choice. Then end the macro. You could use this technique, for instance, to make Alt-F display the Frame menu.

Don't forget that with a keyboard enhancer, the function keys are up for grabs, if you're willing to make their usual function of tagging paragraphs and other shortcuts unavailable or less accessible. By using the function keys you can make various operations available with one keystroke.

USING A RAM DISK

If your computer has extended memory available (at least 1.2 megabytes in all), you'll probably wish to put it to use with Ventura. To do so, you can create a *RAM drive* (or *virtual disk*) and set up Ventura to use it.

In normal operations, Ventura uses your computer's memory to store and manipulate text as you work on it. However, with large chapters, Ventura may run out of RAM. When that happens, Ventura will spill portions of the chapter over to the disk drive (a procedure called *swapping to disk*), and retrieve the material as necessary. Because disk drives contain moving parts, they are slow compared to RAM. Therefore, Ventura's operations can become significantly slower when material spills over.

A RAM drive is a portion of computer memory that you configure so that it operates like a disk drive. With Ventura, you can use extended memory for this purpose. A drive letter is assigned to the memory so that, as far as the program is concerned, this memory constitutes a disk drive. Ventura will use it to hold spillover portions of the chapter as necessary.

To use a RAM drive, you must first create it. To do this, use the software that accompanied the extended memory when you purchased it. With an AT computer and DOS 3.0 and higher, you can use DOS's VDISK command. The size of the RAM drive should be at least 500K.

Next, you must inform Ventura of the RAM drive's existence. You do this by adding a code to the last line of the VP.BAT file, located in the root directory. Use ASCII mode in your word processor to do this (see Chapter 11). The code you add consists of a slash, the letter *O,* and an equal sign, followed by the disk-drive letter assigned to your RAM drive and a colon. Thus, if your RAM drive is drive E, you would add

```
/O=E:
```

(See "Editing the VP.BAT File" earlier in this appendix.)

USING LARGE DISPLAYS

Monitors with large displays, such as the Genius full-page display, usually have several operating modes. Some programs cannot use the complete display, and so these modes regulate the screen as required by the program in use.

When you install Ventura, you specify the monitor you will use. If the monitor operates in several modes, it's important to make sure that it is configured for the full-page display whenever you use Ventura. This can be accomplished automatically by including a line in the VP.BAT file that invokes the proper mode whenever you load Ventura.

With the Genius display, this is accomplished by adding

```
vhr mds
```

to the beginning of the VP.BAT file. Be sure you add the line before the DRVRMRGR command, as this is the command that invokes Ventura.

NETWORKS, OS/2, 3.5-INCH DISKS, WINDOWS

It's not difficult to install and run Ventura from these various environments, assuming you have the correct tools.

To install Ventura for use on a network, obtain the special network version of the program from Xerox. The standard Ventura will not operate from a central file server. Printing over a network with a shared printer is possible with the standard Ventura, but there may be some diminishing of performance.

To run Ventura with OS/2:

1. Begin with the Program Selector screen, which appears when you start up the computer.
2. Use the arrow keys to highlight "MS-DOS Command Prompt," which appears in the second column.
3. Press the Enter key. The DOS prompt appears.

4. Proceed as you would otherwise. To install Ventura, insert the Application disk (#1) and enter **A:VPPREP**; or to run Ventura, enter **VP**.

To install the 3.5-inch version of Ventura, simply obtain the disks. The installation procedures are the same as for 5.25-inch disks. Ventura 2.0 packages are clearly labeled with the type of disks they include.

To install Ventura for use with Microsoft Windows:

1. Insert the Utilities Disk (#5) into drive A.
2. Type

   ```
   COPY A:\VP.PIF C:\WINDOWS\PIF
   ```

   and press Enter.
3. Make sure the PATH statement specifies the location of the VP.BAT file (such as PATH C:\). Usually, this command appears in the AUTOEXEC.BAT file.

Then, to load Ventura from Window's MS-DOS Executive:

4. In the WINDOWS\PIF directory, point to VP.PIF with the mouse and double-click.

APPENDIX
B

Ventura's Sample Documents

APPENDIX B

FIGURES B.1 THROUGH B.20 SHOW THE SAMPLE DOCuments that are provided with Ventura. The samples are copied into the TYPESET directory when you install Ventura.

We have made some changes in the samples as they initially appear on the disk. The samples were apparently designed to achieve their formatting effects on a PostScript printer. Printing them with a different printer, as we did with the Hewlett-Packard LaserJet Series II, can create undesirable changes. For example, dropped capitals are positioned too low and bullets are too tightly placed in the LaserJet versions of the documents. Where these changes have created poor style in the samples, they have been corrected. These corrections are discussed in Chapter 12 and noted in the examples where they were made. We have also used the Chapter menu's Re-Anchor Frames command to reposition the frame in &BOOK-P1, thus avoiding poor figure placement caused by the changed line length on the LaserJet.

You may wish to make additional changes as well. For example, letters touch the rules below many paragraphs (look at the *Digitizers* heading in &LSTG-P2). It would be good design to increase the spacing in order to avoid this.

Chapter files and style-sheet files are paired and presented according to their common main file name; that is, that portion of the file name that precedes the period. The extensions, being the defaults, are assumed; namely, all chapter names end with the CHP extension and all style-sheet names end with the STY extension. When you load chapter and style-sheet files, Ventura automatically assumes the appropriate extension, and filters file names accordingly. Chapter 2 contains further discussion of the system used for naming the samples, and Appendix C examines file filtering.

Along with the printed versions of the samples, Tables B.1 through B.20 list the salient features for each sample. Only those features that are stored with the style sheet appear. By using the same style sheet with your document, you can have these features available.

Each table is divided into two parts. First, there are features that affect the document in general. These are accessible via the Chapter and Frame menus. The Frame settings apply to the underlying-page frame, which must be selected if you wish to change the settings.

Following these general features is a list of the paragraph tags contained within the style sheet. Body Text is always the first tag listed, followed by others alphabetically. The listings do not necessarily contain all tags for the particular style sheet, only those with features of particular interest are listed. You will probably want to explore the samples further.

Some tags occur repeatedly within the various style sheets. Two in particular are the Page Break tag (usually F8) and the Change Bar tag (usually F9). The Page Break tag causes the paragraph that follows it to begin on a new page. If you want to cause a page break, you can press an extra return between paragraphs that you want on separate pages, and then format the extra paragraph mark with the Page Break tag. The Change Bar uses a ruling box around to create a vertical bar to the left of the paragraph so tagged. The technique for creating this format is discussed in Chapter 7. Although the Change Bar tag is not initially applied to any of the sample paragraphs, we have done so in the first two samples to demonstrate this tag in action.

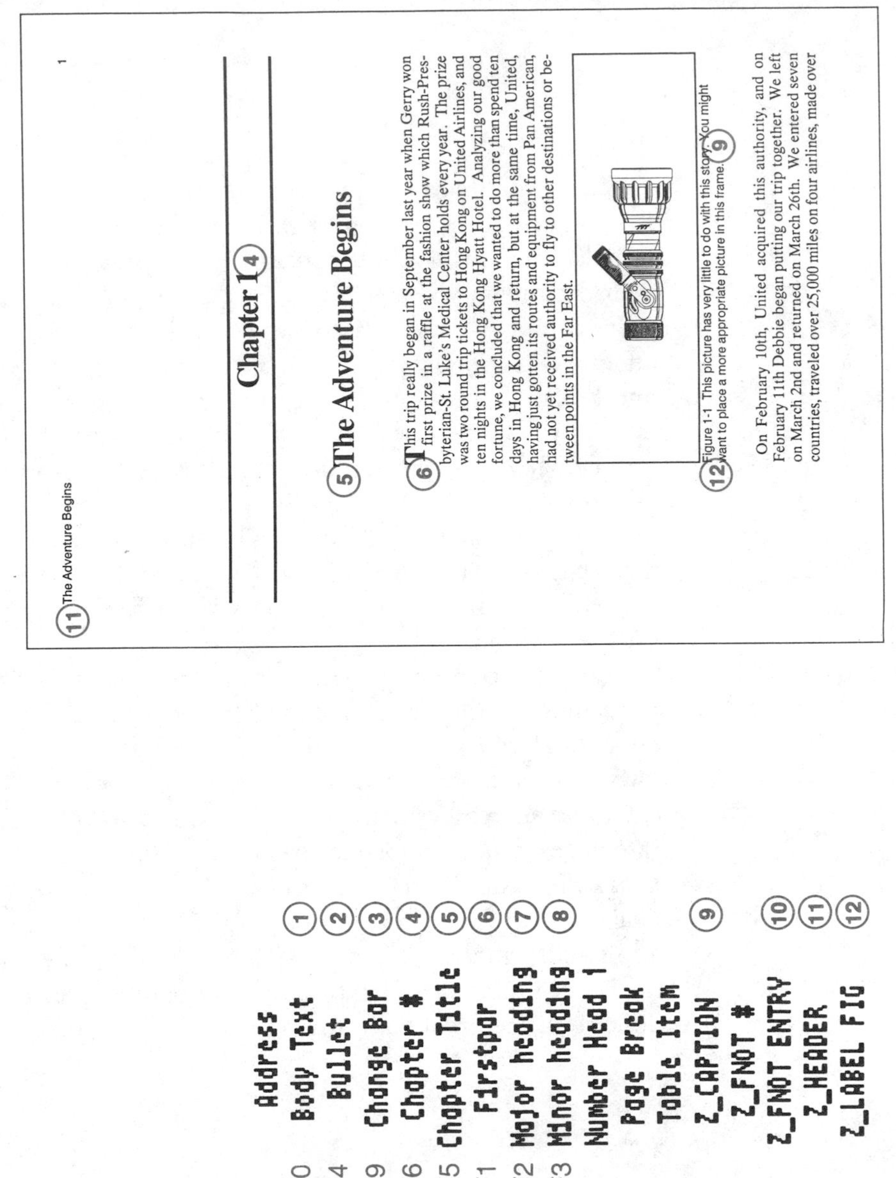

Figure B.1: &BOOK-P1 sample pages

Key	Tag	
	Address	
F10	Body Text	(1)
F4	Bullet	(2)
F9	Change Bar	(3)
F6	Chapter #	(4)
F5	Chapter Title	(5)
F1	Firstpar	(6)
F2	Major heading	(7)
F3	Minor heading	(8)
	Number Head 1	
	Page Break	
	Table Item	
	Z_CAPTION	(9)
	Z_FNOT #	
	Z_FNOT ENTRY	(10)
	Z_HEADER	(11)
	Z_LABEL FIG	(12)

2 Title of the Book

500 Kodachrome® slides, almost 200 Kodacolor® prints, and 5 1/2 hours of color and sound videotape.

(7) **Chicago to Tokyo**

11:03 P.M. Chicago time. 39,000 feet somewhere over the Western Pacific, we are 8 hours and 42 minutes out of Los Angeles with about 2 more hour to go to Tokyo. We were about an hour and ten minutes late out of Los Angeles.

(8) **Travel Log**

So far, it's been a long and interesting day and I guess it's just about half over. We did the following:

(2)
- Arose at 5:30 A.M.
- Left the house at 7:00 A.M.
- Arrived in Los Angeles at 12:35 P.M.
- Arrived in Tokyo at 11:46 P.M.

11:31 P.M. Tuesday, March 4th

It's been a long day, but in many ways really quite fabulous. Let's go back to the beginning. As related above, our trip yesterday was a good one with fine weather, accompanied by underlying clouds much of the way. Our 5400 mile* flight from Los Angeles took us north almost to the Kurile Islands and then down into Tokyo. Letting down through the clouds over a rough sea we saw many fishing boats and other vessels all headed into Tokyo. Our approach into the Narita Airport involved a long, slow descent which, after passing the shoreline (strangely reminiscent of the West shore of Lake Michigan although with some sandy beaches), gave us an opportunity to see many small patches of cultivated ground. Tiny houses, and even small factories. Everything seemed miniature.

At 4:25 P.M.** the sun was fairly high in the sky, but due to what appeared to be smog visibility was probably not more than 5 miles. Quarantine and customs proved no problem, but immigration was slow with much attention to detail. Our 5:15 P.M. limousine – really a rather large bus departed promptly and car-

(10)
* Nautical miles
** Local time

Figure B.1: &BOOK-P1 sample pages (continued)

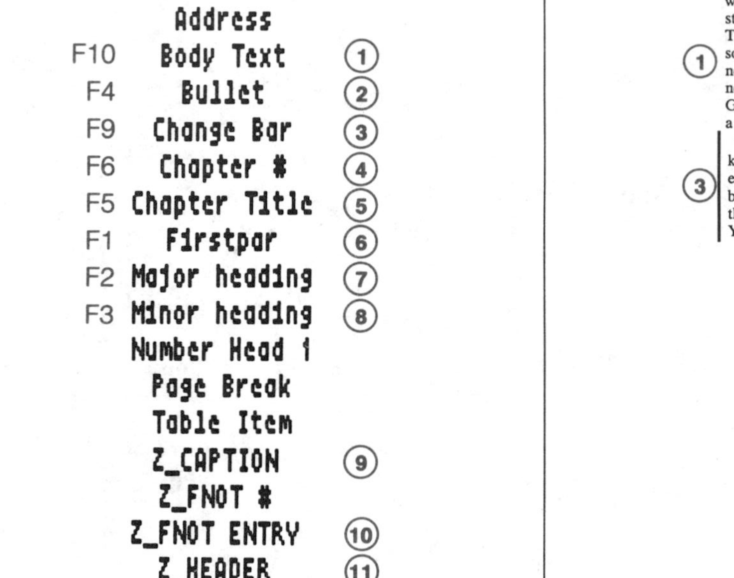

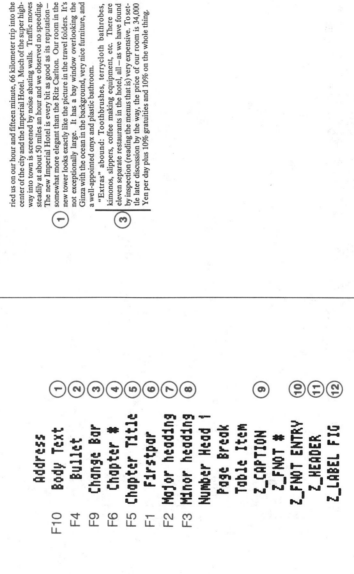

ried us on our hour and fifteen minute, 66 kilometer trip into the center of the city and the Imperial Hotel. Much of the super highway into town is screened by noise abating walls. Traffic moves steadily at about 50 miles an hour and we observed no speeding. The new Imperial Hotel is every bit as good as its reputation – somewhat more elegant than the Ritz Carlton. Our room in the new tower looks exactly like the picture in the travel folders. It's not exceptionally large. It has a bay window overlooking the Ginza with the ocean in the background, very nice furniture, and a well-appointed onyx and plastic bathroom.

"Extras" abound: Toothbrushes, terrycloth bathrobes, kimonos, slippers, coffee making equipment, etc. There are eleven separate restaurants in the hotel, all – as we have found by inspection (reading the menus that is) very expensive. To settle later discussion by the way, the price of our room is 34,000 Yen per day plus 10% gratuities and 10% on the whole thing.

Figure B.1: &BOOK-P1 sample pages (continued)

Table B.1: &BOOK-P1

	MENU	COMMAND	SETTING	
	Chapter	Page Size & Layout	Orientation:	Portrait
			Paper Type & Dimension:	Letter, 8.5 × 11 in.
			Sides:	Double
	Frame	Margins & Columns	# of Columns:	1
			Column Width:	6 in.
			Margins:	Top: 1.5'' Bottom: 1.17'' Left: 1.25'' Right: 1.25''
		Ruling Box Around	Space Above Rule 1:	54.00 fractional points
			Height of Rule:	0.72 fractional points
FIGURE REFERENCE	**TAG NAME AND FUNCTION KEY**	**PARAGRAPH MENU COMMAND**	**SETTING**	
①	Body Text (F10)	Alignment	Firstline:	Indent
			Indent Width:	6 points (.08'')
		Spacing	Inter-Line:	01,02 picas & points
			In From Left:	1.5''
②	*Bullet (F4)	Spacing	Above & Below:	00,03 picas & points
			Inter-Line:	13.98 fractional points
			In From Left:	1.67 inches
③	**Change Bar (F9)	Ruling Box Around	Width:	Custom
			Height of Rule 1:	1.98 fractional points
			Custom Indent:	−6 fractional points
			Custom Width:	1.98 fractional points

Table B.1: &BOOK-P1 (continued)

FIGURE REFERENCE	TAG NAME AND FUNCTION KEY	PARAGRAPH MENU COMMAND	SETTING	
④	Chapter # (F6)	Alignment	Horz Alignment:	Center
		Ruling Line Above/Below	Width: Height of Rule 1:	Margin 1.98 fractional points
⑤	Chapter Title (F5)	Alignment	Horz Alignment:	Center
		Spacing	Above & Below:	03,00 picas & points
⑥	†Firstpar (F1)	Special Effects	Special Effect: Space for Big First Char:	Big First Char Custom, 2 lines
⑦	Major heading (F2)	Spacing	Above: Below:	01,02 picas & points 00,07 picas & points
⑧	Minor heading (F3)	Spacing	Above: In From Left:	01,01 picas & points 09,00 picas & points
	‡Page Break (F8)	Breaks	Page Break:	After

* We increased the Indent After Bullet to 1 pica (see Chapter 12).
** Creates a vertical bar along the left edge of the paragraph (see Chapter 7). We applied this tag to the last paragraph.
† We shifted the dropped capital up 6 points (see Chapter 12).
‡ Causes the next paragraph to begin on a new page.

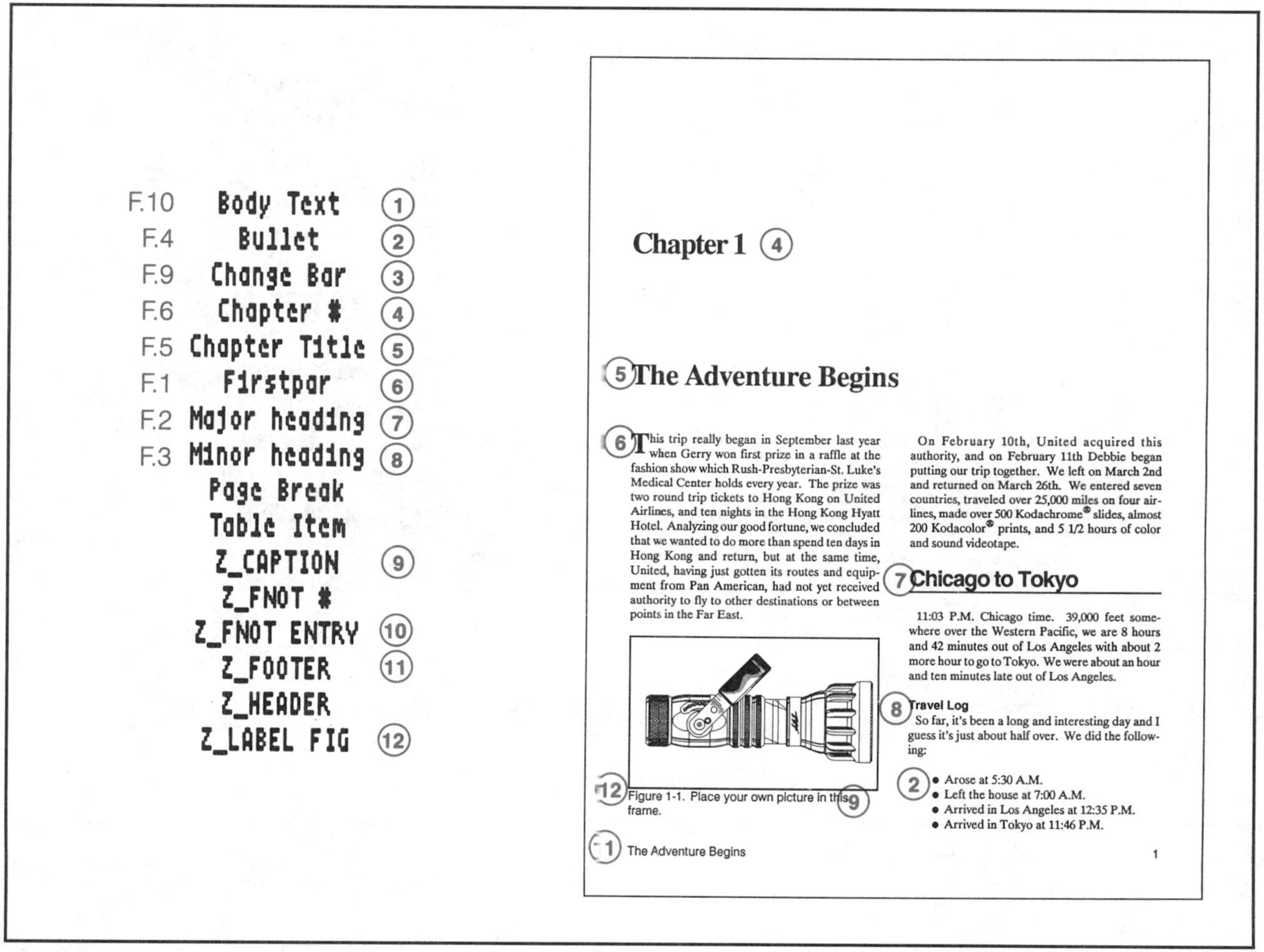

F.10	Body Text	(1)
F.4	Bullet	(2)
F.9	Change Bar	(3)
F.6	Chapter #	(4)
F.5	Chapter Title	(5)
F.1	Firstpar	(6)
F.2	Major heading	(7)
F.3	Minor heading	(8)
	Page Break	
	Table Item	
	Z_CAPTION	(9)
	Z_FNOT #	
	Z_FNOT ENTRY	(10)
	Z_FOOTER	(11)
	Z_HEADER	
	Z_LABEL FIG	(12)

Chapter 1 (4)

(5) The Adventure Begins

(6) This trip really began in September last year when Gerry won first prize in a raffle at the fashion show which Rush-Presbyterian-St. Luke's Medical Center holds every year. The prize was two round trip tickets to Hong Kong on United Airlines, and ten nights in the Hong Kong Hyatt Hotel. Analyzing our good fortune, we concluded that we wanted to do more than spend ten days in Hong Kong and return, but at the same time, United, having just gotten its routes and equipment from Pan American, had not yet received authority to fly to other destinations or between points in the Far East.

(12) Figure 1-1. Place your own picture in this frame. (9)

On February 10th, United acquired this authority, and on February 11th Debbie began putting our trip together. We left on March 2nd and returned on March 26th. We entered seven countries, traveled over 25,000 miles on four airlines, made over 500 Kodachrome® slides, almost 200 Kodacolor® prints, and 5 1/2 hours of color and sound videotape.

(7) Chicago to Tokyo

11:03 P.M. Chicago time. 39,000 feet somewhere over the Western Pacific, we are 8 hours and 42 minutes out of Los Angeles with about 2 more hour to go to Tokyo. We were about an hour and ten minutes late out of Los Angeles.

(8) Travel Log

So far, it's been a long and interesting day and I guess it's just about half over. We did the following:

(2)
- Arose at 5:30 A.M.
- Left the house at 7:00 A.M.
- Arrived in Los Angeles at 12:35 P.M.
- Arrived in Tokyo at 11:46 P.M.

(1) The Adventure Begins 1

Figure B.2: &BOOK-P2 sample pages

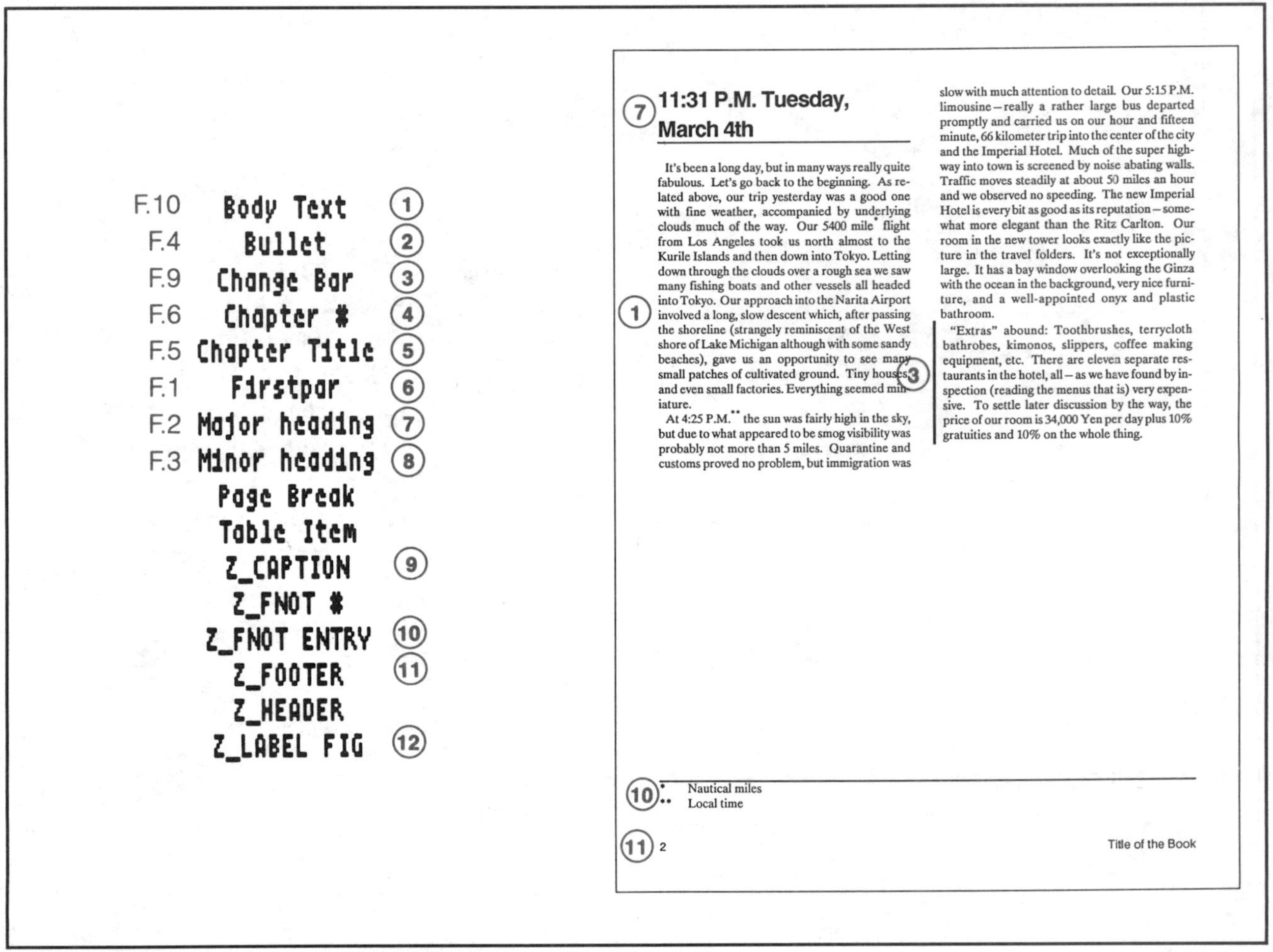

F.10	Body Text	(1)
F.4	Bullet	(2)
F.9	Change Bar	(3)
F.6	Chapter #	(4)
F.5	Chapter Title	(5)
F.1	Firstpar	(6)
F.2	Major heading	(7)
F.3	Minor heading	(8)
	Page Break	
	Table Item	
	Z_CAPTION	(9)
	Z_FNOT #	
	Z_FNOT ENTRY	(10)
	Z_FOOTER	(11)
	Z_HEADER	
	Z_LABEL FIG	(12)

(7) **11:31 P.M. Tuesday, March 4th**

It's been a long day, but in many ways really quite fabulous. Let's go back to the beginning. As related above, our trip yesterday was a good one with fine weather, accompanied by underlying clouds much of the way. Our 5400 mile* flight from Los Angeles took us north almost to the Kurile Islands and then down into Tokyo. Letting down through the clouds over a rough sea we saw many fishing boats and other vessels all headed into Tokyo. Our approach into the Narita Airport (1) involved a long, slow descent which, after passing the shoreline (strangely reminiscent of the West shore of Lake Michigan although with some sandy beaches), gave us an opportunity to see many small patches of cultivated ground. Tiny houses (3) and even small factories. Everything seemed miniature.

At 4:25 P.M.** the sun was fairly high in the sky, but due to what appeared to be smog visibility was probably not more than 5 miles. Quarantine and customs proved no problem, but immigration was slow with much attention to detail. Our 5:15 P.M. limousine—really a rather large bus departed promptly and carried us on our hour and fifteen minute, 66 kilometer trip into the center of the city and the Imperial Hotel. Much of the super highway into town is screened by noise abating walls. Traffic moves steadily at about 50 miles an hour and we observed no speeding. The new Imperial Hotel is every bit as good as its reputation—somewhat more elegant than the Ritz Carlton. Our room in the new tower looks exactly like the picture in the travel folders. It's not exceptionally large. It has a bay window overlooking the Ginza with the ocean in the background, very nice furniture, and a well-appointed onyx and plastic bathroom.

"Extras" abound: Toothbrushes, terrycloth bathrobes, kimonos, slippers, coffee making equipment, etc. There are eleven separate restaurants in the hotel, all—as we have found by inspection (reading the menus that is) very expensive. To settle later discussion by the way, the price of our room is 34,000 Yen per day plus 10% gratuities and 10% on the whole thing.

(10) * Nautical miles
** Local time

(11) 2 Title of the Book

Figure B.2: &BOOK-P2 sample pages (continued)

Table B.2: &BOOK-P2—Formatting Features

MENU	COMMAND	SETTING	
Chapter	Page Size & Layout	Orientation:	Portrait
		Paper Type & Dimension:	Letter, 8.5 × 11 in.
		Sides:	Double
Frame	Margins & Columns	# of Columns:	2
		Column Widths:	2.83 in.
		Margins:	Top: 1.17''
			Bottom: 1.5''
			Left: 1.25''
			Right: 1.25''
	Ruling Box Around	Space Above Rule 1:	54.00 fractional points
		Height of Rule:	0.72 fractional points

FIGURE REFERENCE	TAG NAME AND FUNCTION KEY	PARAGRAPH MENU COMMAND	SETTING	
①	Body Text (F10)	Alignment	Firstline:	Indent
			Indent Width:	.08''
		Spacing	Inter-Line:	01,00 picas & points
②	*Bullet (F4)	Spacing	In From Left:	.17 inches
③	**Change Bar (F9)	Ruling Box Around	Width:	Custom
			Height of Rule 1:	1.98 fractional points
			Custom Indent:	−6 fractional points
			Custom Width:	1.98 fractional points
④	Chapter # (F6)	Spacing	Above:	09,00 picas & points
			Below:	06,00 picas & points

Table B.2: &BOOK-P2—Formatting Features (continued)

FIGURE REFERENCE	TAG NAME AND FUNCTION KEY	PARAGRAPH MENU COMMAND	SETTING	
⑤	Chapter Title (F5)	Spacing	Above & Below:	03,00 picas & points
⑥	†Firstpar (F1)	Special Effects	Special Effect:	Big First Char
			Space for Big First Char:	Custom, 2 lines
⑦	Major heading (F2)	Spacing	Above:	01,00 picas & points
			Below:	00,11 picas & points
		Ruling Line Below	Width:	Column
			Height of Rule 1:	1.02 fractional points
⑧	Minor heading (F3)	Spacing	Above:	01,00 picas & points
	‡Page Break (F8)	Breaks	Page Break:	After

* We increased the Indent After Bullet to 1 pica (see Chapter 12).
** We applied this tag to the last paragraph.
† We shifted the dropped capital up 3 points (as Chapter 12).
‡ Causes the next paragraph to begin on a new page.

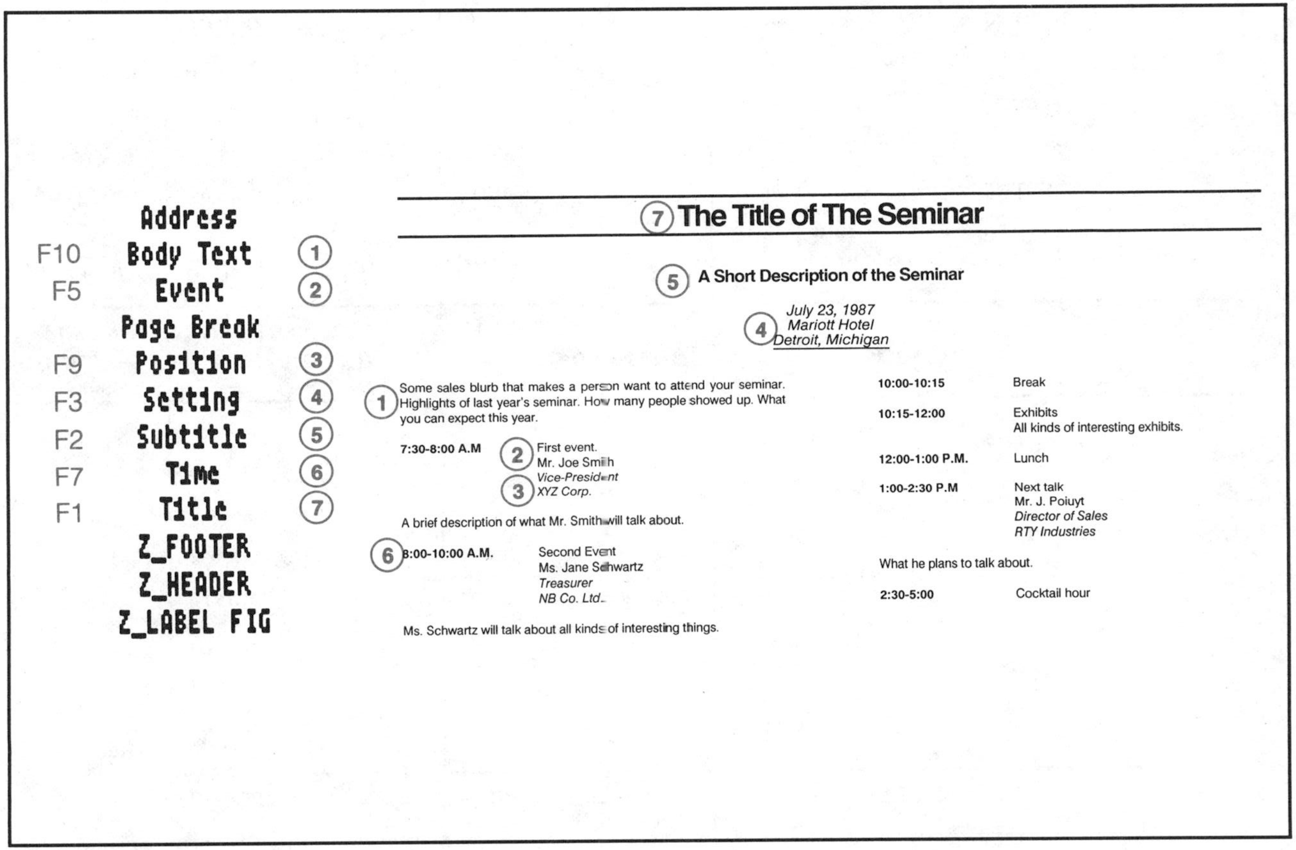

	Address	
F10	Body Text	1
F5	Event	2
	Page Break	
F9	Position	3
F3	Setting	4
F2	Subtitle	5
F7	Time	6
F1	Title	7
	Z_FOOTER	
	Z_HEADER	
	Z_LABEL FIG	

(7) The Title of The Seminar

(5) A Short Description of the Seminar

(4) *July 23, 1987*
Mariott Hotel
Detroit, Michigan

(1) Some sales blurb that makes a person want to attend your seminar. Highlights of last year's seminar. How many people showed up. What you can expect this year.

7:30-8:00 A.M (2) First event.
Mr. Joe Smith
Vice-President
(3) *XYZ Corp.*

A brief description of what Mr. Smith will talk about.

(6) **8:00-10:00 A.M.** Second Event
Ms. Jane Schwartz
Treasurer
NB Co. Ltd.

Ms. Schwartz will talk about all kinds of interesting things.

10:00-10:15 Break

10:15-12:00 Exhibits
All kinds of interesting exhibits.

12:00-1:00 P.M. Lunch

1:00-2:30 P.M Next talk
Mr. J. Poiuyt
Director of Sales
RTY Industries

What he plans to talk about.

2:30-5:00 Cocktail hour

Figure B.3: &BRO-L2 sample page

Table B.3: &BRO-L2

Menu	Command	Setting	
Chapter	Page Size & Layout	Orientation:	Landscape
		Paper Type & Dimension:	Letter, 8.5 × 11 in.
		Sides:	Single
Frame	Margins & Columns	# of Columns:	2
		Column Widths:	4.25 in.
		Margins:	Top: 1.5'' Bottom: 1'' Left: .75'' Right: .75''

Figure Reference	Tag Name and Function Key	Paragraph Menu Command	Setting	
①	Body Text (F10)	Spacing	Above & Below:	01,00 picas & points
			Inter-Line:	01,00 picas & points
②	*Event (F5)	Font	Style:	N-Italic
		Spacing	In From Left:	1.5''
		Breaks	Line Break:	After
	Page Break (F8)	Breaks	Page Break:	After
③	Position (F9)	Font	Style:	N-Italic
		Spacing	In From Left:	1.5''
		Breaks	Line Break:	Before

Table B.3: &BRO-L2 (continued)

FIGURE REFERENCE	TAG NAME AND FUNCTION KEY	PARAGRAPH MENU COMMAND	SETTING	
④	Setting (F3)	Font	Style:	N-Italic
		Alignment	Horz Alignment:	Center
		Ruling Line Below	Width: Height of Rule 1:	Text 1.02 fractional points
⑤	Subtitle (F2)	Alignment	Horz Alignment: Overall Width:	Center Frame-Wide
⑥	**Time (F7)	Breaks	Line Break:	Before
⑦	Title (F1)	Alignment	Horz Alignment:	Center
			Overall Width:	Frame-Wide
		Ruling Line Above/Below	Width: Height of Rule 1:	Column 1.98 fractional points

* Since Event text has no break set before it, it stays on the same line as text formatted with the Time tag.
** The Time tag has no break after it, so that text following it stays on the same line.

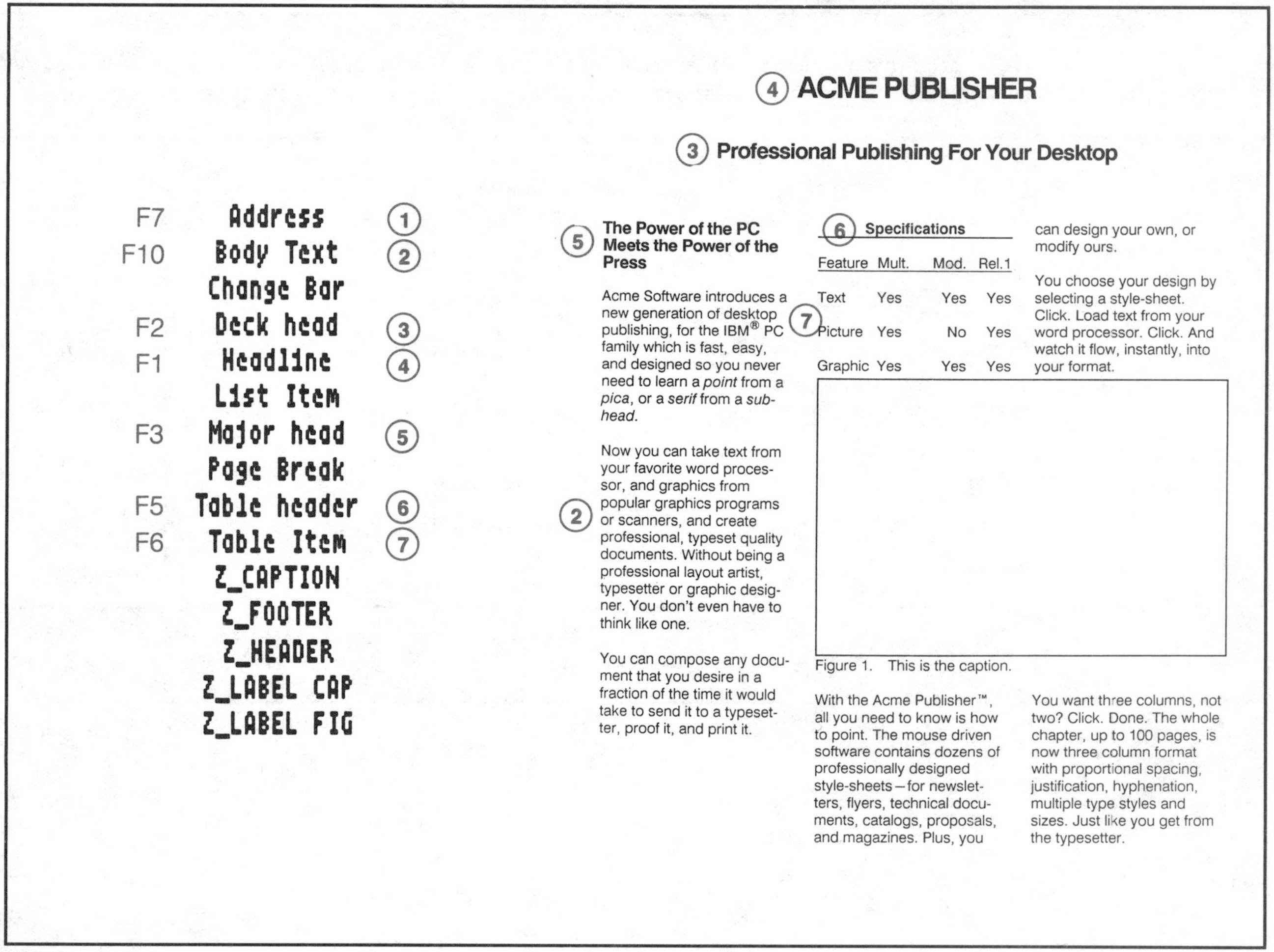

F7	Address	(1)
F10	Body Text	(2)
	Change Bar	
F2	Deck head	(3)
F1	Headline	(4)
	List Item	
F3	Major head	(5)
	Page Break	
F5	Table header	(6)
F6	Table Item	(7)
	Z_CAPTION	
	Z_FOOTER	
	Z_HEADER	
	Z_LABEL CAP	
	Z_LABEL FIG	

(4) ACME PUBLISHER

(3) Professional Publishing For Your Desktop

(5) The Power of the PC Meets the Power of the Press

Acme Software introduces a new generation of desktop publishing, for the IBM® PC family which is fast, easy, and designed so you never need to learn a *point* from a *pica*, or a *serif* from a *subhead.*

(2) Now you can take text from your favorite word processor, and graphics from popular graphics programs or scanners, and create professional, typeset quality documents. Without being a professional layout artist, typesetter or graphic designer. You don't even have to think like one.

You can compose any document that you desire in a fraction of the time it would take to send it to a typesetter, proof it, and print it.

(6) Specifications

Feature	Mult.	Mod.	Rel.1
Text	Yes	Yes	Yes
(7) Picture	Yes	No	Yes
Graphic	Yes	Yes	Yes

Figure 1. This is the caption.

With the Acme Publisher™, all you need to know is how to point. The mouse driven software contains dozens of professionally designed style-sheets – for newsletters, flyers, technical documents, catalogs, proposals, and magazines. Plus, you can design your own, or modify ours.

You choose your design by selecting a style-sheet. Click. Load text from your word processor. Click. And watch it flow, instantly, into your format.

You want three columns, not two? Click. Done. The whole chapter, up to 100 pages, is now three column format with proportional spacing, justification, hyphenation, multiple type styles and sizes. Just like you get from the typesetter.

Figure B.4: &BRO-P3 sample pages

Key	Tag	No.
F7	Address	1
F10	Body Text	2
	Change Bar	
F2	Deck head	3
F1	Headline	4
	List Item	
F3	Major head	5
	Page Break	
F5	Table header	6
F6	Table Item	7
	Z_CAPTION	
	Z_FOOTER	
	Z_HEADER	
	Z_LABEL CAP	
	Z_LABEL FIG	

Chapters can be chained together to form documents as large as your computer hard disk can hold.

Now, add a picture. Move it from graphics programs, such as Autocad™ or Lotus 1-2-3®, or enter it via a scanner. Add a border. Play with its width. You're guided by interactive, easy to understand, drop down menus every step of the way.

(1) Acme Software
125 Main St.
Maintown, CA 90345
(408) 555-1212

Figure B.4: &BRO-P3 sample pages (continued)

Table B.4: &BRO-P3

MENU	COMMAND	SETTING	
Chapter	Page Size & Layout	Orientation:	Portrait
		Paper Type & Dimension:	Letter, 8.5 × 11 in.
		Sides:	Double
Frame	Margins & Columns	# of Columns:	3
		Column Widths:	2.17 in.
		Margins:	Top: .78'' Bottom: .83'' Left: .75'' Right: .75''

FIGURE REFERENCE	TAG NAME AND FUNCTION KEY	PARAGRAPH MENU COMMAND	SETTING	
②	Body Text (F10)	Alignment	Horz Alignment:	Left
		Spacing	Above & Below:	01,02 picas & points
			Inter-Line:	01,02 picas & points
①	Address (F7)	Alignment	Horz Alignment:	Center
③	Deck head (F2)	Alignment	Horz Alignment:	Center
			Overall Width:	Frame-Wide
		Spacing	Above:	01,02 picas & points
			Below:	03,06 picas & points
④	Headline (F1)	Alignment	Horz Alignment:	Center
			Overall Width:	Frame-Wide
		Spacing	Above:	03,06 picas & points

Table B.4: &BRO-P3 (continued)

FIGURE REFERENCE	TAG NAME AND FUNCTION KEY	PARAGRAPH MENU COMMAND	SETTING	
⑤	Major head (F3)	Spacing	Above & Below:	01,02 picas & points
	Page Break (F8)	Breaks	Page Break:	After
⑥	Table header (F5)	Alignment	Horz Alignment:	Center
		Ruling Line Below	Width: Height of Rule 1:	Margin 1.02 fractional points
⑦	*Table Item (F6)	Tab Settings	Tab Number 1: Tab Number 2: Tab Number 3:	Left, 0.67'' Right, 1.67'' Right, 2.17''

* The tab settings are discussed in Chapter 8.

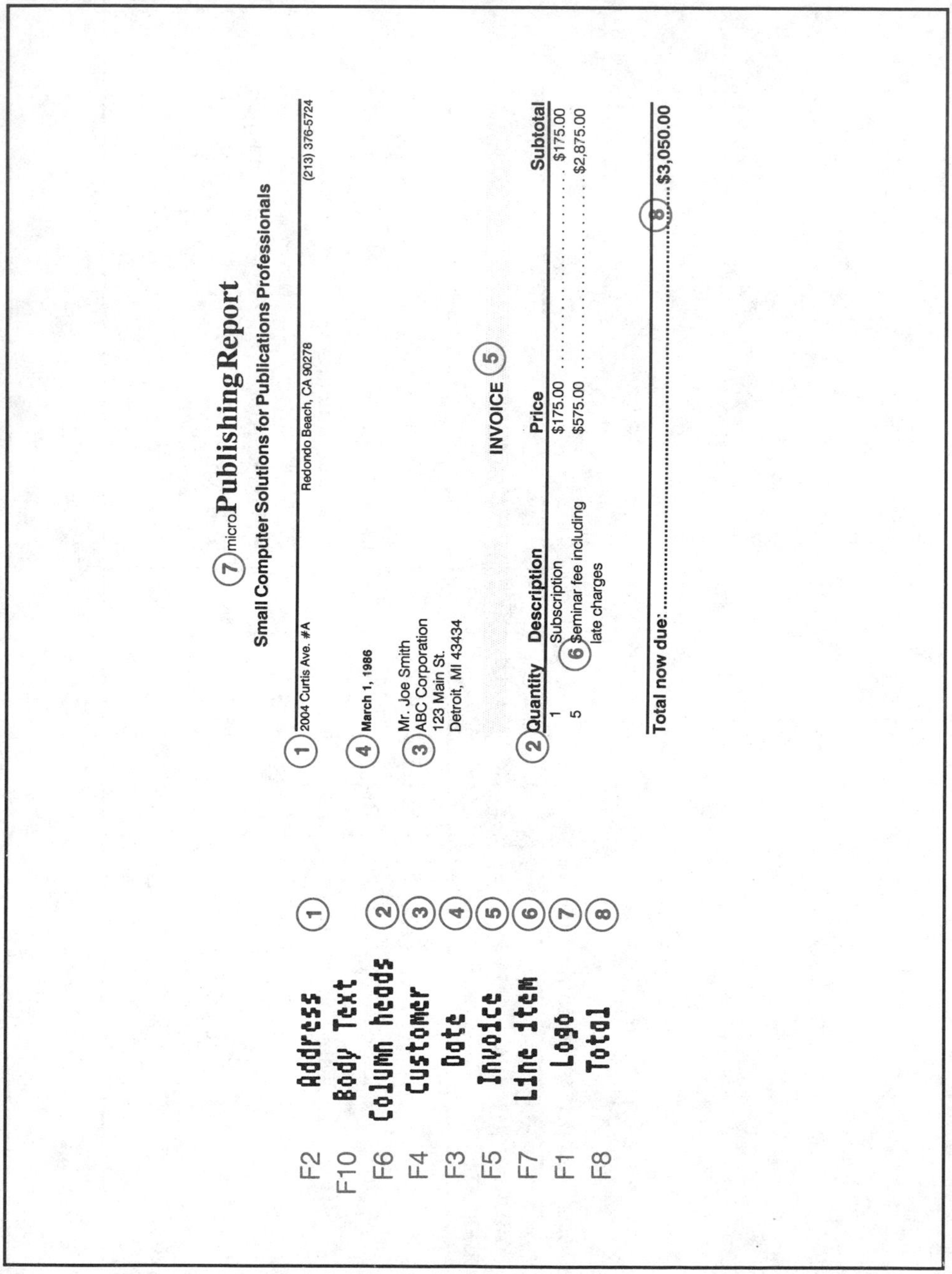

F2	Address	1
F10	Body Text	
F6	Column heads	2
F4	Customer	3
F3	Date	4
F5	Invoice	5
F7	Line item	6
F1	Logo	7
F8	Total	8

(7) micro**Publishing Report**

Small Computer Solutions for Publications Professionals

(1) 2004 Curtis Ave. #A — Redondo Beach, CA 90278 — (213) 376-5724

(4) **March 1, 1986**

(3) Mr. Joe Smith
ABC Corporation
123 Main St.
Detroit, MI 43434

INVOICE (5)

(2) Quantity	Description	Price	Subtotal
1	Subscription	$175.00	$175.00
5	(6) Seminar fee including late charges	$575.00	$2,875.00

Total now due: .... (8) $3,050.00

Figure B.5: &INV-P1 sample page

Table B.5: &INV-P1

Menu	Command	Setting	
Chapter	Page Size & Layout	Orientation:	Portrait
		Paper Type & Dimension:	Letter, 8.5 × 11 in.
		Sides:	Single
Frame	Margins & Columns	# of Columns:	1
		Column Width:	7''
		Margins:	Top: 1'' Bottom: .5'' Left: .75'' Right: .75''

Figure Reference	Tag Name and Function Key	Paragraph Menu Command	Setting	
	Body Text (F10)	Alignment	Horz Alignment:	Left
		Spacing	Inter-Line:	01,00 picas & points
①	Address (F2)	Tab Settings	Tab Number 1: Tab Number 2:	Center, 3.5'' Right, 7''
②	Column heads (F6)	Tab Settings	Tab Number 1: Tab Number 2: Tab Number 3: Tab Number 4:	Left, 1'' Left, 3.33'' Right, 7'' Decimal, 6.67''
⑤	*Invoice (F5)	Ruling Line Above	Pattern: Height of Rule 1: Space Below Rule 3:	1 18 fractional points – 18 fractional points

Table B.5: &INV-P1 (continued)

FIGURE REFERENCE	TAG NAME AND FUNCTION KEY	PARAGRAPH MENU COMMAND	SETTING	
⑥	Line item (F7)	Tab Settings	Tab Number 1: Tab Number 2: Tab Number 3: Tab Number 4:	Left, 1'' Left, 3.33'' Right, 6.7'' Decimal, 6.7''
⑦	**Logo (F1)	Alignment	Horz Alignment: Overall Width:	Center Frame-Wide
⑧	Total (F8)	Tab Settings	Tab Number 1: Tab Display: Leader Char:	Decimal, 6.7 in. Shown as Leader Char ...

* See Chapter 12 for a discussion of shaded text, like that of the word *Invoice.*
** Text attributes change the font sizes and lower the bottom line of text in the sample document.

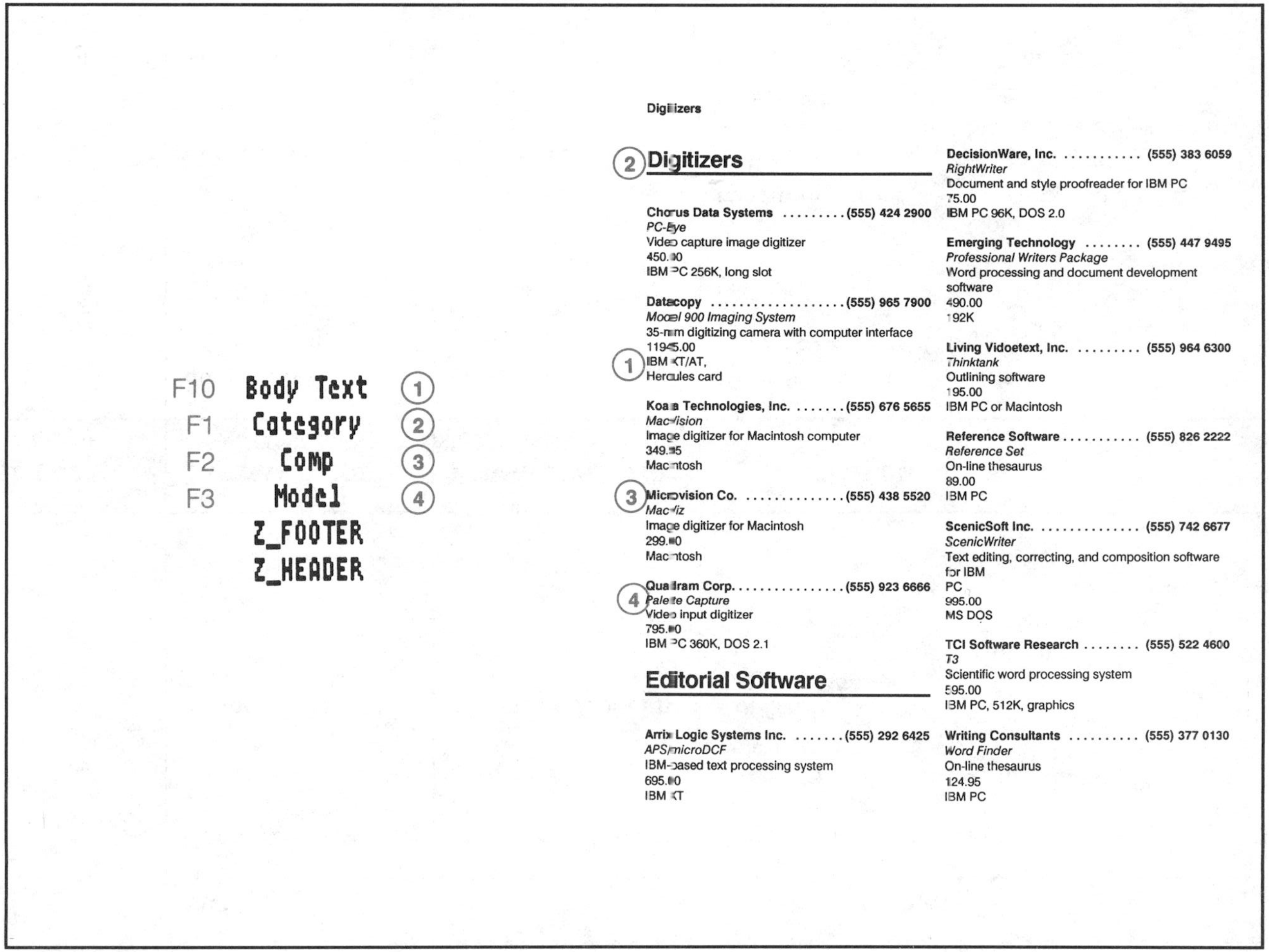

F10 Body Text ①
F1 Category ②
F2 Comp ③
F3 Model ④
Z_FOOTER
Z_HEADER

Digitizers

② Digitizers

Chorus Data Systems ....(555) 424 2900
PC-Eye
Video capture image digitizer
450.00
IBM PC 256K, long slot

Datacopy ....(555) 965 7900
Model 900 Imaging System
35-mm digitizing camera with computer interface
11945.00
① IBM XT/AT,
Hercules card

Koala Technologies, Inc. ....(555) 676 5655
MacVision
Image digitizer for Macintosh computer
349.95
Macintosh

③ **Microvision Co.** ....(555) 438 5520
MacViz
Image digitizer for Macintosh
299.00
Macintosh

④ **Quadram Corp.** ....(555) 923 6666
Palette Capture
Video input digitizer
795.00
IBM PC 360K, DOS 2.1

Editorial Software

Arrix Logic Systems Inc. ....(555) 292 6425
APS/microDCF
IBM-based text processing system
695.00
IBM XT

DecisionWare, Inc. .... (555) 383 6059
RightWriter
Document and style proofreader for IBM PC
75.00
IBM PC 96K, DOS 2.0

Emerging Technology .... (555) 447 9495
Professional Writers Package
Word processing and document development software
490.00
192K

Living Videotext, Inc. .... (555) 964 6300
Thinktank
Outlining software
195.00
IBM PC or Macintosh

Reference Software .... (555) 826 2222
Reference Set
On-line thesaurus
89.00
IBM PC

ScenicSoft Inc. .... (555) 742 6677
ScenicWriter
Text editing, correcting, and composition software for IBM
PC
995.00
MS DOS

TCI Software Research .... (555) 522 4600
T3
Scientific word processing system
595.00
IBM PC, 512K, graphics

Writing Consultants .... (555) 377 0130
Word Finder
On-line thesaurus
124.95
IBM PC

Figure B.6: &LSTG-P2 sample page

Table B.6: &LSTG-P2

Menu	Command	Setting	
Chapter	Page Size & Layout	Orientation:	Portrait
		Paper Type & Dimension:	Letter, 8.5 × 11 in.
		Sides:	Double
Frame	Margins & Columns	# of Columns:	2
		Column Widths:	3.17''
		Margins:	Top: .83''
			Bottom: .83''
			Left: 1''
			Right: 1''

Figure Reference	Tag Name and Function Key	Paragraph Menu Command	Setting	
①	Body Text (F10)	Alignment	Horz Alignment:	Left
		Spacing	Inter-Line:	01,00 picas & points
②	Category (F1)	Spacing	Above:	01,00 picas & points
			Below:	01,10 picas & points
		Ruling Line Below	Width:	Column
			Height of Rule 1:	1.98 fractional points
③	Comp (F2)	Tab Settings	Tab Number 1:	Right, 3.17''
			Tab Display:	Shown as Leader Char
			Leader Char:	...
④	Model (F3)	Font	Style:	N-Italic

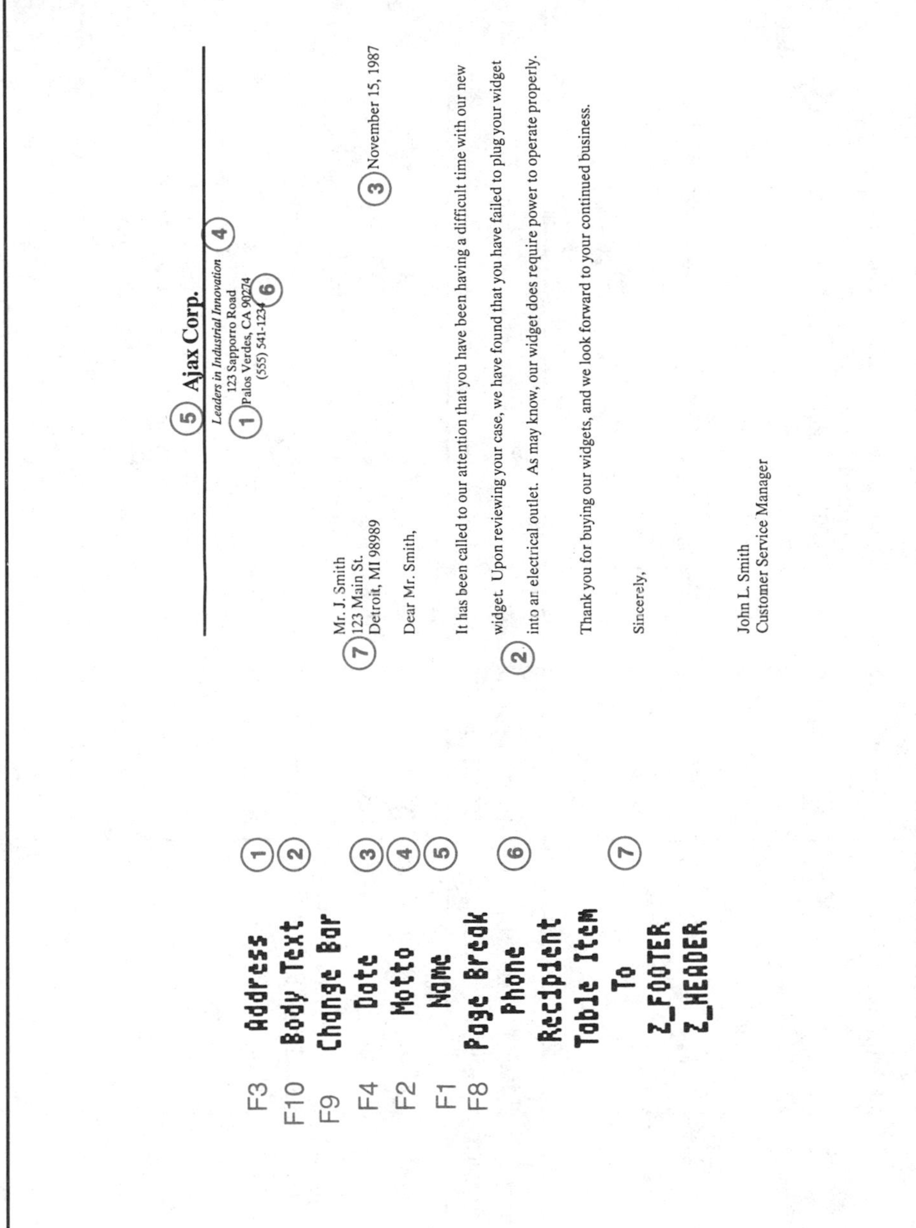

Figure B.7: <R1-P1 sample page

Table B.7: <R-P1

MENU	COMMAND	SETTING	
Chapter	Page Size & Layout	Orientation:	Portrait
		Paper Type & Dimension:	Letter, 8.5 × 11 in.
		Sides:	Single
Frame	Margins & Columns	# of Columns:	1
		Column Width:	6.5''
		Margins:	Top: .58'' Bottom: .5'' Left: 1'' Right: 1''

FIGURE REFERENCE	TAG NAME AND FUNCTION KEY	PARAGRAPH MENU COMMAND	SETTING	
②	*Body Text (F10)	Alignment	Horz Alignment:	Left
		Spacing	Above & Below:	01,02 picas & points
			Inter-Line:	02,04 picas & points
①	Address (F3)	Alignment	Horz Alignment:	Center
	Change Bar (F9)	Ruling Box Around	Width:	Custom
			Height of Rule 1:	1.02 fractional points
			Custom Indent:	–6 fractional points
			Custom Width:	1.98 fractional points
③	**Date (F4)	Alignment	Horz Alignment:	Right
		Breaks	Line Break:	After
			Next Y Position:	Beside Last Line of Prev Para

Table B.7: <R-P1 (continued)

FIGURE REFERENCE	TAG NAME AND FUNCTION KEY	PARAGRAPH MENU COMMAND	SETTING	
④	Motto (F2)	Alignment	Horz Alignment:	Center
		Font	Style:	N-Italic
⑤	Name (F1)	Alignment	Horz Alignment:	Center
		Ruling Line Below	Width: Height of Rule 1:	Frame 1.98 fractional points
	Page Break (F8)	Breaks	Page Break:	After
⑥	Phone	Alignment	Horz Alignment:	Center
⑦	†To	Spacing	Interline:	01,02 picas & points

* The large value in the Spacing menu's Inter-Line setting creates double spacing.
** These settings allow the date to appear at the right on the line on which the previous paragraph ends.
† Keeps single spacing within the paragraph.

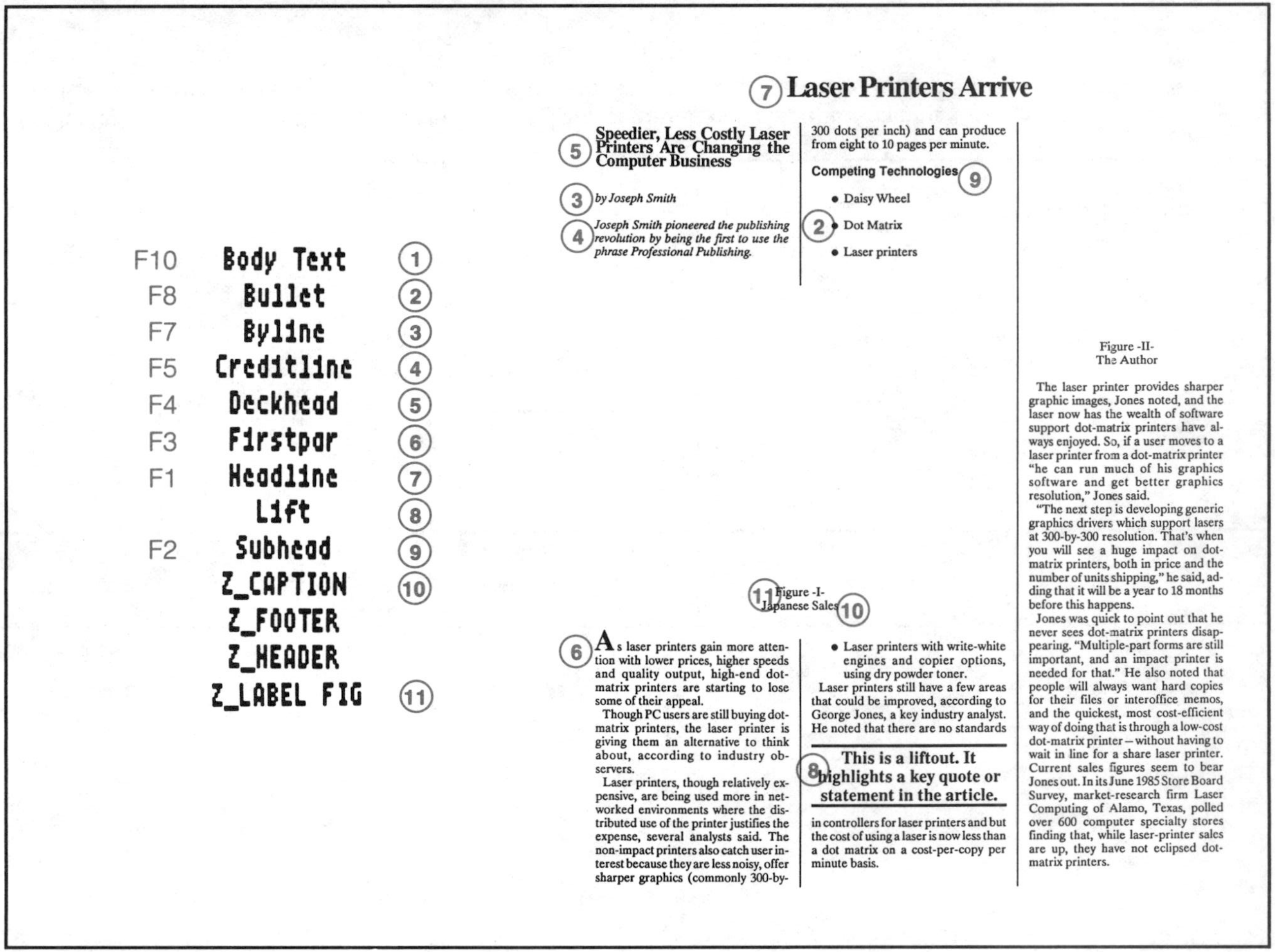

Key	Tag	
F10	Body Text	1
F8	Bullet	2
F7	Byline	3
F5	Creditline	4
F4	Deckhead	5
F3	Firstpar	6
F1	Headline	7
	Lift	8
F2	Subhead	9
	Z_CAPTION	10
	Z_FOOTER	
	Z_HEADER	
	Z_LABEL FIG	11

(7) **Laser Printers Arrive**

(5) **Speedier, Less Costly Laser Printers Are Changing the Computer Business**

(3) *by Joseph Smith*

(4) *Joseph Smith pioneered the publishing revolution by being the first to use the phrase Professional Publishing.*

(11) Figure -I-
Japanese Sales (10)

(6) As laser printers gain more attention with lower prices, higher speeds and quality output, high-end dot-matrix printers are starting to lose some of their appeal.

Though PC users are still buying dot-matrix printers, the laser printer is giving them an alternative to think about, according to industry observers.

Laser printers, though relatively expensive, are being used more in networked environments where the distributed use of the printer justifies the expense, several analysts said. The non-impact printers also catch user interest because they are less noisy, offer sharper graphics (commonly 300-by-300 dots per inch) and can produce from eight to 10 pages per minute.

Competing Technologies (9)

- Daisy Wheel
- (2) Dot Matrix
- Laser printers
- Laser printers with write-white engines and copier options, using dry powder toner.

Laser printers still have a few areas that could be improved, according to George Jones, a key industry analyst. He noted that there are no standards

(8) **This is a liftout. It highlights a key quote or statement in the article.**

in controllers for laser printers and but the cost of using a laser is now less than a dot matrix on a cost-per-copy per minute basis.

Figure -II-
The Author

The laser printer provides sharper graphic images, Jones noted, and the laser now has the wealth of software support dot-matrix printers have always enjoyed. So, if a user moves to a laser printer from a dot-matrix printer "he can run much of his graphics software and get better graphics resolution," Jones said.

"The next step is developing generic graphics drivers which support lasers at 300-by-300 resolution. That's when you will see a huge impact on dot-matrix printers, both in price and the number of units shipping," he said, adding that it will be a year to 18 months before this happens.

Jones was quick to point out that he never sees dot-matrix printers disappearing. "Multiple-part forms are still important, and an impact printer is needed for that." He also noted that people will always want hard copies for their files or interoffice memos, and the quickest, most cost-efficient way of doing that is through a low-cost dot-matrix printer—without having to wait in line for a share laser printer. Current sales figures seem to bear Jones out. In its June 1985 Store Board Survey, market-research firm Laser Computing of Alamo, Texas, polled over 600 computer specialty stores finding that, while laser-printer sales are up, they have not eclipsed dot-matrix printers.

Figure B.8: &MAG-P3 sample pages

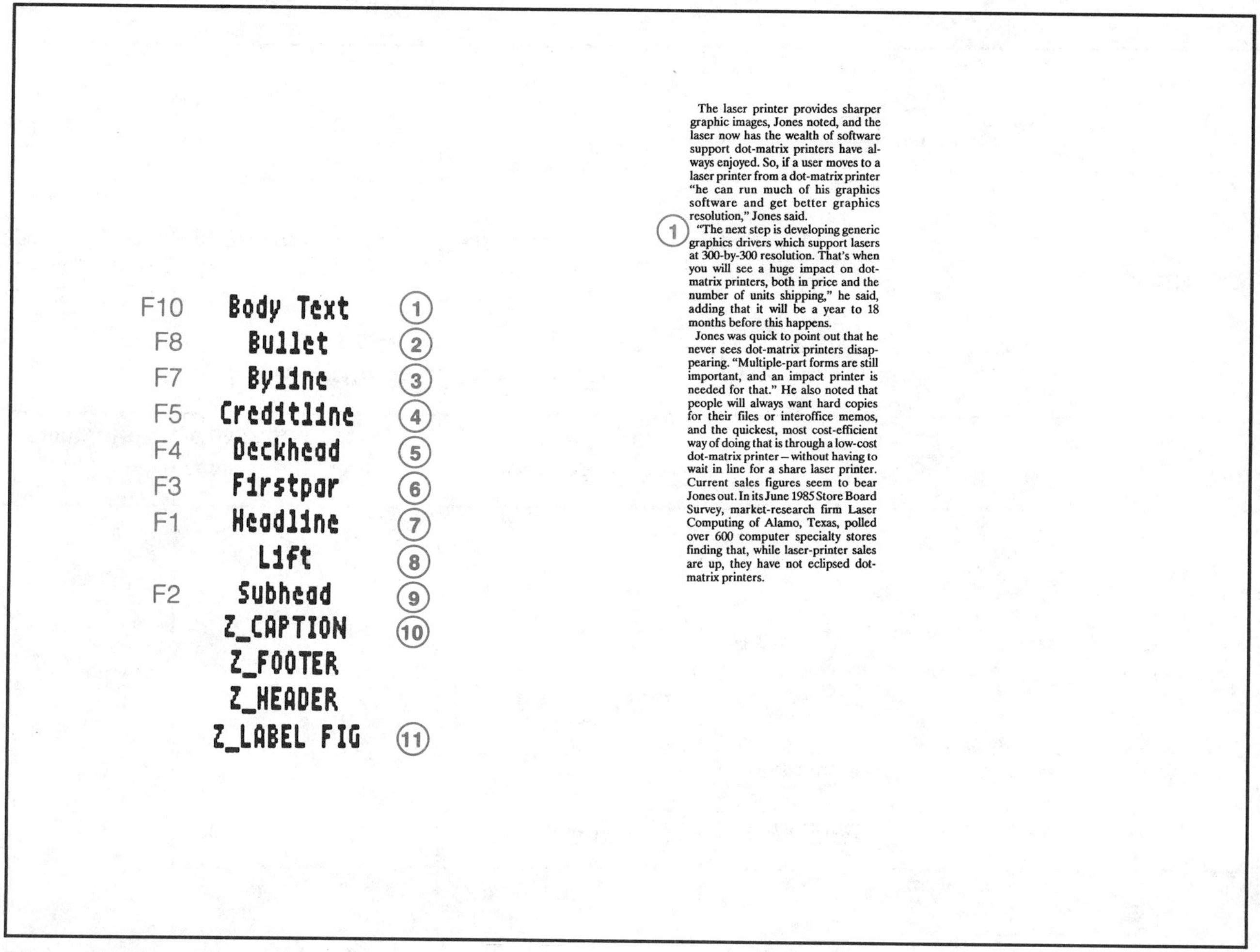

The laser printer provides sharper graphic images, Jones noted, and the laser now has the wealth of software support dot-matrix printers have always enjoyed. So, if a user moves to a laser printer from a dot-matrix printer "he can run much of his graphics software and get better graphics resolution," Jones said.

(1) "The next step is developing generic graphics drivers which support lasers at 300-by-300 resolution. That's when you will see a huge impact on dot-matrix printers, both in price and the number of units shipping," he said, adding that it will be a year to 18 months before this happens.

Jones was quick to point out that he never sees dot-matrix printers disappearing. "Multiple-part forms are still important, and an impact printer is needed for that." He also noted that people will always want hard copies for their files or interoffice memos, and the quickest, most cost-efficient way of doing that is through a low-cost dot-matrix printer – without having to wait in line for a share laser printer. Current sales figures seem to bear Jones out. In its June 1985 Store Board Survey, market-research firm Laser Computing of Alamo, Texas, polled over 600 computer specialty stores finding that, while laser-printer sales are up, they have not eclipsed dot-matrix printers.

F10	Body Text	(1)
F8	Bullet	(2)
F7	Byline	(3)
F5	Creditline	(4)
F4	Deckhead	(5)
F3	Firstpar	(6)
F1	Headline	(7)
	Lift	(8)
F2	Subhead	(9)
	Z_CAPTION	(10)
	Z_FOOTER	
	Z_HEADER	
	Z_LABEL FIG	(11)

Figure B.8: &MAG-P3 sample pages (continued)

Table B.8: &MAG-P3

Menu	Command	Setting	
Chapter	Page Size & Layout	Orientation: Paper Type & Dimension: Sides:	Portrait Letter, 8.5 × 11 in. Double
Frame	Margins & Columns	# of Columns: Column Widths: Margins:	3 2.17'' Top: .75'' Bottom: .75'' Left: .75'' Right: .75''

Figure Reference	Tag Name and Function Key	Paragraph Menu Command	Setting	
①	Body Text (F10)	Alignment	Horz Alignment: First Line: Indent Width:	Justified Indent .08''
		Spacing	Inter-Line:	00,11 picas & points
②	Bullet (F8)	Alignment	First Line: Indent Width:	Indent .19''
		Special Effects	Special Effect: Indent After Bullet:	Bullet .17''
③	Byline (F7)	Font	Style:	N-Italic

Table B.8: &MAG-P3 (continued)

FIGURE REFERENCE	TAG NAME AND FUNCTION KEY	PARAGRAPH MENU COMMAND	SETTING	
④	Creditline (F5)	Font	Style:	N-Italic
⑥	Firstpar (F3)	Special Effects	Special Effect:	Big First Char
			Space for Big First Char:	1 line
⑦	Headline (F1)	Alignment	Horz Alignment:	Center
			Overall Width:	Frame-Wide
⑧	Lift	Ruling Line Above & Below	Width:	Frame
			Height of Rule 1:	1.98 fractional points

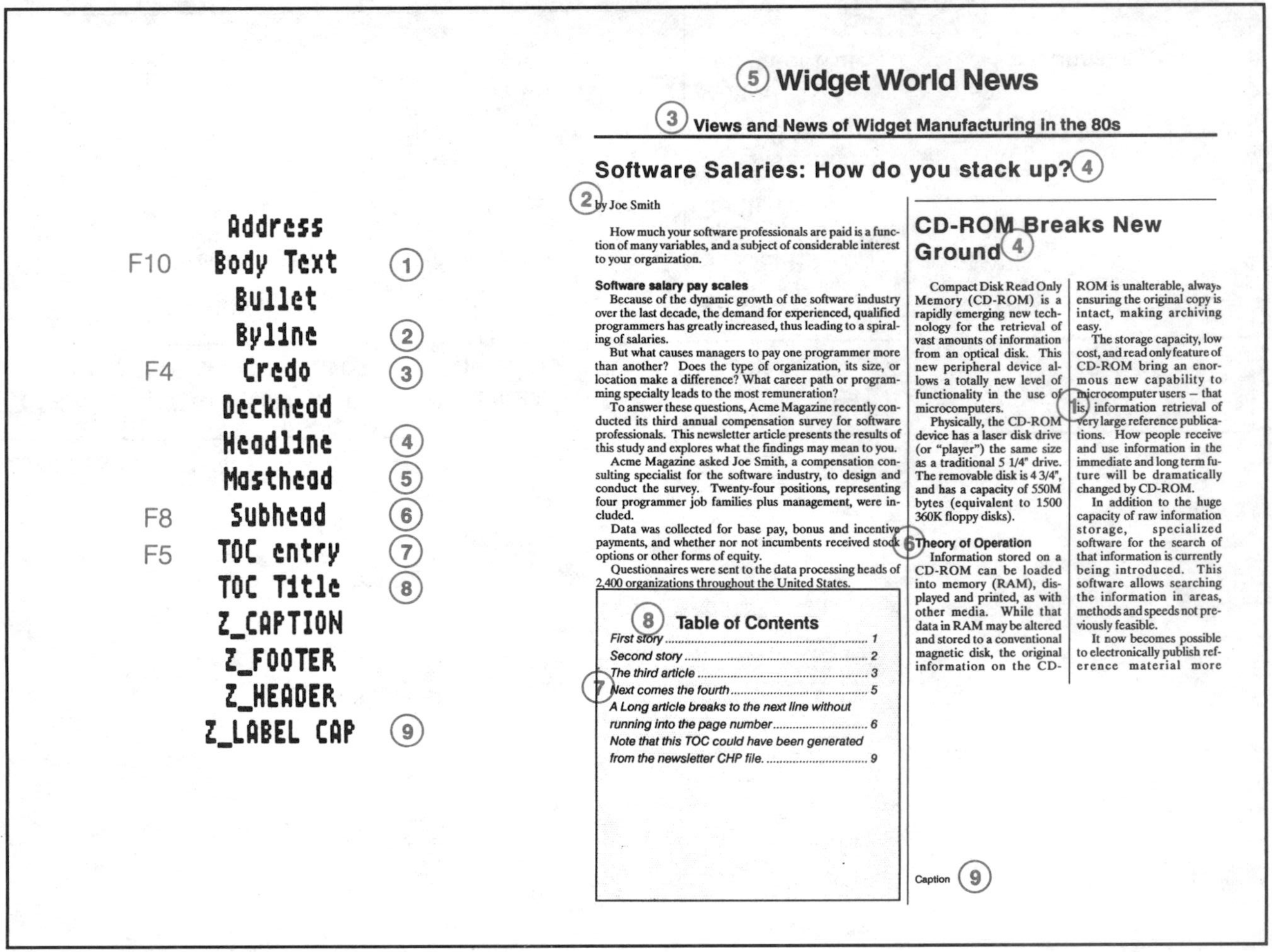
Address
F10 Body Text 1
Bullet
Byline 2
F4 Credo 3
Deckhead
Headline 4
Masthead 5
F8 Subhead 6
F5 TOC entry 7
TOC Title 8
Z_CAPTION
Z_FOOTER
Z_HEADER
Z_LABEL CAP 9
5 Widget World News
3 Views and News of Widget Manufacturing in the 80s
Software Salaries: How do you stack up? 4
2 by Joe Smith
How much your software professionals are paid is a function of many variables, and a subject of considerable interest to your organization.
Software salary pay scales
Because of the dynamic growth of the software industry over the last decade, the demand for experienced, qualified programmers has greatly increased, thus leading to a spiraling of salaries.
But what causes managers to pay one programmer more than another? Does the type of organization, its size, or location make a difference? What career path or programming specialty leads to the most remuneration?
To answer these questions, Acme Magazine recently conducted its third annual compensation survey for software professionals. This newsletter article presents the results of this study and explores what the findings may mean to you.
Acme Magazine asked Joe Smith, a compensation consulting specialist for the software industry, to design and conduct the survey. Twenty-four positions, representing four programmer job families plus management, were included.
Data was collected for base pay, bonus and incentive payments, and whether nor not incumbents received stock options or other forms of equity.
Questionnaires were sent to the data processing heads of 2,400 organizations throughout the United States.
8 Table of Contents
First story 1
Second story 2
The third article 3
7 Next comes the fourth 5
A Long article breaks to the next line without running into the page number 6
Note that this TOC could have been generated from the newsletter CHP file. 9
CD-ROM Breaks New Ground 4
Compact Disk Read Only Memory (CD-ROM) is a rapidly emerging new technology for the retrieval of vast amounts of information from an optical disk. This new peripheral device allows a totally new level of functionality in the use of microcomputers.
Physically, the CD-ROM device has a laser disk drive (or "player") the same size as a traditional 5 1/4" drive. The removable disk is 4 3/4", and has a capacity of 550M bytes (equivalent to 1500 360K floppy disks).
6 Theory of Operation
Information stored on a CD-ROM can be loaded into memory (RAM), displayed and printed, as with other media. While that data in RAM may be altered and stored to a conventional magnetic disk, the original information on the CD-ROM is unalterable, always ensuring the original copy is intact, making archiving easy.
The storage capacity, low cost, and read only feature of CD-ROM bring an enormous new capability to microcomputer users – that 1 is, information retrieval of very large reference publications. How people receive and use information in the immediate and long term future will be dramatically changed by CD-ROM.
In addition to the huge capacity of raw information storage, specialized software for the search of that information is currently being introduced. This software allows searching the information in areas, methods and speeds not previously feasible.
It now becomes possible to electronically publish reference material more
Caption 9

Figure B.9: &NEWS-P2 sample page

Table B.9: &NEWS-P2

	Menu	Command	Setting	
	Chapter	Page Size & Layout	Orientation: Paper Type & Dimension: Sides:	Portrait Letter, 8.5 × 11 in. Double
	Frame	Margins & Columns	# of Columns: Column Widths: Margins:	2 3.42'' Top: .75'' Bottom: .75'' Left: .75'' Right: .75''
Figure Reference	**Tag Name and Function Key**	**Paragraph Menu Command**	**Setting**	
①	Body Text (F10)	Alignment	Horz Alignment: First Line: Indent Width:	Justified Indent .17''
		Spacing	Above & Below: Inter-Line:	0 00,11 picas & points
③	Credo (F4)	Alignment	Horz Alignment:	Center
		Ruling Line Below	Width: Height of Rule 1:	Column 1.98 fractional points

Table B.9: &NEWS-P2 (continued)

FIGURE REFERENCE	TAG NAME AND FUNCTION KEY	PARAGRAPH MENU COMMAND	SETTING	
④	Headline	Alignment	Overall Width:	Frame-wide
⑤	Masthead	Alignment	Horz Alignment:	Center
⑦	TOC Title	Alignment	Horz Alignment:	Center
⑧	TOC entry (F5)	Spacing	In From Left & Right:	.17''
		Tab Settings	Tab Number 1:	Right
			Tab Display:	Shown as Leader Char
			Tab Location:	3.17''
			Leader Char:	...

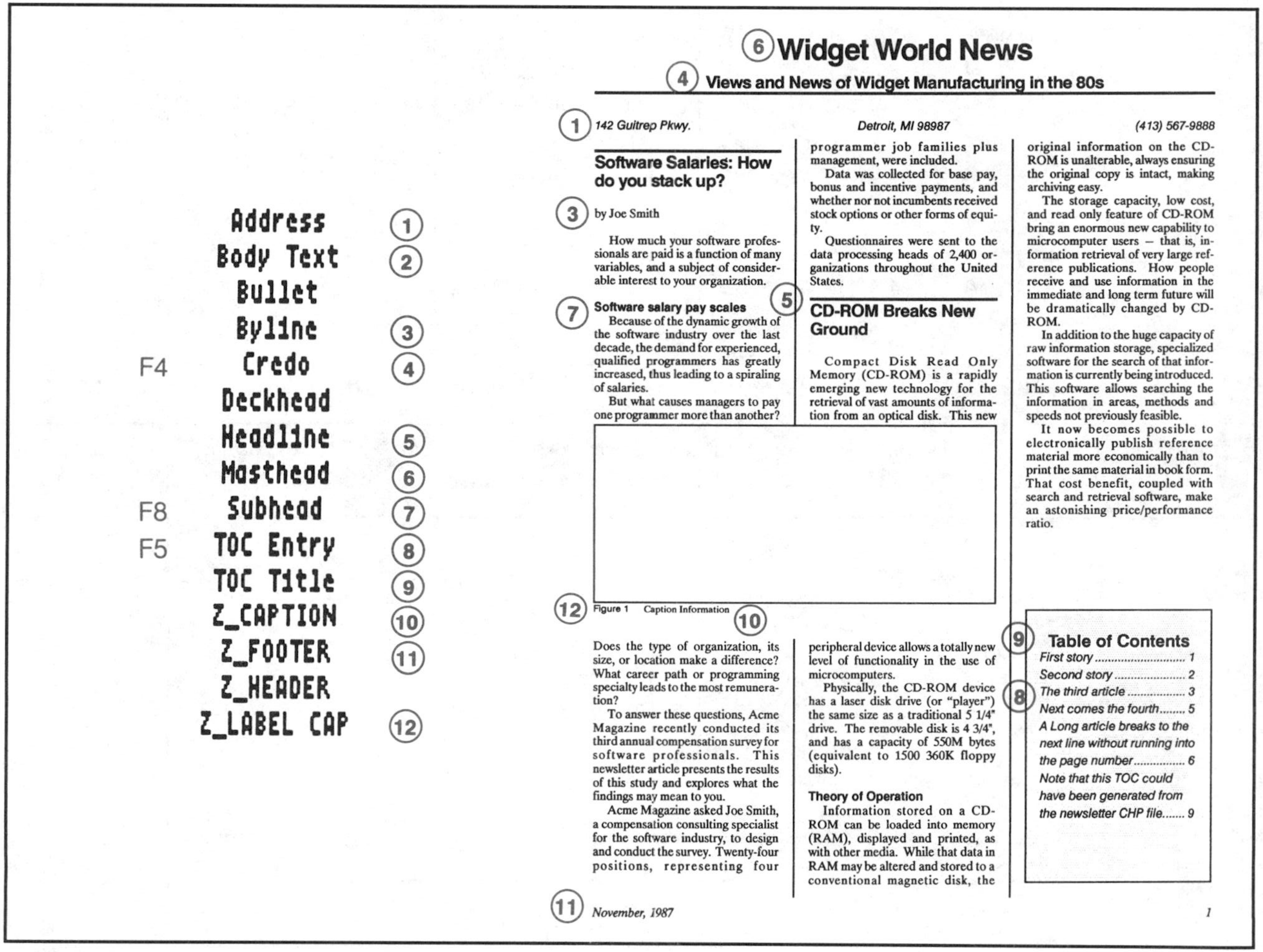

Address (1)
Body Text (2)
Bullet
Byline (3)
F4 Credo (4)
Deckhead
Headline (5)
Masthead (6)
F8 Subhead (7)
F5 TOC Entry (8)
TOC Title (9)
Z_CAPTION (10)
Z_FOOTER (11)
Z_HEADER
Z_LABEL CAP (12)

(6) **Widget World News**

(4) **Views and News of Widget Manufacturing in the 80s**

(1) *142 Guitrep Pkwy.* *Detroit, MI 98987* *(413) 567-9888*

Software Salaries: How do you stack up?

(3) by Joe Smith

How much your software professionals are paid is a function of many variables, and a subject of considerable interest to your organization.

(7) **Software salary pay scales**

Because of the dynamic growth of the software industry over the last decade, the demand for experienced, qualified programmers has greatly increased, thus leading to a spiraling of salaries.

But what causes managers to pay one programmer more than another?

(12) Figure 1 Caption Information (10)

Does the type of organization, its size, or location make a difference? What career path or programming specialty leads to the most remuneration?

To answer these questions, Acme Magazine recently conducted its third annual compensation survey for software professionals. This newsletter article presents the results of this study and explores what the findings may mean to you.

Acme Magazine asked Joe Smith, a compensation consulting specialist for the software industry, to design and conduct the survey. Twenty-four positions, representing four programmer job families plus management, were included.

Data was collected for base pay, bonus and incentive payments, and whether nor not incumbents received stock options or other forms of equity.

Questionnaires were sent to the data processing heads of 2,400 organizations throughout the United States.

(5) **CD-ROM Breaks New Ground**

Compact Disk Read Only Memory (CD-ROM) is a rapidly emerging new technology for the retrieval of vast amounts of information from an optical disk. This new peripheral device allows a totally new level of functionality in the use of microcomputers.

Physically, the CD-ROM device has a laser disk drive (or "player") the same size as a traditional 5 1/4" drive. The removable disk is 4 3/4", and has a capacity of 550M bytes (equivalent to 1500 360K floppy disks).

Theory of Operation

Information stored on a CD-ROM can be loaded into memory (RAM), displayed and printed, as with other media. While that data in RAM may be altered and stored to a conventional magnetic disk, the original information on the CD-ROM is unalterable, always ensuring the original copy is intact, making archiving easy.

The storage capacity, low cost, and read only feature of CD-ROM bring an enormous new capability to microcomputer users — that is, information retrieval of very large reference publications. How people receive and use information in the immediate and long term future will be dramatically changed by CD-ROM.

In addition to the huge capacity of raw information storage, specialized software for the search of that information is currently being introduced. This software allows searching the information in areas, methods and speeds not previously feasible.

It now becomes possible to electronically publish reference material more economically than to print the same material in book form. That cost benefit, coupled with search and retrieval software, make an astonishing price/performance ratio.

(9) **Table of Contents**

(11) *November, 1987* 1

Figure B.10: &NEWS-P3 sample page

Table B.10: &NEWS-P3

	Menu	Command	Setting	
	Chapter	Page Size & Layout	Orientation: Paper Type & Dimension: Sides:	Portrait Letter, 8.5 × 11 in. Double
	Frame	Margins & Columns	# of Columns: Column Widths: Margins:	3 2.11'' Top: .76'' Bottom: .76'' Left: 1'' Right: .5''
Figure Reference	**Tag Name and Function Key**	**Paragraph Menu Command**	**Setting**	
②	Body Text (F10)	Alignment	Horz Alignment: First Line: Indent Width:	Justified Indent 01,00 picas & points
		Spacing	Above & Below: Inter-Line:	0 00,11 picas & points
①	Address	Font	Style:	N-Italic
		Tab Settings	Tab Number 1: Tab Number 2:	Center, 3.5'' Right, 7''
④	Credo (F4)	Alignment	Horz Alignment:	Center
		Ruling Line Below	Width: Height of Rule 1:	Column 1.98 fractional points

Table B.10: &NEWS-P3 (continued)

FIGURE REFERENCE	TAG NAME AND FUNCTION KEY	PARAGRAPH MENU COMMAND	SETTING	
⑤	Headline	Alignment	Overall Width:	Column-wide
		Ruling Line Above	Width: Height of Rule 1:	Column 1.98 fractional points
⑥	Masthead	Alignment	Horz Alignment:	Center
⑧	TOC Entry (F5)	Spacing	In From Left & Right:	.17"
		Tab Settings	Tab Number 1: Tab Display: Tab Location: Leader Char:	Right Shown as Leader Char 1.92" ...
⑨	TOC Title	Alignment	Horz Alignment:	Center

F10 Body Text ①
F1 Phone ②
Z_BOXTEXT
Z_FOOTER
Z_HEADER ③

③ **AST Research Inc.** — **Xerox**

AST Research Inc.	(555) 863 1333
Abaton Technology	(555) 905 9399
Addison-Wesley Publishing Co.	(555) 944 3700
Adobe Systems Inc.	(555) 852 0271
Adserve Media Systems, Inc.	(555) 213 5700
Advanced Technologies Int'l	(555) 748 1688
AFIPS	(555) 620 8926
Airus	(555) 684 3000
Allied Linotype	(555) 434 2000
Allotype Typographics	(555) 577 3035
Alpha Software Corp.	(555) 229 2924
AlphaGraphics	(555) 882 4100
Altertext	(555) 426 0009
American Business Press	(555) 661 6360
Amgraf, Inc.	(555) 474 4797
Amrron Data Services	(555) 859 8333
Apple Computer, Inc.	(555) 996 1010
Applied Publishing Technologies	(555) 872 1190
Archtype	(555) 482 2739
Arrix Logic Systems Inc.	(555) 292 6425
Ashton-Tate	(555) 329 8000
① AST Research Inc.	② (555) 863 1333
Autographix	(555) 890 8558
Autologic	(555) 498 9611
Automatic Fulfillment Services	(555) 366 8722
Autospec Inc.	(555) 649 0890
Award Software Inc.	(555) 395 2773
Beach Media Inc.	(555) 226 6726
Bell & Howell Company	(555) 262 1600
BPAA	(555) 661 0222
Business Systems International	(555) 998 7227
Buttonware Inc.	(555) 746 4296
Canon USA Inc., Printer Div.	(555) 488 6700
Capital Equipment Co.	(555) 829 6220
Cauzin Systems, Inc.	(555) 573 0150
Centram Systems West, Inc.	(555) 644 8244
CF Inc.	(555) 829 4990
Chorus Data Systems	(555) 424 2900
Comm Type Interface Typesetting	(555) 938 8973
Composition Technology Intl.	(555) 848 1010
Compugraphic Corp.	(555) 944 6555
CompuNews, Inc.	(555) 826 1110
CompuScan, Inc.	(555) 288 6001
CompuServe	(555) 457 8600
Computer EdiType Systems	(555) 222 8148
Computing Software Services Inc.	(555) 432 6077
Concept Technologies, Inc.	(555) 684 3314
Creative Strategies Resrch Inter	(555) 249 7550
Cybertext Corp.	(555) 822 7079
Data Transforms	(555) 832 1501
Data Change, Inc.	(555) 441 1332
Data Frontiers, Inc.	(555) 467 3125
Data Recording Systems, Inc.	(555) 293 2400
Data Sytems of Connecticut Inc.	(555) 877 5451
Datacopy	(555) 965 7900
Datalogics Inc.	(555) 266 4444
Datamate Co.	(555) 262 7276
Dataquest Inc.	(555) 971 9000
Datek Information Services, Inc.	(555) 893 9130
DayFlo Inc.	(555) 476 3044
DecisionWare, Inc.	(555) 383 6059
Decision Resources	(555) 222 1974
Desktop Graphics	(555) 736 9098
Dest Corporation	(555) 946 7100
Dicomed Corp.	(555) 885 3000
Diconix Inc.	(555) 259 3100
Digital Equipment Corp.	(555) 884 5111
Digital Technology International	(555) 226 2984
Dunn Instruments	(555) 957 1600
Dunn Technology Inc.	(555) 758 9460
Eastman Kodak	(555) 445 6325
Eikonix Corporation	(555) 275 5070
Electronic Information Technology	(555) 227 1447
The Electronic Publisher	(555) 637 7233
Emerging Technology Consultants	(555) 447 9495
Epsilon	(555) 273 0250
Epson America, Inc.	(555) 534 4500
Ericsson Information Systems	(555) 895 3962
Esgraph Incorporated	(555) 524 0377
Expert Technologies	(555) 621 0818
Flint Hills Software	(555) 841 4503
Form Maker Software, Inc.	(555) 633 3676
Frost & Sullivan Inc.	(555) 233 1080
FTL Systems	(555) 487 2142
Fujitsu America Inc.	(555) 946 8777
Future Computing Inc.	(555) 437 2400
General Binding Corporation	(555) 272 3700
Genesys Systems	(555) 564 3636
Genicom Corp.	(555) 949 1188
Genoa Systems Corp.	(555) 945 9720
Gnostic Concepts, Inc.	(555) 854 4672
Graphic Connections	(555) 251 9750
Graphic Arts Technical Foundation	(555) 621 6941
Graham Software Corp.	(555) 359 1024
GSS	(555) 641 2200
Hammermill Papers Group	(555) 456 8811
Hampstead Computer Graphics	(555) 329 5076
Helena Business	(555) 969 1642
Hewlett-Packard	(555) 323 3869
Xerox	(214) 436 2616

Figure B.11: &PHON-P2 sample page

Table B.11: &PHON-P2

MENU	COMMAND	SETTING	
Chapter	Page Size & Layout	Orientation: Paper Type & Dimension: Sides:	Portrait Letter, 8.5 × 11 in. Single
Frame	Margins & Columns	# of Columns: Column Widths: Margins:	2 3.4'' Top: .75'' Bottom: .75'' Left: .75'' Right: .75''

FIGURE REFERENCE	TAG NAME AND FUNCTION KEY	PARAGRAPH MENU COMMAND	SETTING	
①	Body Text (F10)	Alignment	Horz Alignment:	Left
		Spacing	Above & Below: Inter-Line:	0 00,10 picas & points
		Breaks	Line Break:	Before
②	*Phone (F1)	Alignment	Horz Alignment:	Right
		Breaks	Line Break:	After
③	Z_HEADER	Ruling Line Below	Width: Height of Rule 1:	Frame 1.98 fractional points

* Since the Phone tag does not have a line break before, phones appear on the same line as company names.

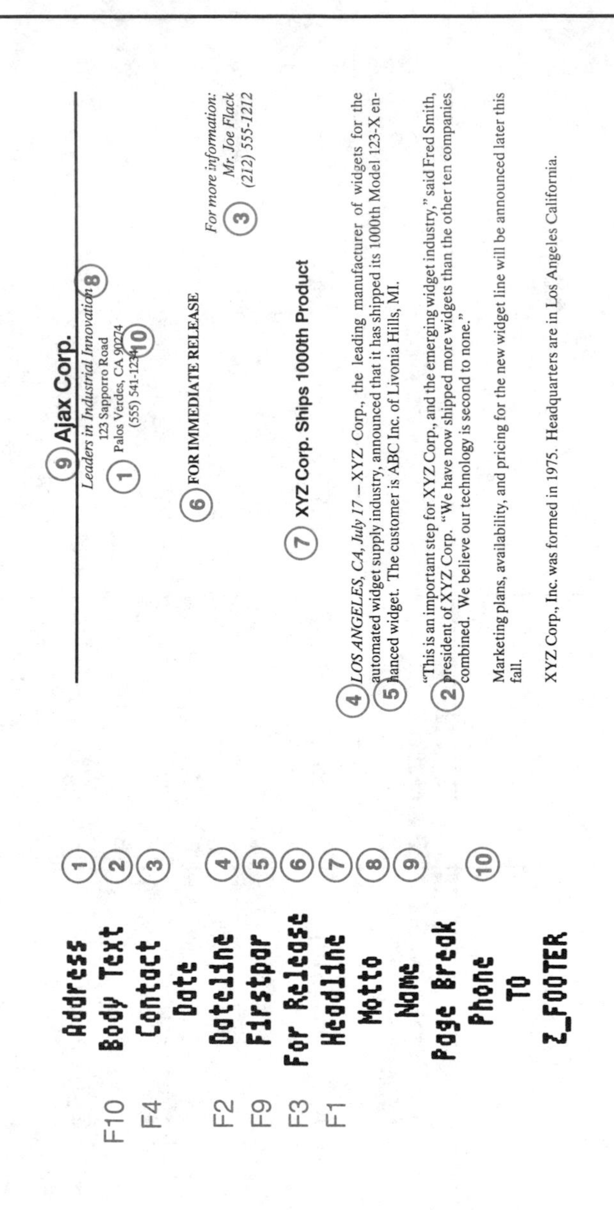

Figure B.12: &PREL-P1 sample page

Table B.12: &PREL-P1

Menu	Command	Setting	
Chapter	Page Size & Layout	Orientation: Paper Type & Dimension: Sides:	Portrait Letter, 8.5 × 11 in. Single
Frame	Margins & Columns	# of Columns: Column Width: Margins:	1 6.5'' Top: .58'' Bottom: .5'' Left: 1'' Right: 1''

Figure Reference	Tag Name and Function Key	Paragraph Menu Command	Setting	
②	Body Text (F10)	Alignment	Horz Alignment:	Justified
		Spacing	Above & Below: Inter-Line:	0 01,02 picas & points
①	Address	Alignment	Horz Alignment:	Center
③	Contact (F4)	Alignment	Horz Alignment:	Right
④	*Dateline (F2)	Font Break	Style: Line Break:	N-Italic Before

Table B.12: &PREL-P1 (continued)

FIGURE REFERENCE	TAG NAME AND FUNCTION KEY	PARAGRAPH MENU COMMAND	SETTING	
⑤	**Firstpar	Alignment	Relative Indent:	On
		Breaks	Line Break:	No
⑥	For Release (F3)	Alignment	Horz Alignment:	Center
⑦	Headline (F1)	Alignment	Horz Alignment:	Center
⑧	Motto	Alignment	Horz Alignment:	Center
		Font	Style:	N-Italic
⑨	Name	Alignment	Horz Alignment:	Center
		Ruling Line Below	Width: Height of Rule 1:	Column 1.98 fractional points
	Page Break (F8)	Breaks	Page Break:	After
⑩	Phone	Alignment	Horz Alignment:	Center

* Allows text with the Firstpar tag to follow on the same line. See Chapter 4.
** No line break and a relative indent causes the text to follow right after Dateline text.

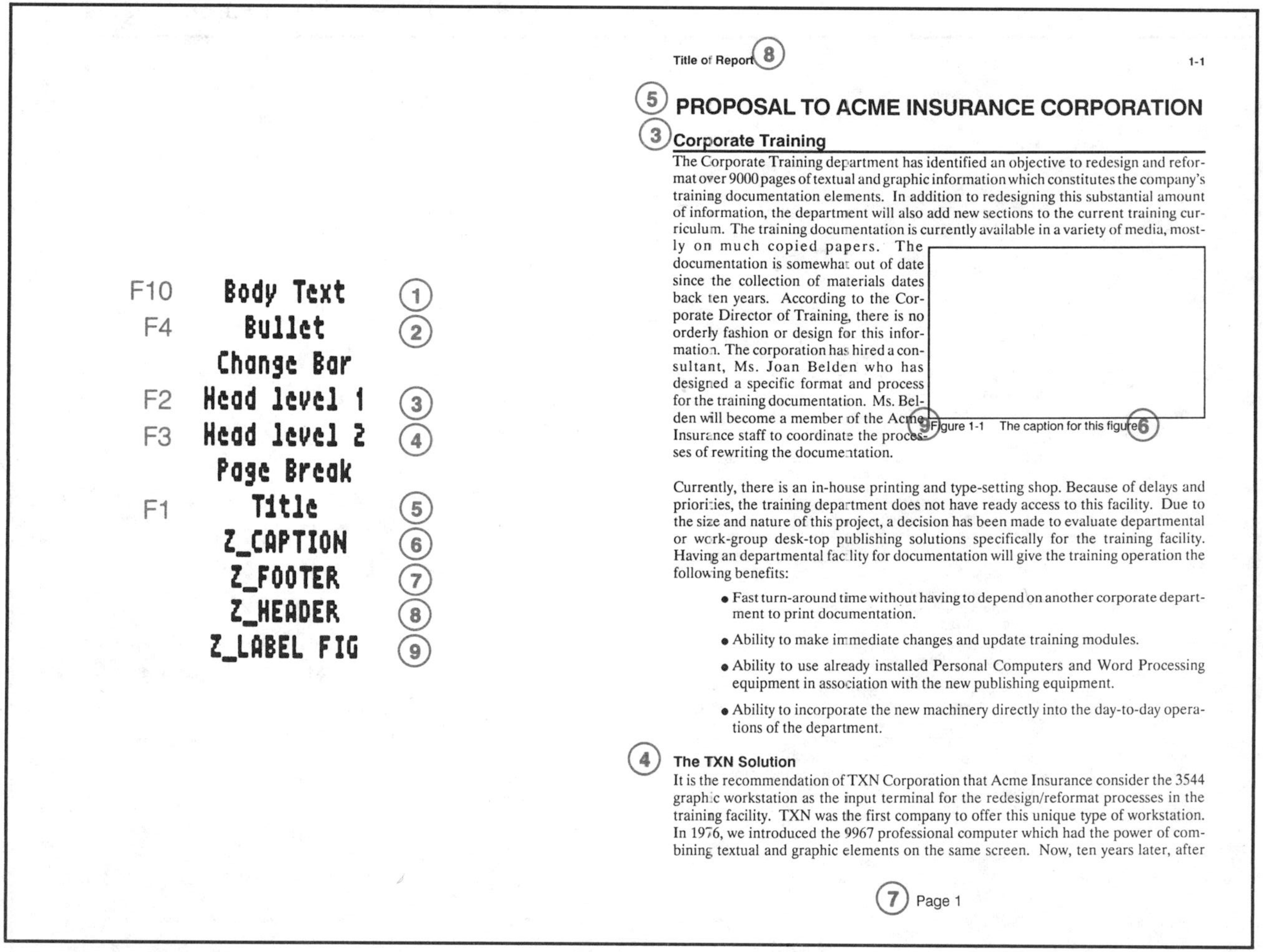

Key	Tag	No.
F10	Body Text	1
F4	Bullet	2
	Change Bar	
F2	Head level 1	3
F3	Head level 2	4
	Page Break	
F1	Title	5
	Z_CAPTION	6
	Z_FOOTER	7
	Z_HEADER	8
	Z_LABEL FIG	9

Title of Report (8) 1-1

(5) PROPOSAL TO ACME INSURANCE CORPORATION

(3) Corporate Training

The Corporate Training department has identified an objective to redesign and reformat over 9000 pages of textual and graphic information which constitutes the company's training documentation elements. In addition to redesigning this substantial amount of information, the department will also add new sections to the current training curriculum. The training documentation is currently available in a variety of media, mostly on much copied papers. The documentation is somewhat out of date since the collection of materials dates back ten years. According to the Corporate Director of Training, there is no orderly fashion or design for this information. The corporation has hired a consultant, Ms. Joan Belden who has designed a specific format and process for the training documentation. Ms. Belden will become a member of the Acme Insurance staff to coordinate the processes of rewriting the documentation.

(9) Figure 1-1 The caption for this figure (6)

Currently, there is an in-house printing and type-setting shop. Because of delays and priorities, the training department does not have ready access to this facility. Due to the size and nature of this project, a decision has been made to evaluate departmental or work-group desk-top publishing solutions specifically for the training facility. Having an departmental facility for documentation will give the training operation the following benefits:

- Fast turn-around time without having to depend on another corporate department to print documentation.
- Ability to make immediate changes and update training modules.
- Ability to use already installed Personal Computers and Word Processing equipment in association with the new publishing equipment.
- Ability to incorporate the new machinery directly into the day-to-day operations of the department.

(4) The TXN Solution

It is the recommendation of TXN Corporation that Acme Insurance consider the 3544 graphic workstation as the input terminal for the redesign/reformat processes in the training facility. TXN was the first company to offer this unique type of workstation. In 1976, we introduced the 9967 professional computer which had the power of combining textual and graphic elements on the same screen. Now, ten years later, after

(7) Page 1

Figure B.13: &PRPTP1 sample pages

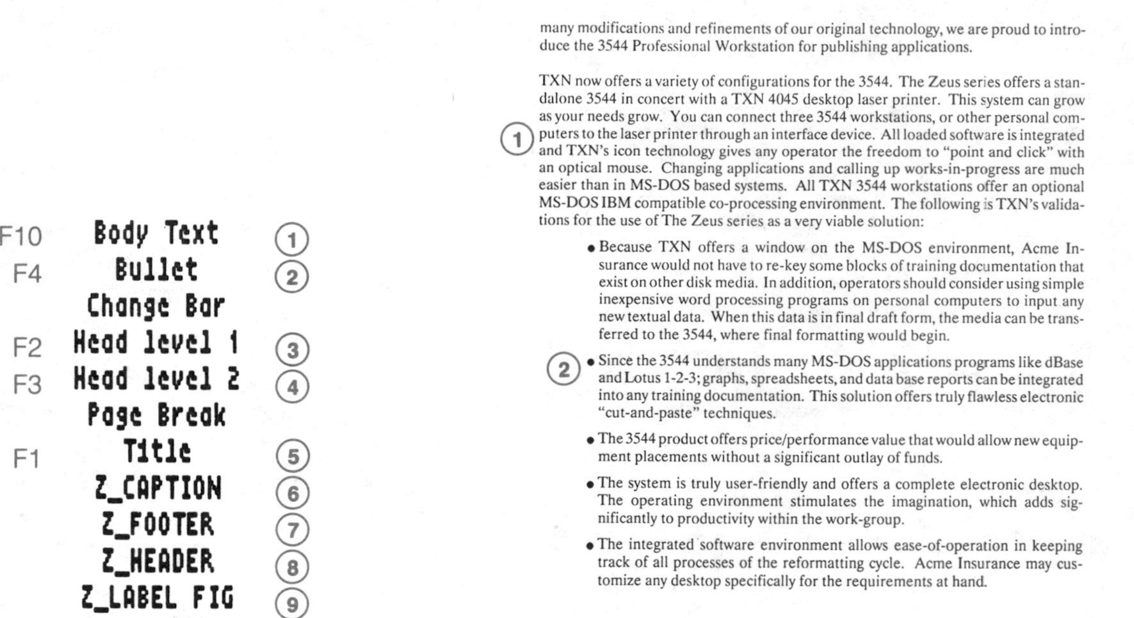

Figure B.13: &PRPT-P1 sample pages (continued)

Table B.13: &PRPT-P1

MENU	COMMAND	SETTING	
Chapter	Page Size & Layout	Orientation: Paper Type & Dimension: Sides:	Portrait Letter, 8.5 × 11 in. Double
Frame	Margins & Columns	# of Columns: Column Width: Margins:	1 6'' Top: 1'' Bottom: 1'' Left: 1.25'' Right: 1.25''

FIGURE REFERENCE	TAG NAME AND FUNCTION KEY	PARAGRAPH MENU COMMAND	SETTING	
①	Body Text (F10)	Alignment	Horz Alignment:	Justified
		Spacing	Above & Below: Inter-Line: Inter-Paragraph:	0 01,02 picas & points 01,02 picas & points
②	*Bullet (F4)	Spacing	Above & Below: In From Left:	00,07 pica & points .5''
		Special Effects	Special Effect: Indent After Bullet:	Bullet .17''
	Change Bar (F9)	Ruling Box Around	Width: Height of Rule 1: Custom Indent: Custom Width:	Custom 1.02 fractional points –6 fractional points 1.98 fractional points

Table B.13: &PRPT-P1 (continued)

Figure Reference	Tag Name and Function Key	Paragraph Menu Command	Setting
③	Head level 1 (F2)	Ruling Line Below	Width: Margin Height of Rule 1: 1.98 fractional points
* Spacing Above and Below creates the space between the bulleted items.			

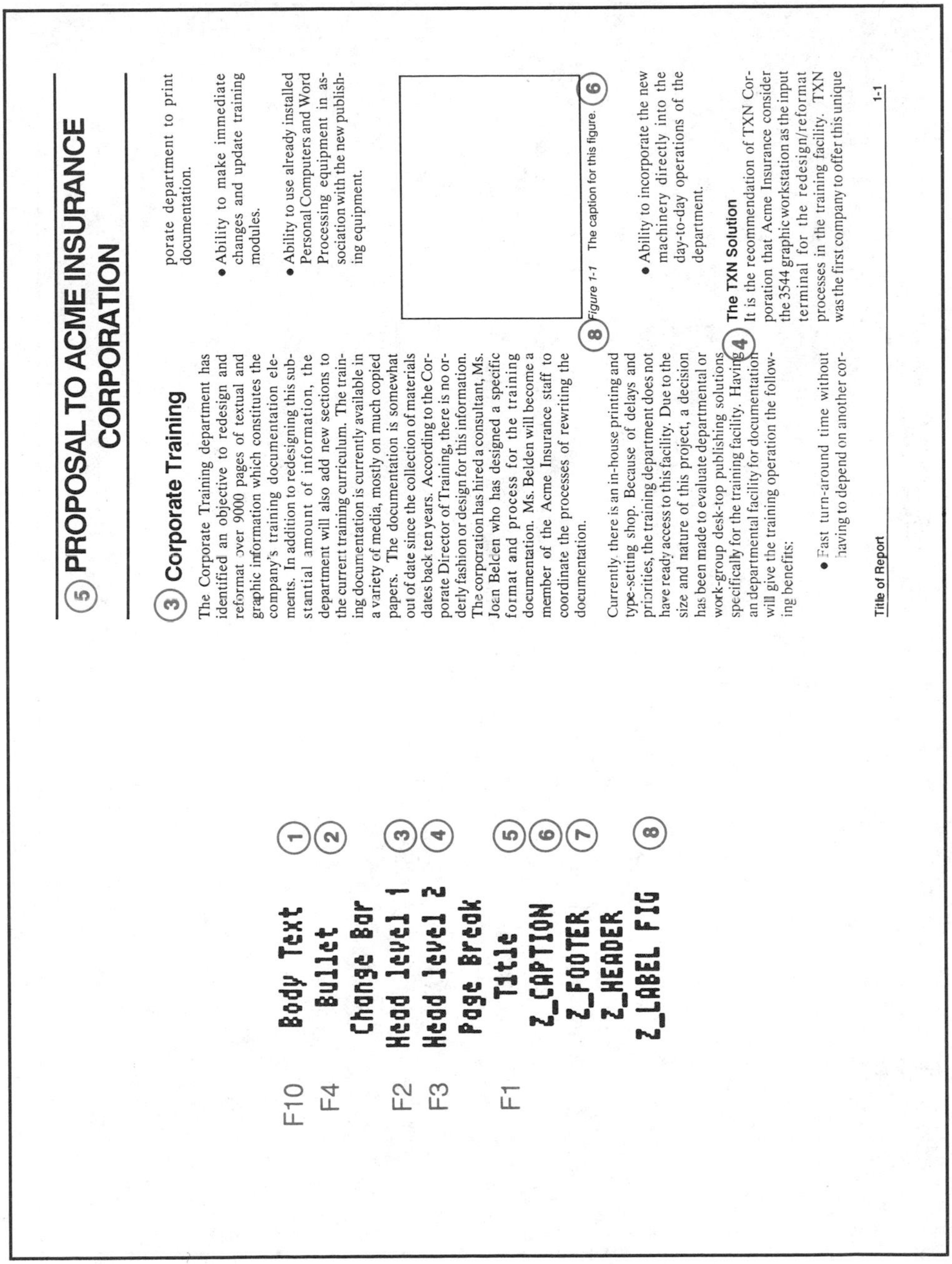

F10	Body Text	1
F4	Bullet	2
	Change Bar	
F2	Head level 1	3
F3	Head level 2	4
	Page Break	
F1	Title	5
	Z_CAPTION	6
	Z_FOOTER	7
	Z_HEADER	
	Z_LABEL FIG	8

(5) PROPOSAL TO ACME INSURANCE CORPORATION

(3) Corporate Training

The Corporate Training department has identified an objective to redesign and reformat over 9000 pages of textual and graphic information which constitutes the company's training documentation elements. In addition to redesigning this substantial amount of information, the department will also add new sections to the current training curriculum. The training documentation is currently available in a variety of media, mostly on much copied papers. The documentation is somewhat out of date since the collection of materials dates back ten years. According to the Corporate Director of Training, there is no orderly fashion or design for this information. The corporation has hired a consultant, Ms. Joan Belden who has designed a specific format and process for the training documentation. Ms. Belden will become a member of the Acme Insurance staff to coordinate the processes of rewriting the documentation.

Currently there is an in-house printing and type-setting shop. Because of delays and priorities, the training department does not have ready access to this facility. Due to the size and nature of this project, a decision has been made to evaluate departmental or work-group desk-top publishing solutions specifically for the training facility. Having an departmental facility for documentation will give the training operation the following benefits:

- Fast turn-around time without having to depend on another corporate department to print documentation.
- Ability to make immediate changes and update training modules.
- Ability to use already installed Personal Computers and Word Processing equipment in association with the new publishing equipment.

(8) *Figure 1-1* The caption for this figure. (6)

- Ability to incorporate the new machinery directly into the day-to-day operations of the department.

(4) The TXN Solution

It is the recommendation of TXN Corporation that Acme Insurance consider the 3544 graphic workstation as the input terminal for the redesign/reformat processes in the training facility. TXN was the first company to offer this unique

Title of Report 1-1

Figure B.14: &PRPT-P2 sample pages

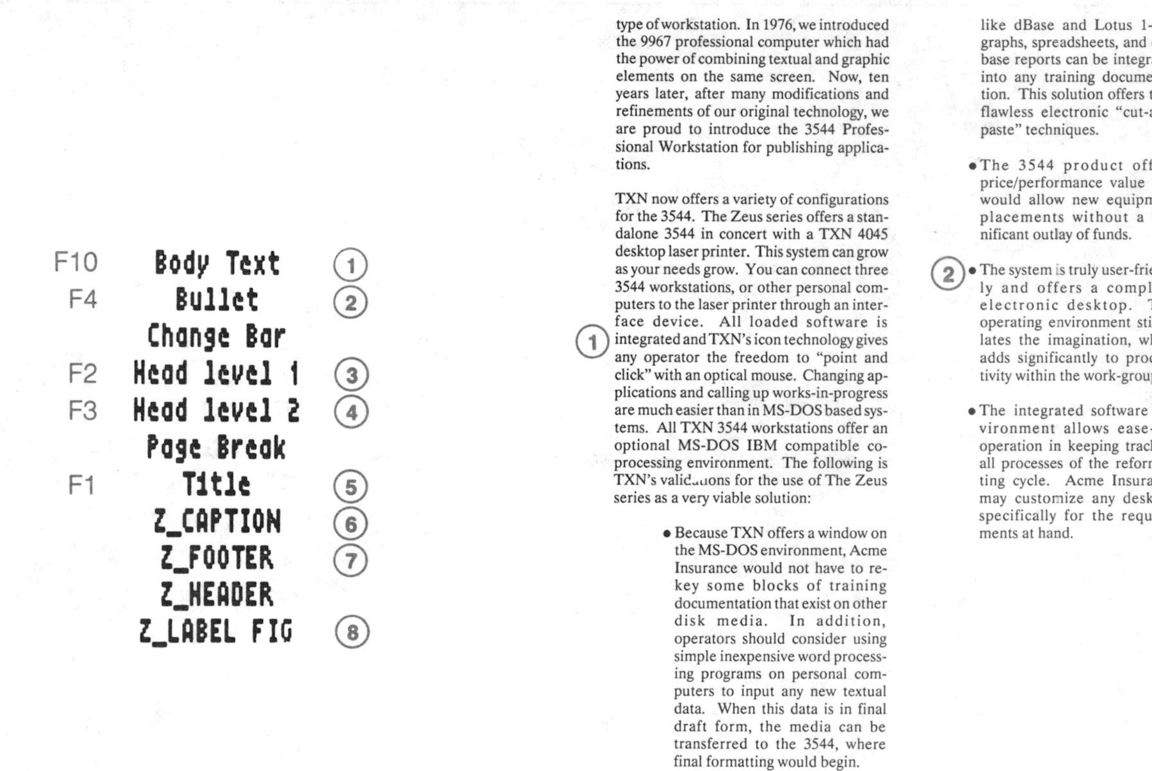

type of workstation. In 1976, we introduced the 9967 professional computer which had the power of combining textual and graphic elements on the same screen. Now, ten years later, after many modifications and refinements of our original technology, we are proud to introduce the 3544 Professional Workstation for publishing applications.

① TXN now offers a variety of configurations for the 3544. The Zeus series offers a standalone 3544 in concert with a TXN 4045 desktop laser printer. This system can grow as your needs grow. You can connect three 3544 workstations, or other personal computers to the laser printer through an interface device. All loaded software is integrated and TXN's icon technology gives any operator the freedom to "point and click" with an optical mouse. Changing applications and calling up works-in-progress are much easier than in MS-DOS based systems. All TXN 3544 workstations offer an optional MS-DOS IBM compatible coprocessing environment. The following is TXN's validations for the use of The Zeus series as a very viable solution:

- Because TXN offers a window on the MS-DOS environment, Acme Insurance would not have to rekey some blocks of training documentation that exist on other disk media. In addition, operators should consider using simple inexpensive word processing programs on personal computers to input any new textual data. When this data is in final draft form, the media can be transferred to the 3544, where final formatting would begin.
- Since the 3544 understands many MS-DOS applications programs like dBase and Lotus 1-2-3; graphs, spreadsheets, and data base reports can be integrated into any training documentation. This solution offers truly flawless electronic "cut-and-paste" techniques.
- The 3544 product offers price/performance value that would allow new equipment placements without a significant outlay of funds.
- ② The system is truly user-friendly and offers a complete electronic desktop. The operating environment stimulates the imagination, which adds significantly to productivity within the work-group.
- The integrated software environment allows ease-of-operation in keeping track of all processes of the reformatting cycle. Acme Insurance may customize any desktop specifically for the requirements at hand.

⑦ 1-2 Title of the Chapter

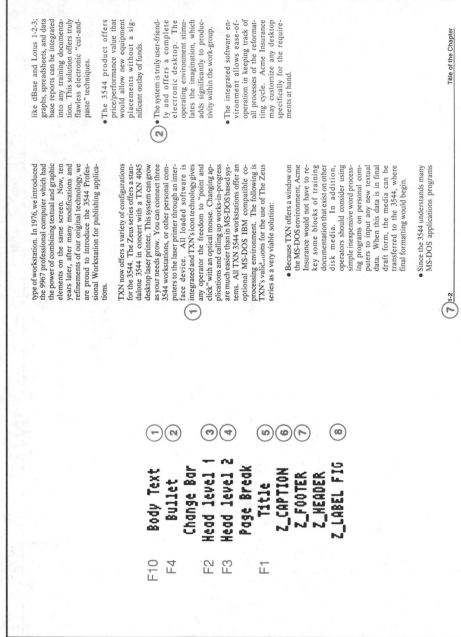

Figure B.14: &PRPT-P2 sample pages (continued)

Table B.14: &PRPT-P2

MENU	COMMAND	SETTING	
Chapter	Page Size & Layout	Orientation:	Portrait
		Paper Type & Dimension:	Letter, 8.5 × 11 in.
		Sides:	Double
Frame	Margins & Columns	# of Columns:	2
		Column Widths:	3'' and 2.83''
		Margins:	Top: .97'' Bottom: .97'' Left: 1.25'' Right: 1.25''

FIGURE REFERENCE	TAG NAME AND FUNCTION KEY	PARAGRAPH MENU COMMAND	SETTING	
①	Body Text (F10)	Alignment	Horz Alignment:	Justified
		Spacing	Above & Below:	0
			Inter-Line:	01,02 picas & points
			Inter-Paragraph:	01,02 picas & points
②	*Bullet (F4)	Spacing	Above:	01,02 pica & points
			In From Left:	.5''
		Special Effects	Special Effect:	Bullet
			Indent After Bullet:	.17''
	Change Bar (F9)	Ruling Box Around	Width:	Custom
			Height of Rule 1:	1.02 fractional points
			Custom Indent:	−6 fractional points
			Custom Width:	1.98 fractional points

Table B.14: &PRPT-P2 (continued)

FIGURE REFERENCE	TAG NAME AND FUNCTION KEY	PARAGRAPH MENU COMMAND	SETTING	
③	Head level 1 (F2)	Alignment	Horz Alignment:	Center
	Page Break (F8)	Breaks	Page Break:	After
⑤	Title (F1)	Ruling Line Above	Width: Height of Rule 1:	Frame 1.98 fractional points
		Ruling Line Below	Width: Height of Rule 1:	Margin 1.98 fractional points

* Spacing Above and Below creates the space between the bulleted items.

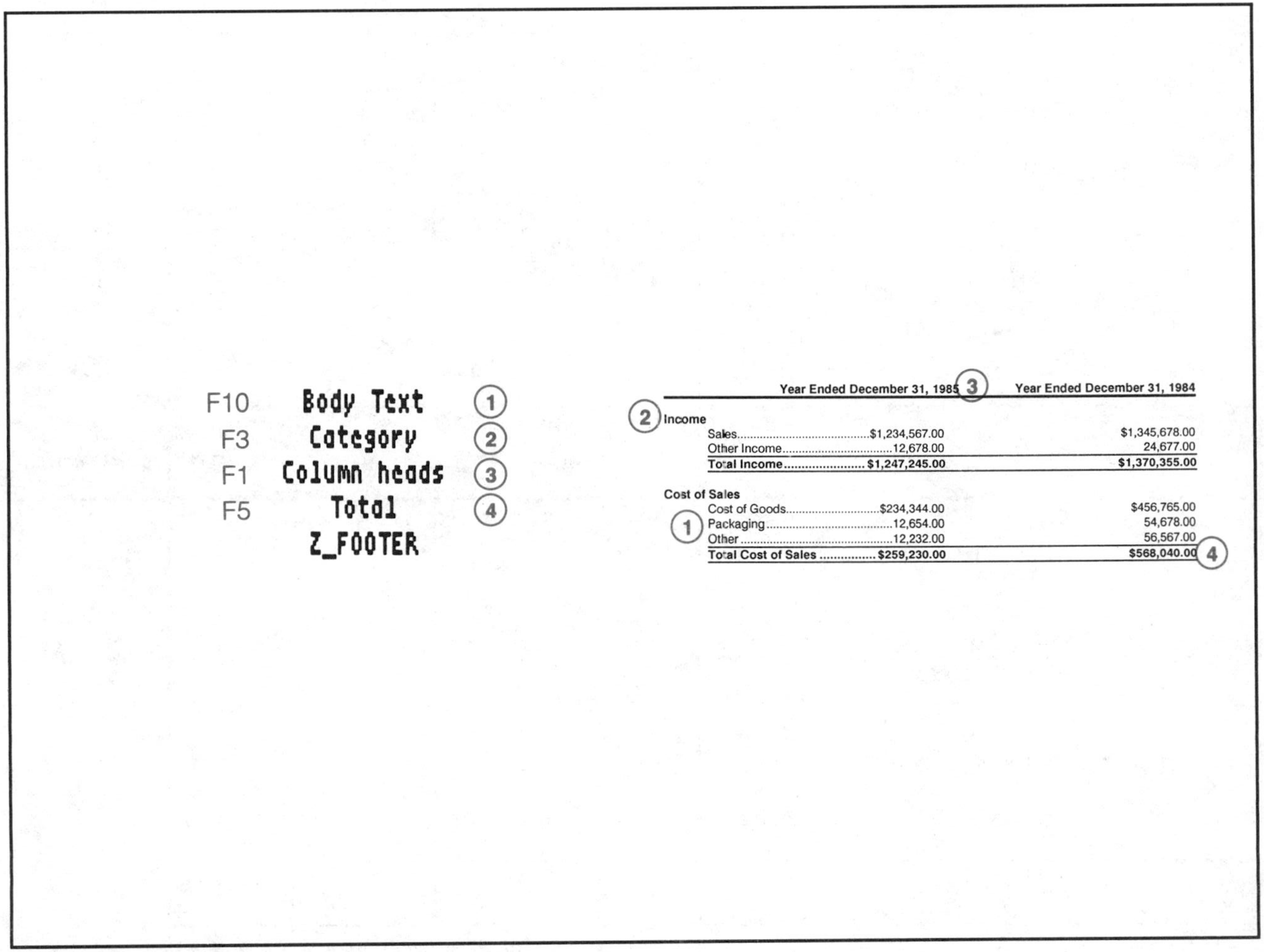

F10	Body Text	(1)
F3	Category	(2)
F1	Column heads	(3)
F5	Total	(4)
	Z_FOOTER	

	Year Ended December 31, 1985 (3)	Year Ended December 31, 1984
(2) Income		
Sales	$1,234,567.00	$1,345,678.00
Other Income	12,678.00	24,677.00
Total Income	**$1,247,245.00**	**$1,370,355.00**
Cost of Sales		
Cost of Goods	$234,344.00	$456,765.00
(1) Packaging	12,654.00	54,678.00
Other	12,232.00	56,567.00
Total Cost of Sales	**$259,230.00**	**$568,040.00** (4)

Figure B.15: &TBL-P1 sample page

Table B.15: &TBL-P1 Formatting Features

Menu	Command	Setting	
Chapter	Page Size & Layout	Orientation:	Portrait
		Paper Type & Dimension:	Letter, 8.5 × 11 in.
		Sides:	Single
Frame	Margins & Columns	# of Columns:	1
		Column Width:	6.5''
		Margins:	Top: .75'' Bottom: .75'' Left: 1'' Right: 1''

Figure Reference	Tag Name and Function Key	Paragraph Menu Command	Setting	
①	Body Text (F10)	Alignment	Horz Alignment:	Left
			First Line:	Indent
			Indent Width:	.5''
		Spacing	Above & Below:	0
			Inter-Line:	01,00 picas & points
		Tab Settings	Tab Number 1:	Decimal, 3''
			Tab Display:	Shown as Leader Char
			Leader Char:	. . .
			Tab Number 2:	Decimal, 5.83''
			Tab Display:	Shown as Open Space

Table B.15: &TBL-P1 Formatting Features (continued)

Figure Reference	Tag Name and Function Key	Paragraph Menu Command	Setting	
③	Column heads (F1)	Tab Settings	Tab Number 1: Tab Number 2:	Center, 2.33'' Center, 5''
		Ruling Line Below	Width: Height of Rule 1:	Text 1.98 fractional points
④	Total (F5)	Tab Settings	*Same tab settings as Body Text*	
		Ruling Line Above & Below	Width: Height of Rule 1:	Text 1.02 fractional points

	Body Text	
F3	Col 1	(1)
F4	Col 2	(2)
F5	Col 3	(3)
F6	Col 4	(4)
	Page Break	
	Rule	
F2	Table header	(5)
F1	Title	(6)
	TOC entry	
	Z_FOOTER	

(6) **Title of this table**

Header for Table	(5) Next Column	Third Col.	Price
(1) **First Entry**	(2) The second column describes some features of the item called out in the first column. Notice that the text for the column is too wide to fit on one line. This type of style might be useful in a comparison chart where flowing text is used.	(3) The third column might expound a bit on the second column. But the fourth column just holds a number, such as price.	(4) $456
Second model.	The next column.	The second model compares quite favorably to the first model described above. There's not as much text here though.	$654
Entry #3	More descriptive text about entry number three. It's called WYSIWYG. It means that as you edit and modify, your screen shows you *exactly what you're going to get when you print it out. No surprises. It's all there in front of your eyes.*	Another column of text.	$66

Figure B.16: &TBL2-L1 sample page

Table B.16: &PRPT-P2

	Menu	**Command**	**Setting**	
	Chapter	Page Size & Layout	Orientation: Paper Type & Dimension: Sides:	Landscape Letter, 8.5 × 11 in. Single
	Frame	Margins & Columns	# of Columns: Column Width: Margins:	1 9'' Top: .75'' Bottom: .75'' Left: 1'' Right: 1''
Figure Reference	**Tag Name and Function Key**	**Paragraph Menu Command**	**Setting**	
	Body Text (F10)	Alignment	Horz Alignment:	Justified
		Spacing	Above & Below: Inter-Line: Inter-Paragraph:	0 01,00 picas & points 01,00 picas & points

See Chapter 8 for a discussion of the tags in this sample.

F10	Body Text	1
F1	Chapter Head	2
F4	Computer Text	3
	Equation	4
F2	Heading 1	5
F3	Heading 2	6
	Heading 3	
	Instruction	
F5	Key Note Text	7
F6	List 1	8
	List 2	
	List 3	
	Page Break	
	Table 1	
	Table 2	
	Table 3	
	Table 4	9
	Table Head 1	10
	Table Head 2	
	Table Head 3	
	Z_BOXTEXT	
	Z_CAPTION	
	Z_FOOTER	11
	Z_HEADER	12

(12) MENU COMMANDS PUBLISHING CHAPTER

PUBLISHING CHAPTER (2)

(5) MENU COMMANDS

Most of Ventura Publisher's functions are controlled through the menus at the top of the screen. This section describes the operation of each of these menus and the options within them. These commands are presented in the order in which they appear on the screen. Use the index for an alphabetical reference to these commands.

(6) Menu Conventions

Often, a menu option will be shown in gray and cannot be highlighted. This usually indicates that the proper function has not been selected. The table below indicates these dependencies. (1)

(10) DESK

(9) Publisher Info . . .	Always available

FILE

New	Must first Open chapter or Load file
Open . . .	Always available
Save	File name must be in title bar
Save As . . .	Always available

FILE MENU

Description/Application

The File Menu controls information flow into and out of Ventura Publisher.

(11) REFERENCE GUIDE 1-1

Figure B.17: &TCHD-P1 sample pages

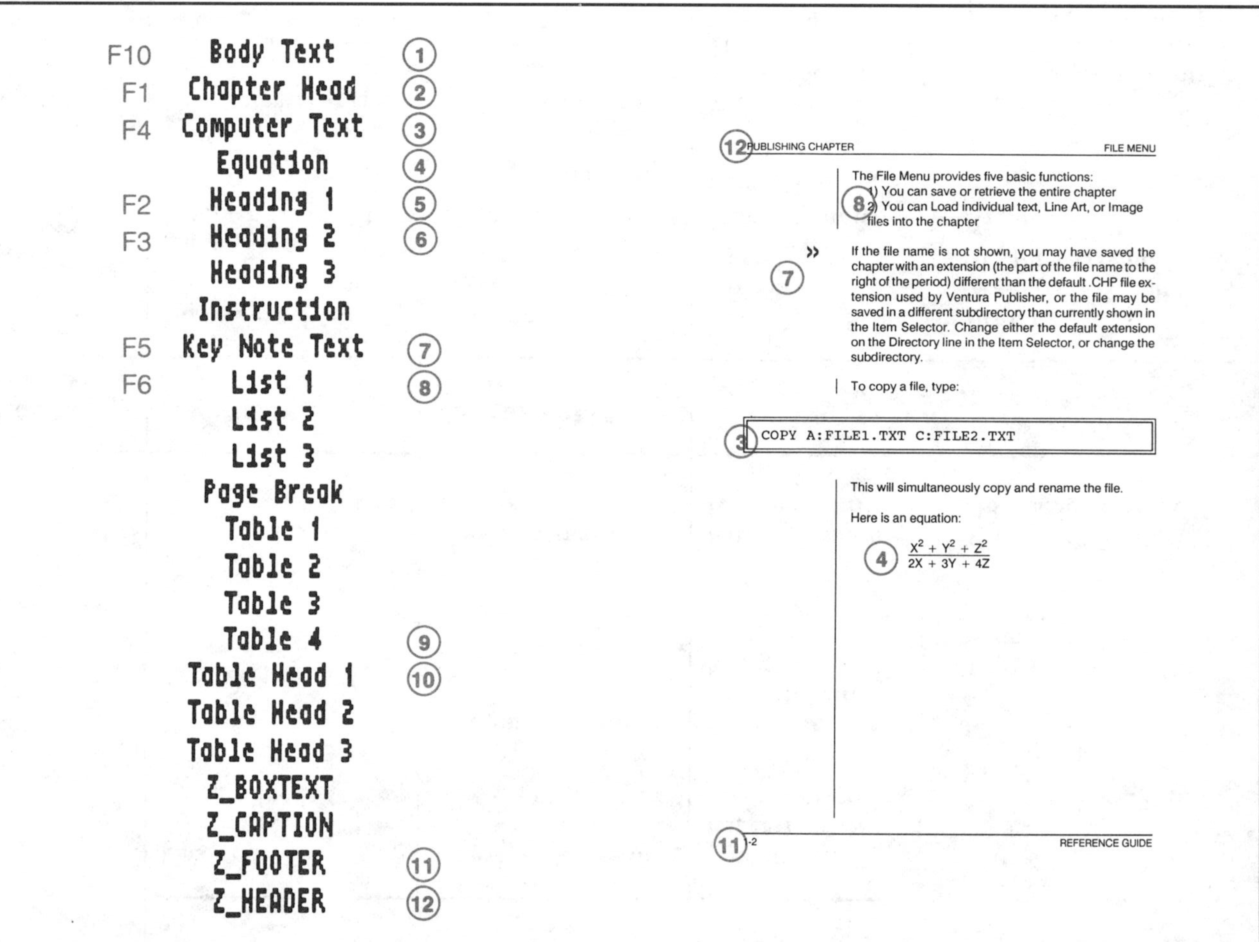

Figure B.17: &TCHD-P1 sample pages (continued)

Table B.17: &TCHD-P1

Menu	Command	Setting	
Chapter	Page Size & Layout	Orientation: Paper Type & Dimension: Sides:	Portrait Letter, 8.5 × 11 in. Double
Frame	Margins & Columns	# of Columns: Column Width: Margins:	1 4.5'' Top: 1.92'' Bottom: 1.92'' Left: 2'' Right: 2''
	Vertical Rules	Rule 1 Position: Rule 1 Width:	3'' .48 fractional points

Figure Reference	Tag Name and Function Key	Paragraph Menu Command	Setting	
①	Body Text (F10)	Alignment Spacing	Horz Alignment: Above: Inter-Line:	Justified 01,00 picas & points 01,00 picas & points
②	Chapter Head (F1)	Alignment	Horz Alignment:	Right
		Ruling Line Below	Width: Height of Rule 1:	Frame 6.00 fractional points
③	Computer Text (F4)	Ruling Box Around	Width: Space Above Rule 1: Height of Rule 1: Space Below Rule 1: Height of Rule 2: Space Below Rule 2: Custom Indent: Custom Width:	Custom 4.74 fractional points .54 fractional points 1.98 fractional points .54 fractional points 4.74 fractional points 6.24 fractional points 28,00 picas & points (4.67'')

Table B.17: &TCHD-P1 (continued)

Figure Reference	Tag Name and Function Key	Paragraph Menu Command	Setting	
④	Equation	Tab Settings	Tab Number 1:	Center, 2.25''
⑤	Heading 1 (F2)	Ruling Line Above	Width: Height of Rule 1: Space Below Rule 1:	Frame 1.98 fractional points 4.02 fractional points
		Ruling Line Below	Width: Space Above Rule 1: Height of Rule 1:	Frame 1.98 fractional points .66 fractional points
⑥	Heading 2 (F3)	Spacing	In From Left:	.67''
		Ruling Line Below	Width: Space Above Rule 1: Height of Rule 1:	Margin 1.98 fractional points .66 fractional points
⑦	Key Note Text (F5)	Special Effects	Special Effect: Show Bullet As: Indent After Bullet:	Bullet » .5''
⑧	List 1 (F6)	Spacing	In From Left:	1.33''
⑩	Table Head 1	Ruling Line Above	Width: Height of Rule 1:	Column .48 fractional points

Key	Tag	
F10	Body Text	1
F9	Bullet	2
F1	Chapter Head	3
F2	Major Heading	4
F3	Minor Heading	5
	Page Break	
F7	System Prompt	6
F5	Table Head	7
F6	Table Item	8
	User Response	
F4	Warning	9
	Z_CAPTION	10
	Z_FOOTER	11
	Z_LABEL FIG	12
	Z_SEC1	13
	Z_SEC2	14
	Z_SEC3	15

(13) 1. USER INTERFACE (3)

(14) 1.1. WYSIWYG (4)

(12) Figure 1-1
(10) This is the caption for the figure. It is anchored below WYSIWYG

(1) Ventura Publisher is designed to provide What You See (on the screen) Is What You Get printed (WYSIWYG). This means that the computer display should match as closely as possible, at all times, what you will see on the final printed page. Of course, the difference between the technology used to display a page on a CRT screen, and the technologies used to print a page on a laser printer or typesetter, do create some unavoidable differences. In particular, becausethecomputerCRTscreencannotproduceanywherenearthesameresolu tion of a printer or typesetter, and because what is displayed is shown in a different aspect ratio (height to width ratio), the space between words and between lines may appear to be bigger or smaller than the printed page under certain circumstances. Several thin ruling lines, with little space between, may show on the screen as one thick line.

(15) 1.1.1 Keyboard Keys (5)

Various keys on the keyboard perform special functions:

- The keyboard Cursor keys control the Text Cursor (The text cursor is displayed as a thin vertical line.)
- (2) The Home key goes to the first page of the document.
- The End key goes to the last page of the document.
- The Pg Up key goes to the previous page.
- The Pg Dn key goes to the next page.

1.2. ITEM SELECTOR

1.2.1 Description

The display shown in Figure 10-2 is called an Item Selector. The Item Selector is used for saving and retrieving files.

(11) 1-A WYSIWYG

Figure B.18: &TDOC-P1 sample pages

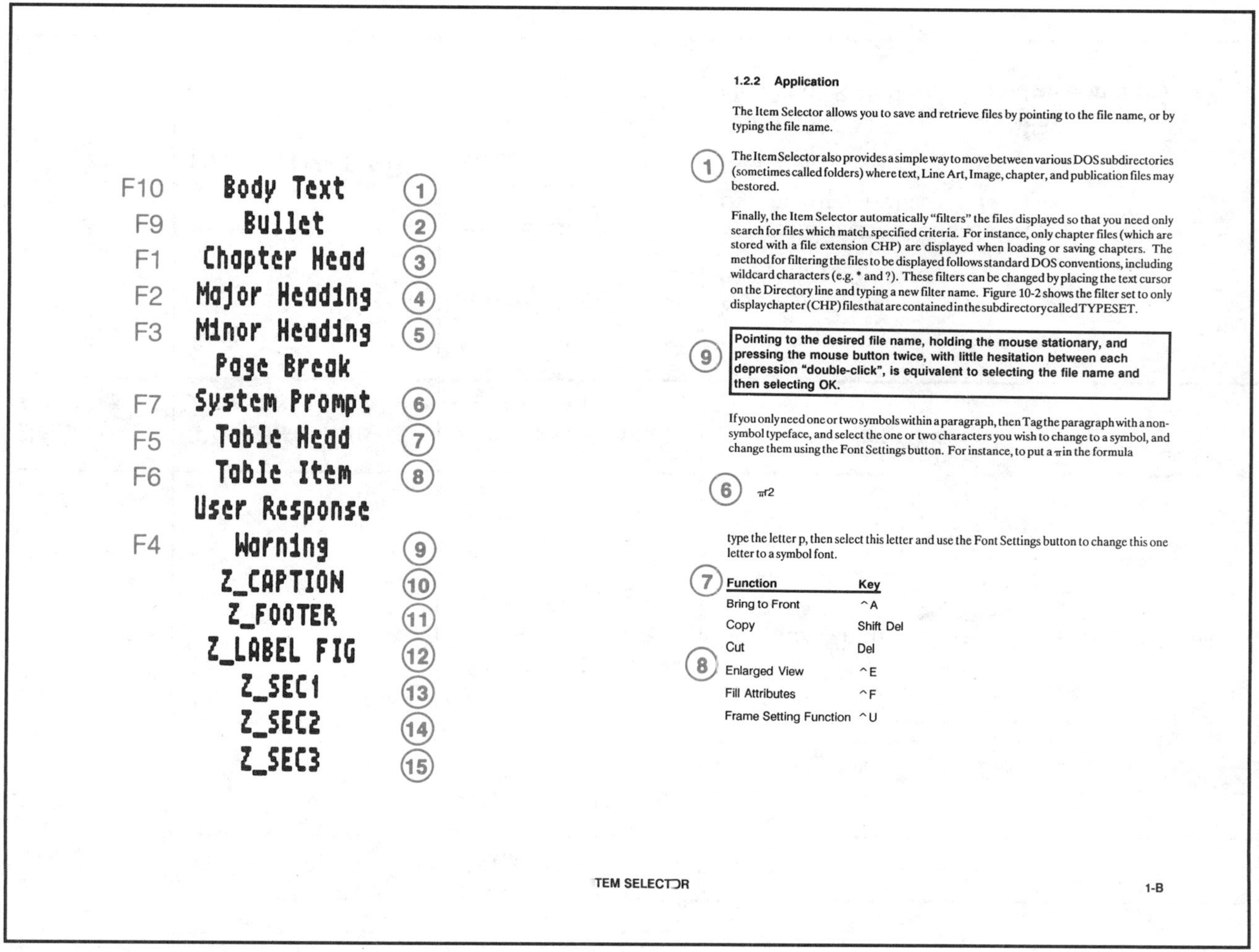

F10	Body Text	1
F9	Bullet	2
F1	Chapter Head	3
F2	Major Heading	4
F3	Minor Heading	5
	Page Break	
F7	System Prompt	6
F5	Table Head	7
F6	Table Item	8
	User Response	
F4	Warning	9
	Z_CAPTION	10
	Z_FOOTER	11
	Z_LABEL FIG	12
	Z_SEC1	13
	Z_SEC2	14
	Z_SEC3	15

1.2.2 Application

The Item Selector allows you to save and retrieve files by pointing to the file name, or by typing the file name.

(1) The Item Selector also provides a simple way to move between various DOS subdirectories (sometimes called folders) where text, Line Art, Image, chapter, and publication files may bestored.

Finally, the Item Selector automatically "filters" the files displayed so that you need only search for files which match specified criteria. For instance, only chapter files (which are stored with a file extension CHP) are displayed when loading or saving chapters. The method for filtering the files to be displayed follows standard DOS conventions, including wildcard characters (e.g. * and ?). These filters can be changed by placing the text cursor on the Directory line and typing a new filter name. Figure 10-2 shows the filter set to only displaychapter (CHP) files that are contained in the subdirectory called TYPESET.

(9) **Pointing to the desired file name, holding the mouse stationary, and pressing the mouse button twice, with little hesitation between each depression "double-click", is equivalent to selecting the file name and then selecting OK.**

If you only need one or two symbols within a paragraph, then Tag the paragraph with a non-symbol typeface, and select the one or two characters you wish to change to a symbol, and change them using the Font Settings button. For instance, to put a π in the formula

(6) πr2

type the letter p, then select this letter and use the Font Settings button to change this one letter to a symbol font.

(7)

Function	Key
Bring to Front	^A
Copy	Shift Del
Cut	Del
(8) Enlarged View	^E
Fill Attributes	^F
Frame Setting Function	^U

TEM SELECTϽR

1-B

Figure B.18: &TDOC-P1 sample pages (continued)

Table B.18: &TDOC-P1

	Menu	Command	Setting	
	Chapter	Page Size & Layout	Orientation: Paper Type & Dimension: Sides:	Portrait Letter, 8.5 × 11 in. Double
	Frame	Margins & Columns	# of Columns: Column Width: Margins:	1 6.5'' Top: 1'' Bottom: 1'' Left: 1'' Right: 1''
Figure Reference	**Tag Name and Function Key**	**Paragraph Menu Command**	**Setting**	
①	Body Text (F10)	Alignment	Horz Alignment:	Justified
		Spacing	Above & Below: In From Left:	0 1.5''
②	Bullet (F9)	Special Effects	Special Effect: Indent After Bullet:	Bullet .17''
③	Chapter Head (F1)	Breaks	Line Break:	After
		Ruling Line Below	Width: Height of Rule 1:	Margin 3.00 fractional points

Table B.18: &TDOC-P1 (continued)

Figure Reference	Tag Name and Function Key	Paragraph Menu Command	Setting	
④	Major heading (F2)	Breaks	Line Break:	After
		Ruling Line Below	Width:	Frame
			Height of Rule 1:	1.98 fractional points
⑤	Minor heading (F3)	Breaks	Line Break:	After
⑨	Warning (F4)	Ruling Box Around	Width:	Margin
			Height of Rule 1:	1.98 fractional points
			Space Below Rule 1:	1.98 fractional points
⑬ ⑭ ⑮	*Z_SEC1, -2, -3	Breaks	Line Break:	Before

* Break settings for section numbers and headings cause the text for these tags to stay on the same line.

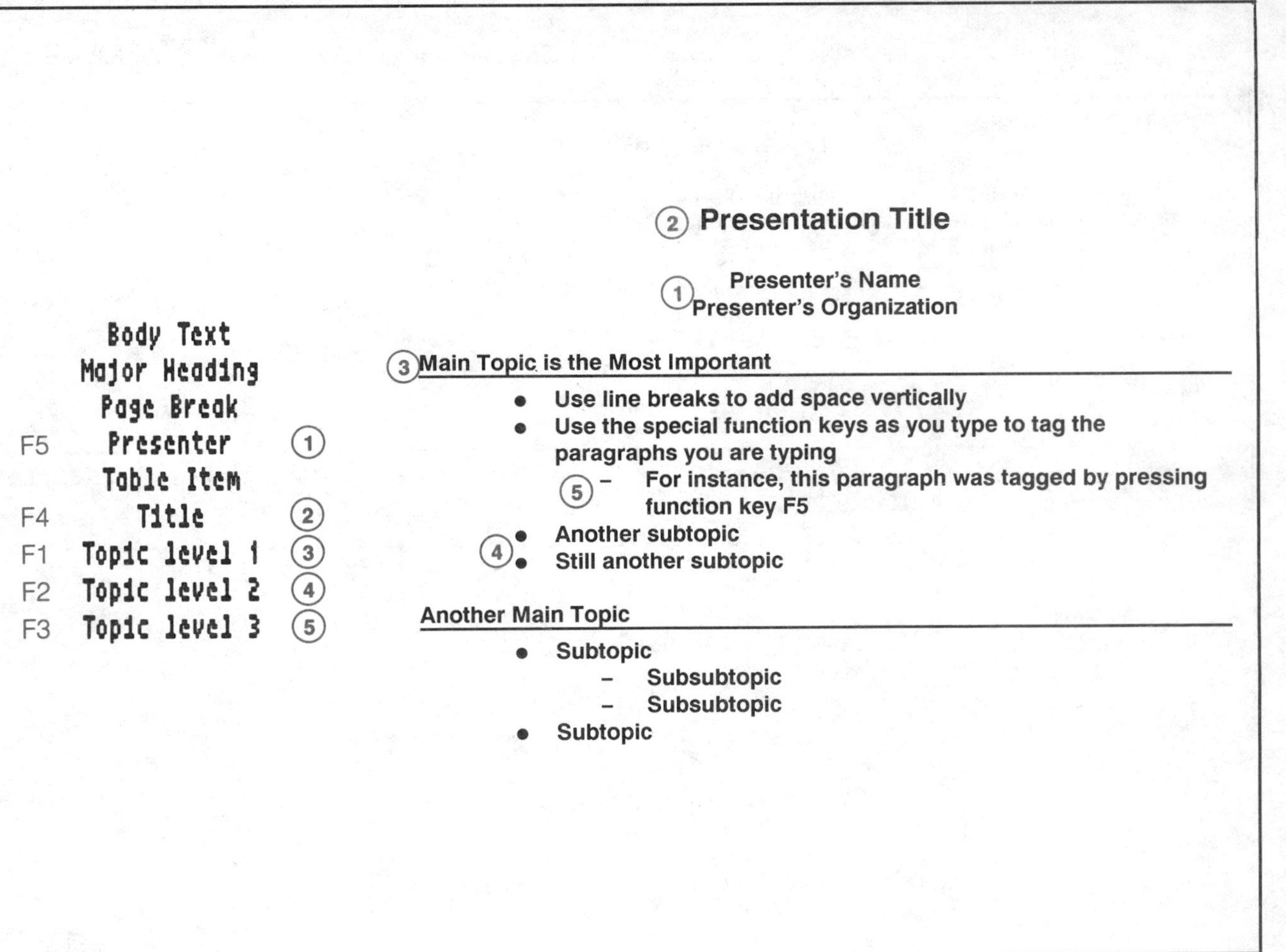

Figure B.19: &VWGF-L1 sample page

Table B.19: &VWGF-L1

MENU	COMMAND	SETTING	
Chapter	Page Size & Layout	Orientation: Paper Type & Dimension: Sides:	Landscape Letter, 8.5 × 11 in. Single
Frame	Margins & Columns	# of Columns: Column Width: Margins:	1 9'' Top: 1'' Bottom: 1'' Left: 1'' Right: 1''

FIGURE REFERENCE	TAG NAME AND FUNCTION KEY	PARAGRAPH MENU COMMAND	SETTING	
	Body Text (F10)	Alignment	Horz Alignment:	Left
		Spacing	Above & Below: Inter-Line:	0 01,10 picas & points
①	Presenter (F5)	Alignment	Horz Alignment:	Center
②	Title (F4)	Alignment	Horz Alignment:	Center
③	Topic level 1 (F1)	Ruling Line Below	Width: Height of Rule 1:	Margin 1.98 fractional points
④	Topic level 2 (F2)	Spacing	In From Left:	1''
		Special Effects	Special Effect: Indent After Bullet:	Bullet .5''
⑤	Topic level 3 (F3)	Spacing	In From Left:	2''
		Special Effects	Special Effect: Show Bullet As: Indent After Bullet:	Bullet – .5''

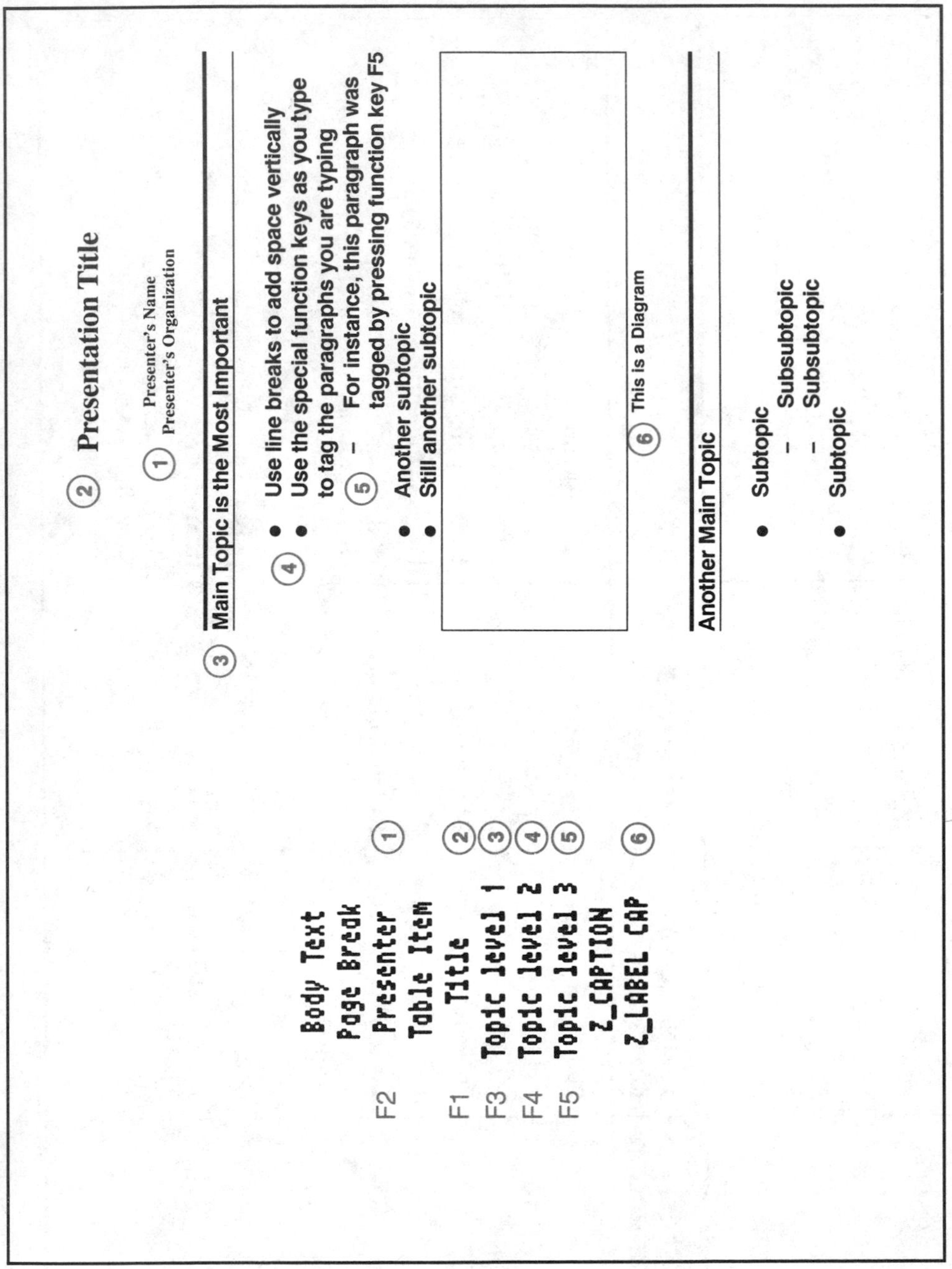

F2 Presenter (1)
Body Text
Page Break
Table Item
F1 Title (2)
F3 Topic level 1 (3)
F4 Topic level 2 (4)
F5 Topic level 3 (5)
Z_CAPTION
Z_LABEL CAP (6)

(2) Presentation Title

(1) Presenter's Name
Presenter's Organization

(3) Main Topic is the Most Important

(4)
- Use line breaks to add space vertically
- Use the special function keys as you type to tag the paragraphs you are typing
  - (5) – For instance, this paragraph was tagged by pressing function key F5
- Another subtopic
- Still another subtopic

(6) This is a Diagram

Another Main Topic

- Subtopic
  – Subsubtopic
  – Subsubtopic
- Subtopic

Figure B.20: &VWGF-P1 sample page

Table B.20: &VWGF-P1

	MENU	COMMAND	SETTING	
	Chapter	Page Size & Layout	Orientation: Paper Type & Dimension: Sides:	Portrait Letter, 8.5 × 11 in. Single
	Frame	Margins & Columns	# of Columns: Column Width: Margins:	1 6.5'' Top: 1'' Bottom: 1'' Left: 1'' Right: 1''
FIGURE REFERENCE	**TAG NAME AND FUNCTION KEY**	**PARAGRAPH MENU COMMAND**	**SETTING**	
	Body Text (F10)	Alignment	Horz Alignment:	Left
		Spacing	Above & Below: Inter-Line:	0 01,09 picas & points
	Page Break	Breaks	Page Break:	After
①	Presenter (F2)	Alignment	Horz Alignment:	Center
②	Title (F1)	Alignment	Horz Alignment:	Center

Table B.20: &VWGF-P1 (continued)

Figure Reference	Tag Name and Function Key	Paragraph Menu Command	Setting	
③	Topic level 1 (F3)	Ruling Line Above	Width: Height of Rule 1:	Frame 3.00 fractional points
		Ruling Line Below	Width: Height of Rule 1:	Margin 1.02 fractional points
④	Topic level 2 (F4)	Spacing	In From Left:	6 picas & points (1'')
		Special Effects	Special Effect: Indent After Bullet:	Bullet .5''
⑤	Topic level 3 (F5)	Spacing	In From Left:	2''
		Special Effects	Special Effect: Show Bullet As: Indent After Bullet:	Bullet – .5''
⑥	Z_LABEL CAP	Alignment	Horz Alignment:	Center

APPENDIX
C

DOS Conventions and Ventura

APPENDIX C

Ventura follows DOS's design conventions for directories and wild cards. This appendix examines these conventions.

DIRECTORIES

Because a hard disk can store so much data, DOS organizes the disk so that it's easier for you to use. Just as you can divide a desk drawer into sections, so too can you divide your hard disk. That way, you can find files when you need them.

At the topmost level, storage for your computer is divided into disk drives. Clicking the Backup button in the Item Selector box repeatedly will ultimately display a list of the disk drives. Disk drives are indicated with a letter (which Ventura always capitalizes) and a colon. Thus, if your system has three disk drives, A, B, and C, they would be indicated like so:

```
A:
B:
C:
```

Disk drives, in turn, are divided into *directories*. By selecting a disk drive, you display its directories. The main directory of a disk drive is the *root directory*. This is the only directory that exists before you divide the disk drive into other directories. The root directory is indicated by a backslash (\) after the disk-drive letter and colon. Thus, the root directory of drive C is indicated by

```
C:\
```

Directories that branch off the root directory are indicated by the name of that directory, following the disk-drive letter, the colon, and the backslash. Thus, your drive C may have a directory for Microsoft WORD, called WORD, in addition to Ventura's VENTURA and

TYPESET directories. These three directories would be indicated like so:

```
C:\WORD
C:\VENTURA
C:\TYPESET
```

Directories themselves can be divided into additional directories, or *subdirectories.* These are indicated with another backslash and the name of the subdirectory. For example, your WORD directory may be divided into MEMOS, REPORTS, and FORMS. These subdirectories would be indicated like so:

```
C:\WORD\MEMOS
C:\WORD\REPORTS
C:\WORD\FORMS
```

WILD CARDS

A DOS wild card, like a wild card in a game of poker, acts as a substitute. Wild cards allow you to "filter" the files that are to be operated upon, based on some criteria you specify. You can filter when using the Item Selector box to open a chapter or load associated files. This decreases the number of files displayed, narrowing your file search. You can also use wild cards to delete matching files with the File menu's DOS File Ops command.

DOS uses two wild cards: the asterisk and the question mark. Ventura honors them both. The asterisk acts as a substitute for any number of characters. By typing an asterisk, a period, and a given extension, for instance, you can select all files that end with the extension you specify. The filter you specify in this manner follows the directory name, separated with a backslash.

For instance, documents created with Microsoft WORD all end with DOC. To filter for WORD documents in the MEMOS directory, you would specify

```
C:\WORD\MEMOS\*.DOC
```

You can also use the asterisk as a substitute for extensions. Thus, if you want to see all the files that begin with the name JONES, you'd use JONES.* as your search pattern. This will display JONES-.DOC, JONES.BAK, JONES.PCX, and so on, depending on what files are present in the indicated directory.

Use an asterisk after an initial letter to display all files beginning with that letter. Thus, specifying J* would display files that begin with J, regardless of the rest of the name or the extension.

The question mark is DOS's other wild card. The question mark acts as a substitute for one character only. You can combine the question mark with the asterisk to create complex search patterns. Thus, to display all files with two-letter extensions beginning with W, you'd specify *.W? for the filter. Again, this filter would be used in conjunction with a drive and directory, as in the following example:

```
C:\MASTERVP\*.W?
```

This filter would display all files ending with WP and WS. It would suppress the display of files with three-letter extensions, such as WOK, as well as files whose extensions begin with letters other than W.

APPENDIX D

Suppliers of Fonts

APPENDIX D

The following companies provide fonts for Ventura. The list provides the name, address, and phone number of the company and indicates whether the fonts they provide include Ventura width tables (WID files), matching screen fonts, and tables with kerning information.

	Width Tables	*Screen Fonts*	*Kerning Tables*
Adobe Systems, Inc. 1870 Embarcadero Road Palo Alto, CA 94303 (800) 83-FONTS	Yes	Yes	Yes
Bitstream, Inc. 215 First Street Cambridge, MA 02142 (617) 497-6222	Yes	Yes	Yes
CES 509 Cathedral Parkway, #10-A New York, NY 10025 (212) 222-8148	No	No	No
Conographic Corporation 16802 Aston Street Irvine, CA 92714 (714) 474-1188	No	No	No
Font Factory 2400 Centro Parkway, Suite J2 Houston, TX 77092 (713) 358-6954	Yes	Yes	Yes

Hewlett-Packard PO Box 3640 Sunnyvale, CA 94088 (800) 538-8787	Yes, on request	No	No
LaserMaster Corporation 7156 Shady Oak Road Eden Prairie, MN 55344 (612) 944-6069	Yes	Yes	Yes
SoftCraft, Inc. 16 North Carroll Street., Suite 500 Madison, WI 53703 (800) 351-0500	Yes	Yes	Yes
StraightForward 3901 Via Oro Avenue Long Beach, CA 90810 (800) 553-3332 (800) 237-9680 (in California)	Yes	No	No
SWFTE International PO Box 5773 Wilmington, DE 19808 (800) 237-9383	No	No	No
VS Software VideoSoft, Inc. PO Box 6158 Little Rock, AR 72216 (501) 376-2083	Yes	Yes	No
VideoSoft, Inc. PO Box 6158 Little Rock AR 72216 (501) 376-2083	Yes	Yes	No
Weaver Graphics Fox Pavilion PO Box 1132 Jenkintown, PA 19046 (215) 884-9286	Yes	No	Yes, on request

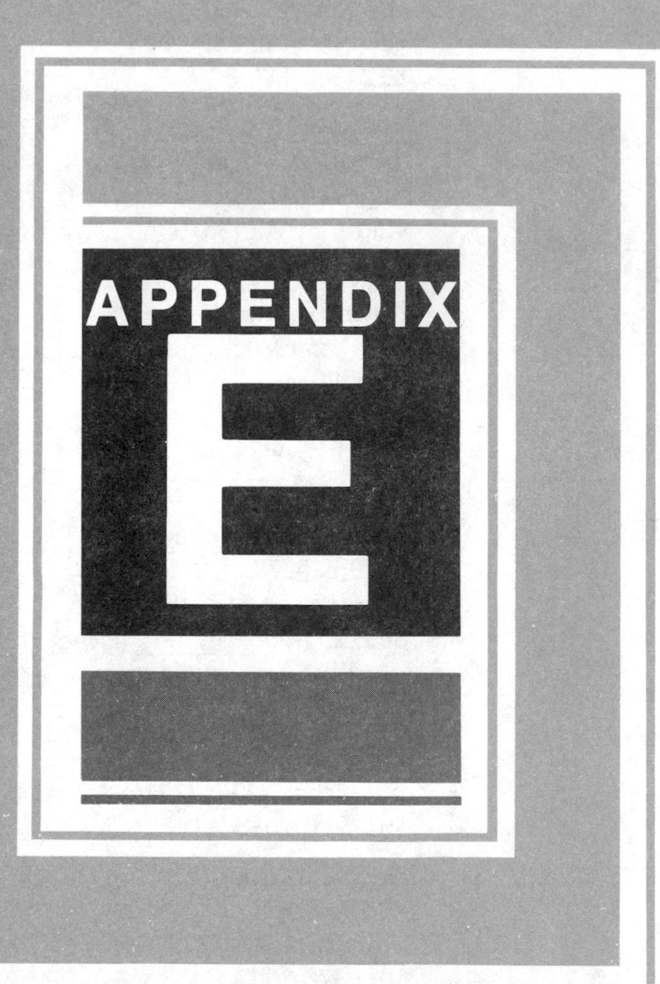
APPENDIX
E

Special Characters and Codes

APPENDIX E

THIS APPENDIX CONSISTS OF TWO PARTS. THE FIRST section is a list of character sets available with Ventura. This section is drawn from the Ventura sample document CHARSET.CHP, located in the TYPESET directory. You can load and print this document yourself. We've added the keyboard shortcuts that appear toward the end of the listing.

Char Set 1 is the character set that Ventura normally uses. Char Set 2 is the set that appears when you format text with the SYMBOL font. The use of this font is discussed in Chapter 12.

The second section of the appendix is a listing of the text codes. These are codes that may appear in the word-processed version of your text files in order to set an effect in place. You can also insert the codes yourself by simply typing them in. The codes are discussed in Chapter 11.

Table E.1: The Ventura Characters Sets

	CHAR SET 1	CHAR SET 2
1-31	not used	
32	space	space
33	!	!
34	"	∀
35	#	#
36	$	∃
37	%	%
38	&	&
39	’	∋
40	(	(
41	)	)
42	*	*
43	+	+
44	,	,
45	-	−
46	.	.
47	/	/
48	0	0
49	1	1
50	2	2
51	3	3
52	4	4
53	5	5
54	6	6
55	7	7
56	8	8
57	9	9
58	:	:
59	;	;
60	<	<
61	=	=
62	>	>
63	?	?
64	@	≅
65	A	Α
66	B	Β
67	C	Χ
68	D	Δ
69	E	Ε
70	F	Φ
71	G	Γ
72	H	Η
73	I	Ι
74	J	ϑ
75	K	Κ
76	L	Λ
77	M	Μ
78	N	Ν
79	O	Ο
80	P	Π
81	Q	Θ
82	R	Ρ
83	S	Σ
84	T	Τ
85	U	Υ
86	V	ς
87	W	Ω
88	X	Ξ
89	Y	Ψ
90	Z	Ζ
91	[	[
92	\	∴
93	]	]
94	^	⊥
95	_	_

Table E.1: The Ventura Characters Sets (continued)

	CHAR SET 1	CHAR SET 2
96	ʻ	‾
97	a	α
98	b	β
99	c	χ
100	d	δ
101	e	ε
102	f	ϕ
103	g	γ
104	h	η
105	i	ι
106	j	φ
107	k	κ
108	l	λ
109	m	μ
110	n	ν
111	o	ο
112	p	π
113	q	θ
114	r	ρ
115	s	σ
116	t	τ
117	u	υ
118	v	ϖ
119	w	ω
120	x	ξ
121	y	ψ
122	z	ζ
123	{	{
124	¦	|
125	}	}
126	~	~
127		
128	Ç	
129	ü	ϒ
130	é	′
131	â	≤
132	ä	⁄
133	à	∞
134	å	ƒ
135	ç	♣
136	ê	♦
137	ë	♥
138	è	♠
139	ï	↔
140	î	←
141	ì	↑
142	Ä	→
143	Å	↓
144	É	°
145	æ	±
146	Æ	″
147	ô	≥
148	ö	×
149	ò	∝
150	û	∂
151	ù	•
152	ÿ	÷
153	Ö	≠
154	Ü	≡
155	¢	≈
156	£	…
157	¥	│
158	¤	—
159	ƒ	↵

Table E.1: The Ventura Characters Sets (continued)

	CHAR SET 1	CHAR SET 2
160	á	ℵ
161	í	ℑ
162	ó	ℜ
163	ú	℘
164	ñ	⊗
165	Ñ	⊕
166	ª	∅
167	º	∩
168	¿	∪
169	“	⊃
170	”	⊇
171	‹	⊄
172	›	⊂
173	¡	⊆
174	«	∈
175	»	∉
176	ã	∠
177	õ	∇
178	Ø	®
179	ø	©
180	œ	™
181	Œ	∏
182	À	√
183	Ã	·
184	Õ	¬
185	§	∧
186	‡	∨
187	†	⇔
188	¶	⇐
189	©	⇑
190	®	⇒
191	™	⇓
192	„	◊
193	…	〈
194	‰	®
195	•	©
196	–	™
197	—	Σ
198	°	⎛
199	Á	⎜
200	Â	⎝
201	È	⎡
202	Ê	⎢
203	Ë	⎣
204	Ì	⎧
205	Í	⎨
206	Î	⎩
207	Ï	⎪
208	Ò	
209	Ó	〉
210	Ô	∫
211	Š	⌠
212	š	⎮
213	Ù	⌡
214	Ú	⎞
215	Û	⎟
216	Ÿ	⎠
217	ß	⎤
218		
219		
220		
221		
222		
223		

Table E.2: Codes for Text Effects

EFFECT	CODE
Color	<C___>
Discretionary Hyphen	<->
Double underline	<C=>
Inserted text:	
Anchor	<$&___>
Footnote	<$F___>
Hidden text	<$h!___>
Index	<$I___>
Italics	<I>
Jump of base line	<J___>
Kerning	<K___>
Line break	<R>
Normal	<D>
Overscore	<O>
Point size	<P___>
Small	<S>
Spaces:	
Em space	<_>
En space	<~>
NoBreak Space	<N>
Thin space	<|>
Figure space	<+>
Strike-thru	<X>
Subscript	<v>
Superscript	<^>

Table E.2: Codes for Text Effects (continued)

EFFECT	CODE
Type weight:	
Bold	<B>
Light	<L>
Medium	<M>
Typeface	<F___>
Underline	<U>

INDEX

G

J

K

L

M

S

T

MASTERING VENTURA Samples Disk

The easiest way for you to use Ventura is by applying style sheets and adapting sample documents. Now, direct from the author, you can receive a disk of professionally prepared style sheets and sample documents.

- Samples include a résumé, letter, memo, book, organizational chart, form, brochure, financial report, newsletter, table, and other formats.
- Features of the formats are listed and clearly discussed.
- Function keys are listed and assigned in a consistent manner, allowing you to switch style sheets easily.
- Tags are carefully organized to allow you to apply them quickly.
- Files are ready to install on your disk, altogether or one by one.

To order, simply fill out this coupon or send the information on a separate piece of paper. Mail to Matthew Holtz, 455 Hyde St. #93, San Francisco, CA 94109. Include a check for $20 each, payable to Matthew Holtz. (California residents please add appropriate sales tax.) Please allow four weeks for delivery.

Please send me __ copies of the *Mastering Ventura* Samples Disk.

____
Name

____
Address

____
City State Zip

____
Phone

SYBEX is not affiliated with Matthew Holtz and assumes no responsibility for any defect in the disk or programs.

TO JOIN THE SYBEX MAILING LIST OR ORDER BOOKS
PLEASE COMPLETE THIS FORM

NAME ______________________ COMPANY ______________________

STREET ______________________ STATE ______ ZIP ______________

☐ PLEASE MAIL ME MORE INFORMATION ABOUT **SYBEX** TITLES

ORDER FORM (There is no obligation to order)

PLEASE SEND ME THE FOLLOWING:

TITLE	QTY	PRICE
______________________	______	______
______________________	______	______
______________________	______	______
______________________	______	______
TOTAL BOOK ORDER	______	$______

SHIPPING AND HANDLING PLEASE ADD $2.00 PER BOOK VIA UPS ______

FOR OVERSEAS SURFACE ADD $5.25 PER BOOK PLUS $4.40 REGISTRATION FEE ______

FOR OVERSEAS AIRMAIL ADD $18.25 PER BOOK PLUS $4.40 REGISTRATION FEE ______

CALIFORNIA RESIDENTS PLEASE ADD APPLICABLE SALES TAX ______

TOTAL AMOUNT PAYABLE ______

☐ CHECK ENCLOSED ☐ VISA
☐ MASTERCARD ☐ AMERICAN EXPRESS

ACCOUNT NUMBER ______________________

EXPIR. DATE ______ DAYTIME PHONE ______________

CUSTOMER SIGNATURE ______________________________________

CHECK AREA OF COMPUTER INTEREST:

☐ BUSINESS SOFTWARE

☐ TECHNICAL PROGRAMMING

☐ OTHER: ______________________

OTHER COMPUTER TITLES YOU WOULD LIKE TO SEE IN PRINT:

____

____

THE FACTOR THAT WAS MOST IMPORTANT IN YOUR SELECTION:

☐ THE SYBEX NAME

☐ QUALITY

☐ PRICE

☐ EXTRA FEATURES

☐ COMPREHENSIVENESS

☐ CLEAR WRITING

☐ OTHER ______________________

OCCUPATION

☐ PROGRAMMER

☐ SENIOR EXECUTIVE

☐ COMPUTER CONSULTANT

☐ SUPERVISOR

☐ MIDDLE MANAGEMENT

☐ ENGINEER/TECHNICAL

☐ CLERICAL/SERVICE

☐ BUSINESS OWNER/SELF EMPLOYED

☐ TEACHER

☐ HOMEMAKER

☐ RETIRED

☐ STUDENT

☐ OTHER: ______________

CHECK YOUR LEVEL OF COMPUTER USE

☐ NEW TO COMPUTERS

☐ INFREQUENT COMPUTER USER

☐ FREQUENT USER OF ONE SOFTWARE PACKAGE:

NAME ____________________

☐ FREQUENT USER OF MANY SOFTWARE PACKAGES

☐ PROFESSIONAL PROGRAMMER

OTHER COMMENTS:

PLEASE FOLD, SEAL, AND MAIL TO SYBEX

SYBEX, INC.
2021 CHALLENGER DR. #100
ALAMEDA, CALIFORNIA USA
94501

SEAL

MENU/SELECTION	EFFECT	PAGE
Anchors & Captions	Allows you to specify a caption for a frame. Also assigns an anchor name to a frame.	247
Repeating Frame	Allows a frame to be repeated on every page. Controls the repeating frame on the current page.	334
Vertical Rules	Places rules between columns of a frame and vertical page rules.	259
Ruling Line Above	Places rules at the top of a frame.	263
Ruling Line Below	Places rules at the bottom of a frame.	267
Ruling Box Around	Places boxes at and within the edges of a frame.	273
Frame Background	Sets the color and pattern of a frame's background.	452
Image Setting	Sets halftoning for gray-scale images.	226
PARAGRAPH		
Font	Controls the font face, size, style and color for a paragraph tag. Also underline, overscore, strike-thru of entire paragraph.	123
Alignment	Sets the alignment, notation, hyphenation, width, first-line indent for a paragraph tag.	136
Spacing	Sets the spacing between paragraphs and lines and the in-from-left/right values.	156
Breaks	Sets the positioning of text when one paragraph ends and another begins.	158
Tab Settings	Assigns the tab type, location, and leaders to a paragraph's tab settings.	297
Special Effects	Sets dropped capitals (big first characters) and bullets for a paragraph tag.	441
Attribute Overrides	Sets placement values for underline, overscore, strike-thru, superscript, subscript, small caps.	466
Paragraph Typography	Sets horizontal spacing between words and characters.	458
Ruling Line Above	Places rules above paragraphs so tagged.	269
Ruling Line Below	Places rules below paragraphs so tagged.	269
Ruling Box Around	Places boxes around paragraphs so tagged.	273
Define Colors	Customizes colors or shades of gray used throughout the chapter.	198
Update Tag List (^K)	Renames, removes tags; saves, prints style sheets; assigns tags to function keys.	164

MENU/SELECTION	EFFECT	PAGE
GRAPHIC		
Show On All Pages	Makes the selected graphic repeatedly appear on all pages.	288
Send to Back (^Z)	Sends a graphic to the back of a graphics pile.	287
Bring to Front (^A)	Brings a graphic to the front of a graphics pile.	287
Line Attributes (^L)	Sets the line thickness, color, and end style of graphics.	282
Fill Attributes (^F)	Sets the fill color and fill pattern of graphics.	284
Select All (^Q)	Selects all the graphics associated with the selected frame.	288
Grid Settings	Defines a grid that positions graphics.	276
OPTIONS		
Set Preferences	Sets generated tag display, greeking, backup files, double-click speed, decimal-tab character, on-screen kerning, automatic adjustments, pop-up symbol, and menu type.	501
Set Ruler	Sets the measurement system and zero point for the screen rulers.	229
Set Printer Info	Sets printer name, screen fonts, output port, and width table.	180
Add/Remove Fonts	Allows you to add and remove fonts and indicate their download/resident status.	191
Show/Hide Side-Bar (^W)	Displays or hides the Side-bar.	503
Show/Hide Rulers	Displays or hides the rulers along the edges of the working area.	504
Show/Hide Column Guides	Displays or hides the edges of columns in the underlying-page frame.	504
Show/Hide Pictures	Displays or hides all pictures on the screen. Also displays or hides selected picture.	504
Show/Hide Tabs & Returns (^T)	Displays or hides tabs, returns, solid spaces, and line breaks, end of file, and other codes.	504
Show/Hide Loose Lines	Displays or hides darkening of lines that exceed the maximum space width, specified with the Paragraph menu's Paragraph Typography.	504
Turn Column Snap On/Off	Turns on or off alignment of frames with columns in the underlying-page frame.	504
Turn Line Snap On/Off	Turns on or off alignment of frames with lines of body text in the underlying-page frame.	504
Multi-Chapter	Allows you to perform operations associated with publications and to copy chapters.	360

MASTERING VENTURA

Book Level
✓ Beginning
✓ Intermediate
Advanced

How-To
Reference

Now completely updated and revised for Version 2, **Mastering Ventura** is the complete guide to desktop publishing on the IBM PC, using Xerox's Ventura Publisher. It's a complex program, and **Mastering Ventura** covers every feature in detail—from exploring the software's menu structure for the first time to putting finishing touches on a complicated publishing project.

No matter what your desktop-publishing needs, this book will get you using Ventura—and adapting it to your own projects—more quickly than you thought possible. And Version 2 enhancements are easy to find with the margin icons. Turn here to learn how to:

- Use Style Sheets to specify margins, columns, fonts, sizes, typefaces, and more
- Understand and use the software's four operating modes: Frame mode, Paragraph mode, Text mode, and Graphics mode
- Design attractive, well-balanced layouts—for anything from single-page letters to multi-column, illustrated brochures
- Import graphs and pictures from Lotus 1-2-3, a variety of graphics programs, and even scanned images
- Create and edit text for Ventura with WordPerfect, Wordstar, Microsoft Word, or your favorite word processing program
- Master every aspect of output and printing—with typesetters, dot-matrix printers, laser printers and more
- Coordinate other programs with Ventura—from keyboard macro generators to dBASE III PLUS
- Choose and add new fonts to the system
- Understand and use the new Professional Extension features

You'll find clear discussions and hands-on tutorials throughout—all centered on concrete examples that show the full range of publishing tasks: *business letters, newsletters, invoices, press releases, brochures, books, technical documents, and more.*

"One of the best guides to Ventura...professional in presentation and content....it conveys useful ideas in an engaging fashion."
—PC Publishing

"More than a standard primer, a very well laid-out course of instruction."
—Computer Literacy

"Complete guide to Ventura. Excellent choice for new users."
—Computer Book Review

About the Author

Matthew Holtz runs a consulting firm that specializes in desktop publishing, and teaches courses in word processing, spreadsheets, and database management in Berkeley, California. His background in business management and employee training makes him especially aware of the computing needs of business. He has written articles and reviews for *PC World* and *Publish!* magazines, and is author of *Mastering Microsoft Word,* from SYBEX.

With *Fast Track* Speed Notes

Fast Track speed notes summarize chapters, list the steps or keystrokes needed to complete specific tasks, and point you to pages on which more detailed explanations appear.

SYBEX books bring you skills—
not just information.
As computer experts, educators,
and publishing professionals,
we care—and it shows.
You can trust the SYBEX label
of excellence.

COMPUTER BOOK SHELF CATEGORY
IBM/PCs: Desktop Publishing

ISBN 0-89588-581-6 U.S. $24.95